Audubon
Wildlife Report
1989/1990

The National Audubon Society, founded in 1905, is dedicated to conserving plants and animals and their habitats, to promoting wise use of land, water, and energy, and to protecting life from the many global environmental problems that now threaten it. With more than half a million members, 510 chapters, 10 regional offices, 5 state offices, and a staff of nearly 400, the Audubon Society is a powerful force for conservation research, education, and action. The views expressed in this book are solely those of the authors.

Audubon
Wildlife Report
1989/1990

William J. Chandler
Editor

Lillian Labate
Associate Editor

Chris Wille
Project Manager

The National Audubon Society
New York, New York

ACADEMIC PRESS, INC.

Harcourt Brace Jovanovich, Publishers

San Diego   New York   Berkeley   Boston
London   Sydney   Tokyo   Toronto

National
Audubon
Society

Academic Press Rapid Manuscript Reproduction.

COPYRIGHT © 1989 BY NATIONAL AUDUBON SOCIETY

ACADEMIC PRESS, INC.
San Diego, California 92101

United Kingdom Edition published by
ACADEMIC PRESS LIMITED
24-28 Oval Road, London NW1 7DX

LIBRARY OF CONGRESS CATALOG CARD NUMBER: 86-643440

ISSN   0885-6044

ISBN   0-12-041003-6   (alk. paper)

PRINTED IN THE UNITED STATES OF AMERICA
89 90 91 92   9 8 7 6 5 4 3 2 1

Contents

Part Three. Case Histories

Part Four. Appendices

Foreword

Before the invention of sophisticated monitoring devices, coal miners used canaries to warn them if the air they were breathing was unsafe. The bird's small lungs and fast breathing made it an excellent indicator of conditions that could not be measured by the technology of the times.

Even today, with our vastly improved technology, we rely on tiny mysid shrimp to test the toxicity of effluents from factories and treatment plants. We do not always know what to measure or how multiple pollutants interact, so we rely on the most sensitive indicators available: living organisms. Often, wildlife is the best indicator of the health of an ecosystem.

And the indications are troubling. Even songbirds, so common to many people that they are often not considered "wildlife," are greatly threatened by deforestation and other changes in their habitat. Every volume of the *Audubon Wildlife Report* brings us the details of such threatened species. And importantly, it also discusses those species that constitute successes in wildlife management. The chapters on federal natural resource agencies and their programs, such as the featured U.S. Army Corps of Engineers, provide in-depth examinations of the government's role in protecting wildlife and habitat.

In the past, the *Audubon Wildlife Report* has focused on important challenges to the continued health of different species and ecosystems. This volume continues that process, furthering the debate on issues such as old-growth forests, the relationship between water and wildlife, and the need to preserve and restore wetlands and grassland range territory.

Now, however, we are challenged by an enormous new threat—global climate change. Not only must we anticipate threats to wildlife in their current habitat, but also predict how populations will respond to changes in climate that in the past occurred over millenia but that now may occur within decades, or at most, centuries.

Unquestionably, significant climate changes will occur, even if we act now to reduce our contribution to the problem. While it is crucial that we develop policies to reduce the overall magnitude or slow the rate of climate change, we must also make sure that we, and the natural systems that ultimately sustain us, can adapt to those changes. Initial studies tell us that we may be able to adapt our infrastructure, albeit at high cost, and that managed ecosystems, such as agriculture, may be able to survive the shifts. Unmanaged ecosystems—wildlife—are in greater danger.

We must respond to this challenge, both for our own sake and because we have a responsibility for stewardship of the Earth and its creatures. This volume of the *Audubon Wildlife Report* is a critical step in that response.

Governor Thomas H. Kean
State of New Jersey

Preface

This is the fifth *Audubon Wildlife Report,* and like earlier volumes, its focus is federal wildlife conservation policy. While the report's focus remains the same, its scope of coverage continues to evolve.

In this volume, the featured federal agency is the U.S. Army Corps of Engineers. The Corps chapter provides a comprehensive overview of the agency: its history, legislative mandate, and key programs that affect the environment.

Also in this volume are nine chapters covering selected problems, issues, and developments affecting fish and wildlife resources. The following subjects are covered:

- Recent federal court decisions that provide new interpretations of federal wildlife law.
- Conservation of coastal wetlands in the Southeast.
- Global climate change and its potential effects on fish and wildlife.
- A monitoring and research strategy for nongame migratory birds.
- Conservation of ancient forests of the Pacific Northwest.
- Restoring public rangelands in the West.
- Discard bycatch in marine fisheries with a special focus on the Gulf of Mexico.
- Trends in western water law and their implications for the environment.
- Appropriations and related congressional policy directives for federal fish and wildlife programs.

These chapters will bring the reader abreast of the latest developments in fish and wildlife policy and provide the comprehensive background material needed to understand the depth and complexity of significant conservation challenges and issues.

The third part of the book contains eight chapters on individual species of plants and animals, selected to illustrate the full range of wildlife management issues faced by professionals today. These case histories are a popular component of the Report, and with good reason: they provide the reader with the latest information on a species's natural history, significance, historical and current status, future prospects, and management needs. This information is valuable to the professional and layperson alike.

Two things caught my attention when I reviewed the species chapters. First, our basic knowledge of many species—including those deemed highly important—is riddled with gaps. Second, the basic conservation needs of some of the species covered are not being met. Indeed, the funds spent on their behalf can only be described as woefully inadequate. These observations raise fundamental questions about the biological research enterprise in the United States, the establishment of wildlife management priorities and budgets, and the overall coordination of research and management to address the nation's most pressing biological conservation needs. Readers' thoughts on these matters would be appreciated as we formulate future topics for treatment in the Report.

Finally, the last part of the Report contains appendices of key fish and wildlife personnel in various federal agencies. The appendices have been expanded in this year's volume to include more individuals and their addresses and phone numbers. The appendices are current as of March 1, 1989; thus, they provide the reader with the most up-to-date listing of federal fish and wildlife contacts likely to be available in 1989.

Correspondence regarding any subject matter in the Report, or lack thereof, should be sent to: Editor, Audubon Wildlife Report, National Audubon Society, 950 Third Ave., New York, New York 10022.

William J. Chandler
Editor

Acknowledgments

Publication of this volume would not have been possible without the generous support of the following:

Robert Winthrop
Olin Corporation Charitable Trust
Union Camp Charitable Trust

The research and writing of this report required the painstaking efforts and expertise of a legion. Thanks go out to nearly every staff member of National Audubon Society. The editors especially appreciate the efforts of those who took time out of their hectic schedules to review and comment on chapter drafts: Dede Armentrout, Hope Babcock, A. D. Chandler, Susan Drennan, Mike Duever, Brock Evans, Lynn Herring, Eugene Knoder, Cynthia Lenhart, Robert Lester, Pete Myers, Jim Pissot, Elizabeth Raisbeck, Scott Reed, Garry Ross, Carl Safina, Sandy Sprunt, Dan Taylor, Larry Thompson, Bob Turner, Fran Spivy-Weber, and Brooks Yeager. Special thanks also go to Susan Parker Martin, Tom Exton, and Diane Nixa for their fundraising efforts; Mary McCarthy, for her computer wizardry; Margaret McWethy, for her swift yet precise production of all the figures in this volume; Fred Baumgarten and Anne Schwartz, for their patience and continued support; Katharine Yagerman, for checking all the law citations; Jean Thomson Black, former liaison with Academic Press, for her hard work and encouragement; and to the staff of Academic Press.

The editors would also like to acknowledge and thank various staff members from the following agencies and organizations: Bureau of Land Management, Bureau of Reclamation, Environmental Protection Agency, U.S. Fish and Wildlife Service, U.S. Forest Service, National Park Service, National Marine Fisheries Service, U.S. Army Corps of Engineers, the U.S. Department of Agriculture, International Association of Fish and Wildlife Agencies, Natural Resources Defense Council, and The Wilderness Society.

Audubon Wildlife Report External Advisory Committee:

Laurence R. Jahn *Wildlife Management Institute*
Scott Feierabend *National Wildlife Federation*
Robert Davison *Professional Staff Member, Senate Committee on Environment and Public Works*
William Molini *Nevada Department of Wildlife*
Thomas Franklin *The Wildlife Society*
Donald Barry *House Merchant Marine Fisheries Committee*

Contents of Previous Volumes

Audubon Wildlife Report 1986

Audubon Wildlife Report 1987

Audubon Wildlife Report 1988/1989

Part One

---◇---

The Featured Agency

Perhaps no other government agency has done more to change the natural face of America than the U. S. Army Corps of Engineers. Best known for its water diversion and control structures, the Corps also has important regulatory functions, such as controlling development in wetlands. The common denominator to all Corps activities is a profound effect on wildlife. *U.S. Army Corps of Engineers*

The U.S. Army Corps of Engineers

Robert B. Smythe

INTRODUCTION

Each year, thousands of visitors to Washington, D.C., first see the city from the air, as they fly over the Potomac River into Washington National Airport. Although many people looking out their airplane window can recognize the Washington Monument, the Capitol dome, the Federal Triangle, the Key Bridge, the Pentagon, and the Tidal Basin, few are likely to know that these features were all constructed by one federal agency—the U.S. Army Corps of Engineers.

Most Americans have at least some passing acquaintance with the Corps of Engineers. Each year millions of people enjoy boating, fishing, or swimming at several hundred lakes impounded by the Corps; many others recognize the Corps' distinctive red flag with the white castle flying at navigation locks on the nation's major rivers, or on bridges over the 12,000 miles of inland and intracoastal waterways maintained by the Corps. Veterans of military service are likely to have some knowledge of the Corps' major role in military construction and in combat engineering. Developers and conservationists are familiar with, and generally hold divergent opinions about, the role of the

Corps in regulating the discharge of dredged or fill material into wetlands and other waters of the United States.

But like the proverbial blind men contemplating an elephant, most people's knowledge of the Corps of Engineers is limited to their own personal experience. Prior to about 1970, the Corps was known primarily for its construction and operation of major civil works projects, including levees, locks, and dams; river and harbor dredging; hydropower; and aquatic recreation and municipal water supplies. During the last twenty years, the Corps has, albeit with considerable reluctance, acquired another role: that of an environmental regulatory agency responsible for protecting the nation's aquatic ecosystems, often from the very types of development activity that the Corps itself has been, and still continues to be, engaged in.

Is the Corps still, as some would describe it, a concrete-pouring, river-channeling beast with an environmental tail grafted on? Or is it a heavy-handed regulatory agency of the federal bureaucracy that stymies legitimate economic development with reams of rule books, permit application forms, and environmental impact statements? Does it serve the public, or the President, or the Pentagon, or Congress? This chapter will explore the basis of such varied questions about the Corps. The following sections provide a brief history of the Corps, a description of its principal activities, and a discussion of the Corps' recent involvement in major legislative and policy issues affecting fish and wildlife and environmental quality.

HISTORY AND LEGISLATIVE MANDATE

Military and Civil Works

Understanding the organization and activities of today's U.S. Army Corps of Engineers requires some acquaintance with its past.[1] The agency's unique combination of military and civil functions has evolved over the past two centuries. The Corps proudly traces its origins back to the American Revolution when, in 1775, General George Washington appointed Colonel Richard Gridley to be the first Chief Engineer for the Continental Army. Gridley's first assignment was to build fortifications at Bunker Hill. A small group of engineer

---

1. Much of the material in this section is drawn from two publications: *A History of Federal Water Resources Programs, 1800–1960,* by Beatrice Hort Holmes, and *The History of the U.S. Army Corps of Engineers,* published by the Corps. For a different and critical perspective, see *Dams and Other Disasters: A Century of the Army Corps of Engineers in Civil Works,* by Arthur E. Morgan. Full citations are given in the list of references at the end of the chapter.

officers and enlisted men were trained by officers from Europe, such as: Thaddeus Kosciuszko, who designed obstructions that delayed General Burgoyne's advance toward Albany; Louis Duportail, who helped design and execute the siege at Yorktown in 1781; and Pierre Charles L'Enfant, best known for his postwar design of the master plan for the new federal city of Washington.

Although the Corps, along with most other army units, was dissolved in 1783, renewed threats of war with Britain and France caused Congress to re-establish a Corps of Artillerists and Engineers in 1794 and, in 1802, to establish a military academy at West Point, New York, to train engineer officers. The U.S. Military Academy at West Point thus became the nation's first engineering school. During the War of 1812, West Point graduates carried out reconnaissance and mapping, and built fortifications to defend coastal harbors, including the Battery in New York City and Fort McHenry in Baltimore. The military academy at West Point remained under Corps of Engineers supervision until 1866, when Congress expanded the scope of training and placed the academy directly under the authority of the Secretary of War.

The War of 1812 demonstrated a need not only for seacoast defenses, but also for an improved system of land and water transportation. The civil works mission of the Corps grew out of a recommendation made in 1819 by John C. Calhoun, Secretary of War. Calhoun urged that Congress direct the Corps to improve waterways navigation to facilitate the movement of the army as well as to enhance national economic development. In 1824, Congress passed a General Survey Act authorizing the President to use army engineers to survey road and canal routes "of national importance, in a commercial or military point of view."[2] Congress then appropriated $75,000 for work on the Ohio and Mississippi rivers. The Corps began removing snags and debris, building wing dams, and dredging channels to facilitate the growing commercial steamboat and barge traffic on the rivers. This work set a precedent for all subsequent civil works activities of the Corps— the combining of military or national security interests with economic development interests to justify a federal role in civilian construction activities.

The Corps' initial civil works role in improving navigation was soon expanded to include repair and construction of the first "national road" west from Cumberland, Maryland, into Ohio, Indiana, and Illinois. The Corps also constructed numerous lighthouses along the Atlantic Coast. Over 40 engineer officers, most trained at West Point, served in the army during the Mexican War. During the 1850s, those

---

2. That same year, the Supreme Court resolved a conflict over the extent of federal authority when it ruled in *Gibbon v. Ogden* that congressional power over navigation extended "within the limits of every state in the Union so far as that navigation may be in any manner connected with the commerce . . ." (22 U.S. 1197).

officers returned to civil works duties. In addition to ongoing river and harbor improvements, their activities included conducting a topographic and hydrographic survey of the lower Mississippi basin, which concluded that levees were needed to control frequent flooding in the region.

In the growing nation's capital, engineer officers supervised the construction of a permanent water supply system for the cities of Washington and Georgetown (part of which is still operated by the Baltimore District of the Corps). In addition, Corps officers reconstructed the U.S. Capitol Building, adding the north and south wings and replacing the old dome with a new one of cast and wrought iron, which stands today as a distinctive work of architectural engineering.

The Civil War provided combat experience for engineer officers on both sides; a number of engineers were promoted to general officers. At Gettysburg, Union generals George Meade and George McClellan faced Confederate generals Robert E. Lee and P.G.T. Beauregard; all four were from the Corps of Engineers. Others remained in the engineer corps, carrying out mapping, intelligence, and siege operations, as well as general military construction duties (Corps 1986).

After the Civil War, the Corps again returned to civil works activities. In the District of Columbia, Corps officers and civilians worked together at the direction of Congress to survey and design Rock Creek Park, to complete the construction of the Washington Monument, and to design and supervise construction of numerous public buildings, including the Library of Congress, the Government Printing Office, the Pension Building, and the State, War and Navy Building (now called the Old Executive Office Building). Corps dredge-and-fill operations on the Potomac River were undertaken for navigation improvement and flood control, but also resulted in the creation of Potomac Park and the Tidal Basin. Corps officials like to point to this work as an early example of the beneficial use of dredged material.

Elsewhere in the country, the Corps undertook an expanded civil works program, again at the direction of Congress. Construction began on a series of locks and dams to improve navigation on the Ohio River. In Michigan, the Corps built a new canal and a state-of-the-art hydraulic lock to allow commercial access between Lake Superior and Lake Huron, which eventually led to construction of the St. Lawrence Seaway in the 20th century.

In 1879, Congress established a Mississippi River Commission to develop and execute a comprehensive plan for flood control and navigation improvements on the lower Mississippi; three of the designated seven members were to be Corps officers. The Mississippi River Commission continues to carry out similar planning and review functions today as an advisory body to the Corps.

These and other assignments gradually led to an ongoing civil works program for the Corps of Engineers. An informal process evolved for undertaking specific projects, in which Congress directed the Corps first to make a survey or an initial investigation of a particular problem, then to report back with plans and recommendations for action. Congress would then authorize a project and appropriate funds to the Corps to carry it out. Usually the construction work would be done by civilians hired and supervised by Corps officers. With some modifications discussed later in this chapter, this is in essence how the civil works program of the Corps operates today.

Beginnings of a Regulatory Program

Although most of the Corps' civil works programs were and still are related to water resources development, Congress gave the Corps another task in the 1870s: to survey and manage the first national park, Yellowstone. Captain William Ludlow and a small survey party mapped the park, constructed roads, and undertook military patrols to protect the park's unique resources from damage by tourists and souvenir hunters. The Corps eventually relinquished authority over the park to the National Park Service after the latter agency's creation in 1916.

Toward the end of the 19th century the practice of dumping garbage, debris, and even animal carcasses from slaughterhouses into the nearest river had become widespread. Building on authority already granted to the Corps to regulate bridge construction and other potential obstacles to navigation, Congress directed the Corps to regulate dumping and filling in the nation's harbors. This authority was greatly expanded with the passage of the Rivers and Harbors Act of 1899. Section 13 of the statute, commonly called the Refuse Act, prohibited the discharge of "any refuse matter of any kind" from either ship or shore "other than that flowing from streets or sewers and passing there from in a liquid state" except by permit; permits for refuse discharges were to be issued by the Corps only when judged by the Chief of Engineers not to be injurious to anchorage and navigation (33 U.S.C.A. 407). This law covered all the navigable waters and tributaries of the United States. The Corps prosecuted numerous violators of the Refuse Act for dumping solid refuse into rivers and lakes, but took the position that most liquid discharges were not covered by the law because they were not obstructions to navigation. It was not until the 1960s that two Supreme Court decisions interpreted the statute to apply to any industrial waste, including liquids (Zener 1974).

The 20th Century—Expanding Missions

In 1904, the U.S. Government took over from a French company the challenge of building a canal across the Isthmus of Panama. Although building the canal was never an official mission of the Corps, engineer officers from the Corps supervised much of the canal's construction. President Theodore Roosevelt appointed Lt. Colonel George W. Goethals as chief engineer and chairman of the Panama Canal Commission. After the excavation of more than 200 million cubic yards of rock and dirt and the construction of a massive dam and several sets of locks, the canal opened ahead of schedule on August 15, 1914. Corps officers served as governors of the Panama Canal Zone, and still continue to be involved in the operations of the canal.

In 1916, the Corps of Engineers was reorganized into three regiments of six companies each. When the United States entered World War I, these units were rapidly expanded to provide combat engineering services to American, British, and French forces. Engineer troops prepared maps, built bridges, railroads, port facilities, barracks, and hospitals, and sometimes were involved in direct combat in places such as Amiens and Belleau Woods. As before, the Corps brought construction and management experience gained in these military operations back to be applied in its civil works programs.

In 1917, Congress passed the first flood control act, which appropriated $45 million for work in the lower Mississippi basin and $5.6 million for the Sacramento River. In 1927, the Corps was authorized to expand its planning functions to conduct comprehensive surveys of river basins throughout the United States and to develop general plans for navigation in combination with hydropower, flood control, and irrigation. Congress thus established in law the Corps' authority to plan for multipurpose water resource projects. That same year, a record flood struck the lower Mississippi, flooding over 25,000 square miles, killing several hundred people, and leaving over half a million people without shelter. In 1928, Congress passed a flood control act that authorized a massive flood-control effort involving levees, dredging, and floodways, including a controversial plan to divert up to half of future Mississippi River flood waters down the Atchafalaya River in Louisiana to the Gulf of Mexico. This plan was considered by a board of engineer officers to be more practical than the alternative of constructing a series of upstream reservoirs to restrain flood waters. The principal elements of this huge regional program, parts of which are still under construction, are outlined later in this chapter.

In the midst of the Great Depression, citizens and their elected representatives looked to the federal government to initiate a wide range of public works projects to provide employment and stimulate the economy. In the Flood Control Act of 1936, Congress assigned the Corps of Engineers nationwide responsibility for federal flood-control projects, to be carried out in cooperation with state and local governments. Aware that this new authority increased the potential for political "pork-barrel," Congress wrote into the statute the requirement that for each project "the benefits, to whomsoever they may accrue, [must be] in excess of the estimated costs" (33 U.S.C.A. 701a). This new requirement was intended to constrain federal involvement to those projects that truly had net national benefits, but a variety of creative accounting methods that diluted this constraint were subsequently employed by the Corps and accepted by Congress. So-called secondary project benefits such as land enhancements, local employment benefits, and value of damage prevented to future development were combined with direct benefits, and low discount rates were set by Congress for computing the present value of future benefits. All these devices had the effect of inflating the benefit side of benefit/cost ratios, which in turn allowed many questionable projects to pass the "net benefits" test. Furthermore, no evaluation of a project's potential adverse environmental effects was required; economic benefits and costs were the only factors considered in the accounting process.

With the approach of World War II, the Corps began a military mobilization that had as its objective providing an engineer combat regiment for each Army division. The military activities of these engineer units during the war were too extensive to discuss in detail here. Some highlights include the defense and eventual retaking of the Bataan Peninsula, road building and mine clearing in North Africa, the assault at Omaha Beach on D-Day, and the capture of the bridge at Remagen, where engineer officers thwarted the German attempt to demolish the bridge and repaired it to allow nine U.S. Army divisions to cross the Rhine. Closer to home, the Corps built the Alcan Highway to Alaska, the naval base at Guantanamo Bay in Cuba, and the facilities at Hanford, Washington, Oak Ridge, Tennessee, and Los Alamos, New Mexico, for the top-secret Manhattan Project, which produced the atomic bomb.

After the war ended, the Corps maintained a presence in both Europe and the Far East, constructing various military facilities. As the Army's engineers, the Corps was soon called on again to provide combat support—first in Korea and later in Vietnam.[3]

Postwar Changes

In the late 1940s and 1950s, the Corps' civil works program was expanded by Congress. Construction was started or resumed on more than 20 previously authorized multipurpose water projects. A rapidly growing economy and population made hydropower and public recreation increasingly important components of those projects. By 1975 Corps facilities were producing more than 25 percent of the nation's hydroelectric power, and Corps recreation areas at reservoirs and other projects were receiving more than 200 million visits per year by people interested in fishing, swimming, boating, and other leisure activities.

3. The Corps' military activities in these conflicts are reviewed in more detail in several publications (Corps 1986).

However, by the early 1960s a number of critics had begun raising questions about the economic and environmental consequences of large-scale structural flood-control and multipurpose water projects, particularly those of the Corps and the Bureau of Reclamation. These projects required the damming of free-flowing rivers and the flooding of productive bottomlands with losses of fish and wildlife habitat. Furthermore, the frequently overstated promises of "permanent" flood protection often encouraged unwise development in floodplains. The Fish and Wildlife Coordination Act (16 U.S.C.A. 611 *et seq.*), first passed in 1934 and amended several times after World War II, required the Corps and other federal water development agencies to consult with the Interior Department's Fish and Wildlife Service regarding the impact of proposed projects on fish and wildlife, and to incorporate wildlife protection and mitigation measures in water project plans where feasible. But these measures were frequently overlooked or only partly implemented when the projects were constructed.

The numerous large water projects authorized by Congress were also requiring an increasing portion of the federal budget, and the Executive Branch had effectively lost control over the process. In 1959, in an attempt to restrain the water projects juggernaut, President Eisenhower vetoed a huge public works appropriations bill. Two years later, President Kennedy sent Congress a water resources planning bill that called for the creation of a Water Resources Council of federal officials to establish uniform standards for the formulation of federal water projects. After considerable debate, the bill was signed into law by President Johnson in 1965 with only minor changes (Hunt 1988). Titled the Water Resources Planning Act (P.L. 89–80, 42 U.S.C. 1961 *et seq.*), the act established a federal Water Resources Council composed of the secretaries of Agriculture, Army, Interior, and Health, Education and Welfare, with a full-time staff and a mandate to establish principles, standards, and procedures for federal water-project planning; to publish a periodic national assessment of the nation's water resources; and to provide support for regional river basin commissions and for the development of state comprehensive water resource plans.

Finally, in response to growing concerns about the nation's environment, Congress passed two major pieces of legislation that brought about fundamental changes in the Corps' civil works and regulatory programs: The National Environmental Policy Act of 1969 (NEPA) (42 U.S.C.A. 4321 *et seq.*) and the Federal Water Pollution Control Act Amendments of 1972 (33 U.S.C. 1251 *et seq.*), usually called the Clean Water Act. NEPA imposed no new technical or economic standards, but required federal agencies to analyze the environmental impacts of their proposed actions. If the impacts appeared to be significant, the project-sponsoring agency had to prepare and circulate for comment a detailed environmental impact statement on the proposed action and reasonable alternatives to it. The statute opened the Corps' planning process to public review; the resulting intense criticism of many projects led to the termination of some and to significant revisions in the design and construction of others.

The Clean Water Act largely supplanted the old Refuse Act by transferring from the Corps to the Environmental Protection Agency the authority to regulate most point-source (end-of-pipe) pollutant discharges into the "waters of the United States." At the same time, Section 404 of the act established a permit program through which the Corps, in an expansion of its traditional authority, was to regulate the discharge of dredged or fill material into U.S. waters. Although the Corps initially interpreted its authority under Section 404 narrowly to apply only to traditionally navigable waters, numerous lawsuits and court decisions have established that most streams, lakes, and wetlands across the United States are subject to regulation under this section. (The Corps' 404 program is discussed in more detail below.)

Other significant statutes enacted during the 1960s and 1970s that have affected the Corps civil works program include the Wild and Scenic Rivers Act of 1968 and the Endangered Species Act of 1973. These two statutes prohibit disruptive projects or other activities in areas that are part of the national Wild and Scenic Rivers System, or that would destroy critical habitat for a list of endangered or threatened species, as determined by the Department of the Interior.

ORGANIZATION, ACTIVITIES, AND BUDGET

Organization of the Civil Works Program

For over 50 years, the Corps of Engineers, with its national, multipurpose civil works program, has been the federal government's largest water-resources development and management agency. The current annual federal budget for this program is in excess of $3 billion. The Corps continues to perform extensive military engineering and construction assignments similar to those summarized above, but the authority and budget for its military work is managed through the Department of Defense. The civil works program, however, remains a separate and direct responsibility of the Corps within the Department of the Army, under the civilian supervision of the Assistant Secretary of the Army for Civil Works. The remainder of this chapter is concerned only with the Corps' civil works activities.

To carry out the extensive civil works mission authorized by Con-

Figure 1. Corps of Engineers Divisions and Districts. Source: Corps of Engineers.

gress, the Corps is organized into 11 geographic divisions, with 36 districts and six laboratories (see Figure 1). Division and district boundaries generally follow the watershed boundaries of major river basins, rather than political boundaries, to allow for more efficient water resource planning and management.

Each district has a staff directed by a district commander (also called the district engineer) who is a Corps officer, usually with the rank of colonel. The district engineer reports through a division commander (usually a brigadier general) to the Director of Civil Works at the Office of the Chief of Engineers in Washington, D.C. The Director of Civil Works is usually a major general; he and his headquarters staff report to the Chief of Engineers and to the Assistant Secretary of the Army (Civil Works).

As a lieutenant general, the Chief of Engineers is the Corps' highest ranking officer and has combined authority for both the military and the civil works programs. This chain of command is derived from the Corps' earliest days; it allows Corps officers to transfer back and forth between civil and military duties, gaining experience in both roles as they advance. This structure also allows the Corps to respond quickly to either military or civil emergencies, integrating its work with other Army or National Guard units when necessary.

However, although Corps officers (also known within the agency as "the green suits") are frequently found presiding over the Corps' public meetings or testifying before congressional committees, they number only about 300 in a civil works program that has approximately 28,000 employees. Civilians have for many years performed virtually all of the planning, construction, operation and maintenance, and regulatory functions of the Corps, with engineer officers serving almost exclusively in top management and supervisory positions. Because Corps officers move through these civil works management positions on a fairly short (three- to five-year) rotation, the career civilian employees are almost always more familiar with the people, the problems, and the projects in Corps districts than are the officers. The Corps has recently adopted a policy that strengthens the relationship between civilian managers and specific Corps projects by "marrying" the managers to their projects for the life of the project, including the planning, engineering, and construction phases. Given the fact that major civil works projects have often taken 15 to 25 or more years to complete, Corps project managers are likely in the future to spend much of their careers on a few assignments in a single district.

Principal Activities

The civil works program has always been primarily concerned with increasing the development and use of the nation's surface water resources. Beginning with navigation improvements, Congress has gradually expanded the Corps' responsibilities to include flood-control and floodplain management, hydropower, and water supply and irrigation; in addition, the Corps has gained recreation, natural resource management, and other functions. All these activities are supported by a multidisciplinary research program. The Corps' major activities are described below.[4]

Navigation. Since the early 19th century, the Corps has completed over 1,500 navigation projects of various types. The Corps now maintains some 12,000 miles of commercially navigable inland and intracoastal waterways. This system serves 41 states and includes 226 navigation locks operated by the Corps. From 1981 through 1986, an average of more than 500 million tons of cargo moved via the inland waterways (see Table 1). Major navigation projects currently under construction include the $950 million replacement of Lock and Dam 26 on the upper Mississippi River, and the $200 million construction of a new lock at Bonneville on the Columbia River east of Portland, Oregon.

4. Unless otherwise indicated, the program descriptions and statistics given here are taken from the Secretary of the Army's Annual Report on Civil Works Activities for fiscal years 1986 and 1987 (Corps 1987, 1988b), and from an unpublished 1988 Corps report to the Council on Environmental Quality obtained from the Office of the Chief of Engineers (Corps 1988c). The latest reported data, usually FY 1987, are used.

Table 1. U.S. Inland Waterway Traffic Total Commodity Movements, 1981 to 1986 (in thousand tons).

Total traffic	1981	1982	1983	1984	1985	1986
Farm products	78,066	85,266	84,732	80,006	70,567	67,565
Metallic ore/prod./scrap	14,812	8,242	8,835	12,537	14,128	14,922
Coal	138,812	131,004	125,811	154,436	147,119	163,127
Crude petroleum	35,290	34,663	35,527	38,664	40,925	43,913
Non-metallic min/prod.	58,761	56,272	59,957	70,253	75,593	75,231
Lumber, Wood prod., & pulp	18,572	16,449	15,690	19,141	17,638	20,073
Industrial chemicals	26,977	23,193	25,315	28,954	29,556	32,895
Agricultural chemicals	8,095	7,269	10,509	12,393	11,225	12,806
Petroleum products	111,073	101,921	98,851	103,521	100,429	107,463
All other commodities	30,211	31,214	21,905	22,598	27,478	22,504
Total	520,669	495,453	487,132	542,503	534,658	560,499

Source: *Waterborne Commerce of the United States.*

The Corps also maintains 88 major commercial harbors (those with 2 million or more tons of commerce annually) and more than 400 smaller harbors. To maintain these channels and harbors, the Corps dredges—and thus must dispose of—more than 300 million cubic yards of material each year. As a comparison, that is 1.5 times the total volume of material excavated to construct the Panama Canal. Or, as a Corps general stated at a recent workshop on beneficial uses of dredged material (Hatch 1987), 300 million cubic yards is enough material to cover the city of Washington, D.C., each year to a depth of five feet.

In the past, this dredged material has often been used to fill wetlands and other flood-prone areas; in Washington, D.C., the land forming the Tidal Basin and the site of the Lincoln Memorial, as well as that of National Airport, is fill material that was dredged from the Potomac River by the Corps. But growing public concern over the continuing loss of wetlands and the water quality impacts of dredged material disposal led Congress to direct the Corps to conduct a five-year, $33 million research program on dredged material and on the physical, chemical, and biological impacts of disposal alternatives. Partly as a result of that research, which was managed by the Corps' Waterways Experiment Station at Vicksburg, Mississippi, the Corps has used dredged material to construct more than 10,000 acres of fresh and salt water wetlands and marshes, and nearly 2,000 coastal islands that provide habitat for birds and other wildlife. The Corps has also revised its regulations for dredging (33 C.F.R. 335–338) to encourage such beneficial uses. A new multiyear dredging research program was begun in 1988; however, controversy continues over selection of specific disposal methods and sites.

Flood Control and Floodplain Management. Since the Flood Control Act of 1936 was enacted, over $13 billion has been spent by the Corps and other federal agencies on structural flood control measures, such as levees and floodwalls, dams and reservoirs, and river channel alterations. By the end of FY 1987 the Corps had completed over 870 such flood control projects. Although they have certainly saved many lives, and protected many billions of dollars of property from flood damage or destruction, these projects also have displaced thousands of residents from their homes, flooded productive farmland, and eliminated natural resources such as native fish populations, bottomland-hardwood forests, and wetlands. As a result, flood-control projects have probably generated more public controversy than any other Corps construction activity.

Nowhere else in the nation have the flood control efforts of the Corps been as ambitious as in the alluvial valley of the lower Mississippi River, from Cairo, Illinois, south to the Gulf of Mexico (see Figure 2a). In order to protect major low-lying urban areas such as Memphis, Natchez, and New Orleans from periodic flooding, the Corps has re-channeled, leveed, and otherwise "engineered" nearly the entire drainage basin to accommodate, in theory, a maximum or "project design" flood greater than the record flood of 1927—a flood that at its peak would discharge about three million cubic feet per second of water into the Gulf of Mexico through four principal outlets (see Figure 2b). Perhaps the most controversial feature of this grand design, collectively called the Mississippi River and Tributaries Project, has been the plan to divert up to half the volume of floodwaters into the huge wetland area of the Atchafalaya River basin, via the West Atchafalaya and Morganza floodways. Before the Corps built the Old River Control Structure above Baton Rouge, the younger Atchafalaya River was gradually, through natural processes, capturing the flow of the Mississippi River. This capture, which had been considered likely to become complete in this century, would have reduced the Mississippi river below its entry point into the Atchafalaya to a tidal estuary, isolating Baton Rouge and New Orleans from access to commercial navigation (Mississipi River Commission 1976). Construction of the Old River Control Structure was authorized by Congress in 1954. During a major flood in 1973, the control structure and the Morganza floodway, another project feature, were used as designed to divert floodwaters into the 800,000-acre Atchafalaya basin.

Levees were also built in the basin during the 1930s and 1940s to establish the Morganza and Atchafalaya floodways. Since the river's sediment load, formerly dispersed throughout the lower basin by floods, was subsequently retained between the levees, the Corps in the 1960s began to dredge a central channel in the lower Atchafalaya to keep the floodway from silting up. But these activities also dried up much of the wetlands surrounding the channel, which eliminated much of the area's commercial crawfish production and encouraged clearing

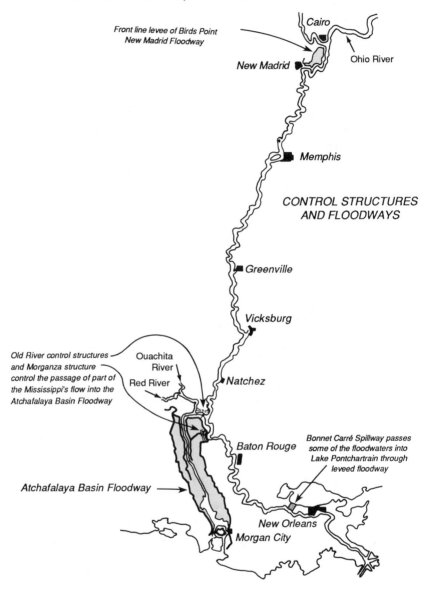

Figure 2a. Corps of Engineers Facilities in the Lower Mississippi River Valley.

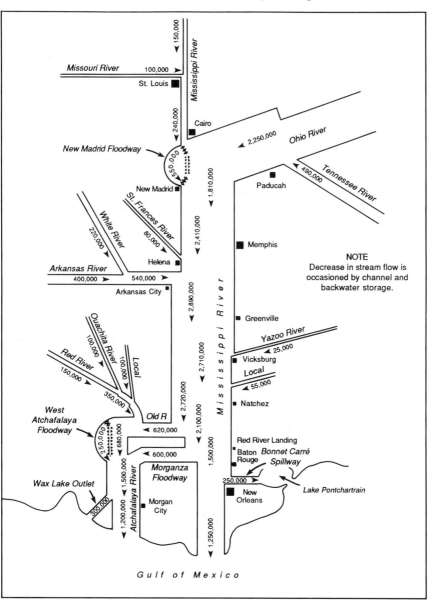

Figure 2b. Project Design Flood for the Lower Mississippi River Valley (flow estimates are in cubic feet per second).

of the land for agriculture and settlement. Amidst growing controversy, the dredging was stopped in 1968.

In 1971 the Corps agreed to prepare an environmental impact statement on the project, and after considerable discussion a federal/state interagency management group was formed in 1972, led by the Corps and including representatives of the Environmental Protection Agency (EPA), the Fish and Wildlife Service, and the state of Louisiana.[5] This group was to conduct studies and develop a multipurpose program for managing the Atchafalaya basin to better protect its flood-control, environmental, recreational, cultural, and economic values (Agency Management Group 1978). Plans were developed to protect large wetland areas in the basin by combining outright purchases with multipurpose easements; after much public debate, the Corps submitted to Congress in 1983 a final environmental impact statement and management plan. In the Water Resources Development Act of 1986 (Public Law 99–662), Congress authorized the environmental elements of the plan; however, only a small fraction of the federal and state funds required to implement these environmental features has been appropriated to date.

Meanwhile, other elements of the Mississippi River and Tributaries project are being funded, including a controversial project, authorized in 1936, to drain a substantial portion of the four-million-acre Yazoo River Delta north of Vicksburg, Mississippi. Much of this area is wetland and bottomland–hardwood forest that serves as winter habitat for migratory waterfowl; part of the Yazoo National Wildlife Refuge already has been drained by the project (Antypas 1988). The Yazoo project was originally authorized to make flood-prone land more suitable for crop production, but draining wetlands for this purpose appears to be inconsistent with more recent federal policies contained in Section 404 of the Clean Water Act and in the "swampbuster" provisions of the 1985 Farm Act; both of these laws are intended to protect wetlands from unnecessary development or alteration. To date, the Corps has spent approximately $1.2 billion on the Yazoo Basin project; the current estimated cost to complete the project as planned is $709 million (Schwartz 1989). Environmental groups and some local property owners are seeking to have the project halted or reformulated to reduce the further loss of wetland and wildlife resources.

Altogether, approximately $6 billion of federal funds have been spent so far on the Mississippi River and Tributaries Project; the Corps estimates that the project has prevented more than $110 billion in flood damages. One may question the accuracy of such estimates, and point out that the natural resource, recreational, and other values lost as a result of the project are usually not considered in the benefit-cost

---

5. See Reuss 1988 for a more detailed historical analysis of the development of the Atchafalaya project.

analysis. Nevertheless, it is a fact that structural flood control measures protect, and even attract, economic development in flood hazard areas. Such projects often reduce the probability of damage from small to moderate floods, but may increase the potential risk to life and property from large infrequent floods that exceed the limits of protection for which the projects were designed.

The obvious alternative to building structures to keep floodwaters away from people and property is to keep people and property away from areas subject to frequent flooding. In order to reduce unwise use of floodplains and to encourage communities to avoid future flood hazards, the Corps has in recent years provided increased flood hazard information, technical assistance, and planning guidance upon request to states, local governments, and individuals. During FY 1986 the Corps responded to over 82,000 inquiries about floodplain development (Corps 1987). The Corps also cooperates with the Federal Emergency Management Agency in conducting joint hurricane evacuation studies for high-hazard coastal areas.

Section 73 of the Water Resources Development Act of 1974 authorizes federal agencies to consider as part of their own project planning the use of nonstructural alternatives to reduce flood damages, including acquisition of floodplain lands for public purposes, floodplain regulation, and relocation of existing structures. However, to date the Corps has fully implemented this approach in only two of its own projects—the Charles River Watershed in Massachusetts, where large wetland areas were purchased to serve as natural storage sites for flood waters, and Prairie du Chien on the upper Mississippi River in Wisconsin, where buildings in an historic, but flood-prone, area were either relocated or purchased and removed to avoid future flood damage. In recent years Congress, in an effort to reduce the federal costs of flood control, has been increasing the percentage of the costs of such projects that must be borne by local beneficiaries. As the local cost-share of federal flood-control projects rises, nonstructural alternatives may become more attractive to local interests because they often can be less expensive and more quickly implemented than large structural projects.

Hydropower. Many of the multipurpose impoundments built by the Corps have included hydropower facilities. In 1986, the Corps operated powerplants at 70 locations with a capacity of 20,000 megawatts; these plants produced nearly 30 percent of the nation's hydropower, or 3.5 percent of the total electric energy generated in the nation that year (Corps 1988b).

Because water can be stored in reservoirs during periods of relatively low power demand and then released quickly to meet peak-period demand, hydropower is being increasingly used as a source of "peaking power" to reduce peak-period demands on plants using fossil and nuclear fuels, thereby allowing them to operate more efficiently as sources of base-load electric power. The demand for hydropower during peak periods led the Corps to advocate construction of pumped-storage facilities at the Dickey-Lincoln School Lakes on the St. Johns River in Maine, the existing Truman Dam in Missouri, and the Richard Russell Dam on the Savannah River between Georgia and South Carolina. Pumped-storage involves two dams: the lower dam retains water released from the upper dam to generate power during peak periods; excess power from other plants is used during low-demand periods (usually at night) to pump water from the lower reservoir back up behind the upper dam, where it is released again during the next peak period.

The rapid fluctuations in reservoir levels at pumped-storage facilities cause shoreline erosion and hamper recreational uses, while the repeated reversing passage of water through turbines and pumps destroys fish caught in the process. After massive fish kills at the Truman Dam in 1982, use of the project's reversible turbines was suspended. The Dickey-Lincoln project was first modified to eliminate pumped-storage and finally de-authorized in 1986. In 1988, several environmental groups and state agencies filed suit to block installation of the pump-turbines at the Russell Dam; the matter is still under legal review. The Corps is now studying ways to protect fish and other aquatic life from damage at pumped-storage hydropower projects.

The Corps has been reviewing other existing dam sites for the feasibility of adding hydropower generation where it does not already exist. In most cases, however, state and local governments and private interests are being encouraged to develop facilities at Corps sites without additional federal financial assistance. In one recent case, at the Town Bluff Dam on the Neches River in Texas, the local power authority contracted with the Corps to add a hydropower plant to the existing dam, after agreeing to pay the full construction costs.

Water Supply and Irrigation. Although the Corps is not authorized to build projects with municipal and industrial water supply or irrigation as their primary purposes, these functions may be incorporated into multipurpose projects. In the West, water for irrigation from Corps reservoirs is available in accordance with the provisions of the Reclamation Act of 1902. In growing urban areas, Corps reservoirs have become increasingly important water sources; members of Congress from these areas are often quite agressive in seeking to have Corps projects with water storage capacity built in their districts. At present, some 115 Corps impoundments can store more than 275 million acre-feet[6] of water for irrigation, municipal, and industrial uses (Corps 1988b). Rapid population growth in urban areas of the Southwest is

---

6. An acre-foot of water is a volume that would cover one acre of surface area to a depth of one foot—or approximately 326,000 gallons.

shifting the demand for water from irrigation to municipal use; as groundwater supplies are depleted by both uses, conflicts will grow over the allocation of limited surface water resources. Surface water already provides about 60 percent of the water used for irrigation nationwide and about 65 percent of public water supplies (Corps 1988b). Pressure on the Corps to impound more surface water will in turn raise environmental concerns about further disturbances of free-flowing rivers, riparian habitat, and their associated recreational and wildlife values.

Recreation and Natural Resource Management. The most popular public benefit provided by the Corps' civil works program is recreation. Like water supply, recreation is a secondary, or "add-on" purpose for Corps projects; but the Corps has established more than 4,400 recreation areas at 472 impoundments and other Corps projects in 42 states. The Corps manages about 2,500 of these areas directly; the rest are managed by other federal, state, or local agencies through cooperative agreements (Corps 1988a).

During each of the last two fiscal years for which data are available (1986 and 1987), approximately 167 million visitor days[7] were recorded at these recreation areas. This level of use, which is more than one-fourth of the total annual visits to all federal lands, makes the Corps the second largest federal provider of recreation in the United States, surpassed only by the Forest Service. The combination of access to water and proximity of many projects to urban areas helps account for the popularity of Corps recreation areas. During FY 1987, Corps projects collected $13.4 million in visitor-use fees (Corps 1988c).

Providing recreational opportunities is only a part of the Corps' natural resources management program. The management objectives for the land and water included in Corps projects include:

- meeting authorized project objectives
- conservation of vegetation, soils, and wildlife
- protection of cultural resources
- protection and development of recreational opportunities

The total amount of land and water managed as part of Corps projects breaks down approximately as follows:

3.4 million acres of water in fee ownership
1.9 million acres of water in easement or river bed
4.2 million acres of land in fee above summer pool levels
1.9 million acres of land in easement above summer pool levels
Total: 11.4 million acres

7. The Corps records recreational use in visitor-hours and visitor-days; each "visit" is roughly equivalent to one person spending 3.5 hours at a recreational facility.

Table 2. Land Management by Type at Corps of Engineers Civil Works Projects (in thousands of acres).

Corps division	Project operations	Intensive recreation	Low density recreation	Natural areas	Wildlife management	Reserve forest	Intensive forest management	Range management
New England	4.45	2.41	38.14	0.002	36.28	24.46	2.84	0.83
North Atlantic	9.07	6.95	26.23	8.72	21.47	21.45	0.0	0.0
South Atlantic	69.22	112.22	102.95	37.65	353.37	169.08	13.52	0.0
Ohio River	61.69	88.28	393.29	9.47	477.40	167.77	0.0	0.0
North Central	2.64	14.83	25.20	1.50	155.73	57.75	1.20	2.18
Lower Mississippi Valley	5.61	53.91	221.09	10.73	347.45	126.04	2.77	0.002
Southwest	105.19	214.47	564.56	65.57	1,107.33	121.87	74.77	47.09
Missouri River	20.24	103.77	191.81	2.55	470.31	75.00	0.04	131.68
North Pacific	26.00	21.63	20.82	9.41	82.47	14.00	0.0	0.0
South Pacific	44.25	24.53	21.83	12.82	28.68	5.00	0.0	5.62
Total: 6901.15	348.36	643.00	1605.92	158.42	3080.49	782.42	95.14	187.40
Percent of total	5.05	9.32	23.27	2.30	44.64	11.34	1.38	2.72

Source: Office of the Chief of Engineers, data as of May 1987 (Corps 1988a).
Note: The total Corps land acreage shown in this table (6.3 million acres) exceeds the total land acreage given in the text (6.1 million acres) because the table includes some areas classified in the text as water.

To manage these land and water resources, the Corps has approximately 2,600 permanent and 1,800 temporary employees. The Corps employs approximately 1,100 rangers and land managers with degrees in natural resources, engineering, and other specialties, and another 800 rangers in temporary or seasonal positions; the remainder of the management staff is in maintenance and support positions. In addition, the Corps benefits from the services of more than 48,000 part-time volunteers who assist the natural resource management program in a wide range of activities, including water safety, interpretation of natural and historic features, tree plantings, and restoration of fish and wildlife habitat (Corps 1988a).

Corps lands are managed for a variety of specific purposes. A breakdown of the approximate acreage in the principal management categories for each of the Corps' 11 civil works divisions is shown in Table 2. This table shows that overall, only about 15 percent of all Corps project lands are intensively used, for project operations, recreation, or forest management; over half the total acreage is managed for wildlife habitat or forest reserves, and nearly one-fourth of project lands is available for low-density recreation.

Regulatory Functions.   The current regulatory program of the Corps of Engineers is based on three primary statutory authorities (see Figure 3 for a schematic representation of the coverage of these laws):

Section 10 of the Rivers and Harbors Act of 1899. Section 10 prohibits placing of structures (such as piers, bulkheads, weirs, jetties, pipelines, or cables) in or over *navigable* waters of the United States without a permit from the Corps (33 U.S.C.A. 403). This statute also regulated the placement of dredged material in open waters and some wetlands before 1972.

Section 103 of the Marine Protection, Research, and Sanctuaries Act of 1972. Also known as the Ocean Dumping Act, Section 103 prohibits transport of dredged or other materials in *ocean* waters for the purpose of dumping without first obtaining a permit from the Corps (33 U.S.C.A. 1401 *et seq.*).

Section 404 of the Clean Water Act of 1972. Section 404 prohibits the *discharge* of any dredged or fill material into *all* waters of the United States without first obtaining a permit from the Corps (33 U.S.C.A. 1344).

The Corps also retains responsibility under Section 13 of the 1899 Rivers and Harbors Act (33 U.S.C.A. 407) to regulate the discharge of refuse into *navigable* waters of the United States. As will be discussed further, the Corps' reluctance to regulate discharge activities pursuant to the broader scope of the Clean Water Act (all waters of the United States) rather than that of the 1899 act (navigable waters) has been a

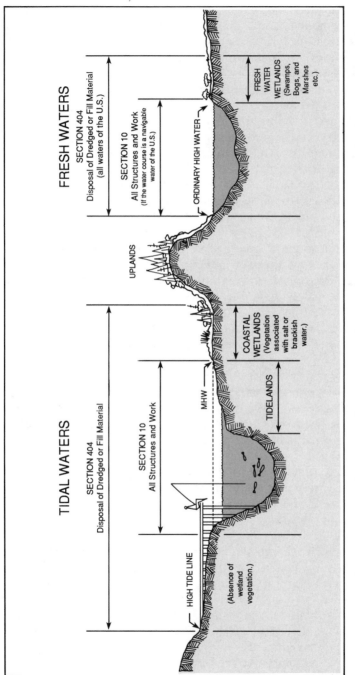

Figure 3. Corps of Engineers Regulatory Jurisdiction. Typical activities requiring permits under Section 10: Marinas, piers, wharves, floats, intake pipes, outfall pipes, pilings, bulkheads, boat ramps, dredging, marine railways, dolphins, fills, overhead transmission lines, etc.; Section 404: Discharge of dredged material, fills, groins, breakwaters, road fills, beach nourishment, rip-rap, jetties, etc.; Section 103: Ocean discharge of dredged material. Source: U. S. Army Corps of Engineers.

source of continuing tension between the Corps and conservation organizations urging federal agencies to provide greater protection of wetlands. There have also been technical disagreements among the Corps, EPA, and the Fish and Wildlife Service regarding the delineation of wetlands for regulatory purposes under Section 404.

Despite the issues of jurisdiction and wetlands definition and identification, the Corps has an active nationwide regulatory program. Measured simply in terms of numbers of individual permit applications received, the program's activity has apparently stabilized at the level of about 15,000 applications per year after declining from a peak of more than 21,000 applications in FY 1977. But this is due in part to the Corps' promotion of the use of regional and nationwide permits for certain activities, such as pipeline and cable crossings, assumed to have insignificant effects on surface waters (33 CFR 330). Regional and nationwide permits are, in effect, published categorical exemptions to the requirement to obtain an individual permit; a discharge activity that meets the conditions specified in the exemption is permitted without the filing of a separate permit application. Corps regulatory program staff in Washington, D.C., estimate that regional permits are utilized (that is, cited as authority for permitting construction activities in wetlands or open waters) about 21,000 times a year and that national permits are similarly utilized about 75,000 times each year.

For activities requiring individual permits, the distribution and trend of applications to the Corps for permits under the three principal statutes is given in Table 3 below. (The tabulated data represent applications for individual permits only; they do not include requests for approval of activities covered by regional or nationwide permits.)[8]

Table 3. Applications Received for Individual Permits.

FY	Section 10 only	Sections 10 and 103	Sections 10 and 404	Section 404 only	Total permits
1977	10,246	36	7,173	3,581	21,036
1978	8,539	24	6,967	3,097	18,627
1979	8,936	38	7,174	3,022	19,170
1980	7,569	19	7,128	2,969	17,685
1981	7,928	58	7,200	3,518	18,704
1982	7,437	101	6,596	3,028	17,162
1983	5,959	52	5,614	2,871	14,446
1984	5,335	41	5,361	2,769	13,506
1985	5,415	59	5,182	3,282	13,938
1986	5,570	53	5,302	3,484	14,419
1987	5,654	50	4,706	3,981	14,391
1988	n.a.	n.a.	n.a.	n.a.	15,402

Source: Office of the Chief of Engineers, December 1988.
  n.a. = not available.

The Corps' annual appropriations for its regulatory program were $55 million for FY 1987, $55.3 million for FY 1988, and $60.4 million for FY 1989. At these levels it is the smallest of the separate line-item programs in the Corps budget (see further budget discussion below). During FY 1987, the regulatory program received 14,391 new individual permit applications, and carried over 5,429 from the previous year. From this combined total of 19,820 applications, 3,323 were withdrawn; 6,931 permits, and 2,752 letters of permission were issued. Only 477 permits were denied; the remaining applications were carried over to FY 1988. In addition, 5,903 alleged violations of permits or otherwise illegal actions were reported (Corps 1988c).

The Corps employs approximately 900 people in its regulatory program. Of this number, 12 are in the Washington office, another 15 work at the division, or regional, level, and all the rest are stationed in the district offices. The number of regulatory program staff per district office is related to the amount of permit activity, and varies from about 6, in the Albuquerque and Tulsa districts, to about 50 in the Jacksonville and New Orleans districts. Many of the Corps' regulatory staff have degrees in biology or related professional disciplines.

In response to the Reagan Administration's efforts to achieve regulatory reforms, the Corps' regulatory program has sought to reduce the average time for processing an individual permit application to approximately 60 days. Corps field staff say that as a result of this effort, less time can be spent reviewing permit applications or negotiating permit conditions that could avoid or reduce the adverse impacts of the activity on streams or wetlands. The related issues of wetland protection and mitigation of adverse impacts are examined further below.

Research and Development. The Corps maintains several research facilities to support its civil works mission. The activities of these research institutions are focused primarily on flood control and navigation, coastal engineering, and water-resources planning. The principal activities of these facilities are summarized briefly here.

Waterways Experiment Station (WES), Vicksburg, Mississippi. This is the Corps' largest research, testing, and development facility. The station has the world's largest hydraulics laboratory, where both physical and mathematical models of waterways and structures are tested. The station also has a structures laboratory that conducts research on technology for repair, evaluation, maintenance, and rehabilitation of existing projects and equipment. Its Environmental Laboratory sponsors a wide range of environmental studies, including work on wetlands and bottomland forest delineation, and on water quality impacts of Corps activities.

8. The Corps does not review or require reporting of the activities covered by nationwide permits; hence, there is no accurate record of the number of wetland-related activities occurring under the "cover" of these general permits.

Field Research Facility, Duck, North Carolina. This facility, operated by WES, conducts a wide range of studies related to the measurement of natural coastal and oceanic processes, including changes that occur during severe storms.

Construction Engineering Research Laboratory, Champaign, Illinois. The laboratory does research on methods of construction management, building design, and project operations management; computer communications and programming applications are also developed there.

Cold Regions Research and Engineering Laboratory, Hanover, New Hampshire. Research at Cold Regions includes a River Ice Management Program and other work on ice problems at navigation locks and on barges. The laboratory also conducts research for the Army on ways to improve its winter transportation and combat capabilities.

Institute for Water Resources (IWR), Ft. Belvoir, Virginia. The institute provides a variety of services to Corps programs, including water resources planning research, navigation analysis, policy studies, training, and technical assistance. Recent projects have included development and application of techniques for risk analysis, and evaluation manuals for estimating benefits from recreation activities and from deep port improvements.

Other Activities.　The Corps performs a variety of civil works activities for other federal agencies and foreign governments. Among the more significant of these efforts is the review of designs submitted to the Environmental Protection Agency by state and local governments for wastewater treatment plants to be funded by the EPA construction grants program. The Corps also provides on-site managers during construction of some of the larger plants.

The Corps also manages much of the design and execution of toxic waste removal actions under EPA's "Superfund" program, and advises EPA on the feasibility of proposed cleanup and removal actions and techniques.

In August 1988, the Army's Toxic and Hazardous Materials Agency, located at Aberdeen Proving Ground in Maryland, was transferred from the Army's Material Command to the Corps. This agency will continue to have dual responsibilities for cleanup of hazardous waste on Army properties and for research and development of new techniques to detect, evaluate, and treat hazardous materials. The facility will also develop and conduct a safety and environmental training program for Army personnel.

Budget

The budget formulation and appropriations process for the civil works program of the Corps is a complex, esoteric, and almost continuous activity. The Corps develops a tentative budget nearly two years in advance, for review and approval by the Assistant Secretary of the Army for Civil Works and by the Office of Management and Budget on behalf of the President. This preliminary budget reflects an aggregation of funding requests from the Corps field offices. Requests are generally grouped into overall "line item" categories: initial project investigations, construction, operation and maintenance, regulatory program, flood control and coastal emergencies, and general expenses. Also, there has been for many years a separate line item for "Flood Control, Mississippi River and Tributaries," which is a tribute to the political clout of former Congressman William Whittington and former Senators John Oucuton and John Stennis.

After negotiations with the Assistant Secretary's office and with the Office of Management and Budget are completed, the Corps' budget request for the upcoming fiscal year (which begins each October 1) is forwarded to Congress each January as part of the President's overall national budget. The Corp's budget request for FY 1990, as submitted by President Reagan shortly before he left office, was for a total of $3.181 billion (see Table 4).

Table 4. Corps Civil Works Budget Request for FY 1990.

General Investigations	$126,108,000
Construction, General	1,201,790,000
Operation and Maintenance, General	1,282,622,000
Regulatory program	69,427,000
Flood Control, Mississippi River and Tributaries	337,000,000
General Expenses	128,000,000
Permanent Appropriations (fees, etc.)	12,000,000
Revolving Fund	23,000,000
Total Appropriations Request	**$3,180,747,000**

The official budget submission shows this $3.1 billion request to be reduced by $41.1 million in offsetting receipts; however, nearly half that amount is contingent upon the enactment of proposed legislation that would increase a variety of user fees. The other half comes from a variety of existing fees and revenue sources.

As aggregate numbers, the funds requested in the above categories do not vary significantly from the amounts appropriated by Congress for the last two fiscal years. However, Army Assistant Secretary Robert Page's testimony before Congress indicated that this budget contained a 20 percent reduction in funds for the operation and maintenance of recreation facilities provided by the Corps (Page 1989). He stated that this reduced funding level would require reductions in recreation services at 654 Corps sites in 41 states, including closure or transfer of 426 of those sites. Congress must now decide whether to accept this reduction. Given the popularity of Corps recreation facilities, and the number of states and congressional districts that would be affected, the recommended reduction is unlikely to be enacted.

The number of "new starts" for water projects proposed in each budget has always been an important indicator to the Corps and to its supporters in Congress of the vitality of the public works program. The 1990 budget request proposes new starts in three categories: under "General Investigations," 31 new project surveys and 31 preconstruction engineering and design studies are listed; under "Construction, General," funds are requested to initiate construction on 10 new projects (and continuing construction on 132 others); under "Flood Control, Mississippi River and Tributaries," one new design study and one new construction start are proposed.

This aggregate budget request, as usual, is accompanied by a bound volume of over 100 pages, in which most of the proposed expenditures are broken down to the level of individual project activities, listed on a state-by-state basis (Department of the Army 1989). The principal purpose of this document is to provide all members of Congress with an indication of how and where the Corps expects to disperse these funds if they are appropriated at the requested levels. Some critics have referred to this publication as the annual best-seller, "Pork-barrel in Paperback."

As an illustration, a review of the funding requests listed on a per-state basis for the categories of Surveys, Preconstruction Engineering and Design, Construction, and Operation and Maintenance, reveals that over $420 million, or approximately 14 percent of the nationwide total budget request for these categories, is for activities in the three contiguous states of Alabama, Louisiana, and Mississippi. It is no coincidence that the chairmen of the relevant Senate and House appropriations subcommittees are from Louisiana and Alabama, respectively. This shows that the Corps of Engineers and the President's Office of Management and Budget both respect Washington's version of the Golden Rule: the ones who distribute the gold make the rules.

However, despite the impressive sum requested for the lower Mississippi region over the past twelve years, if adjusted to correct for inflation, the total funds appropriated for construction have been declining steadily, and since FY 1984 have been less than the amount appropriated for operation and maintenance. This surprising shift is in part an attempt to deal with the enormous budget deficit, and in part reflects the growing need to maintain and rebuild the existing physical infrastructure of civil works projects, including thousands of miles of river channels and levees, many aging locks and dams, and even some heavily used recreation facilities.

Table 5 shows the FY 1987 breakdown of civil works expenditures by region. This table shows a rather broad geographic distribution of

Table 5. FY 1987 Civil Works Expenditures by Division (in thousands of dollars).

Division	General investigations	Construction, general	Operation and maintenance, general	Flood control, Miss. River and tribs.	General expenses	Flood control and coastal emergencies	Permanent appropriations	Rivers and harbors contributed funds	Total
New England	2,277	5,201	24,703	—	673	146	133	596	33,729
North Atlantic	14,765	54,830	126,248	—	5,102	1,182	400	30,158	232,685
South Atlantic	10,235	125,190	199,485	—	5,122	3,014	867	14,069	357,982
Ohio River	12,129	164,452	165,106	—	7,365	1,072	1,867	5,664	357,655
North Central	9,448	54,906	201,569	—	7,768	8,023	267	7,483	289,464
Lower Mississippi Valley	7,734	226,214	131,934	285,597	9,047	3,121	467	3,906	668,070
Southwestern	14,046	95,039	188,528	—	7,140	1,551	3,001	9,754	319,059
Missouri River	3,532	18,189	77,943	—	3,821	3,734	1,267	1,986	110,492
North Pacific	8,649	126,506	161,537	—	5,905	4,667	1,000	245	308,509
South Pacific	18,704	67,226	67,346	—	5,938	12,096	985	12,299	184,594
Pacific Ocean	953	7,545	3,837	—	582	158	0	510	13,585
Headquarters Oversight and Centralized Support	21,783	13,351	20,815	—	54,813	77	6,867	—	117,706
Total	124,255	958,649	1,369,101	285,597	113,276	38,861	17,121	86,670	2,993,530

Source: Corps of Engineers 1988b.

expenditures, with emphasis on construction and operations in the Mississippi and Ohio river basins, followed by the South Atlantic and Southwestern regions.

CORPS PROJECT PLANNING AND CONSTRUCTION

Congress has given the Corps of Engineers continuing authority to undertake certain small-scale activities without specific legislation or appropriations. These activities include emergency assistance during natural disasters, responding to local requests for flood hazard information and floodplain management assistance, and constructing several types of small projects for flood control, navigation, and beach erosion control. This authority was redefined, and dollar limitations specified, in the 1986 Water Resources Development Act (P.L. 99–662). The types of projects covered, and their cost limitations, are summarized in Table 6.

Table 6. Continuing Authorities Program.[a]

Types of projects	Short name	Statutory federal cost limitation per project	Catalog of Federal Domestic Assistance reference number
Flood damage reduction	Section 205	$ 5,000,000	12.106
Snagging and clearing for flood control	Section 208	500,000	12.108
Navigation	Section 107	4,000,000	12.107
Clearing and snagging for navigation	Section 3	None[b]	12.109
Beach erosion	Section 103	2,000,000	12.105
Emergency streambank and shoreline protection	Section 14	500,000	12.105

[a] Under P.L. 99–662, Congress delegated its authority to approve certain projects, up to specified dollar amounts (subject to availability of funds) to the Chief of Engineers.

[b] Annual program limit of $1 million.

All *major* federal water resource projects must receive specific two-part legislative approval by Congress: project authorization and appropriation of funds. The complex process by which major projects are planned and constructed is often a source of considerable confusion and frustration to members of the public seeking to make their concerns known in a way that will have some influence on decisions about proposed projects. Some have described the Corps' approach to public involvement prior to the mid-1970s as being an exercise in which the

Corps frequently told concerned citizens that their comments were too early—until all the decisions were made—after which the Corps told the same parties that their comments were too late.

However, the advent of the National Environmental Policy Act (NEPA) and subsequent changes in Corps policy have made the Corps' planning process much more open to the public. Although every project is in some ways unique, the planning and construction process can generally be understood as occurring in six consecutive stages, each having several steps, as outlined below.[9] With a basic understanding of this process, interested citizens should be better able to participate in the Corps' planning process, particularly in the early stages. As is generally true for public involvement in government activity, participation that is timely and informed is more likely to be received favorably, and therefore more likely to be effective in influencing government agency decisions.

Problem Definition Stage

The development of a major Corps public works project begins when a local government, a business interest, or a group of citizens perceives a need for federal assistance to reduce flood damages, improve navigation, control beach erosion, or meet some other water resource-related need. In response to inquiries, staff in the appropriate Corps district office can carry out an initial reconnaissance investigation to determine whether the proposed purpose is one potentially eligible under existing law for Corps assistance. If the request for assistance appears to be for an eligible purpose, then Corps officials will urge the interested parties to contact their congressional representatives to request authorization for a formal study of the problem and potential solutions. The Corps will not undertake a formal study without specific congressional approval. This policy provides the Corps with an external "filter" that selects from many potential civil works projects those that have significant political support.

Study Authorization Stage

The public works committees of the Senate and the House of Representatives hold the keys to the authorization process for new projects. If there have been previous water resource studies and reports for the area in question, a senator or representative may request the appropriate committee to adopt a resolution authorizing the Corps to review previous reports and determine whether new project recommendations

9. This process is summarized in a somewhat different way in Corps publication EP 1105-2-10 (Corps of Engineers 1987a).

are appropriate. If no previous study and report exist, either public works committee can, for the limited purposes listed in Table 6, directly authorize a study by committee resolution.

For major projects, if no previous study has been made, the committee, after receiving advice from the Office of the Chief of Engineers, must decide whether to seek congressional legislation to authorize a feasibility study. Study authorizations are usually grouped together in an "omnibus" bill, along with authorizations for construction of other projects. A project authorization/study bill is customarily generated in alternate, even-numbered (election) years, providing an opportunity for certain members of Congress to demonstrate the power of incumbency to their constituents. Of course, not every congressional district can have a new water project or study every two years; districts with members of Congress on the relevant public works committees are favored, along with districts represented by others who, for a variety of reasons, have influence with public works committee members. Studies may also be authorized individually in separate legislation, but the usual practice is to combine numerous study and new construction requests in one bill to gain wide congressional support for its enactment. Since the purpose of these studies is to develop information regarding the feasibility of potential projects, an effective role for citizens concerned about project impacts would be to recommend to the Corps and to their congressional representatives that language be included in the legislation to require analysis of specific issues and alternatives of concern.

Feasibility Study Stage

Once a study has been authorized by Congress, the task of carrying it out is assigned by the Chief of Engineers (through the Director of Civil Works) to the appropriate division and district engineer. However, as both beneficiaries and opponents of potential projects have learned, a study cannot proceed until funds for that specific purpose have been appropriated by Congress. Because this is done separately through annual appropriations bills for water resources and energy development, there is usually a lag of one or more years between study authorization and study funding. To actually bring about a study, project proponents must during this stage urge their congressional representatives to persuade the House and Senate appropriations committees to fund it; conversely, project opponents can present arguments to the committees for not doing so, particularly where early evidence exists that a potential project would have serious environmental or economic flaws.

Until 1986, the cost of feasibility studies was borne almost totally by the federal government through direct appropriations. But that year, as part of a larger reform of federal water resources development policy (discussed later), Congress enacted a requirement that no new feasibility study be initiated "until appropriate non-federal interests agree, by contract, to contribute 50 percent of the cost for such study during the period of such study" (P.L. 99–662, Sec. 105[1][a]). Although studies of navigation improvements to the inland waterway system are exempted from this cost-sharing requirement, it applies to studies for all other proposed projects. This provision serves as an additional "filter" for project proposals in the planning stages, by helping to limit the number of projects under study to those for which local sponsors are willing to make a significant "front-end" financial commitment.

Once federal and nonfederal funds have been committed to the feasibility study, the responsible Corps office develops a study design that includes analyses of the engineering, economic, environmental, and social aspects of potential project alternatives. The study must be conducted in accordance with the requirements of numerous laws and regulations, including NEPA, and other statutes. Water project studies also are supposed to be guided by an Executive Branch document containing a set of policies and procedures known as the "Principles and Guidelines" for planning federal water resource development activities (U.S. Water Resources Council 1983). This document states that water development projects should be designed to "maximize national economic development, consistent with the goal of protecting the environment" (47 *Federal Register* 12297, March 10, 1983). These guidelines (known as the "Principles and Standards" prior to 1983) were developed by the Water Resources Council (WRC), a federal interagency coordinating council established in 1965 by Congress in the Water Resources Development Act (P.L. 89–80) to bring greater consistency and efficiency to federal water resource planning and development activities (principally those of the Corps of Engineers, the Bureau of Reclamation, the Soil Conservation Service, and the Tennessee Valley Authority). Although WRC was initially viewed by Congress as a means of facilitating water-resource development, it became the focus of executive branch efforts to bring about reforms in federal water policy and planning. During the Carter Administration, WRC incurred the wrath of Congress by supporting greater nonfederal cost-sharing, converting the Principles and Standards into enforceable rules, and proposing to carry out an independent review of plans for proposed water projects. In 1983, the Reagan Administration directed WRC to revise and convert the Principles and Standards back into nonbinding guidelines, and then obtained congressional approval to terminate the agency.[10] However, several of the cost-sharing reform measures advo-

---

10. For further discussion of the controversy over the "Principles and Standards" versus the "Principles and Guidelines" see Barton 1985.

cated by WRC were later included in the 1986 Water Resources Development Act.

NEPA and the regulations of the Council on Environmental Quality (40 C.F.R. 1500–1508) require the Corps to consider environmental values early in the planning process. If the proposed project is likely to have significant environmental impacts, NEPA requires that the Corps prepare and circulate for comment an Environmental Impact Statement (EIS) on the proposed action and a reasonable range of alternatives to it (including a no-action alternative) during the planning process. At this stage the Corps also initiates planning coordination with other federal and nonfederal agencies, and provides other opportunities for public involvement, usually through one or more public meetings where the proposed project and study plan are presented and comments are requested.

If an EIS is to be prepared, the Corps may hold an initial scoping meeting at which concerned parties are invited to discuss the potential environmental impacts and the range of project alternatives to be analyzed. Because the scoping process usually determines which project alternatives and environmental impacts will be evaluated during the remainder of the planning process, it provides an important opportunity for concerned citizens to participate. Unfortunately, relatively few people do so at this stage—perhaps, ironically, because definitive project plans and environmental analyses are not yet available for review. As the study nears completion, the Corps prepares a project master planning document, usually called either a draft feasibility report or draft definite plan report, and a draft EIS. These documents are circulated for comment by other federal and state agencies, elected officials, and the public; one or more public meetings also are usually held by the Corps at this point to publicize plans for the proposed project and to obtain additional informal public comment.

Most major environmental organizations, as well as many individual conservationists, are active participants in the EIS review and comment process. Many projects have been modified, and some terminated altogether, as a result of comments made on EISs. The most effective comments are those that clearly state specific concerns about potential project impacts and contain reasonable recommendations for project modifications or for additional analysis of significant unresolved issues. Commenters need not provide voluminous technical analyses or supporting data, but should make concise arguments, referring to other laws, policies, or technical information where relevant. The Corps prepares most of its EISs and planning documents in-house, at the district level; Corps planning staff are usually receptive to informal discussion of citizen concerns during the EIS preparation stage, either in person or by telephone, and can often provide additional information in response to questions.

Review and Authorization Stage

After the review and comment period for the draft feasibility report and EIS has closed, the Corps district planning office reviews comments received, prepares responses, and develops a proposed final feasibility report and EIS. The district engineer then forwards these revised documents to the appropriate division engineer's office, where they undergo technical review. After the division engineer determines that the documents are satisfactory, they must be sent either to the Mississippi River Commission (MRC) in Vicksburg, Mississippi, for projects in that region, or to the Washington Level Review Center (WLRC) at Ft. Belvoir, Virginia, for all other Corps projects for review, comment, and recommendation to the Chief of Engineers. The reviewing entity (WLRC or MRC) submits its recommendations and the proposed final project report to the Chief of Engineers. The Chief's office then requests final comments from the heads of federal agencies and the governors of states affected by the project, and seeks to resolve any outstanding issues. During this time the final EIS is filed with the Environmental Protection Agency and released to the public. This is the point at which other federal agency heads may formally refer projects to the President's Council on Environmental Quality for review of controversial environmental issues; it is also the first point at which legal challenges to the adequacy of the EIS may be heard in federal courts.

For projects approved by the Chief of Engineers, there is a final administrative approval step prior to requesting congressional authorization. The project documents and the Chief's report are sent to the office of the Assistant Secretary of the Army for Civil Works; in accordance with Executive Order 12322 (46 *Federal Register* 46561), issued by President Reagan in September 1981, that office then seeks clearance from the President's Office of Management and Budget to submit the final project report and a request for authorizing legislation to Congress on behalf of the President.

Administration approval of new projects has been an issue of considerable controversy for many years. Because each new project authorized by Congress establishes a basis for new expenditures of federal funds, usually in the millions of dollars, recent presidents have often prohibited the official submission of such requests to Congress. However, once completed, project plans become public documents; until the mid-1970s, these documents frequently found their way to Capitol Hill and formed the basis for legislation passed by Congress authorizing new water projects that lacked administration approval. Between 1976 and 1986, threats of a presidential veto restrained Congress from authorizing many new projects; the 1986 Water Resources Development Act (discussed later) authorized many new projects and project studies, but was supported by the Reagan Administration largely because it incorporated numerous policy changes and cost-sharing provisions long sought by the Executive Branch to control the proliferation of "pork-barrel" projects.

Advanced Planning and Design Stage

As with study authorizations, once a Corps project has been authorized by Congress, it must await the appropriation of funds via the annual budget process, and the completion of cost-sharing agreements with local project sponsors. Hundreds of authorized Corps projects remain "on the books" but have never been constructed because one of these two vital steps has not occurred. Although feasibility studies provide the basis for project authorizations, there is usually a great deal of detailed engineering and design work to be completed before acquisition of land and actual construction work can begin. As in the project study phase, Corps districts submit annual budget requests for preconstruction engineering and design funds; the offices of the Chief of Engineers and the Assistant Secretary of the Army then negotiate with the Office of Management and Budget to devise a consolidated budget request that is submitted to Congress each year. Large construction projects may require several years of engineering and design work before the Corps is ready to seek the much larger appropriations required for actual project construction.

As an approximation, planning, engineering, and design costs combined usually amount to less than 10 percent of the total cost of a major Corps construction project. During this advanced design stage, problems sometimes arise that require significant changes in the original project plan (for example, unforeseen geologic or hydrologic characteristics or adverse environmental impacts at a proposed construction site that would require the relocation of a dam or a levee). If the proposed change is of sufficient scale, it may require an amendment to the original legislative authorization, and a revision of, or supplement to, the original environmental impact statement. In this case, the feasibility study and review/authorization phases are in essence repeated to obtain public and congressional approval for a modified project design.

Construction Stage

Project construction, like the study and design stages, requires specific appropriations from Congress. Administration support for appropriations to begin construction has been of vital importance since 1978, when President Carter successfully vetoed the public works appropriations bill for fiscal year 1979 on the grounds that it included funding for more than two dozen water projects that did not meet his minimum economic or environmental standards (Council on Environmental Quality 1979). This action marked the beginning of a reassertion of Executive Branch control over the public works appropriations process, and the beginning of federal water policy reforms that have been continued by successive administrations. Both Presidents Carter and Reagan made the adoption by Congress of rules for increased nonfederal cost-sharing their price for including construction funds to initiate "new starts" for water projects in their annual budgets.

Additional factors influencing congressional priorities for construction funding include public controversy over potential environmental impacts. National and local environmental organizations often provide the appropriations committees with testimony or other analyses of controversial water projects. At this stage, grassroots letter writing and lobbying by constituents from the affected congressional districts can be particularly effective. Faced with growing demands for reduction of the federal deficit, members of Congress are becoming increasingly reluctant to vote in favor of large expenditures for water projects that are seen as having dubious economic or environmental benefits. Even after construction has begun, an effective case can sometimes be made to Congress to terminate or modify major projects. In the early 1970s, public opposition to the Corps' proposed Tocks Island Dam on the upper Delaware River caused Congress to order a restudy of the project, which led to the termination of construction and conversion of lands acquired for the project into a national recreation area administered by the National Park Service.

When administrative and legislative efforts to modify authorized projects have not succeeded, the federal courts have sometimes provided an effective forum for project opponents, particularly where the planning process has failed to meet substantive or procedural standards required by law. The Cross-Florida Barge Canal and a proposed dam and reservoir in the Red River Gorge in Kentucky are both Corps projects that were terminated after suits filed in federal court highlighted major environmental problems. The replacement of Lock and Dam 26 on the Mississippi River near Alton, Illinois, was halted by litigation, and a revised, scaled-down project was subsequently authorized by Congress. But litigation is generally not an effective way to change projects that are simply controversial. Filing suits should not be considered an acceptable substitute for early, active participation in the Corps' planning process, where frank discussion and negotiation can often resolve controversies at far less cost to all parties concerned.

(All Corps district planning and regulatory offices maintain mailing lists for public meeting announcements and notices of proposed project and permit actions; a request to be added to the relevant mailing lists can be made in writing or by telephone to the appropriate Corps office. A list of key Corps district officials and their addresses is contained in Appendix G.)

CURRENT LEGISLATIVE AND POLICY ISSUES

The National Environmental Policy Act

The National Environmental Policy Act (NEPA) had a profound effect on the Corps' project planning process during the 1970s, by opening it to public review and comment and requiring that explicit attention be given to the environmental effects of proposed actions. There was an initial period of "catch-up" during the mid-1970s, when the Corps prepared hundreds of environmental impact statements (EISs) each year for projects in various stages of planning and construction, often in response to court decisions that applied NEPA to Corps projects initiated before the law was passed.[11] In recent years, the number of EISs prepared by the Corps for projects and permits has declined to less than 100 per year (Council on Environmental Quality 1976, 1988). Of the more than 14,000 individual dredge-and-fill permit applications received by the Corps in 1986, EISs were prepared for only 11 (Council on Environmental Quality 1988, appendix B).

The decline in numbers of EISs has not been without controversy. It is in part a reflection of the absence of congressional authorization and funding for new construction projects; however, the Corps also has reduced the number of EISs prepared each year in part by writing Environmental Assessments (EAs) in place of EISs for almost all maintenance and permit actions. EAs are not subject to the same required review and comment period as EISs; their primary purpose is to present sufficient information about a proposal's potential environmental impacts to allow an agency decisionmaker to determine whether an EIS will be needed (see Council on Environmental Quality NEPA Regulations, 40 C.F.R. 1508.9). In the Corps' 1988 revision of its Procedures for Implementing NEPA (53 *Federal Register* 3119–3137; codified at 33 C.F.R. 320 and 325), regulatory actions along with several other activities are listed as "actions normally requiring an EA, but not an EIS"

11. For a widely cited analysis of how federal court decisions in the early years of NEPA interpreted the statute, giving it perhaps more significance than Congress had intended, see Anderson 1973.

(33 C.F.R. 230.7). The regulations state that "the EA normally should not exceed 15 pages" (33 CFR 230.10[c]). Such documents usually contain little information on alternatives other than the one preferred by the agency or, for permits, by the applicant.

If an EIS is not prepared, the Corps prepares a draft Finding of No Significant Impact (FONSI) and, for most proposed projects, circulates the draft FONSI together with the EA and proposed project report for a minimum 30-day review to concerned agencies, organizations, and the "interested public" (33 C.F.R. 230.11). But for permit actions, the regulations do not specify such a minimum review period, and refer only to a "public notice" that "will indicate the availability of the EA/FONSI."

This latest revision of the Corps' NEPA regulations was prompted by recommendations made to the Corps in May of 1982 by President Reagan's Task Force on Regulatory Relief. The Corps' Section 404 regulatory program for dredge and fill activities (discussed in detail later), was one of many programs targeted by the task force for revision in order to reduce paperwork and delay. In response, the Corps in 1984 proposed revisions to its NEPA procedures that, among other changes, narrowed the assessment of environmental impacts of a proposed action, and limited the range of alternatives that must be analyzed. EPA and numerous environmental organizations asserted that the proposed changes would have adverse effects on the 404 regulatory program and formally referred the issue to the Council on Environmental Quality.[12] After receiving public comment on the issue, Council on Environmental Quality in 1987 published recommendations for modifications of the regulations (52 *Federal Register* 22517) and subsequently approved the Corps' revised regulations, which, although still controversial, were issued in February 1988.

Hoskins (1988) offers three general explanations for why so few EISs are prepared by the Corps for permit applications. First, consistent with their revised regulations, the Corps narrowly analyzes the potential impacts of activities requiring permits, excluding related activities not expressly covered by the Corps' regulatory authority. Second, the Corps frequently accepts proposed mitigation measures intended to reduce the significance of potential adverse environmental impacts. Third, Corps decisionmakers often conclude that the proposed activities, if permitted, will not result in significant impacts on the human environment. Hoskins goes on to point out that decisions by the Corps and other agencies not to prepare an EIS have frequently been successfully challenged in the courts, although the standard of judicial review

12. Letter from Lee M. Thomas, EPA Administrator, to A. Alan Hill, Chairman, Council on Environmental Quality, Feb. 25, 1985.

varies among the federal circuits and is thus, in his view, in need of resolution by the Supreme Court.

The Section 404 Permit Program and Wetlands

Overview. Probably the most controversial aspect of the Corps' wetlands-related activities continues to be the permit program to regulate the discharge of dredged or fill material into waters of the United States, as established by Section 404 of the Clean Water Act (33 U.S.C.A. 1344). A variety of issues associated with the Corps' administration of Section 404 have been discussed in previous *Audubon Wildlife Reports* (see Barton 1985, 1986, 1987).

There is no dispute that the United States has lost a substantial portion of the wetlands that existed prior to European settlement. A 1984 study by the Office of Technology Assessment identified the major factors responsible for past and ongoing wetland losses. A more recent report by the General Accounting Office (1988) documented continuing wetland losses throughout the country (see "Conserving Southeastern Coastal Wetlands" in this volume). The central question is whether Section 404 of the Clean Water Act provides an effective—or at least potentially effective—basis for substantially reducing further wetland losses.

Three problems lie at the heart of the continuing controversy over the Section 404 program. First, as stated succinctly by Kilgore (1989), the language adopted by Congress for Section 404 "represents a compromise between those who would have given EPA virtually complete control over the regulation of discharges of dredged and fill material . . . and those who would have favored overwhelming dominion by the Corps of Engineers." Kilgore reviews the process by which the House and Senate developed language that gave EPA a policymaking and oversight role in the program, consistent with its overall responsibilities under the Clean Water Act, while assigning to the Corps the primary administrative responsibility for carrying out the program. The tension created by this arrangement has led to numerous conflicts between the two agencies since the program began in 1972.

Second, the Corps has never accepted a fundamental policy position long since adopted by EPA and most other federal natural resource management agencies—namely, that Section 404 was intended to establish a federal wetlands protection program. The Corps, reflecting its long-established institutional reluctance to assert any general land-use regulatory authority, takes the position that Section 404 is concerned more narrowly with achieving the water quality objectives of the Clean Water Act. Although the word "wetlands" does not appear in the statutory language of Section 404, several federal court decisions have held that the act intended both the Corps and NEPA to assume regulatory jurisdiction over all waters of the United States, wetlands included, to fulfill the act's principal objective: "to restore and maintain the chemical, physical, and biological integrity of the Nation's waters" (33 U.S.C.A. 1251).

Third, the Section 404 program neither establishes federal jurisdiction over all wetlands nor regulates all types of activities that result in wetland losses; these facts are frequently raised by the Corps in support of its narrower interpretation of the program's goals. Much of the extensive clearing of bottomland forests, ditching that drains (without first filling) riparian wetlands, and plowing of isolated prairie potholes are activities that the Corps has considered to be outside its regulatory purview. Although the federal courts have directed the Corps to assert regulatory jurisdiction over some of these activities in some locations,[13] the Corps has continued to take a conservative view of its own authority in most cases where its jurisdiction is uncertain.[14]

After investigating the Corps' 404 program in five districts across the country, GAO (1988) reached the following conclusion regarding the scope of the program's authority:

> The Section 404 program as currently authorized does not provide the Corps with the authority to regulate activities that result in the majority of wetland losses each year. However, the Corps and the resource agencies [EPA, Fish and Wildlife Service, and National Marine Fisheries Service] disagree concerning whether the Corps is doing all it can to protect wetlands under existing program authority.

EPA–Corps Interactions

EPA, as indicated above, has direct authority for several elements of the 404 program. Under Section 404(b)(1) EPA issues guidelines that

13. In 1975 the Corps was ordered to extend its jurisdiction under Section 404 beyond the former narrow definition of "navigable waters" to encompass most of the nation's rivers, lakes, streams, and associated wetlands (*Natural Resources Defense Council v. Calloway*, 39 F. Supp 685 [D.C. 1975]). More recently, courts have found that a 404 permit was required for clearing most of a 20,000-acre tract of bottomland hardwoods (*Avoyelles Sportsmen's League v. Marsh*, 715 F.2d 897, 13 ELR 20942 [5th Cir. 1983]); that the ditching and clearing of several thousand acres of forested wetlands (pocosins) in North Carolina was within the Corps' 404 jurisdiction (623 F. Supp. 1539, 16 ELR 20388 [E.D.N.C.]); and that the Corps was correct to require a 404 permit for modifications by a California ranch owner to a 3000-acre area of human-created wetlands (*United States v. Akers*, 651 F. Supp 320 [E.D. Cal. 1987]). However, other court decisions have limited the Corps' jurisdiction, and the Corps is generally reluctant to assert jurisdiction under 404 in uncertain circumstances.

14. For documentation of the Corps' reluctance to assert its authority under Section 404, see the exhibits of Corps internal memoranda attached to testimony of J. Goldman-Carter (1988) before a subcommittee of the House Committee on Public Works and Transportation.

set the standards for Corps review of 404 permit applications. EPA has authority under Section 404(c) to define areas in which dredge and fill discharges are either restricted or prohibited; this section also provides EPA with the authority to withdraw, or veto, any discharge permit granted by the Corps if EPA determines that the discharge"will have an unacceptable adverse effect on municipal water supplies, shellfish beds and fishery areas . . . wildlife, or recreation areas" (33 U.S.C.A. 1344[c]). These two provisions would seem to give EPA clear authority to impose its perspective on the program. However, in practice the Corps treated EPA's 404(b)(1) Guidelines as advisory, rather than binding, until agreeing to accept them in 1984 as part of an out-of-court settlement of a suit brought by the National Wildlife Federation (49 *Federal Register* 39478–39485 [1984], corrected at 49 *Federal Register* 39843). The Corps was particularly reluctant to apply portions of the Guidelines that impose a strong presumption against approving discharges of dredged or fill material unless the proposed activity is clearly water-dependent and no practicable nonwetland alternative design or location exists.

According to the recent GAO wetlands report, the Corps continues to differ with EPA and other federal resource agencies over the determination of a proposed action's water dependency and of practicable alternatives. The Corps is said to give too much weight to the permit applicant's view of what is a practicable alternative in economic terms, rather than determining whether there is an environmentally preferable alternative that also may be feasible. This criticism reflects the Corps' practice of relying on its own older "public interest review" process (used for Section 10 permits) as the basic framework for the overall evaluation and balancing of factors relevant to permit applications. This process has led to potential adverse environmental impacts being "balanced" against claims of economic benefit, or being downplayed by including mitigation measures, without first applying the tests in the 404(b)(1) Guidelines.

EPA has been criticized by environmental organizations and officials in other federal agencies for rarely invoking its 404(c) veto authority. Information provided by EPA's Office of Wetlands Protection shows that, for all the thousands of permits processed by the Corps since this authority was enacted in 1972, as of January 1989 EPA had initiated only 18 veto actions and had brought only 8 of these to completion. Of the remaining 10, 7 were in progress and 3 were terminated before completion for various reasons. Table 7 identifies the eight completed 404(c) actions, along with the basis for determination of each action. Five of these eight 404 permit vetoes were initiated in one EPA region (Region 4, which is based in Atlanta and covers the Southeast); six of the eight vetoes were initiated after changes in EPA leadership occurred in 1983.

Table 7. Section 404 Permit Veto Actions Completed by EPA (through January 1, 1989).

Project permitted by Corps	EPA findings of unacceptable adverse effects on:	Applicable provision of Section 404(B)(1) Guidelines
North Miami Landfill Site; Municipal landfill in North Miami, Fla.; Reg. 4	Shellfish beds, fishery areas, wildlife due to landfill leachate	—
M.A. Norden Site; fill for recycling plant in Mobile, Ala.; Reg. 4	Fishery areas and shellfish bed due to loss of detrital export; wildlife due to habitat loss; cumulative impacts	230.10(a) alternatives available
Jack Maybank Site; impoundment for duck hunting and aquaculture on Jehossee Island, S.C.; Reg. 4	Fishery areas due to loss of habitat and detrital export; recreational areas; cumulative impacts	230.10(c) significant degradation
Bayou aux Carpes; flood control via levees and pumping in Jefferson Parish, La.; Reg. 6	Shellfish beds due to loss of detrital export; fishery areas and wildlife due to habitat loss; recreation; cumulative impacts	—
Sweeden's Swamp Site; fill for shopping mall in Attleboro, Mass.; Reg. 1	Wildlife due to avoidable habitat loss; mitigation questionable and inappropriate; cumulative impacts	230.10(a) alternative site available when applicant entered market; mitigation not appropriate in lieu of alternative.
Russo Dev. Corp. Site; existing/proposed fill for existing/proposed warehouses in Hackensack Meadowlands, N.J.; Reg. 2	Wildlife due to habitat loss; mitigation inadequate; cumulative impacts	230.10(c) significant degradation; 230.10(a) minimum adverse effects; 230.11(g) deter. cumulative impacts.
Rem, Becker, Senior Corp. sites; rockplowing for agricultural conversion in East Everglades, Fla.; Reg. 4	Wildlife due to habitat loss; cumulative impacts	230.10(c) significant degradation; 230.11(g) deter. cumulative impacts
Lake Alma site; proposed recreational impoundment in Hurricane Creek, Bacon Co., Ga.; Reg. 4	Wildlife due to habitat loss and habitat fragmentation; cumulative impacts	230.10(c) significant degradation; 230.10(d) inadequate mitigation

EPA officials told GAO investigators that, because veto actions require extensive use of limited staff, the agency only uses its 404(c) veto authority as a last resort, after exhausting all other options for resolution. Ironically, in his comments on the GAO report Army Assistant Secretary Page stated that the threat of the 404(c) veto had been effective in persuading applicants to modify their proposals; he further stated,

> The use of the 404(c) "veto" earlier in the application process or in special aquatic areas before applications are even submitted, would save the Corps and the EPA considerable time spent in arguing about decisions (General Accounting Office 1988).

One instance in which EPA exercised its 404(c) veto has led to federal district and circuit court opinions upholding EPA's authority. In 1985, the Corps approved a 404 permit for the construction of a shopping mall in Attleboro, Massachusetts, that would have destroyed 32 acres of a wetland known as Sweeden's Swamp. Although the shopping mall was not a water-dependent activity, and at least one other alternative site was initially available, Major General John Wall, the Corps' Director of Civil Works at that time, took the position that mitigation measures proposed by the developer provided sufficient compensation for the project's adverse wetland impacts. EPA invoked Section 404(c) to veto the permit, on the grounds that the existence of a practicable alternative made the Corps' proposed tradeoff of uncertain mitigation benefits for certain loss of aquatic resources unacceptable. The developer sued EPA; the agency's position was upheld in both the district and circuit courts, giving support to EPA's reliance on the water-dependency test in the 404(b)(1) regulations and on its statutory authority to determine unacceptable adverse effects.[15]

EPA has other authorities under Section 404. EPA regulations define the activities exempted from Section 404 permit requirements in Subsection (f); these activities include "normal" farming, silviculture, and ranching, the construction and maintenance of farm stock ponds or irrigation ditches, farm and forest roads, and other similar activities. EPA also has the responsibility under Subsections (g) through (1) for the approval and oversight of any 404 program to be administered by a state. Although Congress added these provisions in 1977, to date only one state (Michigan) has an approved 404 program. Few other states have expressed interest in assuming the program.

Involvement of Other Agencies

Section 404(q) provides for interagency memoradums of agreement (known as MOAs) between the Corps and other federal agencies, in-

---

15. For a more detailed discussion of the legal and policy ramifications of this precedent-setting permit denial, see Kilgore 1988.

cluding EPA, the Fish and Wildlife Service (FWS) and the National Marine Fisheries Service (NMFS); these memorandums essentially govern the participation of those agencies in the review and comment process for permit applications. The agreements require that the Corps consent to allow issues in dispute to be elevated, placing reviewing agencies in the awkward position of seeking the Corps' permission to pursue objections to Corps proposed actions. The memorandums have been a source of frustration for resource agencies because they restrict the ability of the agencies to unilaterally elevate disputes over permit approvals or conditions to higher levels within the Corps and the Secretary of the Army's office.

The recent GAO report stated that the federal resource agencies infrequently seek to elevate a dispute, in part because of these restrictions, in part because of the staff work involved, but largely because their experience has been that higher-level Corps reviewing officers rarely reverse or significantly modify a district's permit decision. For these reasons, FWS and NMFS field offices generally prefer to negotiate informally with the Corps to attach conditions or modifications to proposed permits. Because these agencies lack the veto option available to EPA, they have limited their attempts to elevate disputes to only a few formal appeals each year. Both agencies have publicly expressed their dissatisfaction with the current elevation process.

Nationwide Permits

In response to criticisms that the 404 program was becoming bogged down in paperwork for trivial actions, Congress included Subsection 404(e) in its 1977 Amendments to the Clean Water Act. This provision allowed the Corps to issue a set of general permits for dredge and fill activities that "are similar in nature, will cause only minimal adverse environmental effects when performed separately, and will have only minimal cumulative adverse effect on the environment" (33 U.S.C.A. 1344[e]). The Corps used this provision to expand a previously developed list of nationwide permits so as to encompass 26 different water-related development activities that are specified in Corps regulations (33 CFR 330.5). Most of these permits can be invoked for land-use activities by individuals or businesses without any notification to the Corps; they authorize such minor activities as placing approved navigation markers, tide gauges, lobster pots and duck blinds, as well as a limited number of activities involving discharge of materials, such as backfilling utility lines, stabilizing riverbanks, or constructing bridge abutments.

Although most nationwide permits have been generally accepted, one has generated considerable controversy. In 1982 the Corps revised its regulations to include nationwide permit 26, covering all discharges into two types of waters: isolated waters such as lakes and prairie potholes, and waters above the headwaters of navigable streams, defined as having a mean annual flow of five feet per second or less. The permit placed no limitation on the amount of dredged or fill material that could be discharged into these areas, which the FWS said could include millions of acres of wetlands.

After the National Wildlife Federation, National Audubon Society, and other conservation groups filed suit over the regulations, the Corps agreed in a settlement to revise them to limit nationwide permit 26 to activities that would cause the loss or modification of less than 10 acres of wetlands. For activities under nationwide permit 26 affecting 1 to 10 acres, individuals are supposed to give the Corps "pre-discharge notification" and wait at least 20 days for a response from the district engineer before proceeding with the discharge. For activities in these areas affecting more than 10 acres, an individual permit is required. Despite the requirement for pre-discharge notification, Corps districts have reported receiving much smaller numbers of notifications than would seem appropriate for the amount of wetland disturbance activities that appear to be subject to this requirement. Furthermore, conservationists have charged that some developers are now partitioning large fill operations into components, each affecting 9.9 acres or less, in order to evade the requirement for an individual permit.

Monitoring and Enforcement

The effectiveness of any regulatory program depends in part on whether there is sufficient monitoring to detect significant unauthorized or unpermitted activities, and whether enough successful enforcement actions are brought to deter potential violators. The 404 program has frequently been criticized for failing on both counts. GAO's investigation found that monitoring and enforcement activities were given low priority by both Corps and EPA officials. The Corps districts visited by the GAO did not routinely perform surveillance to detect unauthorized activities or to ensure that permittees were adhering to permit conditions. Corps officials interviewed by GAO acknowledged that most of their permit staff time and resources were spent on processing permits. One person said that if the staff actively looked for violations, they would not be able to handle the resulting enforcement caseload.

GAO also found that many reported cases of unauthorized filling in wetlands were not investigated for weeks or months (General Accounting Office 1988), and that the Corps' usual methods for resolving violations were either to require violators to restore affected areas or to issue the violator after-the-fact permits, without levying either civil or criminal penalties. For the five districts studied, only six civil actions and no criminal actions were pursued during fiscal years 1984 through 1986; no permits were revoked and only two monetary fines—totaling $12,500—were imposed (General Accounting Office 1988). GAO investigators found that EPA regions varied greatly in their issuance of Section 404 enforcement actions, with some regions being quite active and others deferring enforcement work almost entirely to the Corps.

Wetlands Delineation

The issue of what constitutes a wetland subject to regulation under Section 404 has been a continuing source of interagency disagreement. The Clean Water Act regulates activities in "waters of the United States"; the Corps has published a detailed definition of this term, and of the term "wetlands," as part of its regulations (33 CFR 328, 51 *Federal Register* 41250 [1986]). However, in practice EPA and other resource agencies, including the Soil Conservation Service of the Department of Agriculture, all delineate wetland boundaries differently, with boundaries set by the Corps generally being the most exclusive (encompassing the smallest area as wetlands) and boundaries set by the FWS generally being much more inclusive (delineating a much larger area as wetlands). GAO found several examples of widely disparate estimates of wetlands in the same area among the Corps, FWS, and EPA, particularly in bottomland–hardwood areas. Although EPA has the authority to make wetland boundary determinations for purposes of Section 404, GAO found that EPA has generally deferred to the Corps to do so because EPA lacks the necessary field staff (General Accounting Office 1988).

An interagency task force has been working for some time to develop a joint manual for delineation of wetlands, to be used by EPA, the Corps, FWS, and Soil Conservation Service to establish regulatory boundaries of wetlands under the Clean Water Act. Late in 1988 an agreement was reached; the manual is currently being produced, and will be ready for use by the Corps and other participating agencies later in 1989.

Section 401 Certification

One other avenue for wetlands protection exists in the Clean Water Act, but appears to have been used rarely for that purpose. Section 401 of the act (33 U.S.C.A. 1341) requires any applicant for a federal license or permit that may result in a discharge into waters of the United States, obtain certification from the state in which the discharge will originate that the proposed activity will comply with that state's water quality standards. Although obtaining a state Section 401 certificate is often quite routine, the states are required to include in their standards an anti-degradation policy that could be invoked to limit dredge and fill activities in wetlands. States can place a variety of conditions on their 401 certifications to assure compliance with their standards; in the absence of a 401 certificate, the Corps is prohibited from issuing a 404 permit. In states where concern over wetland loss is high, strict application of state water quality standards in the 401 certification process could provide an additional way to limit further destruction of wetlands. As is the case with federal regulatory agencies, inquiries and comments from concerned citizens to state water quality officials may be instrumental in focusing agency attention on regulatory options for wetlands protection.

Wetlands Policy Initiatives

In late 1988 and early 1989 three documents emerged from different sources that were concerned, at least in part, with protection of wetlands in the United States. The final report of the National Wetlands Policy Forum was released, containing a series of goals and recommendations on how federal, state, and local wetlands policies could be improved. The forum had been convened by the Conservation Foundation in the summer of 1987 at the request of EPA; it consisted of 20 members, including three governors, state and local government officials, and private citizens. The forum's primary recommendation was that:

> . . . the nation establish a national wetlands protection policy to achieve no overall net loss of the nation's remaining wetlands base, as defined by acreage and function, and to restore and create wetlands, where feasible, to increase the quality and quantity of the nation's wetlands resource base (National Wetlands Policy Forum 1988).

Other forum recommendations called for improvements in the consistency and efficiency of the federal Section 404 program, increased delegation of regulatory authority to states, and increased incentives for private efforts to protect wetlands.

The policy of no net loss of wetlands was echoed in "Blueprint for the Environment," a document containing a series of policy and legislative recommendations prepared by a coalition of national environmental organizations for delivery to top officials of the Bush Administration (Project Blueprint 1989). Recommendations to EPA included a legislative transfer of all Section 404 authorities to EPA, and adoption of a "no net loss of wetlands policy," also backed by legislation. Other recommendations included steps to enhance enforcement against illegal filling of wetlands, and the promulgation of biological water quality standards to protect wetlands functions.

The third document, released on January 19, 1989, by outgoing EPA Administrator Lee Thomas, was EPA's Wetlands Action Plan, prepared in response to the recommendations of the National Wetlands Policy Forum. The document adopts the Forum's goal of no overall net loss of remaining wetlands, and sets out seven administrative objectives for EPA (EPA 1989). The agency proposes to work closely with the Corps and other federal agencies to achieve the goal of no net wetlands loss. However, no new legislative initiatives for wetlands protection are recommended in the plan by EPA.

The Water Resources Development Acts of 1986 and 1988

In October 1986, after more than 10 years of conflict between Congress and four consecutive administrations over the future of federal water resources development, during which almost no new projects were authorized for study or construction, the Water Resources Development Act of 1986 (P.L. 99–662) was enacted and signed into law by President Reagan. In addition to authorizing 377 new water projects for construction or study, at an estimated federal cost of more than $12 billion, the act deauthorized nearly 300 old projects, with a total authorized cost of more than $11 billion. Among the projects terminated were the notorious Cross-Florida Barge Canal and the Dickey-Lincoln School Lakes hydropower project in Maine.

The act was made possible because agreement was reached on a number of fundamental policy changes long sought by the Executive Branch. The reforms enacted as part of this law were designed to increase substantially the share of project costs to be paid by nonfederal beneficiaries and to reduce the adverse environmental effects of federal projects through better planning and concurrent funding of fish and wildlife mitigation measures. The following provisions were among the more significant national changes affecting the Corps of Engineers Civil Works program:

- Increased cost sharing by nonfederal beneficiaries, for planning as well as construction of inland waterway projects and harbor navigation projects, should lead to smaller and fewer projects being advanced for authorization as a result of budget constraints on local sponsors. Smaller projects are likely to have reduced adverse environmental impacts in both the construction and maintenance phases.
- Taxes are increased on fuel used by commercial barges in inland waterways, and are imposed for the first time on the value of commercial cargo loaded or unloaded at U.S. ports. Revenues from these taxes are to be placed in inland waterways and harbor maintenance trust funds, and to be used to pay for part of the

cost of operating and maintaining the nation's commercial waterways and harbors.

- All Corps projects submitted for authorization in the future must include either a specific mitigation plan or a determination that the project will have negligible effects on fish and wildlife. Mitigation features for previously authorized and constructed projects costing up to $7.5 million or 10 percent of total project costs may be implemented without sending further specific reports to Congress.

- Fish and wildlife mitigation measures are to be carried out concurrently with construction of other project features; mitigation costs are to be shared by the Corps and project sponsors at the same rate as the project purpose that creates the need for mitigation. This provision will increase the availability of federal funds for some mitigation activities that previously were the primary responsibility of nonfederal sponsors. An Environmental Protection and Mitigation Fund of $35 million is authorized to help pay the federal share of mitigation work in advance of project construction if needed.

- The value of benefits of environmental quality project features such as fish and wildlife enhancement will be considered at least equal to their cost for purposes of benefit-cost analysis. The costs of fish and wildlife enhancement features will be 100 percent federally funded for species of national significance, such as migratory birds, endangered species, and anadromous fish.

- An Office of Environmental Policy is established in the Office of the Chief of Engineers; the office is responsible for the formulation and coordination of environmental policy, and guides and monitors Corps coordination with other agencies.

In addition to these and other policy changes at the national level, the 1986 Water Resources Act included a number of regional or project-specific authorizations, many of which were sought by conservationists to protect or restore environmental resources damaged by previous Corps construction activities. Among them:

- Authorization for the Atchafalaya Basin Enhancement Project, Louisiana, at an initial cost of $223 million, to acquire approximately 315,000 acres of easements and 50,000 acres of fee-title land, all deemed nationally significant and therefore at 100 percent federal cost.

- Authorization of $6 million for wetland creation and restoration projects in the lower Mississippi Valley.

- Authorization of the Upper Mississippi Management Act, with authority for multiyear appropriations totaling over $175 million for environmental studies described in the Corps master plan for managing the Upper Mississippi River Basin.

- Authorization for numerous fish and wildlife mitigation projects to compensate for environmental damage at previously authorized civil works projects, including the following:

1. Tennessee-Tombigbee Waterway, Alabama/Mississippi: 88,000 acres at a cost of $60.2 million
2. Missouri River Mitigation, Missouri, Kansas, Iowa, and Nebraska: 29,900 acres at a cost of $51.9 million
3. Yazoo Backwater Area, Mississippi: 40,000 acres at a cost of $17.7 million
4. Cooper Lake and Channels, Texas: 28,000 acres at a cost of $14.8 million
5. Trinity River, Texas: 10,000 acres at a cost of $10.4 million
6. Richard B. Russell Dam and Lake, Georgia and South Carolina: $20.2 million

The 1986 act's combination of major policy changes and authorizations for funds to be earmarked for fish and wildlife enhancement and mitigation was a major departure from past "pork-barrel" project authorization bills that gave short shrift to economic efficiency and environmental protection. The cost-sharing reforms are already affecting the planning of new water development projects. However, it should be noted that, consistent with previous water development legislation, the 1986 law only authorized (but did not appropriate) funds for the wildlife enhancement and mitigation projects listed above. Subsequent annual appropriations bills (through FY 1989) have allocated relatively modest amounts to these authorized projects, partly on the grounds that some are still in the planning stages. As was true in the past, authorized projects must compete for limited funds in the annual appropriations process.

In 1988, Congress returned to the former pattern of alternate-year water project authorizations, by passing the Water Resources Development Act of 1988. Despite efforts by some interests to repeal or weaken the cost-sharing reforms enacted in 1986, the bill as enacted does not alter the reforms. Rather, it authorizes construction of 16 new projects and modification of 20 others, adds recreation as an authorized purpose for a number of projects in West Virginia, Pennsylvania, and Maryland, and makes minor adjustments in some provisions of the 1986 and earlier water development acts.

MITIGATION OF FISH AND WILDLIFE HABITAT LOSSES

From the beginning of the Corps' civil works activities in the 19th century to the present, the construction and operation of federal water projects has resulted in the loss of millions of acres of wetlands, bottomland forests, and other aquatic and riparian habitats. For at least the past several decades, Congress, in response to criticisms from federal and state fish and wildlife agencies and conservationists, has authorized and encouraged the Corps and other water resource agencies to implement measures to mitigate these losses.

Nevertheless, by any objective measure, relatively little mitigation actually has been accomplished. Despite regular consultation with the FWS during project planning, and the incorporation of mitigation plans in project authorizing documents, the Corps has consistently either failed to fund, or seriously underfunded, actual implementation of significant measures to protect, preserve, and enhance natural ecosystems destroyed during project construction.

Responsibility for the lack of adequate mitigation funds is shared by the Corps, which ranks mitigation low on the priority list for always-limited project funds; the President's Office of Management and Budget, which strongly discourages the Corps from using project funds to acquire any more land than is essential for a project's primary authorized purposes; and Congress itself, which in recent years has *authorized* significant expenditures for mitigation (see the summary above of mitigation provisions in the 1986 Water Resources Development Act), but has consistently failed to *appropriate* funds for the mitigation measures it has authorized.

The Tennessee-Tombigbee Waterway project is exemplary of the mitigation problem. In 1984, the Interior Department found the project's proposed mitigation plan unsatisfactory and referred the issue to the Council on Environmental Quality. The Council recommended that a mitigation plan be developed that "fully replaces the 34,000 acres of bottomland hardwoods lost, through a combination of management and acquisition" to achieve in-kind replacement.[16] In the 1986 act, Congress specifically authorized $60.2 million to acquire up to 88,000 acres of land for mitigation. However, as of March 1, 1989, the Office of Management and Budget has allowed the expenditure of project funds to develop a mitigation plan that would apply only to *existing project lands*; the Office of Management and Budget has not approved the purchase of any new lands to the recommended mitigation.

The 1986 act also authorized $51.9 million to acquire up to 29,900 acres of land for mitigation of habitat lost from past projects along the Missouri River. As of March 1, 1989, no funds have been expended or approved by the Office of Management and Budget to achieve this au-

16. Letter from A. Alan Hill, William L. Mills, and Jacqueline E. Schafer, Council on Environmental Quality, to E. R. Heiberg, III, Chief of Engineers and Richard R. Hute, Deputy Assistant Secretary, Department of the Interior, March 25, 1985. In its letter, the Council on Environmental Quality emphasized that "in-kind" replacement requires acquisition and management of lands to provide natural habitats of the same kind as those lost (for example, forested wetlands for forested wetlands).

thorized objective. Another $223 million was authorized for the acquisition of 365,000 acres of easment and fee-title lands for the Atchafalaya Basin Enhancement Project, to control encroachments in one of the nation's largest freshwater wetlands; as of March 1, 1989, only $24.9 million has been appropriated for this purpose.

Mitigation of losses does not always require compensatory purchase of in-kind lands. The definition of mitigation contained in the Council on Environmental Quality NEPA Regulations, which has been adopted by the Corps, sets out a five-step, sequential mitigation process: (1) avoiding the impact altogether; (2) minimizing impacts by limiting the degree or magnitude of the action; (3) rectifying the impact by restoring the affected environment; (4) reducing or eliminating the action over time by preservation and maintenance operations; (5) compensating for the impact by replacing or providing substitute resources (40 CFR 1508.20).

FWS has criticized the Corps for not applying this sequential process to its own projects or to the review of 404 permit applications, instead, says FWS, the Corps relies too heavily on the compensation form of mitigation, particularly on plans to re-create wetlands. Although the Corps has had some success with establishing wetlands using dredged material, techniques for creating wetlands with both stability and long-term persistence are largely experimental. Furthermore, re-created wetlands appear to require considerable maintenance. EPA and the Corps are in the process of developing a joint mitigation policy that would emphasize the sequential approach outlined above.

FUTURE DIRECTIONS

For two centuries the Corps of Engineers has built an impressive record and reputation as an agency without equal in the role of military and civil works construction for the nation. The Corps' motto "Essayons" (we will try) reflects the professional spirit and attitude of its employees at all levels. However, as the Corps moves into its third century, the challenges it faces are not as great in the area of construction as they are in the area of natural resource management and protection. With management responsibilities for more than 11 million acres of some of North America's most ecologically productive public lands and waters, and regulatory stewardship responsibility for millions of additional acres of the nation's wetlands, the Corps must invoke its motto and apply itself with greater determination to these newer and often more difficult tasks, for which it has widespread public support. As our population continues to grow and become more urban, the Corps' past expertise in flood damage reduction, navigation, and water supply will continue to be important—but this expertise must be applied within the broader framework of maintaining our nation's environmental quality. We face new threats to the purity of our drinking water, increasingly conflicting demands for water-based recreation, and difficult technical problems in containing and disposing of hazardous materials. The Corps is uniquely capable of contributing creative and environmentally sound solutions to all of these problems; the next decade will be a critical period for defining the Corps' role in the 21st century.

REFERENCES

Agency Management Group. 1978. Atchafalaya Basin. Brochure published by New Orleans District, Corps of Engineers. New Orleans, Louisiana.

Anderson, Frederick R. 1973. *NEPA in the Courts: A Legal Analysis of the National Environmental Policy Act of 1969.* Environmental Law Institute. Washington, D.C.

Antypas, Alex. 1988. "Army Corps to drain best duck habitat in Mississippi." *Audubon Activist* 3(1): 1–19. (July/August).

Barton, Katherine. 1985. "Wetlands preservation," pp. 212–264 *in* R.L. DiSilvestro ed., *Audubon Wildlife Report 1985.* National Audubon Society, New York, New York.

———. 1986. "Federal wetlands protection programs," pp. 373–411 *in* R.L. DiSilvestro ed., *Audubon Wildlife Report 1986.* National Audubon Society, New York, N.Y.

———. 1987. "Federal wetlands protection programs," pp. 179–198 *in* R.L. DiSilvestro ed., *Audubon Wildlife Report 1987.* National Audubon Society, New York, New York. Academic Press, Inc., Orlando, Florida.

Corps of Engineers. 1986. *The History of the U.S. Army Corps of Engineers.* EP360-1-21. Office of the Chief of Engineers. Washington, D.C.

———. 1987. Annual Report, FY 1986, of the Secretary of the Army on Civil Works Activities. Vol. 1. Office of the Chief of Engineers. Washington, D.C.

———. 1988a. NRMS Statistics, 1987. Unpublished data on Corps natural resources management program, CECW-ON, Office of the Chief of Engineers. Washington, D.C.

———. 1988b. Secretary of the Army's Report on Civil Works Activities, Fiscal 1987. Vol. 1. Office of the Chief of Engineers. Washington, D.C.

———. 1988c. The Role of the U.S. Army Corps of Engineers in Developed Water Resources and the Environment. Unpublished report to the Council on Environmental Quality. Office of the Chief of Engineers, Washington, D.C.

Council on Environmental Quality. 1976. *Environmental Quality 1976—the Seventh Annual Report of the Council on Environmental Quality.* Government Printing Office. Washington, D.C. p. 132.

———. 1979. *Environmental Quality 1979—the Tenth Annual Report of the Council on Environmental Quality.* Government Printing Office. Washington, D.C. pp. 388–389.

———. 1988. *Environmental Quality 1986—the Seventeenth Annual Report of the Council on Environmental Quality.* Government Printing Office. Washington, D.C. p. 245.

Department of the Army. 1989. Civil Works Budget Request for the U.S. Army Corps of Engineers, Fiscal Year 1990. Office of the Assistant Secretary of the Army (Civil Works). Washington, D.C.

Environmental Protection Agency. 1989. Wetlands Action Plan: EPA's Short-term Agenda in Response to Recommendations of the National Wetlands Policy Forum. EPA Office of Wetlands Protection. Washington, D.C.

General Accounting Office. 1988. Wetlands: the Corps of Engineers' Administration of the Section 404 Program. U.S. General Accounting Office, GAO/RCED-88-110. Washington, D.C.

Hatch, H.J. 1987. Keynote address in Landin, M.C. and H.K. Smith eds., *Beneficial Uses of Dredged Material: Proceedings of the first interagency workshop.* 7–9 October 1986, Pensacola, Florida. Department of the Army Technical Report D-87-1, National Technical Information Service. Springfield, Virginia.

Hoskins, E. David. 1988. "Judicial review of an agency's decision not to prepare an environmental impact statement." 18 *Environmental Law Reporter*: 10331–10347.

Kilgore, Shannon J. 1989. "EPA's evolving role in wetlands protection: elaboration in *Bersani v. U.S. EPA.*" 18 *Environmental Law Reporter*: 10479–10490.

Mississippi River Commission and Corps of Engineers. 1976. Flood Control in the lower Mississippi Valley. Public Affairs Office, Mississippi River Commission and U.S. Army Engineer Division, Lower Mississippi Valley. Vicksburg, Mississippi. p. 36.

Morgan, Arthur E. 1971. *Dams and Other Disasters: A Century of the Army Corps of Engineers in Civil Works.* Porter Sargent. Boston, Massachusetts.

National Wetlands Policy Forum. 1988. *Protecting America's Wetlands: an Action Agenda.* Conservation Foundation, Washington, D.C.

Office of Technology Assessment. 1984. Wetlands: Their Use and Regulation. U.S. Congress, Office of Technology Assessment, OTA-0-206, March 1984. Washington, D.C.

Page, Robert W. 1989. Statement on the Fiscal Year 1990 Civil Works Budget, before the Subcommittee on Energy and Water Development, Committee on Appropriations, U.S. House of Representatives, January 31, 1989. Washington, D.C.

Project Blueprint. 1989. Blueprint for the Environment. Available from the Natural Resources Defense Council, Washington, D.C.

Reuss, Martin. 1988. "Along the Atchafalaya: the challenge of a vital resource." *Environment* 3(4). May 1988. Heldref Publications. Washington, D.C.

Schwartz, Anne. 1989. "Hot tips for budget cutters." *Audubon Activist* 3(3):2.

Zener, Robert. 1974. "The federal law of water pollution control," p. 285 *in* Dolgin, E.L. and T.G.P. Guilbert eds., *Environmental Law.* Environmental Law Institute and West Publishing Company. St. Paul, Minnesota.

Robert B. Smythe, Ph.D., is the principal of Potomac Resource Consultants, an environmental and natural resources firm located in Bethesda, Maryland.

Part Two

◇

Conservation Challenges

Without an understanding of the evolution of western water law, "it is not easy for conservationists to fathom the seemingly irrational affection the old guard has for an antiquated resource allocation system so patently ill-adapted to the broader needs of people, wildlife, and the environment they share." *Photo by Chris Wille*

Western Water and Wildlife: The New Frontier

Christopher H. Meyer

"There are many benefits from a great river that might escape a lawyer's view."

Justice Oliver Wendell Holmes, in
Hudson County Water Co. v. McCarter
(209 U.S. 349, 357 [1908]).

INTRODUCTION

Out West, vast farms, great cities, posh resorts, and many a private fortune have been built on water—and the ability to control it. These occurrences, in a land where sagebrush and cactus once reigned, have required the development of complex water delivery systems and an equally complex system of water laws.

For over a century, water allocation has been controlled by a small group of lawyers, engineers, and bureaucrats who have divvied up among their clients the West's most precious resource. In western parlance they are known as "water buffaloes." They form a club of powerful men (and very few women) who for years have wielded enormous power over what will flourish and what will fail.[1] They do battle and cut deals with each other in a constant cycle of conflict and compromise. And they have tended, as have the high priests of so many orders, to develop an attachment to the system they manipulate, which transcends the purposes for which it originally was developed. Like an old

---

1. The extent of that power is illustrated in the story of Owens Valley, a once prospering agricultural community completely dried up to meet the burgeoning needs of the city of Los Angeles. See W. Kahrl, *Water and Power: The Conflict Over Los Angeles Water Supply in the Owens Valley* (1982); R. Nadeau, *The Water Seekers* (1950).

general grown more fond of the military itself than of its ultimate goals of peace, freedom, and prosperity, it is difficult sometimes for the water buffaloes to comprehend the calls for change that come from conservationists and other "newcomers." Likewise, without an understanding of the central role water law has played in a century of western development, it is not easy for conservationists to fathom the seemingly irrational affection the old guard has for an antiquated resource allocation system so patently ill-adapted to the broader needs of people, wildlife, and the environment they share.

The water allocation system run by the water buffaloes provided security to farmers and their labyrinthine network of ditches, canals, and reservoirs. The system facilitated the development of great cities that sent canals across deserts and tunnels beneath mountains in search of water for bluegrass lawns, swimming pools, and car washes. And the system accommodated the generosity of the federal government, which poured billions into a western "reclamation" program of mammoth proportion. But in doing all this, the system's operators more or less have ignored the needs of the desert environment from which water is extracted.

While declaring as its central premise that water should go to whomever claimed it first ("first in time is first in right"), western water law overlooked the fact that the cutthroat trout, the sandhill crane, and the pronghorn antelope arrived on the scene well before the miner, the rancher, and the homebuilder. The traditional rules of water law served as a catch-22 for wildlife: a right to water was recognized only when water was diverted from a stream. Because fish and wildlife do not build dams, water needed by them was accorded no legal protection whatsoever. Also ignored were fishermen, canoeists, backpackers, and bird watchers—anyone whose enjoyment of the environment depended on water left in the stream.

Today, pressure is growing for fundamental change in the existing water system, change that will recognize for the first time that water is needed for fish as well as farms, birds as well as bulldozers. The ability of western water law to adapt to new demands in order to safeguard environmental values will determine in large part the success or failure of efforts to conserve wildlife habitat across the West. From the Stillwater Basin in Nevada, to the Beaver Dam Mountain Wilderness Area on the Arizona–Utah border, to the Platte River in Nebraska, the single most critical component in wildlife protection efforts is water.

Traditionally, water was not made available to maintain habitat. But state water law is changing. The law of interstate water allocation is in flux. The public trust doctrine is emerging. Federal water rights are being asserted to protect the natural environmental values of federal lands. And federal regulation of private water development is coming increasingly into play. Each of these five developments will be explored in this chapter. The bottom line is that although conservationists are winning many of the legal and political battles, for some species and habitats, the war is far from over. [Editor's note: To better understand this chapter, it is suggested that the reader see Addendum 1, 2, and 3, which contain specific information on water law rules and terminology.]

A SHORT HISTORY OF WESTERN WATER LAW

Rules Well Suited to a Parched Land

In January 1849, gold was discovered in the scourings of the millrace of John A. Sutter's sawmill on the American River in California. The gold rush began, and with it, a rush for water. Pioneers came in droves to the mountains and later settled in what was once called the Great American Desert. They left behind them a land crisscrossed with giant rivers and countless streams, abundant rainfall, and dense forests. Out West, they discovered barren land, hot sun, and trickles of water that they named "rivers."

Mark Twain put the contrast between East and West into humorous perspective in his stories about his travel to Nevada as a young man:

> After leaving the Sink, we traveled along the Humboldt river a little way. People accustomed to the monster mile-wide Mississippi, grow accustomed to associating the term "river" with a high degree of watery grandeur. Consequently, such people feel rather disappointed when they stand on the shores of the Humboldt or the Carson and find that a "river" in Nevada is a sickly rivulet which is just the counterpart of the Erie canal in all respects save that the canal is twice as long and four times as deep. One of the pleasantest and most invigorating exercises one can contrive is to run and jump across the Humboldt river till he is overheated, and then drink it dry (Mark Twain, *Roughing It*, Chapter 27).

The development of western water law began with the arrival of the gold and silver miners in the 1850s.[2] As the miners set up camp along the mountain streams and creeks throughout the Sierra Nevada and Rocky Mountains, they laid claim not just to the valuable ores they found, but to the water they used to flush gold through their sluices.

---

2. These miners were not, of course, the first Europeans to settle in the West. They were preceded by a handful of English and French explorers and trappers who, by and large, left the land untouched and had no occasion to develop either water delivery systems or water laws. Earlier yet, the Spanish established colonies throughout the Southwest. Unlike the early English and French, however, the Spanish were quick to develop elaborate irrigation systems. Southwestern Indian villages to this day hold what are called "pueblo water rights," community rights to water for agricultural and domestic use that were first recognized by the Spanish and Mexican governments.

As more miners showed up, streambeds went dry, and men quarreled. The first disputes were settled with Colt 45s, but soon a principle of frontier law emerged: "First in time is first in right," meaning that those who put the water to use first had priority to continue using it over those who came later. This principle came to be known as the "prior appropriation doctrine." Like all frontier laws, water allocation rules were simple and well-suited to their times. The remarkable thing is that, with very few changes, these rules remain the law today.

The western view of water rights was fundamentally different from that of the East, which inherited its law of "riparian rights" from England. Under the eastern system, each person owning land bordering a waterbody—a lake, stream, or river—shares equal "riparian rights" in that water. He or she does not "own" the water as such, but has a right to its continued flow, and the right to some limited, reasonable use (within the watershed) so long as that use does not unreasonably interfere with the water needs of other riparian landowners. Determining what is reasonable and what is not is left to the courts to sort out as the need arises. But where water is plentiful, few conflicts occur and there is little need to sharpen the rules.

Out West the riparian rights system would never have worked. If everyone shared equally, no one's share would be large enough to be useful. Because there was not enough water to go around, eastern riparian rights were rejected, and the western doctrine of prior appropriation quickly took hold.

Its principles are simple: First, there is no need to own riparian land to gain a right to water. Indeed, many private water rights are obtained from streams on federal land. Second, an individual's "priority date" (when the diversion was initiated) matters more than anything else. If a miner at the lower end of a creek was the first to divert water, his or her water right was "senior" to all others, and miners upstream had to yield to that superior right in time of shortage. This principle is completely unknown to eastern water law where every riparian landowner shares equally regardless of when they or their ancestors appeared on the scene. Third, in the West, a water right can be lost through disuse. This, too, is in stark contrast to the eastern riparian rights doctrine that allows landowners to assert riparian rights even if they have laid dormant for many years. Fourth, the eastern limitation that water must be used within the watershed was eliminated. In the West it is often necessary to construct elaborate delivery systems across hills and even mountains to get water to where it is needed.[3]

3. In Colorado, for example, 80 percent of the water is found on the western slope of the Rocky Mountains, while 80 percent of the people reside on the eastern side of the mountains. Dozens of huge tunnels have been constructed at enormous cost to bring water under the Continental Divide for municipal and agricultural use on the Front Range.

Mines Give Way to Farms

While the mining towns of the West cycled through boom and bust, the land surrounding them was undergoing a more lasting transformation. Sagebrush and tumbleweed gave way to wheat and corn as early pioneers plowed the desert and flooded it with water. Most of the miners eventually left. But the farmers stayed, and kept the water law that the miners had fashioned out of necessity.

In the early years, water was allocated without resort to lawyers, judges, or scholarly treatises. But the formality of the law was not far behind. Every western state came to recognize the prior appropriation doctrine as the official rule, and most of them wrote it into their state constitutions. Nine states with wetter climates[4] grafted elements of the riparian doctrine onto their state water law, but the basic principle of water allocation in the West came to be prior appropriation.

INSTREAM FLOWS

Natural Flows Unprotected

From the earliest days, the purpose of water law in the West has been to get water out of streams. The diversion of water for mining, agriculture, and domestic use was sanctioned by the law. However, water left in the stream—called "instream flow"—was said to serve no one, and was given no legal recognition. This ignored, of course, the vital role natural flows play in the maintenance of riparian habitat.[5] Without legal protection, water for fish and wildlife, swimming, boating, aesthetic enjoyment, and spiritual renewal, was up for grabs to the next diverter.

Conservationists have fought for decades to win the right to protect instream flows. The struggle has been played out in state after

---

4. The "dual system" states are California, Kansas, Nebraska, North Dakota, Oklahoma, Oregon, South Dakota, Texas, and Washington.

5. Water does more than keep fish wet. It is the basic building block of the entire riparian ecosystem. The river environment is shaped by the flow regime, often ranging from a trickle of water in the summer to a torrent in spring. When the natural cycle is disrupted by dams and diversions, river habitat responds dramatically. Peak flows no longer clear vegetation and widen the channel. Sediment no longer feeds the bed and banks. Nutrients are lost from the food chain. Wetlands dry up. And with all this change, the native flora and fauna dependent upon the natural system often disappear. The result is streams that no longer are capable of sustaining the network of life they once supported. Catastrophe then multiplies when mother nature unleashes her occasional deluge on a river no longer resilient. When a real flood hits the narrow, overgrown channels and dried up wetlands left behind by human diversions, the destruction can be enormous.

state, and the battle in Colorado has been one of the most colorful. Take the case of *Empire Water & Power Co. v. Cascade Town Co.* (205 F. 123 [8th Cir. 1913]). No other lawsuit more poignantly captures the inanity of the law's refusal to recognize instream flow rights.

Cascade Town was a small, turn-of-the-century resort set at the base of Pikes Peak in Colorado. The court described vividly the efforts of the town's founders to build a community around a small natural wonder:

> [T]hey have constructed hotels there and built cottages, roads, and trails on its land extending up through Cascade Cañon, through which the stream of the same name flows, improved a small park in said cañon, made a lake and fountain, built a pavilion or auditorium for conventions, and otherwise improved the grounds, thereby adding to the attractions of the place as left by nature. . . . The cañon and falls are rare in beauty and constitute the chief attraction. Without them the place would not be much unlike any other part of Ute Pass. The cañon is about three-quarters of a mile long and very deep; its floor and sides are covered with an exceptionally luxuriant growth of trees, shrubbery, and flowers. This exceptional vegetation is produced by the flow of Cascade Creek through the cañon and the mist and spray from its falls. Some of the falls are as much as 30 feet in height. . . . The vegetation in the cañon and up its sides consists, in part, of pine, spruce, fir, balsam, aspen, black birch, Japanese maple, thimbleberry, wild cherry, choke cherry, and aster, columbine, larkspur, wild rose, the red raspberry, wild gooseberry, ferns, mosses, and many other kinds of trees, shrubs, and flowers (*Cascade Town*, 205 F. at 124–250).

From its beginning the city flourished. Fifteen thousand visitors a year found solace in the canyon's falls. Then, in 1910, the Empire Water and Power Company devised a plan to dam the headwaters of Cascade Creek, divert the entire flow into a tunnel, and generate hydroelectric power.

The town, outraged that this might be done after so much had been invested in the community, brought suit. Cascade charged that it was entitled to a senior water right in the falls, just as a senior irrigator is protected against someone diverting water before it reaches the senior irrigator's headgates. The court expressed sympathy, but declared that it was powerless to protect "the artistic value of the falls." Instead, it said, the court must limit its "inquiry into the effectiveness of the use of the water in the way adopted as compared with the customary methods of irrigation." The court found that using a waterfall to grow canyon vegetation was a rather poor method of irrigation. Consequently, the court allowed the hydroelectric company to proceed with its plans.[6]

6. After winning the court battle, the hydropower company ultimately abandoned its diversion project, and the hamlet of Cascade can still be found a few miles west of Colorado Springs.

The *Cascade Town* case set the stage for decades of struggle by conservationists to find ways to protect water flowing in natural settings. The next Colorado instream flow case also was decided against protection of instream flows. In 1965 the Colorado River Water Conservation District sought an instream water right for "piscatorial purposes," noting (in apparent understatement) that the streams involved "have been a habitat for fish and the propagation and preservation thereof for over 40 years" (*Colorado River Water Conservation Dist. v. Rocky Mountain Power Co.*, 158 Colo. 331, 406 P.2d 798 [1965]). One might have thought that the Conservation District had a stronger case than the town of Cascade, because in 1963 the state legislature specifically authorized the Conservation District "[t]o file upon and hold for the use of the public sufficient water of any natural stream to maintain a constant stream flow in the amount necessary to preserve fish . . ." (Colo. Rev. Stat. Sec. 150-7-5 [10] [1963]).

Despite this explicit legislative direction, the court refused to take the hint and denied the District's request for water rights on three streams in the Colorado River Basin. The court declared, in essence, that it simply could not believe the words it read: "[T]he legislature did not intend to bring about such an extreme departure from well-established doctrine. . . ." The Conservation District's efforts to protect fisheries in western Colorado, it seemed, were doomed by the inflexibility of western water law.

Colorado's Instream Flow Program

Not until 1973 did the Colorado legislature again address the issue of instream flows. Under pressure from a strong grassroots campaign led by Trout Unlimited, the legislature created a special program for instream flow rights to be run by the Colorado Water Conservation Board (CWCB)[7]. CWCB was authorized to acquire water rights for instream flow both by appropriation and by transfer from existing consumptive uses. These new water rights are accorded the same legal protection as water diverted from the stream.

To date, the instream flow program has been a limited success. CWCB has obtained decrees in state water court to protect instream flows in 1,074 segments of streams totalling 6,700 miles (*The Daily Sentinel*, March 29, 1987). This impressive statistic, however, belies the shortcomings of the program. The vast majority of instream flow rights in Colorado range from one to three cfs (cubic feet per second).

---

7. It is not without irony that the task of protecting instream flows was handed to CWCB. This is the Colorado agency charged with promoting the development of Colorado's full share of water through the construction of dams. In other words, the agency charged with making sure that as little water as possible flows out of the state (by building dams) is also charged with the task of increasing and protecting such flows within the state (by not building dams).

One cfs is roughly equivalent to the output of 30 garden hoses discharging at once—not much of a river. The difficulty is that CWCB has approached its task with the timidity of a nervous bureaucrat fearful of doing anything that might offend the conservative water establishment. Consequently, it has translated its legislative mandate "to preserve the natural environment to a reasonable degree," (Colo. Rev. Stat. Sec. 37-92-103 [4] [1974]) into a cautious effort to quantify the minimum amount of water necessary to sustain cold-water fisheries. Although a cold-water fishery often can survive with a fraction of a river's lowest flow, CWCB typically has filed to protect that amount and nothing more.

For 15 years CWCB pursued its limited objectives without interference. While conservationists have complained from time to time that CWCB is not doing enough, their objections have fallen on deaf ears in the state legislature. Instead of expanding or strengthening the instream flow program, the legislature has been content to reiterate that instream flows are the business of CWCB and no one else.[8]

Nine Cases for Instream Rights

Such a narrow legislative outlook finally may be in for change. In the last few years conservationists have been joined by an unlikely collection of other parties to demand that the doors of the state's instream flow program be opened to the public. For example, the city of Fort Collins filed for an instream flow water right to protect flows in the Poudre River, after spending millions improving a downtown park through which the river flows. The city of Boulder, which has just completed a costly riverside bike path and a fish observatory along Boulder Creek, is also exploring what can be done to ensure that the trout that people spot in the observatory are not dead. The nonprofit Greenway Foundation has filed an application for instream flows to protect its kayak route down the South Platte River in the middle of Denver. The city of Salida is concerned that without instream flow rights, upstream diverters may take away water necessary to dilute its treated sewage. The Upper Gunnison River Water Conservation District has filed for instream flow protection of the Taylor River in order to protect the recreation industry that has grown up along its banks. Ranchers along the Colorado River have filed for instream flow water rights to protect fisheries. Homeowners along Crystal Creek have sought to protect their land values by filing for instream flow water rights. The rafting industry is interested in purchasing agricultural water rights and legally converting this water into instream flows in order to increase the number of days the Arkansas River will support

8. Senate Bill 212, 1987 Colo. Sess. Laws ch. 269 at 1305, codified at Colo. Rev. Stat. Sec. 37-92-102(3) (1988 Cumm. Supp.). Other government agencies may make recommendations, but only CWCB may file and hold an instream water right.

white water boating. And the Rocky Mountain Biological Laboratories filed for instream water rights to protect riparian study sites near Crested Butte.

In sum, there has been an explosion of interest in protecting instream flows for a variety of beneficial uses unheard of until recently. And such requests for instream flow rights are being approved. Of the nine requests previously mentioned, three have been granted, one denied, and the rest are pending. Despite a century of dominance of the state legislature by water development interests, it appears that political recognition of the instream flow constituency is gradually occurring.

Similar instream flow protection efforts are under way in virtually every other western state.[9] Growing societal recognition of the importance of instream flow rights for a host of environmental, recreational, and aesthetic objectives is helping to bring western water law up to date.

INTERSTATE ALLOCATION

When the States Go to Court

While most water conflicts pit individual users against each other, sometimes entire states jump into the fray. In the past, these state-versus-state conflicts have focused on water supply for agricultural development. The next decade, however, will see more and more interstate battles fought over water to protect the environment. Indeed, an understanding of interstate water law is becoming essential to the resolution of many wildlife problems.

For over a hundred years, the axiom "first in time is first in right" has reigned unchallenged as the central governing principle of western water law. Anyone who doubted the premise was liable to be charged with spreading "riparian socialism." One might think, then, that this historic principle, so carefully enshrined in the prior appropriation doctrine, would govern disputes between states as well as between people. It does not.

One of the more curious incongruities in western water law is the attitude of western states toward dividing up the waters of a river that flows through several states. If one applied the prior appropriation doctrine, the water would go to whichever state used it first. But it does

9. Nevada joined the ranks of those providing full recognition to instream flows with a state supreme court decision announced last December (*State v. Morros*, 766 P.2d 262 [Nev. 1988]). New Mexico may be the next state to formally protect instream flows. A coalition of conservation organizations in that state has launched a renewed campaign to enact instream flow legislation in the 1989 session, following a narrow defeat in 1987.

not work that way. Instead, water is allocated among states by court decrees or negotiated interstate compacts that often ignore which state began using the water first.

The law of interstate allocation has arisen entirely in this century. In the 1800s, water resources were not sufficiently developed in western states sharing common rivers to generate any cross-border conflicts.[10] Early in the 20th century, however, depletions in some interstate streams became so severe that states took each other to court to fight over what remained.

The first case, *Kansas v. Colorado* (206 U.S. 46 [1907]), was decided in 1907. Kansas sued Colorado charging that extensive irrigation in Colorado was drying up the Arkansas River and restricting the ability of Kansas farmers to launch new irrigation projects. In deciding the case, the Supreme Court had no precedent to go on. The court noted that the Constitution granted it the authority to resolve disputes between the states, and set out with a clean slate to write a new body of interstate allocation law now known as "equitable apportionment."

Had the case arisen today, it is likely that the parties would have documented the environmental consequences of a dried-up Arkansas River. But in 1907 there was no mention of the environment. Instead the court focused its attention on the benefits of irrigated farming. The court determined that it would be inequitable to cut off the water already being used by Coloradans simply to provide more water to Kansas. But the Court did not rule in Colorado's favor simply because its uses were "senior" to uses in Kansas. Rather, the court engaged in a balancing act to determine what allocation of water was "fair" to each of the disputants and concluded that the status quo was "fair." Thus the court allowed Colorado to continue its diversions, with the proviso that Kansas could institute a new suit if Colorado increased its depletions.

Over the years, the Supreme Court has heard 11 cases in which decrees were sought allocating water on interstate streams.[11] No hard and fast rules have emerged from this history of litigation. To the contrary, the Supreme Court has ruled on an *ad hoc* basis, considering whatever evidence on the issue of equity it found appropriate at the

10. Curiously, some of the early interstate water conflicts developed not in the parched West, but on the East Coast as major cities tapped the rivers in neighboring states to satisfy their growing populations.

11. Arkansas River: *Kansas v. Colorado,* 206 U.S. 46 (1907), *prior history,* 185 U.S. 125 (1902), *subsequent history, Colorado v. Kansas,* 320 U.S. 383 (1943).

Bois de Sioux: *North Dakota v. Minnesota,* 263 U.S. 365 (1923).

Chicago River: *Missouri v. Illinois,* 200 U.S. 496 (1906)

Colorado River: *Arizona v. California,* 373 U.S. 546 (1963), *decree entered,* 439 U.S. 419 (1979), *decree modified,* 460 U.S. 605 (1983).

Columbia and Snake rivers: *Idaho v. Oregon,* 462 U.S. 1017 (1983) (dealing with anadromous fish).

Connecticut River: *Connecticut v. Massachusetts,* 282 U.S. 660 (1931).

time. Recently, however, considerations of water conservation and efficiency of use have become a part of the debate.

In the most recent case, Colorado sued New Mexico (*Colorado v. New Mexico*, 467 U.S. 310 [1984]) charging that New Mexico was wasting water taken from the Vermejo River. Although the water uses in New Mexico were longstanding and therefore "senior" to Colorado's potential uses of the river in the future, Colorado asked the Supreme Court to consider the inefficiency of New Mexico's irrigation system. The special master appointed by the court to hear the facts found that "the heart of New Mexico's water problem is the Vermejo Conservancy District," which he considered a failed reclamation project that "quite possibly should never have been built." The court nevertheless determined that Colorado should not be able to force New Mexico to improve the efficiency of the project to free up water for Colorado's use because Colorado had not demonstrated any stronger water conservation program of its own.

This important case demonstrates the possibility that in the future, water may be shifted by the Supreme Court from one state to another on the basis of relative efficiency of use. The case should serve as a prod to all western states to eliminate wasteful water use practices.

Whooping Cranes and Interstate Water

Eighty-two years of equitable apportionment law will soon be put to the test in a conflict over the maintenance of habitat for the endangered whooping crane and other migratory birds in the Big Bend reach of the Platte River. For over a decade, battles have raged between conservation organizations and water developers over the river's waters.[12]

Delaware River: *New Jersey v. New York*, 283 U.S. 336 (1931), *decree amended*, 347 U.S. 995 (1954).

Laramie River: *Wyoming v. Colorado*, 259 U.S. 419 (1922), *decree modified*, 260 U.S. 1 (1922), *new decree entered*, 353 U.S. 953 (1957).

North Platte River: *Nebraska v. Wyoming*, 325 U.S. 589 (1945), *decree modified*, 345 U.S. 981 (1953), *petition to reopen, sub nom.*, *Nebraska v. Wyoming*, No. 108, Original (filed Oct. 6, 1986).

Vermejo River: *Colorado v. New Mexico*, 467 U.S. 310 (1984).

Walla Walla River: *Washington v. Oregon*, 297 U.S. 517 (1936).

12. Platte River litigation to date has centered over four water projects. In each case, conservationists have prevailed: (1) The Grayrocks dam in Wyoming (*Nebraska v. Rural Electrification Admin.*, 12 Env't Rep. Cas. (BNA) 1156 (D. Neb. 1978), *appeal vacated and dismissed upon stipulation*, 594 F.2d 870 [8th Cir. 1979]. (2) The Wildcat Dam in Colorado (*Riverside Irrigation Dist. v. Andrews*, 758 F.2d 508 [10th Cir. 1985]. (3) The Catherland (Little Blue) Project in Nebraska (*Catherland Reclamation Dist. v. Lower Platte North Natural Resources Dist.*, 230 Neb. 580, 433 N.W. 2d 161, slip op., No. 86–692 [Neb., Dec. 16, 1988]. (4) The Enders Project in Nebraska (*Hitchcock & Red Willow Irrigation Dist. v. Lower Platte North Natural Resources Dist.*, 226 Neb. 146, 410 N.W.2d 101 [Neb. 1987].

As western water law slowly evolves to consider the effects of water-allocation systems, conservationists continue to battle for wildlife's right to use water in rivers and streams. The Platte River, pictured here, has been in the center of a longstanding controversy over use of its waters. *National Audubon Society*

Conservationists contend that further depletions in flow will destroy what is left of the river's remarkable migratory bird habitat; developers say the birds can move elsewhere.[13]

From roughly Lexington to Grand Island, Nebraska, the Platte River provides some of the most stunningly awesome waterfowl habitat in the world—what is left of it, that is. Today, 70 percent of the water that once reached the Big Bend no longer nourishes the habitat there. Instead, Platte River water is diverted to irrigate bluegrass lawns planted to replace sagebrush and buffalo grass in places such as Denver, Fort Collins, and Casper. It also grows crops, spins turbines, and evaporates from countless reservoirs under the summer sun.

These depletions have transformed much of what was once wide-open river into a pathetic tangle of rivulets winding through forests of cottonwood and willow. As stream flows have been reduced and sediment caught behind dams, riparian woodlands have grown up in the shrunken remnant of the formerly 2-mile-wide river channel. This dramatic transformation of habitat poses a grave threat to a variety of species dependent upon the natural river system with its open waters, exposed sandbars, and adjacent wetlands. These species include the endangered whooping crane, least tern, and bald eagle; the threatened piping plover; four-fifths of the world population of sandhill cranes; over seven million ducks and geese; and hundreds of other bird species.

The battlefront now has moved to the U.S. Supreme Court. Nebraska has petitioned to reopen an old decree allocating the waters of the North Platte among Colorado, Wyoming, and Nebraska. At first Nebraska hesitated to identify protection of the Big Bend as the reason the court should allow more water to flow into the state. That failure prompted four conservation organizations—National Audubon Society, Sierra Club, Nebraska Wildlife Federation, and the Platte River Whooping Crane Habitat Maintenance Trust—to seek intervention in the case on behalf of the whooping crane and other migratory birds. The conservation groups urged the court to revamp the old decree and allocate water specifically to protect wildlife habitat in Nebraska, as well as for irrigation and municipal use.[14]

It will be years before the Supreme Court ultimately settles the dispute. The outcome will say a great deal about the future course of water development. Will water be allocated and reallocated among western states with an eye to protecting critical wildlife habitat as those needs are identified? If so, this would mark a dramatic change

13. See "Wildlife and Water Projects on the Platte River" in the *Audubon Wildlife Report 1988/1989.*

14. Nebraska later sought to amend its petition to identify clearly the importance of maintaining flows for critical habitat, but not soon enough for the court, which refused to allow the amendment. The court also refused to allow the conservation groups full status as intervenors, but has allowed them to participate as sort of "super *amici curiae*" with opportunity to present evidence and cross-examine witnesses.

in the way the water allocation system has operated for the last hundred years.

PUBLIC TRUST DOCTRINE

Historical Roots in Ancient Rome

While the eastern riparian doctrine has its roots in English history, most westerners assume that western water law can be traced back only to 1849 when gold miners first descended upon California. In fact, the roots of both eastern and western water law reach back over 1,400 years.

In the year 533 A.D., Emperor Justinian handed down his "Institutes," which codified a thousand years of Roman law and articulated the concept of what is now known as the "public trust doctrine." Justinian's words were simple:

> Thus, the following things are by natural law common to all—the air, running water, the sea, and consequently the sea-shore. No one is therefore forbidden access to the sea-shore. . . . On the other hand, all rivers and harbours are public, so that all persons have a right to fish therein (Institutes of Justinian 2.1.1 [Moyle trans. 5th ed. 1928]).

The central premise of the public trust doctrine is that water, and the land under water, are of such vital importance to the public that they must be treated differently from other property. Unlike ordinary property, these resources cannot be rendered entirely private; they always retain a public aspect. In legal terminology, they are "impressed with a public trust."

This idea was taken from Roman law by the English, and from English law by early American courts. (It also followed a route via Spain to the southwestern United States.) Today, the concept that certain resources inherently have public trust values remains deeply ingrained in the law of water allocation throughout the United States—although controversy over its application continues.

The Public Trust Doctrine Comes to America

The first American application of the public trust doctrine came in the 19th century (*Illinois Central Railroad Co. v. Illinois*, 146 U.S. 387 [1892]). In 1869, the Illinois legislature, in an act of incalculable generosity, deeded away virtually the entire lakefront of the city of Chicago to the Illinois Central Railroad. Four years later the legislature thought better of its profligacy and repealed the grant. Central Illinois then sued the state claiming it had no right to take back its gift.

The U.S. Supreme Court sided with Illinois, declaring that the submerged land handed over to the railroad was impressed with a public trust, and declared, "[T]he State holds the title to the lands under the navigable waters of Lake Michigan, . . . [b]ut it is a title different in character from that which the State holds in lands intended for sale. . . . It is a title held in trust for the people of the State that they may enjoy the navigation of the waters, carry on commerce over them, and have liberty of fishing therein freed from the obstruction or interference of private parties" (*Illinois Central v. Illinois* at 452). Thus was born the modern public trust doctrine.

Mono Lake: The Public Trust Doctrine Applied to Water Rights

While the doctrine has been applied with some regularity since that time,[15] it was not until National Audubon Society brought suit in 1979 to protect the waters of Mono Lake that a court made clear that the public trust doctrine may be used to reallocate water rights in order to

15. California: *Ward v. Mulford*, 32 Cal. 365, 372 (1867); *People v. Gold Run Ditch & Mining Co.*, 66 Cal. 138, 4 P. 1152 (1884); *People ex. rel. Webb v. California Fish Co.*, 166 Cal. 576, 138 P. 79 (1913); *Colberg, Inc. v.State ex rel. Department of Public Works*, 67 Cal. 2d 408, 416, 432 P.2d 3, 62 Cal. Rptr. 401 (1967), *cert. denied* 390 U.S. 949 (1968); *Marks v. Whitney*, 6 Cal. 3d 251, 491 P.2d 374, 98 Cal. Rptr. 790 (1971); *Hitchings v. Del Rio Woods Recreation & Park Dist.*, 55 Cal. App. 3d 560, 127 Cal. Rptr. 830 (1976); *People ex rel. Younger v. County of El Dorado*, 96 Cal. App. 3d 403, 157 Cal. Rptr. 815 (1979); *City of Berkeley v. Superior Court of Alameda County*, 26 Cal. 3d 515, 606 P.2d 362, 162 Cal. Rptr. 327, *cert. denied* 449 U.S. 840 (1980); *State v. Superior Court of Lake County*, 29 Cal. 3d 210, 625 P.2d 239, 172 Cal. Rptr. 696,*cert. denied* 454 U.S. 865, *rehearing denied* 545 U.S. 1094 (1981); *State v. Superior Court of Placer County*, 29 Cal. 3d 240, 625 P.2d 256, 172 Cal. Rptr. 713, *cert. denied sub. nom. Lyon v. California*, 454 U.S. 865, *rehearing denied* 454 U.S. 1094 (1981); *National Audubon Soc'y v. Superior Court of Alpine County*, 33 Cal. 3d 419, 658 P.2d 709, 189 Cal. Rptr. 346 , *cert. denied*, 464 U.S. 977 (1983); *Truckee Donner Public Utility Dist. v. County of Nevada*, No. 35920 (Superior Court of Cal. 1988).

Hawaii: *Robinson v. Ariyoshi*, 65 Haw. 641, 658 P.2d 287 (1982), *reconsideration denied* 66 Haw. 528, 726 P.2d 1133 (1983).

Idaho: *Kootenai Environmental Alliance, Inc. v. Panhandle Yacht Club, Inc.*, 105 Idaho 622, 671 P.2d 1085 (1983); *Shokal v. Dunn*, 109 Idaho 330, 707 P.2d 441 (1985); *In the Matter of Application for Permit to Appropriate Water No. 36–7200* (Idaho Department of Water Resources July 22, 1987).

Montana: *Montana Coalition for Stream Access, Inc. v. Curran*, 210 Mont. 38, 682 P.2d 163 (1984); *Montana Coalition for Stream Access, Inc. v. Hildreth*, 211 Mont. 29, 684 P.2d 1088 (1984); *Galt v. State* , 731 P.2d 912 (Mont. 1987).

Nebraska: *Crawford Co. v. Hathaway*, 67 Neb. 325, 351, 93 N.W. 781, 789 (1903); *Kirk v. State Bd. of Irrigation*, 90 Neb. 627, 134 N.W. 167 (1912).

North Dakota: *United Plainsmen Assoc. v. North Dakota Water Conservation Comm'n*, 247 N.W.2d 457 (N.D. 1976).

Oregon: *Morse v. Oregon Div. of State Lands*, 285 Or. 197, 590 P.2d 709 (1979).

South Dakota: *Flisrand v. Madson*, 35 S.D. 457, 152 N.W. 796 (1915).

Utah: *J.J.N.P. Co. v. State*, 655 P.2d 1133 (Utah 1982).

Washington: *Stempel v. Department of Water Resources*, 82 Wash. 2d 109, 508 P.2d 166 (1973); *Caminiti v. Boyle*, 107 Wash. 2d 662, 732 P.2d 989 (1987) *cert. denied*, 108

prevent environmental harm.[16] That decision simultaneously struck fear into the hearts of western water developers across the West, and brought new hope to conservationists striving to protect riparian habitats throughout the West.

Mono Lake is a remarkable sight. California's second largest water body, it sits at the base of the Sierra Nevada escarpment, with strange looking spires and towers rising from its waters. It creates an image more of Mars than Earth.

In 1940 the California Division of Water Resources granted to the city of Los Angeles a right to divert for municipal use virtually the entire flow of four of the five streams feeding Mono Lake. The city went to work building a diversion structure to capture the flow of these tributaries and deliver it to Los Angeles via the Owens Valley aqueduct. With the completion of a second structure in 1970, the city was able to achieve its goal of capturing virtually all the water flowing in those streams for its water supply needs.

When Los Angeles first applied for its Mono Lake water rights nearly 50 years ago, local conservationists vehemently opposed the diversions. They argued that the delicate ecological balance of the lake would be upset if its tributaries were cut off. Though five fresh water streams feed Mono Lake, the waterbody has no outlet, and its deep waters are saline. No fish live in the salty lake, but its waters teem with brine shrimp that feed vast numbers of nesting and migratory birds. The most notable bird is the California gull, whose rookery is located on islands in the middle of the lake. Ninety-five percent of California's gull population (and 25 percent of the worldwide population) nests on these islands.

Conservationists' prediction that the city's planned diversions would damage the scenic beauty and ecological value the lake proved devastatingly true. Since 1940, the water level in the lake has dropped 43 feet, and the lake's surface area has shrunk by one-third, from 85 square miles to 60 square miles. Salts concentrated in the shrunken water body threaten the lake's algae and the brine shrimp and brine flies that feed on it. The increased salinity also interferes with the birds' ability to maintain osmotic equilibrium with their environment, forcing them to spend more time seeking fresh water to drink. Eighteen thousand acres of dry lakebed, now exposed to the air, have become a source of windborne alkali and other minerals that irritate the mucous membranes and respiratory systems of humans and other animals.

S.Ct. 703 (1988); *Orion Corp. v. State*, 109 Wash. 2d 621, 747 P.2d 1062 (1987) *cert. denied*, 108 S.Ct. 1996 (1986).

Wyoming: *Day v. Armstrong*, 362 P.2d 137, 152 (Wyo. 1961).

16. *National Audubon Soc'y v. Superior Court of Alpine County*, 33 Cal. 3d 419, 658 P.2d 709, 189 Cal. Rptr. 346 (1983), *cert. denied*, 464 U.S. 977 [1983]).

In 1979, the lake level dropped so low that Negrit Island, one of the lake's two principle islands, was transformed into a peninsula. As a result, nesting gulls and their chicks became easy prey for coyotes and other predators; ultimately the gulls totally abandoned the former island. Although the lake's devastation was foreseen in 1940, the California Division of Water Resources (as it was then known), which allocated the state's waters, declared that it was powerless to deny Los Angeles' diversion application: "It is indeed unfortunate that the City's proposed development will result in decreasing the aesthetic advantages of Mono Basin but there is apparently nothing that this office can do to prevent it" (Calif. Division of Water Resources Decisions at 7053, Apr. 11, 1940).

Nearly four decades later, National Audubon Society brought suit in state court[17] to stop Los Angeles from continuing its diversions. National Audubon charged that the waters of Mono Lake were impressed with a "public trust"—the same public protection that the U.S. Supreme Court found applied to the shore of Lake Michigan. Audubon's argument was simple: Waters held in trust for the people cannot be conveyed by the state for uses that are inconsistent with trust purposes, and the courts can enforce that trust for the benefit of the people of California at any time. The California Supreme Court[18] ultimately agreed with National Audubon—at least in principle. The court declared that the public trust doctrine was a part of California's water law and announced that public trust purposes must be taken into account in re-examining Los Angeles' water rights.

The court's authority to re-evaluate a city's water rights may sound dramatic or even Draconian. But the principle is no different from that applied in the law of private trusts. When a private citizen places money or property into a trust for the benefit of another, the manager of the trust (the trustee) is always subject to court supervision. If the trustee improperly conveys away the trust property to another person, the court has the power to take the trust property back and restore its benefits to the beneficiary.

In the case of Mono Lake, the trust property is the water of the state. The trustee is the state (and the state agencies that allocate the water), and the beneficiaries are the people. If the water board abused its responsibility to the people of the state by transferring the state's water—the water of Mono Lake—to Los Angeles, the court has the authority to correct the error.

Although the applicability of the public trust doctrine was firmly established by the *Audubon* case, the doctrine's practical effects are

17. The case has bounced back and forth between federal and state court. See footnote 19.

18. Los Angeles sought review by the United States Supreme Court, but its request was denied (*City of Los Angeles Dept. of Water & Power v. National Audubon Soc'y,* 464 U.S. 977 [1983]).

not yet known.[19] The California Supreme Court did not simply declare Los Angeles' water rights invalid, instead it announced that the state water agency (now known as the California Water Resources Control Board) should weigh the relative harm of diversion from Mono Lake against the water needs of the city.

The public trust doctrine is not an automatic bar to water development. As the court said:

> This opinion is but one step in the eventual resolution of the Mono Lake controversy. We do not dictate any particular allocation of water. Our objective is to resolve a legal conundrum in which two competing systems of thought—the public trust doctrine and the appropriative water rights system—existed independently of each other, espousing principles which seemingly suggested opposite results (*National Audubon Society*, 658 P.2d at 732).

The decision makes it clear that the courts bear the ultimate responsibility to ensure that this cosmic balancing takes place. No longer can state agencies dole out water resources blind to the environmental implications of their actions. This does not, however, guarantee that Mono Lake will be saved. It does guarantee that the resource will have its day (or decade) in court.

Presently, the public trust doctrine is being used by conservationists and others in states all across the West to protect habitat and to obtain human access to streams. In every western state in which the issue has arisen—save Colorado[20]—the courts have recognized the public trust doctrine.

Those concerned that the courts have no business changing the traditional rules of water allocation—rules that ignore public value consideration—should be reminded that it was western state courts themselves that overturned hundreds of years of tradition in eastern riparian water law in adopting the prior appropriation doctrine (for example, *Irwin v. Phillips*, 5 Cal. 140 [1855]; *Coffin v. Left Hand Ditch Co.*, 6 Colo. 443 [1882]). It has always been the job of the courts to interpret and apply the common law in the context of contemporary experience. If anything, the public trust doctrine is a stabilizing influ-

19. The California Supreme Court decision did not end the litigation over Mono Lake. That court merely responded to a request from the federal court (where the case is still pending) to explain the relationship between the public trust doctrine and the state water system. Six years later, the case is still working its way through the courts (*National Audubon Society v. Dep't of Water & Power of the City of Los Angeles*, 858 F.2d 1409 [9th Cir. 1988]).

20. Colorado is the only western state to reject the public trust doctrine (*People v. Emmert*, 198 Colo. 137, 597 P.2d 1025 [1979]). That decision is now being challenged by a group of five conservation organizations led by the National Wildlife Federation (*Concerning the Application for Water Rights of the City of Aurora, Colorado, et al.*, Nos. 86-CW-37, 86-CW-202, 86-CW-203, and 86-CW-226 [filed Apr. 29, 1986]).

ence on a water allocation system that, if rigidly conformed to, would be on a collision course with other societal interests. In coming years, it is likely that the doctrine will be applied more often by the courts to ensure that the hard edges of western water law do not undercut the very principles of fairness and stability the law is intended to promote.

FEDERAL WATER RIGHTS

Federal Power Over Water

As recently as 20 years ago, most water lawyers believed that the federal government had no role in the allocation of water. Historically speaking, they were largely correct; legally speaking, they were dead wrong. The federal government has always had the authority to preempt state law when it acts under its delegated powers (for example, the commerce and property powers of the Constitution) coupled with the supremacy clause of the Constitution.[21] In other words, Congress has the power to override any and every aspect of state water law it chooses. This may seem startling, given the history of congressional deference to state water law. But that deference, such as it is, is not based on any constitutional limitation, but rather on congressional self-restraint.

If it determined to do so, Congress could enact a federal water allocation law and do away with state water law altogether. When one considers the broad range of natural resource matters that Congress has subjected to national control—everything from mineral extraction to air pollution—it is perhaps surprising that it has been so reluctant to do likewise with respect to water allocation. Indeed, while Congress has moved aggressively to preempt the field of water *quality* by enacting the Clean Water Act and other statutes, it has given the states relatively free rein with respect to water *quantity* (that is, water allocation).

This dichotomy is not founded in logic or policy, but rather in history. The first settlers in the West were really squatters. The land was owned almost entirely by the federal government. Miners and farmers took what they needed from federal land, and managed to scratch out an existence. When Congress began to actively manage the nation's vast western estate, resource use patterns had been well-established by local custom. Although Congress quickly passed laws controlling (and encouraging) the exploitation of its land resources

21. U.S. Const. art. VI, cl. 2 (supremacy clause); U.S. Const. art. I, Sec. 8, cl. 3 (commerce clause); U.S. Const. art. IV, Sec. 3, cl. 2 (property clause).

through such legislation as the Homestead Act of 1862 (May 20, 1862, ch. 75, 12 Stat. 392 [previously codified in part at 43 U.S.C. Sec. 161–163] [repealed by the Federal Land Protection and Management Act]) and the Hardrock Mining Act of 1872 (General Mining Law of 1872, 30 U.S.C. Sec. 22–39 [1982]), when it came to water, Congress simply acquiesced in the pattern of development established by the settlers.[22] In the language of the day, Congress "severed" the water flowing on public lands from the land itself and made the water subject to appropriation by private parties under state law.

In so doing, Congress washed its hands of any role in allocating water in the West—or at least so thought many western water lawyers. In fact, the federal government's power over water on federal lands was merely dormant. Today, that power is of immense importance to the protection of fish and wildlife habitat throughout the West.

Water for Indians: The First Federal Water Right

Federal power over water was first articulated in a once obscure Indian case handed down by the U.S. Supreme Court in 1908 known as *Winters v. United States* (207 U.S. 564 [1908]). In 1888, the United States entered into a treaty with an Indian tribe that created the Fort Belknap Indian Reservation along the Milk River in Montana. In the court's words, the purpose of the treaty was to convert "a nomadic and uncivilized people" into a "pastoral and civilized people" (*Winters*, 207 U.S. at 576). The Indians, by an earlier treaty, had been granted a reservation covering the entire state of Montana above the Mussel Shell River. This reservation was reduced in size by a subsequent treaty in 1874, and reduced again by the treaty of 1888 to the Indian's new "permanent home." The court found that in so shrinking their reservation, the Indians' former lifestyle was made impossible and their only means of existence was irrigated agriculture. The court then concluded that while the treaty of 1888 failed to reserve explicitly any water rights for the Indians, such a reservation must have been implied in order for the Indians to survive economically.

Federal Water Rights for Parks, Forests, and Refuges

For many decades, westerners viewed the *Winters* case as an anomaly of Indian law, and nothing more. That view was irretrievably shaken in 1963 by the Supreme Court's holding in *Arizona v. California* (373

22. This acquiescence was articulated in three federal statutes. The Act of July 26, 1866, ch. 262, Sec. 9, 14 Stat. 251 (codified at 30 U.S.C. Sec. 51, 52 and note 43 U.S.C. Sec. 661, Sec. 1 [1982]); The Act of July 9, 1870, ch. 235, Sec. 17, 16 Stat. 218 (codified at 43 U.S.C. Sec. 661 [1982]); The Desert Land Act of 1877, ch. 107, 19 Stat. 377 (codified at 43 U.S.C. Sec. 321 [1982]).

U.S. 546 [1963]) that the so-called Winters Doctrine applied equally to all federal "reservations." Suddenly, national parks, forests, and wildlife refuges—any area "reserved" from the public lands—were declared to have federal reserved water rights just like the Fort Belknap Indians won in 1908.

The federal reserved water rights doctrine now has been applied by the U.S. Supreme Court eight times[23] and could be condensed to this simple principle from a 1976 case:

> This Court has long held that when the Federal Government withdraws its land from the public domain and reserves it for a federal purpose, the Government, by implication, reserves appurtenant water then unappropriated to the extent needed to accomplish the purpose of the reservation (*Cappaert v. United States*, 426 U.S. 128 138 [1976]).

Thus, when federal legislation creating reservations is silent with respect to water, the courts will presume that Congress intended to reserve sufficient water to satisfy the purposes of the reservation.

These federal reserved water rights share many of the attributes of private appropriative rights under state law. First and foremost, they fit into the state priority system. They may be quantified in state court proceedings[24] to a specific flow at a particular place with a fixed priority date. In this respect, federal reserved rights bear little resemblance to the loosely defined riparian water rights found in the East.

In other respects, however, federal water rights differ from private appropriative rights. Most importantly, federal reserved rights arise by implication drawn from federal statute, not through compliance with state procedures. As a result they may be "back-dated" by the courts to the time of creation of the federal reservation. This makes them "senior" to any private state water rights that may have arisen subsequent to the creation of the reservation. It is this point which is most troubling to defenders of traditional western water law. The way the reserved rights doctrine evades the priority system—through back-dating—drives western water lawyers crazy.

Since the *Arizona v. California* case was handed down in 1963, western lawyers have fought the doctrine in every forum available, but

23. *Winters v. United States*, 207 U.S. 564 (1908); *United States v. Powers*, 305 U.S. 527 (1939); *Federal Power Comm'n v. Oregon*, 349 U.S. 435 (1955); *Arizona v. California*, 373 U.S. 546 (1963); *United States v. District Court for Eagle County*, 401 U.S. 520 (1971); *Colorado River Water Conservation Dist. v. United States*, 424 U.S. 800 (1976); *Cappaert v. United States*, 426 U.S. 128 (1976); *United States v. New Mexico*, 438 U.S. 696 (1978).

24. In 1952, Congress enacted the McCarran Amendment (43 U.S.C. Sec. 666 [1982]), which waived sovereign immunity and allowed the United States to be joined in state court actions to quantify water rights. The act applies, however, only to general stream adjudications of an entire river basin and not to lawsuits over single water rights.

they have lost the battle over the basic principle. The reserved rights doctrine is now a firmly established part of western water law; what remains to be decided is its scope.

Reserved Water Rights: How Extensive?

While no court has questioned the existence of federal reserved water rights, a great deal of argument has occurred over how extensive those rights are. The pivotal case was decided in 1978. (*United States v. New Mexico*, 438 U.S. 696 [1978]). In *New Mexico* the U.S. Supreme Court was called upon to resolve a dispute over how much water the Forest Service could claim under the reserved rights doctrine for rivers on national forests. The court concluded that reserved rights attached only to the primary, not to the secondary purposes of the reservation, and that only timber production and watershed management were primary purposes of national forests. Consequently, the court rejected the Forest Service's argument that it held reserved rights for instream flows to protect fish, wildlife, and recreation.[25]

While this case constituted in theory a major setback for the protection of instream flows in national forests, its practical effect may not be so bad. Hydrologists for the federal government are now employing the emerging science of fluvial geomorphology in an effort to determine the flows necessary to meet the primary forest purpose of watershed management. In short, they have discovered that it takes a great deal of water to sustain a healthy river course, and their work is equipping conservation advocates with new arguments for federal water rights. In a recent case, the Colorado Supreme Court determined that the federal government must be allowed to present evidence showing the need for peak flows to maintain natural stream channels on national forest land in Colorado (*United States v. Jesse*, 744 P.2d 491 [Colo. 1987]). If the natural stream channel can be maintained, habitat for fish and wildlife will be protected.

How all of this will shake out remains to be seen. But one thing is clear: the key players on this issue are no longer lawyers with treatises, but biologists with hip waders.

Protection of Wilderness Areas and Wild Rivers

While some courts are struggling with the quantification of reserved rights, others are dealing with the question of which federal reservations are entitled to reserved rights at all. When the U.S. Supreme

---

25. It should be kept in mind that the *New Mexico* case was limited to national forests. The primary purposes for national parks and wildlife refuges, for example, clearly include a broader range of goals including fish, wildlife, and recreation.

Court first extended the reserved rights doctrine beyond Indian reservations, it used broad language that applied the doctrine whenever "the Federal Government withdraws its land from the public domain and reserves it for a federal purpose" (*Cappaert*, 426 U.S. at 138). Since that time, however, disputes have arisen over whether the reserved rights doctrine specifically applies to federal wilderness areas and wild and scenic rivers.

The wilderness dispute came to the fore in 1984 when the Sierra Club brought suit in Colorado to force the federal government to claim reserved water rights on existing wilderness areas in that state. Water developers intervened, arguing that, unlike other federal reservations, wilderness areas do not carry with them implicit reserved water rights. The court disagreed (*Sierra Club v. Block*, 622 F. Supp. 842 [D. Colo. 1985] *later proceedings sub. nom., Sierra Club v. Lyng*, 661 F. Supp. 1490 [D. Colo. 1987]). It confirmed the existence of wilderness water rights and ordered the federal government to develop a plan to protect water flows in wilderness areas. The case is now on appeal before the Tenth Circuit.

Meanwhile, a federal court in New Mexico reached the opposite conclusion with respect to both wilderness areas and wild and scenic rivers.[26] No conservation organization participated in the New Mexico litigation, and the ruling issued by the court can fairly be said to be devoid of meaningful legal analysis. Indeed, it overlooks the fact the Wild and Scenic Rivers Act (16 U.S.C. Sec. 1271–1287 [1982 and Supp. 1985], see specifically, 16 U.S.C. Sec. 1284[c] [1982]) is the only organic public land legislation that explicitly creates reserved water rights.

On yet another front, Attorney General Edwin Meese joined with Secretary of the Interior Donald Hodel in issuing a nonbinding advisory opinion on the subject of wilderness water rights during Meese's final week in office in 1988.[27] Meese concluded that in enacting the Wilderness Act, Congress intended to defer to western water law and created no implied water rights. The opinion's major premise is that boiler plate language in the act precludes recognition of reserved water rights. The opinion fails to explain, however, why the same language in the Wild and Scenic Rivers Act does not prohibit reserved rights for those designations (which the opinion concedes exist). It remains to be seen how wilderness water rights will fare under the Bush Adminis-

26. *New Mexico v. Molybdenum Corp. of America*, No. CIV-9780 SC (D. N.M. Report of Special Master filed Feb. 2, 1988, affirmed by the court Feb. 2, 1988, motion for reconsideration denied June 2, 1988) ("Red River Adjudication"); *New Mexico v. Arellano*, No. CIV-76-036-SC (D. N.M. Master's Report filed March 27, 1987) ("San Cristobal Adjudication").

27. Federal Reserved Water Rights in Wilderness Areas, Opinion M-36914, Supp. III (July 26, 1988) (by Solicitor Ralph W. Tarr).

tration. [Editor's note: The latest round has been fired by the Congressional Research Service—*CRS Report for Congress: Wilderness Areas and Federal Water Rights* (Jan. 4, 1989). The report by Pamela Baldwin is a thoughtful rebuttal to the Meese/Hodel opinion.]

The legal battle over wilderness water rights constitutes just one ring in a two-ring circus. In the other ring is Congress, which has been busily at work considering new wilderness designations. In every wilderness bill it has considered, language on water rights has been proposed—running the gamut from claiming reserved rights for all the unappropriated water in the designated wilderness area to disclaiming all water rights. Few of these bills have become law, and the legislative tone for federal water rights largely will be set by the 101st Congress.

Two things are now apparent. First, federal water rights to protect environmental values are here to stay. Second, with the courts increasingly reluctant to read meaning into legislative silence, Congress will be required to be more explicit in defining the terms of these rights.

FEDERAL REGULATION OF WATER USE

Water Rights Versus Water Regulation

Fifty or a hundred years ago, water rights were pretty much all that mattered when it came to figuring out where water would flow. Increasingly, however, the question of who owns the water is proving to be only a part of the water puzzle. Control of water today is a function not just of who owns legal rights to the water, but also of the extent of government regulation of the activities involved.

Over the years, the federal government has enacted a host of environmental laws that significantly affect the allocation of water. While these laws do not create water rights as such,[28] they clearly affect water allocation. Indeed, as a practical matter, federal regulation of a variety of activities on rivers sometimes plays a more important role in protection of riparian habitat than does the matter of who owns the water rights. For example, ownership of the water becomes a moot point if the Corps of Engineers refuses to issue a permit for a proposed water project. Two federal laws deserve special attention: Section 404

28. One legal scholar has suggested that federal laws, such as the Clean Water Act's Section 404 program, should be viewed as creating a new breed of "federal regulatory water rights" (Tarlock, *The Endangered Species Act and Western Water Rights* [20 Land & Water L. Rev. 1 [1985]]. If that argument were taken to its logical extreme, virtually any governmental regulation, from zoning on down, could be viewed as creating property rights. The sounder approach is to maintain the intellectual distinction between property rights and government regulation of property.

of the Clean Water Act (Sec. 404, 33 U.S.C. Sec. 1344)[29] and the Endangered Species Act (16 U.S.C. Sec. 1531–1543 [1982])[30].

The Section 404 Program and Water Law

The Clean Water Act was enacted in present form in 1977.[31] As its name implies, the act deals primarily with water quality. But Section 404 of the act requires that any person wishing to discharge "dredged or fill material" into a waterbody must first obtain authorization to do so from the U.S. Army Corps of Engineers.[32]

This may sound like a rather specialized requirement of little relevance to wildlife habitat protection efforts, but it is not. Simplistically, most everything solid (including a dam) is deemed "fill" and anything wet (including a wetland) is considered to be "navigable waters."[33] Consequently, anyone wishing to place a dam or diversion structure in a river must first obtain a Section 404 permit—even if he or she has

29. Section 404 is by no means the only legal authority for federal regulation of private activities affecting rivers. The Corps' Section 404 authority parallels its authority under Section 10 of the Rivers and Harbors Appropriations Act of 1899 (33 U.S.C. Sec. 403 [1982]). Indeed, the Corps typically issues a combined Section 10/404 permit. Private hydropower projects are licensed by the Federal Energy Regulatory Commission (Federal Power Act, 16 U.S.C. Sec. 791a-825r [1982] as amended by the Electric Consumers Protection Act of 1986, Pub. L. No. 99–495, 100 Stat. 1243 [1986]). Moreover, any water project involving public lands is subject to a variety of controls by the federal land manager.

30. The Endangered Species Act applies both to private development requiring a federal permit (such as Section 404) and to federal water projects (for example, those built by the Corps of Engineers or the Bureau of Reclamation).

31. The precursor to the Clean Water Act was enacted in 1948 (Federal Water Pollution Control Act, ch. 458, 62 Stat. 1155 [1948]). It emphasized state enforcement of water quality standards. The Water Quality Act of 1965 (Pub. L. No. 89–234, 79 Stat. 903 [1965]), marked the first assertion of primary federal authority in national water pollution control efforts. Its approach allowed some pollution, up to ambient standards set by the states. When this approach proved ineffective, Congress enacted the Federal Water Pollution Control Act Amendments of 1972 (Pub. L. 92–500, 86 Stat. 816 [1972]). The amendments adopted direct restrictions on discharges and made it unlawful to discharge a pollutant without obtaining a permit. The amendments also created federal minimum effluent standards. Congress established the goal of "fishable and swimable" waters by the year 1983, and zero discharge by the year 1985. The Act was amended in 1977 (Pub. L. 95–217, 91 Stat. 1567 [1977])—renaming it the Clean Water Act—and again in 1987 (Pub. L. No. 100–4, 101 Stat. 60 [1987]).

32. The act does contains a list of exceptions. For example, various on-going farming, silvicultural, and ranching activities are exempted from Section 404 (33 U.S.C. Sec. 1344[f][1] [1982]). Likewise, the Corps can essentially exempt other activities by issuing what is called a "general permit" for them (33 C.F.R. Sec.325[e][2] [1987]) [regional permits]; (33 C.F.R. part 330 [1987] [nationwide permits]).

33. *United States v. Riverside Bayview Homes, Inc.*, 474 U.S. 121 [1985]; Meyer, *Navigating the Wetlands Jurisdiction of the Army Corps of Engineers*, 9 Resource L. Notes 3 (Nat. Resources L. Center, 1986).

already obtained the necessary water rights under state law. Under the Clean Water Act, the Corps of Engineers[34] is obligated to consider the effect of proposed activities on the broad public interest in determining whether to issue or deny a Section 404 permit. This means that the Corps may prohibit a dam project, the filling of wetlands, the dredging of harbors, or any other activity requiring a 404 permit, if it determines that the project is not in the public interest.

Of course, figuring out what is in the public interest is a rather subjective task. Consequently, courts tend to defer to the Corps' determinations, making it difficult for conservationists to challenge Corps decisions. All this changes, however, when the Clean Water Act is coupled with Section 7(a)(2) of the Endangered Species Act (16 U.S.C. Sec. 1536[a][2] [1982]).

The Endangered Species Act and Water Law

No federal environmental statute is as absolute as the Endangered Species Act. The act requires, without exception, that federal agencies not permit activities that are likely to jeopardize the survival of endangered or threatened species or destroy or adversely modify its critical habitat. There is no room for discretion; the government may not determine that the advantages of a particular project outweigh the potential loss of a species.[35] Consequently, when endangered or threatened species are involved, the Endangered Species Act combines with Section 404 to provide a potent river protection weapon.

A case in point occurred in Colorado a few years ago when the Riverside Irrigation District proposed to build Wildcat Dam on a tributary of the South Platte River. The Corps refused to issue a Section 404 permit for the project because of the potential adverse impact of the dam on downstream whooping crane habitat (*Riverside Irrigation Dist. v. Andrews*, 758 F.2d 508 [10th Cir. 1985]). The Irrigation District sued, claiming that the "Wallop Amendment" to the Clean Water Act[36]

---

34. The Environmental Protection Agency (EPA) is the primary implementing agency of Clean Water Act and logically should have been assigned the role of administering Section 404 of the act as well. However, a political compromise resulted in the Section 404 responsibility being handed to the Corps, while EPA retains a veto power over all 404 permits (Clean Water Act, Sec. 404[c], 33 U.S.C. Sec. 1344 [1982]; 40 C.F.R. part 231 [1987]).

35. Following the celebrated snail darter case, *TVA v. Hill* (437 U.S. 153 [1978]), which blocked construction of the Tellico Dam in Tennessee, Congress amended the act in 1978 to allow an "Endangered Species Committee" of top federal officials to approve projects despite jeopardy to endangered species (16 U.S.C. Sec. 1536[e]; 50 C.F.R. Parts 450–453 [1988]). Despite this authority, the committee (often referred to as the "God Committee" because of its power affecting the life or death of a species), has never exempted a project. Most political analysts doubt the committee ever will.

36. The "Wallop Amendment" provides: "It is the policy of Congress that the authority of each State to allocate water within its jurisdiction shall not be superseded,

prohibited the Corps from interfering with anyone's water rights, and that a Section 404 permit could not be denied just because the water was needed for some other purpose (for example, protection of endangered species). When the Corps waffled in its defense, the National Wildlife Federation intervened.

The court sided with the Federation. It declared that the Wallop Amendment was merely a policy statement that did not override the Clean Water Act's clear and explicit mandate that the Corps regulate the disposal of material in water to maintain the ecological integrity of rivers. The case appears to have put to rest the argument that western water rights are exempt from federal regulation.

Colorado River Endangered Fish Protection

Today, dam projects across the West are coming under increasing federal scrutiny. In project after project, the Corps, and other federal agencies, such as the U.S. Fish and Wildlife Service (FWS), are calling the shots when it comes to water-project development. Having been thrust into the role of river habitat managers, these agencies are struggling—sometimes not so effectively—to develop strategies for fulfilling their new obligations.

A thought-provoking example is found in the Colorado River Basin where three endangered fish reside: the Colorado squawfish (*Ptychocheilus lucius*), the bonytail chub (*Gila elegans*), and the humpback chub (*Gila cypha*). Over a dozen water projects are now planned for the Colorado River (at various stages of seriousness, from far-fetched to ready-to-go). In each case FWS is required under the Endangered Species Act to issue a "biological opinion" indicating whether or not the proposed project is likely to harm endangered species. A so-called "jeopardy opinion" means that the activity is likely to jeopardize the survival of a listed species and cannot go forward.[37]

FWS is developing a recovery plan for the endangered fish of the Colorado River that will enable it to issue "no jeopardy" biological opinions on proposed projects in exchange for payment, which it calls a one-time "depletion charge" of $10 per acre-foot of water. Some water developers call this blackmail. Some conservationists call it a sellout.

---

abrogated or otherwise impaired by this Act. It is the further policy of Congress that nothing in this Act shall be construed to supersede or abrogate rights to quantities of water which have been established by any State" (Clean Water Act Sec. 101[g], 33 U.S.C. Sec. 1251[g] [1982] [enacted in 1977]).

37. FWS serves as an advisor to all other federal agencies with respect to endangered species matters. Although FWS cannot veto a project, federal agencies ordinarily follow its advice. Consequently, a "jeopardy opinion" for all practical purposes means that the activity will not be permitted.

In fact, it is probably a good idea in principle, but has some serious flaws in implementation.

The idea behind the charge is that water project developers should contribute to a fund (supplemented by contributions from federal and state government) that will be used to restore habitat along the river, including the purchase of existing consumptive water rights for conversion to instream flow maintenance. To the extent that enough money is collected, willing sellers are found, instream rights can be legally protected, and the program is properly managed, FWS' initiative represents an exciting new concept in project mitigation. If any one of these assumptions fails to pan out, the depletion charge system becomes unworkable.

The obvious solution is to build into the biological opinions and project permits, conditions that can be adjusted if aspects of the initiative falter or fail. For example, if more water must be purchased than originally assumed, or if water rights cost more than expected, project developers should be required to make up the shortfall. The developers claim they cannot live with such uncertainty. Conservationists counter that the endangered fish may not either. Just where FWS will come out on this is not yet clear, but its decision will help to chart the future course of the federal government's role in river management.

CONCLUSION

Western water law is on the verge of major change, and not a moment too soon. Threats to river environments are mounting daily. The old system of water allocation is simply not up to the task of balancing traditional water uses against new demands for environmental protection. In the coming years, a significant transformation in century-old western water law is likely to occur.

Six forces are at work. First, there is a shift in political strength among water users; old guard agricultural users are losing power to growing cities. Second, there is increasing public awareness of the importance of water to the maintenance of natural ecosystems. Third, there is greater appreciation of the relationship between a healthy environment and a healthy economy. Fourth, there is a growing coalition of "new" user groups advocating river protection: municipalities, homeowners, scientific organizations, and the recreation industry. Fifth, the economic cost of inefficient water use is becoming more fully appreciated. These costs include not only the wasted tax dollars that have gone into subsidized water development, but also the enormous cost of environmental damage correction these projects often require after they are built. Sixth, the states, motivated by the threat of a stronger federal role in water allocation, are taking a more active role in water resources management. This is reflected both in the actions of state legislatures (for example, through instream flow programs) and state courts (for example, via recognition of the public trust doctrine).

The combined effect of these forces all but guarantees that the old rules of water allocation will give way. What remains to be seen is how quickly and in what form the new rules will emerge. For conservationists, the upcoming tug-of-war spells enormous opportunity and urgent necessity.

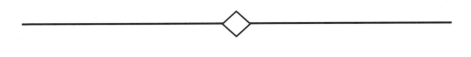

ADDENDUM 1

The Basic Rules of Western Water Law

First Come, First Served.   Water in the West is governed by the "doctrine of prior appropriation." The fundamental principle of this doctrine is that the first person to divert water from a stream has the right to continue his or her use of water in times of shortage. Early water users are "senior," while those who come later are called "juniors." There is no water sharing in time of shortage. If there is not enough water to go around, junior users are cut off one by one starting with the most recent user until there is enough water to satisfy the entire, undiminished shares of the more senior users. The date on which an individual (or his or her predecessor) first began to use the water is known as the user's priority date. The more senior the priority date, the more secure the water right, regardless of where the user is located on the stream.

Water Must Be Applied to a Beneficial Use.   "Waste" of water is prohibited under western water law. But one person's idea of what constitutes waste may differ from another's. For example, irrigating Kentucky bluegrass lawns in cities in the arid West or running volumes of water through leaky unlined canals historically has not been considered waste of water, whereas releasing water from a reservoir to support white-water boating is considered in many jurisdictions to be a wasteful use.

Water Must Be Diverted From the Stream. The traditional rule is that to obtain a water right, the user must "divert the water to a beneficial use." So-called "instream" uses (such as recreation or wildlife habitat protection) flunk both the diversion requirement and the beneficial use requirement. An instream use entails no diversion from a stream, and aesthetic uses of water bodies historically have not been regarded as beneficial. Today, however, many states are changing the rules to provide limited legal recognition for instream water rights.

Water Rights Are Freely Transferable. In most western states, water rights may be bought, sold, and moved around rather freely. Users may change both their "point of diversion" and type of use. For example, a city may find it less expensive to purchase agricultural water rights than to build a new dam. There is one important caveat, however: No change in water rights may "injure" any other user on the stream, including juniors. For example, junior diverters who rely on return flows from upstream irrigation may block any water transfer that would reduce that return flow. In the case of a proposed transfer of water rights by an upstream user, only the water actually *consumed* by the upstream user may be transferred away from the stream. For example, if 60 percent of an upstream user's irrigation water is consumed through evapotranspiration while 40 percent is returned to the stream, the upstream user could sell 60 percent of water he or she diverts, but must allow the remaining 40 percent to reach downstream users. Thus, the downstream users are no worse off after the transfer.

Use It or Lose It. Unlike all other property rights, simple failure to use water for a period of time may result in a permanent forfeiture of the right to use the water in the future. For example, if a farmer stops irrigating for a number of years, he or she will still own the land, but may be deemed to have abandoned the water right. If the farmer later wishes to begin irrigating again, he or she will have lost the senior priority to do so. (Technically, "forfeiture" occurs automatically after a given number of years regardless of intent, while "abandonment" may occur at any moment that the user forms a mental intent to abandon his or her water right.)

Interstate Compacts: A Different Story. The "use it or lose it" rule applies only to individual users within a single state. It is a popular misconception that the rule also applies to water bodies shared by two or more states. In fact, water allocation between states is determined by interstate compacts and court decrees that typically guarantee a portion of the water to each state, thereby ensuring that slowly developing states will not lose out to rapidly developing ones.

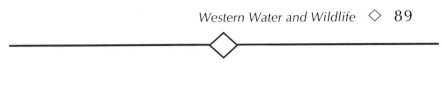

ADDENDUM 2

Water Law Doublespeak

Two key terms in western water law—conservation and waste—have meanings to water lawyers quite different from those understood by most lay persons. The peculiar use of these words provides a useful insight into the nature of western water law.

Consider the word "conservation." While most people conserve water by trying to *use less*, to western irrigators water conservation means building dams in order to *use more*. Likewise, "water conservation districts" function as local dam-building agencies, and are often the primary opponent of environmental conservationists who seek more efficient water use in order that more may be left in free-flowing rivers.

The use of the term "waste" in the West is illustrated nicely by a story sometimes told in water circles about a family of farmers in New Mexico. One Sunday the family went out for a picnic, and settled on a beautiful spot along the Pecos River. Two old men sauntered over to the riverbank, where they stood watching the sparkling river drift by. One farmer let out a long, knowing sigh, turned to the other, and said, "Isn't it just a shame to see all that water going to waste?"

In a simple way, this anecdote captures the difference in perspective over water left in the river, a difference that has driven the conflict over water allocation in the West. All of us appreciate at some level the beauty of a river. After all, the family in this story drove miles to picnic by a river. But there is something deeply ingrained in westerners that makes them think of water as a resource that either serves humans or is wasted. Just as one might exclaim, "Oh, what a waste!" when a bathroom faucet is left running, many westerners view bankfull flows in a river as a waste. This paradoxical notion is evident in the following quotation from a 1950 U.S. Supreme Court decision:

> These dominating rivers [the Sacramento and the San Joaquin in California] collect tribute from many mountain currents, carry their hoardings past parched plains and thriftlessly dissipate them in the Pacific tides. [I]t is sought to make these streams yield their wasting treasures to the lands they traverse.
>
> To harness these wasting waters, overcome this perversity of nature and make water available where it would be of greatest service, the State

of California proposed to re-engineer its natural water distribution. . . . A cost of refreshing this great expanse of semiarid land is that, except for occasional spills, only a dry river bed will cross the plain below the dam (*United States v. Gerlach Live Stock Co.*, 339 U.S. 725, 728–29 [1950]).

The challenge for conservationists today is to mold the law of rivers to fit modern notions of what is waste and what is wonder.

ADDENDUM 3

How a Water Right Is Obtained

People unfamiliar with western water law are often baffled at the concept of a "water right." There is no equivalent in the East. (However, some eastern states are moving toward adoption of permit systems that resemble in some ways the prior appropriation system of western water rights.)

In brief, a water right is a legal right to a certain quantity of water from a certain point on a river (or from a well), during a specified time or season, for application at a particular place. Thus, a farmer might own a water right to divert a total of 300 acre-feet of water per year to apply to 100 acres of land for irrigating crops during the course of the growing season. The right is sometimes expressed in volumetric terms (typically acre-feet) and sometimes as a specific flow (typically, cubic feet per second).

Each western state has its own procedure for obtaining legal documentation of a water right. In all states except Colorado, an individual wishing to obtain a water right must first apply to a state agency, often headed by a state engineer. A hearing is held, objections are considered, and a permit authorizing the diversion of water is either granted or denied. In either case, disappointed parties may appeal the decision through the state courts. (Colorado is unique in clinging to an archaic system wherein a person may create a legal water right simply by going out to a stream and diverting its waters. Then, after the fact, the person may go to a special state water court to have his or her *de facto* water right confirmed. In practice, no one does this anymore. Instead, a potential diverter goes to the water court in advance to obtain a "conditional water right," which, in practical effect, resembles the water use permits issued by other states.)

Most water rights are obtained through this case-by-case process. Western states, however, also conduct proceedings called "general adjudications" in which every person then using water within a specified river basin is required to come forward and establish his or her water rights. (Again, Colorado is the exception. The state has combined its individual water proceedings into something resembling a permanent ongoing general adjudication.[38] These general adjudications are terribly complex and often go on for decades. (See footnote 24 regarding the McCarran Amendment and general adjudications.)

When rivers cross state boundaries, the states themselves often fight over how much water their citizens are entitled to use. If the states are able to work out a compromise, they enter into an "interstate compact." If approved by Congress, these compacts become binding agreements. If, however, no accord can be reached, the states may go directly to the U.S. Supreme Court and request the court to issue an "equitable apportionment decree" dividing up the water. These compacts and decrees do not create individual water rights in themselves. Instead, entire states are guaranteed the right to develop uses for a given quantity of water from a river system. It is then up to each state in accordance with its own law to determine how and by whom its share of water will be developed.

Christopher H. Meyer is an attorney with the National Wildlife Federation's Rocky Mountain Natural Resources Clinic in Boulder, Colorado, where he specializes in western water law.

38. *United States v. District Court of County of Eagle*, 401 U.S. 520 [1971]; *United States v. District Court for Water Div. No. 5*, 401 U.S. 527 [1971]; *United States v. Bell*, 724 P.2d 631 [Colo. 1986].

When loggers first reached the Pacific Northwest, huge evergreen trees were common; now the only sizeable tracts of "old growth" are on public lands, and they are quickly being fragmented. Conservationists claim that we must keep relict stands in order to save the "blueprint" to our native, natural forest. *Oregon Historical Society*

The Pacific Northwest's Ancient Forests: Ecosystems under Siege

Andy Feeney

INTRODUCTION

In just four centuries, most of North America's virgin forests—eons in evolving—have been dramatically altered by the civilization first introduced by European settlers. Some authorities estimate that of the original forests once covering much of the coterminous United States, some 83 to 98 percent have been logged or lost to natural factors since Columbus's time (Thomas *et al.* 1988). Millions of acres of forest land (not all of it virgin forest) have been set aside in parks and designated wilderness areas. But outside these enclaves, as Jack Ward Thomas and others observe, "Management for production of wood fiber is rapidly changing the structure and composition of forests throughout North America." Activities aimed at the "dramatic reduction or elimination of forest stands beyond the age of commercial maturation" have interrupted natural ecological succession on both private and public lands. The result is forest landscapes dominated by relatively young and undeveloped stands of trees (Thomas *et al.* 1988).

Young, managed forests located on public lands, as well as those operated as "tree farms" by giant forest industry companies such as Weyerhaeuser and Georgia-Pacific, have helped the public and the forestry profession regain confidence in the availability of future wood supplies after earlier fears of a coming "timber famine" (Schallau and Alston 1987). But these younger managed forests usually consist of only one or two commercial tree species grown on rotation schedules that allow logging every 40 to 80 years. Moreover, they lack the biological niches for wildlife found in virgin forests, and some researchers question whether they have the "structural and functional diversity" needed to maintain long-run forest productivity (Thomas *et al.* 1988). Furthermore, stands of commercial timber grown on short rotation schedules and logged through clear-cutting lack many aesthetic qualities cherished by the American public. Accordingly, the dispute over the logging or preservation of virgin forests in becoming an important environmental issue throughout the United States.

Patches of virgin forest still exist in many regions of the country, especially where the terrain is relatively rugged and inaccessible. But the Douglas-fir growing area of the Pacific Northwest is the region where controversy over ancient forests has emerged most clearly. This region contains the most diverse coniferous forests in the world and a very wide array of life forms; it is also the source of approximately one-third of the softwood sawtimber cut in the nation (Olson 1988). Particularly in the area west of the Cascade and Sierra Nevada mountain ranges, and stretching from San Francisco north to Canada, immense groves of old trees still stand within the national forests and other public lands. The 12 "westside" national forests where logging of ancient stands is most disputed include the Shasta-Trinity, Six Rivers, and Klamath national forests in California; the Rogue River and Siskiyou national forests straddling the California–Oregon border; the Siuslaw, Umpqua, Willamette, and Mt. Hood forests in western Oregon; and the Gifford Pinchot, Olympic, and Mt. Baker-Snoqualmie forests in western Washington (see Figure 1).

Timber sales on the westside forests garner considerable receipts for the Forest Service. Logging and processing of wood from these forests also benefit the timber industry and provide jobs for loggers and mill workers in Oregon, Washington, and northern California (although the economic significance of the wood-products industry is most marked in Oregon). To some degree, timber exported from the Pacific Northwest to various Pacific Rim markets contributes to the nation's balance of trade. And under federal law, one-quarter of the gross revenues generated by National Forest System timber sales are returned to local county governments in lieu of the Forest Service paying local real estate taxes. Similarly, one-half of the gross revenues generated by the Bureau of Land Management's timber reserves in western Oregon are returned to local counties for roads and schools. This gives Pacific Northwest residents a powerful economic incentive to have the logging of public lands continue.

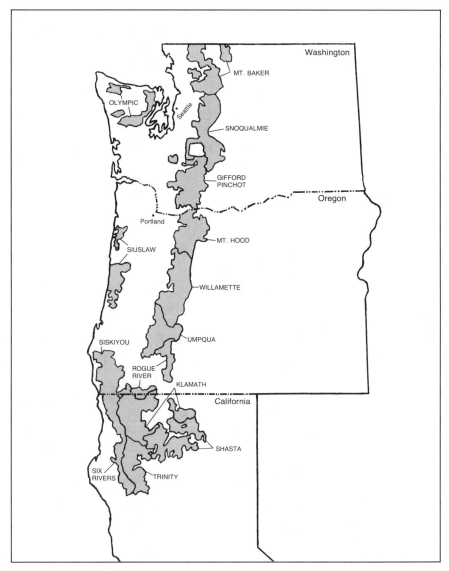

Figure 1. The westside national forests in the Pacific Northwest. National forests in Washington and Oregon are administered by Forest Service Region 6; in California, by Region 5.

At the same time, the Pacific Northwest's virgin forests provide wildlife habitat for numerous species of mammals, birds, amphibians, and invertebrates while helping to regulate runoff in the watersheds important to urban water supplies and the region's salmon industry. The unique scenic values provided by stately and ecologically complex groves of ancient trees, including some individual giants dating back to the days of Chaucer or even Charlemagne, also enchant forest visitors. Rapid liquidation of ancient groves on the region's national forests is thus causing concern in some scientific and government circles and among environmentalists. At stake are also the remaining virgin forests that lie on BLM's "Oregon and California Railroad" lands in southern Oregon. These so-called "O&C" forests are being logged rapidly.

Under a planning process established by the National Forest Management Act of 1976 (NFMA), the Forest Service, timber industry, government officials, and conservationists are currently debating draft management plans for the national forests. While NFMA planning has been controversial across the country, it is particularly so in the Northwest because of the high economic and ecological values of the westside forests.

Meanwhile, in a separate action with implications for forest plans, conservationists have petitioned the U.S. Fish and Wildlife Service (FWS) to list as threatened or endangered two bird species that frequent these forests—the northern spotted owl and the marbled murrelet. Conservationists working on the listing petitions emphasize that both species are worth preserving in and of themselves, quite apart from their connections with ancient forests. But it is widely agreed that if either bird were listed, significant portions of the Pacific Northwest's oldest forests would have to be designated as critical habitat for the species and protected from future logging.

Habitat for the owl occurs on ancient forestlands within 13 of the 19 Pacific Northwest national forests, on both sides of the Cascades. These include the Rogue River, Siskiyou, Deschutes, Gifford Pinchot, Mt. Hood, Siuslaw, Umpqua, Willamette, Winema, Mt. Baker-Snoqualmie, Okanogan, Olympic, and Wenatchee forests in Oregon and Washington. Additional owl habitat exists on several California national forests, including Shasta-Trinity, Six Rivers, and Klamath. The marbled murrelet is a seabird that apparently nests in older forests along the Oregon, Washington, and California coasts. (See the "The Marbled Murrelet" chapter in this volume for more information.)

In addition to petitioning FWS to list the owl, conservation groups have attempted for several years to influence the Forest Service to manage spotted owls as an indicator species for biological diversity under NFMA provisions. Recently, controversy has arisen between conservationists and industry over the Forest Service's final supplemental environmental impact statement for managing the spotted owl. As debate over the fate of the two birds and the NFMA planning process continues, several conservation organizations are challenging Forest Service and BLM timber sales in the courts. State and local governments and the Northwest's powerful congressional delegation also are involved in the fray over ancient forest management. Considering the stakes involved, the controversy is one that should concern conservationists for several years to come—until compromise is reached, until the remaining ancient forests are preserved, or until many of the older stands of trees are logged.

This chapter will explore the forest management controversy in the Northwest in depth. After a background section on the nature of the region's forest resources, the text will cover the wildlife of the forests, controversies between conservationists and industry over the very definition of so-called old-growth stands, other issues relating to the economic importance of timber and other forest resources, the NFMA planning process, the spotted owl and marbled murrelet controversies, the degree to which timber logging on the forests can preserve the stability of mill towns and small communities in the region, and some of the conservation movement's strategies for preserving ancient forests.

THE FOREST RESOURCE

For approximately 80 million years, coniferous or gymnosperm tree species—plants that produce seeds and cones and lack true flowers—have essentially been losing their evolutionary race against rival angiosperms, or flowering trees. Today gymnosperms, such as pines, spruces and hemlocks, still form impressive forest stands in many parts of the world; however, these coniferous forests are mostly confined to ecosystems that are too dry, too cold, too infertile, or otherwise unsuitable for angiosperms. Some of the largest coniferous forests still standing, for example, stretch across the harsh northern latitudes of the Soviet Union and Canada. Elsewhere, as in the American South, certain conifers exist as seral species within forests subject to frequent fires. Generally, however, angiosperms have displaced conifers in the world's richest, most productive forest ecosystems.[1]

There is one exceptional area where large coniferous forests still thrive under conditions of heavy rainfall, fertile soils, and excellent growing conditions. That region is the Pacific Northwest forest province, arguably the site of the "finest conifer forests in the world" (Norse 1988). Here, extremely large conifers belonging to several different species grow in a series of broad ecological bands reaching from the Pacific Coast inland to the Cascade Mountains, and from northern California along the west coast of Canada to southeastern Alaska. Biologists are unsure just why this rich tree-growing area is still dominated by conifers, but some believe the region's dry summers may discour-

1. Much of the information in this section, although not all, is based on the work of Elliot Norse, who is writing a book about the Pacific Northwest's ancient forests. Norse was kind enough to share much of the information below in a lengthy interview with the author in the fall of 1988.

age the growth of the broad-leafed angiosperms, which do most of their growing in the summer, while encouraging evergreen conifers that continue growing slowly even in the "nongrowing season" (Spies 1988). Outside of California's remaining redwood and sequoia forests, the Pacific Forest Province's huge conifer forests are virtually unmatched elsewhere in the world.

In the U.S. Northwest, ancient forest lands are sometimes called "Douglas-fir" forests after Douglas fir (*Pseudotsuga mendezeii*), their most common, economically valuable overstory tree.[2] The name, however, belies the ancient forests' biological complexity. As noted by ecologist Elliott Norse, the land west of the Cascades is profoundly influenced by rainfall from the ocean but is also broken up into numerous distinct ecosystems by smaller mountain ranges that cast large rain shadows across the land. Such mountains —the Olympics in the north, the Coast Range along the west coast of Oregon and Washington, and the Siskiyous and Klamaths to the south—capture moisture on their western slopes but block heavy precipitation on their eastern slopes and in lowland areas within their rainshadows. This causes major precipitation differences throughout the region and gives rise to several distinct forest ecosystems. In addition, the region's mountains display a series of relatively steep gradients, with the timber growing areas rising from near sea level along the Oregon coast to more than 6,000 feet along the tree line in the Cascades, where individual peaks reach to more than 14,000 feet. Changing elevations, by creating differences in temperature, moisture stress and winter snowpack, create a variety of provinces for forest trees.

Because of intersecting ecological factors, Douglas fir is only one of several large conifer trees that dominate different parts of the Northwest forests. According to Norse, 8 or 10 separate ancient forest communities are located in the region (Norse 1988). Charles Sisco (1988), of the National Audubon Society, identifies eight different physiographic provinces; Thomas Spies (1988), of the U.S. Forest Service, finds that the remaining old growth is concentrated in four or five plant communities. Where it is profitable, the timber industry is often reducing these forests to a single forest type: even-aged groves of Douglas-fir grown on land that has first been opened up through clear-cutting.

Sitka Spruce/Western Hemlock Forest

One important forest ecosystem—the Sitka spruce/western hemlock forest—lies in the narrow band of the Washington and Oregon coast between the Pacific Ocean and the Coast Range and extending from southern Oregon to Alaska. This vegetation type extends up major

---

2. Older stands of Sitka spruce may yield timber that is even more valuable than Douglas-fir, but much of the older Sitka spruce already has been logged.

river valleys, following the paths of fog rolling in from the ocean. Here, plentiful rainfall and frequent, heavy fog deliver up to 200 inches of precipitation per year and prevent the thin-barked Sitka spruce from succumbing to summer drought or fire damage. As a result, the land can support ancient forests of relatively fast-growing Sitka spruce intermixed with more shade-tolerant trees like western hemlock and western red cedar. Most of the older Sitka spruce forests outside of Alaska have been cut, due to the great economic value of the species. But where ancient spruce groves do exist, some of the trees can reach ages of 700 or 800 years, heights up to 300 feet, and trunk diameters up to 14 feet (Norse 1988, Spies 1988, Old-Growth Definition Task Force 1986). Western hemlocks growing with the Sitka spruce are a smaller, slower growing, and more shade-tolerant tree, reaching heights of perhaps 175 to 200 feet. However, many of the spruces and hemlocks in this forest province are between 100 and 200 years old as a result of natural fires that occurred within the past two centuries.

Douglas-fir/Western Hemlock Forest

Inland from the coastal area, the Pacific Northwest environment is drier and subject to more frequent fires. In several locations this difference gives rise to dominant Douglas-fir/western hemlock forests, especially in the lower elevations of the Coast Range, within the Puget Lowlands in the rainshadow east of the Olympic and Coast ranges, and on the lower western elevations of the Cascade Mountains in both Washington and Oregon. Douglas-fir replaces Sitka spruce in the canopies of such forests, the Douglas-fir having a thicker bark better able to withstand ground fires. Western hemlock, western redcedar, Pacific silver fir, grand fir, and bigleaf maple are among the larger shade-tolerant trees that make up the forest understory (Old-Growth Definition Task Force 1986). Douglas-fir/western hemlock forests are most common in the northern Washington portion of the Cascades, where much of the remaining Douglas-fir old growth is located (Norse 1988); in the Olympic Mountains, however, Douglas-fir/western hemlock stands may be interspersed with pockets of Sitka spruce (Spies 1988). Old-growth Douglas-fir averages around 500 years in age in most of these forests but can reach ages up to 1,000 years. It may grow to more than 240 feet in height and from 6 to 10 feet in diameter; however, in the highly productive Olympic Peninsula some individual Douglas-firs may reach 14 feet in diameter and 350 feet in height (Spies 1988, Norse 1988).

True Fir Forests

Snowfall is greater, temperatures colder, and fire somewhat less prevalent in the western Cascades above the Douglas-fir/western hemlock zone. Here, dominant trees are likely to be true firs such as Pacific silver fir, noble fir, or perhaps white fir (Norse 1988). Dominant trees grow to more than 150 to 180 feet in height and attain diameters of three to six feet, with some reaching 1,000 years in age or more (Spies 1988).

Mountain Hemlock Forests

Even higher in the mountains, woodlands are dominated by mountain hemlock and, in some cases, ponderosa pine. Growing more slowly than the region's lower elevation forests, older mountain hemlock forests generally reach heights of no more than 100 feet, diameters of no more than three feet, and ages of perhaps 400 to 500 years (Spies 1988). These forests are somewhat less diverse than Sitka spruce, Douglas-fir, or true fir forests and usually less threatened by timber cutting because of their high elevations and the fact that some are in national parks and protected from logging.

Mixed Conifer Forests

The mixed conifer forest type exists further to the south in the dryer and more fire-prone slopes of southern Oregon and northern California. These ancient forest stands are less likely to reach the ages and heights of those to the north. The oldest mixed-conifer stands are around 500 years old, with trees approximately 160 feet to 200 feet in height and trunks up to 6.5 feet in diameter. Although Douglas-fir exists as a dominant tree in such forests, it is accompanied by other coniferous species such as incense cedar, sugar pine, and white fir (Old-Growth Definition Task Force 1986). In fact, Douglas-fir, sugar pine, and ponderosa pine are considered functionally interchangeable as the dominant pioneer species in these forests, according to the Forest Service's Old-Growth Definition Task Force.

Mixed Evergreen Forests

In the Siskiyou and Klamath Mountain complex of northern California and southwestern Oregon much of the Douglas-fir that exists is found in mixed-evergreen forests. An interim report by the Old-Growth Definition Task Force (1986) notes that sugar pine sometimes replaces Douglas-fir as the dominant overstory tree in these forests. Such forests also include a variety of evergreen angiosperm trees, including tanoak, Pacific madrone, and canyon live oak, and may hold ponderosa pine, Port Orford cedar, and grand or white fir as well. They generally do not feature western hemlock in the understory (Norse 1988).

THE ECOLOGY OF ANCIENT FORESTS

There are significant ecological differences among the various types of ancient conifer forests, and it cannot be assumed that the structure found in one type will be duplicated in another. Yet all have certain elements in common, beginning with the presence of large and very old trees. All types support an array of wildlife species.

Complex, Multistoried Canopies

Ancient forests in this region tend to be ecologically diverse and structurally complex, with several layers of forest growth existing beneath a towering overstory. Where the highest level of trees in the forest is unbroken, dense shade may prevent the growth of most other plants along the ground. But usually the canopy is broken when large overstory trees are uprooted by wind or other natural forces. In crashing to earth, these fallen giants create openings in which direct sunlight allows other trees to flourish. As the younger trees grow to maturity, an ancient forest may come to have three or more canopies at different levels. Beneath these canopies, a relatively dense understory of shrubs and small trees may grow along the ground, at least in open patches of forestland. The layered structure of the canopies gives rise to certain important ecological features. Seeds borne in the canopy may support an array of seed-eating birds, including pine siskins and red crossbills (Hall 1988). The canopies also support lichens of the genus *Lobaria*, which fix nitrogen from the atmosphere and replenish the soil when they fall to earth. Although not unique to ancient forests, *Lobaria* seem to do best within the irregular, moist canopies of older coniferous forests (Spies 1988). The upper canopies of ancient forests also provide old, mossy branches and high nesting sites that may be critical to the nesting success of marbled murrelets across the southern part of their range (Marshall 1988). Researchers believe that these canopies are also essential for the survival of the northern spotted owl. This is partly because the ancient forest canopy seems to protect the owl from low temperatures, predation by great horned owls, and competition by barred owls (Advisory Panel on the Spotted Owl 1986). Female spotted owls, which are somewhat smaller than males, do relatively well under a denser overstory, but the males seem to prefer the more open structure afforded by varying levels of big trees.

Large, Downed Logs and Standing Snags

In sunlit gaps of an ancient forest, understory trees and shrubs such as the Pacific yew, vine maple, Oregon grape, and rhododendron may thrive, enhancing the ecosystem's biological diversity. Huge, fallen logs are a critical component of the ecosystem that allows such understory species to thrive. The "dead and down" logs fertilize the forest floor, releasing nutrients and accumulating moisture as their wood decays, becomes spongy, and takes in rainwater and metabolic water produced by bacteria (Maser 1987). According to Maser (1987):

> In our forests in the Northwest, a four hundred year old Douglas-fir usually lasts between two hundred and two hundred and fifty years as a fallen tree. That is before it is recycled. So we're talking about two and one-half centuries. This is a rough average. An 800-year-old Douglas-fir takes about 400 years to decompose and recycle into the system.... After death, it serves an entirely different suite of functions that are necessary to keep the forest going.

Large, rotted logs filled with moisture provide essential habitat for wildlife species such as the lungless Oregon slender salamander, according to Maser. In places, downed trees dam up small streams, creating temporary ponds that provide important habitats for aquatic life. Indeed, some researchers suggest that rotting wood falling into forest streams is important to the survival of salmon (Daniel 1988).

In addition, an ancient forest's dead, standing trees ("standing snags") and dead, fallen trees ("downed logs"), provide hollows and holes used as shelter by certain birds and mammals. For example, as standing snags rot, they create cavities used for nesting by pileated woodpeckers and other birds. As downed logs decay, they provide moist habitats for salamanders, frogs, and other amphibians, while hollow logs provide shelter for foxes and other large mammals (Norse 1988). The soft wood of large rotting logs, by supporting sizeable populations of insect larvae, also provides food for black bears.

Ancient Forests and Mycorrhizal Fungi

Maser suggests that 30 to 40 species of *ectomycorrhizal fungi*, organisms that grow on tree roots in the soil, can be found in the root systems of healthy Douglas-firs. These fungi form a protective mantle around the trees' root tips that prolongs their useful life, while also functioning as "an extension of the tree's root system" for picking up water and nutrients (Maser 1987). Mycorrhizal fungi growing in association with Douglas-fir and western hemlock also contain nitrogen-fixing bacteria. The normal propagation system of these fungi seems to depend on their forming fruiting bodies, or truffles, that are dug up and eaten by mammals, such as northern flying squirrels, Douglas squirrels, shrews, and red-backed voles. The spores of the fungi are then spread throughout the ecosystem in the feces of these animals, assuring a new fungus crop.

Citing the complexity of this system and its importance to forest productivity, Maser argues that maintenance of ecosystems featuring organisms like flying squirrels and mycorrhizal fungi is essential to maintaining healthy forests. In Maser's (1987) view:

> We need ancient forests not for spotted owls only, not for clean water only, not for recreation only, not for spirituality only; we need ancient forests for the survival of our forests . . . (Without them) we will . . . destroy our forests as every other nation has done.

But Charles Meslow, of the Fish and Wildlife Service in Corvallis, Oregon, questions some of Maser's conclusions about whether certain features of ancient forests are essential for their continued productivity. Meslow points out that foresters can mimic some important ecosystem functions—with forest nurseries, for example, routinely inocculating tree seedlings with mycorrhizal fungi in hopes of replicating one function naturally performed by the flying squirrel and other small mammals (Meslow 1988). Maser's response is that while foresters may learn how to perform many functions now provided by nature, they currently lack the knowledge to do so. "We invented the automobile; we designed it, we have a parts catalog, a maintenance manual, and a service station," Maser observes, "Where's the parts catalog, the maintenance manual, the service station for the forests? . . . As we liquidate old-growth forests, we are redesigning the forests of the future. The problem is that we've thrown away Nature's blueprint" (Maser 1987).

Dependent and Associated Wildlife Species

How many wildlife species depend on, or are "closely associated" with, Pacific Northwest ancient forests is unknown. At one time, old-growth forests were considered biological deserts. Only in the last 20 years or so has this view begun to change. Today, it is believed that more than 200 species of vertebrate animals exist within the ancient forests of western Oregon and Washington and northern California. According to David Wilcove (1988) of The Wilderness Society, at least 50 vertebrate species find their greatest distribution and abundance in "old-growth" forests of the Pacific Northwest.

The Forest Service reports that some 19 vertebrate species reach "greatest density for breeding or foraging in old-growth Douglas-fir forests of Western Oregon and Washington." These include the northern goshawk, northern spotted owl, bald eagle, Vaux's swift, pileated woodpecker, Hammond's flycatcher, pine grosbeak, Townsend's warbler, silver-haired bat, long-eared myotis, long-legged myotis, hoary bat, red tree vole, northern flying squirrel, California red-backed vole, coast mole, marten, and fisher (USDA Forest Service 1988).

The Forest Service also notes that several endangered and threatened species inhabit the Northwest's national forests, although they do not necessarily depend on old growth. The NFMA planning process mandates that such species be given special protection, which usually occurs through protection of nesting areas and other necessary habitat. Endangered species of note in the Northwest include the American peregrine falcon (*Falco peregrinus anatum*), brown pelican (*Pelecanus erythrorhynchos*, found in the Siuslaw National Forest near the ocean), Aleutian Canada goose (*Branta canadensis leucopareia*, found in the Siuslaw National Forest), northern bald eagle (*Haliaeetus leucocephalus*), grizzly bear (*Ursus horribilis*, documented on the Mt. Baker-Snoqualmie National Forest), and Oregon silverspot butterfly (*Speyerria zerene hippolyta*, documented on the Siuslaw National Forest) (USDA Forest Service 1988). Protection of most of these species is relatively easy to achieve, according to Meslow, since fairly small amounts of forest must be set aside from logging to accommodate their needs.

According to one source, as many as 1,500 species of insects and other invertebrates live within the canopies of the westside ancient forests. Other sources suggest that "thousands" of invertebrates are present. Many of these species have yet to be identified (Daniel 1988, Franklin 1988). Biologists caution, however, that a large portion of the organisms that live within the ancient forests can exist in other ecosystems, whether or not they enjoy "optimal" habitat conditions under the big trees. Meslow, for example, states that he would list only the northern spotted owl as likely to go extinct if all ancient forests were cut. The marbled murrelet and the bald eagle populations of the Pacific Northwest seem to need ancient forest trees for nesting, Meslow observes, but he believes these species are relatively easy to accommodate, since they require limited stands of large trees for nesting purposes. They do not use forests for foraging, and therefore do not require the preservation of large blocs of old growth for survival (Meslow 1988).

The spotted owl's level of need for old-growth forests has yet to be demonstrated for other species, according to Meslow. Still, as conifer forests age and develop greater structural complexity, certain species do appear that seem specialized in their abilities to exploit such old and stable ecosystems. These include pileated, downy, and hairy woodpeckers; the northern pygmy, northern saw-whet, and flammulated owls; various sapsuckers; tree swallows; purple martins; brown creepers; and various chickadees and nuthatches. Meslow cautions that many of these species rely not on the entire ancient forest, but merely on certain ecosystem features such as large dead snags and logs; therefore, they might be able to survive in more managed ecosystems in which these particular features were preserved (Meslow 1988).

According to other sources, Roosevelt elk are often observed using the edges of ancient forests for shelter in severe winter storms, but whether the elk truly depend on such forests is debatable. Recently, a Roosevelt elk herd took up semi-permanent residence on the devastated slopes of Mt. St. Helens. This may mean that the elk do not need ancient forests for survival—if they are protected from hunting and other disturbances and if grazing habitat is sufficient (Hunthausen 1988).

Recent Research Findings

Many observers believe too little research has been done in ancient forests to state definitively which species depend on this habitat. Furthermore, the studies that have occurred often compared younger, naturally regenerated stands—arising after natural fires of the past two centuries—with older stands. Rarely has the wildlife productivity of ancient forests been compared with that of managed monocultures, labelled by their detractors as "tree farms," that are rapidly replacing them in the region. Unfortunately, research on the wildlife of younger, natural forests may not be relevant to managed tree plantations, because the natural forests may include large downed logs and remnant snags from pre-fire ecosystems that monoculture forests generally lack. Therefore, it is unclear whether existing research fully captures the wildlife values at stake in the debate over ancient forest preservation.

New studies will undoubtedly cast more light on the wildlife significance of these forests. Between 1983 and 1986, for example, a consortium of scientists from the University of Washington, Washington State University, FWS, and the Forest Service surveyed wildlife on 135 different stands of young, mature, and old-growth Douglas-fir forest located in three forest provinces: the western Cascades in Washington, the western Cascades in Oregon, and the Oregon Coast Range. In turn, each of the three provinces was divided into three subprovinces, with 15 Douglas-fir stands studied on each subprovince. Within these 135 stands, researchers sought to identify wildlife species that were closely associated with, or alternatively of uncertain association with, forest groves 200 years old and older.

The results suggest that the Olympic salamander (*Rhyacotriton olympicus*) is highly associated with old growth in the Oregon Coast Range. The Oregon slender salamander (*Batrochoseps wrighti*), found only in the Oregon Cascades, also appears to be highly associated with old growth. So are *Myotis* bats in Oregon and the northern spotted owl throughout the three vegetation provinces studied (Hall 1988). In the wild, Vaux's swift was found to nest in large hollow trees in old-growth Douglas-fir forests. In urban areas, however, this same swift nests in chimneys.

Other species were discovered to be closely associated with older stands of Douglas-fir, although not to the extent of those previously mentioned. These species showing lesser but still significant association include the Olympic salamander in the Cascades; the tailed frog

(*Ascaphus truei*); the Oregon populations of the Pacific giant sala-mander (*Dicamptodon ensatus*); various cavity-nesting birds, includ-ing the pileated woodpecker, brown creeper, and several species of nuthatches; certain seed-eating birds (such as red crossbills, pine sis-kins, and chestnut-backed chickadees), and the northern flying squirrel (Hall 1988).

Similar research, coordinated through the U.S. Forest Service's Pa-cific Southwest Forest and Range Experiment Station, has identified wildlife species that seem dependent on, or closely associated with, older forests in southern Oregon and northern California. Researchers studied 54 forest stands in three Douglas-fir tree provinces: one within an area of California partly managed by The Nature Conservancy and partly by BLM; one in southern Oregon, on both BLM and non-BLM land; and one encompassing parts of the Six Rivers and Shasta-Trinity national forests in California. The stands studied were dominated by Douglas-fir, but also included some redwood, white fir, ponderosa pine, and other conifers.

According to researcher C.J. Ralph (1988), 15 of the 125 bird spe-cies for which representative samples could be obtained were more abundant in older rather than younger forests. However, only the marbled murrelet and, to a much lesser extent Hammond's flycatcher, apparently depended on old-growth stands. Among mammals, only the red backed vole was found to be much more common in old growth, while three reptiles and amphibians were found to be dependent on such stands: the tailed frog, the Olympic salamander, and the Del Norte salamander (*Plethodon elongatus*). The northern spotted owl probably requires old growth in northern California as well.

Additional research on the Andrews Experimental Forest, within the Willamette National Forest of Oregon, concerned the preference of birds for either closed or patchy forest overstories. The results suggest the hermit warbler and golden-crowned kinglet do best in older for-ests. These two species preferred patchy to closed canopies, and an-cient forests tend to have more open canopies than even-aged forests planted after clear-cutting. Eight other species studied apparently pre-ferred closed canopies or had no preference. They included the var-ied thrush, winter wren, western flycatcher, dark-eyed junco, brown creeper, red-breasted nuthatch, chestnut-backed chickadee, and hermit thrush (Hanson 1988).

Biologists caution that more research is needed before species closely *associated* with older Douglas-fir stands can be determined to *depend* on such stands. Conceivably, such research may turn up evi-dence that certain species will be endangered by the loss of old growth. Alternatively, scientists may discover such species have less associ-ation with ancient forest ecosystems than now believed. Species that depend on downed logs or standing snags for nests, for example, may be able to survive in managed forests where logging leaves some very large snags on the land (and some additional trees that will grow to a large size, die, and over several centuries replace the decayed snags with new ones). Therefore, some scientists who favor the preservation of ancient forests warn against basing their protection on the needs of a single endangered species or several such species, arguing that ancient forests should be preserved for their biological diversity and because they are unique, irreplaceable ecosystems.

OTHER NONTIMBER VALUES OF ANCIENT FORESTS

Even apart from the wildlife values at stake, the preservation of westside ancient forests has taken on the aura of a religious crusade for many conservationists and some biologists. The timber industry generally maintains that ancient forests can be replaced by managed forests with no loss in sustainability—a claim some scientists dispute. But in reply to such purely utilitarian thinking, one writer summarizes the conservationist perspective by stating: "We consider these forests to be of inestimable biological, cultural, and spiritual value. We believe that so much old growth has already been lost that . . . further losses are unacceptable." Trying to explain the emotional appeal of ancient forests another way, a second conservationist describes them as "temples" precious to the nation:

> Perhaps it is the awareness of a wild purity, the rare exhilaration of knowing that the forest before you has not been altered by men and women and their machines. It is somehow inspiring to think that a place has changed only according to the patient dictates of succession. . . . Non-Indian Americans have no antiquities, no centuries-old temples or icons that we can touch to pull us back into our history. But we do have these remnants of prehistoric forest, these thick-barked survivors of our natural heritage. The combination of antediluvian grandeur, quiet, incense, filtered light, and chaste vistas makes even the most sobersided visitor to an old-growth forest come away speaking of cathedrals (Wille 1988).

Another conservationist writes, "Some observers have compared the rapid destruction of the Pacific Northwest's forests to the looting of Europe's cathedrals" (Ervin 1988).

Arguably, the spiritual values in ancient forests perceived by conservationists and the competing ethical values and business goals expressed by timber industry supporters are at the heart of the conflict over ancient forests. Bitter social conflict is probably inevitable when one party in the dispute sees westside forests as "ancient cathedrals" while another sees them as raw material for regional sawmills, or as necessary to keep food on the table, or even as renewable resources to be converted into furniture, paper, and houses.

But perhaps because these conflicting values are hard to sort through in a vigorously secular and pluralistic society, conservationists stress that there are also pragmatic economic reasons for preserving ancient forests. To begin with, ecosystems play a significant role in Pacific Northwest watershed management, providing much of the drinking water supply for both Portland and Seattle (O'Toole 1988). According to some sources, domestic water produced in the Mt. Hood National Forest is worth up to $24 million annually (The Wilderness Society 1988). Yet surprisingly, the national debate over westside forest logging has focused relatively little attention on the extent to which replacing old growth with younger forests is (or is not) compatible with municipal watershed management.

The Pacific Northwest's natural salmon industry does seem to be threatened by rapid clear-cutting of ancient trees. Salmon and other anadromous fish often eat insects that thrive in pools formed when dead and downed logs lie across forest streams, creating natural dams. Such pools also shelter anadromous fish from storm run-off and extreme temperatures; some studies indicate that "populations of large salmonids, such as coho salmon and cutthroat trout, are directly related to pool volume on a stream" (Kelly 1988). Thus, some researchers partially link the precipitous decline of the Pacific Northwest's salmon fishing industry following World War I with the contemporaneous destruction of old-growth forests in the Coast Range (Kelly 1988).

Anadromous fish require relatively clear water, and forest logging and road building on steep slopes can trigger landslides and soil erosion that threaten trout and salmon with heavy sedimentation. According to The Wilderness Society (1988), some 60 percent of the erosion now occurring on the roaded portions of the Six Rivers and Willamette national forests comes from logged areas and another 40 percent from forest roads. Within California's Six Rivers and Shasta-Trinity national forests, sedimentation has reportedly caused chinook salmon populations to decline 88 percent and steelhead populations to fall 61 percent compared with previous levels (The Wilderness Society 1988). Thus, The Wilderness Society argues that preserving ancient forests is critically important to preserving salmon resources, adding that "landslides and sedimentation following road building and clear-cutting in sensitive drainages have already decimated anadromous fisheries in some westside forests" (The Wilderness Society 1988).

Compared to younger managed forests, ancient forests may show greater resistance to catastrophic wildfires. This appears to be because of their higher moisture content and the mix of hardwood and conifer species present. While wildfires may sweep easily through a young stand of replanted Douglas-fir, some researchers believe that the moisture and differing chemical content of hardwoods in an older stand will slow such fires and prevent them from reaching the conifers in the older stand. Thus, Oregon State University scientists studying the 1987 forest fires in southern Oregon and northern California found that old-growth forests "resisted damage from the fires to a greater degree than old stands" (The Wilderness Society 1988).

Older Douglas-fir forests also seem to have reduced densities of insect pests compared to younger forests, conservationists add, because their greater ecological complexity supports a variety of predators that prey on pests. Replacing older natural forests with younger, managed ones may thus increase "the likelihood of regionwide pest outbreaks" (The Wilderness Society 1988).

The scenic and recreational benefits of older forest stands, particularly if they are easily accessible to the public, are of considerable economic value to Oregon, Washington, and northern California. In part this is because of the sizeable recreational use of the forests by tourists. In addition, the environmental quality of the Pacific Northwest makes the region an attractive place to live and work, and the preservation of that quality is becoming important to state economic development officials.

DEFINING "OLD GROWTH"

In war, it is said, the first casualty is truth. In the political war under way over forest management in the Pacific Northwest, one important casualty is intellectual consistency. Until a few years ago, the common term used to describe the forests in question was "old growth," a phrase taken from the Forest Service's system for classifying forests according to their annual growth rate and biological productivity. As recently as late 1988, however, the Forest Service and major environmental organizations did not appear to agree on what old growth is, or on how much of it remained in the Pacific Northwest. According to a recent timber industry report, "There is no mutual agreement on the size or age of trees that are referred to as old growth. There is no universal agreement on an ecological definition for a stand of old-growth trees" (National Forest Products Association and American Forest Council 1988).

"Old Growth" and "Ancient Forests"

Partly because of this definitional debate, and partly because environmentalists are beginning to object to "old growth" as a term devised by the forestry profession for economic rather than biological ends, some conservation groups now characterize the oldest trees in the Pacific Northwest as "ancient forests." An "Ancient Forest Alliance" of local and national conservation groups and individual conservationists was formed in the fall of 1988 to preserve this resource (Pissot 1988). However, conservationists do not only want to preserve "ancient forests" and some "mature" forest stands that the forest industry may count as old growth, some also want to preserve large stands of younger sawtimber as well.

Who Defines the Forest?

In 1986 the Old-Growth Definition Task Force of the Forest Service provided an interim definition of old-growth timber that varied somewhat for Douglas-fir/western hemlock, mixed conifer, mixed evergreen, and Sierra mixed-conifer forests. Common to all four types was the requirement that old-growth stands must include at least six trees per acre that are more than 30 to 32 inches in diameter and more than 200 years in age. The stands must have multilayered canopies (except within mixed evergreen forests) and hold minimal amounts of large standing snags more than 20 inches in diameter and fallen logs at least 24 inches in diameter. The task force also characterized old growth as having some trees with deep crowns and broken tops (Old-Growth Definition Task Force 1986).

However, the Forest Service employed somewhat different old-growth definitions in its draft management plans for the 12 westside national forests. In some of these plans, old growth is merely identified as stands of trees at least 21 inches in diameter. In others it must include forests that exceed 200 years or 250 years in average age. In still others, it means "stands of mature and overmature trees" with trunks 21 inches or more in diameter and heights exceeding 50 feet, and so on (The Wilderness Society 1988a).

A Wilderness Society study conducted by forest ecologist Peter Morrison using the Old-Growth Definition Task Force's definition, found the Forest Service's latest old-growth inventory figures "highly suspect" and certain to exaggerate the amount of "true" old growth actually remaining. The use of inconsistent definitions that do not agree with those set by the Task Force, the Society claims, will lead to timber policies that accelerate old-growth logging (The Wilderness Society 1988a). In reply, timber industry representatives have accused The Wilderness Society of distorting the issue, adding that the Forest Service's definition of old growth in the draft plans is "broader" than that used by environmentalists, but "still defensible" (Public Timber Council *et al.* 1988). However, Forest Service Associate Chief George Leonard recently acknowledged that many old-growth figures used in the draft forest plans are based on data at least 10 years old and are therefore somewhat obsolete. Leonard also says the old, timber-oriented definitions used in obtaining the data did not address certain biological aspects of old-growth forests (such as the presence of large, downed snags) that may be essential to these forests as functioning ecosystems (Leonard 1989).

To help clear up conflicting claims about the nature and extent of the old-growth resource, Congress increased the Forest Service inventory budget by $600,000 in the FY 1989 appropriations bill, earmarking the money for work on a more precise definition for old growth and for an inventory of remaining old-growth stands. Congress directed the agency to work with BLM, the National Park Service, and various interest groups in accomplishing these tasks. Until the first part of this work is completed, Leonard says, the Forest Service cannot be said to have adopted the task force's 1986 definition, and it therefore cannot be accused of having violated its own definitions in drawing up the forest plans. Furthermore, Leonard adds that the agency is unlikely to accept the 1986 definition precisely as proposed. Using it for inventory work would require on-site inspection of virtually every stand of large trees in the westside forests—a process the Forest Service finds prohibitively expensive. By the summer of 1989, Leonard predicts, the Forest Service will probably adopt a new definition of old growth that represents a compromise between the task force's definition and other proposals. The new definition will probably enable the Forest Service to do some old-growth inventory work from airplanes (Leonard 1989).

In the meantime, the different definitions have led to varying estimates of how much old growth is left. In 1988, the timber industry said there were 7.5 million acres of old growth in Washington and Oregon alone (National Forest Products Association and American Forest Council 1988). The Forest Service's draft plans (using the outdated inventories previously mentioned) suggest that approximately 4.26 million acres of old growth exist on 11 of the 12 westside forests (Morrison 1988). Morrison's report for The Wilderness Society concluded that in the six national forests studied, old-growth inventories were only 45 percent of those estimated by the Forest Service (Morrison 1988).

ARE ANCIENT FORESTS BEING LIQUIDATED?

At present, the Forest Service estimates, roughly 70,000 acres of old growth are being cut in Washington and Oregon national forests each year. Agency sources say the cut is "predominantly" on the westside forests where Forest Service inventories indicate that 2.2 million of the 3.3 million acres of remaining old-growth trees in Oregon and Washington national forests exists (Delft 1989). The 70,000 acres of old growth logged in 1987 compares to a total clear-cut figure for the region's national forests of 95,000 acres. (In addition, another 80,000 acres of these national forests were subjected to "shelterwood" logging, firewood cutting, and thinning activities, bringing the logging total for the region to 175,000 acres.) (Delft 1989).

The Wilderness Society (1988a) suggests this situation portends the liquidation of the region's ancient forests. The Society, with some other conservation organizations, argues that an insufficient amount of old growth is protected and that the rate at which Pacific Northwest trees are being cut on both public and private lands is not sustainable. The timber industry, however, contends that an estimated 4.5 million acres of old growth is already withdrawn from production and thus constitutes a "protected legacy" in the region. The industry contends that this total includes 1.3 million acres in national parks and on BLM, state, Indian, and private lands; 700,000 acres in low and high elevations formally withdrawn from the timber base in the national forests, and included in wilderness areas and national parks; and another 2.5 million acres proposed for exclusion from timber production in NFMA plans, "to preserve scenic views or to protect sensitive soil and watersheds" (National Forest Products Association and American Forest Council 1988). But an additional Wilderness Society report, Morrison's *Old Growth in the Pacific Northwest: A Status Report* (1988), indicates that on six westside forests, only 352,000 acres of designated wilderness contain "ecologically significant" old growth trees.

Forest Service Associate Chief Leonard explains the situation differently. Leonard states that there are approximately 15.4 million acres of land within the 12 westside national forests. Of this total, 6.1 million acres are excluded from commercial forest acreage in westside forests. This acreage includes grazing lands and lands withdrawn from use as wilderness areas or classified as wild and scenic river corridors, as well as some other land. The remaining 9.3 million acres of national forest is considered "commercial forest land," but of this 9.3 million acres only 6.9 million acres are judged suitable for logging under the region's draft forest management plans. This leaves 2.7 million acres of "commercial" timberland in the westside forests, outside of the region's designated wild and scenic river and wilderness areas, on which no logging is scheduled under the draft forest plans. The 2.7 million acres includes lands on steep slopes and along stream banks where agency regulations preclude logging, as well as other lands set aside for the protection of spotted owls and other indicator species (Leonard 1989).

In response to charges that the Forest Service is liquidating old growth, Leonard replied: "There is and will always be an awful lot of old growth in the Pacific Northwest, much of it set aside in wilderness areas, in which old growth-dependent wildlife species and old-growth trees will continue to exist. We feel that overall, we're addressing the biological diversity needs for the region" (Leonard 1989).

There is at least one point on which industry, the Forest Service and conservationists do agree: much of the remaining old growth in the suitable timber base on the westside forests will be cut within 50 years under current policies. The reason lies in forest economics.

The Rotation Issue

From a management standpoint, many professional foresters view forest land that does not produce a yearly harvest of wood much as business economists view steel factories that do not produce a yearly output of steel. According to Leonard, there are several reasons for this. One is that the Forest Service follows the common business practice of discounting against the future by using inverted compound interest rates to calculate the "net present value" of scheduled timber sales on national forests. Because predicting the future is risky, the net present value of a giant tree that can't be harvested for 200 years is virtually zero, while its value as timber under today's prices can be readily ascertained. Leonard cautions, however, that net present value is only one factor the Forest Service considers in managing the forests and states further that the agency's goal is not to maximize the net present value of its timber, but to maximize the net value of the forests to society—considering both timber and nontimber resources. In the Pacific Northwest, the Forest Service contends that approximately 20 percent of the commercial timber is managed on "long" rotation schedules of 120 years or more, including some rotations of 250 years. But where the Forest Service determines the net present value of timber outweighs other values, national forests will be logged on "economic" rotation schedules that normally do not exceed 100 years (Leonard 1989).

Three additional factors also impel the Forest Service to manage most of the national forests in relatively short rotations, Leonard says. First, certain timber mills and communities depend on timber from the national forests to maintain themselves economically (see the following section on "The Economic Importance of Pacific Northwest Forests"). The Forest Service maintains that reducing the amount of timber flowing from the forests each year would cause many of these communities economic distress, at least in the absence of local economic diversification. Second, the agency generally prefers to maximize wood growth on the national forests, and most foresters contend that growth rates decline once trees reach an age of 80 to 100 years. In managing for a 100-year rotation period, the Forest Service sees itself as maximizing timber productivity. Finally, the agency allows logging in certain areas of the forests where steep slopes require the removal of logs by cable or even helicopter to prevent significant environmental damage. This occurs particularly on old, highly developed soils of the Oregon Cascades, where slopes are steep but a low erosion potential makes logging sustainable with the proper use of technology, Leonard reports. The cost of that technology, however, mandates that the areas in question be managed "relatively close to their productive potential"—that is, on fairly short rotation schedules.

For all these reasons, the agency generally finds it impracticable to manage cutover lands on the 200-year or 500-year rotations necessary to regrow ancient forests, assuming that this can be done at all. Unless new steps are taken to protect ancient forests, such timber-management factors virtually guarantee that old-growth forests judged suitable for timber production will eventually be logged and replaced by short-rotation, managed forests. Some Forest Service officials add that some areas of the westside forests that are not judged suitable for logging, but that are also not officially designated as wilderness or as wild and scenic rivers, are protected only by the agency's regulations. Since the regulations can change, these areas could be logged in the future as technology evolves.

It is a matter of judgment whether this portends the eventual liquidation of old growth, as many environmentalists contend. According to the industry and the Forest Service, what environmentalists call liquidation is merely the setting of a balance, which is more or less arbitrary, between timber and nontimber uses of commercial timber lands. Associate Chief Leonard notes that under the Multiple Use Act, the Forest Service is required to set a balance between managing land for commercial timber production and for other purposes, including outdoor recreation and preservation of undisturbed ecosystems. "Where you set the balance depends on where your values are. There is no right answer," Leonard contends.

Forest Fragmentation

Island biogeography theory predicts the gradual genetic and ecological destruction of isolated ecosystems. Some environmentalists believe the implications of this theory mean that ancient forests in the Northwest face a serious threat from fragmentation. Quite apart from questions of genetics and predator-prey relationships, the fragmenting of old-growth Douglas-fir stands means that they face greater exposure to wind. To prevent damage to watersheds, the Forest Service limits the size of clear-cuts on westside forests to 80 acres or less. Ironically, this disperses clear-cuts throughout the forests, and along with road construction may be exposing the westside's ancient forests to a significant danger from fragmentation.

In his study for The Wilderness Society, Morrison (1988) concluded that approximately 62,000 acres of the estimated 297,000 acres of remaining old growth in the Mt. Baker-Snoqualmie National Forest have been surrounded—and ecologically altered—by clear-cuts, young forest plantations, and nonforested areas. More than 27 percent of the remaining 106,000 old-growth acres in the Olympic National Forest are allegedly exposed to fragmentation as well, and Morrison claims that 55 percent of the 119,000 old-growth acres in the Gifford Pinchot occur in highly fragmented landscapes. Similar fragmentation reportedly affects 37 percent of the 178,000 acres of old growth in the Mt. Hood, 44 percent of the 299,000 old-growth acres in the Willamette, and 66,000 of the estimated 141,000 acres of old growth in the Siskiyou National Forest (Morrison 1988). Conservationists contend that this fragmentation could assure the elimination of most ancient forests as functioning ecosystems within 5 to 15 years.

Some Forest Service biologists admit the fragmentation problem is worrisome, but say the situation is not as dismal as environmentalists paint it. By preserving fairly large blocs of old growth as spotted owl habitat areas and by linking these blocs through wild and scenic river corridors and smaller "stepping stone" patches of old growth, they argue, the Forest Service should be able to preserve a sizeable amount of the ancient forest ecosystem. Jerry Franklin, a leading biological researcher on ancient forests, agrees with the warnings of environmentalists, but suggests that the fragmentation problem might be reduced in scope by changing the Forest Service's rule on maximum clear-cut sizes (Franklin 1989).

Clear-cuts in Williamette National Forest. *Barry Flamm/The Wilderness Society*

THE ECONOMIC IMPORTANCE OF PACIFIC NORTHWEST FORESTS

Approximately one-third of the nation's "softwood sawtimber"— lumber-grade wood from conifers—comes from the managed forests of western Oregon and Washington, which total 21.5 million acres for all ownerships, public and private. Jeffrey Olson, The Wilderness Society resource economist, reports that large, industrial timber companies own about 27 percent; the Forest Service manages about 39 percent; smaller nonindustrial timber owners control 19 percent, and federal and state agencies other than the Forest Service manage about 15 percent (Olson 1988). National forests of the westside account for around 7 percent of the nation's annual timber production and about one-third of the wood taken from the National Forest System (Olson 1988). Much of the westside national forest timber is sold to smaller and medium-sized lumber mills, which differ from industry giants like Weyerhaeuser and Georgia-Pacific in not owning their own timber plantations. This gives the smaller companies a particular interest in continued sales of national forest timber, although commercial timberland held by small nonindustrial forest owners gives the smaller firms one possible alternative source of supply.

The Northwest forests contribute wood to the U.S. housing, construction, paper, furniture-making, and transportation industries. In 1986, a very good year for the timber industry, the total timber taken from all ownerships in western Oregon and Washington amounted to roughly 18 billion board feet. The nine westside national forests of the two states contributed around 3.8 billion board feet of the total, or more than one-fifth (Gorte 1988).

There is some controversy over whether Northwest timber should be processed in the United States, thereby producing profits for small timber companies and jobs for workers in domestic sawmills; or whether logs should be exported in uncut form to sawmills overseas. With this in mind, it is worth noting that in 1986, about 5.2 billion board feet of the Pacific Northwest's private wood production was exported, both in processed and unprocessed forms. The total included some 2.8 billion board feet of uncut logs, about 1.2 billion board feet of "sawn" wood or lumber, 2.28 million short tons of wood chips (equivalent to approximately 1.1 billion board feet of timber), and 542 million square feet of plywood and veneer (equivalent to roughly 106 million board feet of timber) (Gorte 1988).

Timber Dependency of Local Economies

The amount of "timber dependency" shown by the Pacific Northwest economy is significant, especially in southwestern Oregon. According to Associate Chief Leonard of the Forest Service, the agency lists 97 communities in Washington, Oregon, and California as officially dependent on timber from westside national forests (Leonard 1988). These communities generally want old-growth cutting continued— not only to provide jobs for local residents, but also to garner federal payments in lieu of taxes, which amount to 25 percent of the gross receipts from national forests and are budgeted as "payments to states" by the agency. These payments provide county governments with revenues for schools and road construction.

Like other aspects of the ancient forest controversy, the exact degree to which the Northwest's prosperity depends on national forest timber is fiercely debated. One analyst working for democratic Governor Booth Gardner of Washington recently declined to play the numbers game in quantifying his state's timber dependency, saying:

> I don't want to add to the debate. I'm involved in a very sensitive process of trying to get people to sit down on both sides to discuss this issue, and in every meeting I've attended, we can't get to first base because everyone is working from different assumptions (Nichols 1989).

For example, the forest products industry claims that as much as 44 percent of Oregon's economy depends directly or indirectly on timber harvests and that around 20 percent of Washington's economy is similarly timber-dependent (Rey 1988). However, according to The Wilderness Society's Olson, only 4 percent of the total workforce and 20 percent of the manufacturing employment in western Oregon and Washington are directly tied to timber cutting (Olson 1988). State government agencies also have entered the debate with economic estimates of their own.

Figures compiled by the Oregon Department of Forestry, and used by researchers for Governor Neil Goldschmidt, suggest that in 1985, about 35 percent of Oregon's total employment was dependent on timber and timber-related industries, while another 3 percent of Oregon's nonfarm employment depended on the pulp and paper industry (Hoyt 1989). According to an estimate by Jeff Hannum, State Labor Economist for the Oregon Employment Division, some 60 percent of the timber processed in Oregon comes from old-growth stands; when national forest timber alone is considered, probably 80 percent of it is old growth (Hannum 1989).

Partly because of the growth of high-tech industry around Portland, Oregon's urbanized areas are much less dependent on timber than other parts of the state, says Oregon state government researcher Reis Hoyt. But Hoyt notes that in some parts of southwestern Oregon, as much as 70 percent of the economy depends on wood and wood products. Hoyt also reports that nine westside Oregon counties depended on federal payments from national forest timber receipts for at least 20 percent of their revenue in 1985. Of these, Curry, Jackson, and Douglas counties reportedly derived 40 to 49 percent of their revenues from Forest Service payments; Klatsop, Hood River, and Josephine counties received at least 50 percent (Hoyt 1989). Although thousands of timber jobs have been lost statewide since the 1970s, local unemployment rates in these six counties are now fairly low because of the recent timber-industry boom. In 1987 jobless rates ranged from 6.2 percent in Curry County to some 9.1 percent in Hood River County. This compares with 1982 unemployment of 16.3 percent in Curry County and 14.8 percent in Hood River County (Hannum 1989).

In Washington, the economic significance of the timber industry has been somewhat overshadowed by the importance of defense, aerospace manufacturing, wheat farming, apple production, and a growing trade with Pacific Rim nations. According to Washington Employment Department sources, the wood products industry accounted for 39,692 Washington jobs covered by the federal Employment Security Act in 1987—only 2.8 percent of all such jobs in the state. A little more than 16,000 jobs, or less than 1 percent of the jobs in Washington covered by the Employment Security Act, depended on pulp and paper. These totals were down significantly from the 1970s, when the state's wood products industry alone supported more than 55,000 jobs (Blegen 1989).

Still, timber jobs are important in selected rural counties. In 1987, for example, several southwestern Washington counties near the Gifford Pinchot National Forest showed heavy timber dependency, with timber and lumber accounting for an estimated 13 percent of the wage base in Cowlitz County (population 79,200), 18 percent of the wages earned in Lewis County (population 57,100), and 41.8 percent of the wages earned in Skamania County (population 7,800). In Klickitat County, adjoining the Gifford Pinchot on the east side of the Cascades, approximately 27.7 percent of the wage base depended on timber and lumber in 1987 (Blegen 1989). Timber dependency is also significant in certain counties adjoining the Olympic and Mt. Baker-Snoqualmie forests in northwestern Washington, but has diminished in some of these areas due to the growth of metropolitan Seattle. The most timber-dependent counties of the state seem to suffer from economic hardship: 1987 unemployment figures for Lewis County, for example, run to 11.4 percent in contrast with a statewide unemployment rate of 7.6 percent. The 1987 unemployment rates for Klickitat County and Skamania County were 18.7 percent and 20.4 percent, respectively (Blegen 1989).

Disputes over the total number of Washington and Oregon jobs that depend on timber arise partly from different assumptions about how many service sector jobs indirectly depend on timber wages via the economic multiplier effect. However, there is also disagreement over direct timber employment. Direct timber jobs in Oregon are generally put at around the 70,000 mark by conservationists, the Census

Bureau, and state government.[3] Washington state's direct timber industry employment is estimated to be around 40,000 by researchers working for Governor Gardner. The timber industry trade associations, however, have claimed that Oregon's timber industry alone "directly employs 221,000 workers and indirectly supports another 220,000" on both sides of the Cascades (Public Timber Council *et al.* 1988).

Decline in Private Timber Yields Is Forecast

Recently, the Pacific Northwest's private industrial timber producers have been cutting wood from their lands at a rapid and apparently unsustainable rate. According to Ann Nolan Hanus of the Oregon State Office of Economic Analysis, "Most forecasts of private harvests show declines in the next ten to twenty years" (USDA Forest Service 1988). A similar analysis by The Wilderness Society indicates that timber industry lands, with only 27 percent of the commercial forest acreage, supplied more than 53 percent of the softwood sawtimber cut from westside timberlands between 1980 and 1985. The westside national forests, with about 40 percent of the region's forest area and about 43 percent of its sawtimber inventory, contributed only 22 percent of the timber cut (Olson 1988). The disproportionately high rate of logging on private lands has led many to fear future declines in private wood production, which may increase timber demands on the national forests.

The stage is thus set for conflict between environmentalists intent on saving old-growth ecosystems and small communities intent on preserving timber jobs. The timber industry, in its efforts to build political support for continued old-growth logging, is widely perceived by environmentalists as seeking to exacerbate that conflict. The bitterness of the debate is reflected in remarks delivered by a timber industry representative to the Roseburg, Oregon, Chamber of Commerce in 1988:

> The Forest Service is under siege by groups of people who wish to stop harvesting and managing our forest and in essence strangle our economy. These preservationist organizations and their leadership will go to any means to achieve their goals . . . (Church 1988).

Out of similar economic concerns, more than 25 units of state and local government recently joined several state senators and representatives from Oregon, Washington, and California in condemning the

---

3. U.S. Bureau of Census figures for 1986, when the industry was well on its way to recovering from recession, record total Oregon employment in the timber, paper, and forestry occupations at 69,497 jobs, and similar Washington state employment at 48,993 jobs. Other figures that the Oregon Department of Forestry compiled for 1985 put total timber jobs in the state as 70,000. 1987 monthly averages compiled by Governor Gardner's office estimated Washington timber employment at 39,692, and pulp and paper jobs at 16,129.

Forest Service's 1986 draft guidelines for protecting the spotted owl (USDA Forest Service 1988). The Washington Department of Community Development commented that the Forest Service's preferred management strategy for owls, by restricting old-growth timber harvests, could eliminate jobs in eight "economically fragile" counties where unemployment was already averaging between 13 and 22 percent. The Department warned that, "Any action that further reduces the number of employment opportunities threatens the continued existence of these communities and the self-sufficiency of their residents" (USDA Forest Service 1988). Former Oregon Governor Victor Atiyeh also opposed the Forest Service's owl management plan in his comments on the draft guidelines, predicting that the proposed management measures would have "immediate and devastating consequences for many of our communities that have already been hard hit economically" (USDA Forest Service 1988). Oregon state economist Hanus estimated that the direct and indirect employment losses from the Forest Service's proposed spotted owl alternative would total only 1,740 to 4,200 jobs in that state. But in an interoffice memo to Hanus, the Director of Oregon's Economic Development Department stated:

> These jobs are not only some of the highest paid jobs, they are in a sector which has been the economic backbone of many Oregon communities. These jobs will be almost impossible to replace with equally high paying jobs, at least in the short run (USDA Forest Service 1988).

In its comments on the Forest Service's draft environmental impact statement the City of Colville, Oregon, wrote: "We believe that the United States Forest Service obligation (sic) is to intensively manage Oregon's timberland to produce the most jobs possible and ensure a steady non-diminishing supply of timber." The city of Glendale, Oregon, also opposed the Forest Service's owl protection measures, commenting: "This area is *totally* dependent upon the timber industry for its livelihood . . . the proposed plan would have a devastating effect upon the majority of the population" (USDA Forest Service 1988). Under these circumstances it becomes difficult for conservationists to advance their biological and ecological reasons for preserving old growth.

THE COMMUNITY STABILITY DEBATE

Given the economic importance of the Northwest timber industry, a key legal and political argument for logging ancient forests revolves around the perceived need to guarantee "community stability" for timber-dependent communities. The timber industry implicitly argues for logging to preserve community stability when it warns that reductions in old-growth logging will affect jobs in Washington, Oregon, and California. The Forest Service, too, has traditionally asserted its obligation to promote community stability in timber communities. The precise legal basis for this requirement is sometimes questioned, but statements by government officials urging the Forest Service to avoid sudden disruptions in timber supply date back to the agency's earliest days. In part, these statements appear to reflect dissatisfaction with the cut-and-move-on tactics of private timber companies during the 19th century, when the clear-cutting of entire regions was often followed by the appearance of timber ghost towns.

Thus, in a 1905 letter to Gifford Pinchot, the first Chief Forester of the new U.S. Forest Service, Secretary of Agriculture James Wilson stated: "In the management of each reserve local questions will be decided upon local grounds; . . . sudden changes in industrial conditions will be avoided by gradual adjustment after due notice" (Schallau and Alston 1987). In a 1925 article in the *Journal of Forestry*, Chief Forester William B. Greeley claimed:

> The main purpose in most of (the forest management plans) is to avoid a hiatus in timber cut after the old stock has been taken off and a disorganization of industrial and social institutions which depend on a continuous output from a given unit. . . . This is particularly true in the small working circles of a number of Eastern National Forests, where maintaining established local industries or providing woods labor for rural communities are (sic) set forth as definite objects of management (Schallau and Alston 1987).

Somewhat later, Chief Forester Lyle Watts interpreted the passage of the Sustained-Yield Forest Management Act of 1944 (16 U.S.C.A. 583) as an effort to "obtain community stabilization through sustained yield by federal-industry cooperation." Ironically, certain representatives of the timber industry strongly objected to that claim, apparently because of the implications it posed for their freedom to operate without government constraint. One industry official even implied that "conservation" and not the economic stability of lumber towns was the main goal of the law (Robbins 1987). Accordingly, some observers say the few "sustained yield units" the Forest Service established to implement the act have become expensive failures.

In 1963, the Forest Service's timber sales policy provided for "as far as feasible, an even flow of national forest timber in order to facilitate the stabilization of communities and of opportunities for employment" (Schallau and Alston 1987). But some environmentalists and other critics of the agency contend there is little or no legal basis for its emphasis on community stability. Recently, the Reagan Administration's Assistant Secretary of Agriculture, Peter Meyers, insisted that community stability is "an important factor to be taken into account in decisions affecting the national forest timber program," but stated:

"there is limited statutory direction related to the need for the Forest Service to consider community stability" (Feeney 1988).

Is Community Stability Achievable?

Despite past Forest Service policies, a November 1987 national conference on "Community Stability in Forest-Based Economies" has cast some doubt on community stability as an agency goal. One research paper submitted to the conference by economists Ross Gorte of the Congressional Research Service and Julie Gorte of the Office of Technology Assessment indicates that, perhaps because of the boom-and-bust nature of the timber business, lumber mill towns generally average higher unemployment levels than communities dependent on other single industries or mixes of industries. Hence, it is not clear that Forest Service attempts to promote community stability through a guaranteed even flow of timber can succeed (Gorte and Gorte 1987). Professor Dennis Le Master of Purdue University, who helped organize the conference, concluded afterwards: "We will not be able to achieve community stability in the Pacific Northwest because it's a fleeting concept. . . . We live in a market economy, and one thing that's inherent in it is the need for individuals and communities to adapt to change" (Feeney 1988). Similarly, an *Environmental Law* article published by economists Con H. Schallau and Richard M. Alston questioned whether the Forest Service's commitment to community stability is "policy" or "shibboleth." According to Schallau and Alston (1987), past attempts to guarantee an even flow of timber from the westside national forests may have attracted small timber mills to the Pacific Northwest in numbers that cannot be sustained, thus causing instability rather than stability in small communities.

Job Losses and Mill Closures in the 1980s

The large number of layoffs and timber mill closings that occurred in the Northwest during the early 1980s gave rise to further questions concerning the efficacy of attaining community stability through a guaranteed timber supply. Before 1980, Pacific Northwest timber companies faced stiff competition from both Canada and the South because their old mills and highly paid, unionized employees made them "high cost producers" in the competitive market. To alter this situation, the industry decreased its Pacific Northwest workforce from 82,000 to 71,500 between 1980 and 1985, while closing hundreds of mills and automating numerous others (Olson 1988). An estimated 15 percent of the timber industry's landholdings also were offered for sale during this period, according to Olson. In some cases, "unionized mills were closed and sold to independents who re-opened the facilities with nonunion workers." By 1986, when the industry was recovering from recession, the Pacific Northwest timber industry was cutting and selling more wood than in 1979—but with 13 percent fewer workers (Olson 1988). Viewing timber employment another way, the number of Oregon timber workers needed to turn 1 million board feet of timber into lumber fell from 3.9 in 1980 to 2.5 in 1987—a drop of more than 35 percent. The output of the individual worker rose from an average 255,200 board feet per year to 395,500 board feet—nearly a 55 percent increase (Hannum 1989).

As the industry continues to introduce new technology to reduce labor costs and maintain global competitiveness, some observers expect another 26,450 timber jobs will be lost to technology over the next 45 years in Washington and Oregon (Olson 1988). According to Oregon research consultant Harry Lonsdale, additional mill closures will also occur in the state "over the next decade or two" (Lonsdale 1988). Economist Julie Gorte says that nationally, "Timber industry employment is going down, like everything else in manufacturing. I don't see any reason for it to go up" (Feeney 1988).

However, some industry and other observers contend that the wave of job losses linked to productivity improvements has peaked for now. Mark Rey, vice-president of the National Forest Products Association, defends past automation efforts by the Pacific Northwest timber industry as essential to keep the industry competitive. Despite its rhetoric, Rey admits, the timber industry is not in the business to supply jobs but to make money. Yet preserving some timber jobs requires preserving industry profits and competitiveness, he says. He argues further that approximately $5 billion in new capital investments by Pacific Northwest timber producers since 1980 have made these companies the "most efficient, lowest cost timber suppliers in the world" (Rey 1988). It is unclear whether this will enable Pacific Northwest companies to recapture some of the market share they have lost to Canada and the South in recent decades.

Some conservationists contend that because of industry investments in automation, and the inevitable elimination of commercially available old growth in the Northwest should logging continue, economic dislocation must eventually come to many western Oregon and Washington timber communities. The question is whether this will occur while old-growth ecosystems still exist and provide the region with recreational, scenic, and watershed benefits, they say, or whether the transition will come after old growth and its considerable non-timber values have been lost. Says one conservationist, "The timber industry is thinking in terms of next year's profits and the politicians are thinking of elections in two years or six years. But our time horizon is several generations in the future, and that makes conservationists closer to the truth" (Pissot 1988).

The industry and some government officials, however, reject the implications that conservationists draw from arguments about automation and long-term timber availability. They contend that just because timber workers have already lost jobs to automation, there is little reason for such workers to suffer further job losses due to logging restrictions. Oregon State researcher Hoyt also contends that timber communities will probably find it easier to adjust to the end of the old-growth resource over 10 or 20 years—as it is logged and converted to short-rotation forests, to the distress of conservationists—than to face an immediate decline in old-growth availability if large blocks are withdrawn from production for ecological reasons. The question for the timber communities is pain today or pain in a decade or two. Naturally, Hoyt suggests, the communities will choose pain in the future given these alternatives (Hoyt 1989).

Economic Diversification Proposed

Many observers believe economic diversification, along with retraining and economic assistance to displaced workers, will be needed to solve unemployment problems in western Oregon and Washington over the next several years. In the view of some conservationists and government officials, jobs in the recreation and tourism industries, which partly depend on the scenic and undisturbed backcountry resources of ancient forests, might help to replace some timber jobs in various Pacific Northwest communities.

Forest Service Associate Chief Leonard, saying that westside community stability cannot be achieved through timber sales alone, agrees that some timber communities might diversify economically through promoting recreation (Feeney 1988). Forest Service statistics indicate that the national forests of Oregon and Washington already provide more than 19 million "visitor recreation days" each year (one visitor recreation day is equivalent to a visit by one recreationist for 12 hours, or 12 recreationists visiting a forest for one hour). In an effort to increase the economic contribution made by recreation to local communities, the Forest Service has embarked on several ventures to improve recreation opportunities on Oregon and Washington national forests. In addition to studying the feasibility of a computerized information system that would help inform more of the region's visitors to the region about forest recreation opportunities, the Forest Service is working with private groups to improve forest facilities for hikers, cross-country skiers, motorists, and owners of campers and recreational vehicles (Laverty 1989).

Unfortunately, recreation jobs generally pay significantly less than timber jobs, making the transition away from timber difficult to sell politically. Reis Hoyt, examining the economic potential of recreation and tourism for Oregon Governor Neil Goldschmidt, concluded that these industries will help cushion the blow from declining timber availability and the continuing automation of Oregon timber mills. However, she believes recreation is "not the full answer."

The Wilderness Society, meanwhile, suggests that changes in timber industry practices might bring new wood product jobs to the region to counter projected employment losses. According to Olson, a "baseline" continuation of present trends would reduce the Northwest's total timber harvest by 25 percent over the next 45 years, largely because of the coming decline in private timber production. Also, "as in the past, future job losses will be caused by productivity improvement" (Olson 1988). Olson's model indicates that 8,200 jobs could be lost because of harvest reductions and 26,450 jobs lost to productivity improvements, if present logging trends continue. However, the model suggests that an added 13,400 timber jobs could be created in the region by the year 2030 if Oregon and Washington ended their exports of raw logs from state and private lands and instead turned these logs into lumber, plywood, furniture, and other finished products employing local labor in local mills. Increasing the region's domestic manufacturing base in wood products would require "a supply of logs, increased manufacturing capacity, elimination of trade barriers, and successful market development," Olson acknowledges. But he argues that with a curtailment of raw log exports, the creation of 13,400 added jobs could coincide with efforts to reduce timber harvests on westside national forests by 25 percent, thereby protecting the most valuable ancient forests (Olson 1988).

Olson's scenarios also suggest that a net increase of 1,700 timber jobs could be created if investments in new technology helped industry to increase its efficiency in turning raw logs into lumber and wood products. Olson sees less jobs-saving potential in intensified timber management practices, but contends that even this strategy could reduce projected job losses to only 600 by the year 2030, while still preserving the most ecologically significant old growth (Olson 1988).

The DeFazio Log Export Bill

Curtailing log exports as a strategy for preserving mill jobs has also been examined by Rep. Peter DeFazio (D-Ore.), who introduced legislation in 1986 to overturn a Supreme Court decision forbidding states to restrict raw log exports. The export of unprocessed logs cut from the national forests has been prohibited by federal law for some time, but in 1984 the Supreme Court ruled that state restrictions on nonfederal log exports violated the Commerce Clause of the U.S. Constitution.

The ruling had a direct effect on Washington and Oregon, both of which have significant state forests that are cut by industry. The De-Fazio bill would have allowed Congress to delegate some federal powers to the states, allowing them to again restrict log exports from state-owned lands. The measure failed to pass in 1988; it received support from timber unions and smaller timber companies but opposition from the International Longshoremen's Union and the Pacific Rim Trade Association. DeFazio plans to introduce similar legislation in the 101st Congress (1989–1990).

Proposal to End Federal Log Export Ban

Meanwhile, an end to the ban on exporting raw logs from national forests was proposed in the FY 1990 budget submitted to Congress by President Ronald Reagan. According to the proposal, which may be modified by Congress and the Bush Administration, the Forest Service could derive an additional $75 million in revenue each year by allowing raw log exports from national forests. Presumably, approval of this proposal could cause additional job losses for westside mill workers, creating added pressure for logging on national forests. At the same time, lifting the federal log export ban might allow large exporting firms to compete with smaller, local timber companies for more national forest timber. The political implications of such a development are unclear, but it might cause a split between small companies and big exporting firms.

Compensating Timber Workers for Job Losses

Economist Lester Thurow suggests that when society exposes individuals to economic distress by eliminating government subsidies that have protected them, ". . . we have to develop techniques for paying compensation to the individuals who are going to be hurt. . . . It should be generous for the simple reason that if it is not, we will not be able to adopt the policies that the country needs" (quoted in Dixon and Jeulson 1987).

A compensation plan that would help timber workers in the Northwest has been put forward by forest economist Randall O'Toole, in his book-length proposal to reform the Forest Service by "marketizing" it (O'Toole 1988). O'Toole would eliminate timber subsidies across the nation and charge market rates for nearly all uses of the national forests, excluding the protection of endangered species but including such traditionally free or low-priced resources as recreation opportunities. O'Toole believes his proposal would displace as many as 10,000 Forest Service personnel and 30,000 workers in the timber and livestock industries. But he contends that a fund that paid $100,000 per individual could be established to help displaced timber and livestock workers and government employees as they found new work. O'Toole contends that the entire fund could be paid for by just 15 percent of the federal appropriations his proposal would save (O'Toole 1988). A less detailed and less sweeping proposal for saving Pacific Northwest old growth by compensating displaced workers appeared recently in the *Ecologist*, authored by Kenneth R. Dixon and Thomas C. Juelson of the Washington Department of Game (Dixon and Juelson 1987). It is not clear whether significant political support exists for such a compensation program. Wilderness Society Vice-president Syd Butler said in early 1989 that conservationists are thinking about legislation to help displaced timber workers but that they presently lack the expertise to fashion workable proposals (Butler 1989).

THE LEGAL BASIS FOR PRESERVING ANCIENT FOREST ECOSYSTEMS

Federal law provides a somewhat debatable mandate for the preservation of endangered ecosystems. Some protection is mandated under the 1976 National Forest Management Act (NFMA), which directs the Forest Service to "provide for diversity of plant and animal communities based on the suitability and capability of the specific land area" in order to meet "overall multiple-use objectives" within each national forest. Also, in each NFMA forest management plan, the Forest Service must provide "where appropriate, to the degree practicable, for steps to be taken to preserve the diversity of tree species similar to that existing in the region controlled by the plan" (The Wilderness Society 1988). Former Forest Service Chief Max Peterson, however, has said that this law is "deliberately not very specific" and leaves "much room for judgment" (The Wilderness Society 1988c).

NFMA also requires the Forest Service to identify management indicator species to guide the protection of diversity in the national forests. For the Pacific Northwest Region of the National Forest System (Region 6, Oregon and Washington), one indicator species is the northern spotted owl.

In addition, Forest Service planning regulations require the management of wildlife habitats to "maintain viable populations of existing native and desired nonnative vertebrate species" in each national forest (The Wilderness Society 1988c). In some areas of the country, however, Forest Service planners seem to interpret this requirement and NFMA's biological diversity language as justifications for logging that opens up clearings for "desired" species of non-native game animals, even at the expense of less common birds and mammals requiring closed-canopy forests (The Wilderness Society 1988c). This may limit how much real protection is available for westside ancient forests under the NFMA and Forest Service planning regulations.

Still another well-known way to protect ecosystems is to have them designated as critical habitats for endangered or threatened species under the federal Endangered Species Act. In the view of many observers, conservationists have recently tried to protect the westside forests from logging by petitioning the Fish and Wildlife Service to list both the northern spotted owl and the marbled murrelet as threatened or endangered. Some politicians have accused conservation organizations of abusing the Endangered Species Act for this purpose. But although conservationists admit wanting to preserve the westside forests, they also insist that the spotted owl and marbled murrelet are worth preserving for their own sakes.

The Spotted Owl Controversy

Advisory Panel Report on the Spotted Owl. For several years, Northwest timber policy conflicts have been focused in part on the fate of the northern spotted owl, a relatively rare bird listed as threatened by the state of Washington and included on Oregon's threatened and endangered species list. Much of the old growth that once supported this subspecies of spotted owl no longer stands; of the remaining habitat, an estimated 96 percent lies on federal lands. Although two other subspecies of spotted owls exist—one in California and the other extending from the American southwest into Mexico—a 1986 blue-ribbon panel convened by the National Audubon Society, Cooper Ornithological Society, and American Ornithologists' Union concluded that the owl's northern subspecies was in trouble because of timber cutting throughout its range (Advisory Panel on the Spotted Owl 1986).

The panel recommended that enough habitat be preserved to maintain a population of at least 1,500 breeding pairs of owls in Washington, Oregon, northwest California, and the Sierra Nevada mountains. Concluding that the habitat requirements of the owl varied across the region, the panel also recommended the preservation of "home ranges" for pairs of birds totaling 2,500 acres apiece in Oregon, northwestern California, and the Sierra Nevadas, and 4,500 acres per breeding pair in Washington. The Advisory Panel also recommended that the home ranges be connected by corridors of old-growth habitat, to prevent genetic isolation of individual populations, while urging the rejection of the then-conventional wisdom in wildlife biology, which held that the maintenance of 500 breeding pairs was sufficient to prevent extinction in species (Advisory Panel on the Spotted Owl 1986).

Controversy over the Supplemental Environmental Impact Statement. Two years before Audubon's panel issued its report, conservationists appealed a Forest Service regional guide for forest plans in Oregon and Washington as inadequate to protect the spotted owl. Deputy Assistant Secretary of the Department of Agriculture Douglas MacLeery directed the Forest Service to prepare a supplemental environmental impact statement (SEIS) on spotted owl management guidelines. The draft SEIS, released in August 1986, included a number of alternative plans for protecting owls. Its preferred alternative, Alternative F, proposed 550 spotted owl habitat areas in national forests, including 392 habitat areas in areas "tentatively suitable for timber production." Approximately 2,200 acres of old-growth habitat would be designated for each owl habitat area, with 1,000 acres of this being withdrawn from the timber base used by the Forest Service to calculate how much wood may be cut on national forests. The other 1,200 acres of each area would remain in the timber base, but could not be cut within the first 10 to 15 years covered by the relevant forest plan. Owl habitat areas would be allowed to exceed 2,200 acres where habitat was of "lower than average quality" or where this would not interfere with multiple-use objectives such as timber harvests (USDA Forest Service 1986).

The Forest Service received approximately 42,000 comments from the public on the draft SEIS. In addition to letters that criticized the SEIS for inadequate protection of timber jobs, comments received included a letter from the Washington State Department of Game, stating: "Alternative F will not ensure a viable population of spotted owls in the future. It does not meet NFMA requirements or National Environmental Policy Act regulations and should be dropped from consideration" (USDA Forest Service 1988).

Similarly, the Washington Department of Natural Resources criticized the preferred alternative for failing to take the entire owl habitat areas out of the timber base, thus ensuring that overall logging levels could continue, but within smaller areas of forest: the department argued that this would increase logging in old-growth areas that were located outside of designated owl habitat areas (USDA Forest Service 1988). The adequacy of the preferred alternative was also questioned by several conservation groups, the Oregon Department of Fish and Wildlife, and the California Department of Fish and Game, which stated:

> The preferred alternative, as stated, offers only a high probability of persistence over the next 15 years and below a moderate degree of probability of persistence beyond 50 years. Such a preferred alternative indicates that the Forest Service is satisfied with a plan that will not ensure maintenance of Spotted Owls with even a moderate probability of persistence over the next 150 years. We find this position unacceptable (USDA Forest Service 1988).

The Forest Service issued its final supplemental environmental impact statement on the owl in August 1988, but allowed the public an added 30 days to submit comments on the document. The preferred alternative in the final SEIS, again labeled "Alternative F," did not specify the number of owl areas that must be established. It did require that those areas vary in size in different parts of the Northwest, from 1,000 acres in the Klamath Mountains to 2,700 acres in Washington's Olympic Peninsula. It also allowed for the establishment of larger and smaller habitat areas depending on local circumstances; recommended removing all owl habitat areas completely from the timber base; and required the clustering of such areas within the boundaries of national forests and across the boundaries of neighboring forests (USDA Forest Service 1988).

According to the Forest Service, adoption of this preferred alternative would preserve 3.5 million acres of suitable spotted owl habitat at the end of a 15-year period, as opposed to 3.4 million acres if no action were taken. It would affect 348,000 acres otherwise suitable for timber production. On the national forests alone, it would preserve habitat capable of supporting approximately 1,125 pairs of owls, both within and outside of designated owl habitat areas. It would also reduce the "allowable sale quantity" of timber on the 13 affected forests from 3.2 million to 3.0 million board feet annually, eliminate an estimated 455 to 910 timber jobs, and lower timber receipt payments to counties by $11 million (USDA Forest Service 1988).

Projecting further into the future, however, the SEIS indicated that Alternative F would preserve only 2.4 million acres of suitable owl habitat at the end of 50 years and 2.1 million acres after 150 years. It projected a decline in total estimated numbers of breeding pairs of owls—including the owls on national forests, but also including pairs on other public and private lands—from an estimated 2,720 today to approximately 1,540 in 150 years. Summing up the threats to survival that the owl would experience under various management alternatives, including Alternative F, the SEIS expressed only a "moderate" confidence that a well-distributed owl population would continue to exist after 50 years under the Forest Service's preferred management alternative, and said there was a "low" likelihood that such a population would exist after 150 years (USDA Forest Service 1988).

The final SEIS's "moderate" security rating allows "no latitude for catastrophic events affecting the population"—such as volcanic eruptions from Mt. St. Helen's or neighboring peaks in the Cascades—and no latitude for "biological findings that the population is more susceptible to demographic or genetic factors that was assumed in the analysis" (USDA Forest Service 1988). Therefore, conservationists have criticized Alternative F on the grounds that the Forest Service itself admits this strategy has only a low-to-moderate chance of saving the species from local or regional extirpation, if not extinction. Conservationists also objected to the employment and economic projections reached in both the draft and final SEIS, contending that they give an unrealistically high projection of expected job losses.

On the other hand, numerous representatives of the timber industry and timber-dependent communities, as well as some state officials, have observed that much is still unknown about spotted owl population dynamics. The Oregon State Department of Forestry states that adequate data are still lacking concerning the owl's life expectancy, rate of reproduction, frequency in colonizing vacant habitats, average age of reproduction, and competition with barred owls (USDA Forest Service 1988). Timber industry supporters urge the Service to study the species more intensively, or possibly to engage in artificial feeding or propagation of spotted owls, before taking actions to reduce the timber harvest significantly.

Final Record of Decision on SEIS Issued. On December 8, 1988, Forest Service Chief Dale Robertson released a record of decision on the SEIS, selecting the preferred Alternative F but with two significant modifications. First, Robertson increased the size of spotted owl habitat areas in the Olympic National Forest to 3,000 acres to provide greater protection for the bird's isolated population. Second, Robertson ordered a review of spotted owl management provisions in five years to determine their adequacy. The provisions may be modified at that time and timber cutting adjusted up or down as warranted.

The Forest Service says that combined with a special research program on spotted owls, the five-year review provision offers a good chance of preventing the bird's extinction. Also, some, but not all, Forest Service officials contend the SEIS's 50-year and 100-year projections of species viability are virtually meaningless. They reason that the five-year review will allow the projections to be superseded and also that projecting any population trend five or ten decades into the future is inherently difficult. Hence, these officials dismiss concerns about the SEIS showing a dim future for the bird under the preferred management alternative.

Not all scientists agree with that view. For example, one government researcher involved in the controversy criticizes even the final record of decision as failing to ensure owl habitat areas that reflect research findings about the bird's needs. This same scientist is particularly critical of the Forest Service decision because it allegedly fails to consider any special protection for the owl population in the Siuslaw National Forest, which is isolated from the Cascade population and hence subject to particular stress. Conservationists and some timber industry groups have appealed the owl decision, with the timber industry contending that it unduly restricts logging, and conservationists saying that by failing to specify where owl areas must be located, the decision fails to address forest-fragmentation problems threatening the bird.

FWS Listing Decision Leads to Appeal, Lawsuit. Early in 1987, the environmental organization GreenWorld petitioned the Fish and Wildlife Service to list the spotted owl as threatened or endangered under the federal Endangered Species Act. Later in the year, several other national organizations also petitioned for the owl's listing. On Dec. 1, 1987, the Fish and Wildlife Service signed a cooperative agreement with the Forest Service to ensure that Northwest national forests would be managed in a manner to prevent spotted owls from reaching a threatened or endangered condition. On December 17, the Fish and Wildlife Service determined that listing the owl was not warranted. In a December 23, 1987, *Federal Register* notice, the Fish and Wildlife Service referred to the cooperative agreement, among other factors, as a reason the bird did not require listing.

The Sierra Club Legal Defense Fund filed an appeal of the listing decision May 9, 1988 on behalf of the Seattle Audubon Society, National Audubon Society, Sierra Club, Wilderness Society and several local Audubon Society chapters. In the appeal (*The northern spotted owl (Strix occidentalis caurina) et al. v. Hodel et al.*), the plaintiffs alleged that the Fish and Wildlife Service violated the Endangered Species Act by failing to consider biological evidence favoring the listing of the owl; improperly relied on its cooperative agreement with the Forest Service and a 1987 agreement signed with the Bureau of Land Management to avoid listing, in violation of Section 4(b)(1)(a) of the Endangered Species Act; and improperly considered "non-biological factors such as the economic and political impacts of a decision to list" in making its decision.

On November 9, 1988, Judge Thomas Zilly of the U.S. District Court for the Western District of Washington ruled that the Fish and Wildlife Service's decision not to list was "capricious and arbitrary and contrary to law," partly because of the agency's apparent failure to consider listing the owl as "threatened" and partly because the agency could not cite any scientific experts who opposed listing the species. Judge Zilly gave the Fish and Wildlife Service 90 days in which to justify or alter its listing decision. The judge later granted the agency an extension, to May 1, 1989, in order to reopen the court record to recently gathered biological data. Also published in early 1989 is a report by the General Accounting Office on the listing decision. It was requested in 1988 by Representative Gerry Studds (D-Mass.), Chairman of the House Subcommittee on Fisheries and Wildlife Conservation and the Environment. [See Editor's note at the end of this chapter for an update on the spotted owl controversy.]

Controversy on BLM Lands. The debate over spotted owl protection has been extended to BLM's largely forested "O & C" lands in southern Oregon. In the fall of 1987, the Sierra Club Legal Defense Fund and the Western Natural Resources Law Clinic sued BLM on behalf of 11 conservation organizations, alleging that the agency violated various federal laws, including the Migratory Bird Treaty Act, by failing to consider whether its old-growth timber sales might cause the northern spotted owl's extinction. The suit (*Portland Audubon Society et al. v. Hodel*) was denied by the District Court for the state of Oregon in April 1988 on the grounds that a legislative rider attached to the fiscal year 1988 Interior Department appropriations bill prohibited certain legal challenges to BLM and Forest Service management plans.

Plaintiffs appealed to the Ninth Circuit Court in San Francisco and on May 18 were granted an injunction barring BLM from "entering into any new contracts for the sale of timber . . . where such sales would permit logging of Douglas-fir timber older than 200 years." The injunction was later modified to prohibit new sales of trees 200 years or more in age within a 2.1-mile radius of any spotted owl habitat sites identified in the agency's 1987 Spotted Owl Environmental Assessment until the court reached a final decision.

In early January 1989, the timber industry requested the Ninth Circuit Court to lift the injunction, but the request was denied. On January 24, the court issued its opinion, lifting the injunction against timber sales but stating that the rider, regardless of intent, did not prohibit judicial review. The Ninth Circuit determined that the district court should rehear the case and that plaintiffs could seek site-specific relief. The Sierra Club Legal Defense Fund and the Law Clinic then filed with the district court for an emergency injunction against five sales BLM had stated it would conduct.

The Marbled Murrelet

The marbled murrelet is a robin-sized seabird of the family Alcidae whose two subspecies inhabit the coastal area extending from southern California up through Alaska, and from the Sea of Okhotsk and Kamchatka in the Soviet Union south to Korea, Japan and the Kurile Islands (Marshall 1988). According to Marshall, the American subspecies (*Brachyramphus marmoratus marmoratus*), ranges during the summer from the outer Aleutian Islands as far south and east as Santa Cruz County, California, and in the winter from its northern range as far south as San Diego County.

The size of the murrelet population has never been definitively established. Kessell and Gibson (1978) estimated that 250,000 birds may exist off southeastern Alaska. Other observers suggest that 4,400 to 8,300 may fish off the coast of Washington, another 6,000 off the

Oregon coast, and around 2,000 off the coast of California (Marshall 1988).

Only four tree nests for the marbled murrelet have been found to date (two were in Siberia); nests also have been discovered on the ground and in rocky cavities in Alaska. Nevertheless, there are several reasons why some biologists believe marbled murrelets—unlike other alcid birds—nest in trees, and probably in old-growth forests, from British Columbia to southern California. Murrelets have often been observed flying up river corridors at dusk and have been seen—or, more frequently, heard—in old-growth stands in California redwood parks. Murrelets also are known to fly from the ocean to freshwater lakes approximately 45 miles inland in British Columbia and 18 miles inland in Grays Harbor County, Washington. In 1975, a tree surgeon discovered a murrelet nest more than 146 feet from the ground in a Douglas-fir at least 180 feet tall in California's Big Basin Redwoods State Park. The nest contained a young murrelet and was located in a depression in a bright green moss (*Isothecium cristatum*), which often covers the branches of Douglas-firs 150 years old or older.

Historical evidence indicates that murrelet populations have diminished along those sections of the Oregon coast where old-growth cutting is most pronounced. Along the coast of California, the bird is most common opposite parks and other areas where old-growth redwood groves still stand. But whether this indicates that murrelets require any large quantity of old growth is somewhat unclear. Murrelets have short, stubby wings that they must flap very rapidly to stay airborne. This may mean the birds cannot take off or land in dense forests, but need to nest in high trees at the very edges of forests (Marshall 1988).

On January 13, 1988, the National Audubon Society, Portland Audubon Society, Oregon Natural Resources Council, and approximately 40 Audubon Society chapters petitioned the Fish and Wildlife Service to list the marbled murrelet as threatened in Washington, Oregon, and California under the Endangered Species Act. On October 17, 1988, the Service announced in the *Federal Register* that it had found the petition of substance and would consider listing the bird. A 90-day public comment period on the marbled murrelet petition ended December 1, 1988.

The NFMA Planning Process

Delayed Westside Plans. In 1976, partly in response to controversies over clear-cutting, Congress enacted the National Forest Management Act (NFMA). Among other things, the law mandated that nontimber resources such as water quality, recreation, and wildlife habitat receive greater attention in management plans drawn up for the 123 units of the National Forest System. NFMA also required that the plans for these individual forests be revised every 10 to 15 years and that the public participate in their formulation. NFMA plans were supposed to give local communities, citizens, and industry a "bottom-up" chance to influence national forest policy through a complex process that is supposed to integrate these individual forest plans with a nationwide forest-planning document drawn up every five years under the 1974 Forest and Range Land Renewable Resources Planning Act. Partly because of new environmental requirements, NFMA forest plans are expected to be somewhat more protective of Pacific Northwest old growth than the pre-NFMA plans now governing timber production within the Douglas-fir growing region.

Repeated delays in NFMA planning, however, have led some conservationists to question the relevance of the plans. Originally, all first-round NFMA plans were scheduled to be completed by September 1985 (O'Toole 1988). Most plans for national forests in Oregon and Washington were expected to be completed by 1983. But conflicting planning guidelines promulgated in 1979 by the Carter Administration and in 1982 by the Reagan Administration delayed the process. In 1983, all of the draft plans for western Oregon and Washington were scrapped and started anew (O'Toole 1988). The Forest Service further delayed completion of the plans saying that it needed to include final spotted owl guidelines for the region. Also, the timber industry appealed some of the regional environmental protection guidelines for the new plans, creating more delay. Thus, 11 of the 12 draft NFMA plans for westside forests were not available until late 1987; the draft plan for the Klamath National Forest is not expected until late 1989 or early 1990. Final plans for most westside forests are expected in 1989. In the past, however, the timber industry has suggested it may appeal the final plans in the courts, which would allow timber harvests temporarily to proceed under the existing plans.

Interpretations of Draft Plans Vary Widely. The draft westside forest plans, meanwhile, are being interpreted in radically different fashion by the Forest Service, conservationists, state government agencies, and the timber industry. In 1988, the timber industry published a study by the consulting firm CH2M Hill (1988) indicating that the draft plans would reduce timber harvests on the westside by around 20 percent, while also eliminating 13,500 to 18,000 timber dependent and secondary jobs and costing county governments in Washington and Oregon $42 to $56 million in lost timber receipts. Economic analysts for Oregon Governor Neil Goldschmidt also interpret the plans as calling for a 20 percent decline in Oregon timber harvests (Hoyt 1988). However, the Forest Service's Associate Chief George Leonard has claimed that in general, "The national forests in Oregon and Washington are going to be maintaining their historic production levels" under the new NFMA plans (Feeney 1988).

The Wilderness Society published a study in 1988 indicating that the industry, Oregon state government, and Associate Chief Leonard all are mistaken (The Wilderness Society 1988a). According to the original study, timber cutting on the 12 westside forests would actually increase by about 15 percent under the draft NFMA plans; with new figures in hand, The Wilderness Society has since revised this to 10 percent. The report adds: "The CH2M Hill estimates of reduced harvest levels, jobs and economic returns are essentially meaningless" (The Wilderness Society 1988a).

Apart from possible political bias, there are several plausible reasons why the Service, the industry, and conservation groups such as The Wilderness Society can draw radically different conclusions from the same plans concerning future Pacific Northwest timber production. Some of these include:

- *Boom and bust cycles of timber demand.* The region's timber industry is a highly cyclical business whose prices and demand for public timber partly reflect the fluctuating U.S. housing construction market. Also, the timber industry recently has faced significant competition from Canadian timber exports, which have cut into the U.S. market. Both of these factors have caused wide swings in timber demand during the last decade. The housing market and the price of timber, for example, both soared during the inflationary late 1970s, then plummeted during the recession of the early 1980s, and then began to recover in 1984 and 1985. Canadian timber exports to the United States rose to a highwater mark of 34 percent of U.S. total demand, then dropped to 29 percent following a new tariff that the United States imposed on Canadian cedar shingles in 1986 and a tax the Canadians subsequently agreed to place on cedar shingle exports.

  Furthermore, the price of U.S. wood exports in Japanese yen and other foreign currencies was high when the dollar was overvalued during the early 1980s, but has since fallen as the dollar has been devalued. Simultaneously, U.S. timber exports have boomed. The price and demand trends of the last decade are therefore highly ambiguous and can be interpreted to support very different conclusions.

- *Multiple Forest Service statistics for measuring timber harvests, timber sales, and allowable harvest levels.* Under existing forest management plans for the Pacific Northwest, which were drawn up before passage of NFMA, the Forest Service measures the potential productivity of the forests under one set of management rules. It thus derives a fairly high "Potential Yield" for westside forests. But under the new draft NFMA plans, which require greater attention to certain environmental constraints, the potential productivity of these same forests is calculated according to a revised set of management rules. Under these rules, the agency has calculated a new "Long Term Sustained Yield Capacity" (LTSYC) for the region which differs from the old Potential Yield.

Even so, the new LTSYC does not describe the future sales and harvest levels that the agency actually expects on the forests. Instead, draft NFMA plans project sales levels that will be somewhat less than the Long Term Sustained Yield Capacities, and they describe these future sales levels in two different ways. One new measure, called "Allowable Sales Quantity" (ASQ), describes the future levels of timber sales that will be *scheduled* in the forests. But ASQs do not account for additional timber that will probably be removed from the forests and sold to corporations as replanted stands of trees are thinned for management purposes, individual trees are sold for firewood, the Forest Service cuts down trees to create trails and campgrounds, and certain kinds of salvage operations occur. A second new sales measure, "Total Sales Program Quantity" (TSPQ), includes this "nonchargeable" timber as well as the regular sales levels covered by ASQ figures.

As an added source of confusion, it is necessary to distinguish between *sales levels* for a given year and *cut levels* for the same year in the national forests. Generally, timber sold in one year is not actually logged until two or three years afterward. And to accommodate the cyclical nature of the timber business, the Forest Service enforces its limitations on timber logging not year-by-year, but over a 10-year period. New ASQs in draft NFMA plans, then, are *average* figures that may be exceeded by the timber sold (or, separately, the timber cut, which will likely differ from the timber sold) in any given year.

By selectively choosing among these statistics to represent present and future timber supplies and making different assumptions about price and demand trends as well, different analysts can draw radically different conclusions about future westside timber harvests.

- *The Timber Buy Back Program of the 1980s.* During the early 1980s, when national economic recession caused a depression or near-depression in the timber industry, Pacific Northwest companies that had previously contracted to log millions of board feet of uncut timber from the Forest Service defaulted on their contracts. The Forest Service then repurchased the timber and reoffered it for sale once the economy improved in mid-decade. Timber industry sources say that the high level of timber cutting on Pacific Northwest forests that currently alarms environmentalists partly reflects this situation. Although environmentalists may see the westside old growth in danger of being liquidated because of extremely high cutting rates in 1987 and 1988, the industry claims that many trees cut in the past few years were originally scheduled for logging in 1981 or 1982. Thus, the industry partly sees itself as making up for lost time in cutting these trees.

• *Different measures of timber cut.* Cut timber can be described in terms of board feet—the number of one foot by one foot by one inch boards of lumber that can be cut from a given set of logs. Alternatively, it can be measured as total cubic feet of wood present, whether or not that wood can all be cut into one-inch lumber. Because round logs are imperfectly converted into straight, flat boards, a cubic foot of log is not equivalent to 12 board feet of lumber. Large old-growth logs whose circumferences describe a fairly gradual arc may hold up to 9 board feet per cubic foot. But second-growth timber from smaller trees, with tighter arcs of circumference, may hold only 4 board feet per cubic foot.

In projecting future timber harvests, the Forest Service has used cubic feet in its plans, whereas The Wilderness Society has used board feet. If the average diameter of the trees logged on a forest declines over time—as it will if the forest's large old-growth trees are replaced by younger second-growth trees—the number of cubic feet produced by a given section of forest may stay constant. But in the same section, the number of board feet will drop.

Readers interested in seeing how these factors have led the timber industry and The Wilderness Society to radically different conclusions about the future of westside forests should see the addendum to the chapter. Essentially, the addendum indicates that the preferred sale quantities proposed in the draft NFMA plans are about equal to, or even above, the *average* sales and logging levels for westside forests over the past decade. However, the same proposed sales and cut levels are significantly below the *annual* sales and cut levels for these forests during 1986, 1987, and 1989. The difference is due to the surge in timber demand over the past several years.

Thus, the industry is correct in saying that "present" levels of logging on the westside forests would have to decline dramatically under the draft NFMA plans. Yet the Forest Service is also correct in saying that *average* logging levels, as measured over the past decade of boom and bust years, can be maintained. The addendum also indicates that present rates of timber cutting on some westside forests significantly exceed the Forest Service's proposed LTSYC figures for these forests. Thus, the agency's own figures indicate that The Wilderness Society is correct in claiming that present logging rates are biologically unsustainable. And yet because the Forest Service merely maintains *average* sales levels, Associate Chief Leonard can argue that over the next decade, logging levels on these forests will be within the long-term sustained yield capacities.

Do the Draft NFMA Plans Guarantee Sustained Yield?

Under NFMA, the Forest Service is required to manage the national forests for a sustainable yield of timber. Also, agency policy is to maintain a nondeclining, even flow of timber from the forests. Critics say the Forest Service is evading these requirements by measuring the even flow and the sustainable yield in cubic feet. "You make furniture out of board feet, not cubic feet," comments one environmentalist. The industry, however, maintains that the extra biological productivity of cutover forests will make up for their lower output of board feet per cubic foot. According to a 1988 report prepared by the industry,

> Young, newly regenerated forests grow faster than old forests, thus yielding a higher annual volume to be harvested. Consequently, when the Forest Service converts old, decadent (sic) stands to young forests, it increases the productive potential of the forest and increases the quantity which can be removed . . . in perpetuity on a sustained yield basis (Public Timber Council *et al.* 1988).

The Forest Service observes that NFMA actually requires the use of cubic feet in measuring the "culmination of mean annual increment" in a forest—the point at which its annual rate of growth begins to decline. Associate Chief Leonard contends NFMA's legislative history also indicates that cubic feet should be used in measuring "non-declining even flow." Leonard adds that board feet are a very poor measure of forest productivity in general: "When this measure is employed, trees less than 12" in diameter do not appear to have volume at all." And another Forest Service source in Oregon contends that the timber industry already buys trees priced in board feet, but then utilizes their wood by the cubic foot—getting lumber and wood chips out of timber that do not seem to exist when measurement is done by the board foot. For all these reasons the Forest Service defends its use of cubic feet in determining nondeclining even flow. Still, some officials admit that measuring productivity in cubic feet rather than board feet will increase the apparent amount of future timber production on some forests. Whatever the justification, the agency can use a constant output of cubic feet to mask a decline in board feet available to timber purchasers.

Raw logs from state and private lands departing Gray's Harbor in Washington state. *Kathy Kilmer/The Wilderness Society*

Planned Road Construction and Forest Fragmentation

Conservationists argue that forest roads increase the fragmentation and therefore the vulnerability of ancient forests, regardless of the quantity of timber cut. Yet according to The Wilderness Society, "draft plans for the westside national forests clearly demonstrate that the Forest Service intends to retain few of the unprotected roadless areas. In many cases, unroaded lands are targeted for timber management early in the life of the plans" (The Wilderness Society 1988a).

Thus, the Society claims, almost one-half of the remaining available roadless acreage within the westside Oregon and Washington forests will be opened to roads within the first 15 years covered by the NFMA forest plans. By the end of the 50-year planning horizon covered by the plans ". . . 67 percent of the roadless acreage on 11 of the 12 westside forests will lose its unroaded status." In particular, 87 percent of the roadless areas on the Umpqua National Forest will be eliminated within 15 years and 90 percent within 50 years. The North Kalmiopsis roadless area of the Siskiyou National Forest, which conservationists have proposed as a wilderness area or as part of a national park, would largely be dominated by clear-cuts under the forest's draft NFMA plan. Overall, roadless areas within Siskiyou would decline from 314,025 acres today to a planned 13,700 acres in 15 years, for a reduction of 96 percent. The Wilderness Society claims such reductions of roadless acreage will reduce populations of spotted owls, pileated woodpeckers, pine martens, and perhaps deer, elk, and mountain goats (The Wilderness Society 1988a).

However, according to the timber industry:

> It is true that draft plans call for some harvesting in roadless areas that Congress released from wilderness consideration. . . . [But] what is wrong with harvesting roadless areas that were not selected for inclusion in state wilderness bills and were released to general management? Many of these areas rejected for wilderness designation have been found by the Forest Service to be better suited for other purposes, including timber production. That is what forest planning is all about. . . . The Wilderness Society is playing the "heads we win, tails you lose" game: it wants as much acreage as possible to be designated wilderness, and then as much harvesting restriction as possible placed on the remaining, nonwilderness areas (Public Timber Council *et al.* 1988).

Reforestation

Conservationists critical of the draft plans argue that the Forest Service is exaggerating its rate of success in reforesting cutover lands in the Pacific Northwest, and thus including low-productivity cutover areas in the future timber base that should be excluded because of regeneration problems. Under NFMA, the size of the future timber base helps determine how much logging can occur in the present. Thus, critics are implying the agency inflates its regeneration success rate in order to justify higher timber sales. Similarly, forest economist O'Toole (1988) argues that the Forest Service posits unrealistically high levels of wood production that can be achieved through thinning, fertilization, and other management techniques. In this view, the aim again is to exaggerate future wood production levels in order to increase the rate of logging that can occur in the present, without seeming to endanger the sustainability of timber production. National Audubon Society old-growth specialist James Pissot (1988) warns of an inevitable reduction in future wood production on the westside forests that allegedly is being hidden by improper Forest Service planning techniques. Likewise, The Wilderness Society concludes: "Draft plans for the westside forests would result in substantial long-term declines in timber harvest levels. Proposed logging at the beginning of the planning period must be reduced in order to comply with the sustained-yield requirements of the NFMA" (The Wilderness Society 1988b).

The Forest Service admits to past problems with reforestation on certain south-facing mountain slopes in southern Oregon, where exposure to the sun's heat, poor soils, and, in some cases, browsing by deer killed newly planted tree seedlings. However, the agency says it has found new ways to reforest such areas (for example, by partly shading the seedlings and by covering them with wire mesh to prevent their being eaten). Some Forest Service officials in the Northwest say that the region's past problems with regeneration have been solved or recognized by removing problem areas from the timber base. But Oregon conservationists contend that some agency officials are privately alarmed at the high rates of timber cutting being demanded by the timber industry and the Oregon congressional delegation. It is difficult to verify or disprove this claim, but interviews with Pacific Northwest forest officials show some support for achieving more "balance" between timber and nontimber uses of the forests.

NATIONAL AND LOCAL CAMPAIGNS FOR OLD GROWTH PRESERVATION

Both the high stakes in the battle over ancient forests and the many fronts on which it is being waged make predictions of the outcome difficult. Essentially, comments one observer, the conflict is over the rapidly disappearing supply of old growth that remains. Conservationists are trying to preserve as much of it as possible and the timber companies are trying to cut as much as they can before the conservationists succeed. The timber companies generally have local custom and public opinion on their side. But the industry's strength may be waning because of a general spread of conservationist attitudes, the growing economic diversification of Oregon and Washington, and the rising importance of tourism as a source of wages and tax revenues in the region.

To achieve their goals, conservationists must stall the industry's drive to cut old-growth stands long enough for public opinion to shift toward preservation and a new political equilibrium to be established. The industry, to achieve its goals, needs to stall the adoption of new NFMA plans and spotted owl protection guidelines that could reduce current logging rates. Both conservationists and industry need to mobilize public opinion over the long term in support of their positions. Both sides also use lawsuits and political maneuvers in Congress to determine the level of the timber cut, and hence to determine how much ancient forest is saved or liquidated.

This somewhat simplistic model is made more complex by the actions of the Forest Service. The agency has legal responsibilities for managing both timber and non-timber forest resources and appears to have an institutional interest in portraying itself as a neutral referee caught between two quarreling groups of unreasonable extremists. "We're getting criticism from both sides" is a favorite expression used by Forest Service officials, who implicitly justify their agency's existence by speaking of its role in fashioning a "balanced" management strategy for the forests.

Added to the equation, but with different institutional interests than the Forest Service, are state and local governments in Oregon and Washington, who seek to preserve timber jobs and county revenues. For at least some state officials, however, it is important that this occur without sacrificing the scenic beauty and environmental quality that make the Pacific Northwest an attractive region in which to live and conduct business.

The Northwest's ongoing legal and political disputes over NFMA plans, spotted owls, marbled murrelets, wild and scenic river designations, and the legality of individual timber sales are all variations of the same dispute. Playing an important role in determining the outcome of these various subdisputes is the Northwest congressional delegation, and most particularly Oregon's senior U.S. Senator, Mark O. Hatfield. A popular Republican who has displayed considerable ability in working with members of both parties in Congress, Senator Hatfield is a member of the Senate Energy and Natural Resources Committee and is the ranking minority member of the Senate Appropriations Committee, which determines the size of the westside timber cut through the annual appropriations process. Thus, he wields enormous influence over Forest Service policies.

Other important congressional figures in the ancient forest controversy include Representative Les AuCoin, an Oregon Democrat and member of the House Appropriations Committee; Representative Norman Dicks, a Democrat from the Puget Sound area of Washington, who also sits on the House Appropriations Committee; and Representative Thomas Foley, a Democrat from eastern Washington and the current House Majority Leader, the second most powerful official in the House of Representative. In seeking continued old-growth logging, the timber industry appears to be trying to influence public opinion in the Northwest—and hence lawmakers like Hatfield, Dicks, Foley, and AuCoin—to think of the conflict as a "jobs-versus-preservation" issue. Meanwhile, the industry appears to most observers to be using a variety of mechanisms to drag out the NFMA planning process for as long as possible in order to continue logging the national forests under more liberal logging limits of present, pre-NFMA management plans. Conservationists are pursuing a strategy to broaden the old-growth issue. They emphasize that automation, log exports, Forest Service timber policies, and lack of economic diversification are the biggest threats to milltown economies.

Meanwhile, the Oregon Natural Resources Council and the Sierra Club Legal Defense Fund, among others, have brought a host of lawsuits against various Forest Service timber sales. Some conservationists suggest that such lawsuits are essential to slow old-growth cutting while Congress decides the fate of the resource.

Oregon's Governor Goldschmidt and Washington's Governor Gardner have set up special task forces to sift through the competing claims, forge state government strategies for addressing the NFMA and spotted owl issues, and harmonize state government responses to the complex economic and environmental issues at stake. Oregon's task force, in late 1988, proposed an alternative management strategy for the Siskiyou National Forest that sought to increase both wilderness designations and allowable logging levels through intensified forest management. Additional Oregon alternatives to draft NFMA plans for westside forests are expected this year.

At the congressional level, Senator Hatfield has inserted provisions into federal appropriations bills for the past few years restricting the degree to which ongoing BLM and Forest Service management can be challenged in court. In response to one Hatfield-sponsored provision exempting BLM from certain lawsuits, the Seattle District Court last year threw out the conservationist challenge to logging on BLM's O & C grant lands. Conservationists expect that Senator Hatfield will continue his strategy to block lawsuits against BLM and Forest Service timber sales. On the other hand, Senator Hatfield cosponsored the Oregon Wild and Scenic Rivers Act, passed in 1988, that added segments of some 40 Oregon rivers to the national Wild and Scenic River System. Many of these rivers run through national forests, and their designation provides protection for strips of old growth that may serve as ecological corridors for connecting separated blocs of forestland.

The Forest Service, for its part, is continuing to prepare forest management plans under NFMA. In January 1989, the agency published a new appeals procedures designed to shorten the time over which appeals to those plans are resolved and to reduce the number of levels at which citizen appeals must be heard. The agency is also reportedly investigating consensus decision making on the Willamette forest, considered by some as the "flagship" of the entire National Forest System because logging there exceeds that on any other national forest. Final NFMA plans for most, but not all, of the Washington and Oregon forests are expected in 1989. After the final plans have been published, the agency may face industry or conservationist appeals and lawsuits that could keep them from being implemented for several years—although there are indications that some members of the Oregon congressional delegation may try to enact legislation prohibiting such appeals or lawsuits.

The conservationist lawsuit against the Fish and Wildlife Service for not listing the spotted owl, some observers say, could prove politically explosive in 1989. If the Fish and Wildlife Service has to list the owl, there could be an uproar both in the Pacific Northwest and in

Congress. Conservationists note that shortly after the Forest Service published its final decision on the owl, one timber company closed a mill on the Olympic Peninsula on Christmas Eve and dismissed more than 100 employees, citing the spotted owl decision as the reason. If the owl is listed as a threatened or endangered species, similar industry actions may follow. In addition, members of Congress might attempt to revive the so-called "God Committee" established by the 1978 amendments to the Endangered Species Act in response to the Snail Darter/Tellico Dam controversy. The "God Committee" has the power to override the Fish and Wildlife Service's protective efforts if it determines the public interest is better served by *not* protecting a species from development action.

Unlike the timber industry that, with a few exceptions, traditionally presents a united front on national forest logging issues, the local, regional, and national conservation groups working to preserve ancient forests are perceived by some as in disagreement over strategies. Given their somewhat differing constituencies and varying areas of expertise—including prowess at legal battles, lobbying, and economic analysis—this is not surprising. Some specialize in suing the Forest Service and see this legal activity as essential to slowing the logging. Others, like The Wilderness Society, have specialized in challenging draft NFMA plans, often on economic grounds. Some organizations, either because of their constituency base or because of their analysis of the Pacific Northwest political climate, believe that a nationwide campaign to save old growth is needed. Others believe that while a national campaign may induce Congress to play a direct role in preserving ancient forests, little could be achieved over the objections of the Washington and Oregon congressional delegations, particularly if the two are united. Thus some conservation organizations favor smaller, more focused efforts to protect ancient forests with different old-growth stands being protected bit by bit through additions to existing parks and wilderness areas or through inclusion in new wild and scenic river corridors.

National Audubon Society and its many local chapters in the Northwest have adopted a multifaceted strategy on old-growth preservation. National Audubon's Science Department, for example, performs continuing research on the effects of old-growth logging and communicates the results to the public and government agencies. National Audubon's Television Division has produced a one-hour television documentary on old growth that is scheduled for broadcasting in October 1989. The Audubon Chapter Relations Division is working with 33 local Audubon chapters in the Northwest on an "Adopt a Forest" program to help inventory old-growth areas and wildlife habitat areas needing preservation in parts of 29 national forests. The Audubon Litigation Division is working with local conservation activists to bring appeals and lawsuits challenging the logging of particular old-growth tracts. And the Audubon Government Relations Division is involved in the leadership of a national coalition of local and national environmental organizations, the Ancient Forest Alliance, that is promoting the need for congressional hearings on the decline of old-growth forests and on potential legislative remedies.

The Ancient Forest Alliance was formed in September 1988 by a number of national and local conservation groups to coordinate their old-growth preservation efforts. Members of the alliance are likely to support a Washington state Wild and Scenic Rivers bill, probably to be introduced in 1989, and will continue to ask Congress to reduce the overall timber cut in the Pacific Northwest through the appropriations process. Last year, conservationists succeeded in reducing the sales figure for Oregon and Washington forests by 150 million board feet. They failed to persuade the House Appropriations Committee to call for protection of up to 100 "special places" in westside ancient forests, but their efforts did succeed in winning additional funding for the Forest Service's inventory of old-growth ecosystems.

Alliance members and leaders suggest that legislation also will be introduced in 1989 to protect some ancient forest acreage through the expansion of parks and wilderness areas or through special designations of some Pacific Northwest locations as protected areas. Proposals to launch a major national crusade for a large, new "Ancient Forest National Park" or recreation area have not yet gained full acceptance. Whether or not such a proposal is adopted, local and national efforts to win new federal protection for portions of ancient forests are almost certain to engage conservation groups over the next several years.

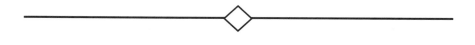

ADDENDUM 1

The Bases for Different Predictions of Westside Timber Cutting Levels

The timber industry's CH2M Hill study compared the theoretical "Potential Yield" of westside forests, under existing pre-NFMA plans, with the "Allowable Sale Quantity" (ASQ) of timber that would be available under the new plans. The results indicated a fall-off in timber availability of about 20 percent.

Forest Service Associate Chief Leonard, however, has stated that partly because of the recession of the early 1980s, the *average* timber sales and actual cut numbers on the westside forests have been significantly below both the old Potential Yield and new ASQ figures. Comparing new ASQ for Oregon and Washington with the average sales experienced from 1977 through 1986, Leonard maintained in 1988 that actual timber cutting on these national forests will remain roughly the same as the average level experienced in the past.

In reply, the industry maintains that Congress has never funded timber cutting in the National Forest System at 100 percent of the potential yield figures. Accordingly, industry studies suggest Congress will fund future sales on westside forests at only 80 percent of new ASQ, causing the timber shortage predicted. This conclusion is disputed by conservationists. First, they say that the old Potential Yield was always a hypothetical maximum-production figure that the agency never expected to achieve. Secondly, they maintain that since the Forest Service earns money on its Pacific Northwest timber sales but tends to lose money on sales in other regions, Congress will likely fund future sales in the region at 100 percent of the ASQ—making the CH2M Hill predictions misleading for westside forests.

A 1988 Wilderness Society study claims that the new ASQs understate the actual level of future logging. This is because ASQs include only "chargeable" timber, from within the designated timber base, that is scheduled for cutting through regular sales. But forests also sell "nonchargeable" timber that includes wood from salvage sales, as well as pole timber and other wood culled during certain kinds of maintenance operations on the national forests. While excluded from ASQ measurements, nonchargeable timber is included in another new statistic called Total Sale Program Quantity (TSPQ).

Comparing the proposed TSPQs for the westside forests with average 1978–1987 logging levels, The Wilderness Society concludes that actual timber cutting on these forests will rise 10 percent. In reply, the timber industry has said that TSPQ figures may be legitimate measures of potential future cutting levels, but it says that since Congress will only fund 80 percent of these potential harvests, the actual harvests achieved will be less than The Wilderness Society assumes. Hence, while The Wilderness Society has used TSPQ figures to show that cutting will increase on most westside forests, the industry uses these same figures (and its 80-percent multiplier) to suggest that the timber cut on most of the forests will fall if the preferred alternatives in the new draft plans are adopted.

Further complicating these rival claims about future westside cutting, are somewhat different calculations of current harvest levels. Wilderness Society figures are lower than industry figures for most of the forests, making the Society's projection of future increases in logging closer to 15 percent than to 10 percent. Sources at The Wilderness So-

170 of 610

Table 1. Past and Projected Sales Volumes and Other Volumes in Region 6 Forests (in billions of board feet of timber).[a]

Average volume 1978–1986	FY 1986	FY 1987	FY 1988	FY 1989 (estimate)	Potential Yield (old plans)	ASQ (new plans)	TPSQ (new plans)	LTSYC (new plans)
3.8	5.05	5.27	5.10	4.95	5.86	4.03	4.64	4.98

[a]Region 6 includes all national forests of Oregon and Washington. Figures for FY 1986–1989 represent congressional funding of timber sales on national forests in the region. "'Average volume" represents timber sales on these forests over the period 1976–1986. "'Potential Yield" is the theoretical maximum level of timber harvest on these forests, given the use of "intensive" forestry techniques, as calculated by existing plans. (For explanations of LTSYC, ASQ, and TPSQ, see text.)

Table 2. Actual Harvest Levels and Projected Total Sale Program Quantities (as calculated by the timber industry and The Wilderness Society).

Westside national forests	Average harvest 1978–1986[a]	Average harvest 1978–1986[b]	1987 harvest[c]	TSPQ[a]	TSPQ x 80 percent[b]	TSPQ[d]
Olympic	258 (241)[e]	258	243.4	206	165	206
Mt. Baker-Snoqualmie	229 (217)	230	296	191	154	192.5
Gifford Pinchot	343 (326)	343	417	427	371	464
Mt. Hood	336 (314)	336	406	347	278	347
Willamette	634 (634)	634	899.5	710	568	710
Umpqua	320 (310)	320	551.9	402	322	402.5
Rogue River	177 (167)	177	203.5	148	118	147
Siskiyou	147 (140)	147	225.2	165	132	165
Siuslaw	292 (282)	292	364	316	253	316
Klamath	181 (187)	187	238.1	222[f]	n/a	n/a
Six Rivers	126	126	177.3	208	149	186
Shasta-Trinity	209 (199)	199	220	247	192	240
Total	3,115	3,249	4,241	3,589	2,702	3,376

[a]Wilderness Society

[b]Industry

[c]Figures for the 1987 harvest are from Forest Service "cut and sold" statistics.

[d]Author's adjustment of industry figures.

[e]Numbers in parentheses show The Wilderness Society's calculation published in "The End of the Ancient Forests," which has since been updated.

[f]Equals allowable sale quantity for Klamath National Forest plus 12 percent additional volume, according to The Wilderness Society.

n/a = not available.

ciety say these figures, based on Forest Service statistics, were revised when another set of Forest Service figures for current timber cutting—essentially agreeing with those cited by the timber industry—became available after publication of The Wilderness Society's "The End of the Ancient Forests." (In an addendum to the report, the Society revised its projections of a future increase in total logging levels from 15 percent to 10 percent.)

It is possible to clear up some of the confusion about the differing visions of the draft NFMA program by comparing the statistics used by the various parties, as in Table 1.

For the region as a whole, we can see that ASQ allowed in the new draft plans exceeds the average sales occurring over the 1978–1986 period, as the Forest Service contends. The proposed TPSQ from the draft plans is even larger. But both ASQ and the TSPQ are significantly below the average sales occurring in fiscal years 1986, 1987, 1988, and 1989, indicating that the industry is correct in saying that the draft plans would not allow "current" logging levels to continue. The Forest Service's proposed LTSYC figure, reflecting the agency's calculation of the cutting levels that are sustainable over the long term on the Washington and Oregon forests, is exceeded by the cut occurring during 1986, 1987 and 1988. Thus conservationists can correctly say that by the agency's own figures, the current cut level—as measured on a yearly basis, although not on an average basis for 1978–1986—is "unsustainable."

Associate Chief Leonard says that the agency regulates timber sales on the basis of 10-year averages, not year to year, so the exceeding of the new LTSYC figure during any given year is not necessarily—in the agency's view—a cause for alarm. If sales in a particular year are very high, he contends, they will be balanced out by a lower sales level during the remainder of the decade-long regulatory period. However, the cyclical history of the timber industry suggests that sales may decline on their own without agency action if, for instance, a rise in interest rates causes new home building to fall off rapidly within the next year or so, thus curtailing demand for Oregon and Washington lumber.

Complicating this analysis somewhat is the existence of more than 6 billion board feet that the timber industry purchased before the 1980s recession, but then defaulted on harvesting. Returned to the government through a special "timber buy back" program enacted by Congress in 1985, this timber has since been largely resold to industry. The high timber sales figures recorded for 1986–1989 include significant quantities of buyback timber, leading the industry to claim that these sales do not, in fact, represent an unsustainable harvest level.

In Table 2, it is clear that average timber harvest levels will decline significantly if the timber industry is correct in suggesting that only

80 percent of TSPQ will be funded. But if conservationists are correct in assuming that Congress will fund Pacific Northwest timber sales at close to 100 percent of the recommended level, the NFMA plans would cause a significant increase over average 1978–1986 timber harvest levels.

However, compared to 1987—when high prices, record timber demand, and the availability of buyback timber all resulted in rapid cutting of both old-growth and second-growth trees—adoption of the new plans would require significant reductions in logging levels. Industry might therefore legitimately claim that the draft NFMA plans would require some reduction in timber industry activity on westside forests. At the same time, of course, conservationists can point to the 1987 harvests as evidence that the timber companies and Forest Service are liquidating ancient forests by allowing cut-levels that exceed the long-term sustained yield capacity of these forests.

REFERENCES

Advisory Panel on the Spotted Owl. 1986. Report of the Advisory Panel on the Spotted Owl. Submitted to the National Audubon Society, April 29, 1986. 75 pp.

Anderson, H. Michael. 1988. "Old growth forests: A conservationist's perspective." *Natural Areas Journal* 8:(1) 13–16.

Blegen, Mark. 1989. Washington State Employment Department. Telephone interview with author, January 1989.

Church, Shawn. 1988. "Timber issue becomes one of 'siege' vs. balance." Roseburg, Oregon *News-Review*. March 8.

Daniel, John. 1988. "The Long Dance of the Trees." *Wilderness* (Spring 1988.):19–34.

Delft, Mark. 1989. Telephone interview with author. USDA Forest Service, Washington, D.C.

Dixon, Kenneth R. and Thomas C. Juelson. 1987. "The political economy of the spotted owl." *Ecology* 68:4; 772–776.

Ervin, Keith. 1988. "Time is running out: federal agencies fail to guard our national living treasure." *Audubon Activist* 2(6). Special Report.

Evans, Brock. 1989. Personal interview with author. National Audubon Society.

————. 1989. We Can Protect Our Remaining Ancient Forests and Maintain a Strong Timber Economy in the Pacific Northwest. National Audubon Society Memo. Washington, D.C. February 3, 1989. 2 pp.

Feeney, Andy. 1988. "In debate over national forest plans, "community stability" emerges as a key issue." *Land Letter* 7:10. Special Report. W.J. Chandler Associates. Washington, D.C.

Gorte, Julie F. and Ross W. Gorte. 1987. Employment and Community Stability in the Forest Products Industries. Paper delivered at a conference on Community Stability in Forest-based Economies. November 1987. Portland, Oregon. 27 pp.

Hall, Patricia. 1988. USDA Forest Service Pacific Northwest Research Station, Forestry Sciences Laboratory, Olympia, Washington. Telephone interview with author.

Hanson, Dr. Andrew. 1988. Hatfield Marine Science Center, Newport, Oregon. Telephone interview with author.

Hannum, Jeff. 1989. Employment Division, Department of Human Resources, State of Oregon, Salem. Telephone interview, February, 1989.

Hoyt, Reis. 1989. Policy Analyst, Governor's Forest Planning Team. Oregon Economic Development Department. Telephone interview with author, February 1989.

Hunthausen, Dr. Richard. 1988. USDA Forest Service Region 6 research biologist. Telephone interview with author.

Kelly, David. 1988. "Guess what else needs big trees: big fish." *Audubon Activist* 2(6). Special Report. (Excerpted from David Kelly, *Secrets of the Old Growth Forest.* Peregrine Smith Books. Layton, Utah.)

Kessel, B. and D.D. Gibson. 1978. "Status and distribution of Alaska birds." *Stud. Avian Biology* l. Cooper Ornithological Society. Los Angeles, California.

Laverty, Lyle. 1989. Recreation Policy, USDA Forest Service, Region 6, Corvallis, Oregon. Telephone interview February 1989.

Leonard, George M. 1987. The Role of the Forest Service in Promoting Community Stability. Speech delivered at a conference on Community Stability in Forest-based Economies, November 17, 1987. Portland, Oregon. 9 pp.

———. 1989. USDA Forest Service, Washington, D.C. Telephone interview with author.

Lonsdale, Harry. 1988. "Can both old-growth trees, timber industry be saved?" *The Oregonian*:B7. April 26, 1988. Portland, Oregon.

Marshall, David B. 1988. "The marbled murrelet joins the old-growth forest conflict." *American Birds* (Summer 1988):202–210.

Maser, Chris. 1987. Ancient Forests, Priceless Treasures. Speech delivered to National Audubon Society Biennial Convention, Bellingham, Washington, August 24, 1987. 14 pp.

Meslow, Dr. Charles. 1988. Fish and Wildlife Service, Corvallis, Oregon. Telephone interview with author.

Morrison, Peter H. 1988. *Old Growth in the Pacific Northwest: A Status Report.* The Wilderness Society. Washington, D.C. November 1988. 58 pp.

National Forest Products Association and the American Forest Council. 1988. Old Growth—A protected Legacy for Future Generations. 9 pp.

Nichols, Robert. 1989. Policy Research, Office of the Governor, Washington State. Telephone interview with author, February 1989.

Norse, Dr. Elliott and Jeffrey T. Olson. 1988. The Wilderness Society, Washington, D.C. Interview with author.

Northwest Forestry Association, National Forest Products Association. 1988. The Environmental Community Should Stop Mischaracterizing the Terms of the National Forest Management Debate. Portland, Oregon, and Washington, D.C. 9 pp.

Old-Growth Definition Task Group. 1986. Interim Definitions for Old-Growth Douglas-Fir and Mixed-Conifer Forests in the Pacific Northwest and California. USDA Forest Service Pacific Northwest Research Station Research Note PNW-447, July 1986. 7 pp.

Olson, Jeffrey T. 1988. *Pacific Northwest Lumber and Wood Products: An Industry in Transition Vol. 4 of National Forests: Policies for the Future.* The Wilderness Society. Washington, D.C. September 1988. 46 pp.

O'Toole, Randal. 1988. *Reforming the Forest Service.* Island Press. Washington, D.C., Covelo, California. 247 pp.

Pissot, James. 1988. Personal interviews with author. National Audubon Society.

Public Timber Council, American Forest Council and National Forest Products Association. 1988. The Real West Side Story: The Wilderness Society Distorts Timber Management on the National Forests. August. 12 pp.

Ralph, Dr. C.J. 1988. USDA Forest Service Southwest Forest and Range Experiment Station, Arcata, California. Telephone interview with author.

Rey, Mark. 1988, 1989. Vice President, National Forest Products Association, Washington, D.C. Telephone interviews with author.

Robertson, Dale F. 1988. Record of Decision. Amendment to the Pacific Northwest Region Guide: Final Supplement to the Final Environmental Impact Statement. December 8, 1988. Washington, D.C.

Robbins, William G. 1987. "Lumber production and community stability: A view from the Pacific Northwest." *Pacific Northwest Journal of Forest History.* October.

Salwasser, Hal. 1989. USDA Forest Service, Washington, D.C. Telephone interview with author.

Schallau, Con H. and Richard M. Alston. 1987. "The commitment to community stability: A policy or shibboleth?" *Environmental Law* 177:429, 429–450.

Simberloff, Daniel. 1987. "The spotted owl fracas: mixing academic, applied, and political ecology." *Ecology* 68:4; 766–772.

Sisco, Chuck. 1988. National Audubon Society staff field biologist, Pacific Northwest region. Telephone interview with author.

Spies, Dr. Thomas. 1988. USDA Forest Service, Pacific Northwest Region. Telephone interview with author.

Thomas, Jack Ward, Leonard F. Ruggiero, R. William Mannan, John W. Schoen and Richard A. Lancia. 1988. "Management and conservation of old-growth forests in the United States." *Wildlife Society Bulletin* 16:252–262.

The Wilderness Society. 1988a. *End of the Ancient Forests: Special Report on National Forest Plans in the Pacific Northwest.* Washington, D.C. June. 75 pp.

———. 1988b. *Protecting Biological Diversity, Vol. 2 of National Forests: Policies for the Future.* Washington, D.C. August. 58 pp.

———. 1988c. *Reforestation Programs and Timberland Suitability, Vol. 3 of National Forests: Policies for the Future.* By Henry H. Carey, V. Alaric Sample, Stephen P. Greenway and Nicholas S. Van Pelt. Washington, D.C. September. 53 pp.

Wille, Chris M. 1988. "In the Pacific Northwest we are cutting the living links with our natural past." *Audubon Activist* 2(6). Special Report.

USDA Forest Service, Pacific Northwest Region. 1986a. Draft Supplement to the Environmental Impact Statement for an Amendment to the Pacific Northwest Regional Guide, Volume 1, Spotted Owl Guidelines.

———. 1986b. Draft Supplement to the Environmental Impact Statement for an Amendment to the Pacific Northwest Regional Guide. Volume 2, Appendices, Spotted Owl G guidelines.

———. 1988a Final Supplement to the Environmental Impact Statement for an Amendment to the Pacific Northwest Regional Guide, Volume 2, Appendices, Spotted Owl Guidelines.

———. 1988b. Final Supplement to the Environmental Impact Statement for an Amendment to the Pacific Northwest Regional Guide, Volume 1, Spotted Owl Guidelines.

[Editor's note: In late February, 1989, GAO released a report, "Spotted Owl Petition Beset by Problems," contending that FWS had altered a draft status review of the owl by deleting a section predicting the bird's eventual extinction under the Forest Service's plan for managing its habitat. GAO added that regional FWS staff working on the listing decision were told that FWS Director Frank Dunkle and other Interior officials "would not accept a decision to list the spotted owl as endangered," and suggested that politics therefore may have played an improper role in the listing decision.

On April 26, 1989, FWS submitted a new finding on the spotted owl's status to the U.S. District Court for the Western District of Washington state. FWS found that the bird warrants listing as a "threatened" species because of ongoing modification and loss of its habitat under the management of the FWS and the Bureau of Land Management. FWS began steps to propose the owl for listing as threatened, but did not immediately draw up a listing proposal.

In the spring of 1989, conservationists won court rulings temporarily halting 165 timber sales on Forest Service lands and 153 sales on BLM lands in Oregon, pending a further decision on whether the sales would endanger spotted owls.]

Andy Feeney is an associate editor of Defenders *magazine in Washington, D.C., published by Defenders of Wildlife.*

Rodenticides containing strychnine are used to kill prairie dogs. Although this poisoning is legal, some 50 species of migratory birds—some endangered—have been killed by strychnine products, a violation of several wildlife statutes. Untangling this legal complication was just one of the important and interesting recent court actions. *Leonard Lee Rue III*

Recent Court Decisions Affecting Wildlife

Michael J. Bean

INTRODUCTION

The courts have come to play an increasingly important role in the development and implementation of wildlife conservation policy. The interpretations placed on conservation laws by the courts can be of critical significance in determining the effectiveness of those statutes. For that reason, individuals interested in wildlife conservation need to stay abreast of judicial developments as well as legislative and administrative ones. This chapter examines some of the most important wildlife cases decided in 1988 and describes their significance for the future implementation of key wildlife conservation programs.

NEW DIRECTIONS IN REGULATING THE "TAKING" OF WILDLIFE

In the history of wildlife conservation laws and programs, restrictions on hunting were among the first measures employed to protect wildlife. In time, however, it became apparent that hunting was but one of

155

many activities that result in the loss, or "taking," of individual wildlife. Effectively regulating the many nonhunting activities that kill wildlife has become a major challenge for conservationists. Several cases recently have been decided that illustrate the importance and complexity of that challenge.

Protecting Endangered Sea Turtles in the Shrimp Fishery

The Endangered Species Act (16 U.S.C.A. 1531 *et seq.* 1985) flatly prohibits the killing of any endangered and most threatened species. Yet each year, more than 11,000 threatened and endangered sea turtles are killed by drowning in the nets of American shrimp fishermen. This carnage is the unintended consequence of towing shrimp nets hours at a time through South Atlantic and Gulf of Mexico coastal waters where shrimp and sea turtles both live. Once caught inside a shrimp net, a turtle is unable to escape and is almost certain to drown, if held under water for more than approximately 90 minutes.

All five species of sea turtles that occur in U.S. coastal waters have been protected by the Endangered Species Act since 1978. Despite that ostensible protection, the act's prohibition against the taking of protected turtles has been impossible to enforce. Literally thousands of shrimp boats ply U.S. coastal waters. The chance that a federal law enforcement officer will be on the scene when a shrimper pulls a dead turtle aboard is virtually nil, for no more than two or three federal officers work in many coastal states. Even if a shrimper were to be observed hauling up a dead turtle, successful prosecution would be hindered by the fact that the hapless shrimper could have done nothing to avoid catching the turtle and was in fact behaving no differently than any other shrimper.

The responsibility for enforcing the Endangered Species Act for sea turtles and other marine species lies with the Secretary of Commerce.[1] By 1987 the secretary had identified a solution to the turtle death dilemma, which was to require shrimp nets to be equipped with a special apparatus, known as a "turtle excluder device," that deflects turtles safely away from capture in a shrimp net. The secretary's requirements were published as regulations in the *Federal Register* on June 29, 1987. Almost immediately, the requirement was challenged in court by the state of Louisiana and a group of fishermen, the Concerned Shrimpers of Louisiana, who believed that their shrimp catch would be reduced if

---

1. Since sea turtles spend part of their lives on land and part in the sea, it was initially unclear whether their protection under the Endangered Species Act was the responsibility of the Secretary of Commerce or the Secretary of Interior. By memorandum of agreement, the two secretaries agreed to share that responsibility. The Secretary of Commerce protects turtles while they are in the water; the Secretary of Interior protects nesting beaches and turtles while they are on land.

they used the turtle excluder devices. The shrimpers did not challenge the secretary's authority under the Endangered Species Act to require the use of particular gear; instead, they challenged the adequacy of the information on which he relied to support the conclusion that this gear was necessary for the conservation of sea turtles. A more frontal assault might have been better advised, for within a few months of each other both the United States District Court and the United States Court of Appeals rejected the challenge in *Louisiana ex rel. Guste v. Verity* (853 F.2d 322 [5th Cir. 1988]). Both courts concluded that the secretary had ample basis to issue the challenged regulations: sea turtles were regularly caught and drowned in shrimp nets in the waters of the Southeast, and use of the excluder devices would virtually eliminate further turtle drownings.

Despite their failure to prevail on the ultimate legal issue, opponents of the turtle regulations did succeed in throwing a monkey wrench into enforcement of the regulations. While agreeing that the Secretary of Commerce had adequate basis for his regulations, the District Court, shortly after the 1988 fishing season began in the Gulf, enjoined enforcement of the regulations pending a final ruling by the Court of Appeals. That injunction remained in effect through August 31, by which time the 1988 fishing season was substantially over. When Congress later in the year passed legislation reauthorizing the Endangered Species Act, it further postponed the regulations by delaying their implementation until the beginning of the spring 1988 fishing season for offshore waters and until spring 1989 for inshore waters. By this action, Congress implicitly ratified the secretary's authority under the Endangered Species Act to regulate the manner in which a particular industry operates in order to reduce the probability that a taking of an endangered species might occur. This was a legislative precedent of potentially great significance, because it affirmed that the secretary can do more than merely prosecute individuals who take an endangered species; if necessary the secretary also can regulate an entire industry to prevent the possibility of unlawful takings.

Preventing the "Taking" of Protected Species by Pesticide Poisoning

Endangered species and other protected species, such as migratory birds, are occasionally killed as a result of pesticide use. Like the drowning of sea turtles in shrimp nets, this is an unintended, but often predictable, consequence of the use of certain pesticides. This fact creates an anomalous situation, for while the Endangered Species Act elevates species conservation concerns above other competing interests, the basic federal law regulating the sale and use of pesticides, the Federal Insecticide, Fungicide, and Rodenticide Act (FIFRA [7 U.S.C.A. 136 *et seq.* 1985]) expressly requires that administrative decisions about pesticide use balance economic benefits against environmental harm. A pesticide may be registered for use if the Environmental Protection Agency (EPA) finds that its use will not cause "unreasonable adverse effects on the environment." However, if FIFRA allows occasional death of endangered or other protected species due to pesticide use, how can these deaths be reconciled with the seemingly absolute prohibitions against the taking of wildlife, as found in the Endangered Species Act and the Migratory Bird Treaty Act? (16 U.S.C. 703 *et seq.*).

Reconciling those disparate provisions of law was the core issue presented in *Defenders of Wildlife v. EPA* (688 F. Supp. 1334 [D. Minn. 1988]). In the case, Defenders of Wildlife and two other groups challenged EPA's continued registration of pesticides containing strychnine for use against prairie dogs, ground squirrels, and meadow mice. About a half million pounds of strychnine are used each year, primarily for rodent control on western range, pasture, and croplands. Strychnine is a nonselective poison that kills anything that consumes enough of it, including predators and scavengers that consume other animals poisoned by the chemical.

With a slowness that is characteristic of regulatory action under FIFRA, EPA began to consider restrictions on strychnine products in 1976. In the intervening years, the U.S. Fish and Wildlife Service (FWS) advised EPA that some 18 endangered species were likely to be jeopardized by the continued use of strychnine. In addition, EPA had information that individuals of nearly fifty species of migratory birds had been killed by strychnine products. Nevertheless, after proposing in 1983 to cancel most strychnine product registrations, EPA concluded its review in 1987 by issuing an order that allowed its continued use, provided only that when used against prairie dogs, a field survey first must be carried out to ensure that no endangered black-footed ferrets are present in the area.

EPA's final decision took the form of an agreement reached with manufacturers and certain users of strychnine; conclusion of this agreement cut short a formal hearing on EPA's 1983 proposal to cancel the registration of all strychnine products. Defenders of Wildlife and the Sierra Club also had been parties to the aborted hearing, but refused to join the agreement. EPA's view was that if Defenders was unsatisfied, it could petition to reopen the matter, effectively beginning anew the eleven-year long process that had just ended. Defenders took another tack, suing in federal court and arguing that the continued registration of strychnine products constituted a taking of protected wildlife in contravention of three wildlife statutes: the Endangered Species Act, the Migratory Bird Treaty Act, and the Bald and Golden Eagle Protection Act (16 U.S.C.A. 668 *et seq.* 1985). The district court agreed with Defenders and ordered EPA to cancel temporarily all strychnine registrations until it had some means of assuring that no unauthorized taking of protected wildlife would occur when the pesticide was used.

The district court's decision was significant for three reasons. First, the court effectively held that FIFRA's provisions requiring the balancing of environmental and economic factors when determining whether to allow a pesticide to be used are overridden by the taking prohibitions in these wildlife protection statutes. Second, by temporarily cancelling are uses of strychnine products outright, the court made sort of an end-run around FIFRA's complex procedures for restricting pesticide use. Normally under FIFRA, a pesticide registration can be cancelled only following a formal—and typically very prolonged—hearing at which the pesticide manufacturer can present evidence in support of continued registration and cross-examine those who offer evidence against continued registration. In this case, the hearing had been obviated as result of the agreement between EPA and the pesticide manufacturer. Thus, the court's decision to halt strychnine use was based solely on a review of EPA's action and of the evidence on strychnine's hazards that principally had been gathered by EPA.

The pesticide manufacturer was unable to challenge the EPA-assembled evidence in court. In the future, the *Defenders of Wildlife v. EPA* decision may deter pesticide manufacturers from bypassing an administrative hearing where they have the chance to make their best argument for product registration, since to do so would undercut their case if a product's registration were challenged in court.

Finally, the relief the court ordered—temporary cancellation of strychnine pending the development of satisfactory assurances that no unauthorized taking of protected wildlife would occur if it were used—is a step that EPA could not have taken under FIFRA. Normally, a pesticide registration can be suspended only upon a finding by EPA that there is an imminent danger to public health or the environment that necessitates acting more swiftly than the normal cancellation procedures allow. Although EPA had found that there was no such imminent danger, the court ordered relief that was tantamount to a suspension of all strychnine products.

Applicability of the Endangered Species Act to Municipal Governments

A third case that explored the nature of the taking prohibition is *United States v. City of Rancho Palos Verdes* (841 F.2d 329 [9th Cir. 1988]). This case arose out of the unfortunate extinction of an endangered California insect, the Palos Verdes blue butterfly. The insect, first listed as an endangered species in 1980, occupied a few coastal scrub sage habitats near Los Angeles. In 1982, the last of these areas, (which FWS had officially designated as critical habitat for the butterfly) was destroyed when the city of Rancho Palos Verdes built a ball diamond and park on the site. Since then, the butterfly has never been seen again and is presumed extinct.

The United States filed a criminal action against the city, charging it with an unlawful taking of the butterfly in contravention of the Endangered Species Act. The city's defense, successfully asserted, was that the act's prohibition against taking applied only to "persons" and that, despite the act's very broad definition of the term "person," a city did not fit within the definition. Whether or not this was a correct interpretation of the act is of only historical interest now, for the Endangered Species Act Amendments of 1988 revised the definition to make clear that, in the future, cities will be subject to the act's provisions.

WETLANDS AND OTHER LAND USE CASES

Broad interpretations by the courts of statutory prohibitions against "taking" wildlife are one way of addressing threats to wildlife. Another equally important method is interpretation of land-use statutes. Several land-use cases with important wildlife conservation implications that were decided in the past year are examined here.

Enforcing Wetlands Easements to Protect Waterfowl

The federal program for waterfowl conservation relies heavily upon acquisition of land or interests in land to protect waterfowl nesting habitat. In the prairie pothole region of the north-central states, FWS has focused on acquiring wetland easements to protect waterfowl breeding habitat. By acquiring an easement, FWS effectively purchases the landowner's promise not to drain, fill, burn, or otherwise destroy wetland areas on a specified parcel of land. An easement represents a perpetual property interest; that is, subsequent purchasers or inheritors of the parcel are bound by the original landowner's agreement. All lands covered by easements held by FWS are managed as part of the National Wildlife Refuge System.

In *United States v. Vesterso* (828 F.2d 1234 [8th Cir.1987]), three members of a North Dakota county water board were charged with damaging federal property—specifically, certain wetland easements —a violation of the National Wildlife Refuge System Administration Act (16 U.S.C.A. 668dd *et seq.* 1985). The water board had undertaken to drain certain wetland areas, including those subject to federal easements, in order to alleviate flooding on adjacent properties. The beneficiaries of the drainage project, the court noted, included two of the three board members, who owned land that benefitted from the drainage project. Among the defenses offered by the board members was one similar to that which had succeeded in the *City of Rancho Palos Verdes* case. Inasmuch as they had acted in their official capacities as county officials, the North Dakotans argued that they should not be considered "persons" subject to the Refuge System Administration Act. Even though the act contains a definition of "person" much narrower than that found in the Endangered Species Act, the court concluded that the three board members were subject to the Administration Act's prohibitions. Rather than fine or jail the defendants, as authorized by the law, the court placed them on probation, which would terminate upon restoration of the easement areas to their former condition.

EPA Veto Authority over Section 404 Permits Issued by the Army Corps of Engineers

The acquisition of wetlands and wetland easements is an important tool in wildlife conservation. However, the effective protection of wetlands depends as well upon a vigorous regulatory program to control the use of privately owned wetlands for development purposes. The most important federal program for regulating private development in wetlands is carried out under the authority of Section 404 of the Clean Water Act (33 U.S.C.A. 1344 [1986]). Section 404 requires that before anyone deposits fill in a wetland, he or she must first apply for and receive a permit from the U.S. Army Corps of Engineers. In deciding whether to issue a requested permit, the Corps must determine that the proposed activity is in the public interest and complies with certain detailed guidelines promulgated by EPA. Although principal responsibility for implementing the Section 404 program lies with the Corps of Engineers, EPA under some circumstances can play a major role as well. An important case, illustrating the respective roles of these two federal agencies and underscoring the potential conservation value of the Section 404 program, was decided by the United States Court of Appeals for the Second Circuit in June 1988: *Bersani v. Robichaud* (850 F.2d 36 [2d Cir. 1988]).

John A. Bersani and his partners sought to build a major shopping center near Attleboro, Massachusetts. The site they selected encompassed a 50-acre, red maple swamp, known locally as Sweedens Swamp. In order to build on the swamp, the developers needed a permit from the Corps of Engineers. Normally, the Corps will not grant permits for development projects that are not "water dependent"; that is, that do not need to be sited in or near an aquatic area to serve their intended purpose. Indeed, the regulations governing issuance of Section 404 permits specify that a developer seeking a wetland permit for a nonwater dependent activity, such as a shopping center, must prove that there is no alternative nonwetland site where the proposed development can be built. In the *Bersani* case, the Corps decided that the developer had met that test because the only alternative site identified had been purchased by a rival shopping center developer shortly before Bersani applied for his Corps permit.

The Corps, however, was not to have the final word on the matter. A seldom-used provision of Section 404 empowers EPA to override a decision of the Corps granting a wetland permit. EPA can use this authority if it determines that the filling of a particular wetland will have "unacceptable adverse effects" on wildlife or other specified natural resources. In the 15-year history of this provision, EPA had used its veto authority approximately half a dozen times.

Sweedens Swamp was surely an unlikely candidate for EPA to defend. The swamp's 50-acre size was not especially large, and although it offered important habitat for local wildlife, it was neither nationally unique nor particularly outstanding. EPA was moved to act, however, less because of the inherent value of the wetland resources at stake than because of its perception that the loss of the swamp could have been avoided entirely. EPA determined that the developer had passed up the nonwetland site prior to its later purchase by a rival developer. The purpose of Section 404, in EPA's view, is to discourage the siting of development in wetland areas, and this purpose can be furthered only by a straightforward rule against development in wetlands by anyone who foregoes the opportunity to site a development in a nonwetland area. Consequently, EPA vetoed the Corps' permit to fill Sweedens Swamp; the veto was challenged by Bersani.

The narrow legal issue decided by the court was whether EPA was justified in concluding that the adverse impacts of the proposed development in Sweedens Swamp were unacceptable because an alternative nonwetland site had been available at the time the developer entered the market in search of a suitable site, even though that site later became unavailable. The court sided with EPA, thus endorsing a very far-reaching scope of authority for EPA and implicitly confirming the primacy of EPA's authority under Section 404 vis-a-vis the Corps. Partly as a result of the Sweedens Swamp controversy, EPA has recently become much more assertive in the use of its Section 404 authority. On December 1, 1988, however, Bersani asked the Supreme Court to review the lower court's ruling. The Supreme Court is likely to decide early in 1989 whether to hear the case or let the lower court's order stand.

Access of Wildlife to Federal Lands

A quite different and unusual case involving wildlife and land use arose out of a Wyoming rancher's efforts to keep antelope from entering onto his private rangeland and crossing onto federal lands where he held grazing rights. As a result of land grants to the Union Pacific Railroad in the 19th century, much of southern Wyoming is characterized by a "checkerboard" pattern of alternating squares of federal and privately owned land. Taylor Lawrence, a Wyoming rancher, owned several squares of the checkerboard and held grazing rights on the adjoining, federally owned squares. Lawrence knew he was not allowed to put a fence on the federal land, but thought he had found a clever way around that prohibition: He erected 28 miles of fence just inside the boundaries of the squares he owned. Whenever his fence reached the corner line of an adjoining, federally owned square, Lawrence would have the fence cross onto his next square precisely at the common corner where four squares meet. As a result, his fence effectively prevented access by antelope to their winter feeding range on some 9,600 acres of federal land.

The United States sued Lawrence to compel him to remove the fence and allow the antelope to cross his property to their feeding range, acting under authority of an 1885 law known as the Unlawful Inclosures of Public Land Act (43 U.S.C.A. 1061 *et seq.* [1986]). This statute had been enacted in response to the "range wars" of the 19th century in which western ranchers sought to keep homesteaders and others off federal lands where they grazed their cattle by erecting fences around those lands. The 1885 law had been upheld by the Supreme Court in an 1897 case involving another rancher who had used a similar scheme to keep homesteaders off federal property that adjoined his land (*Camfield v. United States, 167 U.S. 518* [1897]).

Lawrence sought to distinguish his situation from that of the 1897 case by arguing that his purpose was not to exclude people (his fence included a number of unlocked gates), but rather wild animals. In *United States ex rel. Bergen v. Lawrence*, (848 F.2d 1502 [10th Cir.]), the United States Court of Appeals for the Tenth Circuit ruled that this different purpose did not matter: The law forbade the enclosure of public land whether for the purpose of excluding people or wildlife. Furthermore, the court found that Lawrence's obligation to allow free passage by antelope across his land neither created an "easement" for which he must be compensated nor resulted in a constitutionally impermissible taking on his private property. The case is significant because it represents a clear victory for wildlife and the public in the ongoing struggle over public lands management between public interests and federal grazing permitees who sometimes appear to believe that they, and not the government, are the owners of the federal lands they lease. Lawrence asked the Supreme Court to review the Tenth Circuit's decision, but the court refused to hear the case (*Lawrence v. United States*, 109 S. Ct. 528 [1988]).

ENDANGERED SPECIES ACT CASES

Section 7 Consultation by Federal Agencies

Section 7 of the Endangered Species Act (16 U.S.C.A. 1536) requires all federal agencies to ensure that their actions do not jeopardize the continued existence of any threatened or endangered species or adversely modify their critical habitats. In order to meet its Section 7 obligations, each federal agency consults with FWS about the potential impacts of its planned actions and development projects on listed species or their critical habitats. A consultation may end with the issuance by FWS of a "biological opinion," which expresses its view as to whether the planned action complies with the requirements of Section 7. Though a biological opinion is not legally binding on the agency to which it is issued, as a practical matter it is extremely important because courts give great deference to it in the event of a lawsuit challenging the proposed action. Section 7 was the provision at issue in the famous conflict between TVA's Tellico Dam and the endangered snail darter a decade ago, and is generally considered to be one of the key weapons in the arsenal of environmental litigants.

Consultation Requirements for Onshore Oil and Gas Leasing. In *Conner v. Burford* (848 F.2d 1441 [9th Cir. 1988]), the United States Court of Appeals for the Ninth Circuit considered the application of Section 7 to oil and gas leasing within the National Forest System. Specifically, conservationists challenged the issuance of oil and gas leases by the Bureau of Land Management on some 1.3 million acres of Montana's Flathead and Gallatin national forests.[2] The leases contained a stipulation that reserved to the government the right to limit future surface-disturbing exploration and development activities if it were necessary in order to protect endangered species. Because of that stipulation, FWS' biological opinion included only a limited examination of the impact of the leasing on bald eagles, grizzly bears, peregrine falcons, and gray wolves. Rather than consider the possible impact of leasing and subsequently expected exploration and development ac-

---

2. On national forest lands, the Interior Department's Bureau of Land Management issues oil and gas leases, although the Agriculture Department's Forest Service undertakes most of the related analysis and recommends for or against leasing; its recommendations are generally followed by the Bureau of Land Management.

tivities on the species, the opinion examined only the expected consequences of the leasing itself and concluded that it would not jeopardize
any of the listed species. In so limiting its opinion, FWS was acting
consistently with a series of cases in which a similar incremental,
phase-by-phase review of oil and gas leasing in the Outer Continental
Shelf had been upheld by federal courts (for example, *Village of False
Pass v. Clark*, 733 F.2d 605 [9th Cir. 1984]).

In *Conner*, the Montana Wildlife Federation and two other plaintiffs argued that the rule in the Outer Continental Shelf cases should
not be applied to on-shore leasing; rather, FWS should be obliged, at
the time of leasing, to prepare a "comprehensive biological opinion"
that examined the impact of not just the leasing activities but anticipated post-leasing activities as well. The Tenth Circuit, by a divided
2-to-1 decision, agreed. The court refused to follow the precedent of the
Outer Continental Shelf cases because the legislation governing such
activities expressly provides for sequential regulation of each discrete
stage—leasing, exploration, development, and abandonment—and requires careful environmental review at each stage. Even though the
Montana leases contained a stipulation allowing future review of other
leasing stages, the stipulation was not legislatively required, but added
under the secretary's general administrative authority. Thusly, the
court treated the Outer Continental Shelf cases as unique exceptions
to the general rule that Section 7 compliance must be determined at
the outset of a proposed federal action and not later. This is a very
significant holding because it requires a determination of compliance
with Section 7 before investments are made that are likely to have the
effect of building momentum to carry the action forward to completion
regardless of the impact on endangered species.

Relation of Recovery Plans to Department of Interior Actions.
Grizzly bears were also at issue in *National Wildlife Fed'n v. National
Park Service* (669 F. Supp. 384 [D. Wyo.1987]), a case that grew out of
a controversy over tourist development within Yellowstone National
Park. The Park Service proposed to build a major new visitor complex
within the park, but the question of its impact on the park's threatened
grizzly bear population arose. Initially, FWS, in a biological opinion
issued pursuant to Section 7 of the Endangered Species Act, concluded
that the new facility would jeopardize the continued existence of the
park's bears. In order to avoid that jeopardy, the effects of the new facility would have to be offset by removing the existing Fishing Bridge
Campground, where conflicts between bears and park visitors had long
been a problem. In fact, as long ago as 1974, the Park Service itself had
developed a master plan for the park that called for the restoration of
natural conditions at the Fishing Bridge area because of its superb ecological values and importance for grizzly bears. Nevertheless, strong

local political opposition to the closure of the campground arose and eventually the Park Service proposed to keep the campground open on a reduced scale pending completion of an environmental impact statement.

FWS, in a new biological opinion, approved this change of plans. The National Wildlife Federation, however, believed that the sudden agency reversal reflected political concessions rather than fidelity to the biological requirements of the Endangered Species Act. Accordingly, the federation filed suit, challenging the Park Service's continued operation of the campground while preparing the environmental impact statement. In its decision, the court sided fully with the government. The most noteworthy aspect of its opinion concerns the allegation by the federation that by keeping the campground open the Park Service was acting inconsistently with a formal recovery plan for the grizzly bear that had been prepared under the Endangered Species Act and that—like the Park Service's earlier park master plan—called for closure of the Fishing Bridge facility. The court, however, said that it would "not attempt to second guess the secretary's motives for not following the recovery plan." Thus, without much elaboration of its reasons, the court treated endangered species recovery plans as setting forth discretionary and not judicially enforceable conservation measures. Potentially, this is a very significant holding because it would appear to give the Secretary of Interior unfettered discretion in choosing whether or not to carry out species recovery measures that have been formally identified in recovery plans prepared under the Endangered Species Act and officially approved by the secretary.

Importation of CITES-Listed Species for Commercial Purposes and Applicability of Section 7 Abroad

Two other Endangered Species Act cases deserve brief mention. In *World Wildlife Fund v. Hodel* (Civ. Action No. 88-1276 [D.D.C. June 17, 1988]), World Wildlife Fund–U.S. (WWF) and the American Association of Zoological Parks and Aquariums (AAZPA), a trade association of zoos and aquaria, challenged the importation of a pair of pandas from China for a short-term, nonbreeding loan. Because of their extreme rarity and their enormous value as display animals, pandas have become extremely sought after by many of the world's zoos, which are willing to pay hundreds of thousands of dollars to secure even the temporary right to display a pair of the animals.

In their lawsuit, WWF and AAZPA charged that the essence of the Toledo panda loan was a thinly disguised commercial venture, because the zoo would reap millions of dollars of additional revenue from special admission fees and increased sales of souvenir items. Inasmuch as the Convention on International Trade in Endangered Species of Wild Fauna and Flora (CITES) prohibits the importation of Appendix I species (of which the panda is one) for primarily commercial purposes, the plaintiffs argued that the importation could not lawfully be permitted. Although the plaintiffs failed in their effort to block the importation of the two pandas, they did win a court order prohibiting the Toledo Zoo from charging a separate admission fee to view the panda exhibit. More importantly, however, was FWS' agreement to deny a pending application for yet another panda import and to tighten the criteria under which future panda import requests would be considered.

In *Defenders of Wildlife v. Hodel* (851 F.2d 1035 [8th Cir. 1988]), Defenders challenged FWS regulations that limited the scope of Section 7 of the Endangered Species Act to federal agency actions occurring within the United States or on the high seas. As previously reported (see "Recent Legal Developments Affecting Wildlife Conservation" in *Audubon Wildlife Report 1988/1989*), the district court dismissed the case on the grounds that Defenders lacked standing (that is, the legal right) to challenge the regulations. As anticipated, however, the Court of Appeals for the Eighth Circuit has now reversed that ruling. The case has been remanded to the district court for a decision on the merits of the Section 7 dispute.

MIGRATORY BIRD CASES

Implementation of Interior's Lead Shot Phase-Out Plan

For more than a decade controversy has raged over the use of lead shot in waterfowl hunting. Spent lead shot ingested by waterfowl while feeding causes several million waterfowl deaths annually due to lead poisoning. Nontoxic steel shot can be used in place of lead, but for many years some hunters were reluctant to make the transition.

In 1976, FWS announced a plan to phase out the use of lead shot in selected areas over a three-year period. Opponents of steel shot, however, succeeded in having an amendment, known simply as the Stevens Amendment (for its sponsor, Alaska Senator Ted Stevens), attached each year to the Interior Department appropriations bill. The Stevens Amendment prohibited the department from requiring the use of steel shot within a state unless the state had consented to the prohibition. As a result of the Stevens Amendment and the antipathy toward steel shot by G. Ray Arnett, the Reagan Administration's first assistant Secretary of the Interior for Fish, Wildlife and Parks, little progress was made in reducing the use of lead shot.

Things began to change in the 1980s, however, as evidence mounted that lead pellets were contributing to the mortality of not only waterfowl, but also bald eagles, an endangered species. Eagles were the victims of secondary poisoning due to their consumption of lead-contaminated waterfowl. Pressed by lawsuits from the National Wildlife Federation on this issue, the Interior Department announced its intention to phase out the use of lead shot altogether by 1991. If a state refused to consent to the required use of steel shot, Interior intended to prohibit all waterfowl hunting within that state.

California Fish & Game Comm'n v. Hodel (Civil No. S-87-816 [E.D. Cal. Oct. 29, 1987]), was an unsuccessful challenge to Interior's lead-shot phase-out. The California Fish and Game Commission, joined by the National Rifle Association, contended that the Stevens Amendment prevented Interior from carrying through with its plans. The court disagreed, holding that nothing in the Stevens Amendment diminished Interior's independent authority under the Endangered Species Act, Migratory Bird Treaty Act, and Bald and Golden Eagle Protection Act to close waterfowl hunting seasons. This action probably brings to a close legal efforts to stymie the transition to steel shot.

Arctic-Nesting Geese and Subsistence Hunting

Another long-simmering controversy over migratory birds stems from the taking of Arctic-nesting geese and their eggs in the spring by Alaskan natives. Many of the Pacific Flyway populations of geese have declined dramatically in recent decades, and the largely uncontrolled subsistence taking by Alaskan natives of geese and their eggs during the spring nesting season is thought to be an important factor contributing to this decline. In theory, the solution to this problem is to enforce the Migratory Bird Treaty Act, which prohibits all taking of migratory birds except as authorized by the Secretary of Interior. In practice, however, the federal law enforcement presence in the vast stretches of Alaska where the native harvest occurs is too small to influence Alaska native behavior. Moreover, because the purpose of the harvest is to secure food for subsistence of native peoples who have a long-established tradition of spring bird hunting, the fairness of punishing subsistence users of a resource while at the same time allowing recreational hunters to harvest the same resource in the fall for sport is troubling at best.

The solution embraced by FWS was to sign a cooperative agreement with Alaskan native organizations whereby the subsistence harvest would be voluntarily reduced or eliminated for certain bird species. Enforcement of the agreement was left in substantial part to Alaskan native organizations. The initial agreement was developed in 1984 and was known as the "Hooper Bay" agreement. Not everyone, however, was happy with it. Several Alaskan sportsmen's organizations challenged the agreement (and a successor agreement) as a violation of the Migratory Bird Treaty Act because it authorized hunting of birds in contravention of the 1916 migratory bird treaty between the United States and Canada, which the act is supposed to implement.

In a surprising decision, the district court held that the federal government had no authority whatsoever to regulate the subsistence taking of migratory birds in Alaska because of the long-forgotten 1925 Alaska Game Law 0f 1925, (43 Stat. 739) that ostensibly supplanted the Migratory Bird Treaty Act. The 1925 law authorized the subsistence taking of "animals or birds," which the court interpreted to include migratory birds, thus implicitly repealing the 1916 Migratory Bird Treaty Act. As a result of this curious ruling, the voluntary agreements between FWS and native Alaskans that were the target of the suit were not only not illegal, but they probably represented a bigger concession to bird conservation by the natives than necessary, since the threat of prosecution under the Migratory Bird Treaty Act was rendered without foundation.

The unexpected holding of the district court did not survive the review of the court of appeals. In October 1987, in *Alaska Fish & Wildlife Fed'n v. Dunkle* (829 F.2d 933 [9th Cir.1987], *cert. denied Sub. nom. Alaska Fed'n of Natives v. Alaska Fish & Wildlife Fed'n*, 108 S.Ct. 1290 [1988]), the appeals court held that the Migratory Bird Treaty Act, not the 1925 Alaskan Game Law, controlled the hunting of birds in Alaska. Moreover, the court held that under the Migratory Bird Treaty Act, the Secretary of Interior could be only as permissive of native subsistence hunting as the most restrictive of the four international treaties implemented by the Treaty Act allowed.

As a practical matter, the ruling nullifies the secretary's authority to enter into voluntary bird management agreements like the ones challenged because the treaty with Canada prohibits all game bird hunting between March 10 and September 1 of each year. Thus, the court essentially advised the secretary that the treaty with Canada must first be amended to liberalize native subsistence hunting rules before the secretary can enter into any agreement permitting spring subsistence hunting. This was not quite the same thing as ordering the secretary to prosecute all violators of the Migratory Bird Treaty Act, for the court was at pains to emphasize that the secretary's prosecutorial discretion under the act was beyond judicial review. That is, the secretary cannot be compelled to prosecute a particular individual believed to have violated the Migratory Bird Treaty Act. However, the secretary can be prevented from formalizing a policy of nonprosecution in return for cooperation from native Alaskans on migratory bird management programs.

MARINE MAMMALS

Incidental Taking of Dall's Porpoises in the Japanese Salmon Fishery

Sometimes, a single lawsuit has the power to trigger changes far beyond the specific issues that it decides. Such was the case in 1988 with a lawsuit challenging the issuance by the Secretary of Commerce of a permit under the Marine Mammal Protection Act (16 U.S.C.A. 1361 *et seq.* 1985), which authorized Japanese fishermen to take Dall's porpoises incidental to their salmon gill net fishery off Alaska. Both a coalition of environmental organizations and an Alaskan native fishing group challenged the permit in *Kokechik Fishermen's Ass'n v. Secretary of Commerce* (839 F.2d 795 [D.C. Cir. 1988], *cert. denied sub. nom. Verity v. Center for Envtl. Educ.*, 57 U.S.L.W. 3451 [1988]).

The Japanese salmon gill net fishery is carried out in the north Pacific Ocean and the Bering Sea where hundreds of enormously long plastic nets are set adrift each evening during the summer months. The enormous nets hang like an invisible, vertical wall for distances of up to nine miles each and trap fish that swim blindly into them by entangling their heads and gills in the nets' mesh openings. Unfortunately, it is not just salmon that become entangled in the nets; many marine mammals do as well, particularly the Dall's porpoise, a species common in the North Pacific.

The Japanese applied to the National Marine Fisheries Service and received a permit authorizing the incidental take of more than 6,000 Dall's porpoises in the fishery over a three-year period. The porpoise is the mammal species most commonly taken in the fishery. Other marine mammals, including northern fur seals, were expected to be taken as well, but the permit did not authorize their taking because the National Marine Fisheries Service lacked the basic biological information necessary for fixing a safe level of incidental take.

The plaintiffs challenged the permit on a variety of grounds. The court ruled that because there would be some incidental taking of marine mammal species for which the government lacked the necessary data to issue a permit, it could not lawfully issue a permit for the taking of *any* species, including Dall's porpoises. The federal government contended that it retained the power to impose fines for the prohibited taking of other species, but the court rejected this on the basis that it was tantamount to the government selling a right to harvest species that it was not empowered to grant.

The fallout from the court's decision was immediate and grave, for it called into question not just the Japanese permit, but also permits that had been issued to a number of American fishermen who also incidentally take some of the same species taken by the Japanese in the salmon fishery. The National Marine Fisheries Service announced that when the American fishing permits expired at the end of 1988, it would be unable to renew them unless the law were changed.

The prospect of that action by the National Marine Fisheries Service forced American commercial fisheries interests and environmentalists to the bargaining table. They sought to agree on a new regulatory scheme that would allow U.S. fisheries to continue without fear of violating the Marine Mammal Protection Act, while at the same time assuring effective conservation of marine mammals. With some further changes of its own, Congress embraced the agreement reached by the fishing and environmental interests and enacted them as part of a wholesale revision of the Marine Mammal Protection Act's provisions governing the taking of marine mammals incidental to commercial fishing operations. The amendments, enacted on the final day of the 100th Congress, completely supplanted the prior rules governing the incidental taking of marine mammals with new rules and procedures that emphasize the collection of better data on marine mammals taken by fishermen and the verification of collected data with the use of on-board observers.

LAW ENFORCEMENT CASES

Most wildlife cases in a given year are prosecutions brought by the government against persons charged with violating wildlife conservation laws. A few of these have already been discussed, including the *City of Rancho Palos Verdes* and *Vesterso* cases. This section examines two additional cases that raised noteworthy law enforcement issues.

"Knowing" Violations of Wildlife Laws

In any criminal prosecution, an important issue is the culpability standard against which the defendant's conduct is measured. Under certain statutes, the government need only prove the defendant committed a prohibited act, regardless of whether the defendant knew that the action was illegal or even that it would have the result that it did. This is referred to generally as strict liability; in strict liability crimes, the defendant is held responsible for the consequences of his actions without regard to his state of mind. Other statutes, however, prohibit only so-called "willful" violations, for which the government must prove not only that the defendant did a particular thing but with the knowledge that the act was illegal at the time it was committed. Proving a willful violation imposes a significant burden on the government prosecuting a case because it must prove the defendant's state of mind.

A number of wildlife statutes prohibit only willful offenses or make only willful offenses subject to severe punishment.

In between these extremes is a category of offenses generally described as "knowing" violations. These require that the government prove that the defendant knew what he or she was doing, even though he or she may not have known that it was illegal; in other words, the government need only prove that the defendant had knowledge of the facts, not of the law. This simple rule, however, is not necessarily easy to apply, as illustrated by the case of *United States v. St. Onge* (676 F. Supp. 1044 [D. Mont. 988]). In this action, the federal government charged the defendant with knowingly violating the Endangered Species Act by shooting a grizzly bear, a threatened species. For that offense, the defendant could have been fined up to $20,000 and imprisoned for up to a year.

The defendant in *St. Onge* sought to defend against the charge on the basis that he had made a very significant mistake of fact: he had not seen the bear clearly and in fact thought it was an elk. Thus, he argued, he could not have "knowingly violated" the Endangered Species Act. A 1975 case in the same court involving the Bald and Golden Eagle Protection Act may have buoyed his hope for this defense. In the earlier case, involving the illegal sale of eagle feathers, the court had expounded on the nature of the "knowing" requirement in the Eagle Protection Act, and stated that "a conviction would not be had were a person to sell golden eagle feathers thinking them to be turkey feathers" (*United States v. Allard* [397 F. Supp. 429, 432 (D. Mont. 1975)]).

The court, however, chose to follow a 1987 Florida case, *United States v. Billie* (667 F. Supp. 1485 [S.D. Fla. 1987]). It held that the government "need only prove the [the defendant] knowingly shot an animal that turned out to be a grizzly bear." It was not a sufficient defense to have mistaken the animal for an elk; the "defendant could only claim accident or mistake if he did not intend to discharge his firearm, or the weapon malfunctioned, or similar circumstances occurred." This holding is an important one for enforcing the Endangered Species Act, because proving that a defendant knew which species he or she was taking could be a major hurdle to government prosecutors. That hurdle has been removed by the *St. Onge* decision.

Violation of Indian Tribal Wildlife Laws by Nonresident Indians

A second enforcement case worth noting is *United States v. Big Eagle* (684 F. Supp. 241 [D. S.D. 1988]). The case involved the prosecution under the Lacey Act of a Crow Creek Sioux Indian charged with catching fish with a net and without a license on the reservation of another Sioux tribe and transporting them off the reservation for the purpose of sale. Since it was amended in 1981, the Lacey Act has prohibited the transportation, purchase, or sale of wildlife taken contrary to Indian tribal law, but until the *Big Eagle* case the application of the Lacey Act to an Indian violating the tribal laws of another tribe had not arisen. The decision in the *Big Eagle* case—that the Lacey Act does apply to such circumstances—assures the availability of the act as an important federal backup to enforcement of Indian tribal wildlife laws.

CONSTITUTIONAL ISSUES AND WILDLIFE LAW

State Hunter Harassment Statutes

On January 30, 1986, Francelle Dorman, a Connecticut resident, approached a group of goose hunters in a marsh near her home and urged them to not to kill any waterfowl. They responded by summoning a state law enforcement officer, who arrested her and charged her with violating the state's Hunter Harassment Act, which makes it a criminal offense to "interfere with" or "harass another person who is engaged in the lawful taking of wildlife or acts in preparation for such taking." Under the Connecticut statute—one of a series of such laws that have recently been enacted in about half the states—Dorman could have been fined and imprisoned for three months.

The charges against Dorman eventually were dropped, but she was not content to let the matter rest. Instead, she filed a suit of her own in federal court, attacking the constitutionality of the Connecticut law. On February 1, 1988, the court agreed with Dorman and struck down the law as unconstitutionally vague and overbroad in *Dorman v. Satti* (678 F. Supp. 375 [D. Conn. *aff'd* 1988, U.S. App. LEXIS 17020 [2d Cir. 1988]). This was the first judicial test of a hunter harassment law, and it is likely to be of considerable importance to the future of similar laws.

Two aspects in particular troubled the [Dorman] court about the Connecticut law. First, the law prohibited "interference" with and "harassment" of hunters, but defined neither term. As a result, these proscriptions were at best vague and at worst a limitation that applied equally to speech and physical conduct. Second, these prohibitions applied not only when someone was engaged in lawful hunting, but also when engaged in "acts in preparation for" hunting. Preparatory acts, the court reasoned, might include such far-removed activities as purchasing food or supplies in advance of a hunting trip. Though a state may have an interest in managing and regulating lands for the purpose of wildlife harvest, its interest does not extend to antecedent activities far removed in time and place from hunting itself. Accordingly, the court struck down the law as both unconstitutionally vague and overly broad.

The decision in the *Dorman* case does not necessarily mean that hunter harassment laws in other states are invalid. The court emphasized that these laws vary considerably from state to state and the defects that brought down the Connecticut law may not exist for other statutes. The *Dorman* case does underscore, however, the close scrutiny that such laws are likely to receive in the courts if they touch upon constitutionally protected free speech.

Indian Religious Rights and Wildlife Conservation Laws

A final First Amendment decision from the United States Supreme Court that many expected to shed light on the tension between wildlife conservation restrictions and native American religious rights ended up shedding very little light at all. One of the recurrent legal controversies of the past two decades concerns the scope of state and federal authority to restrict the taking of wildlife by native Americans. Several Supreme Court cases, the most recent of which was *United States v. Dion* (476 U.S. 734, *later proceedings, en banc*, 800 F.2d 771 [8th Cir. 1986]) in 1986, establish at least limited governmental authority over Indian hunting rights that derive from treaties. Sometimes, however, Indians assert a right to kill and use protected wildlife that does not derive from any treaty, but rather from the First Amendment to the Constitution, which guarantees freedom of religion. Neither *Dion* nor any other case has yet resolved the question whether the First Amendment guarantee of religious freedom is paramount to restrictions on the taking of wildlife that are enacted for conservation purposes.

In April 1988, the Supreme Court heard a challenge by Indian groups to a Forest Service plan to build a road and authorize logging activities that would significantly affect areas of California's Six Rivers National Forest that the Indians deemed sacred. A lower court decision had enjoined the Forest Service from carrying out its plans because the effect of those plans would have been to destroy lands that were central to the religious practices of the Indians, and because the government did not have a compelling justification for its land-use plan. In reaching a decision, the lower court thus followed the reasoning of many other circuit courts by trying to strike a balance between two critical factors: how "central" a specific practice is to Indian religious belief and how compelling is the government's justification for its actions that infringe on that practice. Most observers expected these same factors would eventually be used to delimit the government's right to restrict Indian religious practices in order to conserve wildlife.

Instead, the Supreme Court did not attempt to use any balancing analysis. A closely divided court held in *Lyng v. Northwest Indian Cemetery Protective Ass'n* (108 S. Ct. 1319 [1988]), that it was the *form* of the government's restraint on religious practice—and not its practical effect —that determined whether the restraint was constitutionally permissible. A governmental land-use decision, even one that has "severe adverse effects on the practice of their religion," does not contravene the First Amendment rights of native Americans because native Americans are not "coerced by the government's action into violating their religious beliefs," and because its action does not "penalize religious activity by denying any person an equal share of the rights, benefits, and privileges enjoyed by other citizens."

It is difficult to glean much guidance from this opinion for future cases involving the taking of wildlife. It may mean that Indians who kill protected wildlife in order to use them, their feathers, or other parts in religious ceremonies will be unable to assert successfully a First Amendment defense against prosecution under wildlife conservation laws because the taking itself is not "religious activity" and therefore its punishment does not penalize religious activity. On the other hand, where the act of taking wildlife is itself claimed to be a religious practice, it is less clear from the *Cemetery Protective Ass'n* decision whether a state or federal government can constitutionally punish the taking. If such a case ever arises, it may be impossible for the courts to avoid some standard that balances the "centrality" to Indian religion of restricted practices with the governmental interest in restricting those practices to conserve wildlife.

Michael J. Bean is chairman of the Wildlife Program of the Environmental Defense Fund and author of The Evolution of National Wildlife Law.

Most scientists agree that we are altering the climate by pouring polluting gases into the atmosphere. Changes in climate will bring changes in habitat. How will habitat-sensitive species, such as these shorebirds, cope? And what should wildlife managers do about it? *Kenneth W. Gardiner*

Global Warming, Climate Disruption, and Biological Diversity

R.T. Lester
and
J.P. Myers

INTRODUCTION

The gaseous wastes of human activities are now so abundant that they change the physical balance setting the earth's temperature. Since the beginning of the Industrial Revolution humans have pumped carbon dioxide (CO_2) into the atmosphere at such prodigious rates that current levels are about 25 percent higher than they were in 1860. The amounts of other gases also have increased dramatically; some—for example, chlorofluorocarbons—never even existed before the beginning of the 20th century.

By altering the balance of these so-called greenhouse gases, humans have embarked on what two scientists has called a "large-scale geophysical experiment." Carbon dioxide, methane, and chlorofluorocarbons are virtually transparent to incoming solar radiation, yet they are very efficient at trapping the heat that is created after the radiation strikes the earth's surface. This inadvertent warming of the globe caused by changes in the composition of the atmosphere—the Greenhouse Effect—will challenge humanity and the environment in which we live in unprecedented ways.

This chapter examines global warming—what might more comprehensively be called climate disruption—and what is now known and speculated about its consequences for wildlife and biological diversity. The first section provides a basic understanding of the climatology upon which global warming predictions are based. The second then examines what the predictions foretell for the earth's flora and fauna.

Beyond the basic climatological facts and theories that underpin models of climate disruption, much of this chapter deals with predictions and speculations. This begins with attempts to anticipate the rate and magnitude of warming using climatological models and becomes even more speculative when translating these predictions into biological prognostications. The climatic predictions and their biological implications are of such compelling importance to conservation that such speculation is essential.

THE CLIMATE SYSTEM

The Climate Engine

The earth's climate is a vast engine fueled by incoming solar radiation. This incoming energy is balanced by that which is re-radiated to space. It is not, however, equally balanced across the surface of the planet: net gains take place in the tropics while net losses occur at the poles. These temperature differences among latitudinal zones as well as analogous ones between land and sea are the basic driving force behind all meteorological phenomena. Winds and ocean currents redistribute heat from the tropics to temperate and polar latitudes, taking with them dust, nutrients, pollutants, particulate matter, gases, and even plants and animals. Solar radiation also drives the hydrologic cycle and creates the high and low pressure systems that determine regional climates.

Natural Climatic Variation

Climate is not constant. It is influenced by a host of astrophysical, geophysical, atmospheric, and biological forces that together constitute the *climate system* and cause climatic conditions to change through time and across the face of the earth. Some of these forces are external to the climate system, for example, variability in the sun's luminosity. Others involve variations in components of the climate system itself. These *external* and *internal forcings* combine together to cause climatological conditions to vary considerably over the earth, annually, and in multi-annual trends and oscillations. Any change, whether natural or anthropogenic, that affects the earth's radiation balance can cause at least localized changes in climate (Rosenberg 1986).

External Forcing. Changes in the amount and distribution of incoming solar radiation are the primary cause of climatic variation. These vary with changes in the luminosity of the sun and alterations in the astronomical characteristics of the earth's orbit. The luminosity of the sun fluctuates through time because of changes in the nuclear reactions occurring at its surface. Over the lifetime of our solar system, the sun has become about 20 to 40 percent brighter (Henderson-Sellers and Robinson 1986). Solar luminosity is also known to vary by about 0.1 to 0.3 percent over shorter time periods of days and months (Sofia 1984). These variations are associated with "sun spots," slightly cooler regions on the sun's surface that generate powerful magnetic fields. Sun spot activity may be linked to a number of climatic variations on earth but these effects are poorly understood at the present time (Schneider and Londer 1984).

The earth's position in its orbit around the sun and its angle of tilt with respect to the sun determine the amount of solar energy falling to the surface of the earth per unit area per unit time, the so-called "flux density" (Rosenberg 1986). Regular changes in the orientation between earth and sun alter the flux density of solar radiation received by the earth, thereby creating the systematic daily and seasonal changes in climate with which we are familiar.

In addition, longer term, cyclical and quasi-cyclical variations in the earth's orbit and tilt cause changes in the amount of solar radiation received by the earth. These in turn cause changes in climate over several hundred years or more. There are three fundamental orbital variations: changes in the eccentricity of the earth's orbit, changes in its angle of tilt with respect to the sun, and changes in the center of the earth's orbit around the sun. Of these three variations, variation in the eccentricity of the earth's orbit is the only one that actually causes a change in the total amount of solar radiation received. This amount is thought to vary by no more than 0.25 percent on an annual basis (Schneider and Londer 1984). Orbital tilt and changes in the center of the earth's orbit about the sun do not alter the amount of received solar radiation but instead, lead to redistribution of this radiation in time and space. Seasonal differences become more or less pronounced and the temperature gradient between tropics and poles decreases or increases, leading to modifications in global circulation.

Internal Forcing. Natural climatic variations also arise because of changes in the reflective and absorptive characteristics of the earth's surface and/or its atmosphere. Atmospheric gases, aerosols (solid or liquid particles suspended in the atmosphere), clouds, and cover-type all exert effects on local and even global climate by influencing the overall amount of energy absorbed by the earth's atmosphere system. As incoming solar radiation strikes the earth's atmosphere system, it is either absorbed, scattered, or reflected, depending upon its wavelength and the size and nature of the particles that intercept it (Henderson-Sellers and Robinson 1986).

Air consists primarily of nitrogen and oxygen—about 78 percent and 21 percent, respectively, by volume. The remaining 1 percent is composed of small quantities of various gases such as carbon dioxide, methane, and ozone, as well as aerosols like water vapor, dust, and pollen. The most common atmospheric gases—nitrogen and oxygen—do not absorb or scatter much shortwave radiation.

Because solar radiation consists primarily of shortwave radiation, the earth's atmosphere is largely transparent to the sun's rays. However, after solar radiation is absorbed at the earth's surface and re-emitted at longer wavelengths, many of the naturally occurring gases like CO_2, which are present only in small quantities, become strong absorbers of this energy. As they absorb this longwave, terrestrial radiation, they give off heat that warms the lower atmosphere. This is a natural manifestation of the "Greenhouse Effect." Without it, the earth's average temperature would be about 33° C colder than it is today (Hansen *et al.* 1988).

A number of natural gases are efficient absorbers of longwave radiation. The most abundant of these greenhouse gases is carbon dioxide but a number of *trace gases* are even more efficient at absorbing longwave radiation, up to 10,000 times more on a per-molecule basis (Mintzer 1987). These gases include methane, nitrous oxide, ozone, and water vapor. A number of strictly human-made trace gases such as chlorofluorocarbons also contribute to the Greenhouse Effect.

Clouds and natural aerosols cause significant natural variations in climate. Volcanoes are probably the most important source of naturally occurring atmospheric aerosols (Schonwiese 1988). Volcanic eruptions can eject tremendous amounts of particulate matter, including sulfuric acid into the lower and upper atmosphere. The climatic effect of these aerosols is dependent upon their size and altitude, but they generally tend to have a cooling effect because they reflect more solar radiation than they absorb.

Wind-borne dust, marine salts, and biologically produced hydrocarbons and sulfates are also important natural tropospheric aerosols. Their optical properties and hence their climatic effects are poorly understood. However, many of these tropospheric aerosols have an important climatological role because they serve as condensation nuclei for the formation of clouds or because they modify the optical properties of clouds.

Clouds are the most important source of natural changes in incoming solar radiation. They consist primarily of water vapor along with smaller amounts of dust and other aerosols. Because water vapor is such a strong greenhouse gas, clouds are very efficient absorbers of the longwave radiation that produces heat. At the same time, they can also reflect a great deal of incoming solar radiation. Thus their impacts enter on both sides of the earth's radiative balance, and their net effect on local temperature depends upon the specifics of cloud height and shape. In today's climate, clouds appear to exert an overall cooling effect (Ramanathan *et al.* 1989). In contrast, preliminary modeling results of a greenhouse climate suggest that they may further contribute to warming of the earth's surface (Wetherald and Manabe 1988). However, clouds remain one of the biggest uncertainties in modeling studies of future climates, because relatively small changes in cloud cover can produce large changes in the amount of incoming solar radiation (Ramanathan *et al.* 1989).

Local radiation balance is also affected by cover type. Ground covered with snow or ice has a much higher albedo (reflectivity) than does bare ground. It therefore absorbs less sunlight and remains cooler. Changes in the areal extent of snow and ice can have a major effect on the planetary radiation balance, because a large portion of the earth's surface at higher latitudes is covered with snow and ice. Snow and ice can also serve as a sort of thermal blanket by trapping heat in the ground or water they cover. Changes in the amount and type of vegetative cover can also alter local radiation balance and perhaps even global radiation balance, if they occur over a large enough area. Vegetation types differ in the amount of incoming solar radiation they reflect (Dickinson and Hanson 1984), and vegetation can also affect localized heat fluxes through its role in evapotranspiration. As plants transpire, they absorb large amounts of energy, thus cooling the surrounding air. As a result, forested areas are considerably cooler than areas with sparse vegetation.

Climate and Life

The earth's climate has changed continuously over the last 4.5 billion years. In the geologic past, external forces such as increasing solar luminosity and variations in the earth's orbital characteristics generated climatic conditions that were markedly different from those of today. These external factors did not operate alone. Internal forcings such as changes in the composition of the atmosphere—brought about largely by the development of the earth's biota—and alterations in the extent of land and sea ice also played an important role in shaping ancient climates.

Ever since the appearance of the earliest life-forms about 3.5 billion years ago, climate has profoundly influenced the earth's biota. As soon as they reached a significant biomass, these newly diversifying life-forms began, in turn, to affect the earth's climate. This intimate connection between climate and life led to the notion that the two "co-evolved," each shaping and controlling the fate of the other (Schneider and Londer 1984). The association between the climate and life is so strong that fossil plant and animal assemblages are regularly used as proxies for inferring the nature of past climates.

The close connections between climate and life are clearly evident from even a cursory survey of the natural world. The changes in vegetation that accompany the seasons are a simple but eloquent reminder of this relationship. Climate imposes basic physiological constraints on the earth's biota, which in turn, affect a host of reproductive processes and ecological interactions such as competition, trophic relations, and habitat suitability. Because of their dependence on heat-labile enzymes, basic metabolic process like photosynthesis and respiration are highly temperature dependent. Other climatic features such as "date of last frost" and "summer warmth" are also important in determining the reproductive success of many plant and animal species. And finally, many important ecological relationships involve complex but poorly understood climatic controls, which act not only on individual organisms, but on populations, communities, and ecosystems as well. Temperature and humidity, for example, can influence the distribution and abundance of biota by affecting a diverse array of ecological processes and parameters, from population sex ratios (Mrosovsky and Yntema 1980) to the outcome of competitive interactions (Parks 1954).

The response of the biosphere to climate varies through space and time. Pronounced geographic associations between climate and the life-forms of both plants and animals emerge from the climatic sensitivity of basic physiological processes, particularly to temperature, precipitation, and, for plants especially, the amount and quality of solar insolation. Trends in animal morphology follow temperature gradients (James 1970). Broad-scale vegetation types such as moist tropical forest, temperate hardwood forest, boreal forest, and tundra correspond well with latitudinal and altitudinal climate gradients (Woodward 1987). These spatial patterns of vegetation types have shifted through time in response to past climatic changes (CLIMAP 1976, COHMAP 1988, Webb and Wigley 1985).

Unlike plants, animals can respond quickly to changes in climate through alterations in their geographic range. Abrupt climate change has, nonetheless, been implicated as a potentially important mechanism for mass extinction events among many animal taxa in the geologic past (Crowley and North 1988). The most celebrated of these

events occurred about 65 million years ago during the transition between the Cretaceous and Tertiary periods, when as much as one-half
of the earth's biota became extinct (Raup 1988).

In addition to their direct responses to climatic variables, animals
reflect geographic variations in climate indirectly because of their
habitat requirements, for example, dependence upon particular plant
species or plant assemblages for food, shelter, or reproduction. These
effects can reverberate through multiple trophic levels: even carni-
vores not directly dependent upon plants as a food source select predictable habitats linked to prey distributions, which in turn may depend upon amount and quality of vegetation. The ultimate impacts
that future climate changes hold for wildlife populations are likely to
be far more intense through indirect ecological changes of this sort
rather than direct physiological effects.

HUMANS: THE NEW PERTURBATION

Through advances in technology and exponential increases in population, humanity has transformed itself in the last 130 years into a major
agent of change in the climate system. This potential comes principally through alterations in the earth's radiative balance, which is the
ultimate driving force behind the climate engine (see "The Climate
Engine" section, above). Humans exert their main effect on the planetary heat balance by producing greenhouse gases, but changes in land-
use patterns and artificial sources of waste heat can also make a significant contribution, primarily at local scales.

Deforestation, urban development, and large-scale irrigation systems lead to changes in albedo and thus shifts in surface temperatures
(Rosenberg 1986). Removal of vegetative cover also affects temperature
and water balance by reducing evapotranspiration. Such changes can
have widespread effects, as noted for the Amazon Basin (Salati 1986).
Changes in radiation balance are also caused by power plants, cities,
and other sources of waste heat, which warm the ambient air and/or
water. These tend, however, to be significant only at localized scales
(Robinson 1971).

Anthropogenic Sources of Greenhouse Gases

Fossil Fuels. The burning of fossil fuels represents the largest source
of human-produced carbon dioxide. Since the beginning of the Industrial Revolution, the combustion of fossil fuels and deforestation have
together increased the atmospheric concentration of carbon dioxide by
about 25 percent (Mintzer 1987). A number of other greenhouse gases

(GHGs) are also released during the combustion, manufacture, and transportation of fossil fuels. Nitrous oxide (N_2O), carbon monoxide (CO), and oxides of nitrogen (NOx) are released during the combustion of coal and oil, and coal mining and natural gas pipelines release significant amounts of methane (CH_4).

Different fossil fuels release different amounts of carbon during combustion. Natural gas produces about one-half the carbon that coal does for each unit of energy that is produced for consumption; oil falls somewhere in between (JASON 1980). Thus, coal—which constitutes only 35 percent of the world use of fossil fuel energy—produces a disproportionate 41 percent of the world's carbon dioxide from fossil fuels (MacKenzie n.d.). Because they require large energy inputs for their manufacture, synthetic fuels produce even more carbon per unit of delivered energy than direct combustion of natural fossil fuels (that is, oil, natural gas, and coal).

Industrial processes, electric power generation, and transportation each produce 29, 28, and 27 percent, respectively, of the United States' production of carbon dioxide, with the remaining 16 percent produced by homes and businesses (Shepard 1988). The United States produces about one quarter of the world's carbon dioxide emissions from fossil fuels (Shepard 1988). In 1980, North America, western and eastern Europe, and the Soviet Union together contributed about 68 percent of the world's total carbon dioxide emissions from fossil fuels (Shepard 1988). Because of its higher total energy consumption and its smaller population, the industrialized world has a higher *per capita* rate of carbon dioxide emissions than does the developing world.

Deforestation. Together the world's terrestrial vegetation and soils contain approximately two trillion tons of carbon (about 25 and 75 percent, respectively); this is almost three times as much as the atmospheric pool (Trabalka 1985). As forests are cleared and burned, carbon is released immediately into the atmosphere. If the trees are not burned, their decay still releases CO_2 into the atmosphere; this oxidation, however, occurs at a much slower rate.

Greenhouse gases other than carbon dioxide are also liberated as a result of the felling and burning of trees. Recent evidence demonstrates that deforestation may be the principal source of the recent increase in atmospheric methane (Craig *et al.* 1988). The soil underlying newly deforested areas is also partially oxidized, thus contributing further to emissions of carbon dioxide and nitrous oxide (Mooney *et al.* 1987). Deforestation also sets the stage for the release of other greenhouse gases because most deforested lands are converted to agricultural uses that often produce methane or because these newly cleared lands provide good habitat for methane-producing termites (Mooney *et al.* 1987).

Prior to the middle part of the 20th century, forest clearing was probably the major source of carbon dioxide emissions (Olson n.d.). Thereafter the rate of industrialization dramatically quickened and deforestation in Europe and North America stabilized. Today, the tropics are the main source of CO_2 emissions produced by deforestation.

Estimates of the contribution of tropical deforestation to global CO_2 emissions vary considerably, but they probably fall somewhere in the range of 0.4 to 3 petagrams per year (1 petagram = 10^{15} g = 10^9 ton = 1 gigaton) (compare Woodwell *et al.* 1978 to Detweiler and Hall 1988). The uncertainties associated with these figures are due to, among other things, difficulties involved in estimating the global forest conversion rate, vegetation regrowth, the carbon content of various forest types, and the rate of carbon flux between vegetation and the atmosphere.

According to the estimates of one study, tropical America produced 40 percent of the world's CO_2 emissions due to land conversion in the year 1980, while tropical Asia and Africa produced 37 percent and 23 percent, respectively (Postel and Heise 1988). Assuming that land conversion accounted for about 20 percent of the world's annual CO_2 emissions in that year, then deforestation in tropical America alone produced about 8 percent of the world's atmospheric carbon dioxide. This same study also estimates that in 1980, Brazil, Indonesia, Colombia, Cotê d'Ivoire, and Thailand accounted for over 50 percent of the world's CO_2 emissions due to deforestation, with Brazil alone having accounted for 20 percent.

Industrial Processes. Chlorofluorocarbons (CFCs) and halons arise exclusively from human activities. The low boiling point and nontoxic, noncorrosive, and nonflammable nature of CFCs and halons makes them ideal for many uses, including refrigerants, fire extinguishing agents, blowing agents for foam insulation, and cleaners for the electronics industry (Cohn 1987). These gases unfortunately have a very strong greenhouse effect. Furthermore, the long lifetimes of these gases (on the order of 100 years) allows them to persist in their radiative effects long after they are released into the atmosphere. The depletion of ozone by CFCs and halons has also been shown to lead to a cooling of the upper atmosphere, but the potential climatic effects of this phenomenon are not yet understood (Kiehl *et al.* 1988).

Agriculture. Agriculture is an important source of greenhouse gases, most notably methane. Methane is produced by anaerobic bacteria in the anoxic sediments of rice paddies and in the stomach of cattle and other ruminants. Methane concentrations since 1965 have been increasing at the rate of 1.1 percent per year, a rate considerably faster than that of CO_2 (Mooney *et al.* 1987). Much of this increase is attributed to expansion of paddy rice cultivation, increased numbers of domestic ruminants, and other land use changes (Mooney *et al.* 1987). Agricultural activities also indirectly produce CO_2 from fossil fuel inputs, CO_2 and N_2O from biomass burning, and some N_2O from direct application of nitrogenous fertilizers (Mooney *et al.* 1987).

Human Population Growth and Greenhouse Gases

At the root of global warming lies human population growth. As human populations increase, demands for food, energy, and other basic human necessities increase as well. Increased use of fossil fuels and expanded agricultural productivity lead to larger emissions of greenhouse gases.

The world's population is currently about 5 billion and it is expected to double to 10 billion before stabilizing by the end of the 21st century (WRI and IIED 1988). Since the 1950s, population growth rates have increased dramatically. It took more than 100 years for the population to double from 1.25 billion to 2.5 billion by 1950. In contrast, it took a mere 37 years for world population to double again from the year 1950 to 1987 (WRI and IIED 1988). Although average annual population growth rates are falling in most parts of the world, world population continues to grow because of dramatically decreased death rates, increasing numbers of reproductive females, and steady birth rates. Currently, about 85 million people are added to the world's population every year. By the year 2000, this figure is expected to increase to 89 million (WRI and IIED 1988).

Most of the world's population lives in the Third World where population structures are skewed toward younger age groups. These nations are therefore committed to an increase in population growth because of the large numbers of young women entering their childbearing years. Increasing demands for energy, food, and natural resources in the Third World will almost certainly lead to an increase in the production of GHGs in the future.

Emissions of CO_2 and other greenhouse gases are higher in the developed world than they are in the developing world because developed nations generally have a much greater energy usage per capita (Gilland 1988). It has been estimated that a baby born in the United States has 180 times the ecological impact of a baby born in Bangladesh (Ehrlich pers. comm.). Of course, this estimate incorporates more than just greenhouse gas emissions, but the implication is clear: the developed world uses an inordinate share of the earth's resources and produces a disproportionate amount of wastes. However, population growth rates in developed countries are decreasing more rapidly than elsewhere in the world (WRI and IIED 1988).

PREDICTING THE CONSEQUENCES OF CLIMATE DISRUPTION

Scientists predict the effects of global warming using three principal methodologies: simple numerical models, complex sets of computer programs called global circulation models (GCMs), and paleoclimatic reconstructions. Relatively simple numerical models include both the so-called energy balance and radiative convective models. These models simulate the effect of increased GHGs on the earth's temperature balance, but they reduce their result to a single point (that is, a global average), ignoring the effects of latitude, longitude, and altitude on temperature changes. Global circulation models—their vastly more sophisticated cousins—account not only for temperature variations that occur with latitude, longitude, and altitude, but they also take the process several steps further by simulating the effects of temperature changes on precipitation, humidity, soil moisture, cloudiness, and a number of other important climatic variables (see Schneider 1987, Jenne unpubl.). With increasing complexity, however, comes increasing uncertainty and GCMs have a number of important limitations and assumptions (Schlesinger and Mitchell 1987, Schneider 1987). One of their main drawbacks is their inability to realistically link important atmosphere-ocean and atmosphere-biosphere processes. It should be emphasized, however, that GCMs are not necessary to verify the Greenhouse Effect. The basic physics underlying the phenomenon is well known and verified by simple numerical models that have been in use for many years. Despite some of their limitations, GCMs remain one of the best tools for predicting future climate changes. The GCMs most commonly used for climate change impact studies in this country are those that are run by the National Center for Atmospheric Research (NCAR), NOAA's Geophysical Fluid Dynamics Laboratory (GFDL), NASA's Goddard Institute for Space Research (GISS), and Oregon State University (OSU).

To infer past climates, paleoclimatic reconstructions employ a diverse array of physical and biological sources such as ice cores, tree rings, pollen samples, oxygen isotopes, and the distribution of planktonic foramnifera. They depend upon long-term consistency in association between life-form, taxon, and climate. Although these reconstructions are based on real data and not "merely" simulation, many complications interfere with accurate interpretation of these data (Schneider and Londer 1984). Above all, this method assumes that the types of climate changes that occur in the future will be limited to those that have occurred in the past (a shortcoming of GCMs as well). This assumption has important limitations. First, we do not fully understand the ultimate causes of past climatic changes. Second, anthropogenic global warming will involve novel changes in the climate engine. Hence, it is likely that the coming episode of climate change poses many new and unforeseen risks. Still, paleoclimatic reconstructions offer a wealth of information that is useful in inferring the nature of future climates.

Current Predictions

Temperature. Specific scenarios for greenhouse warming are most often based on GCM simulations, with paleoclimatic data generally used to corroborate or provide additional detail to these predictions. GCMs are in broad agreement as to the direction, rate, and magnitude of expected temperature and precipitation changes, but there are many regional differences among these and other variables. For example, compared to the GFDL and NCAR models, the GISS model predicts substantially higher temperature changes over the whole African continent during winter months (see Figure 1). Differences of this sort are due largely to the varied treatment of fundamental climatic processes and differences in the base climates to which the models are calibrated. Discrepancies between models provide useful insights regarding the correct treatment of many of these fundamental climatic processes.

GCM simulations results are generally given in terms of a "double CO_2" scenario ($2XCO_2$). This is the point at which the atmospheric concentration of CO_2 reaches twice its pre-industrial value. In contrast, the control or base climate ($1XCO_2$) scenario uses a CO_2 concentration approximately equal to that of today's climate. Current predictions indicate that a doubling of CO_2 will occur by the middle of the 21st century (Hansen *et al.* 1988). Although some models offer "transient runs" in which trace gas concentrations are gradually increased, most $2XCO_2$ scenarios assume an instantaneously doubled concentration of CO_2 that is already at equilibrium. Double CO_2 scenarios are a convenient but arbitrary convention. Without preventive action, atmospheric CO_2 concentrations could rise well beyond a twofold increase.

Most GCMs predict a mean global warming of 2.5° to 5.5° C for a doubling of CO_2 (Hansen *et al.* 1988). This figure, however, averages considerable spatial variation. All models predict greater changes at high latitudes, as much as 1.5 to 3 times the global average for the arctic (Ramanathan 1988). This polar amplification is due to the positive feedback effects of snow/ice cover at higher latitudes. Despite considerable quantitative agreement among models for changes in global mean surface air temperatures, there are still large discrepancies in the magnitude and seasonality of these changes at the regional scale (Schlesinger and Mitchell 1987).

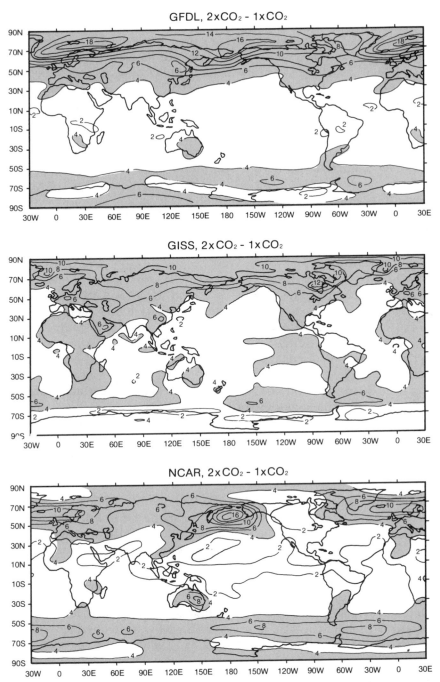

Figure 1. Projected increases in winter (December, January, February) surface air temperature (°C) for three GCMs [$(2 \times CO_2) - (1 \times CO_2)$]. Screen indicates temperature increases larger than 4°C. See text for GCM names. Note the larger temperature increases projected by the GISS model for the African continent. Source: Schlesinger and Mitchell 1987 (© by American Geophysical Union).

Because of the thermal inertia of the earth's oceans, atmospheric temperatures do not respond immediately to increased concentrations of GHGs. A decade to a century or more of lag time is expected before temperatures increase as a result of GHGs already released into the atmosphere (Hansen *et al.* 1988, Ramanathan 1988). Whatever the precise duration of the lag, the full impact of changes in GHG concentrations already wrought is not yet manifest. GCM simulations suggest that emissions to date will force as much as a 1°C warming, despite whatever happens to greenhouse gas productions in the future.

Precipitation and Soil Moisture. Precipitation and soil moisture are secondary effects of temperature and atmospheric circulation patterns, therefore they are more difficult to model than straight changes in temperature. There is an increased degree of uncertainty in predictions of this type (Kellogg and Zhao 1988).

The $2XCO_2$ scenarios of the NCAR, GISS, and GFDL global circulations models predict increases in global mean precipitation in the range of 7.1 to 11 percent over their respective $1XCO_2$ values due to the greater evaporation rates associated with higher temperatures (Schlesinger and Mitchell 1987). While GCM models vary significantly in their prediction of precipitation changes, several points of consensus exist. The largest changes (both positive and negative) occur between latitudes 30° South and 30° North latitude (Schlesinger and Mitchell 1987). Above and below these latitudes, precipitation changes are generally positive in both summer and winter months for all three models (Schlesinger and Mitchell 1987). The GFDL and other models, however, suggest a decrease in summer precipitation rates in continental interiors in northern mid-latitudes (Manabe *et al.* 1981, Mitchell and Warrilow 1987).

A comparison of the the NCAR, GFDL, GISS, OSU, models and the model of the Meteorological Office of the United Kingdom suggests an overall increase in winter soil moisture in the middle and high latitudes of North America, with some decrease in the southern United States and Mexico (Kellogg and Zhao 1988). The comparison also reveals a tendency for dryness in the middle of the continent during the summer, but a possible increase at this same time along the Gulf and West coasts of the United States. This result is roughly consistent with paleoclimatic reconstructions of warm periods in the geologic past in this region (Kellogg and Zhao 1988).

Secondary Effects of Global Warming

Sea Level Rise. Sea levels rise as a result of increases in global ("eustatic") oceanic water levels or localized increases due to subsidence of land or various oceanic-atmospheric events such as El Niño Southern Oscillations (NRC 1987). The difference between the eustatic increase and the localized increase is termed the relative mean sea level rise. Climatic changes in the geologic past have caused world-wide fluctuations in sea level. For example, at the height of the last ice age, about 18,000 years ago, sea levels were approximately 100 meters lower than their current levels (Titus 1988).

Eustatic sea level rises can be produced by increases in the proportion of the earth's water that is in liquid form, for example, by ice-cap melting, or through increases in ocean water temperatures. The latter is due to the thermal expansion of water: when heated, water expands (Wigley and Raper 1987)

As the earth has warmed by approximately 0.5° C over the last 100 years, sea levels have risen about 10 to 15 centimeters (Titus 1988); by the year 2100, sea levels are expected to rise from 1 to 3 meters (Hoffman 1984). Most of this increase will result from the thermal expansion of water, but melting of the West Antarctic Ice Sheet and other smaller glaciers could play an important role as well (Fastook 1984, Peltier 1988).

Intensity and Frequency of Storms and Fires. Global warming will cause changes in the severity and frequency of storms. The energy and frequency of continental storms—which are driven by temperature differentials—could decrease as global warming causes a reduced latitudinal temperature gradient (Richard Wetherald pers. comm.). On the other hand, hurricanes, which are driven by the latent heat of water, are expected to become more frequent and severe due to the increased rate of evaporation that will accompany global warming. Emanuel (1987) has estimated that the destructive potential of hurricanes will increase by 40 to 50 percent for a doubling of CO_2. In addition, global warming will cause a northward shift in the mean track of continental storms (Richard Wetherald pers. comm.).

Fire regimes will also respond to the climatic changes wrought by global warming. Clark (1988) has demonstrated how fire regimes have been affected by past climatic changes in North America, primarily through changes in fuel-load and the periodicity of drought. It would not necessarily take a decrease in precipitation to affect fire regimes. A temperature increase alone could cause a reduction in moisture, which would increase the severity and intensity of fire (Franklin *et al.* in press).

Changes in Ocean Currents. Broecker (1987) has suggested that global warming may cause dramatic changes in oceanic circulation, which, in turn, would trigger abrupt changes in climate. North Atlantic currents presently provide Northern Europe with a relatively mild climate for its latitude. According to Broecker's theory, global warming would initiate changes in oceanic temperatures and salinities that would cause a "shutdown" of these currents. This would send Northern Europe into a cold spell, with temperatures plummeting 6° to 8° C below their current values. Abrupt climatic changes of this type are recognized as a potentially important factor in the mass extinction of species in the geologic past (Crowley and North 1988).

Are the Predictions Correct?

The basic atmospheric physics of the Greenhouse Effect are simple and well-understood. As far back as the 1890s, Svante Arrhenius, a Swedish chemist, anticipated global warming due to fossil fuel use. This deceptively simple impact on the earth's radiative balance will undoubtedly cause major climatic changes, however, the rate at which these changes occur will depend ultimately upon complex interactions between different elements of the climate system, and especially on possible feedback loops that may accelerate or retard the Greenhouse Effect's impact on global temperatures.

Popular Misconceptions

There is quite a bit of confusion as to where the real uncertainty lies in making predictions about future climatic change. The following points attempt to clarify what is and what is not certain in this complex process.

1. *Based on the recent geological past, the earth is headed for an Ice Age.* Whether or not the earth is moving into an ice age is virtually irrelevant to the short-term prospects for global temperature change, because the rate of anthropogenic global warming will be much more rapid than the astrophysical processes that are responsible for causing ice ages. It is estimated that global warming will occur anywhere from 10 to 60 times faster than climatic changes in the geologic past (Schneider 1989).

2. *While average global temperature is increasing, its rate of increase is well below that predicted by GCMs.* The observed temperature increase of about 0.5° C over the last 120 years or so is broadly consistent with some GCM predictions that estimate an increase of anywhere from about 0.3° to 1.1° C for CO_2 warming over the same time period. Thus, the observed warming is consistent with what would be expected given past emissions. The agreement between models and observations is, however, admittedly less impressive when the effects of other greenhouse gases are included as well (see Kerr 1988). A number of factors could account for this discrepancy (Schneider 1989).

3. *Known and unknown feedback loops will counter the effects of global warming.* Undiscovered negative feedbacks might slow the rate of global warming, but they would not prevent it from happening altogether. A recent study of various feedback processes identified a greater number of positive feedbacks, with a greater overall magnitude than negative feedbacks (Lashof in press).

4. *Too much uncertainty exists in several components of the GCMs to make credible predictions.* The Greenhouse Effect is one of the least-controversial and most well-established theories in climatology (Schneider 1989). GCMs are not needed to verify the theory. Simple but no less powerful (for this purpose) numerical models clearly demonstrate the effect of increased concentrations of CO_2 and other GHGs on atmospheric temperatures. What is less certain is how soon this temperature increase will appear and how it will translate into climatic change.

5. *La Niña will cool the earth.* El Niño and La Niña are both part of a periodic, natural weather pattern in the tropical South Pacific known as the El Niño Southern Oscillation (ENSO). The former leads to abnormally high water temperatures in the eastern Pacific, whereas the latter leads to abnormally low water temperatures in the central Pacific. Some climatologists and oceanographers feel that La Niña could postpone the effects of global warming by several decades but the majority of researchers feel that this is an overestimate. In any case, the cooling effect of La Niña would not stop global warming but would only slow its pace. Furthermore, our understanding of ENSO events is still very rudimentary. There is no reason to suppose that global warming itself might not affect the periodicity and strength of ENSO events.

6. *Recent analyses of historical temperatures in the United States failed to show a warming trend.* This is not surprising since the United States covers only a small fraction of the earth's total surface and considerable regional variation is to be expected. The globe as whole could be gradually warming while the United States shows no discernable trend in one direction or another. This is precisely what appears to be happening.

Feedbacks

Feedback loops in the climate engine may dramatically alter the rate of climate change, negative feedbacks suppressing it, positive feedbacks enhancing it. Most GCMs incorporate important, known physical feedbacks, such as water vapor, clouds, and snow/ice albedo. However, the detailed interactions of these feedbacks are poorly understood. No GCM to date incorporates all potentially significant physical or biological feedbacks. Indeed, all possible feedbacks have not even been identified, much less studied.

A recent study by Lashof (in press) reviews a number of important physical and biological feedback processes. Methane hydrates, ocean circulation, and vegetation albedo are identified as the most important positive feedback processes based on their relative magnitude. Methane hydrates are methane molecules locked within a latticed structure of water. They are commonly found in ocean sediments and permafrost, and they remain stable under specific temperature and pressure conditions. As temperatures warm, the appropriate temperature-pressure conditions will cease to be met in many areas and methane (CH_4), which is a strong greenhouse gas, will be liberated as a result.

Changes in the biological productivity and circulation patterns of the world's oceans could also have an important positive feedback effect. Biological activity in the surface layers of the oceans (where light can penetrate) determines the amount of CO_2 that is absorbed from or liberated into the atmosphere. Oceanic currents deliver important nutrients to surface waters and they pump CO_2 into the deep ocean where it is effectively removed from interaction with the atmosphere. Rapid changes in atmospheric CO_2 that accompanied the last glaciation are thought to have been caused by changes in ocean circulation and productivity (Siegenthaler and Wenk 1984). Similar changes in the ocean-atmosphere system may occur as a result of global warming (Broecker 1987).

The large-scale rearrangement of vegetation types (for example, steppe, desert, forest) caused by the poleward migration of many plant species could lead to substantial changes in albedo. If the changes in vegetation type are similar to those that accompanied the transition from glacial to interglacial cycles in the geologic past, then the planetary albedo may decrease, thus leading to increased warming.

Other biological feedbacks also exist, including the accelerated release of carbon dioxide, methane, and nitrous oxide from biological sources (positive feedbacks) and increased sequestering of carbon dioxide by trees and other vegetation (a negative feedback) (see Table 1).

Nonlinear interactions among moderately positive feedbacks can greatly increase the sensitivity of climate to greenhouse warming (Hansen *et al.* 1984). Lashof (in press) estimates that the net impact of various feedback processes could lead to an increase in global mean temperatures of as much as 10° C. While a 1° C warming would represent a great challenge to human society and natural systems, a temperature increase of 10° C would prove catastrophic and would almost certainly preclude adaptation.

Table 1. Potential Physical and Biotic Feedbacks.

Positive Feedbacks (Increased Warming)

Melting of snow/ice reduces Earth's albedo (Hansen *et al.* 1984)

Increased concentration of atmospheric H_2O vapor (a greenhouse gas) from increased evaporation rates (Hansen *et al.* 1984)

Changes in cloud height and cover could promote further warming (Hansen *et al.* 1984)

Decreased CO_2 capacity of ocean surface waters (Lashof in press)

Decreased latitudinal temperature gradient stalls ocean currents and reduces pumping of CO_2 to deep ocean (Broeker 1987, Siegentahler and Wenk 1984)

Thawing of methane hydrates releases methane (Lashof in press)

Thawing of tundra releases CO_2 (Billings 1989)

Net release of CO_2 from plants and soils because respiration rates could exceed photosynthetic rates (Woodwell 1986)

Deforestation and biomass burning releases CO_2 and CH_4 (Mooney *et al.* 1987, Craig *et al.* 1988)

Negative Feedbacks (Decreased Warming)

Increased concentrations of atmospheric CO_2 could stimulate vegetative growth leading to increased sequestering of CO_2 (Strain and Cure 1985)

Changes in cloud height and cover could promote cooling (Hansen *et al.* 1984)

Deforestation could increase surface albedo leading to cooling (Dickinson and Hanson 1984)

Increased nearshore marine productivity could lead to more sequestering of CO_2 (Lashof in press)

Production of dimethylsulfide by phytoplankton increases cloud cover and leads to localized cooling (Bates *et al.* 1987)

A World Without Precedent

Human-induced global warming will differ from all past climatic changes in at least three critical features. First, the projected rates of warming are 10 to 60 times faster than any periods of warming that have occurred since the last ice age (Schneider 1989). Second, the magnitude of this temperature increase will make the earth warmer than it has been anytime in the last 100,000 years (Hansen *et al.* 1988). The rapidity and scale of the change will deter adaptive responses by natural systems and by human institutions.

Third, in a special challenge to biological diversity, these changes will take place upon a landscape that has been massively altered and degraded by human activities. This is Lovejoy's "manscape" (Lovejoy in press). It will impede range shifts and reduce genetic diversity in remaining populations. Habitat and population fragmentation will ensue, placing severe constraints on the ecological and evolutionary processes that shaped the biota's responses during past epochs of change. The likely consequences will involve increased extinction rates, reduced capacity for evolutionary adaptation, and an unprecedented wave of biotic impoverishment.

IMPACTS ON THE BIOSPHERE

Of all the impacts climate disruption may have, its potential effects on biotic resources are the least understood and perhaps most profound. Not only is the biosphere an active component of the climate system, but it is itself a sensitive register of climatic change.

Early in the 20th century, abiotic explanations of plant and animal distributions dominated ecological theory. These gradually gave way to such biotic explanations as competition, predation, and parasitism (Andrewartha and Birch 1954, MacArthur 1972, Ricklefs 1970, Scott 1988). Perhaps spurred by the specter of climatic change, abiotic explanations are once again coming to the fore (Root 1988, Turner *et al.* 1988). The 30- to 40-year hiatus in research that resulted from this shift in perspective has left us with a surprisingly rudimentary understanding of how climatic factors influence plant and animal distributions and a myriad of other ecological relationships.

Peters and Darling (1985) first explicitly addressed the effects of global warming on natural communities. This seminal work stimulated growth of research on the impacts of climate change in unmanaged ecosystems and it remains one of the best reviews on the subject, particularly with respect to conservation.

Mechanisms, Consequences, and Organismic Responses to Climatic Disruption

Anthropogenic climatic change will have pervasive impacts on the biosphere because practically every environmental variable to which plants and animals are sensitive is affected directly or indirectly by climate (see Table 2). Paleoecological studies reveal that climatic changes in the past have been accompanied by profound changes in community structure and composition, by large shifts in the distribution of species, by extinctions, and by evolutionary adaptation to new climates. Organisms living today will likely respond to anthropogenic global warming in the same ways, save that evolutionary adaptation is unlikely to keep pace with the rate of warming (currently predicted to approach 1° C per decade).

Starting with the sensitivity of basic physiological processes to temperature, effects will be manifest throughout the physiology and ecology of the world's biota; community interactions, genetic phenomena, and evolutionary events will not be immune. The simplest yet perhaps most far-reaching impacts for wildlife may begin with the physiology of plant growth, survivorship, and reproduction. Plants take root, survive, grow, and reproduce in climatic zones where on average their photosynthetic rates match or exceed their respiration

Table 2. Some Predicted Consequences of Global Warming for Biological Diversity.

EFFECT

Decreased productivity of arctic sea-ice and benthic communities (Alexander)

Increased temperatures and lower water tables reduce CO_2 uptake in arctic tundra (Billings).

Increased temperatures lead to thermokarst erosion in arctic tundra (Billings)

Computer model predicts that boreal forests will be replaced by northern hardwoods by the middle of the next century (Botkin and Nisbet)

Kirtland's warbler—an endangered species—will face extinction due to habitat loss (Botkin and Nisbet)

Computer model predicts localized extinction of several tree species (Davis and Zabinski)

Trypanosomiasis—the parasite that causes sleeping sickness—will greatly expand its range in Africa (Dobson and Carper)

Forests of the northwest United States will decrease in species diversity and areal extent because of increased fires, storms, and pathogens (Franklin *et al.*)

Northward displacement and isolation of subtropical vegetation types in Florida (Harris)

Increased stream acidity in Rocky Mountains due to changes in the timing of snow melt will cause localized extinction of salamander (Harte and Torne)

Changes in the seasonality of rainfall could alter species composition, population structure, and plant phenology in tropical rainforests (Hartshorn)

The banana slug of California redwood forests would become restricted to patches of humid forest because of moisture-dependence of its food, a mint (Lincoln)

Population declines or extinction of the threatened Bay checkerspot butterfly in the San Francisco Bay Area of California (Murphy and Weiss)

Population declines in arctic migratory shorebirds due to loss of tundra habitat, sea-level rise on wintering grounds, and disruptions in timing of resource phenology along migratory route (Myers and Lester)

Seventy percent of the Cape Hatteras National Seashore might be replaced by low, sandy grasslands (Ray *et al.*)

Changes in relations between social insects because of volatilization of pheromones (Rubenstein)

Population sex ratios in crocodiles, alligators, and turtles will change (Rubenstein)

Drought will cause female elephant bands to fragment; as a result the frequency of copulation with nondominant males will increase (Rubenstein)

Expansion of the thermo-Mediterranean climatic zone in California (Westman)

Soybean looper will be forced to eat more to compensate for higher C/N ratios of vegetation (Lincoln)

Author source: *Proceedings of the Conference on the Consequences of the Greenhouse Effect for Biological Diversity. October 4–6, 1988.* World Wildlife Fund. Edited by R. L. Peters and T. E. Lovejoy. Washington, D.C.

rates. If the temperature increase to which a particular species is subjected surpasses its range of tolerance, then individual plants will die or fail to reproduce or grow. In the remaining plants, physiological responses will alter plant energy balances, stature, reproductive output, and other basic ecological parameters. New species with a different set of climatic tolerances will invade and colonize the area. Competitive balances will shift with ensuing changes in plant community compo-

The climate changes from the Greenhouse Effect will cause major crop-growing areas to migrate. Wheat farming, for example, may be possible farther north. *Doug Wilson/U. S. Department of Agriculture*

sition and dominance and ultimately, where the changes are large, in the life-form of the vegetation.

This process will produce profound changes in the distribution and extent of North American and other biomes. Southern forms (in the Northern Hemisphere) will extend their northern boundaries northward, while withdrawing along their southern edge. Simulation-modeling of forest succession predicts, for example, that the boreal forests of northern Minnesota will be replaced by hardwoods from the south, with changes detectable perhaps as early as 2010 (see Figure 2). The belt of loblolly pine now found across the southeastern United States may find its climatic zone shifted several hundred miles northward by the middle of the 21st century (Miller *et al.* 1987), and sugar maple will migrate northward to the edge of the Hudson Bay (Davis and Zabinski in press).

Elements of the flora and fauna that may not be directly affected by the climatic changes themselves may nonetheless be dependent upon microclimate, nutrients, or food generated by the plants that are sensitive directly. Thus, as the boreal forests migrate and contract, such warblers as the Blackpoll (*Dendroica striata*) and Cape May (*D. tigrini*) will suffer major reductions in breeding habitat. Likewise, tundra fauna will undergo significant contractions in their ranges.

These two examples typify what may be the most widespread impact on wildlife: changes in quality and quantity of suitable habitat. Some habitats will disappear outright, while others will experience a

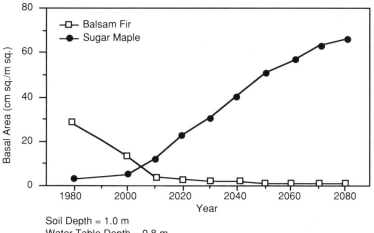

Soil Depth = 1.0 m
Water Table Depth = 0.8 m

Figure 2. Computer model predictions for basal areas of sugar maple (*Acer saccharum*) and balsam fir (*Abies balsamea*) in the Boundary Waters Canoe Area of northern Minnesota under a transient $2 \times CO_2$ scenario. Source: Botkin *et al.*, unpubl.

substantial decrease in the area they occupied. Still others will undergo such dramatic ecological changes that they will evolve into new habitats, completely distinct from their present forms. Certain habitat types will be lost or transformed more quickly than others, because of the different time lags exhibited by their constituent species. Thus, short-lived, herbaceous communities will probably disappear more quickly than forests (Davis 1985).

In some cases, the tables may turn and the effects of global warming on habitat may actually be mediated through wildlife populations. Certain animals such as elephants and other large herbivores exert a profound impact on their vegetative environment. Through continuous grazing and felling of large trees, elephants foster the type of vegetative cover in which many smaller herbivores thrive. In the 100 years following the disappearance of elephants in the Hluhluwe Game Reserve in Natal, several species of antelope have become extinct and populations of open country grazers such as wildebeest and waterbuck have been greatly reduced (Lewin 1987). Global warming could set off a chain of extinction events by eliminating keystone herbivores such as elephants or their functional counterparts in other ecosystems. Such subtle ecological linkages will be among the most difficult to anticipate.

Changes in the structure and composition of natural communities will lead to the formation of new habitat types. Changes in plant and animal productivity occur fairly rapidly (on the order of months) in response to climatic fluctuations. Alterations in many community-level attributes such as species diversity and dominance, however, occur more slowly. Nonetheless, Botkin and Nisbet (in press) have shown through computer simulation that global warming would lead to significant changes in biomass and species composition of specific North American forest communities as early as 2010 (see Figure 2).

Habitat modifications and losses will take place not only because of climate-induced shifts in plant distributions, but also because of sea-level rise. Coastal wetlands in the United States may be reduced up to 80 percent with a doubling of CO_2 (Environmental Protection Agency 1988). The frequency and severity of fires, hurricanes, and similar events could likewise alter many habitats (Emanuel 1987, Clark 1988).

The impacts of anthropogenic climate change will penetrate far beyond those effects mediated directly by temperature. Plants will also respond directly to increased concentrations of atmospheric CO_2, depending upon the specifics of their photosynthetic pathways and the efficiency with which they use water. Under conditions of increased CO_2, photosynthetic rates of the so-called C_3 plants (for example wheat and soybeans) increase considerably; however, this effect is much less pronounced in C_4 plants (for example, sugar cane, corn, and tropical grasses). In contrast, C_4 plants show a dramatic increase in water-use efficiency when exposed to elevated levels of CO_2, but C_3 plants actually exhibit a slight decrease in efficiency if CO_2 levels become too high. Differential physiological repercussions of this type are likely to alter the balance of competitive relationships in many biological communities.

The reproductive physiology of many plants and animals is also influenced by climate. The sex of turtle, lizard, and crocodilian hatchlings is highly dependent upon the incubation temperature of their eggs (Mrosovsky and Yntema 1980) (see Figure 3). Reproductive success in grizzly bears and several species of ungulates can be predicted on the basis of temperature and precipitation data (Picton 1978, 1984). Changes in the seasonality of rainfall are expected to interfere with the fruiting and flowering phenologies of keystone tree species in the tropical rainforests of Panamá (Hartshorn in press).

Both plants and animals will exhibit important physiological responses to secondary effects induced by changes in temperature and precipitation. Increased water temperatures, for example, will decrease

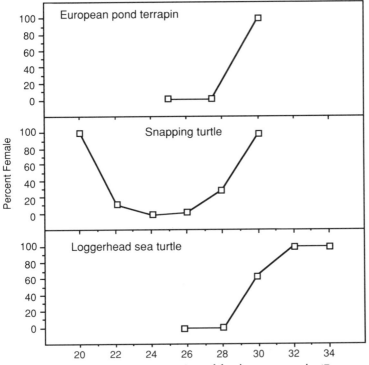

Figure 3. Sex ratios in two species of fresh water turtle (European pond terrapin *Emys orbicularis* and snapping turtle *Chelydra serpentina*) and one species of sea turtle (loggerhead *Caretta caretta*) from eggs incubated at different temperatures. Source: Mrosovsky and Yntema 1980.

the amount of dissolved oxygen available to fish (Meisner *et al.* 1988) and changes in precipitation and run-off could alter salinities and nutrient and pollutant concentrations in aquatic environments.

At an evolutionary scale, climatic disruption threatens to reduce global biotic diversity, most obviously by its exacerbation of extinction, more subtly through the loss of genetic diversity that will beset species suffering major population declines. Many animal and plant populations will experience isolation and fragmentation as a result of climatic changes. This could lead to reduced gene flow among populations, in-breeding, impaired mate selection, and other deleterious genetic effects (Soulé 1986).

Range Shifts

From the discussion above it is apparent that changes in the geography of climate will cause shifts in the distributions of species. By the middle of the 21st century, for example, temperature increases are expected to shift temperate biotic zones several hundred kilometers poleward. Specific predictions for particular species become problematic, however, because other factors will constrain the pace of range shifts. One fundamental observation is that plant and animal species will respond individualistically to changes in climate rather than *en masse*. Each species will move, adapt, or succumb to extinction at its own pace (Davis 1985, Graham 1985). Pleistocene biotas, for example, consisted of species that today live in widely separated areas, and thus many habitats from this epoch have no modern-day analogs (Graham 1985). The communities that develop in response to global warming may therefore consist of novel assemblages for which there are no contemporary counterparts.

Maximum dispersal rates in plants and some animals will be controlled by the vectors (for example, winds and currents) that carry their propagules. Many tree species have maximum dispersal rates on the order of 10 to 40 kilometers per century (Davis and Zabinski in press), but this rate will be insufficient to keep pace with projected shifts in biotic zones of several hundred kilometers per century. Furthermore, plants can only migrate to areas with proper soil types, while animals depend to varying degrees on specific plant assemblages or vegetation structures for food, shelter, and breeding. Those with specialized requirements will be constrained by the movement rates of their critical habitats. In fact, Davis (1985) has even suggested that because of the unstable nature of Quaternary climates, a selective advantage may have been conferred on those organisms that were able to easily dissociate from the communities of which they were a part.

Requirements for the successful dispersal of even highly mobile creatures like birds will be difficult to assess. Seemingly insignificant obstacles like small stretches of unforested areas could prevent some animals like deep-forest, tropical birds from successfully dispersing (Peters and Darling 1985). Furthermore, many natural and human-made barriers such as mountains, oceans, and areas of intense human development will represent significant obstacles to migration.

Animals and plants responded to climatic fluctuations in the past by migrating up and down altitudinal gradients in a manner analogous to latitudinal migration (LaMarche 1973, van der Hammen 1984). A 3°F temperature rise would cause montane communities to shift upward about 1000 feet along an elevational gradient (MacArthur 1972). As species migrate up mountains, they may experience extinctions due to lack of alternative habitat, fragmentation, and isolation; the distributions of many montane species will likely be reduced to isolated mountain-top refugia.

The isolation, fragmentation, and habitat loss experienced by many montane populations will leave these species vulnerable to many genetic pressures. Furthermore, montane biotas are known to be centers of endemism (Terborgh and Winter 1982); thus it is more likely that global warming will lead to not merely localized but global extinction of species.

Phenological Considerations

Global climate change will shift the timing of meteorological events and critical temperature thresholds to different phases in the annual cycle. Spring will come earlier and autumn later. Precipitation patterns will change. These changes in seasonality will directly or indirectly affect the timing of varied biological phenomena, such as the fruiting or flowering of plants, the emergence of insect blooms, and the long-distance migrations of animals. The impacts may involve complex interactions with other anthropogenic problems. For example, stream acidity in the Rocky Mountains is dependent upon the rate at which spring snowmelt occurs and acidity is the primary characteristic determining the existence of the tiger salamander (*Ambystoma tigrinum*) (Harte and Hoffman in press). If spring snows melt quickly, then there is more runoff and less absorption by the soil, which has a number of acid-neutralizing compounds. As a result, the quicker the snowmelt, the more acid the runoff and vice versa. The salamander disappears from local streams at a pH below 5. Its existence is thus dependent upon the timing of spring snowmelt, which is, in turn, dependent primarily upon temperature.

Global warming could interfere with the timing of animal migrations that have arisen in response to the sporadic distribution of food and other resources in time and space. For example, the migration of shorebirds along the U.S. East Coast—a pathway for birds moving

The eggs of the horseshoe crab are the main food source for many migratory shorebirds, such as this sanderling, that stop over in Delaware Bay to refuel. Global warming will disrupt the seasonal timing of annual migrations and available food sources. *Kenneth W. Gardiner*

between tropical or temperate wintering areas and arctic breeding ground—depends critically upon the timing of horseshoe crab (*Limulus polyphemus*) spawning in Delaware Bay relative to the timing of insect emergence in the Canadian arctic. The eggs of the horseshoe crab are the principal food source for shorebirds during their stopover in the Bay (Myers 1986); they are laid in early May as temperatures rise. Global warming will advance the emergence of both horseshoe crabs and tundra insects, but the latter more than the former because of the greater impact of global warming at high latitudes.

Special Cases

Certain communities and populations will be especially vulnerable to global warming by virtue of their geographical location or genetic make-up and the nature of the expected changes in climate.

Coasts and Wetlands. A rise in sea level of anywhere between one and three meters is expected by the middle of the next century or sooner (Hoffman 1984). Rising sea levels will affect wetlands, barrier islands, and other coastal habitats by inundation, saltwater intrusion, and erosion. These ecosystems serve as critical habitat to many bird and fish species and countless other animals, as well as barriers to coastal erosion and sinks for a variety of pollutants. With slow sea level rise, coastal wetlands respond over the long-term by migrating upward and landward. Many existing wetlands, however, will be incapable of migrating at a rate fast enough to keep pace with the rate of sea level rise caused by global warming. By the middle of the 21st century, this rate is expected to approach one centimeter per year (Titus 1988). As a result, many wetlands will be partially or totally converted to open water.

The slope of the wetlands and adjacent uplands will control the extent of wetland loss to sea level rise (Titus 1988). For example, many marshes in New England and along the Pacific Coast are situated just below steep cliffs. As sea level rises, these marshes will be completely inundated because the cliffs restrict inland migration. Low coastal profiles do not ensure protection either: vast areas of wetlands in Louisiana and elsewhere lie within one meter of mean sea level; a relatively small rise in sea level will therefore translate into wetland inundation that will penetrate far inland. The United States is expected to experience a net loss of about 25 to 80 percent of its coastal wetlands by the year 2100 as a result of sea level rise (Environmental Protection Agency 1988). Human developments—either those that are in place now or those that will be built to protect investments—will exacerbate this loss.

Vegetation communities in many wetlands will change as rising sea level forces the disappearance of salt-intolerant species. The general effect will be to reduce the area of freshwater coastal wetlands, such as cypress swamps in the southeast United States. Whether these freshwater habitats are replaced by saltwater marshes will depend upon local wetland topographies; many will revert to open water (Titus 1988).

Wetlands, barrier islands, and mainland beaches will all experience increased erosion rates as sea levels rise. Increased erosion will be most important for barrier islands and beaches since most wetlands will be flooded long before they are eroded. Approximately 90 percent of all U.S. beaches experience erosion rates of anywhere between two and five feet per year; sea level rise is expected to double or even quadruple these rates (Leatherman 1987, 1988). Erosion of sandy beaches will lead to a decline in habitat for shorebirds, terns, gulls, and other coastal species, as well as loss of unique ecological communities dependent upon barrier islands.

Rising sea levels will not be the only effect that global warming has on coastal communities. Changes in temperature may also alter nearshore circulation and upwelling patterns that are critical for supporting a host of organisms from microscopic primary producers to the largest marine mammals. The warmer water temperatures that accompanied the 1982–1983 El Niño interfered with normal upwelling patterns and caused mass mortalities of seabirds, pinnipeds, marine iguanas, seaweeds, and corals, as well as encouraging the migration of warm-water forms into temperate waters (LaCock 1986, Merlen 1984). Fisheries will also undergo many negative changes as a result of global warming, adding further to difficulties of managing this already beleaguered resource (Frye 1983).

The immense biological productivity of arctic waters is maintained by complex upwelling patterns and sea ice (Alexander in press). The greater temperature increases expected to occur at higher latitudes will lead to melting of sea ice that serves as critical habitat for the primary producers at the base of the arctic, marine food chain. Increased temperatures and changes in seasonality will also affect the occurrence of "polynyas," large holes in the sea ice that stay open all year long and support an immense amount of biological productivity, including large populations of mammals and seabirds (Alexander in press).

Tropical, marine ecosystems such as coral reefs will not escape the effects of global warming unscathed, despite the fact that temperature changes in these latitudes are expected to be considerably smaller than they are for other regions. Because tropical marine organisms live at temperatures closer to their upper thermal limits, they might prove to be more sensitive to a given temperature change than their temperate counterparts (Johannes and Betzer 1975). Furthermore, rapid sea level rise could favor the development of many fast-growing staghorn and elkhorn corals (*Acropora* spp.) at the expense of major frame-building species such as star coral (*Montastrea* spp) (Ray *et al.* in press). This type of shift in species composition could have a significant impact on reef-associated biota. In addition, the increased frequency of hurricanes expected to accompany global warming (Emanuel 1987) could have major implications for reef successional processes.

Arctic and Boreal Communities. Because of the greater temperature increases predicted for higher latitudes, arctic and boreal communities face special risks from global warming. Tundra and taiga (boreal forest) communities are especially important from the perspective of global warming because they contain between 10 and 27 percent of the world's terrestrial carbon reserves (Oechel and Riechers 1986). As atmospheric temperatures increase due to global warming, much of this carbon will be released, thus creating a powerful positive feedback loop.

Permafrost covers about 20 percent of the world's land surface (Ives 1974). It consists of polar and high-mountain regions that remain below 0° C for more than two consecutive years (Harris 1987). A global warming of 5° C would lead ultimately to a melting of permafrost in all regions of the Nearctic, except for the northernmost portions of the Canadian mainland, the Arctic islands, and the northern half of Greenland (Harris 1987). As permafrost melts, it creates surficial depressions, flooding, and eventually erosion. This condition—known as thermokarst—is self-reinforcing because the lower albedo of water promotes increased heat absorption, which, in turn, leads to the formation of more thermokarst. The flooding that results from thermokarst formation is known to have a large impact on wildlife such as shorebirds and waterfowl because it alters the heterogeneous patterns of water and terrestrial microsites (Walker *et al.* 1987). The large temperature increases expected at higher latitudes are likely to cause considerable thermokarst formation that will directly or indirectly affect wildlife. Another impact may be felt in low coastal areas currently dominated by permafrost. Melting may lower the surface of the land sufficiently to make it vulnerable to sea level rise (P. J. Webber pers. comm.). How significant a problem this may be is not currently understood, but it could challenge major areas of coastal plain tundra such as Alaska's North Slope.

Summer warmth is one of the most important factors limiting the growth of vascular plants in the arctic (Edlund 1986). The 13° C mean July isotherm, for example, coincides closely with the limit of the boreal forest in North America (Edlund 1986). Latitudinal climatic gradients also control the height and growth form of woody plant species. Plants become increasingly stunted and prostrate with increasing latitude (Edlund 1986, Walker 1987).

Global warming will result in a northward shift of the mean July isotherm and a significant change in the distribution and growth forms of many woody plant species. For example, extrapolating the distribution of different Holdridge Life Zones based on warming caused by doubling CO_2, Emanuel *et al.* (1985a, 1985b) predicted that the areal extent of boreal forests would decline by 37 percent. The actual changes in biome distribution that take place will be influenced by more complexity than can be incorporated in Holdridge Life Zones, especially the availability of suitable soil types and moisture regimes (Edlund 1986). Nonetheless, they will undoubtedly be dramatic.

Although little is known about the migration rates or seed banks of individual species of tundra plants, preliminary results suggest that the tundra biome as a whole faces severe threats from global warming. At worst, Emanuel *et al.*'s (1985) work with Holdridge Life Zones suggests that a doubling of CO_2 will result in a 32-percent decline in the areal extent of the tundra biome. Localized extinctions of both vascular and nonvascular species of plants are likely on many of the arctic islands, given the relatively large distances of open water, which would prevent successful migration.

Genetically Depauperate Species and Geographic Considerations.
As global warming causes latitudinal and altitudinal shifts in climatological conditions, several attributes related to the genetic make-up
and geographic spread of species will interact to determine its susceptibility to extinction (see Peters and Darling 1985):

1. Currently localized species are less likely to have populations
   in suitable habitat after climatic change compared to more
   widely distributed forms, even if their starting populations are
   large and vigorous. This applies especially to animal populations restricted to national parks and other "habitat islands."
2. Small and/or isolated populations may lack sufficient genetic
   diversity to respond by evolutionary adaptation to changed climatic conditions.
3. Populations on the retreating edge of their range will be more
   susceptible to global warming than those on the leading edge or
   in the center of their range.

POLICY RESPONSES

The prospect of global warming requires two complementary strategies: amelioration and adaptation. Amelioration will require slowing,
stopping, and reversing increases in the atmospheric concentrations of
greenhouse gases. It is of paramount importance because of the pervasive biotic and social disruptions that would accompany full-blown
global warming.

It will not be sufficient, however, because greenhouse gases already in the atmosphere guarantee a warming of at least 1° C. Major
efforts will be required to adapt to this warming already under way.
How far it goes will depend upon our effectiveness at amelioration.
Both policy responses will be difficult to design and to implement because they ultimately may disrupt many accepted life-styles and economic practices.

The challenge to achieve effective policy responses will be heightened by competing interests: indeed, if analyzed in isolation some economic sectors and even whole national economies may anticipate
benefit from warming. To the degree that policies focus on adaptation,
moreover, severe conflicts will arise between steps taken to protect
human investments and those needed to ensure the persistence of critical habitats, wildlife, and biological diversity, especially in coastal
zones. The natural world will take it on the chin—a one-two assault
first from climatic disruption itself and then from self-centered human
efforts to mitigate and adapt. Coastal ecosystems, for example, may
suffer many unanticipated negative effects from the construction of

fortifications (for example, sea walls and groins) built in response to rising sea levels, or wildlife may be displaced as previously uncultivated lands come under the plow.

Amelioration

Policies to slow the trajectory of global warming will focus on stabilizing atmospheric concentrations of greenhouse gases, both through reductions in their production as well as through increases in the rate at which they are removed from the atmosphere. Most of these fixes concentrate on energy policy (reduced production of CO_2), elimination of trace gas production (for example, chlorofluorocarbons) or reforestation (removal of atmospheric CO_2). The available options, discussed below, are especially logical because they would provide a number of benefits to society, independent of their ameliorative effects on global warming (Schneider 1989).

Additionally, a number of high-tech fixes have been proposed. These make attractive illustrations in popular science magazines, but otherwise involve either such enormous leaps in technology or such prodigiously intrusive chemical manipulations as to warrant consideration only as desperate last resorts.

Enhanced Energy Efficiency

Increasing the efficiency of energy production and use provides the most sensible, cost-effective method for beginning to reduce CO_2 emissions. Since 1973, improvements in efficiency throughout the world have saved more energy than was gained from all new sources in the same time period (Flavin and Durning 1988).

According to one calculation, a two percent annual reduction in CO_2 emissions would keep the atmospheric concentration of CO_2 at about 463 parts per million by volume by the year 2075, and this in turn, would hold the global mean temperature to within about 1° C of its present value (Flavin and Durning 1988). Energy efficiency can be attained not only through conservation and technological improvements, but also through removal of inefficient subsidies, financial disincentives, and a fundamental restructuring of industrial and transportation systems.

Energy efficiency varies by sector and country, and attempts to enhance energy efficiency must recognize these differences. For example, in Third World and centrally planned countries, the industrial sector is generally the most energetically inefficient, whereas, in most industrialized nations, this sector usually requires less attention than others (Flavin and Durning 1988). Improved efficiency in the transportation sector is important for almost all countries, especially in the United

States, where it represents more than 63 percent of all oil consumed (EESI 1988).

Renewables and Other Energy Sources

Global warming now makes weaning humanity from a largely fossil fuel energy diet a global imperative. This is especially true for coal, for two reasons: (1) it contributes inordinately to global warming per unit of energy produced because of its high carbon content; and (2) it contributes large absolute amounts of carbon because of its widespread use. Natural gas and other fuels with relatively low carbon content will play a crucial role in the transition to renewable energy sources.

Many underutilized renewable energy technologies exist: photovoltaics, wind power, hydropower, wave and tidal power, geothermal energy, biomass, and more. In the future these must fulfill a significant portion of the world's energy demands if CO_2 stabilization is to be obtained. Not all are equally desirable though; many have other detrimental consequences for the environment. Their potential costs must be weighed against their contribution to atmospheric stabilization.

The development of renewable energy technologies in the United States has been greatly impeded by the lack of government support for research and development and the removal of many important investment tax credits. With proper federal support, renewable energy sources could become the principal source of energy for the future. Greater federal responsibility for the development of renewables should include a significantly expanded research and development budget, public–private cost sharing, financial incentives, and the provision of subsidies equivalent to those given to fossil and nuclear fuels (Moomaw 1988).

Nuclear power remains the only other energy source besides renewables that does not result in the net production of greenhouse gases. Yet the present generation of nuclear reactors has proven in the public's eye to be uneconomical, unsafe, and, as a result, untenable. A new generation of reactors, deemed "inherently safe," holds some promise for operational safety, although they fail to solve the troubling fuel disposal and proliferation problems that have vexed the current generation. These remain in early stages of research and lack feasibility demonstrations. Further research and development of inherently safe reactors is warranted as an insurance policy against unexpected problems in developing renewable energy sources.

Stop Deforestation and Promote Reforestation

The earth's vegetation and soils represent an enormous pool of carbon, roughly three times that stored in the atmosphere. Current rates of deforestation probably account for about 20 percent of all anthropogenically produced CO_2 emissions. Curbing the rate of deforestation could thus contribute significantly to reducing the rate of global warming.

Reforestation removes atmospheric carbon by sequestering it as biomass. It would take approximately 1.28 to 1.65 billion acres of new plantation forests to sequester five gigatons of carbon per year, an amount roughly equal to annual emissions to the atmosphere (Marland 1988). This would require an area of land greater than one-half the size of the United States (Dudek 1988). Clearly, reforestation by itself would be impractical as a policy to curb the rate of global warming; even more modestly scaled efforts would run into problems of competition with food and cash crops and difficulties associated with growing such large acreages in monoculture.

Postel and Heise (1988) have calculated that reforestation measures adopted as a result of the United States Food Security Act of 1985 (also known a the 1985 Farm Act) might change North America from a net source to a net sink of carbon within the next couple of decades. Dudek (1988) has developed an economically feasible plan whereby a provision of this same act would be used to promote reforestation on retired farmland. This plan would sequester enough carbon to offset CO_2 emissions from new electric utilities proposed for construction between 1987 and 1996.

Taken together, efforts to curb deforestation and promote reforestation could have a significant effect on slowing the rate of global warming. It is estimated that by planting 300 million acres of trees and halving deforestation rates in the four countries with the highest rates of deforestation, net carbon emissions from terrestrial ecosystems could be reduced by two-thirds (Postel and Heise 1988).

Research, Education, and Legislation

Policy responses to global warming will only be as good as the science on which they are based, and they can only hope to be effective if they have a broad base of support in the scientific and policymaking communities and in the public eye. A major government commitment to research and education is thus an essential ingredient for any strategy to cope with global warming.

Research needs include better global circulation models with greater resolution and more realistic representation of ocean-atmosphere and biosphere-atmosphere coupling; better understanding of the sources and sinks of methane and other greenhouse gases; improved knowledge of oceanic circulation and its relation to climate, continued study to assess the impacts of global warming on social and biotic systems, and greatly enhanced basic ecological research and monitoring. The latter cannot be overemphasized. Compared to many other scientific disciplines, ecology is handicapped by the paucity of basic research needed to make sound predictions. The National Science Foundation should be encouraged to re-evaluate its funding practices to include more of the long-term research that is required of investigations on climate change.

More than any other environmental problem, global climate protection requires a strong base of international cooperation. Industrialized nations will need to take the lead in calling for an international convention to protect the global climate. They will also have to assume much of financial burden of reforestation schemes, investments in renewables, energy efficiency, and the like.

Adaptation and Its Implications for Biological Conservation

To the degree that the general circulation models are accurate, some global warming is inevitable: changes already effected in atmospheric GHG concentrations will produce at least a 1° C increase. The longer the delay in instituting effective policies for amelioration, the greater this rise will become. Policies for adaptation—for minimizing the impact—thus become a necessary part of the global response to climate change. They become critical to world conservation strategies, moreover, because of the implications for biotic diversity that loom in global warming. Not only do these implications challenge wildlife directly, they also stand to undermine many current conservation efforts.

There are two fundamental challenges: First, the pace of extinction is likely to accelerate. Conservation will be hard-pressed to respond effectively, if for no other reason than the sheer volume of species and places that will need attention. Second, our most basic approach—identifying land that merits protection and then setting it aside—will enter a phase of dubious application. Protected lands will become uninhabitable by the very species, habitats, and communities they were designated to preserve because of the shifting climatic conditions (Peters and Darling 1985).

Protected Areas. With climatic change pushing habitats and their component species poleward, inland, and up mountains, what criteria and practices will be useful to guide design, placement, and management of protected areas? Peters and Darling (1985) have suggested several general guidelines. Whether they can be implemented in any meaningful way will depend upon particulars of each case:

1. Maximize flexibility in reserve design. The ideal would be reserves whose boundaries could change. Since this is not practical, the need for flexibility can be met probably only by maximizing the amount of land available for future protection.
2. The conservation merits of specific areas under consideration for protection will change: some areas of great value now will

become less valuable, while other currently unattractive areas will become more desirable in the future.

3. Large pieces of land are more likely to retain biological value than small ones. This is a consequence of geographic shifts in climate zones. It places a premium on major land acquisitions, for example, current efforts led by The Nature Conservancy to acquire the Gray Ranch in New Mexico.

4. Heterogeneity in soil type, topography, vegetation, and other habitat-defining parameters will increase the likelihood that the biological communities of interest will either persist or be successful in establishment.

5. Every effort should be made to preserve natural habitat corridors, particularly those that run north-south, span major altitudinal variation, or extend inland from coastal marshes. These will be necessary to allow for the distributional shifts that will be required to keep pace with shifting climates.

6. When evaluating the merits of acquisitions to preserve specific habitats or species, sites at the northern or altitudinal upper-edge of the habitats' or species' distribution will be preferable to sites at the southern or lower edge.

In the face of global warming, natural lands management must become increasingly intrusive if it is to achieve preservation of the diversity of communities and species extant today. Mitigating the effects of climatic disruption may require species or habitat transplantation programs, selective breeding, off-site storage of germplasm, irrigation, and other manipulative techniques (Peters and Darling 1985); a host of new procedures may emerge under the rubric of "salvage ecology."

This new mandate for increased manipulation will undoubtedly spawn philosophical debates in the conservation community: what balance should be struck between letting evolutionary and biogeographic processes unfold versus artificial maintenance of species and systems? At what point do these techniques so transgress being "natural" that they are unacceptable? What is the management target: species preservation, ecosystem preservation, or maximizing the likelihood that natural processes can take place?

The risk of these debates is that they may diffuse and delay substantive conservation efforts. Appeals to "naturalness" and to "preserving process" are attractive intellectually but become managerially quixotic: If future climate predictions are correct and the next several decades witness major climatic disruption, then arguments favoring natural processes are moot. The changes will be too rapid to permit a replay of the ecological and evolutionary adaptations that carried flora and fauna through previous episodes of climate change.

To respond to this challenge, conservation must become increasingly proactive in its strategies. Single-site acquisitions should be evaluated for their contribution to regional systems designed to provide corridors for habitat migration and provide new sites for displaced biota. Regional habitat networks should be formed out of available natural patches; high priority should be assigned to research that investigates the variables that will affect the functioning of these networks, for example, dispersal rates, patch sizes, and inter-patch gaps. Efforts on this front might build on the successes and failures of the Forest Service to build a habitat network for the spotted owl (U.S. Forest Service 1988). High priority should also be given to elements of restoration ecology that will enable the creation of new habitat patches at critical positions in these networks.

Endangered Species. Approximately 500 threatened and endangered species have been identified in the United States, 150 of which are plants (Fay 1988). Another 3,800 species are currently being reviewed for addition to the federal Endangered Species List (Fay 1988). Recent surveys suggest that even without climatic disruption, this number is likely to grow very rapidly (Center for Plant Conservation 1988). The endangered status of more than a few of these is directly attributable to over-specialization or dependence upon habitats that in the past had much more extensive geographic distributions, for example, "Pleistocene relics." These species will be at an immediate disadvantage when challenged by new and drastic climate changes because of their limited and isolated distribution and their genetically depauperate status.

The combined impact of species already at risk and those threatened by climate change will heighten existing challenges to endangered species policy and management. It is already impossible to meet the needs of each species acknowledged to be legally endangered or threatened; further additions to the list would make a bad situation utterly untenable. If any coherent and meaningful strategy emerges, it will necessarily incorporate much more strategic thinking on where investments for endangered species management should be placed. In the future, conservation priorities will depend in part upon the likelihood that a species will survive climatic change.

CONCLUSION

Given the uncertainties of rate and magnitude inherent in climatic predictions, the even greater unknowns in estimating what these changes mean for flora and fauna, and the rising tide of challenges these predictions, however imprecise, foretell for biological diversity, the pathway for conservation's response to climate change is not yet clear. There is an immense and immediate need for research and development of flexible conservation strategies that allow for climate disruption. This need encompasses basic ecological research to better understand the impacts of climate change on species, habitats, and ecological communities, development of management techniques that can increase the likelihood that species will persist through episodes of rapid climate change; and policy research to evaluate the utility of current programs in the face of climate change, and to identify and prioritize conservation investments for the future.

More than research, however, the prospects for climate change require action. This action must embrace both amelioration and adaptation, with a clear emphasis on the former, reserving the latter for aspects of climate disruption we cannot forestall or avoid. For the near-term, amelioration means energy efficiency, eliminating the production of greenhouse gases, and stopping deforestation. Over the long haul it will entail alternative, climate-neutral energy sources, reforestation, and rational limits to human population growth. The wildlife conservation community will participate with many other sectors of human society to achieve these goals.

Wildlife, and biological diversity in general, will confront special needs for adaptation, needs that will conflict with efforts to protect human investments. Wildlife managers must begin now to evaluate their own particular mandates in resource management and ask how their responsibilities will change with the climate. It is not too soon to begin developing on-the-ground implementations of pilot programs to explore different methods for adapting to climate change: management plans for protected lands that give explicit attention to rising sea levels, warming temperatures, and changing precipitation; habitat transplant procedures; habitat corridors or networks; and species' salvage techniques. The sooner this stage of response to the challenge of climate change begins, the more effective will be the conservation effort.

REFERENCES

Alexander, V. 1989. "Arctic marine ecosystems," *in* Peters, R. L. and T. E. Lovejoy eds., *Proceedings of The Consequences of the Greenhouse Effect for Biological Diversity.* October 4–6, 1988. World Wildlife Fund. Washington, D.C.

Andrewartha, H. G. and L. C. Birch. 1954. *The Distribution and Abundance of Animals.* University of Chicago Press. Chicago, Illinois.

Bates, T. S. et al. 1987 "Evidence for the climatic role of marine biogenic sulfur." *Nature* 329(6137): 319–321.

Billings, W. D. 1989. "Effects of predicted climatic warming on arctic tundra ecosystems on the Alaskan North Slope," *in* Peters, R. L. and T. E. Lovejoy eds., *Proceedings of The Consequences of the Greenhouse Effect for Biological Diversity.* October 4–6, 1988. World Wildlife Fund. Washington, D.C.

Botkin, D. B. and R. A. Nisbet. 1989. "Projecting the effects of climate change on biological diversity in forests," *in* Peters, R. L. and T. E. Lovejoy eds., *Proceedings of The Consequences of the Greenhouse Effect for Biological Diversity.* October 4–6, 1988. World Wildlife Fund. Washington, D.C.

———. et al. n.d. "How soon will forests respond to CO_2 induced climate change? Unpublished.

Broecker, W. S. 1987. "Unpleasant surprises in the greenhouse?" *Nature* 328: 123–126.

Center for Plant Conservation. 1988. *CPS Endangerment Survey.* Center for Plant Conservation. Boston, Massachussetts.

Clark, J. S. 1988. "Effect of climate change on fire regimes in northwestern Minnesota." *Nature* 334: 233–235

CLIMAP. 1976. "The surface of the Ice-Age Earth." *Science* 191: 1131-1137.

COHMAP. 1988. "Climatic changes of the last 18,000 years: observations and model simulations." *Science* 241: 1043-1052.

Cohn, J. P. 1987. "Chlorofluorocarbons and the ozone layer." *Bioscience* 37: 647–650

Craig, H. et al. 1988. "The isotopic composition of methane in polar ice cores." *Science* 242: 1535-1539.

Crowley, T. J. and G. R. North. 988. "Abrupt climate change and extinction events in earth history." *Science* 240: 996–1002

Davis, M. B. 1985. "Climatic instability, time lags, and community disequilibrium," pp. 269–284 *in* Diamond, J. and T.J. Case eds., *Community Ecology.* Harper and Row. New York, New York.

Davis, M. B. and C. Zabinski. 1989. "Rates of dispersal of North American trees: Implications for response to climatic warming," *in* Peters, R. L. and T. E. Lovejoy eds., *Proceedings of The Consequences of the Greenhouse Effect for Biological Diversity.* October 4–6, 1988. World Wildlife Fund. Washington, D.C.

Detweiler, R. P. and C. A. S. Hall. 1988. "Tropical forests and the global carbon cycle." *Science* 239: 42–47.

Dickinson, R. E. and B. Hanson. 1984. "Vegetation-albedo feedbacks" pp. 180–186 *in* Hansen, J. E. and T. Takahashi eds., *Climate Processes and Climate Sensitivity, Geophysical Monograph 29, Maurice Ewing Volume 5.* American Geophysical Union. Washington, D.C.

Dudek, D. J. 1988. *Offsetting New CO_2 Emissions.* Environmental Defense Fund. New York, New York.

Edlund, S. A. 1986. "Modern arctic vegetation distribution and its congruence with summer climate patterns," pp. 84–99 *in* French, H. M. ed., *Proceeding of the Impact of Climate Change on the Canadian Arctic, March 3–5, 1986, Orillia.* Ontario, Canadian Climate Program. Ottawa, Canada.

EESI. 1988. Energy Policy Statement: A Call to Action for the Next President and Congress. Environmental and Energy Study Institute. Washington, D.C.

Ehrlich, P. 1988. Personal communication with J. P. Myers.

Emanuel, K. A. 1987. "The dependence of hurricane intensity on climate." *Nature* 326: 483–485

Emanuel, W. R. et al. 1985a. "Climatic change and the broad-scale distribution of terrestrial ecosystem complexes." *Climatic Change* 7: 29–43.

———. 1985b. "Response to comment climatic change and the broad-scale distribution of terrestrial ecosystem complexes." *Climatic Change* 7: 457–460.

Environmental Protection Agency. 1988. The potential effects of global climate change on the United States, Vol. 2: National studies. Washington, D.C.

Fastook, J. L. 1984. "West Antarctica, the sea-level controlled marine instability: past and future," pp. 275–287 *in* Hansen, J. E. and T. Takahashi, eds., *Climate Processes and Climate Sensitivity, Geophysical Monograph 29, Maurice Ewing Volume 5.* American Geophysical Union. Washington, D.C.

Fay, J. 1988. Remarks to the Climate Institute's Symposium on the Impact of Climate Change on Wildlife. January 21–22, 1988. Washington, D.C.

Flavin, C. and A. B. Durning. 1988. "Building on success: The age of energy efficiency." *Worldwatch Paper* 82. Worldwatch Institute. Washington, D.C.

Franklin, J.F. et al. In press. "Effects of global climate change on forests in northwestern North America," in Peters, R.L. and T.E. Lovejoy eds., *Proceedings of the Consequences of the Greenhouse Effect for Biological Diversity.* October 4–8, 1988. World Wildlife Fund. Washington, D.C.

Frye, R. 1983. "Climatic change and fisheries management." *Natural Resources Journal* 23: 77–96.

Gilland, B. 1988. "Population, economic growth, and energy demand, 1985–2020." *Population and Development Review* 14(2): 233–244.

Graham, R. W. 1985. "Response of mammalian communities to environmental changes during the late quaternary," pp. 300–313 in Diamond, J. and T. J. Case eds., *Community Ecology.* Harper and Row. New York, New York.

Hansen, J. et al. 1984. "Climate sensitivity: Analysis of feedback mechanisms," pp. 130–163 in Hansen, J. E. and T. Takahashi eds., *Climate Processes and Climate Sensitivity, Geophysical Monograph 29, Maurice Ewing Volume 5.* American Geophysical Union. Washington, D.C.

———. 1988. "Prediction of near-term climate evolution: what can we tell decision makers now?" *Proceedings of the first North American Conference on Climate Change: A Cooperative Approach October 27–29, 1987, Washington, D.C.* Government Institutes, Inc. Rockville, Maryland.

Harris, S. 1987. "Effects of climatic change on northern permafrost." *Northern Perspectives* 15: 7–9.

Harte, J. and E. Hoffman. "Possible effect of acidic deposition on a Rocky Mountain population of the tiger salamander *Ambystoma tigrinum*." *Conservation Biology.* In press.

Hartshorn, G. 1989. "Effects of Global Warming on Tropical Forest Bio-Diversity," in Peters, R. L. and T. E. Lovejoy eds., *Proceedings of The Consequences of the Greenhouse Effect for Biological Diversity.* October 4–6, 1988. World Wildlife Fund. Washington, D.C.

Henderson-Sellers, A. and P. J. Robinson. 1986. *Contemporary Climatology.* John Wiley and Sons, Inc. (Longman Scientific and Technical, United Kingdom). New York.

Hoffman, J. S. 1984. "Estimates of future sea level rise" pp. 79–104. in Barth, M. C. and J. G. Titus eds., *Greenhouse Effect and Sea Level Rise: A Challenge for this Generation.* Van Nostrand Reinhold Company. New York.

Ives, J. D. 1974. "Permafrost," pp. 159–194 in Ives, D. D. and R. G. Barry, *Arctic and Alpine Environments.* Methuen, London.

James, F. C. 1970. "Geographic variation in birds and its relationship to climate." *Ecology* 51: 365–390.

JASON. 1980. "The long term impacts of increasing atmospheric carbon dioxide levels." Prepared for the U. S. Department of Energy, SRI International, JSR-79-04. Arlington, Virginia.

Jenne, R. L. 1988. Data from Climate Models; the CO_2 Warming. National Center for Atmospheric Research. Boulder, Colorado. Unpublished.

Johannes, R. E. and S. B. Betzer. 1975. "Introduction: Marine communities respond differently to pollution in the tropics than at higher latitudes." in Ferguson Wood, E. J. and R. E. Johannes eds., *Tropical Marine Pollution.* Elsevier Scientific Publishing Company. Amsterdam.

Kellogg, W. W. and Z. Zhao. 1988. "Sensitivity of soil moisture to doubling of carbon dioxide in climate model experiments. Part I: North America." *Journal of Climate* 1: 348–366.

Kerr, R. 1988. "Is the Greenhouse here?" *Science* 239: 559–561.

Kiehl, J. T. et al. 1988. "Response of a general circulation model to a prescribed Antarctic ozone hole." *Nature* 332: 501–504.

LaCock, G. D. 1986. "The Southern Oscillation, environmental anomalies, and mortality of two southern African seabirds." *Climatic Change* 8: 173–184.

LaMarche, V. C. 1973. "Holocene climatic fluctuations inferred from treeline fluctuations in White Mountains, California." *Quaternary Research* 3: 632–660.

Lashof, D. A. In press. "The dynamic Greenhouse: feedback processes that may influence future concentrations of atmospheric trace gases and climatic change." *Climatic Change.*

Leatherman, S. P. 1988. "Effects of sea level rise on beaches and coastal wetlands." *Proceedings of the first North American Conference on Climate Change: A Cooperative Approach, October 27–29, 1987, Washington, D.C.* Government Institutes, Inc. Rockville, Maryland.

———. 1988. Impacts of the Greenhouse Effect on Coastal Environments: Marshlands and Low-lying Population Areas. Presented before the U.S. Senate Committee on Energy and Natural Resources.

Lewin, R. 1987. "Domino effect invoked in Ice Age extinctions." *Science* 238: 1509–1510.

Lovejoy, T. E. "Conference overview," *in* Peters, R. L. and T. E. Lovejoy eds., *Proceedings of the Conference on the Consequences of the Greenhouse Effect for Biological Diversity.* October 4–6, 1988. World Wildlife Fund. Washington, D.C.

MacArthur, R. H. 1972. *Geographical Ecology: Patterns in the Distribution of Species.* Harper and Row. New York, New York.

MacKenzie, J. J. n. d. Breathing Easier: Taking Action on Climate Change, Air Pollution, and Energy Insecurity. World Resources Institute. Washington, D.C.

Manabe, S. and R. T. Wetherald. 1987. "Large-scale changes of soil wetness induced by an increase in atmospheric carbon dioxide." *Journal of Atmospheric Sciences* (April 15): 1211–1235.

Marland, G. 1988. The Prospect of Solving the CO_2 Problem through Global Reforestation. Oak Ridge Associated Universities, Institute for Energy Analysis. Oak Ridge, Tennessee, DOE/NBB-0082.

Meisner, J. D. et al. 1988. "The role of groundwater in the impact of climate warming on stream salmonines." *Fisheries* 13: 2–7.

Merlen, G. 1984. "The 1982–83 El Niño: some of its consequences for Galápagos wildlife." *Oryx* 18: 210–214.

Miller, W. F. et al. 1987. "Effect of rising carbon dioxide and potential climate change on loblolly pine distribution, growth, survival, and productivity," pp. 157–187 *in* Shands, W. E. and J. S. Hoffman eds., *The Greenhouse Effect, Climate Change, and U.S. Forests.* The Conservation Foundation. Washington, D.C.

Mintzer, I. 1987. A Matter of Degrees: The Potential for Controlling the Greenhouse Effect. World Resources Institute. Washington, D.C.

Mitchell, J. F. . B. and D. A. Warrilow. 1987. "Summer dryness in northern mid-latitudes due to increased CO_2." *Nature* 330: 238–240.

Moomaw, W. R. 1988. Proposed Near-Term Congressional Options for Responding to Global Climate Change. World Resources Institute. Washington, D.C.

Mooney, H. A. et al. 1987. "Exchange of materials between terrestrial ecosystems and the atmosphere." *Science* 238: 926–932.

Mrosovsky, N. and C. L. Yntema. 1980. "Temperature dependence of sexual differentiation in sea turtles: Implications for conservation practices." *Biological Conservation* 18: 271–280.

Myers, J. P. 1986. "Sex and gluttony on Delaware Bay." *Natural History* 95: 68–76.

NRC. 1987. Responding to Changes in Sea Level: Engineering Implications. National Academy Press. Washington, D.C.

Oechel, W. C. and G. H. Riechers. 1986. "Impacts of increasing CO₂ on natural vegetation, particularly the tundra," pp. 36–41 *in* Rosenzweig, C. and R. Dickinson eds., *Climate-Vegetation Interactions. Proceedings of a workshop held at NASA/Goddard Space Flight Center, January 27–29, 1986. Greenbelt, Maryland.* Office for Interdisciplinary Earth Studies. Boulder, Colorado.

Olson, J. S. n. d. The Role of the Biosphere in the Carbon Cycle. Oak Ridge Associated Universities, Institute for Energy Analysis. Oak Ridge, Tennessee.

Parks, T. 1954. "Experimental studies of interspecies competition. II. Temperature, humidity, and competition in two species of Tribolium." *Physiological Zoology* 27: 177–238.

Peltier, W. R. 1988. "Global sea level and Earth rotation." *Science* 240: 895–901.

Peters, R. L. and J. D. S. Darling. 1985. "The Greenhouse Effect and nature reserves." *BioScience* 35: 707–717.

Picton, H. D. 1978. "Climate and the reproduction of grizzly bears in Yellowstone National Park." *Nature* 274: 88–889.

———. 1984. "Climate and the prediction of reproduction of three ungulate species." *Journal of Applied Ecology* 21: 869–879.

———. et al. 1986. "Climate, carrying capacity, and the Yellowstone grizzly bear." *Proceedings-Grizzly Bear Habitat Symposium, April 30-May 2, 1985, Missoula, Montana.* U.S. Forest Service General Technical Report.

Postel, S. and L. Heise. 1988. "Reforesting the Earth." *Worldwatch Paper* 83. Worldwatch Institute. Washington, D.C.

Ramanathan, V. 1988. "The greenhouse theory of climate change: A test by an inadvertent global experiment." *Science* 240: 293–299.

———. et al. 1989. "Cloud-radiative forcing and climate: results from the Earth radiation budget experiment." *Science* 243: 57–63.

Raup, D. M. 1988. "Diversity crises in the geological past," pp. 51–57 *in* Wilson, E. O. ed., *Biodiversity.* National Academy Press. Washington, D.C.

Ray, G. C. *et al.* In press. "Overview of coastal-marine systems," *in* Peters, R. L. and T. E. Lovejoy eds., *Proceedings of The Consequences of the Greenhouse Effect for Biological Diversity.* October 4–6, 1988. World Wildlife Fund. Washington, D.C.

Ricklefs, R. E. 1970. "Stage of taxon cycle and distribution of birds on Jamaica, Greater Antilles." *Evolution* 24: 475–477.

Robinson, G. D. 1971. "The major pollutants: their emission and role in the atmosphere," pp. 156–166 *in* Matthews, W. H. *et al.* eds., *Man's Impact on the Climate.* MIT Press. Cambridge, Massachusetts.

Root, T. 1988. "Energy constraints on avian distributions and abundances." *Ecology* 69(2): 330–339.

Rosenberg, N. J. 1986. "A primer on climatic change: mechanisms, trends and projections." Resources for the Future (Renewable Resources Division). Washington, D.C.

Salati, E. 1986. "Amazon: forest and hydrological cycle," pp. 110–114 *in* Rosenzweig, C. and R. Dickinson eds., *Climate-Vegetation Interactions. Proceedings of a workshop held at NASA/Goddard Space Flight Center, January 27–29, 1986, Greenbelt, Maryland.* Office for Interdisciplinary Earth Studies. Boulder, Colorado.

Schlesinger, M. E. and J. Mitchell. 1987. "Climate model simulations of the equilibrium climatic response to increased carbon dioxide." *Reviews of Geophysics* 25: 760–798.

Schneider, S. 1987. "Climate modeling." *Scientific American* 256(5): 72–80.

———. 1988. Implications of Climate Change for Humanity. Talk given at the Climate Institute's Symposium on Climate Change and Economic Growth. June 13, 1988. New York, New York.

———. 1989. "The Greenhouse Effect: science and policy." *Science* 243: 771–781.

———. and R. Londer. 1984. *The Coevolution of Climate and Life.* Sierra Club Books. San Francisco, California.

Schonwiese, C. D. 1988. "Volcanism and air temperature variations in recent centuries," pp. 20–29 in Gregory, S. ed., *Recent Climatic Change.* Belhaven Press. London, England.

Scott, M. E. 1988. "The impact of infection and disease on animal populations: implications for conservation biology." *Conservation Biology* 2(1): 40–56.

Shepard, M. 1988. "The Greenhouse Effect: Earth's climate in transition." *EPRI Journal* (June): 5–15.

Siegenthaler, U. and Wenk, Th. 1984. "Rapid atmospheric CO_2 variations and oceanic circulation." *Nature* 308: 624–626.

Sofia, S. 1984. "Solar variability as a source of climate change." pp. 202–206 in Hansen, J. E. and T. Takahashi eds., *Climate Processes and Climate Sensitivity, Geophysical Monograph 29, Maurice Ewing Volume 5.* American Geophysical Union. Washington, D.C.

Soulé, M. E. 1986. *Conservation Biology: The Science and Scarcity of Diversity.* Sinauer Associates. Sunderland, Massachusetts.

Strain, B. R. and J. D. Cure. 1985. Direct Effects of Increasing Carbon Dioxide on Vegetation. Department of Energy. DOE/ER-0238. Washington, D.C.

Terborgh, J. and B. Winter. 1982. "Evolutionary circumstances of species with small ranges," pp. 587–600 in Prance, G. ed., *Biological Diversification in the Tropics. Proceedings of the Fifth International Symposium of the Association for Tropical Biology, Macuto Beach, Caracas, Venezuela, February 8–13, 1979.* Columbia University Press. New York, New York.

Titus, J. G. 1988. Greenhouse Effects, Sea Level Rise and Coastal Wetlands. Environmental Protection Agency. Washington, D.C.

Trabalka, J. R., (ed.). 1985. Atmospheric Carbon Dioxide and the Global Carbon Cycle. Department of Energy. DOE/ER-0239. Washington, D.C.

Turner, J. R. G. et al. 1988. "British bird species distributions and energy theory." *Nature* 335: 539–541.

U. S. Forest Service (Pacific Northwest Region). 1988. The Final Supplement to the Environmental Impact Statement for an Amendment to the Pacific Northwest Regional Guide: Spotted Owl Guidelines. U.S. Department of Agriculture. Washington, D.C.

van der Hammen, T. 1984. "Paleoecology of Tropical South America," pp. 60–66 in Prance, G. ed., *Biological Diversification in the Tropics. Proceedings of the Fifth International Symposium of the Association for Tropical Biology, Macuto Beach, Caracas, Venezuela, February 8–13, 1979.* Columbia University Press. New York, New York.

Walker, D. A. et al. 1987. "Height and growth rings of *Salix lanata* ssp. *richardsonii* along the coastal temperature gradient of northern Alaska." *Canadian Journal of Botany* 65: 988–993.

———. 1987. "Cumulative impacts of oil fields on northern Alaskan landscapes." *Science* 238: 757–761.

Webb, T. and T. M. L. Wigley. 1985. "What past climates can indicate about a warmer world," in MacCracken, M. C. and F. M. Luther eds., *Projecting the Climatic Effects of Increasing Carbon Dioxide.* Department of Energy. DOE/ER-0237. Washington, D.C.

Webber, P. J. 1988. Personal communication with J. P. Myers.

Wetherald, R. 1988. Personal communication with R. T. Lester.

———. and S. Manabe. 1988. "Cloud feedback processes in a general circulation model." *Journal of the Atmospheric Sciences* 45(8): 1397–1415.

Wigley, T. M. L. and S. C. B. Raper. 1987. "Thermal expansion of sea water associated with global warming." *Nature* 330: 127–131.

Woodward, F. I. 1987. *Climate and Plant Distribution.* Cambridge University Press. Cambridge.

Woodwell, G. M. et al. 1978. "The biota and the world carbon budget." *Science* 199: 141–146.

————. 1986. "Global warming and what we can do about it." *Amicus Journal* (Fall): 8–12.

WRI and IIED. 1988. *World Resources 1988–89*. World Resources Institute and International Institute for Environment and Development, Washington, D.C. (In collaboration with the United Nations Environmental Programme). Basic Books. New York, New York.

Robert Lester is an environmental policy analyst in National Audubon's Science Division.
J.P. Myers, Ph.D., is National Audubon Society's senior vice-president for Science and Sanctuaries.

The eight coastal southeastern states have rich wetland resources that are part of their environmental, economic, and cultural foundations. These wetlands are being destroyed at a pace that dismays all but the most optimistic of conservationists. Some of the states are acting aggressively to stem the loss. *South Florida Water Management District*

Conserving Southeastern Coastal Wetlands

Anne D. Southworth

INTRODUCTION

It is well documented that the United States is experiencing significant wetland losses nationwide. Today there are fewer than 95 million acres of wetlands left in the coterminous United States, about 45 percent of the wetlands present at the time of European settlement. The United States continues to lose some 300,000 to 500,000 acres of inland and coastal wetlands each year. Even more troubling is the fact that the large majority of wetland losses are concentrated in the southeastern part of the country, the region that includes 83 percent of all remaining coastal wetlands in the coterminous United States (Alexander *et al.* 1986). From the mid-1950s to the mid-1970s, North Carolina, South Carolina, Georgia, Florida, Alabama, Mississippi, and Louisiana experienced a combined loss of 312,000 acres of estuarine wetlands—5.6 percent of the estuarine wetlands in the lower 48 states (Hefner and Brown 1985).

Coastal wetland loss is critical because the marshes and swamps that line the South Atlantic and Gulf coasts are extremely valuable; they boast high net primary productivity, provide habitat for significant populations of migratory waterfowl, and serve as important nursery and spawning grounds for numerous fish and shellfish species. Wetland losses diminish the coasts' natural ability to lessen flood and storm damage, minimize erosion, and improve water quality. Losses in the Southeast are particularly significant because coastal wetlands are less common than their inland counterparts and are subject to severe development pressures.

Congress and a number of state legislatures have developed a variety of regulatory and nonregulatory programs to protect wetlands. The Clean Water Act Section 404 program, the Coastal Zone Management Act, state coastal wetland laws, planning programs, restoration programs, taxation and acquisition programs, and a variety of other efforts have slowed losses and at least helped bide time. These programs, however, have not been able to stop losses, largely because their statutory objective does not mandate "no loss" of wetlands, or even "no net loss" of wetlands. Existing wetland laws are unable to provide comprehensive protection because they require that wetland protection be balanced with development needs. While this approach has resulted in the preservation of some of the region's remaining wetlands, no one is able to determine exactly how many acres have been saved because most agencies administering wetland regulatory programs have not kept inventories to measure what the laws have achieved. As the Southeast begins to assess more rigorously its wetlands problem, it must stand back and determine the nature of wetland losses and the effectiveness of programs that have an impact on wetlands.

STATUS OF SOUTHEASTERN COASTAL WETLANDS

The Resource

The eight coastal southeastern states from North Carolina to Texas are rich in coastal wetland resources; they have 2,799 miles of coastline with 29,900 miles of tidal shoreline (Shalowitz 1964, Orlando *et al.* 1988). The region's relatively flat coastal plain and abundant rainfall of 40 to 60 inches per year have been conducive to wetland formation. In addition, much of the South Atlantic and Gulf coast is shielded from storms by barrier islands. These islands deflect the brunt of the wave action that hits the coastline, and their inland side provides sheltered, saline environments where wetland vegetation thrives.

Coastal counties in the Southeast contain a mixture of saltwater and freshwater wetlands. Estuarine emergent wetlands,[1] or salt

---

1. Tidal wetlands characterized by erect, rooted, herbaceous hydrophytes, excluding mosses and lichens. The vegetation is usually perennial (Cowardin *et al.* 1979).

marshes, are particularly characteristic of the region. The marshes are dominated by rooted, herbaceous hydrophytes such as smooth cordgrass (*Spartina alterniflora*), saltmeadow cordgrass (*Spartina patens*), saltgrass (*Distichlis spicata*), black needlerush (*Juncus roemerianus*), and in less saline areas by Olney threesquare (*Scirpus olneyi*) and saltmarsh fleabanes (*Pluchea* spp.). Also common are estuarine scrubshrub wetlands[2] and estuarine wooded wetlands,[3] including all of the nation's 400,000 to 650,000 acres of mangrove swamp (Odum *et al.* 1982).

Freshwater wetlands also are present in coastal areas, primarily along tidal rivers and bays. Palustrine emergent wetlands[4] (freshwater marshes) are particularly abundant in the Mississippi delta of Louisiana, where thousands of acres of cattails (*Typha* spp.), wild rice (*Zizania aquatica*), pickerelweed (*Pontederia cordata*), and spatterdocks (*Numphar* spp.) grow. Freshwater swamps, including wooded and shrub swamps, are found in southeastern coastal counties but are typically considered inland wetlands rather than coastal wetlands.

Acreage Statistics

The precise quantity of existing wetlands is unknown because wetland acreages are constantly changing, and existing mapping techniques have a slight margin of error. Since 1976, the U.S. Fish and Wildlife Service (FWS) has been locating, classifying, and mapping wetlands in the United States under the National Wetlands Inventory. While the South Atlantic and Gulf coasts have been mapped completely, FWS is remapping parts of southern Louisiana to obtain more accurate estimates of the area's wetland acreage.

The most recent estimates of coastal wetland acreage in the Southeast are found in two studies: Hefner and Brown (1985) and Alexander *et al.* (1986). Acreage estimates in Hefner and Brown (1985) are based on 2,221 of the 3,635 stratified random plots identified and used by FWS to determine wetland status and trends in the coterminous U.S between the mid-1950s and the mid-1970s (Frayer *et al.* 1983). In contrast, Alexander (1986) compiled wetland inventory data from coastal counties. Alexander's data were gathered from the National Wetlands Inventory, academia, and a variety of federal, state, and local agencies and then used to estimate acreages of salt marsh, fresh marsh, tidal

2. Tidal wetlands characterized by woody vegetation less than 20 feet tall. Vegetation may be a successional stage leading to forested wetlands; common plants include tree shrubs, young trees, and trees whose growth is stunted by environmental conditions (Cowardin *et al.* 1979).

3. Tidal wetlands characterized by woody vegetation that is 20 feet or taller (Cowardin *et al.* 1979).

4. Nontidal wetlands characterized by erect, rooted, herbaceous hydrophytes (Cowardin *et al.*).

flats, and swamp. Where possible, Alexander *et al.* excluded freshwater wetlands that were not influenced by coastal processes.

Hefner and Brown's study reports that, in the mid-1970s, approximately 4.07 million acres of estuarine wetlands were present in the southeastern states, excluding Texas. This figure includes 3.09 million acres of intertidal emergent wetlands and 565,000 acres of intertidal scrub-shrub and forested wetlands. The authors calculated palustrine wetland acreage but did not differentiate between coastal and inland regions.

The Alexander study concluded that the 106 coastal counties that comprise most of the South Atlantic and Gulf coasts have approximately 9.4 million acres of wetlands (see Table 1). States with the greatest coastal wetland acreages include Louisiana, 2.9 million acres; North Carolina, 2.4 million acres; and Florida, 2.2 million acres. Swamps register as the most common wetland type (4.3 million acres), largely because the study could not differentiate noncoastal swamps from coastal swamps. As a result, coastal acreage estimates for North Carolina, which has a good deal of freshwater swampland, are certainly overestimated.

Neither study included estimates of sea grasses, which are even more difficult to map than wetlands because they are usually submerged. According to the National Marine Fisheries Service, most of the nation's sea grasses are located in the Southeast. Like associated wetlands, this aquatic vegetation provides valuable fisheries habitat. If counted with wetlands, seagrasses would increase total marine vege-

Table 1. Wetlands in Southeastern Coastal Counties (wetland acres [100s]).

State	Salt marsh	Fresh marsh	Tidal flats	Swamp	State total	Percent of wetlands in U.S.[a]
North Carolina	1,588	920	n/a	21,075	23,583	20.8
South Carolina	3,695	645	n/a	n/a	4,340	3.8
Georgia	3,743	315	95	2,860	7,013	6.2
Florida	5,272	4,609	n/a	12,297	22,178	19.6
Alabama	146	106	n/a	1,513	1,765	1.6
Mississippi	640	40	n/a	760	1,440	1.3
Louisiana	17,486	6,888	n/a	4,372	28,746	25.4
Texas	3,904	787	n/a	403	5,094	4.5
South Atlantic subtotal	9,985	5,714	95	26,525	42,324	37.3
Gulf subtotal	26,489	8,596	0	16,755	51,840	45.9
Southeast subtotal	36,474	14,310	95	43,280	94,164	83.2

Source: Adapted from Alexander *et al.* 1986.

[a]Coterminous United States.

tation habitat acreage by at least 40 percent (Mager and Ruebsamen in press).

Wetland Losses

The Southeast is losing wetlands at an alarming rate. While certain local areas within the region are gaining wetlands through wetland creation and restoration projects, these additions are not sufficient to offset wetland losses. Hefner and Brown (1985), using data from the FWS' wetlands status and trends report (Frayer *et al.* 1983), estimate that between the mid-1950s and the mid-1970s, the Southeast, excluding Texas, lost a total of 312,000 acres of estuarine wetlands, including 301,000 acres of saltmarsh and 17,000 acres[5] of estuarine scrub-shrub and forested wetland. This represents a 7-percent loss of the then-existing total estuarine wetland resources in the Southeast. The most severe wetland losses occurred in coastal salt marshes in Louisiana (183,000 acres) and Florida (15,000 acres) (Frayer *et al.* 1983).

In Louisiana, wetland losses may have escalated to as high as 32,000 acres (50 square miles) annually, compared to 20,000 acres (31 square miles) in the late 1970s (Gagliano 1981, 1984). If losses continue at that rate, four of Louisiana's parishes[6] will become submerged within a century; one of them, Plaquemine Parish, will disappear within 50 years.

As mandated by Congress in the Emergency Wetlands Resources Act of 1986 (16 U.S.C.A. 3931), FWS is working to provide a new estimate of wetlands status and trends for the nation. FWS' report, which will include new loss statistics, must be submitted to Congress by September 30, 1990. When published, the report will contain the most accurate estimate of wetlands status and loss in the Southeast.

Causes of Wetland Losses

Coastal wetland losses in the Southeast are caused by both natural and human activities. Hefner and Brown (1985) report that approximately two-thirds of estuarine wetlands lost in the Southeast between the mid-1950s and the mid-1970s can be attributed to forces that convert wetlands to deepwater habitat.[7] The remaining one-third was attributed to urban development. This statistic is somewhat misleading as it suggests that wetland submergence was chiefly responsible for coastal wetland loss in most states. In fact, this has been true only in Louisiana. In other states, coastal wetland loss has been caused prin-

5. The standard error of the estimate is equal to or larger than the estimate.
6. The Louisiana term for county.
7. Deepwater habitat is defined as permanently flooded lands where water is too deep to support emergent wetland vegetation (Cowardin *et al.* 1979).

cipally by urban development and loss rates have been correlated with an increase in population density (Gosselink and Baumann 1980).

Coastal wetland loss is to be expected, given the increased development and resource extraction activities in coastal regions since World War II. Between 1960 and 1985, the population living within 50 miles of the U.S. coast increased from 92.7 million people to 125 million people—52 percent of the population in the coterminous United States. Population increases have been particularly rapid in Florida and Texas; Florida's population has increased more than 400 percent since 1950 (U.S. Department of Commerce 1988). Clearly, coastal settlement is attractive; coastal areas are often scenic and ideal locations for increasingly popular outdoor recreation. The attraction of the coast has been particularly strong because there have been relatively few severe hurricanes and winter storms in the South Atlantic and Gulf in the past half century to discourage settlement.

As coastal settlement has boomed, there has been a commensurate increase in the number of wetland acres dredged, filled, and drained. Coastal wetlands also have been drained to meet demands for more agricultural land. Industrial interests have been drawn to the coast because of the region's wealth of natural resources including fisheries, oil, gas, phosphate, sand, and minerals, and abundant water supply that can be used for cooling water and for waste disposal. To gain access to many of these resources, industry and the U.S. Army Corps of Engineers have carved thousands of miles of canals through coastal marshes. These canals disrupt the hydrology of wetlands and may result in saltwater intrusion. The problem is exacerbated over time as canals widen due to erosion and more wetlands are displaced by open saltwater.

Coastal development has also required the construction of more flood-control structures. Nowhere has this been more apparent than in Louisiana where today only the Atchafalaya branch of the Mississippi is allowed to flow naturally to the Gulf. Levees, dikes, dams, seawalls, and other control structures have increased wetlands loss by preventing nutrient and sediment-laden water from replenishing wetland resources. In southern Louisiana, for example, levees have prevented the Mississippi River from depositing its sediment on the river delta as it has for thousands of years. With no place to settle, some 183 million tons of sediment per year are being channeled out into the Gulf and dropped over the continental shelf. As a result, the delta is gradually sinking.

In Louisiana, and to a lesser extent in other states, wetlands have been converted to deepwater habitat because accretion in wetland areas has been unable to keep pace with sea level rise and coastal subsidence. Sea level rise has had an important but minor impact on wetland loss since the rate of rise is relatively slow, estimated at approximately 1.2 millimeters per year (Fish and Wildlife Service 1982). Its impact will undoubtedly increase, however, if the global climate continues to warm and polar ice caps melt at an accelerated rate (see "Global Warming, Climatic Disruption, and Biological Diversity" in this volume). Although it is hard to isolate the effects of sea level rise from those of subsidence, recent studies suggest that 80 to 90 percent of the relative sea level rise (the cumulative effect of sea level rise and coastal subsidence) that occurs in southeastern Louisiana may be attributed to subsidence of the coastal plain (Louisiana Department of Natural Resources 1987). Subsidence is a natural process that occurs as marsh sediments and vegetation become heavy and compact, driving out the water between clay and silt particles. Humans, however, have greatly increased the rate of subsidence by extracting oil, gas, and groundwater from coastal areas. A study of an industrial area near Baton Rouge, Louisiana, found that the area sank an average of three feet between 1964 and 1969, a period when the community was extracting 110 million gallons of water from the ground each day (Wintz 1970).

Other natural forces also adversely affect wetlands. Wave action breaks up and de-roots wetland vegetation and erodes wetland soils. The impact of waves is particularly severe during storms and hurricanes when waves are highly energized and the ocean floods less saline areas. In 1988, for example, hurricanes Florence and Gilbert eroded 50 to 100 feet of shoreline along barrier islands south of New Orleans, despite the fact that the brunt of the storm did not hit the Louisiana coast. In addition, musk rats, nutria, and other animals have been known to decimate acres of coastal wetland by eating large quantities of wetland vegetation.

Impacts on Fish and Wildlife

Experts generally agree that significant wetland losses have a notable effect on fish and wildlife, particularly resident species, because habitat is severely altered or destroyed. Unfortunately, the precise impact of wetland losses on particular species may be difficult if not impossible to determine. In as much as the loss of wetland habitat is one of many factors that may affect a fish or wildlife population, it may not be the sole reason for the population's decline. To date, scientists have hypothesized a correlation between the decline of certain species and wetland destruction and identified species that are threatened with extinction due to loss of coastal habitat. Some examples:

Fish and Shellfish. Most estuarine fish and shellfish depend on wetlands during at least one phase of their lifecycle. Wetlands are particularly valuable nursery and spawning grounds because they produce large amounts of organic detritus. Estuarine fish scientists estimate that about 96 percent of the commercial, and 70 percent of the recreational, fishery resources in the Southeast are estuarine-dependent (Mager and Ruebsamen in press), including such species as menhaden (*Brevoortia tyrannus*), Atlantic croaker (*Micropogonias undulatus*), red drum (*Sciaenops ocellatus*), blue crab (*Callinectes sapidus*), brown shrimp (*Penaeus aztecus*), white shrimp (*Penaeus setiferus*), and eastern oyster (*Crassostrea virginica*). The value of wetlands to shellfish is clearly seen in a study demonstrating a direct correlation between shrimp production and the expanse of coastal marsh (Turner 1977). Moreover, areas with a high marsh to open water ratio have proven to have particularly high menhaden yields (Cavit 1979). Fish and shellfish industries are often key components of local economies. Between 1981 and 1985 commercial landings in the Southeast totalled 13.6 billion pounds of fish and shellfish with a dockside value of $3.8 billion (National Marine Fisheries Service 1983, 1985, 1986). In 1985, recreational fishermen spent $3.4 billion on saltwater angling in the Southeast (Schmied and Burgess in press).

Waterfowl. More than half of the migratory waterfowl that travel through the Mississippi Flyway depend on wetlands in the Gulf for shelter, roosting, and feeding during fall and winter. Unfortunately, the marshes that provide the most valuable vegetation to wintering waterfowl are disappearing the fastest. FWS biologists believe that a number of waterfowl may have changed their wintering areas as a result of significant habitat loss along the Mississippi Flyway, settling for less adequate habitats. This may well be the reason that a number of waterfowl are returning to breeding grounds in poor physical condition, which in turn affects breeding. If such trends continue, waterfowl production could be affected (Bidwell 1988).

Because of its critical habitat value to wintering waterfowl, large parts of the Southeast, including coastal areas in Texas, Louisiana, Mississippi, South Carolina, and North Carolina have been identified as waterfowl habitat requiring protection under the North American Waterfowl Management Plan. Decreased waterfowl production would be a great financial as well as biological loss. Waterfowl hunting in the Mississippi Flyway alone is currently valued at $58 million yearly (U.S. Army Corps of Engineers 1988).

Other Birds. Southeastern coastal wetlands support numerous other migratory birds, including clapper rail (*Rallus longirostris*), king rail (*Rallus elegans*), sora (*Porzana carolina*), common snipe (*Capella gallinago*), and purple ganule (*Porphyrula martinica*). Nonmigratory birds are also abundant. More than 874,000 colonial waterbirds, representing

Wetland-dependent birds, such as this white ibis, have suffered dramatic declines in the southeastern states due to habitat degradation. *Manuel A. Rodriguez*

26 species, nest in the saltwater marshes and barrier islands of Louisiana, Alabama, and Mississippi (Portnoy 1977).

Furbearers. Coastal wetlands in the Southeast support nutria, muskrats, and other furbearers—animals that are both economically and ecologically valuable. Louisiana has become the largest fur-producing state in the nation; each year it produces 40 percent of the nation's wild furs and hides, worth some $17 million annually (U.S. Army Corps of Engineers 1988). Most of these furbearing animals inhabit wetlands.

Endangered Species. Southeastern coastal wetlands support a number of federally endangered and fish and wildlife species, including red wolf (*Canis rufus*), Florida manatee (*Trichechus manatus latirostis*), Key deer (*Odocoileus virginianus clavium*), American peregrine falcon (*Falco peregrinus anatum*), whooping crane (*Grus americana*), eskimo curlew (*Numenius borealis*), American alligator (*Alligator mississippiensis*), American crocodile (*Crocodylus acutus*), and shortnose sturgeon (*Acipenser brevirostrum*).

Plants. A number of rare plant species also occur in southeastern wetlands. These include: Long's bullrush (*Scirpus longii*), a rush found in marshes along the Atlantic coast; sensitive jointvetch (*Aeschynomene virginica*), a herbaceous plant found in tidal marshes of North

Carolina; and skullcap (*Scutellaria thieretii*), a herbaceous plant found in the brackish marshes of Louisiana.

FEDERAL REGULATORY PROGRAMS

Clean Water Act Section 404 Program

Section 404 of the Clean Water Act (33 U.S.C.A. 1344) authorizes the principal federal regulatory program with a direct impact on wetlands. Under the law, the Army Corps of Engineers regulates the disposal of dredge or fill material in waters of the United States, including the deposition of such material in wetlands. Landowners wishing to undertake an activity in their wetland involving the discharge of dredged or fill material must first obtain a permit from the Corps. The Section 404 program, however, does not regulate all activities that adversely affect wetlands; activities such as draining, channelization, excavation, clearing of wetland vegetation, excavation of wetland soils, and wetland flooding do not require a permit unless there is a discharge of dredged or fill material into the wetland associated with these activities.

The Corps administers the Section 404 program jointly with the Environmental Protection Agency (EPA). Before a Corps district office issues a permit, it conducts a "public interest review" to ensure that the proposed activity is in the public interest. In its review, the district office considers a wide range of factors, including "conservation, economics, aesthetics, general environmental concerns, wetlands, cultural values, fish and wildlife values, land use, navigation, shore erosion and accretion, recreation, water supply and conservation, water quality, energy needs, safety, food and fiber production, mineral needs, and in general, the needs and welfare of the people" (33 C.F.R. §320.4[a][1]). According to its regulations, the Corps also must take into account the cumulative impact of wetland conversions in deciding whether or not to grant a permit.

The Corps must follow EPA's 404(b)(1) Guidelines (40 C.F.R. §230), which set environmental standards for proposed projects. The guidelines prohibit the discharge of dredge or fill material unless there are no "practicable alternatives" to the proposed activity. They also require the Corps to deny the permit if actions are not taken to minimize adverse environmental effects, or if the Corps determines that the activity will significantly degrade the aquatic ecosystem or violate other laws, such as the Endangered Species Act or state water quality laws. Without a permit, the landowner or other party is unable to deposit fill legally. However, denial of a permit does not permanently protect the resource. Conceivably, a developer could later propose a new project to develop the same site. At that time, the Corps would reinitiate its public interest review.

EPA, FWS, and the National Marine Fisheries Service (NMFS) are generally given notice of permit applications and may submit recommendations to the Corps based on the potential impact on wildlife habitat and fisheries resources. EPA's authority goes even further: if the agency finds that granting a proposed Corps permit will have an unacceptable adverse effect on water supplies, shellfish beds, fisheries (including spawning and breeding areas), wildlife, or recreational areas, it can use its authority under Section 404(c) to veto the Corps' permit decision. The Corps and EPA are also given authority to take enforcement actions against those who discharge without a permit or who violate permit conditions. They may revoke or suspend a 404 permit; require restoration of an illegally altered area; seek criminal, civil, or administrative penalties; or pursue a number of these alternatives simultaneously.

While the success of the program in protecting wetlands has not been precisely quantified, estimates suggest that Section 404 may save as few as 50,000 acres of wetlands from conversion each year (Office of Technology Assessment 1984). This is due in part to the existence of Section 404(f), which exempts ongoing agriculture and silviculture, the construction of drainage ditches, road maintenance, and other activities from regulation. The Corps' often narrow interpretation of its jurisdiction to regulate certain wetlands or activities may be a factor as well. The agency also makes use of a number of "general permits" for activities that are substantially similar in nature, but which individually or cumulatively have a minor impact on the environment. Unfortunately, the impact of many of the projects that are allowed under the general permits can, in fact, be substantial.

In the end, while a number of projects are redesigned in the permitting process, relatively few permits (individual or general) are actually denied. The Office of Technology Assessment (1984) estimates that less than 3 percent of permits are denied nationwide and as few as 0.64 percent are denied in Louisiana (Houck 1988).

In FY 1986, for example, the Corps district office in Jacksonville, Florida, considered permit applications that would have converted a total of 1,557 acres of wetland; ultimately, the Corps authorized the conversion of 1,187 acres. To mitigate these losses, the Corps required applicants to create a total of 168 new wetland acres. Thus the net loss was over a thousand acres. In addition, the Corps required applicants to enhance 3,998 acres of existing wetlands (General Accounting Office 1988).

Acreage statistics compiled by NMFS are somewhat more positive. Mager and Ruebsamen (in press) report that 169,029 acres of the

Table 2. Acres of Habitat Involved in NMFS Reviews of Corps Permit Applications (primarily Section 404 and Rivers and Harbors Act Section 10 permits) in the Southeast, 1981 to 1987.

Year	Number of permits sampled	Acres proposed for alteration	Acres not challenged by NMFS	Acres rejected by NMFS	Acres of mitigation required
1981	811	7,949	2,868	5,081	2,471
1982	1,059	81,184	21,831	59,353	7,910
1983	825	20,778	8,658	12,120	26,775
1984	888	8,606	3,981	4,625	54,050
1985	1,802	65,670	11,161	54,509	19,200
1986	969	90,559	70,838	19,721	49,713
1987	1,054	21,755	8,135	13,620	7,139
Total	7,408	296,501	127,472	169,029	167,258

Source: Mager and Ruebsamen in press.

296,501 acres of coastal wetlands that permit applicants proposed to alter between 1981 and 1987 were conserved. An almost equal number of wetlands acres were either created or restored to compensate for losses (see Table 2).

In September 1988, the General Accounting Office released a report on the Corps of Engineers' administration of the Section 404 program. Data for the report were collected from five Corps districts. The report, and related testimony presented before the House Committee on Public Works and Transportation, Subcommittee on Investigations and Oversight,[8] highlight many of the problems that occur in administering the 404 program in the Southeast.

In its report, the General Accounting Office notes that the program's capacity to protect wetlands is limited because jurisdiction is limited. In addition, the Corps often does not follow the 404(b)(1) Guidelines; if it does, it uses the guidelines as only one factor to consider in its public interest review. In a May 1987 memo to the EPA Office of Wetlands Protection, EPA Region VI[9] stated: "In our experience for the majority of cases we have seen, the Corps practice is to issue permits for whatever the applicant wants with very little consideration to the "test" within the Guidelines that address prohibition and alternatives, or EPA stated concerns" (General Accounting Office 1988). EPA, FWS, and NMFS all believe that the Corps does not give enough consideration to practicable alternatives to proposed development projects or to the cumulative impacts of individual projects on natural resources.

The General Accounting Office found that while the Corps always considers the recommendations of the resource agencies, it does not

8. Hearing before the House Committee on Public Works and Transportation, Subcommittee on Investigations and Oversight, September 14, 1988.

9. Region VI includes Texas, Louisiana, New Mexico, Oklahoma, and Arkansas.

always accept and implement them. Since 1981, NMFS has tracked the number of its recommendations on 404 permit applications that the seven Corps offices in the Southeast[10] have accepted, partially accepted, or denied. In 1987, Corps districts issued permits for filling eight percent more wetlands acres than NMFS accepted for conversion. Agreement between NMFS and the Corps on the acres that could be converted varied widely between Corps districts, ranging from total agreement in the Wilmington district to agreement on less than 20 percent of the permits in the Mobile district (Mager and Ruebsamen in press). In particular, resource agencies have noted a significant decline in the number of their recommendations accepted by the Corps in the Jacksonville district since 1982, when the Corps instituted Reagan Administration regulatory reforms requiring offices to speed up permit processing (General Accounting Office 1988).

While the resource agencies often disagree with Corps permit decisions, they seldom appeal them. Appeals are time consuming and resource intensive; furthermore, permit decisions are rarely overturned. As a result, resource agencies have generally preferred to work with the permit applicants to mitigate losses rather than to chance an unsuccessful appeal. EPA has completed only four 404(c) veto actions involving projects in coastal wetlands of the Southeast as of January 1, 1989, and the number of acres of coastal wetlands actually saved by these actions has been minimal.

Another point of controversy is the Corps current practice of compensating for wetland losses. The majority of the 404 permits issued in the Southeast contains mitigation conditions. While this practice in itself is not a problem and is often necessary, the Corps moves much too readily to offsite compensation—wetlands enhancement, restoration, or creation—as the preferred mitigation technique. As a result, the Corps often fails to fully address the impact of the activity on the site. EPA and FWS have consistently held that compensation for adverse impacts to wetlands should only be used as a *last resort* where impacts cannot be *avoided* or *minimized*. NMFS has cautiously supported wetlands compensation as a mitigation alternative in an attempt to offset allowed conversions. In 1987, NMFS offices in the Southeast recommended that 7,301.8 acres be mitigated to compensate for the 7,515.7 acres that it agreed could be converted (Mager and Ruebsamen in press). In doing so, however, the agency cautions that habitat creation is a relatively new, experimental technique that should be studied and used with care until perfected.

EPA and the Corps also give relatively low priority to monitoring and enforcement activities in the Southeast despite the fact that 20 percent of permit holders violate permit conditions in the region (Ma-

10. Wilmington, North Carolina; Charleston, South Carolina; Savannah, Georgia; Jacksonville, Florida; Mobile, Alabama; New Orleans, Louisiana; and Galveston, Texas.

ger and Thayer 1986). The Corps' Jacksonville district typically spends only five percent of the time that it allocates to the entire 404 program work on surveillance activities. As a result, it has only inspected 0 to 15 percent of the projects undergoing construction and 0 to 30 percent of the projects that have completed construction (General Accounting Office 1988).

Primarily because there are so few compliance inspections, the Corps rarely revokes or suspends a permit. To date, the Corps and EPA have taken few enforcement actions. An EPA official in Region VI claims that there has essentially been no functioning 404 enforcement program in the region over the last year and that the office is only just starting to issue administrative orders (General Accounting Office 1988). Enforcement efforts in Region IV [11] have also been minimal because of personnel changes and shortages, and limited support from the Office of Regional Counsel. Between FY 1984 and FY 1988, Region IV issued 16 administrative orders and no administrative penalty orders, [12] and referred only one civil and one criminal case to the Department of Justice (Munson 1988). EPA and the Corps are working to increase their wetland enforcement efforts in the Southeast as seen in ongoing efforts to train employees in Section 404 enforcement. However, until a strong enforcement program is in place, violations are likely to continue.

Clean Water Act Section 401

The Section 401 Water Quality Certification program is another tool that can be used to protect southeastern coastal wetlands. Under Section 401 of the Clean Water Act (33 U.S.C.A. 1341), states have the authority to review federally licensed or permitted activities that may result in a discharge to waters of the United States. If the state finds that a proposed activity may not meet state water quality standards, and the applicant for the required license or permit is unwilling to modify the activity to meet those standards, the state can refuse certification and thereby prevent the license or permit from being issued. It may also place conditions on a 401 certification.

Theoretically, Section 401 is a powerful tool for protecting wetlands in that it provides the broad authority of the Clean Water Act to

11. Region IV includes North Carolina, South Carolina, Georgia, Florida, Alabama, Mississippi, Kentucky, Tennessee, and the Canal Zone.

12. An administrative order is an order that requires the violator to comply with the conditions of the Section 404 program. It is issued by the Regional Administrator under authority of Section 309(a) of the Clean Water Act. Authority for administrative penalty orders under Section 309(g) of the Clean Water Act was added to the agencies' arsenal of enforcement authorities under the Water Quality Act of 1987 (Pub. L. No. 100–4, 101 Stat. 7 [1987]).

protect the chemical, physical, and biological integrity of U.S. waters (Ransel and Fish 1988). However, it only applies to activities that require a federal license or permit, including activities regulated by Section 404 of the Clean Water Act, Section 402 of the Clean Water Act, Section 9 or 10 of the Rivers and Harbors Act, and the Federal Power Act.

In the Southeast and other parts of the country, water quality certification has been used primarily in conjunction with Section 404 permits. In South Carolina, for example, 95 percent of the certifications issued by the Department of Health and Environmental Control's Division of Water Quality involve Section 404 permits; the remainder involve Section 10 permits, Coast Guard permits and Federal Energy Regulatory Commission licenses (Cowles *et al.* 1986).

Although the Section 401 program has been in existence since the Federal Water Pollution Control Act was passed in 1972, southeastern states have rarely used it to protect wetlands. Few states even have kept track of the number of times they have used their Section 401 authority to condition or deny activities that involve wetlands; as a result, there is no database on the program.

According to some 401 certification personnel, failure to meet state water quality standards is almost never the reason for denying a federal permit for an activity involving wetland alteration, and is only occasionally the reason for modification of a proposed project. Part of the problem is that state administrators often do not look on Section 401 as a wetlands protection tool. As one Louisiana official stated, "[We're] not in the wetlands protection business, that's not what 401 is all about" (Cowles *et al.* 1986). This viewpoint has been aggravated by the fact that none of the southeastern states has adopted state water quality regulations in which wetlands are specifically defined as surface waters of the state. Because of the absence of the term wetlands from the definition of state waters, state decisionmakers may argue that wetlands are outside the purview of the 401 water quality certification process.

Section 401 certification managers also have been known to rely on the federal resource agencies to compile data and convince the Corps to modify projects that do not meet state water quality standards. But if the federal agencies fail to act, or are unsuccessful at convincing the Corps to modify or deny a permit, the state has in essence waived its right to condition or deny certification to a project because it did not act within the one-year time period allocated for certification.

While Section 401 has been used sparingly, interest in the program has grown tremendously in the past year, due largely to the efforts of EPA's Office of Wetlands Protection and the Environmental Law Institute. With the help of the Institute, EPA has convened state managers and created a handbook for states entitled *401 Certification and Wetlands: Opportunities and Guidelines* (Ransel and Fish 1988). As a result of these initiatives and growing concern over wetland losses, some states are considering strengthening their 401 programs. South Carolina, for example, is in the process of drafting regulations for its 401 program. Concerned over the number of acres of marsh that are being filled, North Carolina officials are planning to use Section 401 more frequently to deny "after-the-fact" Section 404 permits (permits that are issued by the Corps after a site has been converted without a permit).

Like Section 404, Section 401 was not designed to provide comprehensive wetlands protection. By providing the states the opportunity to condition or deny permits, however, it increases the probability that proposed projects requiring a federal license or permit will be more carefully scrutinized and be less damaging to wetland resources.

STATE REGULATORY PROGRAMS

Background

The eight states that line the South Atlantic and Gulf coasts have established a number of programs that regulate activities in coastal wetlands. These programs vary greatly from state to state both in their intent and scope, but all offer some kind of protection to wetlands. With the exception of Georgia and Texas, all states developed their coastal wetland programs with the assistance of Coastal Zone Management Act funds. North Carolina, Georgia, Florida, and Mississippi have programs that regulate discharge of dredge or fill materials or other activities in coastal wetlands. South Carolina, Alabama, and Louisiana have incorporated wetlands protection regulations into broader coastal programs that also regulate activities affecting estuaries, dune systems, and other valuable coastal resources. Florida is the only southeastern state with wetland regulations for both inland and tidal wetlands.

The jurisdiction of state programs also varies. In most states, wetland programs cover both public and private coastal wetlands. Exceptions include Mississippi, where jurisdiction is limited to public tidelands,[13] and Texas, where dredge and fill activities are only regulated at the state level on state-owned coastal lands. North Carolina, South Carolina, Alabama, and Florida have procedures to designate selected

13. See discussion of *Phillips Petroleum v. Mississippi* in the legal issues section of this chapter.

sites as areas of particular environmental value or concern and to submit permits affecting these sites to more stringent review.

State wetland programs are frequently administered in conjunction with the Section 404 program. In Florida, Georgia, Mississippi, and South Carolina, for example, state agencies process state dredge and fill permits jointly with the Corps of Engineers. In North Carolina, the Corps automatically issues a Section 404 permit if the state Coastal Resources Commission and Division of Coastal Management issues a Coastal Area Management Act permit.

Activities covered by permits vary as well. The Alabama and Mississippi programs, for example, require that the proposed activity depend on its proximity to a water resource. In Alabama, Mississippi, Georgia, and South Carolina, a permit is required for any activity that alters the natural topography or habitat, or damages existing flora or fauna (Cowles *et al.* 1986).

To complement state wetland programs, some counties and municipalities have established separate local permitting programs, zoning, or by-laws that provide further protection for coastal wetlands. These, however, will not be discussed in this chapter.

Wetlands Regulation in Four States

To gain a better understanding of state regulation in protecting wetlands, several state programs are described here in greater depth. The following sections cover coastal regulatory programs in North Carolina, Florida, Louisiana, and Texas—states that have used somewhat different approaches to regulation and are responsible for the bulk of wetland losses in the Southeast.

North Carolina. Coastal wetlands are regulated in North Carolina under the Dredge and Fill Act and the Coastal Area Management Act of 1974. The Dredge and Fill Act (N.C. GEN. STAT. §§113–229), is a permitting program that covers dredge and fill activities that may affect estuarine tidelands, marshes, and lakes in coastal counties. The act is administered by the Coastal Resources Commission and the Department of Natural Resources and Community Development's Coastal Management Division. In 1978, the Dredge and Fill Act was merged with the Coastal Area Management Act (N.C. GEN. STAT. Sec. 113A-100); as a result, dredge and fill permits are now issued jointly by the state under the act's program and the Corps under the Section 404 program.

The Coastal Area Management Act program, also administered by the Commission and the Coastal Management Division, regulates development in 20 coastal counties. Before developers can alter the regulated area, they must obtain either a "major" or "minor" program permit. Projects are approved only if they comply with the Commission's development standards, the local land-use plan, and the local development regulations. A large number of activities are regulated under the act, including construction or enlargement of structures; ditch-building on nonagricultural lands; excavation; dumping; removal of clay, silt, sand, gravel, or minerals; bulkheading; driving pilings; clearing or altering lands as an adjunct of construction; and altering waterway or wetland bottoms. If activities require a federal permit, they are reviewed by the Coastal Management Division to determine if they are consistent with the state's Coastal Zone Management program.

According to North Carolina officials, the Coastal Area Management Act program has been relatively successful; few coastal marshes have been lost and federal-state joint permit processing works well (Cowles *et al.* 1986). The commission's development standards for work in wetlands are relatively strict. For example, the location, design, and construction of a project must give highest priority to the conservation of coastal wetlands. Similarly, the site and design of the project must cause the least possible damage to the productivity and integrity of coastal wetlands. Work on the project must be timed to minimize the impact on wetlands. Among other requirements, projects must be water dependent; give high priority to promoting biological, economic, and social values; do the least possible damage to fish and wildlife; not violate water quality standards; not increase siltation or create a stagnant water body; not damage valuable archeological resources; and not impede navigation.

Florida. In Florida, wetlands protection is provided under the state's dredge and fill permitting program, the Warren S. Henderson Act of 1984 (FLA. STAT. §§403.91–403.929). Under the program, the Department of Environmental Regulation reviews permits for dredge or fill activities in surface waters of the state and its adjacent wetlands. To receive a permit, activities must not be contrary to the public interest or violate state water quality standards. If the activity occurs in designated "Outstanding Florida Waters" it must be judged to be in the public interest. Today, more than five percent of the state is classified as Outstanding Florida Waters. Additional areas, including aquatic preserves, areas of critical state concern, and areas subject to resource management plans adopted by the Administrative Commission, also receive more stringent permit review and enforcement. The department's review of dredge and fill applications includes thorough consideration of cumulative impacts; it considers the cumulative impacts of existing projects as well as the impacts of projects that are under review. The department has authority to delegate permitting responsibilities to local governments. Local governments that accept delegation receive state oversight.

The program also authorizes special protection for mangroves (FLA. STAT. §§403.93–403.938). All projects that alter mangroves in waters that are regulated under the Henderson Act require a second permit, and consequently undergo extra scrutiny.

Department of Environmental Regulation officials are relatively pleased with the state program. To a certain extent, the program has been able to ward off development pressures. Between October 1, 1987, and September 30, 1988, the department issued permits authorizing the destruction or temporary disturbance of 1,518 acres of wetlands on proposed project sites. To compensate for these losses, 28,408 acres of wetlands were created and 87,885 acres were improved (Department of Environmental Regulation 1989).

Louisiana. Wetlands protection is provided at the state level under the Louisiana State and Local Coastal Resources Management Act of 1978 (LA. REV. STAT. ANN. §§49.213.1–49.231.21 [1978]). The act sets up the Coastal Use Permit program administered by the Department of Natural Resources' Coastal Management Division. The act regulates activities that may have a significant impact on waters in the coastal zone below the five foot contour line, including dredge and fill activities; wetlands drainage; levee construction; freshwater diversion; and marsh management activities.

To receive a permit, an activity must meet the criteria set out in the state's Coastal Zone Management program guidelines. Projects, for example, must "recognize the value of special features of the coastal zone such as barrier islands, fishery nursery grounds, recreation areas, ports and other areas where development and facilities are dependent upon the utilization of or access to coastal waters, and areas particularly suited for industrial, commercial, or residential development and manage those areas so as to enhance their value to the people of Louisiana" (LA. REV. STAT. ANN. §49:213.8[C][4]). Activities exempted under the act include the construction of single-family residences, construction of navigational aids, and activities in state-designated offshore oil port special management areas.

Louisiana parishes with coastal management programs may help the Coastal Management Division by processing permits that involve activities with minor impacts on the environment. For example, parishes often review dredge and fill projects, residential development, bulkhead construction, and channel maintenance. Such local participation gives the division more time to review major projects.

Overall, the program has seen results: there has been a decrease in the average number of acres disturbed per permit (Cowles *et al.* 1986).

Program success is limited, however, because so many permit applications are related to oil and gas exploration and production, and these are rarely denied. Between 1980 and 1982, for example, 73 percent of the permits issued involved access channel dredging, canal dredging, and other activities associated with the oil and gas industry. Because Louisiana's economy is dependent upon oil and gas production, the Coastal Management Division often finds that it is not practicable or in the public interest to deny such permits. As a result, although some permits have conditions attached, few are actually denied.

Texas. Texas has perhaps the least-developed wetlands program in the Southeast. It has no federal or state coastal zone management program and no state wetland protection statute. However, two programs—the Sand, Shell, Gravel and Marl Program and the Texas Public Lands Management Program—provide some measure of protection for wetlands. The Sand, Shell, Gravel and Marl Program (TEX. PARKS & WILD. CODE ANN. §§86.001–86.020) requires the Texas Wildlife and Parks Department to administer a permitting program for activities that involve the disturbance or taking of any bay-bottom or stream-bed material. Before the department can issue a permit, it must balance the needs of industry and the value of the material to the state against the potential damage or injurious effect of the proposed project on the aquatic environment. The Texas Public Lands and Management Act (TEX. NAT. RES. CODE ANN. §§31, 32.001–33.176), requires the General Land Office School Board to regulate dredge and fill activities on state owned coastal land by reviewing coastal projects and granting easements for selected dredge and fill activities.

The ability of these programs to protect wetlands is limited because their regulatory scope is limited. Clearly, the Sand, Shell, Gravel and Marl Program would be more effective if it also covered dredge and fill activities. While the Public Lands and Management Act regulates dredge and fill activities on state lands, these constitute only a small amount of the coast. According to the Texas Parks and Wildlife Department, the Sand, Shell, Gravel and Marl Program has been able to prevent a number of poor projects from proceeding; however, the program generally suffers from lack of personnel (Cowles *et al.* 1986).

NONREGULATORY PROGRAMS

Coastal Zone Management Act

A number of federal, state, and local agencies and organizations in the Southeast have begun to implement land- and resource-planning programs. The largest of these is the Coastal Zone Management Program. In 1972, Congress passed the Coastal Zone Management Act [CZMA] (116 U.S.C.A. 1451 *et seq.*) to provide coastal states with federal funds for natural resources management, including the management of wetlands. Basically, the act authorizes 80 percent matching grants to coastal states to help them develop "management programs for the land and water resources of the coastal zone." Once a state has established a coastal zone management plan that outlines the objectives of the program, it may apply for additional 80 percent matching grants to implement the program. States or their political subdivisions may use these federal funds to acquire valuable coastal land and to develop and implement land or water use regulations that provide more comprehensive protection for coastal resources.

CZMA also requires that any federal activity or activity that requires a federal license or permit, which occurs within the designated coastal zone, must be consistent with the state's coastal zone management plan. If the activity fails to meet the criteria of the plan, it cannot be undertaken.

In 1980, Congress amended the act to authorize additional funding. States may now apply for resource management improvement grants to preserve or restore coastal areas of particular value, revitalize urban waterfronts, and provide access to public beaches. Funds may be used for acquisition, rehabilitation, shoreline stabilization, public education, and other activities that further those goals.

Today, all but two states (Texas and Georgia) in the Southeast have federally approved Coastal Zone Management Programs. By funding a variety of regulatory programs and acquisition and restoration efforts, coastal management programs help protect wetlands; however, protection efforts are limited because CZMA requires states to balance resource protection with economic growth. Also, in addition to protecting wetlands, states have other protection objectives including shorelines, dune systems, and uplands.

Despite these limitations, states have used CZMA funds with some success. North Carolina, for example, has used its federal money to revise and update local land-use plans, which identify areas of environmental concern, including wetlands. South Carolina has used some of its funds to pay for a management plan for the Shem Creek area of Charleston Harbor. This plan has helped steer development away from wetlands areas, which support local commercial fishing and seafood industries. CZMA funds also have been used in South Carolina to fund a high school social studies course on coastal problems and resource management.

In amending the act, Congress encouraged the development of Special Area Management Plans: comprehensive plans that balance resource use with resource protection in a limited geographic area by designating land and water uses and setting standards and conditions for development. In theory, the plans increase the coordination and consistency of federal and state agency actions and address the cumulative impacts of development projects. While there has been a great deal of discussion on the use of Special Area Management Plans, few have been implemented in the Southeast.

Advance Identification

The Advance Identification planning process, set out in the Clean Water Act 404(b)(1) Guidelines, has been used more frequently in southeastern coastal regions than special area management planning. Under this program, EPA and the Corps identify and delineate the wetlands in a given area; determine those locations experiencing the greatest resource pressures; and determine the relative functions and values of the wetlands within the area. Using this information, EPA and the Corps may then identify the sites where it may be both appropriate and inappropriate to place fill material. The agencies may also identify activities that might not meet the Section 404(b)(1) Guidelines. In addition, EPA may use its authority under Section 404(c) of the Clean Water Act to designate waters of particular value or concern as areas ineligible for Section 404 permits, although it has yet to do so.

Advance identification has been used at three sites in the Southeast: at the Bolivar Flats in Texas, along the Pearl River as it flows through Mississippi, and at Burr Drive in Florida's East Everglades. According to EPA officials, the program gives the regulated community a better idea of what to expect in the course of the permitting process. This tends to minimize confusion and delays, and increases the overall efficiency of the Section 404 program.

State Planning Programs

States also have initiated planning programs over and above their coastal zone management programs. Florida, for example, has a relatively comprehensive program in place under the Environmental Land and Water Management Act (FLA. STAT. §380). This law authorizes the state Department of Community Affairs to designate areas of critical state concern if, among other reasons, the area has a significant impact on, or encompasses, natural resources or historical/archeological sites of regional or statewide importance. Once the Department of Community Affairs has designated an area, the governor appoints a Resource Planning and Management Committee to collect and evaluate data on the given area; the committee then develops a comprehensive management plan that identifies and attempts to resolve current and future areas of conflict. The committee is responsible for having the plan incorporated into local land-use plans; if it is unable to do so, the state designates the area as an area of critical state concern and develops its own management plan.

Designated area of critical state concern programs and Resource Planning and Management programs are in place in many coastal areas, including the Florida Keys, the Apalachicola Bay Area, the Charlotte Harbor Area, Hutchinson Island, and the northwest Florida Coast. These management plans address wetlands as well as water supply, wastewater treatment, emergency evacuation in case of a hurricane, and shellfish production. Because many of these plans have only been completed within the past five years, it is difficult to determine their effectiveness.

Coastal Barrier Resources Act

The Coastal Barrier Resources Act of 1982 (16 U.S.C.A. 3501-3510) affects wetlands indirectly by discouraging development of lands included in the coastal barriers resource system; 186 undeveloped coastal barriers on the Atlantic and Gulf coasts are included in the system. The act prohibits the federal government from financing projects and programs that develop or encourage development in the barrier system. Privately funded development on lands within the system is allowed, but such development is ineligible for such benefits as federal flood insurance and federal grants for water projects and road construction.

While the Coastal Barrier Resources Act may help to slow the development of coastal barriers and related wetlands, it may inadvertently displace development onto adjacent lands, with equally fragile wetland ecosystems. The act loses much of its effectiveness as a wetland protection tool because many human activities are exempted under the act. Among other activities, oil and gas development and the maintenance of channel improvements, jetties, and roads, are still allowed and continue to cause significant coastal wetland losses.

Acquisition Programs

Federal, state, and local governments, and private interests have been able to protect specific wetlands by acquiring them. Since 1965, the federal government has provided funds, generated primarily from the sale of offshore oil and gas leases, for acquisition of open space areas under the Land and Water Conservation Fund (16 U.S.C. §§4601.4–4601.11). Monies in the fund are allocated to federal land management agencies and to state and local governments (on a matching basis). Under the Emergency Wetlands Resources Act of 1986 (16 U.S.C. §3921), each state must prepare a Statewide Comprehensive Outdoor Recreation Plan to receive Land and Water Conservation Fund grants. This plan must assess the importance of wetlands as an outdoor recreation resource and include a wetlands priority plan for acquisition.

While there has been no accounting of the acres of wetlands that have been preserved using LWCF monies, the amount is undoubtedly extensive. These monies have been used by federal agencies to purchase national wildlife refuges, national seashores, and numerous other open spaces that contain wetlands.

Southeastern coastal states have devised a variety of acquisition programs that vary in their funding sources, administration, and resources or areas covered. Typically, acquisition programs in the Southeast are administered by the state fish and wildlife department. Funds are obtained primarily from the Land and Water Conservation Fund and state income tax check-offs, and used to purchase land outright or to acquire conservation easements. Generally, a state can generate between $50,000 and $100,000 for acquisition in income tax check-offs each year (Cowles *et al.* 1986). States also acquire some land through donations.

Other funding sources for land acquisition have been used. In Louisiana, for example, the Department of Wildlife and Fisheries has purchased over 500,000 acres of wetlands statewide with profits from oil and gas production on state-owned lands and the sale of oil and gas licenses. Acquisition in South Carolina and Florida is funded partially through a documentary stamp tax. Private organizations, the most prominent of which is The Nature Conservancy, have been extremely supportive of state acquisition efforts. These groups have provided technical assistance to identify valuable lands and help set priorities for acquisition, purchased and protected lands until states could buy them, and acquired land and managed nature reserves themselves.

Two Florida acquisition programs, the Conservation and Recreation Lands Trust Fund (CARL) and the Save Our Coasts Program, have been particularly effective in acquiring coastal wetlands. Administered by the Department of Natural Resources, the CARL Trust Fund provides up to $40 million per year for land acquisition—especially the acquisition of wetlands, floodplains, and fragile beach lands—from severance taxes on oil, gas, solid minerals, and phosphate rock. A bond issue authorized by the state legislature in 1986 should provide an additional $54.5 million dollars over the next 10 years.

To make the most efficient use of this money, a committee composed of the heads of six state agencies—Department of Natural Resources, Department of Environmental Regulation, Game and Fresh Water Fish Commission, Department of Community Affairs, Division of Forestry, and Division of Historical Resources—evaluates possible acquisition sites and places them on a priority list. The CARL committee generally gives high priority to resources that are not well protected under existing state or federal regulations.

The Save Our Coasts Program has provided additional funds for the acquisition of Florida's beaches and associated wetlands. With revenues from state bonds and a documentary stamp tax, the Florida Department of Natural Resources has been able to acquire 344,000 acres of state parks and preserves. The department makes a concerted effort to pick lands most worthy of acquisition and manage them appropriately after they are acquired. It solicits site recommendations from local governments, landowners, conservation groups, and researchers familiar with a project site, and develops and implements a management plan once the lands have been acquired.

Not all states have had the success that Florida has had. On paper, the Texas Coastal Wetlands Acquisition Act (TEX. NAT. RES. CODE ANN. §§33.231–33.238) looks ideal. Under the act, the General Land Office is given the authority to identify and designate coastal wetlands of significant public interest; the Texas Department of Parks and Wildlife is then authorized to acquire these areas. Unfortunately, the program is inactive and, as a result, the state has had to rely on monies raised by its Waterfowl Stamp Program to fund wetland acquisition. To date, no coastal wetlands have been acquired under the act because the state has yet to appropriate funds to the program and the department has no funds from the sale of state lands. According to Cowles *et al.* (1986), acquisition programs in Georgia, North Carolina, and South Carolina also suffer from inadequate funding. In addition, North and South Carolina officials have complained about limited public awareness and support for existing acquisition programs (Cowles *et al.* 1986).

Restoration and Management Efforts

In recent years, the public and several federal and state agencies have begun to realize the need to actively restore wetlands. At the federal level, the need for restoration was recognized in the passage of the Water Resources Development Act of 1986 (33 U.S.C. §2211). The act authorizes funding for the Corps of Engineers to restore wetlands or other fish and wildlife habitat degraded by completed or ongoing water development projects. The Corps may receive up to $30 million per year to mitigate damages to fish and wildlife habitat, but may spend no more than $7.5 million dollars per project.

The act clearly provides authority and opportunity for the Corps to become involved in restoration efforts. To date, however, the Corps has been unable to proceed because Congress has not appropriated funds. A number of critics claim that the Corps will be unable to carry out restoration efforts even if funds come through, because the expense of such projects is far greater than accounted for in the act. In addition, local governments or other nonfederal parties may be unwilling or unable to shoulder 25 percent of the project's costs as the law requires if the benefits are not national (Houck 1988).

Nowhere is the need for restoration greater than in Louisiana. In 1986, a group of environmental activists, scientists, recreational and commercial fishermen, and concerned landowners formed the Coalition to Restore Coastal Louisiana, a group dedicated to working cooperatively to develop and implement a plan to restore the state's tidal wetlands and other coastal resources. A year later, the coalition released an action agenda calling for controlled diversion of river sediments, restoration of degraded wetlands and barrier islands, and restrictions on the construction and use of navigation canals.

To accomplish these goals, the coalition proposed that the Corps make controlled breaks in the levees along the Mississippi River to allow the sediment to flow out of its confined channel and rebuild the river delta. Replenished by sediments, the delta could support more wetland species. Wetlands could also be restored by dismantling spoil piles and filling abandoned canals in order to re-establish the natural hydrology of the area. The coalition hopes to slow wetland erosion by encouraging the oil and gas industry to use alternative technologies— including directional drilling, hovercrafts, and helicopters—to gain access to hydrocarbon.

In response to the coalition's recommendations, the state of Louisiana has moved its Coastal Restoration Unit into offices within the Department of Natural Resources, and upgraded its status from a section to a division. The governor also has appointed a technical coordinator of coastal activities, who will work closely with the governor and state and federal agencies to promote and coordinate restoration efforts. While these efforts are a strong first step, the office's restoration initiatives are limited by a lack of funds. The state assembly has been reluctant to impose a pipeline and navigation fee on industry; as a result, there is little money in the State Coastal Restoration Fund. Congress has not funded eligible Louisiana restoration projects under the Water Resources Development Act.

Despite these setbacks, the coalition remains active and determined to implement its restoration action plan. And there is reason for hope. Two years ago there was little discussion of coastal restoration. Now, perhaps in part because of the decline of the oil industry, the coalition has begun to see increased interest in restoration as the public begins to reassess the value of its other natural resources (Wille 1988). This interest is reflected in the significant increase in membership in Louisiana wetlands coalitions and in the formation of two new groups: a subcommittee of the state legislature's Natural Resources Committee, and an association of state legislators called Fresh Outlooks on Coastal U.S., or FOCUS. (At the national level, a new coalition called Fishermen Involved in Saving Habitat, or FISH, has formed to unite sport and commercial fishermen, conservationists, fisheries scientists, fisheries managers, and fish processors and distributors on wetlands conservation issues.)

On another front, for several years, NMFS has conducted studies to determine the functional values of mitigated and created habitats in order to develop and evaluate habitat creation techniques. For example NMFS is presently conducting two pilot habitat restoration/creation studies with the Corps of Engineers—one in Wilmington, North Carolina, and the other in Galveston, Texas. In Wilmington, the agencies have recontoured three islands made of dredged material and, with the help of North Carolina State University, have planted saltmarsh and seagrass vegetation. They are now monitoring the sites to evaluate their potential to control erosion and their habitat value to such species as shrimp, menhaden, mullet, spotted and gray sea trout, red drum, croaker, spot bluefish, and blue crabs. In the Galveston Bay pilot project, the agencies have constructed access channels in transplanted *Spartina alterniflora* marsh in an effort to increase the density of marine organisms. Ultimately, such projects should lead to greater knowledge on the best means of creating and restoring wetland habitat.

LEGAL ISSUES

Legal developments in 1987–1988 have raised numerous questions on the extent to which government agencies in the Southeast may regulate wetland properties. Two major U.S. Supreme Court decisions, *First English Evangelical Lutheran Church of Glendale v. County of Los Angeles* (107 S.Ct. 2378, 17 ELR 20797 [1987]) and *Nollan v. California Coastal Commission* (107 S.Ct. 3141, 17 ELR 20918 [1987]), followed by presidential Executive Order 12630,[14] give government agencies new reason to give greater scrutiny to the development and application of regulatory programs that might result in a taking of private property. However, on another front, the U.S. Supreme Court appears to have given governments greater leeway in regulating coastal wetlands by expanding the scope of the public trust doctrine (*Phillips Petroleum Co. v. Mississippi*, 108 S.Ct. 791, 18 ELR 20483 [1988]).

14. 53 *Federal Register* 8859.

Takings

Under the Fifth and Fourteenth Amendments of the U.S. Constitution, the government is prohibited from taking private property for public use without just compensation. The government must balance the need to protect the environment with the need to respect a landowner's property rights. Government laws and regulations that regulate wetland use in the Southeast must meet the court's "takings test"; if they do not and go too far in denying a landowner reasonable use of his property, these laws and regulations may be found to constitute a taking of property for which compensation must be paid. In the 1978 landmark takings case *Penn Central Transportation Co. v. New York* (438 U.S. 104 [1978]), the U.S. Supreme Court identified three major factors to be considered in determining whether a specific law or regulation constitutes a taking: (1) the character of the government action; (2) the economic impact of the action on the claimant; and (3) the extent to which the action interfered with the reasonable investment-backed expectations of the owner.

In 1987, the U.S. Supreme Court issued two decisions that may make government agencies think twice before strictly regulating wetland property. In *First English Lutheran Evangelical Church of Glendale v. County of Los Angeles*, the court ruled that a local floodplain ordinance that denied the church the right to rebuild structures on the floodplain after a flood could not simply be invalidated. Compensation would have to be available as a remedy if a taking was found to have occurred, even temporarily. In the second case, *Nollan v. California Coastal Commission*, the court found that a taking had occurred when the commission conditioned a permit to build a beach home by requiring the landowners to provide public access across their property to the public beach. The decision was based on the finding that the government action did not "substantially advance" a "legitimate state interest" and that the required contribution of the private property owner to help solve the beach access problem was "disproportionately" large.

Citing concern over the implications of these cases, namely the possibility that federal agencies might be required to pay for takings, President Reagan signed an Executive Order drafted by the President's Task Force on Regulatory Relief. Published on March 15, 1988, Executive Order 12630 requires federal agencies to review their actions to ensure that they do not inadvertently create a taking of property where it is not intended and to budget for actions that necessitate a taking.

The Executive Order and the accompanying guidelines prepared by the Department of Justice, essentially embrace and, according to some critics, go substantially beyond the holdings of *First English* and *Nollan* (Jackson and Albaugh 1988). Before commencing an action that might infringe upon a landowner's use of his or her private property, federal agencies must conduct a takings implication analysis. The federal agency must make sure that there is a nexus between police power and the advancement of the public interest, and that the regulation is not "disproportionate to the degree to which the individual's property use is contributing to the overall problem." Agencies must also make a thorough evaluation of the action's economic impact and its potential interference with reasonable investment-backed expectations. The order goes on to require that federal agencies that enact regulations to protect public health and safety must have evidence that the absence of regulations would result in a risk to public health and safety. Drawing tangentially on the *Nollan* decision, the order requires that agencies avoid undue delays that could, in theory, result in a temporary taking.

The precise impact of Executive Order 12630 and the two U.S. Supreme Court decisions on wetland regulations in the Southeast, remains to be seen. But initial commentary suggests the *First English* and *Nollan* decisions will not restrict or significantly change existing regulatory programs. It is still difficult to prove a regulatory taking, particularly if the government regulates for a valid public purpose, evaluates impacts of the regulation on the affected owner's entire property, and does not deny the use of the entire property (Kusler and Meyers 1987).

The Executive Order itself may have greater impact. Jackson and Albaugh (1988) and McElfish (1988) both argue that the order has unreasonably expanded the stated judicial intent of the *First English* and *Nollan* decisions. If anything, the order will increase delays in the administration of programs like the Section 404 program and give landowners more ammunition to challenge the federal government (Jackson and Albaugh 1988). Ironically, the federal government does not appear to need the guidance of the Executive Order in its regulatory actions to ensure that takings do not occur and remedies need not be paid; in fiscal years 1985, 1986, and 1987, there were no court findings of regulatory takings by agencies subject to the Executive Order (McElfish 1988).

Public Trust Doctrine

In February 1988, the U.S. Supreme Court issued another decision with significant implications for southeastern coastal wetlands. The decision, *Phillips Petroleum v. Mississippi*, involved the public trust doctrine, an arcane legal doctrine that gives states certain rights and responsibilities to use waters and the lands beneath them for the benefit of the public. Whether or not, under what circumstances, and to what extent "public trust" waters can be privately owned are still matters of debate.

The controversy arose when the Phillips Petroleum challenged Mississippi's claim to title in certain tidal lands in order to prevent the state from issuing gas leases on those lands. The Mississippi state court found that certain portions of these tidal lands were, in fact, subject to the public trust doctrine and that the state owned them subject to the doctrine. The U.S. Supreme Court affirmed the lower courts, finding that the state gained title to all tidelands when it entered the Union in 1817. In its ruling, the court for the first time clarified the scope of the doctrine beyond navigable water to include non-navigable tidelands.[15]

The court also ruled that the areas subject to the public trust should be determined by state law. The property in question was found to be included in the public trust area because Mississippi courts have consistently held that all lands influenced by the ebb and flow of the tide are state-owned.

The implications of *Phillips* are likely to be extremely variable. States have defined their public trust lands and responsibilities in different ways. Some states, for example, have conveyed some of their tidelands to private parties; others have considered tidelands to lie outside the public trust altogether. Even so, by expanding the scope of what constitutes public trust lands, the U.S. Supreme Court appears to have given states more ammunition to control coastal wetland activities (Kosloff 1988).

CONCLUSION

Evidence is irrefutable that the Southeast is losing its coastal wetlands at a devastatingly rapid rate, yet existing programs are unable to halt or significantly slow the conversion. Federal and state programs designed to help protect wetlands have been stymied by legislative compromises and limited funding. Even under the best of circumstances, the region's regulatory programs are unable to provide comprehensive protection because they speak to multiple public interests, not just to wetlands protection. Nonregulatory protection efforts have been able to slow the rate of loss, but are too limited to counter the losses not stopped by regulatory programs; they also cannot compensate for losses that result from activities that occurred in the past, such as channelization of the Mississippi River.

The situation is not new; for years those involved with wetland management, on both the federal and state level, have debated the effectiveness of existing wetland protection programs. Policymakers and

15. All areas subject to the ebb and flow of the tides.

wetland managers have made numerous recommendations on how to increase the administrative efficiency and scope of protection of these programs, but few of these recommendations have been adopted because they were proposed by disparate interests and had limited political appeal.

In 1987, at the request of the Environmental Protection Agency, the Conservation Foundation convened the National Wetlands Policy Forum, a group representing diverse interests dedicated to adopting a policy and action agenda to manage and protect the nation's wetlands. Released on November 15, 1988, the forum's report has received much praise because of its stated commitment to a goal of no-overall-net-loss of wetlands in the short run, and an increase in total wetlands acreage in the long run. While a number of environmentalists believe that the recommendations do not go far enough to protect wetlands and should include more decisive protection measures, most agree that implementing the forum's action agenda is an important first step. EPA has already responded by adopting the no-net-loss goal and committing to many of the forum's recommendations in an agency Wetlands Action Plan released in January 1989.

To prevent further wetlands loss, the Southeast must strengthen its regulatory approach by making existing programs work to their full potential and by establishing new provisions or programs that provide more comprehensive protection for wetlands. The Section 404 program, for example, could be improved by having the Corps work more closely with EPA, FWS, and NMFS during the permitting process to consider the practicable alternatives to wetlands conversion and the cumulative impacts of proposed activities.

The National Wildlife Federation and several other groups have suggested that the Corps turn over the administration of the Section 404 program to EPA, which would be more likely to enforce the 404(b)(1) Guidelines. The forum steered clear of this proposal, recommending instead that states with the legal authority and capability to achieve the no-net-loss goal assume the responsibility of the 404 program. EPA would retain its 404(c) authority in states that have assumed regulatory primacy and oversee those state programs. The forum also suggested that activities covered under the Section 404 program be expanded to include removal or excavation of soils, drainage or flooding, destruction of plant life, and the driving of pilings or the placement of other structures. Similarly, states could strengthen their Section 401 programs. Since Section 401 has seldom been used in the Southeast, its ability to protect wetlands has yet to be tested.

New programs could also help slow wetland losses. The forum recommended that Congress develop legislation like the Coastal Barrier Resources Act to eliminate federal subsidizes for development activities in valuable wetland areas. Such legislation might not stop all losses in the designated areas, but would certainly discourage conversion of wetlands. Other, more ambitious recommendations include the establishment of some form of coastal zoning (Houck 1988), which would control coastal development in wetland areas but allow some sort of passive economic activity to occur so that a regulatory "taking" would not be deemed to have occurred.

Because of the inherent limitations of regulatory programs, the majority of the forum's recommendations focused on *nonregulatory* approaches to protecting wetlands. It recommended that each state prepare a State Wetlands Conservation Plan to determine the best means of managing and protecting it wetlands. Federal activities must then be consistent with these plans. At a national level, the forum suggested that Congress authorize the establishment of a Wetlands Preservation Trust and an Agricultural Wetlands Reserve Program. Landowners could donate wetlands to the trust in exchange for tax benefits. By transferring permanent easements on agricultural land to such a trust, farmers would be eligible for special subsidies.

To prevent further losses, the Southeast must not only slow wetlands conversion, but also increase its wetland restoration and creation efforts. To achieve this goal, the forum recommends that public and private organizations cooperate to establish a National Restoration Initiative. At least to begin with, the initiative's restoration efforts would focus on the Louisiana coast. To assist in this effort, the forum suggests that the National Academy of Sciences appoint a committee to provide technical guidance on restoration. The committee could build on research conducted by NMFS, the Corps, and other groups, and ultimately help develop criteria for wetlands restoration and creation.

Expanded education and training efforts that focus on the functions and values of wetlands and on the administration of wetland protection programs are needed as well. Such programs would help increase public interest in wetlands and enable existing programs to run more smoothly.

Finally, the Southeast needs to increase its acquisition efforts. Acquisition programs like Florida's CARL program should be established in other states. In addition, there must be greater coordination between different levels of government and between the public and private sectors to identify the wetlands that should be acquired first.

The forum's recommendations will clearly require greater government funding for wetland programs. Funds could be obtained from the proposed American Heritage Trust Fund (which would replace the Land and Water Conservation Fund), state initiatives such as the documentary taxes in Florida and South Carolina, increased development permit fees, and increased federal and state budget appropriations (National Wetlands Policy Forum 1988).

Money alone, however, will not solve the problem; the Southeast must make a firm commitment to wetlands protection and the no-net-loss goal. Public and private sectors must begin to think of wetlands as water resources that are part of our common heritage and worthy of protection, rather than land that can be altered at will. Whatever recommendations policymakers and wetlands managers decide to adopt to slow or stop wetland losses, they must implement them swiftly and emphatically; each day of delay results in further loss.

REFERENCES

Alexander, Charles E. and Marlene A. Broutman. 1986. An Inventory of Coastal Wetlands of the U.S.A. National Oceanic and Atmospheric Administration, U.S. Department of Commerce. Washington, D.C.

Bidwell, Duane. 1988. "Louisiana goes out to sea." *The Leader*. National Wildlife Federation. Washington, D.C. December 1988.

Cavit, M.H. 1979. Dependence of Menhaden Catch on Wetland Habitats: A Statistical Analysis. NSTL Station, MS: U.S. Fish and Wildlife Service, Office of Biological Services, National Coastal Ecosystems Team. Unpublished report submitted to U.S. Fish and Wildlife Service, Ecological Services Field Office. Lafayette, Louisiana. 12 pp.

Cowardin, L.M., V. Carter, F.C. Golet, and E.T. LaRoe. 1979. Classification of Wetlands and Deepwater Habitats of the United States. U.S. Fish and Wildlife Service, Department of the Interior. FWS/OBS-79/31.

Cowles, C. Deming, Lisa Bennett Haas, Glenn J. Atkins, William Britt, Terry Huffman, and Amy Wing. 1986. State Wetland Protection Program—Status and Recommendations. U.S. Environmental Protection Agency, Office of Wetlands Protection.

Department of Environmental Regulation. 1989. Report to the Legislature on Permitted Wetlands Projects, October 1, 1987–September 30, 1988.

Frayer, W.E., T.J. Monahan, D.C. Bowden, and F.A. Graybill. 1983. *Status and Trends of Wetlands and Deepwater Habitats in the Coterminous United States, 1950s to 1970s*. Department of Forest and Wood Sciences. Colorado State University. Ft. Collins, Colorado.

Gagliano, S.M. 1984. Comments on the Socio-economic and Environmental Influences of Off-shore Oil and Gas Activity on the Louisiana Coastal Zone. Subcommittee on the Panama Canal-Outer Continental Shelf. U.S. House of Rep., Comm. Merch. Mar. Fish., Huoma, Louisiana, March 9.

Gagliano, S.M., Meyer-Arendt and Wicker. 1981. "Landloss in the Mississippi Deltaic Plain." *Transactions of the 31st Annual Meeting, Gulf Coast Association of Geologic Societies*: 295.

Gosselink, J.G. and R.H. Baumann. 1980. "Wetland Inventories: wetland loss along the United States coast." *Z. Geomorph. N.F. Suppl. Bd.* 34: 173–187.

Hefner, J.M. and J.D. Brown. 1985. "Wetland trends in the southeastern United States." *Wetlands* 4: 1–11.

Houck, Oliver. 1988. "Ending the war: A strategy to save America's coastal zone." *Maryland Law Review* 47(2):385–405.

Jackson, Jerry and L.D. Alaugh. 1988. "A Critique of the Takings Executive Order in the Context of Environmental Regulation." *Environmental Law Reporter* XVIII (11): 10463.

Kosloff, Laura H. 1988. "Nonnavigable tidelands subject to the public trust doctrine." *National Wetlands Newsletter* 10(3):9.

Kusler, Jon and Erik J. Meyers. 1987. "The taking issue and land regulation in the U.S. Supreme Court." *National Wetlands Newsletter* 9(4):9–11.

Louisiana Department of Natural Resources. 1987. Public information release on wetlands loss.

Mager, Andreas, Jr. and Rickey Ruebsamen. In press. "National Marine Fisheries Service habitat conservation efforts in the coastal coutheastern United States for 1987." *Marine Fisheries Review*.

———. and Gordon W. Thayer. 1986. "National Marine Fisheries Service habitat conservation efforts in the southeastern region of the United States from 1981 through 1985." *Marine Fisheries Review*. 48(3) 1–8.

McElfish, James M., Jr. 1988. "The takings Executive Order: constitutional jurisprudence or political philosophy?" *The Environmental Law Reporter* XVIII(11):10474.

Munson, Ethel. 1988. Memorandum of June 29, 1988 to Director, Regulatory Activities, Office of Wetlands Protection, U.S. Environmental Protection Agency regarding Clean Water Act enforcement mechanisms.

National Marine Fisheries Service. 1983. *Fisheries of the United States, 1982*. U.S. Department of Commerce, NOAA, National Marine Fisheries Service, Current Fish Statistics. 117 pp.

———. 1985. *Fisheries of the United States, 1984*. U.S. Department of Commerce, NOAA, National Marine Fisheries Service, Current Fish Statistics. 121 pp.

———. 1986. *Fisheries of the United States, 1985*. U.S. Department of Commerce, NOAA, National Marine Fisheries Service, Current Fish Statistics. 121 pp.

National Wetlands Policy Forum. 1988. *Protecting America's Wetlands: An Action Agenda*. The Conservation Foundation. Washington, D.C.

Odum, W.E., C.C. McIvor, and T.J Smith III. 1982. The Ecology of the Mangroves of South Florida: A Community Profile. U.S. Department of the Interior, Fish and Wildlife Service, Office of Biological Services. Washington, D.C. FWS/OBS-81/24.

Office of Technology Assessment. 1984. *Wetlands: Their Use and Regulation*. Office of Technology Assessment. Washington, D.C.

Orlando, S.P., F. Shirzad, J.M. Schuerholz, D.P. Mathieux, and S.S. Strassner. 1988. Shoreline Modification, Dredged Channels and Dredged Material Disposal Areas in the Nation's Estuaries. U.S. Department of Commerce, NOAA, Washington, D.C. 18 pp.

Portnoy, J.W. 1977. Nesting Colonies of Seabirds and Wading Birds—Coastal Louisiana, Mississippi, and Alabama. U.S. Fish and Wildlife Service. FWS/OBS-77/07. 126 pp.

Ransel, Katherine and Dianne Fish. 1988. 401 Certification and Wetlands: Opportunities and Guidelines. Revised Draft. Office of Wetlands Protection, U.S. Environmental Protection Agency.

Schmied, R.L., and E.E. Burgess. In press. "Marine recreational fisheries in the southeastern United States—a descriptive overview." *Marine Fisheries Review*.

Shalowitz, A.L. 1964. *Shore and Sea Boundaries*. Vol. 2. U.S. Coast Geod. Surv., Public. 10–1. 749 pp.

Turner, R.E. 1977. "Intertidal vegetation and commercial yields of penaeid shrimp." *Transactions of the American Fisheries Society* 106: 411–416.

U.S. Army Corps of Engineers. 1988. *Crisis on Louisiana's Coast: America's Loss*. New Orleans District. Published in cooperation with the state of Louisiana.

U.S. Department of Commerce. 1988. Statistical Abstract of the United States. Bureau of Census.

U.S. Fish and Wildlife Service. 1982. "Future sea level changes along the Louisiana coast," pp. 165–171 *in* Boesch, D. ed., *Proceedings of the Conference on Coastal Erosion and Wetlands Modification in Louisiana: Causes, Consequences and Options*.

U.S. General Accounting Office. 1988. Wetlands: The Corps of Engineers' Administration of the Section 404 Program. GAO/RCED-88-110.

Wille, C.M. 1988. "Massive loss of coastal wetlands shrinks Louisiana." *Audubon Activist* 3(2):1,15. National Audubon Society. (November-December).

Wintz, W. 1970. "Subsidence and groundwater offtake on the Baton Rouge areas." *Louisiana Water Resources Research Institute Bulletin* No. 6.

Anne Southworth is editor of the National Wetlands Newsletter, *published by the Environmental Law Institute, Washington, D.C.*

Billions of pounds of "nontarget" fish are caught by commercial fishermen and thrown overboard. This "bycatch" represents a tremendous waste of fisheries resources and has unknown, but probably significant, effects on the ecosystem. Of special concern are sea turtles and other endangered animals that are inadvertently caught and killed. *Michael Weber/Center for Marine Conservation*

Discarded Catch in U.S. Commercial Marine Fisheries

Eugene C. Bricklemyer, Jr.,
Suzanne Iudicello,
and
Hans J. Hartmann

INTRODUCTION

When white settlers first came to the Columbia River in the middle of the 19th century, the white sturgeon (*Acipenser transmontanus*) was extremely abundant. Prior to commercial exploitation that began in the early 1880s, sturgeon were inadvertently caught in large numbers in the Columbia River salmon fishery. Strong and persistent, sturgeon were considered a nuisance because they clogged salmon gillnets and the webbing of traps, were caught in seines and fish wheels, and often damaged fishery gear because of their armored side plates and large size (many weighed more than 1,000 pounds). Salmon fishermen deliberately killed and discarded sturgeon by the thousands; in fact, so many were killed that during the salmon season the shores of the river were littered with sturgeon carcasses.

Eventually, sturgeon have been recognized as a valuable resource, but it has taken almost a century for the species to recover from the massive discard practice of the late 1800s, a succeeding decade of overexploitation, and substantial human-made changes to their habitat. Even today in the strictly managed sturgeon fishery in the Colum-

259

bia River, where stocks below the Bonneville Dam are considered "healthy," individual sturgeon weigh only a fraction of the 150 pounds they averaged before the turn of the century, and harvest tonnage still is far below the historic high (Parks 1978, Jans 1988).

Sturgeon were wantonly wasted in the 1800s because they were considered worthless to the fishermen who caught them while pursuing other economically valuable species. Unfortunately, this practice, and the underlying economic view that justifies it, continues to affect many other species in commercial marine fisheries today.[1] For example, in the northwest Atlantic, large but unquantified numbers of dogfish (*Squalus acanthias*), are discarded by New England fishermen.[2] Like sturgeon in the 1870s, dogfish are considered a nuisance in the groundfish fishery because they become entangled in the mesh of nets and have no economic value in the New England fishery. Comparable in size to the very groundfish sought by the fishery, dogfish represent 30 to 40 percent of the total catch per haul in some locations during the summer. In order to be sure that dogfish do not foul the nets again, fishermen either cut off their heads, slam them against the deck or hull before they are thrown back, or sometimes leave them on deck until it is clear that they are dead (Murphy interview). Some fishermen also believe that dogfish prey extensively on species that are commercially valued, thereby offering further justification for destroying them.

In Alaska, in the groundfish fisheries of the Bering Sea and Gulf of Alaska, trawlers discard hundreds of thousands of pounds of cod and pollock because it is not profitable to retain them. Alaska trawlers also discard halibut and crabs because they are prohibited by regulation from harvesting them. However, the same regulatory bodies that prohibit groundfish trawl fishermen from retaining crab and halibut make allowance for the groundfish fleet's discards of these species: They allocate to the groundfish fleet the amount of crab and halibut that the trawlers catch and discard, then make a commensurate reduction in the amount of these species that crab and halibut fishermen are allowed to catch in the directed fishery. In short, the discard of halibut and crab in the groundfish fishery is viewed by fishery managers and the fishing industry as an unavoidable, permissible "cost" of catching groundfish.

Yet another cost of fishing, from Kodiak to San Diego, from Galveston to Tampa, and from Miami to Bar Harbor, is the incidental capture and discard of other marine species in addition to nontarget fish. Those species adversely affected each year include, among others:

---

1. While recreational sport fishermen also discard unwanted fish, the total level of discard is of a much smaller magnitude and is not discussed in this chapter.

2. The dogfish is a slow-growing shark and is often a target species elsewhere in the world.

- nearly one million seabirds each year from at least 20 different species (for example, tufted and horned puffins, crested auklets, murres, and short-tailed shearwaters);
- more than 6,000 seals and sea lions;
- more than 10,000 cetaceans, from the smallest belugas and dolphins to a few members of the great whale species; and
- thousands of endangered and threatened sea turtles, including the critically endangered Kemp's ridley sea turtle.

Altogether, the world's commercial marine fishermen annually catch and throw overboard an estimated 12 billion (Saila 1983) to 20 billion pounds of sea life.[3] The higher estimate is based upon a compilation of views of government officials and other observers who believe that the combination of minimal reporting, underestimates of discard, and the nonreporting of discard species other than finfish and crustaceans (for example, turtles, marine mammals, seabirds) makes the lower figure unrealistic (Wooster pers. comm., Smith interview, Evans interview). Even the lower 12 billion pounds estimate constitutes at least 10 percent of the total catch of fish and shellfish removed from the world's oceans each year (Saila 1983, Brown 1985). Most discarded organisms are dead, dying, or in such a weakened state they are vulnerable to predators (Saila 1983).[4]

The world shrimp fishery, for example, with its very effective but nonselective trawl gear has discard of all types: shrimp below minimum size, valuable finfish, protected endangered species, and massive quantities of other marine organisms that have neither protected status nor currently recognized economic value. Total worldwide shrimp landings in 1985 were 4.4 billion pounds (U.N. Food and Agriculture Organization 1986a). Estimates of annual, worldwide bycatch in the shrimp fishery range from 10 to 42 billion pounds; in some places the ratio of bycatch to shrimp catch is 30 to 1. At least one-quarter to one-half (6 to 10 billion pounds) of the bycatch is discarded (Saila 1983). The Food and Agricultural Organization (FAO) of the United Nations has called for improved use of all caught species because of a predicted 20 percent shortfall between global demand and supply of fish in the year 2000 (U.N. Food and Agricultural Organization 1986b). FAO estimates that as much as 20 percent of all fish annually landed on deck worldwide never reaches the consumer; the huge discard waste of

3. Nonselective gear, while it is the cause of the bycatch, is not always the reason for the discard. In some cases fishery regulations mandate that a vessel throw away bycatch of certain valuable species that the harvester otherwise could retain and market.

4. In some cases discarded catch survives. This occurs in certain pot (for example, crab) or longline (for example, sablefish) fisheries. It also may occur in various trawl fisheries if the tow is not too long in duration and the fish is hardy, if it is not crushed by the weight of the catch and if it is rapidly returned to the sea.

shrimp trawls cited as a major reason (Robinson 1982). Exact figures are unavailable for the percentage of fish harvested in U.S. waters that is discarded, but the total annual discard certainly exceeds several billion pounds (Saila 1983, Tarnas 1986).

Fishermen who must sort discards from retained catch lose fishing effort and time. Fishermen who may want to harvest the discarded species could suffer reductions in fishing opportunity because of declining populations of target species. Consumers may lose potential food products. And, the marine ecosystem is being affected by discard in ways not well understood because the disruptions caused by discard are not monitored or assessed. By ignoring the adverse impacts of discard, fishery managers may be missing a critical element in the wise management of the nation's resources. Clearly, there are no quantified *benefits* of discard waste—yet the practice continues.

This chapter examines the discard problem in U.S-managed waters. It also examines the mechanisms for regulating fisheries, and the reasons why U.S. fishery managers, for the most part, do not apply those mechanisms to reducing discard. This chapter explores how the practice of discard has become institutionalized to such a degree that managers in effect sanction waste by counting discards against the catch quotas of directed fisheries that wish to take and use the very species discarded. It questions whether this policy of allocating catch levels first to a fishery that must discard this take is in keeping with a stated national policy of wise use of marine resources.

For illustrative purposes, the chapter will examine in detail the shrimp-trawl fishery in South Atlantic and Gulf of Mexico waters. There, the politics of discard catch have embroiled different fishing constituencies—the environmental community, federal agencies, state governments, and the public—in a heated controversy for the last decade. [Editor's note: Readers are strongly advised to first read Addendum I at the end of this chapter.]

THE DISCARD PROBLEM

Discard and Its Ecological Effects

The way managers view discard has been influenced heavily by the practices of traditional fisheries management. Generally, U.S. fishery managers treat individual fish stocks as single biological units rather than as components of a larger ecosystem in which all organisms play significant roles.[5] Each stock is managed to bring a maximum eco-

5. The principal federal fishery management statute, the Magnuson Fishery Conservation and Management Act (16 U.S.C.A. 1801–1882) defines a "fishery" as "one or

nomic return, an end that may or may not take into account the need to conserve a certain portion of the stock because of its role as predator or prey for other marine species. Indeed, federal fishery regulations boldly state this economic bias.

For example, because of the nature of the trawl gear and fishery techniques used in the Gulf of Alaska groundfish fishery, tons of bycatch are scooped up annually. In National Marine Fisheries Service (NMFS) regulations applicable to foreign fisheries, the agency names one category of "nonspecified species." NMFS describes this part of the bycatch, which includes all forms of sea life not in some other category, as "a residual category of species of no current or foreseeable economic value or *ecological importance*" (emphasis added) (50 C.F.R. §611.92 [b][4][1987]). This bycatch is normally discarded, but no information whatsoever is collected about the discard—what species, how many, what size, age class, and so forth—hence it is impossible to determine the status and condition of discard species, or the effects of the discard on the ecosystem as a whole.

In the few instances where discard catch is a concern, it is usually characterized as a narrow problem such as waste of a potential food source, interference with fishing operations, or excessive kills of highly valued commercial (for example, prohibited species) or protected species. In fact, discard also may affect the productivity of target species in indirect ways, and may have as yet undetermined consequences for their habitat. The present system of managing fisheries does not provide for consideration of discard as a potential interference with the ecosystem as a whole, and thus does not allow consideration of the response of the ecosystem.

Certain stocks of commercially exploited species are directly affected by discard mortalities. In the Alaska groundfish fishery, for example, the bycatch of juvenile halibut and crab (prohibited species) clearly reduces the likelihood that the bycatch individuals will be caught in the directed halibut and crab fisheries to which they are allocated. Discard mortality of reef fish by shrimp trawlers affects the government's ability to manage those fish successfully for use by reef fishermen, particularly if the take by shrimpers is undocumented and therefore unaccounted for in overall allocation strategies. When species such as king crab, whose take is prohibited because of current population problems, wind up as discard catch, the effects of discard are even more significant because population decline is further exacerbated by this incidental mortality.

The discard of undersized individuals of a target species has a direct effect on the future of the target fishery itself. For example, in the

more stocks of fish which can be treated as a unit for purposes of conservation and management." The act permits NMFS and the fishery management councils to consider interrelated stocks or species in the ecosystem.

Bering Sea during the 1960s the Japanese groundfish fleet took substantial quantities of juvenile halibut. This bycatch caused the historic low harvest levels experienced by the directed halibut fishery in the 1970s. Although the bycatch occurred primarily in the Bering Sea, the subsequent collapse of halibut stocks was felt along the entire West Coast (Cotter pers. comm.). In another instance, four flounder species that constitute an average of 12 to 57 percent by weight of each tow haul in the Gulf of Maine groundfish fishery are discarded because of their small size (Langan and Howell 1984). Investigators have generally acknowledged that excessive incidental take and subsequent discard of undersized target fish in fisheries such as the Gulf of Maine may have contributed significantly to the decline of groundfish harvests (Saville 1980).

If species with no present commercial value are taken as bycatch and discarded without knowledge of their population dynamics, the potential for using that species in the future when it may become valuable can be reduced or eliminated. The decline of the white sturgeon is an example from the past, and the dogfish may be an example for tomorrow.

There is a third effect that is not taken into account when certain bycatch species are discarded. Seabirds and certain marine mammals have neither present nor potential future economic value as harvested species, but are considered valuable for other reasons, both biological and aesthetic. The immediate ecological effects of the removal of these species from the marine environment through incidental take in fisheries is just beginning to be examined. They may be indicator species that signal declines in the quality of the overall marine environment. They may consume fish that are harvested or may prey upon species that are either predators or prey of the harvested fish. Thus far, however, fishery managers and policymakers have resisted including in fishery management decisions consideration of the role of birds and mammals in the marine ecosystem. All efforts at regulating bycatch of these species in fisheries take place because of specific statutes protecting birds, marine mammals, and endangered species.

Ecologists who study marine species admit that there is no species for which sufficient information is available to understand all the factors that affect its distribution and abundance (Andrewartha and Birch 1984). While ecologists may be able to pinpoint the effects on populations of changes in food supply, habitat, and predation, the effects of other indirect factors such as bycatch are less well documented. At the very least, studies have shown that discarded catch affects ecosystem dynamics in two major ways: (1) Interference with predator-prey dynamics. Continuous, selected removal of certain organisms from the ocean alters predator-prey and competitive interactions and may significantly modify ecosystem structure and function. Discarded organisms are transformed from active participants in the predator-prey cycle to passive, highly vulnerable prey, or more commonly, into carcasses and detritus. (2) Recycling of dead organic matter. Return of carcasses into the marine environment enriches the detritus-based food web, attracting scavengers and decomposers. This changes community structure and diversity, and enhances energy turnover, nutrient release, and biochemical oxygen demand.

These effects of discard, though they have the potential to affect the productivity of commercially valuable stocks of fish and how those stocks are managed, have yet to be included in the fishery management plans that guide the management of fish and shellfish resources in the U.S. Exclusive Economic Zone (EEZ), where the federal government and federally established fishery management councils have jurisdiction.[6]

Fishery Management Law and Discard

The legal mechanisms available to address the discard problem are ambiguous at best. The waste of biological resources by discarding bycatch is not expressly prohibited or even mentioned by the Magnuson Fishery Conservation and Management Act (FCMA or Magnuson Act [16 U.S.C.A. 1801 *et seq.*]), the principal federal law that governs how fisheries are managed, regulated, and allocated in the EEZ.[7]

The Magnuson Act.   FCMA was passed in response to U.S. concerns over the growing exploitation of fishery resources by foreign fleets and the perception that international agreements were not conserving fish stocks sought by U.S. fishermen. The goal of the act is to prevent overfishing while achieving the optimum yield from each fishery. The act also requires that fish stocks must be managed to ensure continued reproduction sufficient to yield desired harvest levels.

While the act did not preempt existing state management authority over fishing activities within the territorial sea, it changed significantly the role of the federal government in managing, regulating, and allocating fishery resources of the United States from the seaward boundary of each coastal state to 200 miles offshore.[8] Declaring that

6. The U.S. Exclusive Economic Zone is that area of the ocean that falls between a line drawn along the U.S. coast 3 miles seaward from the shoreline and another such line drawn 200 miles seaward.

7. For a general discussion of the Magnuson Act, see the *Audubon Wildlife Report 1987*; a detailed review of the background of the act and its provisions can be found in *The Evolution of National Wildlife Law* by Michael Bean (1983).

8. The coastal waters of a state generally extend three nautical miles from shore. Texas, the Florida Gulf Coast, and Puerto Rico have fishery jurisdiction extending to nine nautical miles offshore. Preemption of state management authority by the Secretary of Commerce is possible under limited circumstances (16 U.S.C.A. 1856).

its purpose was to "take immediate action to conserve and manage" U.S. fishery resources, Congress created a fishery conservation zone (now called the Exclusive Economic Zone, or "EEZ"), expanded the role of the National Marine Fisheries Service to one of research and industry support to one of fishery regulation and management, and created a system of regional fishery management councils with federal, state, and private members to share the responsibility of management and allocation of fishery resources within the EEZ.

In promulgating a comprehensive national fishery policy for the first time, Congress stated that in managing finite and valuable fishery resources, managers were to use the best scientific information available, promote efficiency, and initiate measures that were workable and effective. The underlying management standard is *optimum yield*, defined as the amount of fish that will provide the greatest benefit to the nation, considering not only biological, but also relevant economic, social, or ecological factors. In allowing consideration of these external factors, Congress attempted to give fishery managers a flexible, dynamic management system that could be adjusted to reflect changing values and conditions, not only among fishermen, but also in their communities, among consumers, and recreational users (Jacobsen and Davis 1983). Finally, the act allowed consideration of elements heretofore considered unrelated to managing a discrete fishery stock, such as incidentally taken unregulated stocks, other marine species, and the marine environment as a whole (50 C.F.R. 602.11[2][3]).

The act established eight regional fishery management councils to regulate and manage resources in their respective geographical areas. The objective of the councils is to balance demands to harvest fish against the need to conserve stocks. The most significant provision of the act is its requirement that Fishery Management Plans (FMPs) be developed for species harvested commercially in the EEZ. The plans are prepared by the regional councils, but must ultimately be approved by the Secretary of Commerce. Each regional fishery management council is to devise its FMPs with the assistance of its own scientific advisors (especially NMFS fishery scientists), the states, the fishing industry, other user groups, consumer and environmental groups, and the general public.

The development of a FMP is a complex, time-consuming process that goes through several stages of scientific documentation, planning, technical and legal review, public comment, and administrative review before approval by the director of NMFS. Each fishery plan must incorporate "conservation and management" measures consistent with seven national standards enumerated in the act. The standards require that such measures:

1. prevent overfishing and assure optimum yield;
2. be based on the best scientific information available;
3. provide for the management of stocks as a unit;

4. be nondiscriminatory;
5. promote efficiency;
6. allow for contingencies; and
7. minimize costs.

The Standards and Bycatch.   With only a few exceptions, the phrase "conservation and management measures" has been interpreted by NMFS and the councils to mean the development of FMPs that include conservation and management measures only for commercially valued fish and shellfish species. (One exception is the joint billfish plan for the Atlantic and Gulf coasts and the Caribbean, where billfish were allocated solely for recreational use.) Despite the demonstrated reluctance to consider the conservation requirements of noncommercial species, some segments of the industry and NMFS think that FMCA provides the basis for dealing with the amount and effects of discard in fishery management plans. Thus, conservationists argue that discard—as waste, as a biological impact, and as an allocative dispute—ought to be considered in fishery management decisions.

Others argue that the act's standards compel consideration only of economics and efficiency, and where controlling or limiting discard effects efficiency, efficiency must come first. Since the underlying fishery management principle is optimum yield to the harvester, conservation and management of nontarget species, or of the ecosystem as a whole, appears to be of little concern. Adding further to the economic bias is the fact that many of the nongovernmental members of the regional councils are primarily representatives of the commercial fishing industry. Although the act specifically mentions that environmental interests are to be part of the community that helps devise a fishery management plan, no environmental organization was represented on any of the eight regional councils as of January 1, 1989. Faring better, especially on the Gulf and South Atlantic councils, are recreational fishing interests, which have two or more representatives on all but one of the eight councils. Sport fishing representatives often focus their efforts on allocation disputes between commercial and recreational users of the same species; in several instances they also have been successful in requiring the council plans to address the effects of commercial discard of species valued by sport anglers.

The North Pacific Fishery Management Council has dealt most directly with bycatch. The council has allocated crab and halibut as bycatch to the groundfish trawl fisheries that must discard these species. The crab pot fisheries and halibut longline fisheries receive their allocation of crab and halibut as target species, but their allocations are reduced by the amount given first to the trawlers. Spokespeople for these fisheries have argued that at least four of the national standards can be applied to regulating discard (Kronmiller pers. comm.).

The first standard states that appropriate measures must be taken to prevent overfishing and at the same time achieve an optimal yield. The second requires that these measures be based upon the best scientific information available. The third, and perhaps the one most directly applicable to bycatch and discard, provides that individual stocks must be managed as a unit, but that interrelated stocks be considered part of that unit. Finally, the fourth requires that allocations among fishermen be fair and equitable, and not discriminatory.

Representatives of the Alaska Crab Coalition argue, for example, that "conservation" is defined as wise use, "and that avoidance of waste is an important conservation objective" (Kronmiller pers. comm.). They claim further that achieving an optimal yield does not necessarily mean that a fishery must be allowed to take the entire estimated optimal yield, especially when doing so would produce wasteful levels of bycatch. Groundfish trawlers argue that conservation only means preventing harvest at levels that would harm the resource, and that tighter restrictions on bycatch would violate the requirements in the national standards that fisheries be conducted efficiently and that allocations be equitable and fair. The groundfish industry characterizes bycatch as a type of "utilization," and urges that consideration be given only to comparing the worth of the groundfish harvest (given a certain allowable level of bycatch) to the worth of the crab and halibut discarded if it were harvested instead (Alaska Data Bank *et al.*, pers. comm.).

Don Bevan, a participant in the council process since its inception, suggests the real question is one of controlling waste. "I would define waste as catching more bycatch than was necessary to take a target species or discarding marketable fish. Of course, we mandate the latter by regulation. Waste of fish at sea is a bit like pornography—everyone can recognize it when they see it but it is very difficult to define by law or regulation. If an extraordinarily large bycatch comes aboard, I am sure that every skipper knows whether it was due to the deployment of his vessel or if it was due to normal random variation. I am also certain that his observer is not capable of making the same distinction. It is even a step further removed for a council to determine what is an appropriate number." (Bevan interview).

Lee Alverson of Natural Resources Consultants in Seattle has long been involved in fisheries management, and he has strong feelings on the bycatch issue. According to Alverson, there are responsible, concerned trawlers in the North Pacific "who believe that bycatch is not just an allocation, but also a conservation issue, and one that deserves immediate attention" (Alverson interview, Highliners Assoc. pers. comm.). However, he says, "While nonselective gear causes some of the problems, the regulatory structure is equally to blame. If we were to redesign fisheries management in the North Pacific instead of trying to repair a patchwork quilt of often out-dated rules, we probably would not come up with a system that requires trawlers to throw away perfectly good, highly desirable fish. We would not reserve a species for harvesting by only one type of gear when we knew it was inevitable that other gear types would catch that same species." But, he adds, the reason that no resolution can be reached is that "everyone is pointing the finger at everyone else."

Jay Johnson, deputy general counsel for the National Oceanic and Atmospheric Administration (NOAA), says that FCMA provides ample authority for the councils to address bycatch in fishery management plans and that they have done so in the past. Such action can be based on the fair allocation or the conservation standard, or both, Johnson says, and can apply not only to species with current economic value but also to fish that have no presently recognized commercial value. "We are responsible for preserving all fish stocks for future use under the Magnuson Act's definition of conservation and management," says Johnson, "and in fact what may be a 'trash fish' today may provide the cure for cancer tomorrow" (Johnson pers. comm.). Johnson believes that there is a substantial amount of authority in the Magnuson Act to regulate bycatch which has yet to be tested (Johnson interview).

David Cottingham, director of NOAA's Office of Ecology and Conservation, believes "there is sufficient authority to deal with the bycatch issue if the interest exists." As an example, he points to a recent action by the South Atlantic Fishery Management Council. The council prohibited the use of trawl gear in the snapper/grouper fishery in a certain portion of the grounds between Cape Hatteras, North Carolina, and Cape Canaveral, Florida. This was done in order to prevent damage to the limited live bottom habitat that supports the directed snapper/ grouper fishery and to stop further overfishing of vermillion snapper, which has resulted of substantial trawl harvest of extremely small fish (Cottingham interview).

Larry Cotter has chaired the bycatch committee of the North Pacific Fishery Management Council. His prognosis is pragmatic if not optimistic: "There is no way you are going to get the councils to address bycatch of species that are not commercially valuable. And once a species is commercially valuable, they won't be discarded, assuming they are of marketable size and not prohibited to that gear type: they'll be kept and sold. You can't look for the councils to interpret the Magnuson Act in a way just to save fish" (Cotter interview).

Johnson disagrees, noting that the Atlantic coral plan attempts to protect coral as an essential part of the ecosystem by prohibiting the use of certain types of fishing gear that would otherwise damage the coral. As another example, he cites the Pacific anchovy plan that preserves some anchovies as prey for sport fish species (Johnson pers. comm.).

Wildlife Protection Laws and Discard

In the absence of aggressive action by NMFS to deal with the discard problem, environmental organizations have successfully used several wildlife protection statutes to control the take by fishermen of nontarget marine birds, mammals, and turtles in various fisheries. These laws include the Endangered Species Act, the Marine Mammal Protection Act, and the Migratory Bird Treaty Act.

Endangered Species. The Endangered Species Act (16 U.S.C.A. 1531 *et seq.*) prohibits the "taking" of any endangered species by any person subject to U.S. jurisdiction. The term "take" includes kill, trap, harass, pursue, hunt, shoot, wound, capture or collect, or to attempt to engage in any such conduct (16 U.S.C.A. 1532). Thus, if an endangered animal were accidentally entangled in a fishing net—even if it were released alive—the entanglement would be considered a "taking" for purposes of the act (Bean 1983). Section 7 of the Endangered Species Act requires all federal agencies to ensure that any action carried out by them does not jeopardize the existence of listed species or adversely affect their designated critical habitat. "Actions" can include promulgation of regulations, such as fishery management plans.

The Endangered Species Act has been applied in three instances to modify fisheries practices where commercial fishing operations resulted in bycatch of listed species. In California in the early 1980s, scientists documented the entanglement and drowning of large numbers of threatened California sea otters in halibut set nets off the coast. In response to pressure from federal agencies and environmental groups to have the act's prohibitions enforced, the California legislature enacted changes in the state fisheries code to create areas closed to set net fishing within state-managed waters.

The critically endangered monk seal occurs in areas in Hawaiian waters where a spiny lobster fishery also takes place. The monk seal population is at such a low level that measures to reduce fishery/monk seal interaction were included in the lobster FMP. Also, after many years of effort and the filing of a federal lawsuit, NMFS declared certain parts of the monk seal's range as critical habitat under the Endangered Species Act.

Finally, in the Gulf of Mexico and Southeast Atlantic, shrimp trawls capture an estimated 48,000 sea turtles yearly, with an estimated annual mortality of more than 11,000. One of the species caught, the endangered Kemp's ridley sea turtle, is thought to have an adult breeding population of fewer than 600 females worldwide. Environmentalists invoked the Endangered Species Act to bring shrimpers and NMFS to the negotiating table in 1986 to discuss the possibility of regulations that would require the use of a device in shrimp trawls designed to exclude sea turtles from shrimp trawl nets. Congress ultimately approved use of the gear. (Further details on sea turtle protection in the shrimp fishery are provided in the case study in the next section of this chapter.)

Marine Mammals. The Marine Mammal Protection Act of 1972 (MMPA [16 U.S.C.A. 1361 *et seq.*]) was enacted to protect marine mammal species "of important national and international significance," including whales, porpoises, seals, sea lions, walruses, sea otters, polar bears, and manatees. The statute prohibits the "taking" of any marine mammals by persons subject to U.S. jurisdiction. However, this prohibition on taking (("taking" includes hunting, capturing, killing, or harassment) is waived under four circumstances. In addition to an exemption granted to coastal Alaskan Natives to take marine mammals for subsistence purposes, the Secretary of Commerce or Interior may grant permits for the incidental take of marine mammals during commercial fishing operations;[9] allow incidental takes of small numbers of animals during other activities, such as oil and gas exploration; and issue permits for the collection of marine mammals for public display or scientific research.

Environmental groups and concerned fishermen successfully used MMPA to prevent Japanese driftnet fishermen from taking marine mammals as bycatch in the North Pacific salmon fishery. In 1987, NMFS renewed a three-year incidental-take permit for the Federation of Japan Fishery Associations allowing its driftnet fleet to take more than 5,000 Dall's porpoise and other marine mammals, including depleted Northern fur seals in the course of salmon fishing operations. Environmentalists and some Alaska fishermen challenged the agency action in June 1987, claiming NMFS could not, under MMPA, issue a permit allowing the incidental take of a marine mammal unless the agency could make certain specific findings (*Kokechik Fishermen's Association, et al. v. Secretary of Commerce, et al.*, 679 F. Supp. 37 [D.D.C. 1988], aff'd, 839 F.2d 795 [D.C. Cir. 1988] *cert denied*, Jan. 1989). The federal court agreed, ruling that because the government lacked the information necessary to safely include an allowable take of fur seals in the permit, it could not lawfully issue a permit for the taking of *any* marine mammals. (See "Recent Court Decisions Affecting Wildlife" in this volume for further details of the case.)

While the lawsuit was aimed only at the foreign driftnet fishery, it had consequences for U.S. fishermen as well. In 1984, NMFS issued eight, five-year permits to domestic commercial fisheries on the West Coast, allowing a total annual take of more than 6,400 marine mammals. Those permits were up for renewal in 1988, but the agency said

---

9. Public Law 100–711, signed by the president on November 23, 1988, reauthorized the Marine Mammal Protection Act and granted commercial fishermen a five-year exemption from the permit requirements of the act.

it could not renew them because American fishermen took some of the same marine mammals as the Japanese, and the same considerations that flawed the foreign permit would bar issuance of the domestic permits unless MMPA were changed. Environmentalists and fishermen spent several months negotiating proposed changes to MMPA that would allow domestic commercial fishing to continue, yet would provide protection for marine mammals, then submitted their ideas to Congress. On the last day of the 100th Congress, legislators approved amendments to MMPA that replaced the incidental take permit provisions with a five-year exemption program allowing incidental takes to continue. However, during this period, NMFS is required to gather adequate information about interactions between commercial fishermen and marine mammals so that a long-term plan for regulating these interactions can be established. The plan must be ready for implementation by October 1, 1993.

Seabirds. The United States has treaties with Great Britain, the U.S.S.R., Mexico, and Japan to protect shared migratory birds. While these treaties are primarily aimed at regulating the hunting of migratory waterfowl, the Migratory Bird Treaty Act, which implements the treaties in the United States, has been used for broader conservation purposes. The treaty with Japan demonstrates the potential applicability of the act to entanglement of seabirds during fishing operations.

The agreement with Japan, the Convention for the Protection of Migratory Birds and Birds in Danger of Extinction and Their Environment (25 U.S.T. 3329, T.I.A.S. 7990 [1972]), was based on a recognition by both countries that migratory birds were a "natural resource of great value." Article II of the convention defines the migratory birds covered by the treaty, and protected species are listed in Annex I. Article III of the convention prohibits the taking of any of the listed species. Of the 21 species taken in high seas driftnets in the North Pacific, 18 are listed in Annex I.

The Migratory Bird Treaty Act (16 U.S.C. sec. 703 *et seq.*) implements the convention with Japan. The law provides that "unless and except as permitted by regulations . . . it shall be unlawful at any time, by any means, or in any manner, to pursue, hunt, take, capture, kill, attempt to kill, attempt to take, capture, or kill . . . any migratory bird . . . included in the terms of the conventions." This prohibition against the taking of migratory birds has been broadly construed by the courts to include any taking, whether intentional or not (*U.S. v. Corbin Farm Services, Inc.*, 444 F. Supp. 510 [D.C. Cal. 1978], *aff'd* 578 F.2d 259).

The Secretary of the Interior is authorized to determine whether it is appropriate to adopt regulations allowing the take of birds protected under the convention with Japan. Currently, allowed takings include only those for recreational hunting of game birds, takings for scientific purposes, and for depredatory bird eradication; none of these allowed takings is applicable to seabirds taken as bycatch in fisheries.

Bycatch of birds occurs with documented regularity in gillnet fisheries, particularly in the high-seas driftnet fisheries of the North Pacific. Studies have documented the ensnarement and drowning of hundreds of thousands of marine birds of 21 different species. Large numbers of birds also have been taken in U.S. fisheries off the coast of California and with increasing frequency in Washington coastal fisheries.

Conservationists have unsuccessfully sought to have bycatch of seabirds considered during permit proceedings for foreign fisheries in the U.S. EEZ, but have been thwarted by NMFS' insistence that it has no authority to manage seabirds, claiming those species are the responsibility of the Department of the Interior (52 *Federal Register* 19874, 1987). Yet, the Department of Interior appears to have taken the position that it does not have the legal authority to exercise jurisdiction beyond the limit of U.S. territorial waters (Fish and Wildlife Service 1980, 1981).[10]

The Migratory Bird Treaty Act has been employed successfully by conservationists to limit bird kills by marine fishermen in at least one instance in state waters. In 1985 and 1986, seabird biologists in California documented an alarming decline in the Farallones population of common murres. After tracking possible causes ranging from oil spills to the effects of the El Niño current warming event on the murres, they concluded that thousands of the birds were being entangled and drowned in halibut and croaker set nets off the central California coast. Environmentalists brought the bird mortality to the attention of the state fish and game agency and the Fish and Wildlife Service, and cited the prohibitions of the Treaty Act as a means of stopping this bycatch of seabirds.

While no fishermen actually were prosecuted for the illegal bird takes, the Fish and Wildlife Service and the California attorney general acknowledged the applicability of the law to such takings. The threat of legal action by conservation groups provided the impetus for a series of meetings among government fish and wildlife agencies, fishermen, and environmental groups, which resulted in changes to California

10. An opinion of the Interior Department's solicitor asserts that while the Migratory Bird Treaty Act is applicable to foreign fishermen in U.S. territory, "territorial waters" for purposes of the Treaty Act do not encompass the EEZ. In *Blueprint for the Environment* (1988), a coalition of environmental groups challenges the correctness of the 1975 solicitor's opinion, and urges that incoming Interior officials interpret the Migratory Bird Treaty Act to expand its application to 200 miles offshore.

fishery management laws. The new provisions regulate the halibut gillnet fishery by zone, depth, and timing so as to essentially eliminate its adverse impact on common murres.

Gear Control Laws

Frustrated by unsuccessful attempts to get NMFS to use its authority to reduce, or even document, the significant mortality of marine animals in foreign fisheries in the North Pacific Ocean and the Bering Sea, in 1986 environmentalists took their concerns to Congress.[11] Their testimony on S. 62, a bill introduced by Senator Ted Stevens (R-Alaska), revealed what scientists had known for several years: North Pacific fisheries, employing free-floating panels of driftnet from 9 to 20 miles long, were killing not only the salmon and squid they sought, but everything else that came into the path of the driftnet, including hundreds of thousands of seabirds and thousands of marine mammals (U.S. Senate 1987). Although the Stevens bill failed to pass in 1986, a similar measure did succeed in 1987, when it was added as a separate title of the Marine Plastic Pollution Control Act. (See *Audubon Wildlife Report 1988/1989* for further details on plastic debris and wildlife.)

Referred to as the Driftnet Impact Monitoring and Control Act, this law requires the Secretary of Commerce, in consultation with the secretaries of State and Interior, to initiate negotiations with foreign governments whose nationals conduct driftnet fishing operations in waters outside the EEZ that have an impact on U.S. marine resources. The negotiations are intended to result in agreements that will allow U.S. observers aboard the foreign vessels to document the bycatch of U.S. fish, seabirds and marine mammals. The first such negotiations occurred in 1988 to address the Korean high-seas squid fishery, but no observer agreement was reached. A report to Congress on the results of the first year's talks with Japan, Korea, and Taiwan is due in early 1989. Negotiations also must be undertaken to improve the enforcement of other laws governing driftnet fishing operations, and any nation that fails to implement such an agreement by June 30, 1989, may face U.S. embargoes on its fish products.

The Driftnet Act also called for studies on the nature and extent of driftnet fishing operations and their impacts on marine resources, an evaluation of alternative driftnet materials, feasibility of driftnet tracking systems, and methods of retrieving derelict driftnets. NMFS is conducting this research.

11. Greenpeace presented testimony concerning the impacts of pelagic driftnets on fish, marine mammals, and birds on behalf of the Animal Protection Institute, the Humane Society of the United States, the International Wildlife Coalition, the Society for Animal Protective Legislation, and the Whale Center; the Center for Marine Conservation presented testimony on driftnet effects on seabirds.

DISCARDED BYCATCH IN THE SOUTHEASTERN U.S. COMMERCIAL SHRIMP FISHERY: A CASE STUDY

Shrimp Fleet Discard

The vast majority of U.S.-harvested shrimp is caught in the South Atlantic and Gulf of Mexico. The shrimp fishery, with its very effective but nonselective trawl gear, has discard of all types: shrimp below minimum size, valuable finfish, protected endangered species, and massive quantities of other marine organisms that have neither protected status nor recognized economic value.

In the United States, the shrimp industry's discard problem results from the use of the otter trawl, a nonselective, meshed net pulled along the ocean bottom. Like all trawl nets, the otter trawl is wide at the opening and funnels back to a narrow end. It is extremely efficient in taking virtually everything in its path. Concerns over the use of otter trawls in the Gulf of Mexico have been expressed at least since the 1930s (Lindner 1936). But the bycatch issue received attention only very recently, largely because of the estimated 48,000 sea turtles that are annually caught by Gulf and South Atlantic shrimp fishermen. Sea turtles, which must surface to breathe, often drown when caught in the trawls. NMFS estimates annual sea turtle mortality at more than 11,000 (NOAA/NMFS 1987).

Reducing Sea Turtle Bycatch

It has been known for decades that substantial numbers of sea turtles, including the critically endangered Kemp's ridley sea turtle, are killed by shrimp fishermen each year.[12] After years of urging by conservationists, NMFS began development of devices to exclude turtles from shrimp nets in 1978; a successful model was produced by 1981 (Saila 1983, NOAA/NMFS 1987). Refinement and testing continued until an effective, lightweight, and inexpensive NMFS Trawling Efficiency Device (or TED) was available in 1985. The TED (also called the Turtle Excluder Device), was proven effective by NMFS researchers in more than 10,000 hours of field trials in the Gulf and South Atlantic. It reduced by 97 percent the bycatch of sea turtles without significantly reducing the amount of shrimp caught. Also, the NMFS TED excluded from the trawl other commercially undesirable organisms such as horseshoe crabs, jelly balls, loggerhead sponges, and fat grass, and

---

12. Species of marine turtles incidentally caught in shrimp trawls in the Gulf of Mexico include: loggerhead (*Caretta caretta*), green (*Chelonia mydas*), Kemp's ridley (*Lepidochelys kempi*), hawksbill (*Eretmochelys imbricata*), and leatherback (*Dermochelys coriacea*).

could easily be modified to decrease finfish bycatch by 50 to 70 percent (NOAA/NMFS 1987).[13] Because of its ability to exclude unwanted organisms, the TED has the potential for increasing the economic efficiency of shrimp fishing. Although NMFS undertook an education campaign to acquaint shrimpers with the TED and promote its use, by 1986 only about a hundred of the thousands of vessels in the U.S. shrimp fleet had adopted it. Most other shrimpers did not believe the device worked, and probably more importantly, did not want the government dictating gear modification.

After determining that NMFS would not *require* the use of TEDs, the conservation community agreed to mediate negotiations with the U.S. shrimp industry.[14] These negotiations concluded at the end of 1986 with an agreement requiring a phase-in of TED use over three years. While the industry participant from Louisiana immediately repudiated the agreement, and was responsible in large part for generating an unsuccessful lawsuit by the state of Louisiana seeking to block it, in 1987 NMFS issued regulations under the Endangered Species Act that required either use of approved TEDs (several designs have been certified), or 90-minute tow times with conventional trawls, depending upon the area, the time of year and the length of the vessel involved.[15] Although technically in effect for a few days in September 1988, implementation of the regulations (except in the Cape Canaveral area, where they went into effect in 1987) was delayed until 1989 by a provision added to the Endangered Species Act (Pub. L. 100–478) and went into effect May 1.

The use of TEDs will save thousands of turtles from drowning, but solves only a very small, albeit important, part of the shrimp trawl discard problem. The practice of the removal of billions of live finfish and the return of that biomass as billions of pounds of carcasses continues. This is because shrimp fishermen are permitted to use any TED that excludes 97 percent of all sea turtles encountered. While the NMFS TED also excludes significant numbers of other species from a trawl's bycatch, other certified TEDs are much less effective in this

13. The current version of the NMFS TED is collapsible, weighs only 30 pounds, costs about $350, is installed in a webbing extension, and eliminates 50 to 60 percent of finfish bycatch (Seidel interview).

14. Led by the Center for Marine Conservation, the negotiating team included representatives from the Environmental Defense Fund, Greenpeace, Monitor International, and the Fund for Animals. The team, however, also represented the interests of a larger national coalition, made up of groups including the Sierra Club, National Audubon Society, and HEART.

15. During TED testing NMFS gathered data on mortality of turtles related to the length of time in a trawl tow. There was no mortality up to 45 minutes, but mortality took a sharp rise after 65 to 75 minutes. At 90 minutes, approximately 25 percent of the captured turtles succumbed, and beyond 90 minutes the rate rose dramatically (NOAA/NMFS 1987).

One agency estimates that 20 percent of the fish caught worldwide is discarded. *Michael Weber/Center for Marine Conservation*

regard. The waste of nontarget biological organisms is especially great in the Gulf of Mexico shrimp fishery. Of the more than 18,000 commercial boats and vessels in the Southeast shrimp fishery, almost 80 percent operate in the Gulf. Gulf vessels are larger, more powerful, and often pull four trawls instead of two; they stay on the fishing grounds for weeks and generally pull for long periods of time per tow (NOAA/ NMFS 1987). In 1986 and 1987 Gulf of Mexico fishermen caught 304 and 257 million pounds of shrimp, respectively, valued at $563 and $469.2 million. South Atlantic fishermen by comparison landed 23 million pounds of shrimp in 1986 (worth $59.5 million) and 22.9 million pounds in 1987 (worth $46.3 million) (NMFS 1988).

At least 115 species of Gulf finfish are taken along with shrimp (Bryan *et al.* 1982). In some areas of the Gulf, more than 21 pounds of fish are landed for every pound of shrimp; the Gulf average of finfish to shrimp is over 10 to 1 (Pellegrin *et al.* unpubl.), while the average ratio in the South Atlantic is 2.8 to 1 (Pellegrin 1982). Almost all of the bycatch is thrown back, either dead, dying, or likely to be consumed in its weakened state by predators such as gulls and pelicans that follow the shrimp boats. Using the 10 to 1 ratio and a 90 percent discard rate, an estimated 2.7 billion pounds of Gulf of Mexico finfish were dumped overboard in 1986 and 2.3 billion pounds in 1987; approximately 58 million pounds were discarded in the South Atlantic in each of those years.

Up to 70 percent of this discard by weight is commercially recognized groundfish species such as croaker, sea trout, and spot.[16] Reef fish, such as valued red snapper and grouper, also are discarded. The fishery management plan for reef fish estimates that 78 million juvenile red snapper are caught annually by shrimpers (Gulf of Mexico Fishery Management Council 1981).[17] By comparison, commercial landings in 1986 totalled 3.8 million pounds of red snapper with 1.4 million pounds harvested by the recreational fishery (Leary interview).

Such losses not only deny potentially harvestable fish to other commercial fishermen, but to recreational fishermen as well. Croaker, spot, snapper, and grouper are especially sought by recreational fishermen. There are more recreational boats in the Gulf of Mexico than in the rest of the United States combined, and they are used for an average of 20 million saltwater fishing trips each year (NOAA 1987).

Ecological Effects of Discarded Bycatch

It is clear that such monumental discards by shrimp fishermen affect other users, such as sport fishermen and the commercial reef fisheries.

---

16. One estimate, based upon less shrimping effort than is currently occurring, is that 3.3 billion croaker are caught by commercial shrimpers in the Gulf yearly. The vast majority of these are very small fish, in their first year of life. Thus, those which are lost as bycatch will not spawn or be recruited to the fishery (Pellegrin *et al.* unpubl.).

17. More recent estimates are that 12 million snapper are discarded, all younger than the first year class, but the Gulf Council has not revised its 78 million estimate (Nichols *et al.* 1987).

What is less clear is how and to what extent discard mortality affects the discarded species and the Gulf ecosystem. Several scientists and a natural resources economist believe that the impact of the shrimp fishery on the groundfish resource has been significant—severe enough to raise the issue of overfishing from an economic point of view (Stokes pers. comm.). Other NMFS scientists say that some species affected by discard are under stress and are decreasing in abundance. While croaker stocks seem healthy in terms of the number of fish, the individual average size of croaker in the Gulf continues to decrease. This is a classic sign of overfishing—and the only large-scale fishing going on is the bycatch of the shrimp fleet (Seidel interview). Reports on the reef fish fishery indicate a decline in the red snapper catch in the directed fishery, as well as a decrease in size per fish caught (Pellegrin *et al.* unpubl.). Government scientists predict that a reduction in shrimp bycatch might increase red snapper yield in the fishery by as much as 90 percent (Powers *et al.* 1987).

Ecosystem effects of discard can be looked at in terms of predator-prey relationships and the impacts of detritus on marine communities. Information on predator-prey interactions is limited, because there are only a few long-term studies documenting significant changes. The vast majority of the relevant work done has concentrated on the shrimp fishery because of its high level of discard.

Through use of an energy-flow model for the Gulf of Mexico shrimp fishery, the potential effects of excessive bycatch discard on groundfish populations and shrimp/groundfish predator-prey interactions have been examined (Browder 1981). The data indicate that the rate of groundfish kill through shrimp bycatch is equal to the natural predation rate. The model predicted that it was possible that groundfish stocks could be adversely affected by the shrimp fishery. More importantly, however, the model showed that the natural predation rate on shrimp was three times greater than the harvest rate, and that bycatch increases predation pressure on shrimp by removing disproportionate numbers of other, similar-sized species, such as juvenile finfish, from the predators' potential menu. Increased predation on shrimp could reduce shrimp stock size and harvest levels. These findings are corroborated by a long-term field study of the German North Sea shrimp fishery (Tiews 1978a, 1978b).[18]

The return of discards into the marine food web may also affect ecosystem relationships in more indirect ways. Incapacitated organisms, carcasses, body pieces, and tissue may be consumed by large and small predators. Discards that are not consumed immediately

18. Other, short-term field studies have been less conclusive (for example, a four-year investigation of the discard of small redfish in the Newfoundland shrimp fishery) (Atkinson 1984).

reach the sea floor and become part of the benthic food web, attracting scavengers such as crab species and decomposers such as worms. Artificial additions of detritus may cause changes in community structure and diversity by increasing the number of resident scavenger and decomposer species. If certain members of the pelagic and benthic communities thrive and grow rapidly at times when shrimp fleet discards are abundant, then their predation on commercially valuable species could increase during times when discard deposits decrease. Yet, there is no substantial research being done on the problem at this time.

Addressing the Finfish Discard Problem

It is generally acknowledged that the discard catch of finfish in the Gulf and South Atlantic shrimp fishery will have to be dealt with, sooner or later. But, the Gulf of Mexico Regional Fishery Management Council is not likely to address the problem. For example, in late 1988, the council amended its shrimp management plan and did nothing to address finfish bycatch (Gulf of Mexico Regional Fishery Management Council 1988). Yet, the council has recognized the magnitude of the problem since approval of the original shrimp management plan in 1981. The original plan states that bycatch is a source of conflict with the reef fishery (for which there is a management plan) and with the groundfish fishery (for which there is a draft plan). For this reason the council concluded that bycatch by shrimpers should be minimized "where appropriate." To reach this objective, the shrimp plan states that the council will "encourage research on and the development of shrimping gear in order to reduce the incidental catch without decreasing the overall efficiency of shrimping or excessively increasing the cost of gear" (Gulf of Mexico Regional Fishery Management Council 1981). The council is in the process of preparing an amendment to its reef fish plan, but at this point it seems unlikely that it will arrive at any solution to the shrimp discard problem (Leary interview).

NMFS' Role. NMFS officials, especially research staff at the Pascagoula laboratory (who developed the TED, and worked hard to design a device that also would decrease finfish bycatch), continue to be optimistic that somehow the agency will confront the problem of finfish discard. In the meantime, shrimpers are most likely not to use NMFS' TED model—the only device that substantially reduces bycatch in addition to excluding turtles— but rather one of the five other approved TEDs developed by private industry.[19] The most most-favored TED is

19. The approved TEDs are the Cameron TED, the Matagorda TED, the Georgia TED, the Morrison TED, and the Parish TED; the last two are referred to as "soft" TEDs because they have no rigid parts and are made of net webbing (52 *Federal Register* 24244 [1987]; 52 *Federal Register* 37152 [1987]; and 53 *Federal Register* 33820 [1988]).

the "Georgia Jumper," a simple, oval, barred device that is an adaptation of what is called a "jelly ball shooter," a contraption that shrimpers have used for decades to get rid of jellyfish that sometimes are so dense on the grounds that they clog the trawls. In addition to being cheaper ($300 to $400 per pair), lighter, of a more simple construction, and more easily installed and used than the NMFS TED, the Georgia Jumper has the additional appeal of having been developed and manufactured by a Georgia shrimper—not the government (Oravetz interview, Seidel interview).

In 1989, NMFS' southeast regional office launched a three-year effort to study shrimp bycatch. The study involves developing a comprehensive economic model of the Gulf shrimp fishery that would examine how bycatch and the regulation of it affects fishermen's decisions to enter or leave the fishery. The costs of regulation would be compared to estimated benefits to the public of reducing bycatch in the shrimp fishery (Ward interview). The agency also has proposed a three-year, $700,000 gear development and education project to get a fish separator device perfected for the Gulf shrimp fishery (Seidel interview).

Wil Seidel of the NMFS Pascagoula lab, who with John Watson worked on the TED project from the outset, says that the government must resume work on gear design (Seidel interview). For years NMFS labs experimented with and developed new fish harvesting gear as an integral part of the agency's role in developing the use of U.S. fishery resources. But by the early 1980s nearly all of that work was phased out because of budget cuts and because the agency received criticism that the research was subsidizing industry. Fishing gear research continued at reduced levels in Pascagoula, mainly because of the shrimp-turtle situation. Based on their perception of the continuing importance of bycatch problems, NMFS officials in 1985 proposed the establishment of a conservation engineering program. The program was envisioned as employing 10 full-time technical staff with a modest $2 million addition to the NMFS budget (NMFS unpubl.). Although supported by the former director of NMFS, William Gordon, the plan did not make it into the final budget request submitted in 1985. Seidel believes that gear development to reduce bycatch is a necessary and proper role for the agency (Seidel interview).

Views of Other Fishermen. The commercial fishermen who are adversely affected by the discard of their target species have not been effective lobbyists on the issue. In the case of the groundfish industry, there are only a few boats fishing and these are selling their catch for pet food. A new pilot plant for surimi production, a joint venture with the Japanese, could increase demand for groundfish, however. One natural resource economist has shown that the discard of croaker alone could be wasting more than $6 million worth of commercially useable

Table 1. Comparison of Annual Bycatches with Average Recreational Catches, Gulf of Mexico 1972–1985 (in millions of fish).

Species	Estimated bycatch	Recreational catch
Croaker	1,500	11
Spot	156	0.2
Sand seatrout	89	7.2
Sea catfish	43	19
King mackerel	0.2	0.5
Spanish mackerel	1.3	2
Red snapper	12	3.1

Source: Nichols *et al.* 1987.

groundfish each year (Stokes pers. comm.). New markets might affect the balance of power in the Gulf fishing industry.

Sports fishermen are better organized, although just beginning to use their influence on a national scale. Perhaps the most vocal of these groups in the Gulf and South Atlantic states is the National Coalition for Marine Conservation. The organization came out in 1986 in support of requiring the TED for turtles and believes that the discard issue must be faced head on:

> No one is out to put shrimpers out of work. But they seem to forget that they make their living catching and selling a public resource, something that belongs to everybody, not just to them. The shrimp belong to everybody, the turtles belong to everybody, and the fish belong to everybody. . . . To the extent that shrimp trawling routinely kills and wastes substantial numbers of fish, turtles, and other marine life . . . the public has a right to insist that shrimpers use [TEDs] to eliminate the waste (National Coalition for Marine Conservation 1987).

Coalition Executive Director Ken Hinman poses this question: "If someone came along today and said that they had this great new way to fish—and introduced the shrimp trawl—would it be allowed? I think people would say 'no way' " (Hinman pers. comm.).

Four million residents from the Gulf states alone fished for recreation in the Gulf in 1985, harvesting 145 million fish. Sport fishermen have good reason to be disturbed by shrimp trawl practices. Shrimp vessels in many cases catch and discard more of the species sought by recreational fishermen than are caught by the sport fishermen themselves (see Table 1).

As David Rockland of the Washington, D.C.-based Sport Fishing Institute says, "Sport fishermen are very concerned about bycatch, and sea turtles have brought the issue to the fore. What is missing now is to require the use of the NMFS TED or another device that would eliminate the significant waste of important sport fisheries species now occurring due to shrimp trawling." The Institute and other groups

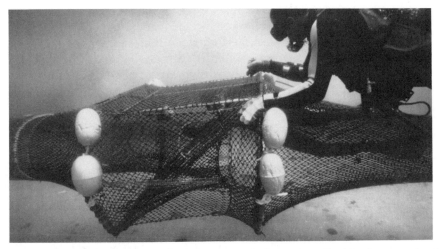

A diver checks a Trawling Efficiency Device that is installed in the mouth of a shrimp seine. The TED allows sea turtles and large fish to escape, while shrimp pass through into the net. *John Watson/NMFS*

will be working on this issue during reauthorization of the Magnuson Act in 1989 (Rockland interview).

Shrimp Association Views. The Texas Shrimp Association, which took part in the TED negotiations, believes that not much of the discard has time to decay because it is rapidly consumed by predators; and in any case, such organisms enrich marine waters and should not be considered waste. Ralph Rayburn, the association's executive director, says shrimpers would rather catch only shrimp in their nets, but money for gear innovation is dependent on the economic health of the industry. Shrimp profits are erratic at this point, not increasing each year, a situation that makes fishermen reluctant to invest in new technology or take the risk of gear innovation. Nonetheless, the association is planning to focus membership attention on the problem. Rayburn says his objective is to keep the discard issue from becoming another turtle crisis because no one wins in those situations. "[T]here are responsible fishermen who are trying to reduce the impact of their operations on other interests. This is not a new issue, but it's one that needs to be dealt with sensibly, sensitively, and now." Rayburn adds, however, that he does not believe "the NMFS TED is the answer to the offshore industry bycatch issue" (Rayburn pers. comm.).

Shrimpers elsewhere cannot fail to be aware of the problem. During field trials of the NMFS TED in South Carolina in 1983, a demonstration ship had a TED installed on the starboard trawl and no TED on the port trawl. Toward the end of a 90-minute tow, as the port net was being hauled in, the captain, seeing the substantial wake on the port side commented that it looked like he had caught a whale. In fact, he had caught thousands of fingerling-sized fish, many blue and horse-shoe crabs, numerous other unidentified crabs, a dozen "jelly balls" (softball- to basketball-sized jellyfish), a fair-sized shark, a number of large fish, some fatgrass, and a handful of shrimp. By the time the shrimp were sorted and the rest pushed overboard, all of the bycatch organisms were dead except some crabs. Similar events occur on a daily basis in the shrimp fleets from North Carolina to Texas.

Role of Conservation Organizations. The conservation community's role in solving the bycatch problem is unclear. Its first priority is to see that TED regulations are properly implemented. Furthermore, it may not be willing to take on the shrimp industry again so soon after the battle over TEDs during the 1987–1988 reauthorization of the Endangered Species Act. The reauthorization of the Magnuson Act in 1989 offers the earliest opportunity for the national conservation community to debate the issue. Only a very small segment of the conservation community has shown an interest in fisheries matters, and the positions of these groups are often dependent on one or two individuals. Greenpeace, while consistently involved in fisheries management, has worked mostly in the North Pacific. Jan Johnson of Greenpeace's southeast regional office says bycatch must be addressed, and that the shrimp industry must be made more accountable—through regulations under current law, or if necessary, through changes in the Magnuson Act. Bycatch waste will be one of the southeast office's priorities for the next several years (Johnson interview). Michael Weber of the Center for Marine Conservation, a key player in obtaining TED regulations, notes that the conservation community highlighted bycatch in *Blueprint for the Environment*, a list of recommendations for the Bush Administration. The Center will be working on the Magnuson Act reauthorization and may attempt to focus greater attention on the issue (Weber interview).

What is certain is that optimism is not rampant among conservationists. It took 10 years to get NMFS to protect endangered sea turtles, and to this day the Gulf of Mexico Fishery Management Council consistently avoids dealing with the larger bycatch issue. Conservationists can only wonder how long it will take to get NMFS policymakers to address massive discards in the Gulf of Mexico when the agency is on record stating that it considers species of no economic value to be environmentally insignificant as well.

RECOMMENDATIONS

Under current fishery management practices, bycatch of marine life is controlled in only two instances: where the bycatch contains species that are specifically protected under a nonfishery statute, or where the bycatch contains species that are highly valued by other fishermen who pursue them in a commercial or recreational fishery. This leaves unregulated the ongoing waste of billions of pounds of fish and other sea life annually. Bycatch could be addressed now—technologically, scientifically, and legally. In addition, conservationists could pursue changes to the Magnuson Fishery Conservation and Management Act in the 1989–1990 reauthorization process to more clearly focus the statute on ecological issues such as bycatch waste.

Fish in the waters of the United States, as our wildlife, trees, lands, and other public trust resources, are supposed to be conserved and managed for the overall public benefit. To some, the concept of conservation embodies enhancement, protection, putting something by for the future. To others, it may mean wise use—use up to a point that approaches, but does not exceed, the ability of the resource being conserved to recover and reproduce so that it will continue to be available in the future. Fisheries management policy as set forth in the Magnuson Act and driven by the goal of "optimum yield," reflects both of these viewpoints.

Yet FMCA's pursuit of harvest efficiency and economic return to the harvester makes it difficult for fishery management councils to address the bycatch problem. For species of bycatch that are not yet considered commercially valuable, the councils see no reason to set limits or make attempts to conserve these stocks. Any attempt to do so may reduce the efficiency of a directed fishery managed by the councils. Thus, discard is treated as a cost of doing business.

The regulation of species of bycatch that are commercially valuable is viewed by the fishery making the discard as unfairly affecting its competitive position. This further complicates decision-making for the councils because they must, according to the Magnuson Act, allocate fairly among users. Limiting bycatch in the nontarget fishery is seen as an allocation issue—an issue of which fishermen get to catch and market valuable stocks—not a question of protecting the resource.

The National Standards and Bycatch

The present language of the Magnuson Act could be interpreted to afford a basis for regulating bycatch—not only of commercially valuable species, but others as well. Fishermen in fisheries that discard bycatch have used national standards 4 and 5 to argue against regulation because, they say, these standards mandate economic efficiency and fairness in allocation. In the authors' view, however, those same standards could be used to justify bycatch regulation. Standard 4 of the Magnuson Act says that "conservation and management measures shall not discriminate [among fishermen] . . . and allocations shall be fair and equitable and reasonably calculated to promote conservation." The objective of this standard is to avoid promulgating management regulations that benefit one user group to the detriment of another. Federal fishery regulations provide that there may be instances where hardships may be imposed on fishermen by allocation decisions if the hardships are outweighed by the total benefits to the nation. Further, promotion of conservation is a recognized reason for allocating fishing privileges (50 C.F.R. 602.15 [c][3][B]). In cases where discard of bycatch is depressing target stocks, altering predator-prey relationships in ways that will affect target stocks, or affecting an interrelated stock of fish, this standard compels an examination of conservation measures—even if such measures impose burdens on the required fishery. Any imposition on the regulated fishery is outweighed by total conservation benefits to that user group in the future (for example, preserving juveniles for later recruitment to the fishery), or to other user groups in the present (for example, making species that would be discarded and wasted available for harvest and use by other fishermen).

Making a species available to a fishery that would harvest it instead of to one that discards it has been criticized as "economic allocation." Some argue this would be counter to Standard 5, which requires that conservation and management measures "promote efficiency in the utilization of fishery resources." One could question, however, whether the current practice of allocating a portion of the annual optimum yield to fisherman who waste it as discarded bycatch is really "efficient" use of that resource. One long-term participant in the council process described it this way: "You allow a certain take of the resource, first by people who are not allowed to sell it, and then—only after that—you establish a quota for those who are allowed to catch and sell that species. It makes little sense" (Bevan interview).

To fishery managers, efficient utilization of the fishery stocks means achieving the greatest biologically allowable level of catch at the least possible cost. Utilization encompasses harvesting, processing, and marketing. While the Magnuson Act and NMFS regulations recognize that the goal of promoting efficiency may conflict with other legitimate social or biological objectives of fishery management, the regulations point out that Standard 5 "highlights *one way* a fishery can contribute to the nation's benefit with the least cost" (emphasis added). Furthermore, measures that would reduce efficiency, if they contribute to the attainment of other social or biological objectives, are permissible (50 C.F.R. 602.15 [b][2][ii]).

Therefore, if gear changes or other changes in how a fishery is conducted would reduce bycatch, they could and should be considered by the councils even if such measures would reduce somewhat the efficiency of the fishery creating the discard. For example, where technology offers the principal means of solving the bycatch problem, as in the shrimp trawl fishery, gear changes should be imposed: NMFS could require the use of its TED, or other models with comparable ability to exclude finfish. The agency could also require that crabbers, for instance, substitute a larger mesh when replacing worn-out pots that would allow the escape of crabs below the legal size. NMFS should resurrect the idea of a full-fledged "conservation engineering" program as proposed in 1985. Such a program would continue work on turtle excluders, methods of catching tuna fish without causing the deaths of dolphins, and more work on the crab excluder project begun in 1988 to explore ways of reducing the capture of crabs in bottomfish trawls. NMFS regulations state that "conservation constitutes wise use of all resources involved in the fishery, not just fish stocks" (602.15 [b][2]).

In order to implement regulatory measures to reduce bycatch waste, an examination of species other than target species must be included in the development of fishery management plans. Conservation of interrelated ecosystems must become part of the biological, ecological, and social objectives of the fishery management plan, and the effects of bycatch and discard must be considered in subsequent allocation and management decisions. Managing a fishery without knowing the ecological effects of discard leaves a large gap in the scientific information base.

Standard 1 requires that conservation and management measures prevent overfishing while obtaining an optimum yield from each fishery. According to NMFS regulations, the optimum yield need not be a number or weight of fish, but can be expressed as a quota by user group or gear type, by season, minimum size of shellfish, or any other specification that expresses how economic, social, or ecological factors were taken into account (16 U.S.C.A. §1802[18][A]; 50 C.F.R. 602.11[e][2]). What is required, according to the courts, is a good faith effort by the council and NMFS to gather and use available information, examine options, consider the relevant factors and reach a reasoned conclusion on what the harvest level should be for a particular stock, at a particular time, by a particular fishery (*Pacific Coast Federation of Fishermen's Associations v. Secretary of Commerce*, 494 F. Supp. 626, 635 [D.C. Cal. 1980]).

In order to consider ecological factors, the councils must know something about them. Standard 2 requires that conservation and management measures must be based upon the best scientific information available, and existing information on bycatch effects should be considered by the councils. Scientific information includes not only fishery data, but also ecological, economic, and social information. Just because scientific information is incomplete, a council is not prevented from preparing a fishery management plan (50 C.F.R. 602.12[b]). Further, if there are conflicting facts or opinions among the data presented, a council may choose among them as long as it justifies the choice (50 C.F.R. 602.12[b][2]).

The councils should include existing information in the development of FMPs. In fisheries where bycatch is known to occur, NMFS should study the effects of discards on the discarded species, the target species, and the ecosystem. The agency should begin to examine the magnitude of discard, and the proportion of discard to retained catch in terms both of numbers of organisms and biomass. Predator-prey relationships and interactions, as well as the effects of discards on associated communities and ecosystems, also should be studied.

Finally, even though the Magnuson Act does not specifically declare that fishery managers must address the fate and impact of marine organisms dumped overboard by the ton, Standard 3 demands that managers consider the interrelationships of fish stocks: "To the extent practicable, an individual stock of fish must be managed as a unit throughout its range, and interrelated stocks of fish must be managed as a unit or in close coordination" (16 U.S.C.A. 1851[a][3]). Since councils have the flexibility to set not only harvest limits, but also management units, their decisions about what stocks are "interrelated" should be guided by ecological factors as well as harvest factors. The regulations state, for example, that a management unit can be organized around "species that are associated in the ecosystem" (50 C.F.R. 602.13[d][1][vi]), and, further, that "a management unit may contain, in addition to regulated species, stocks of fish for which there is not enough information available to specify . . . optimum yield or to establish management measures, so that data on these species may be collected under the FMP" (50 C.F.R. 602.13[d][2]). This language provides the basis for studying bycatch species that now are caught and discarded, but may later be found to affect the fishery subject to the FMP, or species that may form the basis for valuable fisheries in the future as market tastes change.

Needed Changes to Law and Regulations

During reauthorization of the Magnuson Act, environmental groups should seek changes to make clear that its focus extends beyond managing just those fishery stocks deemed commercially valuable to the conservation and management of marine ecosystems. Elements of a reform effort could include the following actions.

1. Require that all domestic fisheries be subject to 100 percent observer coverage to document both directed take and bycatch in situations where the vessel size and fishery operations make on-board observers possible; devise alternative verification programs in other situations. As one commentator says, "running fisheries without observers is like running a bank without an audit" (Bevan interview). Parties who profit from the enterprise should pay for the observer program, either directly or through a tax assessed on landings.

2. Require that fishery management councils include members from both consumer and environmental organizations.

3. Add specific language to the statute defining discard as "waste" and make it clear that waste must be eliminated or reduced.

4. Amend reporting regulations to require that *all* species landed or caught and released be documented.

5. Force "cleaner fishing" through a combination of statutory and regulatory changes. Fishing gear can be modified by requiring the use of new devices or changes in mesh size to exclude bycatch. Fishing in zones where a large bycatch is known to occur should be regulated by a combination of time, season, and area closures. All bycatch that is alive and appears to have a chance of survival should be returned immediately to the sea. Vessels must retain all fish caught and deliver them to market. Proceeds from species not allocated to the vessel that catches them should be used to fund research programs in the region. In those instances where it is impossible to retain all fish caught because of ship capacity, or where proper disposal of those fish on shore would be impractical, discards should be allowed, but a tax should be levied on the discard to provide industry incentives to reduce it.

Bycatch can also be addressed indirectly by use of other existing laws. The National Environmental Policy Act should be used as a tool to work in conjunction with FCMA national standards to ensure that fishery management councils consider the full range of environmental impacts of fishery management plans. Also, since logs dumped into Alaskan marine waters are considered a "discharge" that requires a National Pollutant Discharge Elimination System permit under the Clean Water Act, there is reason to speculate that the dumping of tons of dead fish may also require a discharge permit from the Environmental Protection Agency.

Although fisheries management is gradually emerging from the single-species focus of the past, it is still driven by the economic demands of the most powerful fishing interests. Slowly but surely environmentalists have addressed the the incidental take of specially protected species. It will take an even greater effort to confront the issue of discarded finfish bycatch. Conservationists must forcefully use FCMA in its current form while seeking relevant changes to it. They must pursue imaginative remedies using other federal environmental laws. In the meantime, it is important that groups with marine conservation goals attend council meetings, comment on proposed FMPs or amendments, and generally become much more involved in fishery management decisions and actions. Until very recently, the councils have heard only from industry, recreational fishermen, and regulators because broader-based public interest groups with a stake in ocean conservation have failed to make their positions known. Bycatch and its effects on the marine environment have received little attention to date. If the problem is to be solved, especially for species with no current market value, a new force for change must come from outside the fishing industry.

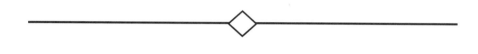

ADDENDUM 1

Discard: A Landlubber's Primer

For those who do not know red drum from a red herring, fisheries management terminology can be extremely confusing. In order to understand "discard," it is helpful to understand not only the terminology used to describe commercial fishing operations, but also something about the process of fisheries regulation in the United States.

Commercial fisheries generally are organized by the type of fish sought, the gear used to catch them, and the area and season in which fishing occurs. For example, "Bering Sea groundfish trawl fishery" describes a fishery that seeks to capture groundfish such as pollock and cod by using trawl nets in the Bering Sea. State and federal regulation of fisheries mirrors fishery characteristics. The regulating agency sets seasons, limits the numbers of fish that may be caught, prescribes the type of gear that may be used, defines who may fish, and establishes other rules for commercial fishing.

In addition to basic fishery regulations, state and federal regulatory bodies also *allocate* fishery resources. Through a combination scientific-economic-political process, fishery management agencies decide which fishermen get how much of which fishery resources. For example, salmon are caught in gillnets, seines, and on troll lines. Different groups of fishermen may harvest from a particular run of salmon in the ocean, at a river mouth, or in the spawning stream. The process whereby the regulatory agency decides how to divide among ocean trollers, coastal seiners and river gillnetters the number of salmon that may safely be taken from the run (allowing some to go upstream to spawn) is called *allocation*. The fish that are divided among users are called *allocated species* or *regulated species*. In deciding how to allocate the harvest, regulators consider scientific information on the size and health of the stock, the economics of the various fishermen that want to catch fish from this stock, and testimony from users regarding their desired share.

Once the allocation decision is made, a fisherman within the user group receiving a harvest allocation may catch those species up to the limit allowed. (To fishermen not within the user group, these same fish are considered *prohibited species*, and they have no right to catch them.) The effort to catch allocated species is called a *directed fishery* or *target fishery*, and the allotment of the fish a harvester is trying to catch is called his or her *directed take* of target species. In a fishing vessel's daily take from the sea, or *catch*, there normally is a mix of *target* and *nontarget* species. Nontarget species are the organisms unintentionally captured in the process of harvesting the target species; all caught, nontarget species are collectively referred to as *bycatch*. Usually the fisherman does not want bycatch species, but he may decide to retain some of the nontarget species if they are marketable, if applicable laws and regulations allow him to keep them and sell them, or if separating them from his target catch is not too much trouble.

Discard (or *discard catch*) is that portion of the total catch including both target and nontarget species that is released, never landed, or most commonly, thrown overboard. It should be noted that with rare exception, discarded organisms are almost always dead before being dumped overboard; those that do survive capture and deck exposure are weakened and highly vulnerable to predation after being returned to the water.

Discard from a vessel might include, for example, target species such as:

- fish or crustaceans too small to process (juveniles);
- individuals under or over the legal size limit;
- in fisheries where a maximum allowable limit has been set, that part of the catch that exceeds the maximum take limits for the period; and

- fish lost during fishing (for example, gillnet dropouts), purposefully not landed, or released in order to protect fishing gear from damage.

The discard almost always includes nontarget species such as:

- prohibited species which all but select fishermen are forbidden to take (species such as salmon, halibut, king and Tanner crabs);
- species whose take is not prohibited, but that are not considered economically valuable by the fishermen catching them even though they may be considered valuable by other fishermen (for example, finfish caught by shrimp trawlers);
- species with no current commercial value (for example, certain species of bottomfish, such as sculpins, that are not presently desired by consumers); or
- protected species with recognized special status, such as marine mammals (seals, dolphins), endangered species (sea turtles), or migratory birds (seabirds in the North Pacific), whose take by fishermen is highly restricted or forbidden.

REFERENCES

Alaska Data Bank, Alaska Factory Trawl Association, American High Seas Fisheries Association, Arctic Alaska Seafoods, Inc., Association, Golden Age Fisheries, Inc., Highliner's Association, Marine Resources, Inc., Midwater Trawlers Association, North Pacific Fishing Vessel Owners Association, Northern Deep Sea Fisheries, Inc., Pacific Independent Trawlers Association. 1988. Position Paper to John Peterson, Chairman, North Pacific Fishery Management Council Relative to 1989 Bycatch Limits for Bering Sea-Aleutian Islands Trawl Fishery. October 24.

Alverson, Lee. Interview with author Bricklemyer. Seattle, Washington. January 30, 1989.

Andrewartha, H.G. and L.C. Birch. 1984. *The Ecological Web: More on the Distribution and Abundance of Animals.* University of Chicago Press. Chicago, Illinois.

Atkinson, D.B. 1984. "Discarding of small redfish in the shrimp fishery off Port au Choix, Newfoundland 1976–1980." *Journal of Northwest Atlantic Fisheries Science* 5:99–102.

Bean, Michael. 1983. *The Evolution of National Wildlife Law.* Praeger. New York, New York.

Bevan, Donald. Interview with author Bricklemyer. Anchorage, Alaska. December 7, 1988.

Browder, J.A. 1981. "Use of an energy flow model to evaluate alternative harvesting strategies in a multispecies fishery." pp. 571–583 in *International Symposium on Energy Ecology Modeling.* Louisville, Kentucky.

Brown, Lester R. 1985. "Maintaining world fisheries," pp. 73–96 *in* Linda Starke ed., *State of the World 1985.* W.W. Norton. New York, New York.

Bryan, C.E., T. Cody and G. Matlock. 1983. "Organisms captured by the commercial shrimp fleet." *Texas Parks and Wildlife Department Technical Series* 31.

Cotter, Larry. Interview with author Bricklemyer. Anchorage, Alaska. December 7, 1988.

———. Written comments to author Bricklemyer. January 27, 1988.

Cottingham, David. Interview with author Bricklemyer. Washington, D.C. January 12, 1989.

Evans, Dale. Interview with author Bricklemyer. Anchorage, Alaska. December 7, 1988.

Fish and Wildlife Service. 1980. Memorandum from Assistant Solicitor. December 11, 1980.

———. 1981. Memorandum from Assistant Solicitor, March 27, 1981.

Gulf of Mexico Fishery Management Council. 1981. Fishery Management Plan for the Shrimp Fishery of the Gulf of Mexico, United States Waters. Tampa, Florida.

———. 1988. Amendment Number 4 to the Fishery Management Plan for the Gulf of Mexico, United States Waters. Tampa, Florida.

Highliners Association. Letter to author Bricklemyer. December 20, 1988.

Hinman, Ken. Letter to author Bricklemyer. January 31, 1989.

Jacobsen, J. and K. Davis. 1983. *Federal Fisheries Management*. Ocean & Coastal Law Center. Univ. of Oregon Law School. Corvallis, Oregon.

Jans, Nick. 1988. "The hardy sturgeon makes a rebound." *National Fisherman* (December 1988): 22–24, 40.

Johnson, Jay. Interview with author Bricklemyer. Washington, D.C. November 29, 1988.

Johnson, Jan. Interview with author Bricklemyer. Washington, D.C. January 12, 1989.

———. Written comments to author Bricklemyer. January 23, 1989.

Knowles, Tony. Interview with author Bricklemyer. Anchorage, AK, December 7, 1988.

Kronmiller, Ted. 1988. Memorandum of November 30, 1988 to John G. Peterson, Chairman, North Pacific Fishery Management Council.

Langan, R. and W.H. Howell. 1984. Commercial Trawler Discards of Four Flounder Species in the Gulf of Maine. Unpublished manuscript. University of New Hampshire Marine Program contribution.

Leary, Terry. Interview with author Bricklemyer. Washington, D.C. February 14, 1989.

Lindner, Milton J. 1936. "A discussion of the shrimp trawl—fish problem." *Louisiana Conservation Review* l(4).

Murphy, Tara. Interview with author Bricklemyer. Washington, D.C. March 14, 1985.

National Coalition for Marine Conservation. 1987. "TEDs: Waste is the real issue." *Marine Bulletin* 27:1–3.

National Marine Fisheries Service. 1988. *Fisheries of the United States, 1987*. Washington, D.C.

———. 1987. *Fisheries of the United States, 1986*. Washington, D.C.

———. Unpubl. Conservation Engineering: A Program Development Plan for the National Marine Fisheries Service.

National Oceanic and Atmospheric Administration/National Marine Fisheries Service. 1987. Final Supplement to the Final Environmental Impact Statement Listing and Protecting the Green Sea Turtle, Loggerhead Sea Turtle, and Pacific Ridley Sea Turtle Under the Endangered Species Act of 1973. Washington, D.C. 48 pp and appendices.

Nichols, Scott, Arvind Shah and Gilmore Pellegrin. 1987. Estimates of Annual Shrimp Fleet By-Catch for Thirteen Finfish Species in the Offshore Waters of the Gulf of Mexico, Report of the Southeast Fisheries Center, Mississippi Laboratories, National Marine Fisheries Service.

O'Hara, Kathryn J. 1988. "Plastic debris and its effects on marine wildlife," pp. 395–437 in Chandler, W.J. ed., *Audubon Wildlife Report 1988/1989*. National Audubon Society and Academic Press, Inc. New York.

Parks, Norman B. 1978. "The Pacific Northwest commercial fishery for sturgeon." *Marine Fisheries Review* 40(7): 17–20.

Pellegrin, Gilmore J., Shelby B. Drummond and Robert S. Ford. Unpubl. The Incidental Catch of Fish by the Northern Gulf of Mexico Shrimp Fleet. Report of the Southeast Fisheries Center, Mississippi Laboratories, National Marine Fisheries Service.

———. 1982. "Fish discards from the southeastern United States shrimp fishery," in *Fish By Catch . . . Bonus from the Sea: Report of a Technical Consultation on Shrimp By-*

Catch Utilization held in Georgetown, Guyana, 27–30 October, 1981. International Development Research Centre. Ottawa, Canada.

Powers, Joseph E., C. Phillip Goodyear and Gerald P. Scott. 1987. The Potential Effect of Shrimp Fleet By-Catch on Fisheries Production of Selected Fish Stocks in the Gulf of Mexico. Report of the Southeast Fisheries Center, Mississippi Laboratories. National Marine Fisheries Service, Coast Resources Division, Contribution No. CRD-87/88–06.

Rayburn, Ralph. Interview with author Bricklemyer. Washington, D.C. November 29, 1988.

———. Letter to author Bricklemyer. February 3, 1989.

Robinson, M.A. 1982. Prospects for World Fisheries to 2000. United Nations Food and Agriculture Organization Fisheries Circular No. 722, Rev. 1. Rome, Italy. 16 pp.

Rockland, David. 1989. Interview with author Bricklemyer. Washington, D.C. January 12.

Saila, S.B. 1983. Importance and Assessment of Discards in Commercial Fisheries, UN Food and Agriculture Organization Fisheries Cir. No. 765. Rome, Italy. 62 pp.

Saville, A. 1980. "The assessment and management of pelagic fish stocks: discussion and conclusion of symposium." *Rapports et Proces verbaux des Reunion du Conseil International pour L'Exploration de la Mer* 177: 513–517.

Seidel, Wil. Interview with author Bricklemyer. Washington, D.C. February 14, 1989.

Smith, Tim. Interview with author Bricklemyer. Seattle, Washington. April 8, 1985.

Stokes, Robert L. Memorandum to author Bricklemyer, September, 1986.

Tarnas, David. 1986. Discard of Marine Fishes by the Gulf of Mexico Shrimp Fleet. Memorandum prepared for E.C. Bricklemyer. School of Fisheries. University of Washington. Seattle, Washington.

Tiews, K. 1978a. "Non-commercial fish species in the German Bight: records of by-catches of the brown shrimp fishery." *Rapports et Proces verbaux des Reunion du Conseil International pour L'Exploration de la Mer* 172: 259–265.

———. 1978b. "The predator-prey relationship between fish populations and the stock of brown shrimp (*Crangon crangon* L.) in German coastal waters." *Rapports et Proces verbaux des Reunion du Conseil International pour L'Exploration de la Mer* 172: 250–258.

United Nations Food and Agriculture Organization. 1986a. *State of World Fisheries Resources.* Rome, Italy.

———. 1986b. *Development of International Trade in Fishery Products 1960–1985.* Unpublished. Rome, Italy.

U.S. Congress, Senate Committee on Commerce, Science and Transportation, National Ocean Policy Study. 1987. Hearings on S. 62, the Driftnet Impact Monitoring, Assessment and Control Act. Series No. S.Hrg. 100–204.

Ward, John. Interview with author Bricklemyer. Seattle, Washington. February 9, 1989.

Weber, Michael. Interview with author Bricklemyer. Washington, D.C. January 13, 1989.

———. 1987. "Federal marine fisheries management," pp. 267–344 *in* Di Silvestro, R.L. ed., *Audubon Wildlife Report 1986.* National Audubon Society. New York, New York.

Wooster, Warren. Letter to author Bricklemyer. March 7, 1985.

Bo Bricklemyer is managing director of the Aquatic Resources Conservation Group in Seattle and counsel to Greenpeace USA's Ocean Ecology Campaign.

Suzanne Iudicello was a legal associate at the Center for Marine Conservation (formerly the Center for Environmental Education) in Washington, D.C., at the time this article was

written. She is now associate director for fisheries and the environment in the Washington, D.C. office of the Alaska governor.
Hans Hartmann is a post doctoral fellow at the Groupe de Protistologie et Zoologie, Universite Blaise Pascal de Clermont Ferrand, France, and a partner in the Aquatic Resources Conservation Group.

The authors wish to thank the Schools of Law and Fisheries at the University of Washington for support during the years 1984–1987, when early research on this article was accomplished.

The U. S. Fish and Wildlife Service, which is responsible for managing 815 species of birds, concentrates its efforts on the 58 species that are hunted. There is not enough known about so-called "nongame" birds, such as this sharp-shinned hawk, to manage them effectively. *Leonard Lee Rue III*

Conserving Nongame Migratory Birds: A Strategy for Monitoring and Research

Judith Gradwohl
and
Russell Greenberg

INTRODUCTION

The federal government has been legally responsible for the conservation and management of all migratory bird species in the United States since 1918. Implementation of that authority is the responsibility of the U.S. Fish and Wildlife Service (FWS), an agency within the Department of the Interior. Presently, FWS is responsible for 757 nongame bird species and 58 species that are hunted.[1]

The federal mandate to protect migratory birds evolved from a series of bilateral international treaties and congressional acts prompted by the overexploitation of waterfowl, shorebirds, and other species. Prior to federal regulation of migratory bird hunting in 1918, any species large or tasty enough to constitute a meal was legal game.

Within the past 60 years it was further recognized that habitat protection was critical to protecting migratory birds, particularly wa-

---

1. Approximately 600 to 650 of these 815 species regularly occur within the United States. The total number of federally protected species fluctuates yearly depending on various administrative, regulatory, and treaty changes.

297

terfowl dependent upon diminishing wetlands. Consequently, FWS' responsibility was expanded to include monitoring and conserving migratory bird species and their habitats. Although the initial impetus of migratory bird legislation was the conservation of all overexploited migratory birds, the overwhelming emphasis of federal management has been gamebirds, particularly waterfowl.

Nongame bird conservation programs at FWS have never received equivalent staff or funding equivalent to the programs oriented toward game species. However, lawmakers have attempted to address this imbalance in recent years. Concern over the lack of emphasis on nongame species in the 1970s led to the passage of the Fish and Wildlife Conservation Act in 1980, which authorized federal grants to states for the development of plans, programs, and projects to conserve nongame vertebrates. Unfortunately, Congress has never funded the act.

Resurgence in the concern for nongame birds led to congressionally initiated budget increases for nongame bird activities in fiscal years 1988 and 1989 totalling $1.75 million, the release by FWS of "Nongame Bird Strategies" (U.S. Department of Interior 1988b), and the passage of the Mitchell Amendment in 1988. The Mitchell Amendment requires FWS to monitor all nongame birds and their habitats and to identify needed management actions before any particular species becomes threatened or endangered. To pay for this monitoring, FWS either must reallocate existing funds or request new sums from Congress. The Mitchell Amendment and the budget "add-ons" of $1.75 million are a strong message from Congress to FWS that it is time to re-examine programs and establish new priorities for nongame species.

This chapter outlines the major conservation problems facing many migratory bird populations,.examines the strengths and limitations of existing FWS nongame bird activities, and outlines a 10-year strategy of monitoring and research for songbirds and shorebirds.

Although FWS has a legal mandate to monitor and protect migratory birds and a steady source of funding to carry out its charge, it suffers from inherent problems. First, there is an acknowledged lack of interest within FWS in nongame species. This is reflected in the allocation of funding. Rough estimates provided by FWS show that nongame species receive around one-sixth of the funding (not including monies spent on rare and endangered species) allocated to game bird species for monitoring and research. The Office of Migratory Bird Management estimates that only 10 percent of its $8 million annual appropriation (FY 1989) goes for nongame work. There also has been considerable apathy within FWS toward the "Nongame Bird Strategies" statement released by the Office of Migratory Bird Management in May 1988. A second major problem is that nongame species do not receive attention or priority until they are considered threatened or endangered with extinction; tremendous amounts of funding are then allocated toward often hopeless recovery efforts.

WHY PROTECT COMMON SPECIES?

The pitfalls of putting too much emphasis on threatened or endangered species are not as obvious as the relative lack of funding for nongame species, but they will result in similar problems. Two separate but complementary arguments can be advanced for focusing conservation efforts on common species of migratory birds. First, recovery programs for threatened and endangered species are expensive and often ineffective because the management system is too slow to respond until the species requires emergency action. A second, and perhaps even more important reason, is that environmental problems often affect large numbers of species that share similar habitats or ecological roles. These general problems may cause chronic population declines long before individual species reach the brink of extinction. The expensive and often futile nature of recovery programs is illustrated here with two case studies.

The Dusky Seaside Sparrow

The case of the dusky seaside sparrow (*Ammodramus maritima nigrescens*) illustrates the pitfalls of delaying conservation measures until a species reaches a crisis state. The dusky's extinction is the first known extinction of a North American subspecies of bird protected by the Endangered Species Act. The sparrow, although restricted to marshes on one island and the mainland in Brevard County, Florida, was locally abundant until the 1950s. Dusky populations were first devastated by exposure to DDT used for mosquito control. In the mid-1950s marshes were impounded and flooded, and the sparrows lost most of their breeding habitat. In 1968 the Department of Interior purchased land and created a national wildlife refuge to help protect the subspecies, but the island population disappeared in 1976 and the mainland habitat (still privately owned) was decimated by development, draining, and wildfires (Kale 1977, Sykes 1980). The last female dusky seaside sparrow died in 1976; in 1980 only four wild males remained. These were captured for a breeding program to back cross them with females of another race of seaside sparrow. After a successful cross in 1980 the program was halted when the FWS refused to issue permits to continue the breeding program. In 1983 when permits were again issued, the males were 6 to 10 years old and no further successful breeding occurred (Kale 1983). The last male died in captivity in June 1987 (Council on Environmental Quality 1988).

The cost for this unsuccessful effort was approximately $5 million (Kale interview). Although FWS did respond appropriately by identifying lack of suitable habitat as a major problem, and by establishing a national wildlife refuge, the action came too late to save the dusky seaside sparrow. Captive breeding is extremely expensive; despite the growing body of research conducted by zoos, breeding techniques are not well established for wild species. If the breeding program had been successful the population would likely have suffered from genetic problems associated with inbreeding in small populations.

The dusky seaside sparrow case illustrates another compelling reason to apply early management action. Lack of appropriate habitat is the most common cause of declining bird populations (Fish and Wildlife Service 1987). The acquisition and regeneration of suitable habitat can take many years. If appropriate natural habitat is not available, it may be necessary to obtain and improve land with marginal habitat.

The Piping Plover

The conservation problems that faced the dusky seaside sparrow were in some senses easy to solve compared with those of an endangered species that performs annual migrations. In the case of the sparrow, the survival of the population depended upon the correct management of a single habitat within a single region. Current efforts to conserve the piping plover (*Charadrius melodus*) underscore the danger of allowing a population of wide-ranging migratory birds to decline to low numbers (Haig and Oring 1987). Threats to the plover can be identified in a variety of breeding localities ranging from the Atlantic Coast to the Great Plains. Loss of wintering ground habitat in the Gulf of Mexico and the southern Atlantic coast of the United States adds another layer of complexity.

When a migratory bird's population declines due to habitat problems at various sites, the ability of small surviving groups to successfully migrate to specific safe habitats becomes improbable. This type of situation may have exacerbated declines in Bachman's warbler (*Vermivora bachmani*) (Hamel 1987) and the eskimo curlew (*Numenius borealis*). Current efforts to protect declining piping plover populations are expensive, costing from $500,000 to $1 million annually, according to informed sources; FWS provides half of this cost.

THE CHALLENGE OF CONSERVING NONGAME MIGRATORY BIRDS

The growing recognition of the conservation needs of all migratory birds is reflected in the language of the Mitchell Amendment, which calls for FWS to study and monitor migratory bird populations to prevent common species from becoming threatened. The practical implications of fulfilling this legislative mandate are daunting. The task calls for a major change in priorities of the migratory bird progams of

FWS, changes that are all the more difficult for two reasons: the sheer diversity of nongame species involved and the array of independent organizations and programs that deal with various aspects of migratory bird conservation with less than adequate coordination.

Complexity of Monitoring Many Species

The 757 nongame bird species in North America cover a vast taxonomic range. They include large raptors at the top of the food chain as well as tiny seed-eating birds. The group includes colonial-nesting waterbirds, songbirds, shorebirds, cosmopolitan species such as peregrine falcon (*Falco peregrinus*), geographically restricted species such as tricolored blackbird (*Agelaius tricolor*), and species that occur far from the North American mainland, on islands off Alaska, in Hawaii, Guam, and Puerto Rico. The habitats required to maintain these species include northern deciduous and coniferous forests, tundra, grasslands, mudflats, riparian forest, desert, and tropical forest.

Migration makes the problems more complex. For example, the tiny blackpoll warbler (*Dendroica striata*) flies from boreal coniferous forests as far north as Alaska to diverse tropical forests of the Amazon Basin. Each of these habitats faces different threats of degradation and destruction.

Monitoring a diverse group of migratory species may require many different census techniques conducted throughout the year and careful data collection and analysis. Each species of migratory bird has its unique distribution and set of habitat preferences that result in unique conservation problems. The only way to effectively approach problems facing all migratory birds is to recognize ecologically similar groupings of species facing similar threats. Several major groups of migratory birds are discussed here.

Forest Passerines. Unlike other migrant groups, forest passerines rarely concentrate but are widely distributed throughout forests or woodlands covering large areas of the eastern United States. Songbirds that live in western woodlands are more often restricted to regionally uncommon habitats, such as riparian woodlands that cover much less than one percent of the land surface of the western states (Knopf *et al.* 1988). Also, forest migrants have a limited number of migration stopover sites along the Gulf Coast and in western arid lands.

Despite the relatively great extent of forests in the Americas and the Caribbean, current trends in land-use patterns suggest threats to songbird populations, particularly for the approximately 120 species that migrate to the tropics. Arguably, the greatest single change in our perception of habitat needs of migratory birds has come from recent studies of the effects of habitat fragmentation on forest bird communities. A number of studies on the relationship between forest patch size and bird community composition have shown that the clearing of temperate forests results in the loss of Neotropical migrant birds (Robbins *et al.* ms, Lynch and Whitcomb 1984). Fragmentation appears to have no negative effect on a number of short-distance migrants or temperate zone residents. These large scale surveys have established that forest interior migrants are often "area sensitive," occurring only in large woodland patches of a minimum size.

Approximately two-thirds of the bird species that breed in the forests of the eastern United States winter in the tropical areas of the Greater Antilles, Mexico, Central America, and northern South America. Although a lower percentage of western birds migrate to the tropics, a large number do (particularly those in riparian habitats).

It is in the tropical areas that the greatest amount of deforestation is occurring. Many areas already are left with only relict stands of the original forest cover (Janzen 1986, Estrada and Coates-Estrada 1988, Sader and Joyce 1988). The most commonly quoted annual rates of tropical forest loss are 1 to 4.5 percent for most of the nations of the Caribbean Basin and Andean regions (Lanly 1982). These figures are almost certainly out of date; more realistic figures based on remote sensing are generally higher (Gradwohl and Greenberg 1988). Increasingly, the proximate cause of deforestation is conversion of lowland forests to cattle pasture, a land use that is generally thought to reduce the amount of available secondary fallow forest as well (Nations and Komer 1982). Localized studies in the tropics indicate that certain species became regionally rare or absent when forest was cleared (Rappole and Morton 1985). The severity of habitat destruction for forest migrants depends on the intensity of clearing and the degree to which development is balanced by forest conservation (Askins *et al.* in press).

Shorebirds. Shorebirds are legally game birds, but with the exceptions of American woodcock (*Philohela minor*) and common snipe (*Capella gallinago*), the 49 species of shorebirds that breed in North America, have been protected from hunting since 1927. Shorebirds are perhaps the most threatened by habitat alteration in North America because many species depend upon coastal marshes and wetlands. The nationwide loss of original coastal and inland wetlands is estimated to be 54 percent in the lower 48 states, with some state and regional losses known to be higher (Tiner 1984). The few species that rely upon grasslands are also being hard hit by development. Agricultural cultivation has claimed half of the original 770,000 square kilometers of upland grassland in North America.

Encroachment by human populations will have other harmful repercussions. It will bring shorebirds in closer proximity to potentially harmful pesticides used on crops and for mosquito control in marshes.

Even alternative forms of mosquito control such as digging ditches and ponds for predatory fish will affect the quality of shorebird habitat. Shorebirds also seem particularly vulnerable to human disturbance. Disturbance of nesting efforts on sandy beaches is implicated in the decline of piping plovers in North America (Senner and Howe 1984). Grassland breeding shorebirds such as killdeer (*Charadrius vociferous*) are also disturbed or killed by farm machinery (Higgins 1975). North American shorebirds could suffer greatly from a catastrophic oil spill such as the Exxon Valdez spill in Alaska's Prince William Sound in March, 1989. The concentration of shorebirds into staging areas during migration and on the wintering ground exacerbates all of these. During certain times of the year, the entire North American population of a given species may be dependent upon a single site, and thus a localized problem could affect an entire species (Myers *et al.* 1987).

Raptors. Raptors are large-bodied birds at the top of the food chain that require large areas for breeding and are particularly susceptible to dangerous chemicals that accumulate in their prey. Because of delayed maturity and low annual productivity, raptors also are slow to recover from population declines. Hunting, particularly between 1900 and 1950, and the use of DDT until the 1970s, contributed to declines in many raptor populations (Cade *et al.* 1988). Six of the 50 species of raptors that breed in North America are listed as endangered, and the California condor (*Gymnogyps californianus*) survives only in captivity.

Role of Other Organizations

The second factor that complicates FWS' role in migratory bird management and research is the involvement of many other government and private organizations in the field. The activities of all parties require careful coordination and communication to avoid duplication of effort. More importantly, FWS should focus its limited resources on the national and international aspects of migratory bird conservation, rather than try to do too much with too little.

Federal Agencies. FWS directly controls the management of 90 million acres of refuge land, of which 17 million is in the 48 coterminous states. Other federal agencies, such as the National Park Service, U.S. Forest Service, Bureau of Land Management, and Department of Defense, control much more land. FWS could play a major role in influencing habitat management and protection for migratory birds by other federal agencies. The Park Service, for example, is charged with keeping more than 74 million acres of land in a relatively pristine state, but currently has no research or management program oriented toward migratory birds. Yet, even pristine ecosystems require management and study. Questions, for example, regarding the degree to which vegetation is allowed to succeed into uniform climax stages, will become increasingly important.

The Forest Service manages 191 million acres for timber supply, watershed protection, grazing, recreation, energy development and mining, as well as wildlife conservation. The traditional emphasis of the Forest Service's wildlife program has been managing big-game species for hunting. Recent legislation has directed the Forest Service to preserve biological diversity and manage for nongame as well as game species (Norse *et al.* 1986). The Forest Service is further charged with managing and protecting endangered species that occur on Forest Service lands. Current research emphasis is on rare species and, to a lesser extent, on monitoring birds in endangered habitats such as western riparian woodlands and old-growth forest (Verner interview). Because of its emphasis on timber management the Forest Service is unlikely to play a major role in protecting expanses of habitat for nongame species that are not threatened or endangered, but research conducted on habitat use could contribute significantly to bird management plans for other lands.

State and Private Organizations. A considerable amount of land is controlled by state conservation agencies and private organizations such as The Nature Conservancy. The Nature Conservancy has programs in all 50 states and currently manages approximately 600,000 acres of land. Although not specifically oriented toward migratory birds, the Conservancy identifies habitats of unique biological concern and often protects critical habitat for birds. There are a large number of other, smaller private land conservation organizations that are potentially important stewards of habitat for migratory birds. However, most have local interests and many need to balance habitat preservation with numerous other uses.

FWS is not the only organization that conducts basic and applied research on the ecology of migratory birds (see Table 1). National Audubon Society has a strong national program of habitat conservation and research on migratory nongame birds. Field research has focused on wetland birds, although population monitoring efforts, particularly the Christmas Bird Count and Breeding Bird Census have a wider scope.

A number of observatories, such as Manomet Bird Observatory and Point Reyes Bird Observatory, conduct population censusing and monitoring. The orientation of most of these efforts is necessarily local, with the exceptions of the International Shorebird Survey run by Manomet Bird Observatory and the maintenance and analysis of certain national data bases (Christmas Bird Counts, Nest Card records, and

Table 1. Annual Research Budgets and Activities for Nonendangered Migratory Birds.

Organization	Approximate budget	Activities
Fish and Wildlife Service[a]	$2,000,000	Monitoring and research on landbirds and shorebirds nationwide
National Audubon Society[b]	$1,500,000	Population studies of wetland and shorebirds and their habitats; Neotropical migrant habitat use; biology and management of coastal seabirds; Christmas Bird Counts
Point Reyes Bird Observatory[c]	$300,000	Shorebird censuses; landbird banding; ecological studies of California birds
Manomet Bird Observatory[d]	$250,000	Shorebird censuses; studies of coastal birds and habitats; landbird banding in Massachusetts and Central America
Cornell Laboratory of Ornithology[e]	$200,000	Analysis of existing bird population data sets, including Breeding Bird Census, Christmas Bird Counts
Illinois Natural History Survey[f]	$70,000	Population studies of forest migrants
World Wildlife Fund[g]	$40,000	Survey work; ecological studies in Neotropics

[a] Cummings pers. comm.
[b] Myers interview.
[c] DeSante interview.
[d] Leddy pers. comm.
[e] Butcher interview.
[f] Robinson interview.
[g] Freese interview.

Breeding Bird Censuses) by the Cornell Laboratory of Ornithology in cooperation with National Audubon. The existence of a large number of amateur ornithologists interested in participating in monitoring efforts provides a tremendous opportunity for an organization, such as the FWS, to coordinate national monitoring efforts. This opportunity has been exploited successfully in the agency's Breeding Bird Survey Program, but much less extensively for other monitoring programs.

FWS Responsibilities and Role. FWS is reponsible for maintaining a global perspective on habitat needs for migratory birds, and for seeing that critical habitats are preserved and more commonplace habitat managed to ensure healthy populations of migratory birds. This places primary importance on nationwide monitoring of bird populations and habitat, as well as conducting basic research on the factors that impact populations and habitat. If it is to develop a comprehensive program on migratory bird conservation, FWS will have to take a leadership role in coordinating efforts that already exist in North America and abroad. To live up to treaty obligations to conserve and protect migratory birds throughout the Western Hemisphere, FWS will also need to take a leading role in establishing research projects and continue its training efforts in Latin America (Raffaele interview).

PROBLEMS FACING THE ADMINISTRATION OF NONGAME PROGRAMS IN THE FISH AND WILDLIFE SERVICE

Beyond the institutional lack of interest in nongame bird species and the skewed allocation of funds between game and nongame species, there are further barriers to nongame bird programs at FWS. The decentralized nature of FWS nongame bird activities works against effective administration of nongame programs. In addition, the bureaucratic separation of research on nongame species and population monitoring discourages the analysis of monitoring data. Finally, FWS lacks truly long-term planning for nongame species conservation.

The development of a program on migratory birds that is carefully coordinated with other organizations can only follow the establishment of such a program within FWS itself. Decentralized implementation of FWS priorities acts against nongame species by making it difficult to build a comprehensive program throughout the agency (Senner 1986). Lacking a specific nongame bird unit, FWS' present programs are small branches of larger programs oriented toward game birds. Decisions about nongame bird management priorities are made on a regional basis, and FWS' national policymaking divisions can do little more than produce white papers and suggest changes. This is evident in the nongame strategy statement, which states that FWS personnel consider many nongame activities as minor responsibilities.

FWS separates research on nongame species under Region 8 (Research and Development) from population monitoring work, which is coordinated by the Office of Migratory Bird Management. This distinction seems artificial and tends to discourage the analysis of data gathered by the monitoring programs. Monitoring data should be woven into the core of any research program on nongame bird populations.

FWS lacks a clear overall vision and direction for its programs on nongame bird species. The recently published "Nongame Bird Strategies" outlines current efforts to research and monitor nongame species. Although it claims to be a five-year plan, the strategy document describes current programs, with little indication of future plans or directions. The document was circulated in draft form both within and outside FWS. Comments from outside groups have generally been critical of the lack of any clear priorities in the document (either in funding or in staffing).

Table 2. Fish and Wildlife Service Nongame Bird Activities Funded by $1 Million Congressional Add-on Appropriation for FY 1988.

REGION 1, PORTLAND, OREGON ($140,000)
  Marbled murrelet status surveys
  Oregon seabird colony survey
  Loggerhead shrike: impacts of land-use changes
  Impacts of USDA grasshopper spray program on grassland birds
  Old-growth forest inventory
  Protection of white pelican nesting island in Oregon
  Assess impacts of Bird Depredation Order in California
  Financial support for "Oregon Wildlife Viewing Guide"
REGION 2, ALBUQUERQUE, NEW MEXICO ($20,000)
  Stabilization of dredge-spoil islands on Brazoria National Wildlife Refuge
  Habitat requirements of tamaulipan birds on Santa Ana National Wildlife Refuge
  Restoration of tamaulipan vegetation on Santa Ana National Wildlife Refuge
REGION 3, TWIN CITIES, MINNESOTA ($120,000)
  Preparing status reports on 14 species of management concern
  Coordination with states to investigate ecology/management needs of species of manage-
      ment concern (15 projects in 8 states):
    Breeding bird atlases/population monitoring—4
    Candidate species (loggerhead shrike)—3
    Wetland dependent species—3
    Raptors—2
    Other—2
  Conducted regional workshop on nongame bird management
REGION 4, ATLANTA, GEORGIA ($20,000)
  Conduct snowy plover surveys in Florida and Alabama
  Investigate black rail census techniques
  Marsh burning: Impacts of summer burns on wading and shorebirds at Lake Woodruff Na-
      tional Wildlife Refuge
  Burning of pine savannah study: Summer vs. winter burns at Okeefenokee National Wildlife
      Refuge
REGION 5, NEWTON CORNER, MASSACHUSETTS ($20,000)
  Species uses not identified
REGION 6, DENVER, COLORADO ($20,000)
  Implement redistribution plan for trumpeter swan in tri-state area
REGION 7, ANCHORAGE, ALASKA ($20,000)
  Assess population status and habitat requirements of bristle-thighed curlew on Yukon Delta
      National Wildlife Refuge
REGION 8, DIVISION OF WILDLIFE RESEARCH ($500,000)
  Population status and habitat requirements of the bristle-thighed curlew
  Development of techniques for surveying/monitoring shorebirds and raptors
  Migratory shorebird use of wetlands in the southern Great Plains
  Study forest fragmentation effects on wintering areas and its impact on breeding birds
REGION 9, OFFICE OF MIGRATORY BIRD MANAGEMENT ($140,000)
  Christmas Bird Count analysis of population trends for 13 species of management concern
  Publication of Breeding bird censuses and winter-bird population studies
  Study mortality of seabirds in high seas drift-net fisheries of the North Pacific
  Develop population trend estimates using data from the International Shorebird Survey
  Radio-telemetry study of loggerhead shrike winter mortality
  Financial support of Raptor Research Foundation annual meeting
  Prepare and distribute new brochure on winter bird feeding
  Co-sponsored with Research and Development a workshop on population trend analysis for
      migratory birds

The major recommendation of the report is to suggest additional staff positions of nongame coordinators in each of the agency's regional offices. The regional offices are most likely to interact with state and private conservation organizations interested in nongame birds. However, because resources and staff interests differ among regions, central direction from the national office is necessary if a coordinated nongame program is to be established. Furthermore, FWS should set conservation priorities at a national level. A potentially profound conservation problem for a local bird population or habitat might be seen as less significant if the next county or state has a healthy population or extensive tract of habitat.

One indication of the patchwork nature of the nongame programs at FWS is the allocation of the $1 million FY 1988 congressional budget add-on. As shown in Table 2, the distribution of funds is unequal between regions and the resulting eclectic research program includes large amounts spent on single species.

The effectiveness of the FWS migratory bird program will depend on its ability to command a national and international perspective on the problems. The highest priority should be given to monitoring populations and problems that will have large-scale impact on migratory bird populations, such as chronic destruction and degradation of habitat. The rest of this chapter will focus on some of the existing programs that address these priorities and introduce some specific suggestions for linking these smaller projects into a coordinated and centralized program.

EXISTING FISH AND WILDLIFE SERVICE NONGAME BIRD PROGRAMS

Monitoring

Any attempt to manage bird populations should be based on up-to-date census information. FWS has recognized this principle in its waterfowl management program. Consisting of an extensive program of aerial surveys, the Waterfowl Breeding Population and Habitat Survey, forms the backbone for current efforts to establish a long-term strategy for waterfowl conservation in the North American Waterfowl Management Plan (Fish and Wildlife Service 1986, 1988a). The survey has been conducted each year since 1955. The spring portion of the survey is particularly extensive, covering some 3.5 million square kilometers of habitat. Data on waterfowl population trends are published annually for 20 species or species-groups of ducks, 5 species of geese, and 2 species of swans.

Waterfowl breeding-ground censuses are supplemented by mid-winter surveys that are not designed to measure population trends so much as the distribution of waterfowl across habitats. Nevertheless, the winter survey supplements the spring and summer efforts by providing population estimates for some species that are not counted in breeding season surveys (most notably the black duck [*Anas rubripes*]).

Similar population trend data do not exist for continental estimates of population for the vast majority of migratory birds (see Table 3). However, through its Breeding Bird Survey (BBS), FWS does attempt to measure gross increases and declines in nongame land birds that can be censused from roadways. But considerable question remains as to whether the BBS can be relied upon as the sole census program for even the roughly 600 species it is designed to cover. Currently, no comprehensive program in FWS exists for monitoring populations of shorebirds, colonial waterbirds, raptors, or seabirds. Moreover, there has been little success in focusing FWS' bird-banding efforts towards a monitoring function.

This section provides an overview of some of the major programs for monitoring nongame bird populations on a large scale (a more complete list can be found in Table 3). However, first it is necessary to briefly examine some underlying problems in monitoring programs. A dichotomy exists between detailed local efforts and broad-brushed regional surveys. Local censuses will continue to produce more accurate and repeatable bird density estimates for a specific habitat, but may lack generality. Regional surveys will lose resolution, but are more likely to detect large-scale or continent-wide increases or declines in populations.

The ability to detect global trends may be critical in assessing the effect of current wide-scale alteration and destruction of tropical non-breeding habitat for migratory birds. Reduction in populations due to disturbances in that habitat will probably be evident over a large portion of the breeding grounds. At any one location a breeding population will be strongly influenced by local breeding-ground factors, including inclement late-spring weather, insect outbreaks, pesticide spraying, and local habitat changes (see Holmes and Sherry 1988). The detection of persistent regional declines caused by nonbreeding-season events can be likened to a radio signal that must be detected through the background noise generated by this large number of local effects.

Two strategies have been employed to detect a hypothetical non-breeding-season effect on a population: long-term censuses of plots in "pristine" habitats and continent-wide surveys such as the BBS. The long-term censuses will presumably reduce the anthropogenic noise by focusing on plots that are mature (not undergoing succession) and remote (not experiencing fragmentation). These plots are still subject to natural sources of local fluctuations. These could be dampened by

Table 3. Migratory Bird Monitoring Programs in the United States.

Program	Taxa	Geographic scope	FWS involvement
Breeding Bird Survey[a]	landbirds—377 species	continental	Coordination data analysis
Breeding Bird Census[b]	landbirds	continental	Some support for publication
Colonial Waterbird Surveys[c]	gulls, terns, and wading birds	continental	May initiate new censuses along Great Lakes
Colonial Waterbird Register[d]	gulls, terns	continental	None
Hawk Migration Counts[e]	raptors	Eastern United States	Partial support since 1979
International Shorebird Survey[f]	shorebirds	U.S. East Coast and Central Flyway	Assistance in testing of methods and data analysis
Landbird Banding Stations[g]	landbirds	continental	Data storage and permit issuance
Christmas Bird Counts[h]	all birds	continental	Some analysis
Breeding Bird Atlas[i]	all birds	continental	None

[a] Droege interview.
[b] Engstrom pers. comm.
[c] Erwin interview.
[d] Erwin interview.
[e] Senner *et al.* Ms.
[f] Howe Interview.
[g] Dawson interview.
[h] Butcher, G. in press.
[i] Robbins in press.

making the censuses truly long-term and conducting them over at least 15 to 20 years (Hall 1984, Wilcove 1988, Holmes and Sherry in press). The second strategy consists of selecting random census points over a large area. This should also dampen a large amount of local variation, but may fail to distinguish between large-scale declines due to non-breeding-ground effects and regional changes in breeding-ground habitat. Only with a clever blending of these two strategies can we hope to detect actual population declines due to problems outside the breeding grounds. Given the number of factors that could affect the survey data, it is likely that only strong trends are detected. Therefore, any interpretation of BBS or long-term census data should recognize the inherently conservative nature of the trend estimates.

Breeding Season Monitoring

Breeding Bird Survey. Population monitoring is the cornerstone of current FWS nongame bird programs. Conducted along nearly 50,000 miles of roads each year, the agency-coordinated BBS is the only census program that is continental in scope. Because of this scale it is able to provide population trend estimates for a large number of migratory landbirds. Currently, census sample sizes are sufficient for the analysis of population trends for approximately 377 species. It is not surprising that "Nongame Migratory Bird Strategies" features BBS as the primary FWS effort in the management program.

BBS was first applied on a continent-wide scale in 1966 (Robbins *et al.* 1986). Its establishment was largely a response to concerns over the possible effects of pesticides on songbird populations (Carson 1962). That the BBS has survived and grown during the ensuing 22 years makes it a model for how a large number of volunteers can be used to mount a major research program with a minimal amount of bureaucratic overhead. The BBS currently involves nearly 2,000 bird watchers censusing 24.5-mile routes (Droege and Sauer 1988). Even the administration of the program is largely done by volunteers; at the state level, volunteers coordinate the cadres of censusers. FWS staffing for the program consists of a single coordinator and the part-time efforts of statisticians who analyze the data collected. This is approximately the same level of effort FWS provides for the nationwide Mourning Dove Survey—an effort that is focused on a single game species.

It is impossible to expect a single survey to provide adequate data to track all migratory bird populations. BBS provides data for over 600 species, roughly two-thirds of the landbirds that commonly breed in North America. Its major drawback is that sample sizes for many of these species (for example, Swainson's Warbler [*Limnothlypis swainsonii*]) are marginal or inadequate for statistical analysis. Much of the western United States is poorly covered as are other habitats such as tundra, which lack extensive roads. Furthermore, certain extremely localized species are missed by the survey.

Nevertheless, the BBS has proven its usefulness in monitoring bird populations. The survey has documented declines and recoveries of certain short-distance migrants such as Carolina wren (*Thryothorus ludovicianus*) and eastern bluebird (*Sialia sialis*) that were negatively affected by severe winters like that of 1977. Insectivorous forest birds that are associated with widespread caterpillar outbreaks, such as the spruce budworm specialists, bay-breasted (*Dendroica castanea*), Cape May (*Dendroica tigrina*), and Tennessee (*Vermivora peregrina*) warblers (MacArthur 1958) and the two species of cuckoos (yellow and black billed [*Coccyzus americanus* and *Coccyzus erythropthalmus*]) show distinct population patterns that correlate with known budworm outbreaks.

Recently, more patterns have emerged with important implications. BBS has shown a substantial population decline for 70 percent of the forest-breeding Neotropical migrants over the past 11 years, that follows a period of general increase. No similar pattern can be found in birds that remain in the temperate zone throughout the year. This implies that the decline is due to wintering ground conditions; a further examination shows that those species that winter in Neotropical forests are showing the most consistent decline (Robbins *et al.* ms).

The discovery of this pattern underscores another problem with BBS as it is currently administered: the slowness with which data are analyzed and interpreted. The general decline in Neotropical migrants is apparent in the data of the 1970s, yet it was not until 1987 that the general analysis of trends was published for the period through 1979. Discussions of tropical migrant conservation are still focused on conclusions drawn from the 1966–1979 period (Hutto 1988), even though data has been collected and stored for succeeding years.

It is no simple task to analyze BBS data—the data base is large and the necessary analysis (for example, Geissler 1986) is complicated. Much to the credit of FWS staff involved with BBS, the data are open for use by outside researchers. Still, as a practical matter, it is extremely difficult for people outside of the BBS office to manipulate the data to answer specific questions. Thus, BBS data have not been adequately explored to answer more detailed questions regarding the regional patterns of declines. The publication output from the program is modest in comparison with the potential of the data to illuminate processes of both theoretical and applied concerns. In particular there appears to be great potential in pursuing single-species studies in conjunction with data on habitat preference, local land-use patterns on the breeding range, wintering ground habitat changes, and potential exposure to pesticides and contaminants. It is probably impossible to conduct such analyses using existing FWS research staff, but creative ways should be explored to bring in outside researchers.

The reliability of BBS data has been challenged by some. Although a great deal of effort has been put into standardization of technique and sampling effort, variation will be found in any monitoring program that involves large numbers of people. Factors causing variation include the effects of weather, changing observers, the changing skill of individual observers, the exact dates within permissible periods that the census is conducted, and so forth. Some of these problems, such as the role of observer variation can be partially ameliorated by the statistical methods used for data analysis.[2] Most of these problems will sim-

---

2. These methods could include using the individual observer as a co-variable in the statistical model, or classifying observers by skill level.

ply force cautionary statements about interpretation of the data, but not preclude its use. It is particularly important to bear the variation in mind when statistically significant trends are not found, because most of the bias is not systematic but works to decrease the power of statistical tests to detect real trends.

Other potential problems are characteristic of the survey technique. The fact that field observations are made along secondary roads is a problem because roads do not pass through all representative habitats. It would be difficult and expensive, however, to design an extensive program that did not census habitat close to roadways. The biggest problem is that roadside habitat may be changing at a greater rate than randomly selected areas. Therefore the actual population trends may be more influenced by local breeding ground events than nationwide changes. This problem could be partially ameliorated if habitat evaluation were conducted on a sample of routes, with particular attention paid to habitat changes. Another area of contention is the ecological significance of counting only singing males. It should be possible to study how well the number of singing males correlates with population health by conducting a complementary research program on intensively censused plots (see below).

Breeding Bird Census. In 1937, long before the BBS was devised, amateur and professional ornithologists began site-intensive surveys based on spot mapping singing male birds (Butcher 1986, Engstrom interview). Initiated by National Audubon Society, these censuses, referred to as the Breeding Bird Censuses (BBC), were published in an annual issue of *Audubon Field Notes* and, until 1984, in *American Birds*. In addition, a smaller number of winter population censuses began in 1948. Because these censuses are based on repeated visits to a small plot, the counts correspond more closely to the actual density of birds. In addition, vegetation is sampled (with standard plant sampling techniques introduced in 1970), and censuses are conducted in areas of known and uniform vegetation type. However, because it is a labor-intensive survey, sample sizes are often quite small for all but the most common species. Furthermore, the actual distribution of census plots in time and space is up to the initiative of individuals. Although it was hoped that BBC would yield long-term information, in reality few areas were censused for more than a decade (Askins *et al.* in press). In the eastern deciduous forest there are only about 10 long-term censuses, of which only four are in areas of extensive forest. BBC has provided the grist for a number of papers on bird ecology and biogeography, but the program has hit upon hard times as the censuses are no longer published, but are simply filed. Current efforts focus on resurrecting the program by renewing publication of the results in the *Journal of Field Ornithology*. This effort is spearheaded by the Cornell Laboratory of Ornithology and the National Audubon Society. FWS provides modest financial support ($16,000 over 5 years), which will only cover a portion of the publication cost. At present there are no specific plans to design a series of breeding bird censuses that would be the focus of site-intensive, long-term monitoring. There is some discussion among several private and governmental groups about conducting long-term surveys on undisturbed lands in national parks or on sites selected for long term ecological research by the National Science Foundation (Council on Environmental Quality 1988).

Migration Counts

During migration, a large number of birds can be censused in a short period of time. In some groups (notably raptors and shorebirds), and in certain areas, large portions of the global population funnel through particular flyways or gather at specific staging grounds. Migration is an exciting time for bird watching and it is easier to convince amateurs to participate in censusing or banding programs at this time of year. Migration census data have been collected for hawks and shorebirds, and censuses have been proposed for migratory land birds.

Raptor Migration Counts. Migration counts of raptors have been conducted on a regular and long-term basis at 29 localities from the Iron Range of Minnesota to Hawk Mountain, Pennsylvania, and Chincoteague Island, Virginia (Roberts 1984). Recent attempts to determine concordant trends among the stations have met with some success (Senner pers. comm.). Long-term data, for example those reported from Hawk Mountain, show a decline and recovery of populations of bald eagles (*Haliaeetus leucocephalus*) and peregrine falcons (*Falco peregrinus*), which corresponds with periods prior to and after the ban on DDT in 1972 (Senner *et al.* ms). Indications of declines have been found more recently in broad-winged (*Buteo platypterus*) and red-shouldered hawks (*Buteo lineatus*) and golden eagles (*Aquila chrysaetos*) in the Northeast (Senner *et al.* ms). Migration counts are more appropriate for detecting global or regional declines than for pinpointing problems in particular areas or times of year. Efforts to analyze migration data are being supported by private organizations and through staff time of FWS research personnel; funding has been provided by the U.S. Army for analysis of data on peregrine falcons.

International Shorebird Survey. The outlook for monitoring coastal shorebird populations by migration counts is encouraging. In fact, the International Shorebird Survey (ISS) has been censusing shorebirds at sites along the Atlantic Coast and in the central United States since 1972. Some preliminary analyses show that consistent declines can be detected for several species of shorebirds, although the error estimates surrounding these trends suggest that only very large population changes could be detected reliably (Howe interview). FWS is cooperating with an analysis of whether the assumptions of the ISS monitoring program are valid. The effort, led by Manomet Bird Observatory, will apply trend analysis statistics to the data and focus the censusing effort on the most representative stopover sites. There is considerable need for FWS to increase support for this program and expand to the West Coast and interior United States where no long-term regional shorebird census program exists today.

Bird Banding. Leg banding birds is another activity that is conducted by non-FWS amateurs and professionals under the administrative control of the FWS. The FWS nongame bird strategy statement explicitly recognizes the scientific value of the banding program, and calls for the continued issuance of permits and collation of data as a major contribution to this effort by FWS. FWS therefore acts primarily as a coordinating agency and central data bank (for a subset of the data gathered on banded birds). It plays a role in standardizing field techniques and assuring safe handling of birds as well as in the publication of banding manuals and monitoring of banding returns.

Currently, FWS plays a minor role in directing or encouraging specific types of research conducted by banding stations. This has not always been the case. From 1964 to the late 1970s FWS established and coordinated the ambitious "Operation Recovery," which was an effort to map the migration routes of land birds based on the recovery of individual birds (Dawson interview). The lack of a significant number of inter-station recaptures quickly depressed enthusiasm for the migration route focus of the program. However, the banding stations remained in contact and published summaries of annual captures for a number of years (Dawson interview). Perhaps the major contribution of this program was the development of criteria for determining the sex and age of birds, which has proven invaluable for research on avian demography.

There is a great deal of appeal to establishing a network of banding stations to conduct population monitoring. Birders are often sensitive to observed changes in migration volume over the years—a perception that can be tested with standardized and quantified data. Also, banding stations provide a focus for the activities of serious amateurs and can generate an enormous amount of data. Late breeding season mist-netting has already been used with some success for monitoring the reproductive output of locally breeding landbirds (Desante and Guepel 1987).

A cogent argument for expanding the role of banding stations is that large data bases of banding records, as well as systems for record-keeping, are already well established. It should be noted, however, that most net capture data are subject to a large amount of statistical "noise" (for example, the effects of weather) and are very sensitive to local effects (for example, vegetation at the banding station and in the area around the banding station). Also, it is difficult to combine the data from a number of stations to look for geographic consistency of trends because it requires competing stations to cooperate. FWS is giving minor support to research projects that examine the possibility of analyzing data from a number of stations (Dawson and Sauer ms). However, this effort has not yet been coordinated with similar standardization efforts at individual bird observatories.

BASIC ECOLOGICAL RESEARCH

Natural History Studies

One might ask why money and effort should be expended on studying basic ecology when urgent conservation action is needed to counteract massive population declines. In fact, effective conservation strategies cannot be established without basic information about the ecological needs of the target species. Simple monitoring and survey work alone cannot provide the background information and understanding needed to define factors that might contribute to population declines. Census work should be fully complemented by research into the natural history and population ecology of a species, particularly focusing on the classic ecological question: Which factors contribute to the patterns of distribution and abundance of species? The need for more basic biological information is particularly true of the approximately 150 Neotropical migrant species for which our understanding of life history is particularly poor (Greenberg 1985).

This objective is fully consistent with the current structure of scientific research at FWS, which directs population monitoring through its Office of Migratory Bird Management, and supports basic and applied research through Region 8 (Research and Development). In practice, however, most of the agency's basic ecological research is focused on game birds or threatened and endangered species.

The classification "Species of Management Concern" has been used by FWS to focus attention on bird species showing serious declines (Fish and Wildlife Service 1987). These species are highlighted as potential subjects of future research in the event that funds for nongame migratory bird research increase. In fact, one of these species, the bristle-thighed curlew (*Numenius tahitiensis*), is already the focus of a major research effort (see Table 2).

However, current research on migratory bird ecology has focused on threatened, endangered, or other species of management concern almost to the exclusion of other migratory species. While this focus is understandable, the reasons for conducting research on other species while they are abundant, is compelling. Understanding the causes of a population decline often requires information on the basic demography and natural history of a species. This type of information becomes difficult to obtain for species that are declining or rare. An extreme example is the Bachman's warbler (*Vermivora bachmanii*), whose natural history is summarized by Hamel (1986). During at least one period of recorded ornithological history (1890 to 1920), Bachman's warbler was a reasonably widespread and common species. Yet the reports we have today on habitat preference, foraging behavior and a variety of other features of its natural history are mostly fragmented and anecdotal. Furthermore, it is impossible to obtain needed data today. (See "The Bachman's Warbler" chapter in the *Audubon Wildlife Report 1988/1989* for more information.)

If any one of the 52 species of migratory wood warblers were to decline rapidly in the next decade, our understanding of the bird's basic ecology would be similarly limited. In terms of population ecology, factors contributing to the decline of a species cannot be evaluated without baseline information on demography under more favorable conditions. Furthermore, as a matter of practicality, even with completely adequate monitoring systems in place—which is not the case—a species could undergo a tremendous decline before FWS considered it to be in trouble.

In general, the understanding of life history parameters for migratory bird species requires careful study with marked birds throughout the year. It may prove impossible to conduct such studies for most of the species of North American nongame birds. However, studies of representative species and community-level studies of the population dynamics of species in various habitats needs to be a future priority for basic ecological research. An example of this can be found in the riparian program conducted by staff at FWS' National Ecology Center (Knopf interview). Various studies have selected focal species such as orchard oriole, yellow warbler, and willow flycatcher. These species are not rare, but are representative of distribution abundance patterns found in other species. Detailed research is determining which factors affect geographic limits and identifying seasonal events that regulate populations.

More extensive research on migratory bird ecology may be difficult to initiate because these studies fall between disciplines. Autecological studies of population dynamics and habitat requirements have been more frequently conducted by students in wildlife programs focusing on wildlife species. Zoology programs have traditionally fostered research that is more theoretically oriented. We know much

Amateur bird watchers have compiled massive amounts of data on song-birds such as this female eastern bluebird, but comprehensive population-monitoring strategies are needed. *Irene Vandermolen/Leonard Lee Rue III Enterprises*

more about the basic demography of a variety of communally breeding bird species around the globe than we do about some of the most common North American woodland species that have less remarkable social systems. This situation would change rapidly if funding and employment for students were oriented toward basic research on migratory nongame birds.

Land-Use Practices and Management

Habitat loss is generally considered the most significant threat to most bird populations (Senner and Howe 1984, Rappole *et al.* 1983, U.S. Department of the Interior 1986, 1988b). Carrying capacity for many bird species is directly related to the amount of suitable habitat available. The effects of habitat destruction can be assessed by monitoring the amount of habitat that remains, using a composite of local information or a system of global monitoring (for example, remote sensing). FWS cooperates with other agencies to produce a detailed inventory of wetland habitat (Tiner 1984). However, no similar effort is directed toward terrestrial habitats.

Habitat degradation due to small changes can be as devastating as habitat destruction but is more difficult to detect. Habitat that appears superficially to be suitable for a particular species can suffer greatly from logging, grazing, isolation, fragmentation, unnatural flooding regimes, ditching and draining, and so on. The assessment of these potential causes of habitat-related population declines requires a research program beyond the inventory of existing habitat. FWS is mandated to protect critical habitats through research and monitoring where species are endangered. Current FWS programs concerning several key areas of habitat loss or degradation are discussed here.

Forest Fragmentation in the United States. FWS-supported research in the mid-Atlantic states has played an important role in developing a basic description of the effects of forest fragmentation. The emphasis in forest fragmentation research has shifted to mechanisms. Originally, the problem was cast entirely in terms of island biogeographic theory. Small forest patches were seen as suffering high extinction rates that were not balanced by colonization due to the low dispersal rate of long-distance migrants. Currently, most research is more ecologically deterministic in its focus. The hypothesis is that there is some feature of migrant Neotropical bird breeding ecology that reduces survival in small forest patches. Some support has been garnered for the fact that nest predation and brood parasitism rates are higher in forest fragments, and that Neotropical migrants have nesting and demographic characteristics that make them more sensitive to these encroachments (Wilcove 1987, Askins *et al.* ms). FWS is conducting some research on factors affecting nesting success of migratory birds in habitat patches of different sizes. In addition, censuses are being conducted in areas before and after fragmentation occurs. Although a large number of studies to date record the effects of fragmentation, the magnitude and distribution of fragmentation and forest loss has not been well documented.

Deforestation in the Tropics. FWS has only recently funded research into the effects of wide-scale habitat conversion on the large number of forest-wintering migratory species. At first the funding came from the Office of International Affairs and was allocated under the authority of the Western Hemisphere Convention, which established that the conservation of populations of migratory birds is a major objective for signatory nations. The convention's implementing legislation requires FWS to identify conservation measures, but not to implement them. Despite some congressional support for more research on wintering ground ecology, according to FWS sources there remains considerable resistance to such research within FWS; obtaining permission for foreign travel needed to conduct this research is frequently difficult and unpredictable.

The primary research focus of FWS in the tropics has been to study the role of forest fragmentation. This research is an extension of work conducted on the breeding grounds and was designed to examine the quality of relict wood lots and small forest patches for forest-interior birds on their wintering grounds. The research has been conducted in several different countries, representing the major regions for Neotropical wintering landbirds, including Jamaica, Puerto Rico, Costa Rica, and Venezuela. Local students were often involved, so the projects had the secondary role of training Latin American scientists. The research consisted of a short-term survey of paired plots in large continuous and fragmented forests. The project was generally unable to detect an effect of forest fragmentation on forest interior migrants (Robbins *et al.* 1987).

This research does not address the potential effects of forest conversion. Often forest fragments of any size are difficult to locate in a deforested tropical landscape, so the fragmentation question becomes moot. The effects of converting forest to various agricultural activities is being studied in a similar broad-scale mist-netting program. Complementary to this research is a project contracted to nongovernmental ornithologists to determine the density of "mist-nettable" migrants in habitats that are mapped by remote sensing imagery. This project was initiated on a small scale in northeastern Costa Rica and will expand in 1989 to include a portion of Belize. These projects provide rudimentary baseline information on migratory bird populations that can be manipulated to estimate the effects of future habitat conversion. Although FWS projects in the tropics rely heavily upon mist-netting as a survey technique, many tropical ornithologists consider this too labor intensive and biased to be reliable (Remsen and Parker 1983, Askins *et al.* in press).

The National Ecology Center is sponsoring research on Neotropical migrants that is designed to examine the fate of forest migrant birds in cleared forest land. The initial focus of the project is the Sian Ka'an Biosphere Reserve in the Yucatan Peninsula in Mexico. The research has the additional "spin-off" effect of encouraging basic ecological research on terrestrial systems in this newly established tropical reserve.

The recent interest in basic research on the effect of habitat conversion in the Neotropics does not appear to be shared by the FWS Office of Migratory Bird Management. For example, tropical deforestation is largely discounted as a factor contributing to the decline in "species of management concern" (U.S. Department of the Interior 1987). Over the past 25 years the Neotropical migrant cerulean warbler (*Dendroica cerulea*) has declined at a rate of over three percent per year. However, the agency does not consider intensive forest clearing in the foothills of the Andes a possible contributing factor. Furthermore, tropical deforestation is not featured as a major concern in the "Nongame Bird Strategies" document (U.S. Department of the Interior 1988b).

Shorebird Habitat. Because shorebird habitat is often located in areas of intense human activity and economic development, the identification of critical migration and wintering sites and their protection and management should be high priority activities. FWS sponsors research on migration ecology of shorebirds at several key areas, including Cheyenne Bottoms in Kansas and a number of areas in Alaska.[3] Other organizations, notably the Manomet Bird Observatory, Canadian Wildlife Service, World Wildlife Fund, and National Audubon Society, have taken leadership roles in developing a comprehensive effort to identify and coordinate the protection of critical shorebird habitat. This effort is being spearheaded by the Western Hemisphere Shorebird Reserve Network, which calls for the identification of critical staging areas, the designation of lands already under some form of protection as units in the system, development of management priorities for these lands, and the identification of additional lands that should be protected (Myers *et al.* 1987).

RESEARCH AND MANAGEMENT STRATEGY FOR SONGBIRDS AND SHOREBIRDS

"Nongame Bird Strategies" provides a concise outline of current agency activities, but it is otherwise a conservative document that offers little vision for what could be accomplished with a new and adequately funded program. This conservatism is by design, according to FWS officials, because it was believed that a limited program would be

---

3. The Alaska program dates back to the Outer Continental Shelf Environmental Assessment Program, related to proposed petroleum development.

easier to accomplish and would renew credibility for nongame research. The tone of the document partly is a response to the criticism of the earlier draft strategy statement circulated in 1982–1983 (Dwyer interview); that draft was attacked for being an unrealistic wish list. The new strategy calls for an increase in coordination both within FWS and between government agencies, but has few specific recommendations regarding how such coordination will be accomplished, to what ends, or at what cost. FWS does recommend creation of nongame coordinators in each of the seven regional offices—currently only Region 1 (Portland, Oregon) has such a coordinator.

The magnitude of the conservation problems facing migratory birds, particularly Neotropical migratory species, calls for a more comprehensive attack that is designed from the bottom up. It appears that the potential for increased funding is promising in light of recent congressional interest in nongame migratory bird conservation. In addition to the creation of a comprehensive program for monitoring and investigating migratory bird populations, clear priorities within the program need to be established so that funds are spent effectively.

It is beyond the scope of this chapter to draft an alternative, comprehensive, national strategy statement, but a suggested strategy for monitoring and research on songbirds and shorebirds is provided. The program could easily be extended to include other groups such as seabirds and colonial waterbirds. The proposed program has an approximate price tag of $1.5 million per year for the next 10 years. Although the recommended strategy is the invention of the authors, it is based on the priorities and concerns of a number of ornithologists.

Recommended 10-year Program

I. MONITORING: Most ornithologists believe this to be the most important function of FWS' migratory bird program. The landbird monitoring needs to be enhanced by increased publication and other use of existing Breeding Bird Survey data and complementary studies of large tracts of different habitat types. The shorebird census program needs to expand its coverage and refine its censusing and analytical techniques.

A. Breeding Bird Survey
    1. *Goals:* Complete every 10 years a population trend analysis, support specific research projects conducted on species and regions, and increase data use by outside researchers.
    2. *Program:* Increase FWS staff by one senior scientist for analyzing data and preparing papers for the ornithological literature. Increase junior staff to complete statistical analysis and trend and map preparation. Provide grants and run visiting scientist programs to

encourage innovative use of data. Incorporate habitat variables into census and analysis.
3. *Implementation*: Immediate.
4. *Budget*: $150,000/year.
B. Benchmark Census Program
1. *Goals*: Establish 10 long-term plots on undisturbed sites in extensive tracts of habitat that will be censused annually by territorial spot-mapping techniques. Support basic research on population ecology.
2. *Program*: Hire senior scientists for each site to establish and coordinate efforts, and to sub-contract to bird observatories and non-governmental organizations to provide skilled assistants to conduct monitoring activities.
3. *Implementation*: Plots should be phased-in over the first five years so that problems of protocol can be corrected. Year one should include a workshop for interested researchers from within and outside FWS, and establishment of a pilot plot.
4. *Budget*: $250,000/year.
C. International Shorebird Survey
1. *Goals:* Establish censuses at all major stopover sites in North America (at least all lower 48 states). Continue local studies to evaluate the significance of census results. Create one or two senior positions devoted to monitoring shorebirds and related research.
2. *Program*: Contract with bird observatories and local and national groups to provide labor and coordinate efforts.
3. *Implementation*: Phase in by region over 5 years.
4. *Budget*: $150,000.
II. HABITAT INVENTORY: Because habitat is critical to conservation efforts, a regular program of surveying and collating existing data on the distribution and condition of habitat, similar to the National Wetlands Inventory, should be established.
A. North America
1. *Goals*: Assess forest cover and the degree of fragmentation for North America every 10 years. Conduct detailed analysis of extent of critical habitats.
2. *Program*: Create senior position of habitat inventory coordinator and several junior positions to review and analyze existing data, and cooperate with other federal agencies to conduct satellite imagery studies. Contract with local geographers and organizations to prepare maps for key areas.
3. *Implementation*: Immediate.
4. *Budget*: $100,000/year.
B. Caribbean and Latin America
1. *Goals*: Assess forest cover and degree of conversion of wintering habitat (forest and agricultural fields) every 10 years.

2. *Program*: Create one senior position to cooperate with other organizations concerned with tropical land use. Use satellite imagery to assess habitat changes.

3. *Implementation*: Establish cooperative relationship with other organizations such as NASA with remote sensing analysis capabilities. Phase in as quickly as possible.

4. *Budget*: $100,000/year.

C. Western Hemisphere Shorebird Reserve Network

1. *Goals*: Support Western Hemisphere Shorebird Reserve Network to locate and preserve critical areas for conservation. Incorporate existing FWS refuge lands into program, and manage water levels to accomodate migrating shorebirds.

2. *Program*: Contract with Network for one senior and two junior scientist positions to conduct habitat surveys and develop management recommendations.

3. *Implementation*: Immediate.

4. *Budget*: $100,000/year.

III. NONGAME BIRD RESEARCH: Although basic research can suffer from too much bureaucratic control, general priorities for the next 10 years can be outlined. These should include considerably more Neotropical field work in forests, wetland and coastal habitats. Carefully coordinated basic ecological field work would amplify knowledge gained by an enhanced monitoring program.

A. Assess local population responses to habitat changes in tropics

1. *Goals*: Establish five, two- to three-year study sites associated with nature reserves in the Caribbean, Mexico, Central and northern South America. Train Latin American and Caribbean students to assist in conducting research.

2. *Program*: Each site would be staffed by a senior contract researcher and several assistants for entire winters. Research focus on long-term changes in migratory and resident bird populations and resources in a representative array of habitat types.

3. *Implementation*: Sites would be phased in and out so that no more than two to three would be operating simultaneously. Senior staff would continue to ensure use of standardized research techniques.

4. *Budget:* $200,000.

B. Research on Songbird and Shorebird Ecology

1. *Goals*: Conduct basic studies on species in the benchmark study plots. Continue to support research on features that control nesting success in disturbed and undisturbed habitats. Continue to study specific causes of declines such as brood parasitism, and forest edge-induced nest predation, and how such problems can be ameliorated.

2. *Program*: Increase contract funding to support graduate student and senior academic research on FWS-sponsored benchmark study plots.
3. *Implementation*: Immediate.
4. *Budget*: $500,000.

CONCLUSION

Although FWS is charged with the study and protection of all migratory birds, in practice a small number of game bird species have received almost all of the agency's attention. The few nongame species that do receive help usually are the focus of expensive recovery efforts. This relegates the vast majority of over 750 species of North American birds to "minor responsibility" status.

Recent interest in nongame bird conservation has resulted in congressional budgetary add-ons of $1.75 million over fiscal years 1988 and 1989 to fund research and management activities. In addition, FWS released the "Nongame Bird Strategies" statement, which outlines a five-year plan for conservation of migratory nongame birds and their habitats. All this would suggest that major positive steps have been taken to rectify the past imbalances in FWS resources and effort toward game versus nongame bird species. However, the additional funding has been used neither to evaluate the effectiveness of existing programs nor to establish a more carefully integrated program on migratory bird conservation. Research and management actions are still being implemented on a single species or case-by-case basis, and little effort has been put toward identifying wide-scale environmental problems that affect many species.

There is no question that increased support and improved coordination are needed to provide better coverage of monitoring and research on migratory nongame birds. However, wise allocation of funds should support a strong conservation program addressing critical issues, rather than the present scatter-shot approach that funds many unrelated projects. The development of such an integrated program may require major changes in the administration of nongame bird programs within FWS. Under the present decentralized administrative structure it will be more difficult to implement a hemisphere-wide bird conservation program. With a growing number of private groups supporting research and monitoring of migratory nongame birds, it will require careful coordination and cooperation to make the most out of every dollar and every hour of volunteer effort spent on bird conservation. If FWS is unable to coordinate research and monitoring efforts within the agency it will be hard-pressed to cooperate effectively with outside organizations. Whether FWS is able to make the fundamental changes in internal structure and priorities and act as a coordinating body for other smaller organizations remains a critical issue for migratory bird conservation in the 1990s.

REFERENCES

Askins, R. Interview with authors, Washington, D.C., October 18, 1988.

Askins, R.A., J.F. Lynch and R. Greenberg. *Current Ornithology*. In Press.

Butcher, G. 1986. "Breeding bird censuses and winter bird population studies: An update." *American Birds* 40: 67–68.

———. In Press. Audubon Christmas Bird Counts. FWS Biological Report.

———. Phone interview with R. Greenberg, February 2, 1989.

Carson, R. 1962. *Silent Spring*. Houghton Mifflin. New York.

Council on Environmental Quality. 1988. "Birdlife of the United States," in *Environmental Quality 1986*. Washington, D.C.

Cummings, E. Letter to the authors, August 20, 1988.

Dawson, D. Phone interview with R. Greenberg, August 20, 1988.

———. and J. Sauer, MS Symposium on trends.

DeSante, D. Phone interview with R. Greenberg, January 16, 1988.

———. and G.R. Guepel. 1987. "Landbird productivity in Central Coastal California: the relationship to annual rainfall and reproductive failure in 1986." *Condor* 89: 636–654.

Droege, S. and J. Sauer. In press. The North American Breeding Bird Survey. FWS Biological Report.

———. Phone interview with R. Greenberg, September 6, 1988.

Dwyer, T. Interview with the authors, Washington, D.C., August 20, 1988.

Engstrom, T. Phone interview with R. Greenberg, September 5, 1988.

———. Letter to the authors, September 19, 1988.

Erwin, M. Interview with the authors, Patuxent, MD, October 7, 1988.

Estrada, A. and R. Coates-Estrada. 1988. "Tropical rainforest conservation and perspectives in the conservation of wild primates (*Alouata* and *Ateles*) in Mexico." *Amer. J. Prim.* 14: 315–327.

Freese, K. Phone interview with J. Gradwohl .

Gradwohl, J. and R. Greenberg. 1988. *Saving the Tropical Forests*. Island Press. Washington, D.C. 210 pages.

Greenberg, R. 1985. "Competition among migratory birds in the nonbreeding season." *Current Ornithology* 3 : 281–307.

Geissler, P.H. 1986. "Estimation of animal population trends and annual indices from a survey, call-counts or other indications." *Proceedings of the American Statistical Association*.

Haig, S.M. Interview with the authors, Washington, D.C., September 5, 1988.

Haig, S.M. and L.W. Oring. 1987. "The Piping Plover.," *in* R. Di Silvestro, ed. *Audubon Wildlife Report 1987*. National Audubon Society and Academic Press. New York.

Hall, G. 1984. "Population decline of Neotropical migrants in an Appalachian forest." *American Birds* 38: 14–18.

Hamel, P. 1987. *The Bachman's Warbler: A Species in Peril*. Smithsonian Press. Washington, D.C.

Higgins, K.F. 1975. "Shorebird and game bird nests in North Dakota croplands." *Wildlife Society Bulletin*. 3: 176–179.

Holmes, R. T., and T. Sherry. 1988. "Assessing population trends in New Hampshire birds: local vs. regional patterns." *Auk* 105:756–768.

Howe, M.A. Interview with the authors, Patuxent, MD, October 7, 1988.

——., P.H. Geissler, and B.A. Harrington. 1986. Population Trends of North American Shorebirds wintering in Central and South America. Nineteenth World Conference International Council on Bird Preservation. Kingston, Ontario, Canada.

Hutto, R. 1988. "Is tropical deforestation responsible for the reported declines in Neotropical migrant populations?" *American Birds* 42: 375–380.

Janzen, D. 1986. *Guanacaste National Park: Tropical Ecological and Cultural Restoration.* Editorial Universidad Estatal Distancia. San Jose, Costa Rica.

Kale, H.W. 1977. "Endangered species: Dusky Seaside Sparrow." *Florida Naturalist* 50: 16–21.

——. 1983. "A status report on the Dusky Seaside Sparrow. *Bird Conservation.* 1: 128–132.

——. Phone interview with J. Gradwohl, November 15, 1988.

Knopf, F.L. Phone interview with R. Greenberg, October 14, 1988.

——., R.R. Johnson, T. Rich, F.B. Samson, and R.C. Szaro. 1988. "Conservation of riparian ecosystems in the United States." *Wilson Bulletin.* 100: 272–284.

Lanly, J. P. 1982. Tropical Forest Resources. Food and Agriculture Organization. Rome.

Leddy, L. Letter to authors, August 28, 1988.

Lynch, J.F. and R.F. Whitcomb. 1984. "Effects of the insularization of the eastern deciduous forest on avifaunal diversity and turnover," *in* A. Marmelstein, ed., *Classification, inventory and analysis of fish and wildlife habitat: Proceedings of a Symposium.* U.S. Fish and Wildlife Service OBS-78/76, Washington, D.C.

MacArthur, R. 1958. "Population ecology of some warblers of northeastern coniferous forest." *Ecology* 39: 599–619.

Myers, J.P. 1988. "The sanderling," pp. 651–666 *in* Chandler, William J. ed., *Audubon Wildlife Report 1988/1989.* National Audubon Society and Academic Press, Inc. New York.

——. Phone interview with J. Gradwohl.

——., R.I. Morrison, P.Z. Antas, B.A. Harrington, T.E. Lovejoy, M. Sallaberry, S.E. Senner and A. Tarak. 1987. "Conservation strategy for migratory species." *American Scientist* 75: 19–26.

National Oceanic and Atmospheric Administration. 1980. The Federal Coastal Programs Review: Report to the President. U.S. Department of Commerce. Washington, D.C.

Nations, J. and D. Komer. 1982. *Rainforest, Cattle and the Hamburger Society.* Center for Human Ecology. Austin, Texas.

Norse, E.A., K.L. Rosenbaum, D.S. Wilcove, B.A. Wilcox, W.H. Romme, D.W. Johnston and M.L. Stout. 1986. Conserving Biological Diversity in Our National Forests. The Wilderness Society. Washington, D.C.

Powell, G.V.N. and J.H. Rappole. 1986. "The hooded warbler," pp. 827–853 *in* Di Silvestro, R.L. ed., *Audubon Wildlife Report 1986.* National Audubon Society. New York.

Raffaele, H. Interview with J. Gradwohl by phone

Rappole, J., E. Morton, T. Lovejoy III, J. Ruos. 1983. Nearctic Avian Migrants in the Neotropics. U. S. Fish and Wildlife Service, Washington, D.C.

Remsen, J.V., T.A. Parker III. 1983. "Contribution of river-created habitats to bird species richness in Amazonia." *Biotropica* 15:223–231.

Robbins, C.S. In press. Potential of Breeding Bird Atlases for Monitoring Bird Populations. FWS Biological Report.

Robbins, C.S., D. Bystrack and P.H. Geissler, 1986. The Breeding Bird Survey 1965–1979: The First Fifteen Years. U.S. Fish and Wildlife Service, Washington, D.C.

——., B.A. Dowell, D.K. Dawson, J. Coln, F. Espinoza, J. Rodriguez, R. Sutton and T. Vargas. 1987. "Comparison of Neotropical winter bird populations in isolated patches versus extensive forest." *Acta Oecologia.* 8:285–292.

————., J.R. Sauer, R.S. Greenberg and S. Droege. Recent declines in populations of North American birds that migrate to Neotropical forests. Ms.

Roberts, P.M. 1984. "Why count hawks? A continental perspective." *Hawk Mountain News.* 62:47–51.

Robinson, S. Phone interview with R. Greenberg, February 2, 1989.

Sader, S.A. and A.T. Joyce. 1988. "Deforestation rates and trends in Costa Rica, 1940–1983." *Biotropica* 20:11–19.

Senner, S.E. 1986. "Federal research on migratory non-game birds: Is the Fish and Wildlife Service doing its job?" *American Birds* 40:413–417.

————. 1988. "Saving birds while they are still common." *Endangered Species Update* 5:1–4.

————. Interview with the authors.

————. and M. Howe. 1984. "Conservation of nearctic shorebirds," *in* J. Burger and B. Olla, eds, *Shorebirds: Breeding Behavior and Populations.* Plenum Publishing Corporation.

————., D. Klem, L.J. Goodrich and J.C. Bednarz. Migration Counts at Hawk Mountain, Pennsylvania as Indicators of Population Trends, 1934–1986. Ms.

Sykes, P.W. 1980. "Decline and disappearance of the dusky seaside sparrow from Merritt Island, Florida." *American Birds.* 34:728–737.

Tiner, R.W. Jr. 1984. Wetlands of the United States: Current Status and Recent Trends. U.S. Fish and Wildlife Service National Inventory. Government Printing Office. Washington, D.C. 59 pages.

U.S. Department of Interior, Fish and Wildlife Service. 1986. North American Waterfowl Management Plan. Washington, D.C.

————. 1987. Migratory Birds of Management Concern in the United States. Office of Migratory Bird Management. Washington, D.C.

————. 1988a. Final Supplemental Environmental Impact Statement: Issuance of Annual Regulations Permitting the Sport hunting of Migratory Birds. Washington, D.C.

————. 1988b. Non-game Bird Strategies. Office of Migratory Bird Management. Washington, D.C.

Verner, J. Phone interview with R. Greenberg, September 5, 1988.

Wilcove, D. 1988. "Changes in the avifauna of the Great Smoky Mountains: 1947–1983." *Wilson Bulletin* 100:256–271.

Judith Gradwohl is an environmentalist in the Office of Assistant Secretary for Research of the Smithsonian Institution. Russell Greenberg is an ornithologist who works for the Department of Zoological Research, National Zoological Park, Smithsonian Institution.

This chapter benefitted greatly from discussions with the individuals who generously provided personal communications. We are particularly grateful to William J. Chandler, Sam Droege, J.P. Myers, and Stanley Senner for their insightful comments on various drafts of the manuscript.

According to the agency's own studies, 59 percent of BLM-administered public rangeland is not in good condition, mostly because of overgrazing. The effects of overgrazing are especially deleterious in riparian areas, where cattle quickly degrade wildlife habitat. While there is some agreement on the nature of the problem, there is no consensus on the politically sensitive solution. *Karen Copeland*

Restoring the Ravaged Range

Charles Lee Atwood

> No single activity or combination of activities has contributed more to the deterioration of plant and animal life than the nibbling mouths and pounding hooves of livestock. When the land was grazed by bison and other wild animals, little injury was done. The grazing was intermittent and widespread.
>
> Richard and Jacob Rabkin,
> *Nature in the West* (1981)

INTRODUCTION

Over the years Americans have been remarkably indifferent to the fate of the nation's arid brush and grasslands, which constitute about 750 million acres of land in 16 western states and receive 20 inches or less annual precipitation (see Figure 1). The mindless slaughter, almost to extinction, of the buffalo aroused popular sentiment and provided grist for the new American conservation movement in the late-19th century (Viola 1987). But somehow pity for the buffalo did not translate into public demand to conserve the buffalo's habitat. Americans mythologized the cowboy/rancher while steadfastly ignoring the ecological devastation wrought by his cattle and sheep.

Now there are signs that all this may be changing. Indifference seems to be giving way to concern. Concern for the denizens of the arid brush and grasslands—creatures as varied as the desert tortoise, the kit fox, the wild horse, the jaguarundi, the sage grouse, and the cutthroat trout. Concern for the riparian areas of the arid West upon which so much life depends. Also, a new appreciation of the value of native

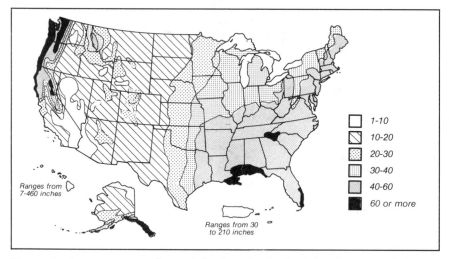

Figure 1. Average annual precipitation (in inches) in the United States. Source: U. S. Department of Agriculture.

grasses can be detected. Increasingly, the virtues of native grass cover are being extolled: grassland acts like a great sponge, soaking up the all-too-scarce rainfall so it does not run off the land in one big rush; it enables springs and streams to stay alive year-round; and it shields the life-nurturing soil from the erosive force of wind and rain.

This chapter examines some of the encouraging developments in arid lands conservation. These include the restoration of some riparian areas, removal of livestock from certain critical habitat areas, and the re-establishment of permanent vegetation cover on millions of acres of highly erodible land that have been removed from dryland crop production. Before treating those subjects, however, it is important to recall what a century of indifference—from the great cattle boom in the 1880s and 1890s to the present—has produced.

THE CONSEQUENCES OF INDIFFERENCE

The major consequences of public indifference include millions of acres of ecologically impoverished brush and grasslands, huge subsidies for a politically powerful special interest group—the livestock industry—and poor stewardship of public resources. Each of these is discussed here.

Impoverished Rangelands

Until recently, no systematic assessment of the condition of the nation's rangelands existed. However, national resources inventories, conducted in 1977 and 1982 by the Department of Agriculture's Soil Conservation Service, and information collected by the Bureau of Land Management (BLM) for court-ordered environmental impact statements, have changed that.

The 1982 National Resources Inventory (U.S. Department of Agriculture 1987), the most comprehensive inventory ever made of the nation's nonfederal soil, water, and related resources, revealed that 61 percent of the nation's nonfederal rangeland—247 million acres—*is in less than good condition* (see Figure 2). Specifically, some 69 million acres of private and state-owned rangeland—an area larger than the states of Pennsylvania and New York combined—are in "poor" condition. Poor condition means that less than 25 percent of the present plant communities on those lands is climax vegetation (the vegetation that evolved there over millenia) (U.S. Department of Agriculture 1987). In other words, as a result of overgrazing, the perennial grasses and forbs have given way to invaders, annuals such as cheatgrass (brome), filaree (erodium), and tumbleweed, or to bare ground. Poor rangeland is considered unstable rangeland. Its productivity (in the full ecological sense of the word) is declining and its soil is eroding faster than nature can regenerate it.

Another 178 million acres of private and state-owned rangeland is in "fair" condition. Fair means that 26 to 50 percent of the present plant communities is climax vegetation. Rangeland classified as fair may or not be unstable, depending on local conditions, but it is considered "unsatisfactory" by both the Soil Conservation Service and

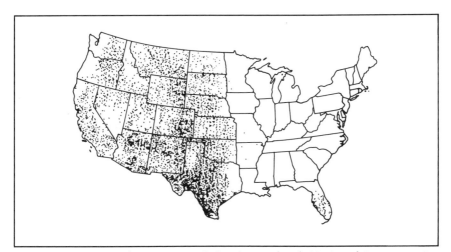

Figure 2. Range condition on nonfederal rangeland (National Resources Inventory 1982). Each dot = 50,000 acres of rangeland in fair or poor condition. Source: U. S. Department of Agriculture/Soil Conservation Service, National Resources Inventory.

Table 1. Condition of BLM-managed Public Range.

Source	Condition class (percent)				
	Excellent	Good	Fair	Poor	Unknown
NRDC/NWF[a] (1985)	1.9	27.1	42	29	0
BLM range managers (GAO 1988)	6	23	31	12	28
Official BLM report (1986)	4	30	41	18	7

[a] Natural Resources Defense Council and National Wildlife Federation. Based on an analysis of the grazing environmental impact statements done by BLM between May 1978 and June 1985, covering about 118 million of the 165 million acres of public rangeland administered by BLM.

Table 2. BLM Rangeland Condition by State.

State	Percent of total BLM range by condition class			
	Excellent	Good	Fair	Poor
Arizona	3.4	22.1	48.1	26.4
California	0.2	38.7	49	12.1
Colorado	0.2	11.4	48.9	39.5
Idaho	1.2	19.2	32.1	47.6
Montana	7.6	64.8	26.6	1
Nevada	1	19.5	35.3	44.2
New Mexico	0.5	22	51.6	25.9
Oregon	0.7	27.2	54.6	17.5
Utah	2.7	29.6	48.9	18.7
Wyoming	5.8	50.9	34	9.4
Total acreage in class (in millions)	2.3	32.1	49.7	34.4

Source: National Wildlife Federation and Natural Resources Defense Council.

BLM. Overgrazing on this rangeland may be historical or ongoing, or both. Whenever the overgrazing occurred, it made these acres less productive.Figure 2 only shows *nonfederal* rangeland in poor or fair condition. If the federal rangeland administered by BLM were included, another 98 to 117 million acres of range in poor to fair condition would have to be added (General Accounting Office 1988, Wald and Alberswerth 1985).

An analysis by the Natural Resources Defense Council and the National Wildlife Federation of 116 of 144 court-ordered environmental impact statements prepared by BLM on its grazing plans as of 1985 indicates that 71 percent of BLM-administered public land is not in good condition (see Tables 1 and 2). According to BLM's official (1986) estimate, 59 percent of BLM-administered public rangeland—about 98 million acres—is not in good condition. Of this, about 30 million acres—an area larger than the state of Virginia—are in "poor" condition, and 68 million acres are in "fair" condition.

Unfortunately, comparable figures are not available for the roughly 100 million acres of public rangeland administered by the Forest Service because this agency uses a different classification system than the Soil Conservation Service and BLM. The Forest Service compares the present condition of the plant community with "the potential natural community" that would ultimately become established in the absence of human interference under present environmental conditions. Generally, Forest Service-administered public rangelands tend to be found at higher elevations in the West where rainfall is more abundant, and they are considered to be in somewhat better condition than BLM-administered rangelands.

It is interesting to note that it does not seem to make much difference who owns the rangeland. In terms of the percentages of acres in poor, fair, good, or excellent condition, private, state-owned, and federal (BLM-administered) rangelands are quite similar (see Figure 3). The reason for this is simple: The ranchers whose sheep and cattle graze state and federal range think of that land as part of their own property. Indeed, a rancher's so-called "grazing allotment" on the public land is considered part of his equity capital when he goes to the bank for a loan or into the market to sell his property. Hence, the same profit and loss considerations of the stock owner rule over private and public rangelands alike.

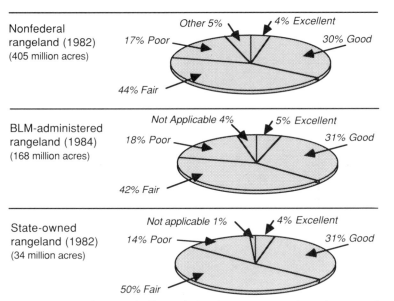

Figure 3. Condition of all nonfederal, state-owned, and BLM-administered rangelands. Source: U. S. Department of Agriculture, *Second RCA Appraisal*, July–August, 1987.

Desertification

"Desertification" is the word scientists use to describe the impoverishment of arid land ecosystems by human actions (Dregne 1983, Sheridan 1981). The major causes of desertification worldwide are (1) overgrazing, (2) dryland cropping, and (3) poor irrigation practices. In his pioneering study of desertification in North America, Texas Tech soil scientist Harold Dregne calculated that some 464 million acres of rangeland (all owners) in the United States had undergone some degree of desertification. He noted that "overgrazing has left a lasting imprint on the arid lands of North America, and little has been accomplished to restore the land to its original productivity" (Dregne 1983). All of the areas designated as "very severely" desertified by Dregne in Figure 4 have been overgrazed and so too have most of the "severely" desertified areas.

"By the 1870s and 1880s," Dregne observes, "a radical and frequently permanent deterioration in vegetation cover had been brought about by the excessive numbers of cattle being fattened—at little cost—for eastern markets." He adds:

The impetus for cattle herd expansion came from the profitability of meat production when newly constructed railroads provided transportation connections with population centers in the East. Overgrazing continued in the following decades, especially at the end of a series of wet years and the beginning of the inevitable series of dry years that followed. By the 1920s, moderate to severe desertification was prevalent nearly every-

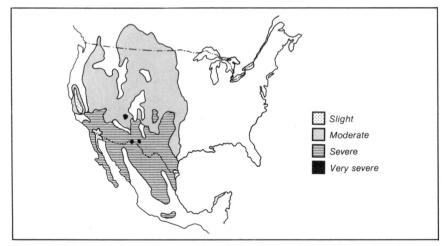

Figure 4. Status of desertification in arid regions of North America. Source: Council on Environmental Quality 1981.

where and range productivity had reached a minimum. Improvement since then has been very slow (Dregne 1983).

Why has progress been so slow? Because, as Dregne notes, "the single-most difficult step to take in restoring abused ranges to a high level of productivity is the first and most essential act: reduce livestock numbers" (Dregne 1983). The reason so much rangeland today is in fair to poor condition is because overgrazing, while not as bad as it once was, still persists (U.S. Department of Agriculture 1987, General Accounting Office 1988). The rancher either has too many sheep or cattle on the land or allows his livestock to graze too long in one spot (U.S. Department of Agriculture 1987, Sandvig 1983, Goodloe 1969, 1988, McMillan 1988, Dregne 1988).

Poorly Managed U.S. Rangeland

The Soil Conservation Service's appraisal of the 1982 National Resources Inventory data indicates that about 136 million acres of nonfederal rangeland are being "adequately" managed (U.S. Department of Agriculture 1987). This means that some 270 million acres are being *inadequately managed*, especially in terms of the numbers of livestock on the land or the duration of the grazing (see Table 3). The General Accounting Office, the congressional watchdog agency, estimates

Table 3. Inadequately Managed[a] Nonfederal Rangeland.

State	Percent	Acreage (in millions)
Texas	77	73.4
New Mexico	72	29.4
Arizona	80	24.5
Colorado	74	24.2
Montana	55	20.8
Wyoming	69	18.6
California	65	11.8
Oklahoma	63	9.5
South Dakota	41	9.3
Kansas	53	9
Oregon	88	8.3
Utah	87	7.4
Nebraska	31	7.1
Nevada	71	5.6
Idaho	78	5.3
Washington	73	4.1
North Dakota	31	1.1

Source: U.S. Department of Agriculture 1987.
[a] In terms of number of livestock and duration of grazing, and control of weed and brush invaders.

that one of every five acres of public rangeland administered by BLM is overstocked (General Accounting Office 1988). Curiously, the land grant universities of the West graduate thousands of range managers and range scientists each year. American range experts go all over the world to advise developing countries about how they should manage their rangelands. And yet, over 300 million acres of private and public U.S. rangeland—an area twice the size of Kenya—are being inadequately managed. How can this be?

The experience of conservationist-rancher Ian McMillan sheds some light on this question. A lifelong rancher in the rolling hills of east San Luis Obispo County, California, McMillan inherited a piece of land on the arid westside of the San Joaquin Valley in Kern County, California. The land was in awful shape, so McMillan arranged for an on-the-ground consultation with the county agricultural extension service agent to discuss how to restore it. "In full view was a broad slope gullied by recent rains and bare from intensive grazing," McMillan recalls. "I showed the young official a few remaining stubs of the native saltbush that prior to the damage had grown abundantly on the area as the key species of a stable arid-land ecosystem. I pointed out areas of bare hardpan on exposed locations where removal of the protective vegetation had allowed wind to carry off the topsoil."

For a considerable time, the young farm advisor said almost nothing. McMillan assumed "that faced with such an extreme state of devastation he was at a loss for what to recommend." Finally, the young range expert told McMillan: "You really have no problem here. The range has always been like this. All you need is rain. The filaree [an invader annual grass, which as its Latin name, erodium, implies, thrives in overgrazed areas] will come right up. If you don't clear it off, it will all go back to ripgut grass [a term that ranchers use to describe a number of different native arid land plant species]" And the young expert added: "We don't like the word overgrazing." While he and McMillan gazed upon the barren slope, the young range expert concluded: "Our research has produced no evidence that grazing has caused range depletion in this region" (McMillan 1976, 1988).

McMillan decided to fend for himself. He planted saltbushes and radically altered the grazing practices of the leasee whose sheep grazed the land. McMillan allowed the leasee to put sheep on the land only after the annual grass, mostly brome, had started to grow and required the leasee to remove them before the annual grass matured. In this way, the sheep do not browse the saltbushes. Over the years, McMillan has seen this piece of once-overgrazed, arid rangeland stabilize and slowly recover (McMillan 1988).

In McMillan's view, the young range expert's attitude was symptomatic of what has happened to the discipline of range science. McMillan believes that the academic leaders in range science who were critical of overgrazing were replaced by advocates of maximum range use, or "full utilization" as it came to be known. "Steadily," McMillan says, "the new research produced findings that fitted the argument and range practices as well as the political whims of the grazing interests." He adds: "And the universities produced a new type of range technician to spread the gospel of full utilization" (McMillan 1988).

Big Subsidies for Ranchers

Another consequence of public indifference to what is happening out on the arid brush and grasslands of the West is the establishment of a system of subsidies for the special interest group whose livestock graze the public land. As the General Accounting Office has pointed out, BLM's grazing management program—which involves everything from installing livestock watering facilities on the public land to destroying unwanted brush and weeds, to planting crested wheatgrass for consumption by cattle—cost taxpayers $39 million in 1986. In return, the government collected $14.6 million in grazing-fee receipts from the ranchers whose stock grazed the public land. That amounts to a federal subsidy of about $1,200 per year for each rancher with a grazing permit—or about $12,000 per rancher over the 10-year life of the grazing permit. In the Forest Service's grazing management program, there is comparable gap between outlays and receipts, hence ranchers with permits to graze Forest Service-administered lands are subsidized at roughly the same rate (Committee on Government Operations 1986).

That is only part of the subsidy received by ranchers with federal grazing permits. The federal government (BLM and Forest Service) actually charges ranchers three to four times *less* for public forage than its market value. (The government currently charges $1.86 per animal-unit-month or AUM), which is the amount of forage required to sustain a 1,000-pound cow, a horse, or five sheep for one month. Cattle account for about 90 percent of the livestock forage consumed on public land.) Even assuming a very conservative average market value for forage—$5.20 per AUM—the federal charge of $1.86 represents an annual subsidy of about $60 million. The figure comes to about $3,000 for each rancher per year—or $30,000 over the life of the permit.

The combined subsides for ranchers with public grazing permits add up to about $4,200 per rancher per year—or about $42,000 over the life of the permit. It should be noted, however, that these are not the total subsidies received by the ranchers. They also benefit from other federal government programs. The Department of the Interior, for example, for years operated a predator control program, the so-called "gopher chokers" program, for the benefit of western ranchers as well as pest eradication programs, especially in overgrazed areas infested with

The General Accounting Office estimates that one in five acres of public rangeland is overstocked. Ranchers are able to lease federal grasslands at prices significantly lower than market value and critics argue that the Bureau of Land Management is subsidizing the deterioration of public lands. *Karen Copeland*

grasshoppers. The predator control program was shifted to the Department of Agriculture in FY 1986. In addition, the ranchers whose livestock graze the public lands also are eligible for various Department of Agriculture assistance programs. Probably the most significant of these are the low-interest loans of the Farmers Home Administration and the Agricultural Stabilization and Conservation Service's emergency feed program, which during times of drought subsidizes farmers' and ranchers' purchase of feed for their livestock. In 1988, some 380 million pounds of feed were purchased under this program at a cost to the taxpayer of about $140 million (Agricultural Stabilization and Conservation Service 1989).

What do the taxpayers get in return for all these subsidies, aside from depleted brush and grasslands? In terms of the subsidies directly related to grazing the public lands, the answer is: surprisingly little. Only one out of six western ranchers enjoys the privilege of a federal grazing permit. Only seven percent of the forage consumed nationally by cattle and sheep comes from the public lands (U.S. Department of the Interior 1989). As one Department of Agriculture economist told this author: "If we phased out grazing on the public lands over, say, a 10- to 15-year period, I don't think it would cause even a blip in the price of beef or lamb. We are not talking precious metals here. The supply of livestock feed in the United States is very elastic. The market could adjust to a seven percent loss in supply, spread out over a number of years, without any problem at all. The effect on the consumer would probably be imperceptible."

Of course, the local communities in the vicinity of the public rangelands do benefit from the subsidies, along with ranchers who hold public grazing permits. In evaluating the "no grazing option" in the environmental impact statement prepared for 2.4 million acres of public rangeland in southwestern Idaho and north-central Nevada—the Bruneau-Kuna Resource Area—BLM estimated that grazing on the public land generated an annual income of about $1.6 million for the area (U.S. Department of the Interior 1982). The environmental impact statement for 4 million acres of public rangeland in northwestern Nevada—the Paradise-Denio Resource Area—estimated that grazing on the public land generated an annual income of about $11.3 million for the local economy (U.S. Department of the Interior 1981). If BLM and Forest Service grazing programs were put on a pay-as-you-go basis and ranchers were charged the market value for the public forage their livestock consume, those local income figures would certainly be reduced. But why then should the taxpayers subsidize Denio, Nevada, or Bruneau, Idaho?

Lax Management of Public Resources

Public indifference has also encouraged lax management of public resources, especially by BLM. Evidence of lax management goes beyond the unsatisfactory condition of the public rangeland. A 1986 audit of BLM's grazing management program by the Department of the Interior's Office of Inspector General concluded: "BLM does not have an effective trespass monitoring program to detect and prevent grazing, is not diligent in pursing and resolving the trespass cases that are reported, and is not recovering all costs associated with trespass" (Sheehan 1986).

Apparently, little has changed. Consider the recent experience of a General Accounting Office (GAO) investigation team at Tabor Creek, near Deeth, Nevada, in the northeastern part of that state (General Accounting Office 1988). On the way to inspect BLM's restoration of the Tabor Creek riparian area, BLM officials explained that the area had improved dramatically ever since a stretch of the creek had been fenced off from cattle. While the surrounding rangeland remained in poor condition, the vegetation inside the enclosure was rejuvenating and the stream bank stabilizing. Tabor Creek, BLM officials said, is now a "showcase."

But when the GAO team arrived at Tabor Creek they found something very different. A large number of cattle had broken the enclosure

fence and grazed the once protected area to "a desert-like condition."
GAO reported:

> Essentially all of the regenerated grass in the area was eaten or trampled
> and most of the area was reduced to dust. BLM officials expressed their
> surprise and dismay with the trespass. They stated, however, that such
> trespass is not uncommon and they would try to work more closely with
> the permittee to gain assurance that the incident would not be repeated.

It is common knowledge that BLM employees who pursue trespass
cases against local ranchers too vigorously will find themselves in hot
water with their bosses—the BLM district manager and the state director. And if the employee persists, he or she may be found shuffling
papers in a windowless office far away, probably Alaska. A rancher
whose cattle have trespassed repeatedly into a no-grazing area does not
forfeit his grazing permit. As rancher Jim Clapp, who has worked for
BLM and is founder of the Wild Horse Sanctuary in Shingletown, California, observes: "You have to remember what the BLM is. It's a bunch
of cattlemen running the public land" (Toussaint 1989).

The Inspector General's report also found that some grazing permittees actually were subleasing their allotments on the public lands
to other ranchers. And needless to say, they were not charging the government AUM rate. In other words, the permittees were leasing the
land from the government at the subsidized rate and then subleasing it
to another rancher at the much higher market rate, thereby making a
tidy profit in the deal (Committee on Government Operations 1986).
It is illegal to sublease a public grazing allotment and the subleasee is
considered a trespasser, under federal law, but BLM has failed to halt
the practice.

Furthermore, the Inspector General found that BLM was doing a
poor job of collecting the grazing fees owed it by the ranchers. Its review of 205 billings by five BLM field offices revealed that permittees
were delinquent in paying 56 percent of their billings (Sheehan 1986).

But the clearest indication of lax management was revealed in a
recent GAO report (1988). GAO sampled BLM range managers in the
field to see how conditions on the ground squared with what BLM was
saying back in Washington, D.C. BLM range managers surveyed admit-
ted to GAO that they were not aware of the range condition on about
28 percent of the rangeland under their "management." Applied BLM-
wide, those results would mean that BLM managers do not know the
condition of some 47 million acres of public land—an area about the
size of North Dakota.

To summarize, imagine you are a private landowner and the agent
you hired to look after your property:

- allows renters to abuse that property on a regular basis;
- charges those renters three to four times less than the market
  rate;

- fails to keep trespassers off the property;
- does not collect over half the rents on time; and,
- is unable to tell you the condition of one-fourth the property.

This situation would obviously be intolerable to the private land-owner, yet the U.S. public finds itself in such a predicament with the 165 million acres of rangeland that it owns and BLM manages.

HEALING SOME WOUNDS

Restoring Riparian Areas on Public Lands

Both the Forest Service and BLM have become more aggressive in re-cent years in trying to stop the destruction of riparian areas by live-stock and restoring them to their natural state. And for good reasons. Riparian areas—those ribbons of green along streams and rivers are enormously important. They provide wildlife with food, water and shade—all scarce commodities in the arid West. Moreover, riparian areas filter the runoff that flows into streams and rivers, removing sedi-ment; during downpours they dissipate the energy of flood waters, thereby reducing both the gully and arroyo-cutting force of the water as well as the flood peaks downriver.

Cattle trample streambanks, which causes cave-ins and sloughing. A lot more sediment ends up in the stream and it smothers the areas where fish have laid their eggs, so that fish reproduction suffers. Cattle also devour streamside vegetation, which reduces fish food supply, es-pecially insects, and eliminates the shade that keeps water tempera-tures within the tolerance level of native trout and other fish (U.S. Department of the Interior 1982). The damage done by cattle can also render riparian habitats unfit for other creatures as well—river otters, pronghorn antelope and deer, bighorn sheep, raptors, waders, and hummingbirds.

Roughly 1.5 million acres of riparian areas in the arid West have been seriously damaged by livestock (Brouha 1988). Only a tiny frac-tion of these riparian areas have been saved from further livestock damage and restored. Nonetheless, the efforts to do so are very encour-aging, and they involve not only the Forest Service and BLM but also conservation organizations such as the American Fisheries Society, state fish and game departments, and some private landowners, includ-ing ranchers. Usually, riparian restoration entails putting up fences to keep the livestock out, sometimes laying rock rip-rap on streambanks to stop erosion, and building rock or wood structures in the stream to help raise the water table and create pools. Sometimes, vegetation is planted on the denuded riparian land, but often it is left to come back on its own.

Riparian restoration is *the* hot topic today in western conservation and natural resource management circles. Fortunately, not all the actual restoration projects have ended up like Tabor Creek, Nevada. Following are some projects that have, under different circumstances, succeeded. They are drawn from a GAO assessment (1988) and represent a beginning.

Huff Creek, Wyoming.   Huff Creek runs for about 5.5 miles through grassland in western Wyoming. About 3.8 miles are on public land. The creek is part of the Thomas Fork drainage of the Bear River and it provides habitat for the rare Bear River cutthroat trout. According to the Wyoming Game and Fish Department, Huff Creek's trout population dropped from 222 fish per mile in 1958 to 93 per mile in 1978. A BLM study attributed the decline to excessive livestock grazing and herbicide use.

Together with the Wyoming Game and Fish Department, BLM employees formulated a habitat management plan for the Thomas Fork Drainage. Along Huff Creek, about 40 acres were fenced off and stream stabilization work was undertaken. The project required the cooperation of the permittee—the Smith's Fork Grazing Association. The association agreed to defer grazing of cattle along all of Huff Creek until August each year, and it employed a range rider to keep the cattle from grazing too long in any one part of the unfenced part of the riparian area. By 1984, the trout population was up to 444 trout per mile, a 377 percent improvement.

In the case of Huff Creek, the continuing control of the cattle's grazing by the range rider proved as effective as the fencing. By 1987, conditions outside the fenced off area were virtually as good as those inside it.

Texas Creek, Colorado.   Texas Creek flows through 25 miles of rough, brushy terrain in south-central Colorado. Some of the land along it is private, some is administered by BLM and some by the Forest Service. Noting that unrestricted livestock grazing was causing the creek's brown trout population to decline and its banks to erode and collapse, BLM began a restoration project in 1977. The condition of the creek's riparian areas at that time was rated as "poor." What was particularly interesting about this effort was that BLM divided the project's 20 acres into three equal segments and implemented different restoration techniques in each. On segment 1, livestock grazing was deferred for a time and then allowed. No structural improvements were made. In segment 2, livestock were excluded entirely and intensive structural improvements were made. In segment 3, livestock were excluded; no structural improvements were made. By 1987, segment 2 had improved the most, going from a habitat rating of "poor" to "excellent," and its brown trout population grew fivefold—from 13 trout per 500 feet of stream to 71. Segment 1's habitat rating improved from "poor" to "good." And segment 3 went from 'poor' to 'fair.' The trout population in both segments 1 and 3 tripled.

BLM reports that initially it was difficult to gain the cooperation of the permittee. But in 1981 a new permittee took control of the allotment. According to BLM, he was cooperative because his overall AUMs were not reduced on the allotment and because forage and water remained available in the upland areas, hence the permittee had no need to graze his cattle in the project area.

Mahogany Creek, Nevada. The "before" pictures of Mahogany Creek in northern Nevada are not pretty. Over many years of heavy grazing, cattle had stripped its grasses, leaving only some old, decaying aspen trees. Mahogany Creek is in a BLM resource district in which some 326 stream miles of riparian habitat are in "poor" condition (U.S. Department of the Interior 1981).

In 1974, BLM started a restoration project for Mahogany Creek because it is one of only two areas where the rare Lahontan cutthroat trout reproduces naturally. Extensive trespass grazing occurred in the project area between 1974 and 1976, however, and conditions did not improve. Therefore, in October 1976, during a period when the allotment was being transferred between permittees, BLM fenced off most of the creek and its watershed.

By 1986, Mahogany Creek's flow had increased by 400 percent, its depth by 50 percent, and its banks had stabilized. The area's grasses and aspen had regenerated, and the creek's trout population had burgeoned. BLM officials involved with the project concluded that significant riparian habitat improvements in this area were made only after the complete removal of livestock.

Prognosis for BLM Riparian Restoration

GAO cautions that BLM's ongoing efforts to restore livestock-damaged riparian areas will progress slowly because BLM officials are very reluctant to proceed without the approval of the ranchers who hold grazing permits on the riparian areas that are in need of restoration. GAO adds:

> From our discussions with livestock industry representatives, it is apparent that an increasing number of ranchers are coming to accept the benefits healthy riparian areas can bring to their operations. It is also apparent that many more ranchers remain unconvinced about the value of riparian improvement initiatives. . . . Future progress will therefore have to be won on allotments where permittees may not voluntary cooperate. This will probably require a greater willingness to mandate cooperation as a condition for continued use of the land.

Restoration of Private Riparian Areas

Riparian restoration efforts are also occurring on private rangelands. While these efforts are not as well documented, the following example shows that an entire watershed can benefit when grazing is properly controlled.

Rocky Creek, Texas. The Rocky Creek watershed is in the rolling brush and grassland of west-central Texas. Five ranches covering about one-half the watershed began an extensive range improvement program in the early 1960s. By 1970, springs dormant since the 1930s had begun flowing again on all five ranches and the watershed's overall water yield increased markedly. Today, West Rock Creek, which is part of the restored area but comprises only three percent of the entire watershed, supplies approximately seven percent of the water supply of San Angelo, 20 miles away (U.S. Department of Agriculture 1987).

The Nature Conservancy Initiatives. Founded in 1951, The Nature Conservancy is a private, nonprofit organization that buys land in order to save the habitat of rare and endangered species and ecosystem types. Although the majority of the Conservancy's projects are in the eastern United States, in the past decade the organization has become an important force in the conservation of arid land ecosystems. The Conservancy's recent initiative in the Carrizo Plain in eastern San Luis Obispo County, California, is illustrative.

In 1886, a visitor to the Carrizo Plain described it as follows: "In the spring, native bunch grasses, reaching as tall as the side of a horse, grew thick on the undulating land turning to naturally cured hay in the summer. Wild horses, elk, deer and antelope were abundant on the Plain" (Smith 1988). Today's Carrizo Plain bears no resemblance to that description. One hundred years of overgrazing have taken their toll. The native perennial bunch grasses, interspersed with flowering native annuals, are very scarce. The European invaders—filaree and brome—now reign. Carrizo Plain has a desiccated look, even in the spring. And the California condor is gone; this was once one of its major habitats. The condor was done in by hunting and more recently by chemical poisons put out by ranchers to kill predators. But the Carrizo Plain has remained remarkably isolated and undeveloped, so that some creatures have survived. These include the endangered San Joaquin kit fox, the giant kangaroo rat, and the blunt-nosed leopard lizard. In January 1988, the Conservancy, in a joint project with BLM, purchased eight contiguous ranches on the Carrizo Plain—85,000 acres altogether— that will be the core of a 180,000-acre nature reserve. The Conservancy will develop the reserve and then eventually sell the bulk of the land to BLM, with some small parcels going to the California Department of Fish and Game (Wiley 1988, 1989).

The challenge facing the Conservancy is to restore the native bunch grasses and flowering annual forbs and push out the invaders. Ken Wiley, the Central Coast Area Manager of the Conservancy, reports that most of the plain has been severely overgrazed and the grassland is in poor shape. The Conservancy will allow continued livestock grazing on the land it has acquired, under leasing arrangements with four ranchers who live nearby, but under a much stricter grazing management regime than has prevailed in the past. A three-pasture rotation system will be used. During the four winter months when the invader annual grasses are green, one-third of the range will be grazed and the other two-thirds rested. No grazing will be allowed anywhere during the other eight months. It is hoped the grazing will serve two purposes: one political, solidifying local support for the project, and the other ecological. The Conservancy expects that by putting increased pressure on the invader annuals through livestock grazing, it will give the native perennials a better chance of returning. Grazing, in other words, will be used as a positive management tool (Wiley 1988, 1989). "What we'd like to see eventually on the Carrizo," says Wiley, "is a wide-open plain, with healthy herds of antelope and Tule elk, vast acreages of saltbush shrubland, a grassland-forb community made up largely of native species, and a growing population of kangaroo rats and kit foxes" (Wiley 1988).

The Nature Conservancy has also taken over ranch properties in other western states. In Arizona, for example, it now has 11 preserves, almost all of which were once overgrazed ranch land. Ken Wiley's major responsibility before taking on the Carrizo Plain project was setting up a long-term protection program for the long overgrazed Muleshoe Ranch in the southeastern part of Arizona near Willcox. The ranch itself was about 4,400 acres, but it came with came grazing permits to about 50,600 acres of public land, half of which is managed by the Forest Service, half by BLM. Within the total 55,000 acres are over 17 miles of perennial streams bordered by fairly intact riparian forest that provide major habitat for the rare black hawk, zone-tailed hawk and gray hawk. Perennial streams and their riparian habitats are precious resources in this part of the state (Wiley 1988, Hoffman 1989).

"It was obvious early on," Wiley notes, "that continued grazing of cattle would have a detrimental effect on the Muleshoe." He adds:

> It was very dry, very rugged, and, as a result, the cattle, of course spent the majority of their time during the long hot Arizona summer in the riparian zone. While the riparian forests appeared superficially healthy, we learned that their extent had been dramatically decreased over the years due to flooding, apparently caused by denuding of the upper watersheds.

There was essentially no reproduction of the major tree species because the young seedling cottonwoods, sycamores, willows, walnuts, and ash were grazed off every summer by the cattle (Wiley 1988).

The Conservancy terminated all livestock grazing on the Muleshoe ranch. It also convinced the Forest Service to retire the Muleshoe grazing permits on the land it administered, and persuaded BLM to agree to a five-year moratorium on grazing for the Muleshoe allotments it administered.

With no grazing, the Muleshoe's riparian areas have made "a dramatic comeback," according to Preserve Manager Dona Howell.

The riparian understory—grasses and young willow and cottonwoods saplings—is returning, and stream conditions have improved in Bass Canyon as well as in Hot Springs and Redfield Creeks for the five species of native fish we have here. Only Double R Creek has shown no improvement. Its streambed had been so badly scoured by past floods that water just roars through it. Small weir dams will probably have to be constructed to slow down the flow and create pools, and the stream banks will have to be cut down by earth-moving equipment to allow flood waters to spread out as they once did (Howell 1989).

What concerns the Conservancy most about the Muleshoe today is whether BLM will allow livestock grazing back onto the land that it manages. The agency is under pressure from local ranchers to do so. The five-year grazing moratorium was linked to the preparation of a new Resource Management Plan (RMP) by BLM. The RMP is now in draft form and is subject to change, but as BLM Area Manager Meg Jensen explains: "Right now we are considering allowing grazing on Soza Mesa and nowhere else in the Muleshoe Preserve, especially not in any of the riparian areas. Soza Mesa constitutes 3,000 acres in the southwestern part of the Muleshoe; it's geographically separate and in good condition." Jensen says that she is abundantly aware that BLM has to do a better job of managing watersheds: "We tend to concentrate on the stream channel only, she says, and need to pay more attention to the upper portion of the watershed" (Jensen 1989).

The Nature Conservancy and BLM are involved in protecting another important riparian area in Arizona—Aravaipa Canyon. The Conservancy has acquired about 6,000 acres at either end of the canyon; BLM has put together a large block of land in between and manages it as a wilderness area. The only grazing still allowed in Aravaipa Canyon is on part of the Conservancy's preserve; in acquiring the land it inherited an existing 10-year grazing lease (Jensen 1989).

Of course The Nature Conservancy has its limitations. The total number of acres it can save at any one time are small—it currently owns about 0.5 million acres nationwide. But by acquiring ranch properties that contain rare or endangered species habitat and rare ecosystem types, the Conservancy is playing a major conservation role in the arid West because it either ends livestock grazing entirely on these land or installs a radically different grazing regime. Certainly the Carrizo Plain project is a valuable experiment in the restoration of badly overgrazed shrub and grassland; it will be watched closely by conservationists and natural resource managers throughout the West. Indeed, it could become something of a model. With 99 to 117 million acres of private, state, and BLM rangeland in poor condition, models are badly needed.

Re-establishing Grass Cover on Highly Erodible Land. Next to overgrazing, the major cause of desertification is the plowing up of dryland in order to grow crops. A major effort is now under way in the United States to convert highly erodible cropland back into grass or some other permanent cover. Launched by the Conservation Title of the Food Security Act of 1985, otherwise known as the 1985 Farm Act, this effort is nationwide in scope. While the Farm Act says nothing about combatting desertification, if fully implemented it should do more to conserve arid land wildlife, water, and soil resources than any program since the Dust Bowl days.

The sodbuster provision of the 1985 Farm Act makes farmers who plow up highly erodible grassland (without first having a Soil Conservation Service-approved conservation plan that substantially reduces soil loss) *ineligible* for most Department of Agriculture benefits. Benefits are lost not just on the highly erodible part of their land but their entire farm (U.S. Department of Agriculture 1986). Among the benefits a farmer could lose for "sodbusting" are:

- price and income supports
- crop insurance
- Farmers Home Administration loans
- Commodity Credit Corporation storage payments
- Farm storage facility loans
- Conservation Reserve Program annual payments

Sodbuster represents a powerful economic *disincentive* for farmers who are considering the conversion of grassland on highly erodible soil into cropland. In the past, western farmers have responded to market increases in commodity prices by plowing up millions of acres of marginal dry lands to plant wheat, barley, and so on. The Department of Agriculture's commodity and drought relief programs provided them with additional economic incentives to farm arid lands (Sheridan 1981). For example, the tilling of marginal grasslands occurred after the grain price surges in World War I and immediately after the big Russian wheat deal in the early 1970s; terrible soil erosion resulted.

Soil erosion on the western Great Plains (see Figure 5) far exceeds

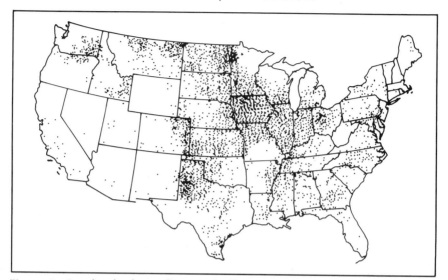

Figure 5. Cropland where sheet and rill erosion or wind erosion is greater than "T" (see text). Each dot = 50,000 acres. Source: U. S. Department of Agriculture/Soil Conservation Service.

the soil tolerance rate or "T." "T" is the maximum average annual soil erosion by wind or water that can occur without affecting productivity over a sustainable period. It is based on an estimate of how fast a given topsoil can regenerate. Since different topsoils form at different rates, the "T" value can vary from area to area. Usually, though, "T" ranges from two to five tons per acre per year.

Wind erosion is the great threat on the western Great Plains. Cropland on the dark-brown glaciated plains of northwestern North Dakota are losing, on average, 11.8 tons of soil per acre per year to wind erosion. Cropland on the central high plains of eastern Colorado and Wyoming and western Nebraska are losing 9 tons per acre per year to the wind. And croplands on the southern high plains of southwestern Oklahoma, west Texas, and eastern New Mexico are losing 21.3 tons per acre per year. The sandy loams of the southern high plains are especially vulnerable to wind erosion after they have been stripped of their native blue grama and buffalo grasses in order to grow wheat, barley, grain sorghum, and cotton (U.S. Department of Agriculture 1987).

The erosion rates from rangelands in these very same regions are noteworthy. Rangelands on the glaciated plains of North Dakota and the central high plains of Colorado, Wyoming, and Nebraska are eroding at a rate of less than one ton per acre per year, which is less than "T." Rangelands on the southern high plains of Oklahoma, Texas, and New Mexico are eroding at a rate of 3.7 tons per acre per year, which is less than "T" in some areas and more than "T" in others, but seven or more times less than the cropland erosion rates. In other words, livestock grazing is a far superior land use on the western Great Plains (even inadequately managed livestock grazing), than dryland cropping from a soil conservation perspective. Of course private landowners do not base their land-use decisions on soil erosion rates, but rather on which use generates the most income in the short run. By this measure, crops such as wheat and cotton usually win out over cows, at least until such time as the basic resource—the topsoil—is exhausted.

Western farmers have plowed up steeply sloping shrub and grasslands in the arid West in their pursuit of increased income. By so doing, they have opened the way for both wind and water erosion. For example, cropland on the Nebraska Sand Hills is losing 1.8 tons per acre per year to sheet and rill erosion and 6.5 tons to the wind. Cropland on the eastern plateaus of Idaho—the watershed for the Bear, Portneuf, Blackfoot, Snake, and Teton rivers—is losing 9.8 tons per acre per year to sheet and rill erosion and 5 tons to the wind. Cropland on the rolling, loess hills of the Palouse River Basin in eastern Washington are losing less than 1 ton per acre per year to wind erosion but 11 tons per acre per year to sheet and rill erosion. The rangeland soil erosion rate in all three of these regions is less than 2 tons per acre per year (U.S. Department of Agriculture 1987).

Until the 1985 Farm Act, the government's farm support programs strongly encouraged these ecologically unsound practices. After only two years of producing a crop on a field, despite how susceptible the soil was to wind or water erosion, a farmer was able to qualify that acreage as part of his base acreage for price supports and other benefits. So even if the yields from the land were low—and they often were very low in the inevitable drought or flood years—the farmer kept those lands in crop production in order to continue to collect government benefits. Throughout the arid West, this practice was common and it came to be known as "farming the farm program" (McMillan). For example, the Carrizo Plain Reserve contains some 40,000 acres that had been dryland farmed, mainly for barley, even though the Carrizo averages less than 10 inches of rainfall per year. The plain's farmer/ranchers were clearly farming the farm program. (The Nature Conservancy has retired this acreage from crop production and is revegetating it with permanent cover [Wiley 1988].)

It is too early to tell how effective the sodbusting provision of the 1985 Farm Act will ultimately be. In the short run, it seems to be working, but the real test is yet to come. Another bad drought on the Great Plains like that of 1988 could reduce U.S. grain supplies sufficiently to cause a surge in prices. Then it will be seen whether western farmers are willing to risk loss of government supports for short-term profits by cropping grasslands, or whether under intense political pressure, Congress will encourage the Soil Conservation Service to rubber-stamp the conservation plans of would-be sodbusters even though the plans do not reduce soil loss. Alternately, some suspect Congress might simply waive the sodbuster provision for the duration of the drought.

The 1985 Farm Act also created the Conservation Reserve Program (CRP). Under CRP, the government pays the farmer an annual rental to retire from production for 10 years those lands the Soil Conservation Service classifies as highly erodible. Currently, the annual rental payments are averaging $47.90 per acre (U.S. Department of Agriculture 1988). Twenty-eight million acres have been enrolled in CRP as of January 1989 (U.S. Department of Agriculture 1989); the enrollment goal is 45 million acres (see Table 4). Also, the government pays half the cost of establishing permanent vegetation—grass, trees or wildlife plantings—on the highly erodible land.

CRP seems to be faring well in the arid West, although the percent of eligible acres that are enrolled in the program varies considerably from state to state. North Dakota leads the way with 78.6 percent of eligible acres enrolled. In Table 4, note the sharp decrease in erosion rates for the acreage enrolled in the the program. It is also interesting to note that three out of every five CRP-enrolled acres are in the West.

According to the Agricultural Conservation and Stabilization Service, 58 percent of CRP acreage has been covered with non-native grasses; 26 percent with native grasses; 6 percent with trees; 4 percent

Table 4. Conservation Reserve Program in the Arid West.

State	Acreage in CRP (as of January 1989)	Percent of eligible acres enrolled in CRP	Erosion rate (tons/acres/year) Before enrollment	After enrollment
Arizona	0	0	—	—
California	170,479	22.2	15.3	1.3
Colorado	1,748,117	30.9	28.5	3.1
Idaho	714,307	30.6	17.7	1.6
Kansas	2,385,454	34.3	18.8	1.8
Montana	2,264,770	26.7	14.7	1.4
Nebraska	1,159,689	32	25.4	1.8
Nevada	2,343	1.2	14.8	1.8
New Mexico	468,310	54.7	44.4	3
North Dakota	2,175,123	78.6	16.9	1.2
Oklahoma	1,017,301	33	25.3	1.7
Oregon	497,622	41	12.9	1.6
South Dakota	1,222,860	60	14	1.3
Texas	3,457,007	25.2	38.6	2
Utah	227,357	49	19.4	2.5
Washington	870,230	35.3	14.8	1.2
Wyoming	222,606	58	14.7	1.5
Total	18,603,845			

Source: U.S. Department of Agriculture 1989.

with wildlife plantings; and the rest with field windbreaks or other acceptable cover (U.S. Department of Agriculture 1988).

If fully implemented, CRP should prove a boom to wildlife (Berner 1988). In some states such as Colorado and Kansas, there are already reported increases in the populations of upland game birds—ring-necked pheasants, bobwhites, and scaled quail (Misztal 1988, Dick 1988).

Over the long term, many other bird species are expected to prosper as a result of CRP, including the greater prairie chicken, the lesser prairie chicken, the sharp-tailed grouse, and the upland plover (Oetting 1988, Caster 1988). Gary Krapu, a biologist with the Fish and Wildlife Service's Northern Prairie Wildlife Research Center, thinks that in the long run raptors may benefit most of all from CRP because it will expand the habitat of prey species (Krapu 1988). Other animals that should benefit from the increase in permanent vegetative cover include elk, pronghorn antelope, white-tailed deer, coyotes, foxes, rabbits, and a host of small mammals (Misztal 1988, Oetting 1988).

Whether CRP realizes its full potential will depend on (1) how the program is administered, and (2) what happens after the 10-year contracts run out (Tidd 1988, Cacek 1988). During the drought of 1988 farmers in drought-stricken areas were allowed by the Department of Agriculture to hay their CRP acreage in order to feed their livestock. As Krapu (1988) notes, that decision greatly reduced the wildlife benefits of the the CRP. "The haying turned the CRP land into a death trap for groundnesting birds," he reports.

CRP is expensive, costing over $1 billion per year. The great worry among conservationists is that budget pressures will force Congress to make deep cuts in the program in the future. The first big test for CRP will be the 1990 Farm Bill (Benbrook 1988). Congress will have to decide what to do about CRP lands after the contracts run out, what financial commitment to make to the program in the 1990s, and whether to expand it beyond the 45 million acre goal. The 1982 National Resources Inventory indicates that there is much more to do. Some 105.8 million acres of U.S. cropland—about 25 percent of the total—is undergoing sheet and rill erosion at a rate that exceeds "T," and some 67.5 million acres—or about 16 percent—are undergoing wind erosion rates greater than "T" (U.S. Department of Agriculture 1987).

There is likely to be tremendous political pressure to "open up" CRP acreage if drought-caused crop failures drive up commodity prices. However, the federal government has paid farmers to idle twice as many acres to control supply (and prop up prices) under the annual set-aside program than have been idled for conservation purposes under CRP. This annually set-aside land could be brought back into production. For example, farmers growing winter wheat in 1987–1988 were required to idle 27.5 percent of their winter wheat acreage in order to remain eligible for commodity supports. In 1988–1989, they only had to set aside 10 percent. There is, in other words, a reserve of productive land that can be used to increase crop production rather than bringing CRP lands back into production (Gray 1988).

OUTLOOK FOR MAJOR NEW INITIATIVES

With the 1985 Farm Act, the U.S. government executed a dramatic mid-course correction in its cropland conservation policy. For the first time, a program with real financial incentives was established to take cropland out of production specifically for the purpose of saving the soil (rather than reducing surpluses). The act also included the powerful concept of "cross-compliance," that is, it linked eligibility for government farm program benefits to required land-use practices. The question today is whether the time is ripe for a comparable mid-course correction in rangeland conservation.

The Taylor Grazing Act

In 1934, Congress passed the Taylor Grazing Act, which ended uncontrolled grazing on what are today BLM-administered public lands. (Unrestricted grazing ended on Forest Service-administered rangeland in 1906, when a grazing permit system was introduced.) The Taylor Grazing Act was a major policy initiative launched in response to the 1930s Dust Bowl. Under the extreme erosion conditions that prevailed at that time, neither the American public nor Congress could ignore what ranchers and farmers had done to the nation's native brush and grasslands. Like the privately owned arid crop and rangelands, the public range was in terrible shape. In addition, the Great Depression had put the usually-resistant-to-change livestock industry into a receptive mode. The industry was especially receptive to the Taylor Grazing Act, which promised to end the free-for-all on the public range, which was essentially an unregulated commons providing established ranchers with long-term grazing privileges at a low cost (Voight 1976).

Like most pieces of legislation having to do with the management of the public lands, the Taylor Grazing Act had a little something for everyone. For conservationists, it had the stated intent "to stop injury to the public grazing lands by preventing overgrazing and soil deterioration." For the ranchers whose livestock graze the public lands, it promised "to stabilize the livestock industry dependent on the public range." More than 50 years after the act's passage, some 97 to 117 million acres are still in fair to poor condition. This suggests that the Taylor Grazing Act has been something less than a roaring success. However, are things better now than back in the Dust Bowl days?

The answer is yes. The range condition data from the 1930s are rather fuzzy, making exact comparisons impossible, but certainly there has been improvement in the condition of the public range. The steady upward growth in the pronghorn antelope population throughout the West is but one indication of this improvement (Yoakum 1988). Overall, a careful analysis of the grazing environmental impact statements and GAO reports reveal that while the Taylor Grazing Act failed to restore the public range to anything resembling its former productivity—in the full ecological sense—it has led to the stabilization of many millions of acres, albeit at a lower level of productivity.

Some Encouraging Signs

The prospects for a major change in public rangeland policy look increasingly bright. First of all, thanks to the efforts of GAO, numerous professional employees of the Department of the Interior, and various conservation organizations, especially the Natural Resources Defense Council, the message is starting to get through to Washington. As the title of a congressional committee report proclaims: "Federal Grazing Program: All Is Not Well On The Range" (Committee on Government Operations 1986). Moreover, in these times of tight federal budgets and painful deficit control measures required by the Balanced Budget and Emergency Control Act of 1985 (Gramm-Rudman-Hollings), any revenue-generating program that covers only 35 percent of its costs becomes increasingly indefensible (Committee on Government Operations 1986, General Accounting Office 1986). The proposition that ranchers should pay full market value for public forage and at least share the cost of range capital improvements now makes very good fiscal and political sense on Capitol Hill.

There are some other factors at work that encourage change. For example, a growing proportion of Americans seem to care passionately about wild animals, especially mammals. There have been numerous manifestations of this phenomenon, but probably none more dramatic than the strong public opposition in the United States to commercial whaling. And as any congressional aide will tell you, a growing number of Americans care enough about animals in the wild—from wild horses to river otters—to petition their elected representatives to have the animal's saved. One staffer for a western Congressman reports: "Why they're [the public] even against killing the damn coyotes."

The growing urbanization of the West is another factor. This urbanization puts increasing recreational pressure on the public lands. Almost 96 percent of the people who live in California now reside in metropolitan areas, 82 percent in Nevada, 82 percent in Colorado, 77 percent in Utah, and 75 percent in Arizona. A growing number of these people want somewhere to hike, camp, and fish—somewhere nice to get away from it all—and these needs can clash with the ranchers' demand for cheap public forage, especially in riparian areas. Rose Strickland, the head of the Sierra Club in Nevada, is convinced that it is the urbanization of the West itself that "will ultimately break the hammerlock the grazing interests have had on the public land decisionmaking process—from Congress on down through the state BLM offices to the local BLM manager" (Strickland 1988).

Finally, beef is losing some of its appeal to American consumers, and this will probably affect the politics of public lands. Per capita consumption of beef is declining. The beef industry has actually had to launch an expensive nationwide advertising campaign, targeted at younger consumers, especially young women, to sing the praises of beef: "Real Food for Real People." Meanwhile, medical authorities continue to caution the public about eating too much beef because of its high cholesterol content, compared to chicken, fish, tofu, and so on, and the risk cholesterol poses for heart disease.

Fortunately, though, for western ranchers another economic opportunity has emerged. Studies show that a growing number of Americans would like to vacation on a ranch. In Colorado, for example, one ranch in five has now diversified into tourism, and tourism is now *the* growth industry in the big ranching states of the Rocky Mountain region (U.S. Department of Agriculture 1987). It seems that while the chief product of ranches—beef—has lost some of its magic, more Americans than ever want to experience "the magic of a ranch environment," as the travel brochures say.

But before conservationists begin to celebrate victory, they should keep in mind the words of rancher-conservationist Ian McMillan: "The political power of the western grazing interests is enormous" (McMillan 1988). It is a myth that public rangeland primarily benefits "the small rancher" as BLM and other defenders of the current grazing program would lead one to believe. Fifty-eight percent of the public forage goes to large ranch operations, that is, those that own 500 or more animals; 32 percent goes to medium-sized operations—100 to 499 animals. Only 10 percent of the public forage goes to the small rancher who owns less than 100 animals. Big ranchers will not give up their subsidies without a battle, and their political leverage, from state legislatures to the United States Congress and the White House, has been amply demonstrated over the years (Voight 1976, Lash 1984, Luoma 1986).

Despite the popular sentiments for a healthy environment, including abundant wildlife, conservationists still must overcome the concentrated political power of a well-entrenched vested interest—the western livestock industry. BLM bulletins about grazing on the public lands still read as if they were written by the National Cattlemen's Association (U.S. Department of the Interior 1989). It should be remembered that the U.S. whaling industry was long dead before citizens convinced their government to take action against commercial whaling.

Private Rangeland Conservation

Whether sufficient political sentiment is developing to change *private* rangeland conservation policies is much less certain. Although, the 1982 National Resources Inventory clearly shows that the majority of private range is in unsatisfactory condition—in no better shape than the public range administered by the BLM. Conservationists have focused much less attention on private lands, however, this may be changing.

Mac Gray, head of strategic planning for the Soil Conservation Services, notes: "Since the 1985 Farm Act, most of our attention, of necessity, has been concentrated on cropland conservation. Frankly, rangeland conservation has kind or fallen through the cracks. I think you will see that changing very soon." Gray says that the Soil Conservation Service will become much more aggressive in the immediate future in helping private rangeland operators meet their conservation needs. "I think there is widespread awareness that we and they have to do a better job" (Gray 1988).

There are, however, some nagging questions regarding private rangeland conservation that need answering: Are the government's current conservation programs adequate, especially with regards to watershed and riparian conservation? Do some government support programs such as the emergency feed program actually encourage ranchers to overgraze their land? Should cross-compliance be applied to ranching as it has been to farming? For example, should ranchers who chronically overgraze their land or whose range is in poor condition be denied eligibility for government farm benefits? Should ranchers be provided specific financial incentives to retire badly damaged range from grazing and to restore it?

In the years ahead, it will be interesting to see how the booming arid sunbelt's growing need for water will affect range conservation. Well-managed range greatly enhances a watershed—increasing perennial streamflow and recharging groundwater aquifers. With groundwater supplies shrinking (see Figure 6), major surface sources such as the Colorado River already overused (Sheridan 1983), and diminishing political support for big new water projects, rangeland conservation becomes more important than ever. In some especially water-short areas, ranches may become more valuable for their water rights than for their output of cattle or sheep. In such cases, water utilities or bro-

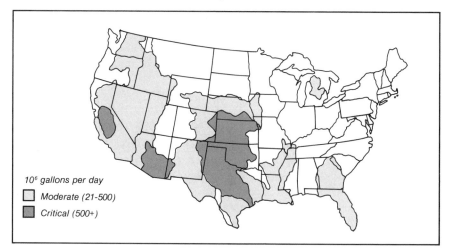

Figure 6. Groundwater overdraft. Source: U. S. Department of Agriculture/ Soil Conservation Service.

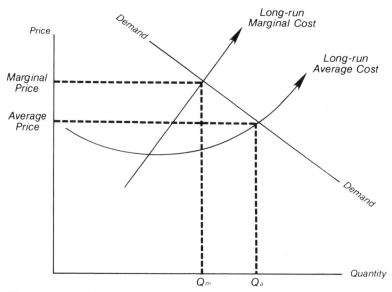

Figure 7. Equilibrium prices and quantities with average cost and marginal cost pricing rules. Source: H. J. Vaux, Jr., Growth and Water in the South Coast Basin of California (draft paper for the World Resources Institute, April 1986).

kers may simply buy these lands and retire them from production, leaving the rangeland free of livestock. In fact, this has already begun to happen near Tucson and Phoenix (Lindsey 1987).

There has been considerable discussion in recent years concerning the development of a free market in water in the arid West and marginal cost pricing of water as ways of dealing with the region's water problems (see Figure 7) (El-Ashry 1986). These could have a profound effect on rangeland conservation, perhaps providing ranchers with an added economic incentive to practice good range conservation or to abandon livestock grazing altogether in some areas. At this time, how such a water market might evolve is highly speculative. It seems likely, however, that as the region's growth outstrips its water supplies, serious consideration will be given to marginal (rather than average) cost pricing, and this will both make water more valuable and conservation more economically appealing.

MAJOR RANGELAND REFORMS ARE STILL NEEDED

Years of tinkering with the present public land grazing management system have not accomplished much. Earl Sandvig, veteran grazing consultant and retired Forest Service official, explains why: "The system is designed and operated for the rancher's needs to take precedence over the physiological requirements of the plants. Destructive grazing practices are always justified in terms of meeting the rancher's needs." Sandvig adds:

> Dozens of experiments have been tried over the past five or six decades in an effort to find a system of range management or range improvement that would eliminate the ugly, harsh necessity of reducing livestock grazing to improve overgrazed, depleted, degraded or denuded rangeland. Many years and much money has been wasted in trying to find the panacea. The result? One band-aid treatment after another for the land's running, open cancerous types of sores (Sandvig 1983).

Great hopes were held out for the Carter Administration's Public Rangeland Improvement Act of 1978. Its commitment to public investment in range "improvement" projects such as the installation of livestock watering facilities was supposed to greatly reduce overgrazing. It did not. The act's new formula for calculating grazing fees was supposed to raise them to fair market value. It did not. The act's Experimental Stewardship Program was supposed to (1) forge a new "partnership" between BLM and permittees, (2) lead to "innovative' range management practices, and (3) improve conditions on the grazing allotments. It did none of these (General Accounting Office 1988).

Scrap the Existing Grazing System

Clearly, the present grazing system is a fiscal and ecological failure; scrapping it is probably the only realistic option. Both the Forest Service and BLM should, as the current grazing permits expire, go to a competitive bidding system for those allotments that are designated suitable for grazing. (The Department of Defense already operates a competitive bidding system for grazing on some of its lands.) An allotment that is classified in "poor" condition is, *ipso facto*, not suitable for grazing. An allotment in "fair" condition, may or may not be suitable for grazing. The decision should be made on a site-by-site basis. Riparian areas in "fair" condition are unsuitable for grazing. So too are upland areas that are experiencing soil erosion in excess of "T" or excessive water runoff as manifested by gullying, arroyo-cutting, or channel destabilization downstream. Also unsuitable for grazing are "fair" areas in which livestock are outcompeting native species of wildlife such as desert tortoises (Campbell 1988) or quail (McMillan 1988) for forage or cover.

If none of the grazing bids reflect the market value of the forage, then no permit should be issued. Any citizen should be eligible to bid for a grazing permit so long as they are able to pay the fee, even if they have no intention of grazing the land. In this way, nongrazing interests such as conservation organizations or hunting and fishing groups can participate in the process if they choose to protect certain nongrazing values on public lands.

Permits should be issued for three to five years; they should specify the time of year the grazing can occur, the duration of the grazing on different segments of the allotment, and the number of livestock allowed. Failure to live up to these specifications should constitute trespass and automatic forfeiture of the grazing permit.

Under the proposed new system, ranchers whose livestock graze the public lands would share 50–50 with the government the cost of range capital improvements directly related to livestock grazing. BLM and the Forest Service would maintain all fences, gates, cattleguards, and so forth, however, and manage access to the allotment so that the permittee's livestock are secure and the forage undamaged. Access management is especially important in terms of the land management agencies restricting off-road vehicles (ORVs) to designated trails and roads (Goodloe 1988). Both BLM and the Forest Service have done a poor job of this in the past. They have allowed ORVs to run at will over public rangeland where these machines have done considerable damage to soil, vegetation and streambeds and disrupted wildlife and livestock alike (Sheridan 1979, Goodloe 1986).

Most importantly, in creating a new grazing management system for the public lands, Congress has, once and for all, to make its priorities clear instead of leaving it up to the land management agencies to resolve vague conflicting objectives in the law. *The primary purpose of the new system should be the long-term conservation of the public rangeland's wildlife, water, vegetation, and soil resources.* All decisions relating to livestock grazing or other uses of the public rangeland must be compatible with this primary objective. Stabilizing the livestock industry dependent upon the public range should *not* be an objective of the new system. To try and use a public land management program to serve such an objective is both economically inefficient and ecologically unsound. There are other means of economically assisting these ranchers through the Department of Agriculture.

Overhauling Private Rangeland Conservation

A special task force should be assembled under the direction of the Secretary of Agriculture to re-asses existing private land conservation programs in light of the findings of the 1982 National Resources Inventory. Are the government's farm assistance programs, such as the emergency feed program, working at cross-purposes with its conservation programs? Is more than fine-tuning of existing conservation programs needed? Should a major private rangeland conservation program be established? Among existing programs, what is working, what not? These are the kinds of questions that need to be pursued.

It is especially important that disciplines in addition to range science are represented on the task force—biology, hydrology, soil science, economics, and public administration. The National Agricultural Research and Extension Service should also play a major role in the task force. This should not be an academic exercise; the task force should come up with specific policy and program suggestions.

CONCLUSION

Many of the proposals made in this chapter may seem radical, even impolitic. But the fact remains that the majority of the vast acreage of arid brush and grasslands in this country is impoverished—a status totally unacceptable to anyone who values the creatures and other natural resources of the lands. Band-aids, as Earl Sandvig said, will not suffice. And this author remembers that, when he and others in the late 1970s put forth such ideas as making sodbusters ineligible for farm benefits and paying farmers to retire high erosion land from crop production they were told that these proposals—which are now law—were too radical and politically impossible. Indeed, during the Carter Administration, the conclusion of a draft report for the President's Council on Environmental Quality, which recommended these proposals, was dropped solely because these ideas were too controversial and might offend some members of Congress. However, yesterday's radical proposals have a way of becoming tomorrow's conventional wisdom, especially when the politically safe programs of the day are such obvious failures.

Walter Clay Lowdermilk, one of America's pioneer soil conservationists, once said that "a civilization writes its record on the land." Fortunately, Americans still appear to have time to rewrite their record on the nation's arid lands.

REFERENCES

Benbrook, Charles M. 1988. "The environment and the 1990 Farm Bill." *Journal of Soil and Water Conservation* 43(6):440–443. (November/December)

Berner, Alfred. 1988. "The 1985 Farm Act and its implications for wildlife," pp. 437–465 in Chandler, W.J. ed., *Audubon Wildlife Report 1988/1989*. Academic Press, Inc. and National Audubon Society. New York, New York.

Brouha, Paul. American Fisheries Society. Interview with the author. Washington, D.C. October 25, 1988.

Cacek, Terry. 1988. "After the CRP contract expires." *Journal of Soil and Water Conservation* 43(4):291–293. (July/August).

Campbell, Faith Thompson. 1988. "The desert tortoise," pp. 567–581 in Chandler, W.J. ed., *Audubon Wildlife Report 1988/1989*. Academic Press, Inc. and National Audubon Society. New York, New York.

Caster, Dewey. Biologist, Fish and Wildlife Enhancement Office, Fish and Wildlife Service, Kansas State University. Interview with the author. Manhattan, Kansas. October 20, 1988.

Dick, Donald. Biologist, Kansas Fish and Game Department. Interview with author. Manhattan, Kansas. October 19, 1988.

Dregne, Harold. 1983. *Desertification of Arid Lands*. Harwood Academic Publishers. Chur, Switzerland.

———. Interview with the author. Lubbock, Texas. July 27, 1988.

El-Ashry, Mohamed T. and Diana C. Gibbons. 1986. *Troubled Water: New Policies for Managing Water in the American West*. World Resources Institute. Washington, D.C.

Goodloe, Sid. 1969. "Short duration grazing in Rhodesia." *Journal of Range Management* 22(6):369–373. (November).

———. "A separate view: Off-road vehicle damage to public lands," pp. 43–46 in *Appraisal of the Proposed 1987 Budget for Food and Agricultural Sciences*. National Agricultural Research and Extension Users Advisory Board. Washington, D.C.

———. The Diamond A Cattle Company. Interview with the author. Roswell, New Mexico. October 18, 1988.

Gray, Mac. Soil Conservation Service. Interview with author. Washington, D.C. October 20, 1988.

Howell, Dona. Manager, Muleshoe Preserve, The Nature Conservancy. Interview with the author. Safford, Arizona. February 12, 1989.

Jensen, Meg. Area manager, Bureau of Land Management. Interview with the author. Willcox, Arizona. February 13, 1989.

Krapu, Gary. Biologist, Northern Prairie Wildlife Research Center, Fish and Wildlife Service. Interview with the author. Jamestown, North Dakota. October 18, 1988.

Lash, Jonathan, Katharine Gillman, and David Sheridan. 1984. *A Season of Spoils: The*

Story of the Reagan Administration's Attack on the Environment. Pantheon Books. New York, New York.

Lindsey, Robert. "Booming cities buy up 'water ranches' in Southwest." *New York Times*: E-5. August 16, 1987.

Luoma, Jon R. 1986. "Discouraging words." *Audubon* 88(5):87–104. (September).

McMillan, Ian. 1976. "How the experts teach ranchers to overgraze." *Earth's Advocate* (August):1–4. Environmental Center of San Luis Obispo County. San Luis Obispo, California.

———. Interview with the author. Shandon, California. July 27, 1988.

Misztal, Adam,. Staff specialist-planning, Refuges and Wildlife Office, Fish and Wildlife Service. Interview with the author. Denver, Colorado. October 20, 1988.

Oetting, Robert. Assistant director, Northern Prairie Wildlife Research Center, Fish and Wildlife Service. Interview with the author. Jamestown, North Dakota. October 20, 1988.

Rabkin, Richard and Jacob. 1981. *Nature in the West.* Holt, Rinehart and Winston. New York, New York.

Sandvig, Earl. Interview with the author. Portland, Oregon. April 17, 1983.

Sheehan, Thomas. 1986. Testimony of the Acting Inspector General, Office of Inspector General, U.S. Department of the Interior, before the Environment, Energy and Natural Resource Subcommittee of the Committee on Government Operations, U.S. House of Representatives. Washington, D.C. January 8.

Sheridan, David. 1979. *Off-Road Vehicles on the Public Lands.* Council on Environmental Quality. Washington, D.C.

———. 1981. *Desertification of the United States.* Council on Environmental Quality. Washington, D.C.

———. 1983. "The Colorado—An engineering wonder without enough water." *Smithsonian* 13(11):44–45. (February).

Smith, Gayle McMillan. 1988. "The miracle of the Carrizo Plain." *Cal Poly Today* (Fall):12–13.

Strickland, Rose. Sierra Club. Interview with the author. Reno, Nevada. October 28, 1988.

Tidd, Peter. Director, Land Treatment Program Division, Soil Conservation Service. Interview with the author. Washington, D.C. October 17, 1988.

Toussaint, Danielle and Laura Moretti. 1989. "Wild, wild horses: Westerners rally to save the last roaming herds." *Utne Reader* (January/February):100–101.

Committee on Government Operations, U.S. House of Representatives. 1986. Federal Grazing Program: All Is Not Well On The Range. House Report 99–593. Washington, D.C.

U.S. Department of Agriculture. 1986. What Sodbuster Means To You. Fact Sheet. Washington, D.C. December.

———., Soil Conservation Service and Iowa State Statistical Laboratory. 1987. Basic Statistics 1982 National Resources Inventory. Washington, D.C.

———. 1987. The Second RCA Appraisal: Soil, Water and Related Resources on Nonfederal Land in the United States, Analysis of Conditions and Trends. Washington, D.C.

———., Agricultural Stabilization and Conservation Service. 1988. Conservation Reserve Program. May 31.

———., Soil Conservation Service. 1989. The Conservation Reserve Program. News Release. January 5.

U.S. General Accounting Office. 1986. Rangeland Management: Grazing Lease Arrangements of Bureau of Land Management Permittees. GAO/RCED-86-168BR. Washington, D.C.

———. 1986. Rangeland Management: Profiles of Federal Grazing Program Permittees. GAO/RCED-86-203FS. Washington, D.C.

———. 1988. Rangeland Management: More Emphasis Needed On Declining And Overstocked Grazing Allotments. GAO/RCED-88-80. Washington, D.C.

———. 1988. Public Rangelands: Some Riparian Areas Restored but Widespread Improvement Will Be Slow. GAO/RCED-88-105.

U.S. Department of the Interior, Bureau of Land Management. 1981. Paradise-Denio Grazing Environmental Impact Statement. Winnemucca, Nevada.

———. 1981. Lakeview Grazing Management Environmental Impact Statement. Portland, Oregon.

———. 1982. Bruneau Kuna Grazing Environmental Impact Statement. Boise, Idaho.

———. 1989. Information Bulletin No. 89–93. Washington, D.C. January 6.

Viola, Herman J. 1987. *Exploring The West.* Smithsonian Books. Washington, D.C.

Voight, John. 1976. *Public Grazing Lands: Use and Misuse by Government and Industry.* Rutger University Press. New Brunswick, New Jersey.

Wald, Johanna and David Alberswerth. 1985. Our Ailing Public Rangelands: Condition Report—1985. Natural Resources Defense Council and National Wildlife Federation. San Francisco, California and Washington, D.C.

Wald, Johanna. Natural Resources Defense Council. Interview with the author. San Francisco, California. July 25, 1988.

Wiley, Ken. 1988. Letter to Ian McMillan. July 20.

———. Interview with the author. San Luis Obispo, California. October 28, 1988.

———. 1989. Letter to the author. January 25.

Yoakum, Jim. 1988. "The American pronghorn," pp. 637–648 *in* Chandler, W.J. ed., *Audubon Wildlife Report 1988/1989.* Academic Press, Inc. and National Audubon Society. New York, New York.

Charles Lee Atwood is a freelance writer based in Washington, D.C.

Part Three

Case Histories

The monarch butterfly's annual two-way migration is a unique phenomenon in the insect world. However, the butterfly faces several threats: development of its habitat; timber cutting and firewood collection; the uses of insecticides, herbicides, chemical fertilizer, and biocontrol agents; and removal of milkweed, its major food source. *Christopher D. Nagano*

The Monarch Butterfly

Christopher D. Nagano

Natural History Museum of Los Angeles County

and

Walter H. Sakai

Santa Monica College

SPECIES DESCRIPTION AND NATURAL HISTORY

The migratory monarch butterfly (*Danaus plexippus*) is perhaps the most well-known and widely recognized butterfly in North America. The monarch's body is black with thick mink-like dark hair on the upper rear portion of the thorax. The adult's wings are colored tawny to mandarin orange with black veins and wide borders with numerous white spots on the edges. The male, with its thinner wing veins and a scent pouch on each of the hind wings, is distinct from the female. The wingspan ranges from 2.5 to 4.5 inches (6.4 to 11.4 centimeters), making the monarch one of the largest butterflies on the continent.

The monarch is known as a milkweed butterfly (Danainae) (Ackery and Vane-Wright 1984) because milkweed (Asclepiadaceae) is the sole foodplant of monarch caterpillars. Milkweed contains cardiac glycosides that make the butterfly distasteful or even poisonous to many predators, including birds and other insectivores (Brower 1969, Brower and Calvert 1985).

All members of the Danainae are basically tropical butterflies that die when exposed to prolonged freezing weather. Thus, the migratory behavior allows it to exploit milkweed in extensive areas of North America, all the while escaping fatal winter temperatures.

Range

The monarch butterfly is one of the most widespread butterfly species in the world. It inhabits North and Central America; the Pacific region, including New Zealand, Australia, the Moluccas and New Guinea; the Atlantic region including, the Azores, Canary Islands, and Bermuda (Hilburn 1988); the British Isles; and the island of Mauritius. However, only the populations in New Zealand, Australia, and North America are known to form wintering colonies.

Generally, the Continental Divide separates the monarch butterflies of North America into two populations that have distinct migratory routes and wintering areas (see Figure 1) (Urquhart 1960, 1976, Urquhart and Urquhart 1976, 1977, 1979a, Williams *et al.* 1942).

Each autumn approximately 100 million monarchs that reside east of the Rocky Mountains migrate from as far north as southern Canada and New England to the mountains of central Mexico, where

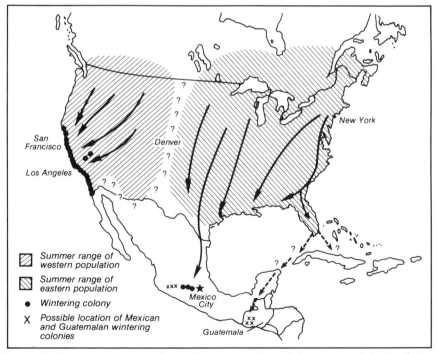

Figure 1. Summer range and overtime roost sites of the monarch butterfly in North America. Source: F. Urquhart, Entomological Society of Canada.

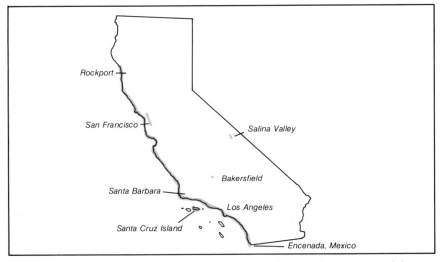

Figure 2. Range of the monarch butterfly wintering colonies in California. Source: Nagano and Sakai, unpublished manuscript.

they occupy an area extending from approximately Mexico City to as far west as the states of Colima and Jalisco and western Guatemala (Calvert and Brower 1986, Nagano unpubl. notes, Urquhart 1976, 1987, Urquhart and Urquhart 1976, 1979b). The nine known monarch colonies are formed in the transvolcanic mountain range at altitudes between 10,000 to 11,000 feet (254 to 280 meters) and vary in size from ¹⁄₁₀ of an acre to 10 acres (.40 to 4 hectares) (Brower and Calvert 1986).

The western population migrates through the Great Basin, the Pacific Northwest, the Southwest, and portions of western Canada to an archipelago of colonies stretching along the California coast from northern Mendocino County southward as far as the Ensenada region of Baja California, Mexico (see Figure 2) (Nagano and Lane 1985, Nagano and Sakai 1988, unpubl., Urquhart and Urquhart 1976). Colonies have been recorded on Santa Cruz Island, the southern San Joaquin Valley, and in a few canyons in the Mojave Desert near Death Valley (Giuliani 1977–1984, Nagano and Lane 1985). Little is known of the inland sites as they do not form every year. The number of monarchs wintering in California probably ranges from a low of about one million to a high of approximately five million butterflies.

Breeding

The female monarch lays a single egg on the underside of a milkweed leaf. The larvae hatch within a few days and grow rapidly through five successive molts or "instars." The larval stage lasts from three to five weeks, depending upon air temperature and other environmental factors. The monarch caterpillar then forms a gold-spotted, jade-green-colored chrysalis that lasts about 10 days. Four to five generations are hatched every year. The spring and summer generations each survive about a month and mate throughout their adult life span. Monarchs that winter at the colonies live six to nine months, with the majority of mating taking place from January through March.

Migration

The shortening periods of daylight and cooler air temperatures of August and September result in reduced levels of juvenile hormone in the monarch butterflies (Brower 1985). Courtship, mating, and egg laying then cease as the butterflies feed heavily on flower nectar, which increases the insects' store of lipids. By mid-September, fat constitutes one-third of their body weight. Monarch butterflies from all over North America begin migrating in August and September in a highly directional flight to the wintering colonies (Baker 1984, Schmidt-Koenig 1979, Urquhart 1987).

The butterflies ride thermal air currents to gain altitude and then glide effortlessly on tail winds for many miles (Gibo 1981, Gibo and Pallet 1979). Gibo (1981) reports that migrating monarchs have been observed by glider pilots at altitudes of 3,280 to 3,937 feet (83 to 100 meters). Some butterflies have been documented as traveling as far as as 80 miles in a single day (Baker 1984). Feeding heavily on nectar along the migration routes, the insects arrive at the wintering colonies with extensive fat reserves. An adequate supply of lipids is crucial for survival, as the amount of nectar at the colonies is often insufficient to sustain all the butterflies for the entire season.

Research indicates that the monarch butterfly navigates using the position of the sun (Hyatt and Kreithen 1986), or possibly the earth's magnetic field (Schmidt-Koenig 1979), to reach the general vicinity of the roosts. The insect then seeks out specific temperature and humidity regimes (Brower 1985, 1988, Nagano unpubl.). Various naturalists have speculated that the butterflies "mark" the wintering colonies with distinctive odors or scents that enable following generations to locate the sites. There, however, have been no experimental studies to investigate this claim.

With the start of migration, the butterflies begin to gather at "temporary bivouacs" near the Pacific Ocean in California or at sites along their migratory pathways. A site is especially likely to be used when it has the only stands of trees in the area, possesses an abundant nectar supply, is protected from adverse weather, and receives the morning sun. The insects spend anywhere from a few hours to weeks in bivouac sites before moving on. Bivouacs persist because there is a constant stream of monarch butterflies entering and leaving (Nagano and Sakai unpubl.). Bivouacs may last through the winter if conditions are mild, or disappear in a few weeks. Some sites are used every fall. For example, a single silver maple (*Acer saccharium*) in Iowa has been used regularly for at least 50 years (Swander 1974). Other sites may be used only once, or at highly unpredictable intervals.

During November, the butterflies begin to form "permanent roosts" where they will usually spend the entire winter. The roosts are characterized by long periods of residency and often by large numbers of butterflies. The monarchs begin to mate in January; by March they have left the colonies during the spring migration. Some sites on the coast are temporary in some years, but permanent in others (Nagano and Sakai unpubl.). Despite their geographic distance, the roosts in Mexico and California bear many similarities to each other. The monarchs cluster in groves with trees of various heights and an understory of shrubby vegetation. The trees and understory comprise a "thermal blanket" that maintains wind, temperature, and relative humidity at optimal levels (Calvert and Brower 1982, Calvert and Cohen 1983, Calvert *et al.* 1982, 1983).

Both temporary bivouacs and permanent roosts are located in groves of native and introduced trees. In California these include oaks (*Quercus*), western sycamore (*Plantanus racemosa*), and alder (*Alnus*), as well as introduced tree species, such as gums (*Eucalyptus*) and palms (Palmae). Species used for bivouacs in eastern North America are equally diverse, including maple (*Acer*), willow (*Salix*), and spruce (*Picea*) (Urquhart and Urquhart 1979a). Oyamel fir (*Abies religiosa*) is the tree most often used as a permanent roost in Mexico.

Within the groves, the butterflies gather in clearings, and clusters ranging in height from 6 inches (very rare) to 74 feet or more (Nagano and Sakai unpubl.). The monarchs roost on different branches or different trees as the season progresses and as environmental factors change. Wind protection is critical and provided by tree cover and topography. Drinking water is also essential for successful winter survival and is provided by dew (the butterflies sometimes use streams, ponds, or even grass lawns in urban regions) (Brower *et al.* 1977, Nagano and Sakai unpubl.). Flowering plants growing in and near the colonies supply nectar to supplement internal fat reserves. At the California site the nectar is supplied by gum trees, mule fat (*Baccharis*), wild mustard (*Brassica*), and numerous other native and cultivated species.

The sites must be cool and humid enough to keep the butterflies from using up internal fat reserves—needed for the spring migration inland, yet warm enough to prevent freezing to death. It is important to recognize that it is the *location* of the groves rather than specific tree species that supplies the proper environmental conditions for wintering monarch butterflies.

In the West, fall migrating monarchs increase in weight after they reach the California coastline and begin feeding on nectar sources (Nagano and Sakai unpubl.). Tuskes and Brower (1978) found a considerable decrease in average lipid content as the winter season progressed. The distance monarchs are able to fly in the spring may be directly related to the amount of accumulated lipid reserves (Calvert and Lawton in press).

As the end of the wintering season approaches and the days become longer, sexual maturation, courtship and mating, and spring migration occur (Hill *et al.* 1976). In California, female strategies consist of both short and long distance spring movements to inland regions (Nagano unpubl.). Tagging studies by Nagano and Sakai indicate that a number of females leave the colonies before the males in order to deposit their eggs on local milkweeds, while other female monarchs migrate greater distances to the west slope of the Sierra Nevada or even further inland to lay their eggs. The males move inland to hold territories at milkweed patches or travel between wintering colonies. Both of these activities are strategies that maximize access to female monarch butterflies. Brower (1985) found that in Mexico both sexes leave together during the spring migration.

Cockrell *et al.* (1986) found that the butterflies from the Mexican colonies fly to the Gulf region before laying their eggs and dying. Each succeeding generation moves farther north until the end of summer when the migration south is repeated. A similar strategy is employed in western North America, although the numerous mountain ranges, extensive valleys, and deserts make the spring migration far more complicated. Tuskes and Brower (1978) found some of the colonies in California last longer along the central Pacific coast than those in the South. In contrast, Nagano and Sakai (unpubl.) determined that the breakup period varies greatly, not only between different areas of the coast, but also between adjacent roosts.

SIGNIFICANCE OF THE SPECIES

The annual migration of hundreds of millions of monarch butterflies is considered to be one of the epic phenomena of the animal kingdom. It is comparable to the large mammal migrations of the African Serengeti, the vast flocks of passenger pigeons that once covered eastern North America, or the great herds of bison that populated the Great Plains.

The monarch is the only butterfly with a documented annual two-way migratory behavior. Other lepidopterans that have regular migrations include the Australian bogong moth (*Agrotis infusca*:Noctuidae)

(Common 1954), the Island of Rhodes tiger moth (*Euplagia quadri-punctaria*:Arctiidae) (Sbordoni and Forestiero 1984), and many tropical (Parson pers. comm., Haber 1986) and several temperate butterflies. Although many other insects migrate, they do so probably only in response to unpredictable environmental conditions.

The monarch butterfly is one of the most studied butterflies in the world. In particular, studies of mimicry in the monarch have become classical studies in ecology (Brower 1969). Proof of the tremendous interest in this insect was clearly demonstrated when 70 scientists from eight countries gathered at the Second International Conference on the Monarch Butterfly to present papers on their studies of the physiology, biochemistry, ecology, and conservation of the species (Norman 1986).

Monarch wintering colonies have been a tremendous attraction for tourists for at least 50 years in California (Sims 1942). During an average season, an estimated 70,000 sightseers visit the colonies at Natural Bridges and Pismo state beaches to enjoy the spectacle of the monarch (D. Ackerman 1987, J. Ortiz pers. comm.). The popularity of the butterfly is seen in the number of coastal inns and motels named after them, as well as the endless array of souvenirs inscribed with monarch motifs.

Monarca, a private international conservation organization, has led efforts to attract tourists to the Mexican wintering colonies and has created a substantial economy for local residents (Freese pers. comm.). The colonies were visited by 50,000 tourists in 1985–1986 and the number continues to increase (Nagano and Freese 1987). Tourism may encourage the protection of the mountain forests from logging and firewood collection that will otherwise eliminate the wintering roosts.

A number of California wintering colonies are located in groves composed of *Eucalyptus*, which was introduced from Australia beginning in 1853 for timber, firewood, and for ornamental use (Friedman 1988). Its highly invasive nature and toxic oils, which eliminate native plants and prevent herbivory, have made eucalyptus an extremely successful competitor with native vegetation. The presence of monarch butterflies has complicated the plans of resource ecologists and park managers who are attempting to restore natural ecosystems (Anonymous 1988c, Boyd 1988, Nagano and Sakai 1988).

HISTORICAL PERSPECTIVE

The range of the North American wintering colonies before European colonization is uncertain. Vane-Wright (1986) proposed that migration began only a few hundred years ago and not during the Pleistocene Epoch as is generally believed (Brower 1988). This hypothesis is based on the increase in available open-field habitat for the milkweed as a result of extensive cutting of the hardwood forests of North America; the total lack of records of any clustering prior to the mid-19th century, and the abrupt period of range expansion of the monarch into the Pacific and Atlantic regions. There are no written records of Mexican wintering colonies from Europeans or native Americans prior to the 1970s (Calvert and Brower 1986), although local Indians seem to have known of their presence for hundreds of years. However, Malcolm and Brower (1987) presented several arguments for a greater age of the migration. The range of the California wintering colonies prior to the mid-19th century is also uncertain.

There is considerable speculation, but no hard data, on the wintering range of the California colonies. One school of thought has suggested that the monarch butterfly utilized groves of pines (several species of *Pinus*) that extended from northern California to the central coast, and expanded its wintering range farther south when *Eucalyptus* was introduced in the 19th century. A second hypothesis proposes that the colonies were present on native trees in coastal canyons and drainages within the current wintering range and that the butterfly began to utilize introduced species when the indigenous vegetation was destroyed by development.

The first report of a North American wintering colony was made by Hans Beher, a pioneer California entomologist, who in 1862 reported a site on Telegraph Hill in San Francisco (Lane pers. comm.). Sporadic anecdotal stories about monarch roosts continued (Bush 1881, Shepardson 1914) until more detailed investigations were made of the ecology and migratory behavior of the butterflies (Lane 1984, 1985, Urquhart 1960, Urquhart *et al.* 1965, Williams *et al.* 1942). The first comprehensive survey of the wintering colonies was recently completed with the assistance of the World Wildlife Fund-U.S. (Nagano and Lane 1985).

The 40-year search by F.A. Urquhart of the University of Toronto for the monarch's wintering colonies of eastern North America has become legend (Urquhart 1976, 1987). In the 1930s, Urquhart began to suspect that the butterflies migrated south each fall rather than passing the winter by lying dormant. Using bird-banding studies as a model, Urquhart realized the need to track individual monarchs in order to determine precise movement patterns. At first the insects were marked with various dyes and paints. After several unsuccessful years, he developed self-adhesive paper tags bearing individual numbers and a return address. Over three decades, Urquhart and his associates tagged 400,000 monarchs. In 1974, Kenneth Brugger, an assistant of Urquhart, discovered some of the wintering colonies located northwest of Mexico City (Urquhart 1976).

CURRENT TRENDS

Monarch butterfly colonies in California have been destroyed by urban and agricultural development (Nagano and Sakai 1988a) and cutting of trees for timber and firewood in Mexico (Menzel 1983, Nagano and Freese 1987, Snook 1986). These activities also cause adverse changes in the stringent environmental conditions required by the monarchs (Calvert and Brower 1982, Calvert *et al.* 1982, 1983). Wintering sites are particularly vulnerable during the spring and summer, when their significance to the monarch may be neither evident nor ascertainable. For example, 16 colonies are known to have been eliminated by development activities in California (Nagano and Sakai unpubl.) and a number of sites have been lost in Mexico (Brower 1988, pers. comm.).

The use of insecticides, herbicides, chemical fertilizers, and biocontrol agents are extremely serious threats to all stages of the monarch (Brower 1986). Many California wintering colonies are located in urban areas with excessive pesticide use. The butterflies often drink water from lawns near roosts and may ingest herbicides and fertilizers containing toxic chemicals (often labeled as "inert ingredients"). The use of nematode worms as biocontrol agents of insect pests is also of great concern (Anonymous 1988). It is possible that these nematode worms can parasitize and kill monarch caterpillars along with other native (and beneficial) insects. Unlike pesticides, nematode worms and other biocontrol agents reproduce and thus continue to threaten other insects after their release. The worms are available to the public and their use is not regulated by the Environmental Protection Agency.

Modern agriculture, with its monocrops and intense use of herbicides, thus limiting the diversity and abundance of wildflowers and milkweed growing on the edges of fields and roadsides (Brower 1988), reduces the monarch butterfly's source of nectar to fuel migration. Ironically, the less toxic milkweeds may be increasing at the expense of the more poisonous species. For example, the northeastern milkweed (*Asclepias syriaca*) is now more abundant since it grows well in forest clearings and along roadways (Brower 1988). The butterflies that eat this species are less toxic than those that eat other milkweeds, making them more susceptible to predators. Monarchs that winter in Mexico are four times less poisonous on average than those in California (Brower 1988). This may increase the mortality of the butterflies because greater numbers of insectivorous birds are able to feed on them (Calvert *et al.* 1979, Brower *et al.* 1982, 1984).

The wintering colonies in Australia have significantly decreased in size during the past 20 years (Smithers 1965, James 1986). The removal of milkweed by ranchers, because of its adverse effect on cattle, is believed to be the cause of the decline. No information is available

The monarch butterfly's migratory behavior makes it the most-studied butterfly in the world. *Christopher D. Nagano*

on the colonies in New Zealand, although the number of individuals decreased at one of the three known colonies (Wise 1980).

A lack of active management of monarch habitat by government agencies and private landowners is among the greatest threats to the California colonies. Trees and understory vegetation should not be allowed to grow too tall and dense, or to die off, as this will alter the precise environment the monarchs need to survive the winter. Dry leaves and dead wood encourage wildfire. Monarch colonies in Ellwood, near Santa Barbara and also at Pacific Grove, will soon be eliminated unless restoration of the sites is undertaken in the near future. Management plans have been made for only two roosts (Nagano and Sakai 1987).

There is a critical need to conserve all the colonies of both the eastern and western populations. Studies along the California coast have found that there is a tremendous amount of butterfly movement between the sites. For example, during the extremely hot and dry weather of winter 1986–1987, nearly all butterflies within two localities in southern California moved to an adjacent site possessing more optimal conditions. Thus, monarch mortality rates could be substantially increased over time by the destruction of the colony sites, even when the localities are not being fully used at the time of destruction. In addition, the number of butterflies using a site may vary greatly from year to year or even within a single season. For example, 10,000 monarchs may use the site one winter, none the next, and several hundred individuals the third year. Colony instability greatly complicates the enactment of protective measures by government officials and wildlife managers.

Unsupervised sightseers pose a constant danger to the wintering colonies (Nagano and Sakai 1987). Careless visitors have been observed damaging understory vegetation by trampling. Failure to remain on established trails not only destroys living plants but damages the protective ground cover of leaf litter and the smaller understory as well. In addition, vistors sometimes shake monarchs loose from low-laying branches thus exposing them to higher predation rates by rodents and death from adverse environmental conditions and take dead or even live butterflies as souvenirs (Nagano unpubl.). Visitor rules must be established where the public has access to a site.

MANAGEMENT

In the past few years interest in and concern for the monarch butterfly has increased at a geometric rate (Ackerman 1987, Anonymous 1987, 1988a, Menzel 1983, Wolfe and Nagano 1988). The International Union for the Conservation of Nature and Natural Resources (IUCN) in 1976 made the protection of Mexican colonies a top priority; in 1981, IUCN added the California roosts to its protection priorities (Wells *et al.* 1983). No statutory protection was provided, but by these actions, IUCN focused considerable attention on the wintering sites.

The monarch butterfly is also the only insect listed on the Convention for the Conservation of Migratory Species of Wild Animals (the "Bonn Convention") (Collins 1986). However, because the butterflies do not travel through any of the signatory nations, protection is largely symbolic.

In 1980, Mexico's President Lopez Portillo officially recognized the importance of the Mexican wintering colonies (Brower 1988). In 1985, the state of Michoacan expropriated more than 190 acres (77 hectares) of private land at Rosario, one of the largest colonies (Nagano and Freese 1987); in 1986, an ecological reserve was created by presidential decree to protect six colonies. The Secretary of Urban Development and Ecology purchased more than 1,700 acres (689 hectares) of forest containing some of the most important colonies. The department prohibited logging and agricultural development in more than 11,000 acres (4,455 hectares) at the core of the colonies and restricted forest cutting and other activities on another 29,000 acres (11,745 hectares). Nonetheless, there is an imminent need to secure permanent protection and management for the Mexican colonies. Snook (1986) discovered evidence that the Oyamel forests continue to be degraded by biotic threats such as bark beetles and parasitic mistletoe, as well as threats of tree cutting for timber and firewood, grazing, and agricultural conversion.

Efforts are under way to designate the monarch as the national insect of the United States. Like the IUCN priority designation, this would not provide any specific protection, but would instead focus considerable attention on the importance of the wintering colonies. Although monarchs are not specifically protected under federal or state law in California, they can be indirectly conserved under statutes dealing with natural resources and the environment (Nagano and Eng 1984). The California Department of Parks and Recreation has taken the lead in managing a significant number of wintering colonies.

In June 1988, the Wildlife, Coast, and Parks Initiative was passed by the voters of California. The initiative, funded by bonds, will earmark $776 million for statewide programs to restore natural habitats, to purchase significant ecological areas, and to manage various species of plants and animals; $2 million is included for the acquisition of monarch butterfly wintering colonies.

In 1987, State Assemblyman Byron Sher (D) introduced a bill that officially "recognized" the California wintering colonies; it was signed into law by Governor George Deukmejian in the fall of that year. The law directs the California Department of Fish and Game to prepare a management plan for the roosts and marks the first time that the state has recognized the positive environmental significance of *any* of its insects.

Several coastal counties in California are taking specific actions to protect the wintering colonies under their jurisdiction. Santa Barbara has enacted statutes that prohibit deliberate destruction of wintering colonies (Welch pers. comm.). For example, in 1987 an avocado farmer who heavily damaged a monarch site was ordered to restore the roost. Two county environmental planners responsible for protecting the Santa Barbara monarch populations were sent in 1987 to the Mexican colonies for intensive training by monarch ecologists (Anonymous

1988c). The county of San Luis Obispo is attempting to conserve sites in the Morro Bay area, where a number of significant colonies exist. One roost had been heavily damaged by urban development and others are threatened by proposed housing tracts and removal of the eucalyptus groves for aesthetic reasons.

At the local level, Pacific Grove has a municipal code that protects monarch butterflies from harm. The effectiveness of this ordinance is questionable as no protection is given to the wintering colonies, especially the trees on which the butterflies cluster. At least one major wintering site has been lost since the law was enacted (Lane pers. comm.), and the private lands where a second site is located have been proposed for urban development. A third colony located at a city park may soon disappear unless active management of the trees and understory vegetation is undertaken (Nagano unpubl.).

Entomologists from the Natural History Museum of Los Angeles and Santa Monica College are also working to conserve the monarch butterflies of western North America (Nagano and Sakai 1988). They are surveying the coast to locate and map the wintering colonies, attempting to determine the precise environmental conditions required by the butterflies, and tagging the insects to measure population sizes and movement patterns and map migration routes. For the last three years, they have worked closely with environmental planners, ecologists, park rangers and federal, state, and local government agencies to protect and manage colonies. The group publishes *Danaus*, a newsletter about monarch butterfly conservation.

PROGNOSIS

The long-term outlook for the monarch butterfly in North America has gone from absolute uncertainty to one of guarded optimism. The increased awareness of the threats this species face has drawn greater attention from state, national, and international agencies, as well as private organizations.

It is clear that ever expanding human population growth will continue to place tremendous pressure on the wintering colonies in both California and Mexico. It is critical, however, to emphasize that the monarch is a widespread butterfly that is found throughout much of the world and itself is not endangered as a species. It is the migratory phenomenon and the wintering colonies in North America that are clearly threatened. The three major factors affecting the species are due to: (1) the loss of milkweed and nectar sources throughout the species' summering range in Canada and the United States; (2) the decline in the number of roost sites of the western population, due to the astronomically high value of coastal real estate and the resulting developmental pressure; and (3) the imminent threats to the Oyamel fir forests of Mexico from timber cutting, agricultural conversion, and firewood collection.

If the efforts by conservationists in both California and Mexico are successful, the monarch will continue to grace fields and gardens across North America for decades to come.

RECOMMENDATIONS

The following steps should be taken to safeguard the monarch butterfly in North America:

1. Since the monarch has such a wide distribution, at this time it is neither desirable nor advisable for federal or state authorities to list the monarch as endangered, threatened, or rare. Both the United States and California, however, should follow the lead of IUCN by designating the winter colonies as a "Threatened Phenomenon." Statutes should be enacted to provide significant penalties for deliberate destruction or damage of monarch sites.

2. Comprehensive surveys should be conducted throughout the California coast and appropriate regions of Mexico and Guatemala to locate and map additional wintering colonies. This should be undertaken from September until March for at least five years as some sites may not be used every winter.

3. Studies should be undertaken to measure and document the environmental conditions at the wintering colonies. The specific factors that are required by the monarchs should be determined in order to assess the effects of urban development and other site alterations.

4. Every fall and winter a detailed investigation should be conducted on the status of the colonies in Mexico and California. The number of butterflies, fall and spring migration routes, intercolony movement patterns, and other ecological factors, should be measured.

5. Specific management plans should be developed and implemented for all the wintering colonies in California. The California Department of Parks and Recreation should be given this responsibility as some 50 percent of the wintering colonies in western North America are under their jurisdiction.

6. The threats from agriculture and development to the milkweed plant and nectar sources throughout North America should be investigated.

7. Pesticides, herbicides, and chemical fertilizers used in the vicinity of the wintering colonies should be short-term agents; their use should be prohibited when the butterflies are present.

8. Sightseers should be allowed only into colonies with designated trails, interpretive signs, and guards. Understory vegetation and soil cover should be protected from trampling. Sites for camping, picnicking, and parking should be carefully selected and monitored.

9. An extensive program to educate the public and government officials about the monarch butterfly and the threats to the migratory phenomenon should be initiated.

10. All colonies in California should be protected and actively managed though easements, registration, and direct purchase by the California Department of Parks and Recreation or the National Park Service. Major permanent sites should be designated as National Natural Landmarks or state nature reserves.

11. Management efforts at the Mexican wintering colonies must continue to address the socio-economic needs of the local human population. Promotion of tourism and other sources of income instead of timber harvesting must be encouraged.

REFERENCES

Ackerman, D. 1987. "Mass meeting on the coast. The glorious off-season of the Monarch butterfly." *Life* 10(5):21–27.

Ackery, P.R. and I. Vane-Wright. 1984. *Milkweed Butterflies: Their Cladistics and Biology.* Cornell University Press. Ithaca, New York. 425 pp.

Anonymous. 1987. "Tracking the monarch's secret." *Los Angeles Times Editorial.* January 15, 1987.

———. 1988a. Business Section. *Time* 131(18):57. May 2, 1988.

———. 1988b. *Morro Bay State Park General Plan.* California Department of Parks and Recreation. 152 pp. + 4 maps.

———. 1988c. "Significant steps taken to protect and manage California wintering colonies." *Danaus* 1:2–4. February 1988.

Baker, R.R. 1984. "The dilemma: When and how to go or stay," pp. 279–296 in R.I. Vane-Wright and P.R. Ackery eds., *The Biology of Butterflies.* Symposium of the Royal Entomological Society of London 11. Academic Press. London, United Kingdom.

Boyd, D. 1988. "Introduction," pp. 1–15 in D. Boyd ed., *Focused Environmental Study. Restoration of Angel Island Natural Areas Affected by Eucalyptus.* California Department of Parks and Recreation. Santa Rosa, California.

Brower, L.P. 1969. "Ecological chemistry." *Scientific American* 220(2):22–29.

———. 1977. "Monarch migration." *Natural History* 86:40–53.

———. 1985. "New perspectives on the migration ecology of the Monarch butterfly, *Danaus plexippus* L," pp. 748–785 in *University of Texas Contributions in Marine Science 27.* (Supplement).

———. 1986. "Commentary: The potential impact of DIPEL spraying on the Monarch butterfly overwintering phenomenon." *Atala* 14(1):17–19.

———. 1988. "A place in the sun." *Animal Kingdom* 91(4):42–51.

Brower, L.P. and W.H. Calvert. 1985. "Foraging dynamics of bird predators on overwintering Monarch butterflies in Mexico." *Evolution* 39:852–868.

———., W.H. Calvert, L.E. Hedrick, and J. Christian. 1977. "Biological observations on an overwintering colony of Monarch butterflies (*Danaus plexippus* Danaidae) in Mexico." *Journal of the Lepidopterist Society* 31:232–242.

———., J.N. Seiber, C.J. Nelson, S.P. Lynch, M.P. Hoggard, and J.A. Cohen. 1984. "Plant-determined variation in cardenolide content and thin-layer chromatography profiles of Monarch butterflies, *Danaus plexippus* reared on milkweed plants in California. 3. *Asclepias californica.*" *Journal of Chemical Ecology* 10(12):1823–1857.

———., J.N. Seiber, C.J. Nelson, S.P. Lynch, and P.M. Tuskes. 1982. "Plant-determined variation in the cardenolide content, thin-layer chromatography profiles, and emetic potency of Monarch butterflies, *Danaus plexippus* reared on the milkweed, *Asclepias eriocarpa* in California." *Journal of Chemical Ecology* 8(3):579–633.

Bush, A.E. 1881. "Trees attractive to butterflies." *American Naturalist* 15:572.

Calvert, W.H. and L.P. Brower. 1982. "The importance of forest cover for the survival of overwintering Monarch butterflies (*Danaus plexippus* Danaidae)." *Journal of the Lepidopterist Society* 35L216–225.

———. 1986. "The location of Monarch butterfly (*Danaus plexippus* L.) overwintering colonies in Mexico in relation to topography and climate." *Journal of the Lepidopterist Society* 40(3):164–187.

———. and J.A. Cohen. 1983. "The adaptive significance of crawling up into foliage for the survival of grounded overwintering Monarch butterflies (*Danaus plexippus*) in Mexico." *Ecological Entomology* 8:471–474.

———., L.E. Hendrick, and L.P. Brower. 1979. "Mortality of the Monarch butterfly (*Danaus plexippus* L): avian predation at five overwintering sites in Mexico." *Science* 204(4395):841–851.

———. and R.O. Lawton. In review. "Comparative phgenology of size, weight, and moisture of eastern North American Monarch butterflies (*Danaus plexippus* L) at five overwintering sites in Mexico."

———., W. Zuckowski, and L.P. Brower. 1982. "The impact of forest thinning on microclimate in Monarch butterfly (*Danaus plexippus* L.) overwintering areas of Mexico." *Boletin de la Sociedad Botanica de Mexico* 42:11–18.

———. 1983 "The effect of rain, snow and freezing temperatures on overwintering monarch butterflies in Mexico." *Biotropica* 15:42–47.

Chaplin, S.B. and P.H. Wells. 1982. "Energy resources and metabolic expenditures of Monarch butterflies overwintering in California." *Ecological Entomology* 7:249–256.

Cockrell, B.J., S.B. Malcolm, and L.P. Brower. 1986. "The spatial and temporal distribution of Monarch generations in eastern North America," in J.P. Donahue ed., *Abstracts of the Second International Conference on the Monarch Butterfly (MONCON-2).* Natural History Museum of Los Angeles. California. 21 pp.

Collins, N.M. 1986. Insect Protection and International Conventions. Third European Congress of Entomology. Amsterdam, Netherlands. May 19–24, 1986.

Common, I.F.B. 1954. "A study of the ecology of the adult Bogong Moth, *Agrotis infusca* (Boisduval) (Lepidoptera:Noctuidae), with special reference to its behavior during migration and aestivation." *Australian Journal of Zoology* 2:223–263.

Friedman, R. 1988. "Strangers in our midst." *Pacific Discovery* 41(3):22–31.

Gibo, D.L. 1981. "Altitudes attained by migrating Monarch butterflies *Danaus plexippus* (Lepidoptera:Danaidae) during the summer migration in southern Canada." *Canadian Journal of Zoology* 59:571–572.

———. and M.J. Pallett. 1979. "Soaring flight of Monarch butterflies *Danaus plexippus* (Lepidoptera:Danaidae) during the summer migration in southern Canada." *Canadian Journal of Zoology* 58:1393–1401.

Guiliani, D. 1977–1984. "Monarch butterflies," in *Waucoba News* 1 (1977, no. 1,2); 2 (1978, no. 1,2); 4 (1980, no. 1); 8 (1984, no. 1).

Haber , W.A. 1986. "Seasonal migration of Monarchs in Costa Rica, Central America," in J.P. Donahue ed., *Abstracts of the Second International Conference on the Monarch butterfly (MONCON-2)*. Natural History Museum of Los Angeles. California. 21 pp.

Hilburn, D. 1988. "Bermuda's monarchs." *Danaus* 2:2–4. September 1988.

Hill, H.F., A.M. Wenner, and P.H. Wells. 1976. "Reproductive behavior in an overwintering aggregation of Monarch butterflies." *American Midland Naturalist* 95:10–19.

Hyatt, M.B. and M.L. Kreithen. 1986. "Monarchs use sky polarization for migration orientation," in J.P. Donahue ed., *Abstracts of the Second International Conference on the Monarch butterfly (MONCON-2)*. Natural History Museum of Los Angeles. California. 21 pp.

James, D.G. 1986. "Migration biology of the Monarch butterfly in Australia," in J.P. Donahue ed., *Abstracts of the Second International Conference on the Monarch butterfly (MONCON-2)*. Natural History Museum of Los Angeles. California. 21 pp.

Lane, J. 1984. "The status of Monarch butterfly overwintering sites in Alta, California." *Atala* 9:14–16.

Malcolm, S.B. and L.P. Brower. 1987. "White monarch." *Antenna* 11(1):2–3.

Menzel, P. 1983. "Butterfly armies now under guard in annual bivouac." *Smithsonian* 14(8):174–182.

Nagano, C.D. and L.L. Eng. 1984. Insects and Environmental Protection in the State of California, United States of America. Paper presented at the XVII International Congress of Entomology. Hamburg, Federal Republic of Germany.

———. and C. Freese. 1987. "A world safe for Monarchs." *New Scientist* 1554:43–47.

———. and J. Lane. 1985. A Survey of the Location of Monarch butterfly (*Danaus plexippus* [L.]) Overwintering Roosts in the State of California, U.S.A: First year 1984/1985. Report to the World Wildlife Fund-U.S. 108 pp.

———. and W.H. Sakai. 1987. The Monarch Butterfly (*Danaus plexippus* [L.]) Wintering Colonies in the Ellwood Area of Santa Barbara County, California, U.S.A. Report to the California Coastal Conservancy and the Santa Barbara County Department of Resource Management. 17 pp.

———. and ———. 1988. "Making the world safe for Monarchs." *Outdoor California* 49(1):5–9.

Norman, C. 1986. "Mexico protects overwintering Monarch butterflies." *Science* 233 (4770):1525–1253.

Sbordoni V. and S. Forestiero. 1984. *Butterflies of the World*. Times Books. New York, New York.

Schmidt-Koenig, K. 1979. "Directions of migrating Monarch butterflies (*Danaus plexippus*; Danaidae; Lepidoptera) in some parts of the eastern United States." *Behav. Proc.* 4:73–78.

Shepardson, L. DeWolf. 1914. *The Butterfly Trees*. Hearald Printers. Monterey, California. 32 pp.

Sims, B. 1942. *The Miracle of Pacific Grove*. Tide Publishing Company. Pacific Grove, California. 23 pp.

Smithers, C.N. 1965. "A note on overwintering in *Danaus plexippus* (Linnaeus) (Lepidoptera:Nymphalidae) in Australia." *Australian Zoology* 13:135–136.

Snook, L.C. 1986. "Conservation of the Monarch butterfly reserve in Mexico: A forester's perspective," *in* J.P. Donahue ed., *Abstracts of the Second International Conference on the Monarch Butterfly (MONCON-2)*. Natural History Museum of Los Angeles. California. 21 pp.

Swander, M. 1974. "A Monarch butterfly roosting tree in Iowa." *Proceedings of the Iowa Academy of Science* 81:100–101.

Tuskes, P.M. and L.P. Brower. 1978. "Overwintering ecology of the Monarch butterfly, *Danaus plexippus* L., in California." *Ecological Entomology* 3:141–153.

Urquhart, F.A. 1960. *The Monarch Butterfly*. University of Toronto Press. 361 pp.

——. 1976. "Found at last: the Monarch's winter home." *National Geographic* 150:160–173.

——. 1987. *The Monarch Butterfly: International Traveler*. Nelson-Hall Publishers. Chicago, Illinois. 232 pp.

——. and N.R. Urquhart. 1976. "The overwintering site of the eastern population of the Monarch butterfly (*Danaus p. plexippus*: Danaidae) in southern Mexico." *Journal of the Lepidopterist Society* 30:153–158.

——. and ——. 1977. "Overwintering areas and migratory routes of the Monarch butterfly (*Danaus p. plexippus*, Lepidoptera: Danaidae) in North America with special reference to the western population." *Canadian Entomologist* 109:1583–1589.

——. and ——. 1979a. "Breeding areas and overnight roosting locations in the northern range of the Monarch butterfly (*Danaus plexippus plexippus*) with a summary of associated migratory routes." *Canadian Field Naturalist* 93:41–47.

——. and ——. 1979b. "Aberrant autumnal migration of the eastern population of the Monarch butterfly, *Danaus p. plexippus* (Lepidoptera:Danaidae) as it relates to the occurrence of strong westerly winds." *Canadian Entomologist* 111:1281–1286.

——., P. Beard, R. Brownlee. 1965. "A population study of a hibernal roosting colony of the Monarch butterfly (*D. plexippus*) in northern California." *Journal of Research on Lepidopteran* 4:221–226.

Vane-Wright, R.I. 1986. "White Monarchs—Did dispersal come before migration?" *in* J.P. Donahue ed., *Abstracts of the Second International Conference on the Monarch Butterfly (MONCON-2)*. Natural History Museum of Los Angeles. California. 21 pp.

Wells, S., R.M. Pyle, and N.M. Collins. 1983. *The IUCN Invertebrate Red Data Book* International Union for the Conservation of Nature and Natural Resources. Gland, Switzerland. L&633 pp.

Williams, C.B., G.F. Cockbill, M.E. Gibbons, and J.A. Downes. 1942. "Studies in the migration of lepidoptera." *Transactions of the Royal Entomology Society of London* 92:101–283.

Wise, K.A.J. 1980. "Monarch Butterfly dispersal in New Zealand." *Rec. Auckland Institute Museum* 17:157–173.

Wolfe, G. and C. Nagano. 1988. "Migratory Monarchs wintering on California's coast." *California Scenic* 2(1):20–23.

Christopher Nagano is a research associate in the Entomology Section of the Natural History Museum of Los Angeles County and a member of the Butterfly Specialist Group, Species Survival Commission of the International Union for the Conservation of Nature and Natural Resources (IUCN).

Walter Sakai is a professor in the Life Sciences Department at Santa Monica College.

The authors wish to thank Curtis Freese of the World Wildlife Fund-U.S. and Charles L. Hogue of the Natural History Museum of Los Angeles County who kindly reviewed this chapter and offered many helpful suggestions. The chapter is dedicated to California Assemblyman Byron Sher, a leader in protecting Monarch butterfly colonies of western North America.

Humpback whales are best known for their "songs." As the largest creatures on earth, they compel our awe and respect. Ironically, human activities pose the greatest threats to their existence. *Fred Felleman/Center for Marine Conservation*

The Humpback Whale

Steven L. Swartz

Center for Marine Conservation

SPECIES DESCRIPTION AND NATURAL HISTORY

The humpback whale (*Megaptera novaeangliae*) is a member of the family Balaenopteridae, or Rorquals, which includes six species of mysticete or baleen whales. The largest member of this family is the blue whale (*Balaenoptera musculus*), which has been reported to exceed 103 feet (31 meters) in length (Gaskin 1982). In contrast, the humpback is shorter and stouter than other rorquals, with the female humpback reaching a length of 53 feet (16 meters) and the male up to 50 feet (15 meters). Weight is estimated at approximately 24 to 30 tons (Winn and Reichley 1985). Sexual maturity is reached at 4 to 6 years and physical maturity at 12 to 15 years of age (Chittleborough 1965, Nishiwaki 1959). As with all mysticetes, females are larger than males (Winn and Reichley 1985).

The humpback is more robust than the other rorquals and is distinguished by its long, winglike flippers, which may equal one-third of body length and often have knobs or bumps on the leading edges. There is some indication that the majority of Southern Hemisphere humpback whales have flippers that are darkly pigmented, while those of the Northern Hemisphere have lighter-colored flippers. The humpback's head is broad and rounded, similar to that of the blue whale and other rorquals, but shorter. The dorsal fin is located slightly less than one-third of the body length from the notch of the tail flukes and can vary in size and shape (Winn and Reichley 1985). The dorsal fin frequently includes a step or hump, which is accentuated when the animal arches its back to begin a dive, and from which the species derives its common name (Leatherwood *et al.* 1983).

Humpbacks have characteristic rounded, fleshy "tubercles" or dome-shaped protuberances in rows on the margins of their upper and lower jaws and chin, from which short, stiff hairs protrude. The name "rorqual" comes from the long ventral grooves, or pleats, that extend from the chin to the belly; these grooves allow the whales to expand their throats while feeding. Humpbacks possess 14 to 35 broad ventral grooves (Leatherwood *et al.* 1983). Despite the two pairs of openings, or "nares," in its blowhole, the spout of the humpback is seldom bifurcate and is usually lower (6 to 12 feet [2 to 4 meters]) and rounder than the tall thin blowhole of other rorquals.

The body color of humpbacks ranges from black to charcoal gray, with a white region of varying extent on the throat and belly in adults. Newborn calves are light gray. Individually distinctive white and black pigment and scar patterns are found on the flippers, the belly, over much of the body, and on the ventral surfaces of the tail or flukes. The flukes are broad and butterfly shaped, marked on the rear margin by serrations and frequent irregularities, and may be deeply notched in the center (Winn and Reichley 1985). The dorsal surface ranges from black to dark gray, while the ventral side may range from white to black or a distinctive combination of the two. The characteristic markings on the flukes have been widely used for photoidentification research on population abundance and behavior (Katona *et al.* 1979).

Taxonomy

Differences in humpback whale coloration and size may be seen among individuals, but scientists still classify them as one species. Although the humpback has the characteristics of the rorqual family (Balaenopteridae), other notable anatomical differences have persuaded taxonomists to place it in its own subfamily—the Megapterinae Gray (1868) (Barnes and McLeod 1984).

Distribution and Migration

Humpback whales occur in all of the world's oceans ranging from tropical breeding grounds to the edges of polar ice zones (see Figure 1). Like all baleen whales, humpbacks migrate annually between summer feeding grounds in higher latitudes, where productivity is high, and

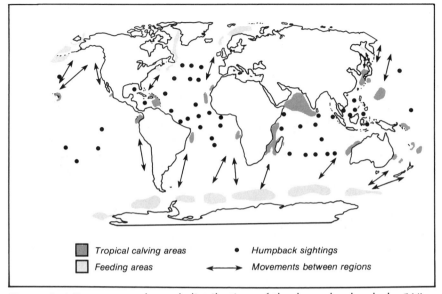

Figure 1. Migratory cycle and distribution of the humpback whale (Winn and Reichley 1985).

temperate-to-tropical winter grounds that are conducive to reproduction. The annual migratory cycles of the Northern and Southern Hemisphere populations differ by six months, but is in phase with the climatic cycle (Winn and Reichley 1985). Unlike other rorquals, humpbacks seek out coastal areas and islands for feeding and breeding, while their migrations take them across vast ocean basins. In winter, humpbacks in both latitudes appear to prefer shallow waters, with their greatest concentrations occurring in waters less than 600 feet (200 meters) deep and in oceanic banks or shallows near islands at latitudes of less than 25 degrees (Chittleborough 1965).

It is assumed that large populations of humpbacks once frequented the coast of West Africa, the islands of the eastern tropical Atlantic, and the reefs of the central and western Pacific; however, because of relentless hunting and, perhaps, some changes in migration patterns, whales are no longer seen in those areas. Today, humpback whales are divided into three discrete populations that appear to be reproductively and geographically isolated: the Southern Hemisphere or Antarctic stock (which may be made up of additional substocks), the North Pacific stocks, and the North Atlantic stock (see Figure 1) (Winn and Reichley 1985, International Whaling Commission 1986).

Antarctic Population.   Seven largely isolated stocks are recognized in the southern oceans (International Whaling Commission 1986); however, limited exchanges between feeding and breeding grounds have been demonstrated to some degree by "discovery tagging"[1] studies conducted during whaling activities (Winn and Reichley 1985). These studies have indicated that Antarctic humpbacks winter in the waters off Brazil, West Africa, Madagascar, and western Australia; in the Coral Sea; near New Zealand to the Tonga Islands; and off Chile, Peru, and Ecuador, as far north as the Galapagos Islands (Leatherwood *et al.* 1983). Because discovery-tag studies require the killing of the whale to recover the tag buried in its body, the dynamics of whale movements from season to season, and the rate of exchanges between areas, are not well-known. In the future, nonlethal photoidentification studies may elucidate migrations in the southern seas.

North Pacific Population. The North Pacific population has been divided into three stocks: Mexican, Hawaiian, and Asian. These divisions are based on the discreteness of the humpbacks' wintering areas (National Marine Fisheries Service 1988). The results of photoidentification studies suggest that there is some mixing among stocks.

The summer feeding range of the North Pacific humpback population includes the continental shelf waters from Point Conception, California, around the Pacific Rim to the Kamchatka Peninsula, and northward into the Bering and Chukchi seas (National Marine Fisheries Service 1988). From late spring to early winter, humpbacks occur throughout Alaskan waters, concentrating in southeastern Alaska (Baker *et al.* 1985); Prince William Sound; the central Gulf of Alaska (Rice and Wolman 1983); the western Gulf of Alaska near Kodiak Island (Rice and Wolman 1982, Leatherwood *et al.* 1983); south of the Alaska Peninsula between the Shumagin and Semidi islands; and off eastern Aleutian Island and the Bering Sea (Leatherwood *et al.* 1983). Humpbacks occur seasonally off Oregon and Washington from spring through fall, presumably while migrating between more northerly summer feeding areas and southern breeding grounds.

Summer concentrations of humpbacks are found along the central California coast, centering near the Farallone Islands west of San Francisco (Cubbage *et al.* 1988). Photoidentification studies suggest that a subpopulation of humpbacks may feed off the coast of California and breed in Mexico near the Revillagigedo Islands and Islas Marias below Baja California (Cubbage *et al.* 1988). Humpbacks are seen traveling through the southern California bight in the spring and fall

1. "Discovery tags" are stainless steel tubes fired from shotguns into the whales' blubber. Each tag contains information on the location and date that each whale was tagged. The tags are retrieved, or "discovered," when the whales are killed and processed at whaling stations, enabling researchers to determine the movements of the whales from the site of tagging to the site of their capture.

as they migrate to and from their wintering grounds in Mexico. Humpbacks wintering in Mexico are found off the west coast of Baja California, the mainland coast of Mexico from southern Sonora to Jalisco, and the far offshore Islas Revillagigedo (National Marine Fisheries Service 1988).

The Hawaiian population appears around the islands as early as October, but the primary season begins in December, with numbers peaking in February (Herman *et al.* 1980). The majority of the whales appears to prefer the 100 fathom isobath around the islands of Maui, Molokai, Lanai, Kahoolawe, and the Penguin Bank, although some are seen off the islands of Niihau and Hawaii (Herman *et al.* 1980, National Marine Fisheries Service 1988).

The winter distribution of humpbacks in the western North Pacific is not well known, but winter sightings of whales are reported in the vicinity of the Marianas Islands, the Bonin Islands, the Ryukyu Islands, and Taiwan (Ivashin and Rovnin 1967).

North Atlantic Population. The largest winter aggregation of humpbacks in the Atlantic Ocean is found in a region of shallows north of the Dominican Republic on the margin of the Antillean Island arc, south through the Caribbean Archipelago to Venezuela (Stone 1987). The center of the winter distribution is Silver Bank, an extensive complex of coral reefs approximately 45 miles (75 kilometers) in diameter. From mid-December to mid-April, the majority of the humpback whales from the North Atlantic is believed to mate and calve in this area. Silver Bank, along with adjacent Navidad, Mouchoir, the more distant Borinquen Bank off Puerto Rico, and Virgin Bank, appears to be where whales from the North Atlantic feeding grounds mingle (Mattilla *et al.* 1989).

North Atlantic humpback whales migrate north each spring to widely separated high-latitude feeding areas along the margins of ocean basins and in the vicinity of oceanographic conversions (where different water masses meet). In the western North Atlantic there are at least four regions where humpbacks go for the spring, summer, and fall feeding period (Katona and Beard 1988). Each region is believed to support a distinct stock that remains faithful to its geographic ranges and seldom mixes with whales of other regions during the feeding season—these are the Greenland, Newfoundland–Labrador, the Gulf of St. Lawrence, and the Gulf of Maine stocks. Early arrivals begin to reach Stellwagen Bank and the southern edge of Georges Bank by early March. Humpbacks continue to move northward throughout the spring and summer until they reach their respective summer feeding grounds. Between mid-November and late December, the whales begin their return migration to the Antilles (Mayo *et al.* 1985).

Behavior

Perhaps the most gregarious of the rorqual family, humpbacks are often seen during the summer months in close associations of two or more while swimming, feeding, or resting. While feeding, "cooperative" groups display coordinated behavior to herd prey (Winn and Reichley 1985) (see "Diet and Feeding"). They occasionally vocalize in these social groupings by making relatively free-form sounds that vary in frequency, volume, and duration. These sounds may include loud wheezing blows, broadband pulses (covering a wide frequency range), grunts, yelps, moans, and shrieks. It has been suggested that a series of pronounced blasts, or "trumpets," indicates agonistic behavior in humpback whales (Watkins 1967, Watkins and Wartzok 1985). These social sounds do not appear as organized complex patterns, and may be heard throughout the humpbacks' range. Although there is no evidence that humpbacks use sound to echolocate, the lower-frequency sounds may be important in orientation and navigation, or in locating schooling prey (Winn 1972, Norris 1969).

Humpbacks are by far the most animated and acrobatic of the large whales. Although they are not particularly fast swimmers (generally traveling at between 3.2 and 6.5 miles [6 and 12 kilometers] per hour),

Characteristic markings on flukes are helpful in photoidentification studies of humpback whales. *Steven Swartz/Center for Marine Conservation*

they frequently "breach," or leap clear of the water in a dramatic, often twisting display ending with a tremendous splash. Humpbacks have been known to breach repeatedly, and in at least one instance up to 55 consecutive times (Swartz pers. observ.). They often raise a flipper and slap it against the water, or "lobtail" by raising the tail high into the air and slamming it down onto the water with a loud crash. Similarly, humpbacks will often lie at the surface, upside down with one or both flippers raised in the air.

Breeding

During the winter breeding season, groups of several animals may form (Darling 1983), and "escort" whales commonly accompany females with calves. Escorts are aggressive towards other humpbacks. Identified escorts have been males, suggesting that the male stays with the female in order to mate with her. However, neither copulating humpbacks nor birthings have ever been witnessed (Winn and Reichley 1985).

Humpback whales are believed to be polygynous (Wittenberger 1981). Apparent competition between males, presumably for access to females, often turns into intense physical "shoving" matches that frequently draw blood as individuals rub their head, flukes, and dorsal fins raw on each other (Darling 1983). Males often attempt to displace male escorts that accompany female-calf pairs by butting and shoving with their head and flukes. Underwater, humpbacks often blow screens of bubbles during aggressive encounters.

Social sounds made during the summer season are different from the long, complex, and highly structured songs produced by males during the winter breeding season. The humpbacks' song is composed of a series of discrete notes or units; a consecutive series make up a theme, and a predictable series of themes makes up a song (Payne and McVay 1971). Because singing occurs primarily during the breeding season, it has been hypothesized that the songs serve some reproductive function, perhaps to attract females, to ward off competing males, or to maintain spatial distance between male singers (Darling 1983). Songs, or songlike themes, have occasionally been recorded on Alaska and Cape Cod feeding grounds (Jurasz and Jurasz 1979, Winn and Winn 1980), notably at the ends of the feeding and breeding seasons (Mattilla *et al.* 1987).

Humpbacks reproduce in semitropical and tropical waters. Although females occasionally give birth in successive years (Glockner-Ferrari and Ferrari 1988), they normally reproduce at intervals of two or more years (Clapham and Mayo 1987a,b). Following an 11- to 12-month gestation period, adult females produce a single calf. The calf is about 15 to 16.4 feet (4.5 to 5 meters) long at birth, averages 2 tons, and is suckled for approximately 6 to 10 months (Winn and Reichley 1985). The humpbacks' milk has a fat content of approximately 20.4 to 41.3 percent, and thus is very rich and nutritive. The calf may consume up to 95 pounds (43 kilograms) of milk daily (Winn and Reichley 1985).

As with all whales, calf growth is rapid during the lactation period. Most calves are weaned when they reach 27 to 30 feet (8 to 9 meters) in length, although there have been observations in Hawaiian waters of yearling calves accompanying their mothers with newborn calves (Glockner-Ferrari pers. comm.). Whether the older calves are still nursing has not been determined.

Diet and Feeding

Instead of teeth, all mysticete whales have racks of baleen plates growing from the roofs of the mouth in two rows along the margins of the upper jaw. In the humpback whale, 270 to 400 black-to-grayish plates form a fringed curtain that filters planktonic prey from the water. The largest baleen plates are up to 27.5 inches (70 centimeters) long and 12 inches (30 centimeters) wide (Leatherwood *et al.* 1983). Baleen growth is reported to increase dramatically with weaning as young whales begin to feed on marine prey. Humpback whales feed on krill (small pelagic shrimps [Euphausiacea]) (Gaskin 1982) and small schooling fish (Wolman 1978). Because they feed by engulfing schooling prey, humpbacks are known as "swallowers" or "gulpers" instead of "skimmers" (for example, right and bowhead whales) (Nemoto 1970).

Humpbacks are known for their specialized feeding technique of blowing bubble nets and clouds, presumably to concentrate their prey. The whales typically dive below a school of fish or krill and encircle it while emitting a stream of bubbles and ascending slowly to the surface. When the prey are "confined" in this bubble net, the whale or group of whales charge through the net, mouths open, and engulf them. A great volume of food and water is taken into the mouth and the throat pleats and "gullet" become extremely distended with water and prey. While at the surface, the whale begins to "drag," or swim slowly while contracting the musculature of the throat, thus forcing the water out through the rows of baleen plates. The krill and fish are retained on the fringed baleen curtain. Photographs of feeding whales clearly show that as they surface open-mouthed, the mandible unhinges in a manner similar to many reptiles (Gaskin 1982).

Other feeding techniques include *tail slashing, flick feeding,* and *inside loop* behavior, where the whale creates turbulence in the water by slashing its tail or by making a 180-degree roll and returning to lunge-feed through the disturbance (Hain *et al.* 1982).

When food is dense and near the surface, the humpback will swim rapidly toward the surface and "lunge" with its mouth agape to consume prey. When lunging in groups, the members tend to be synchronous, with each individual's movements slowed and orchestrated so that it avoids the others (Jurasz and Jurasz 1979, Hain *et al.* 1982).

SIGNIFICANCE OF THE SPECIES

Large whales are "batch feeders," feeding on large quantities of mackerel plankton and other schooling fish. Because their prey consists of organisms that occupy low trophic levels in marine food chains, whales are critically dependent on the availability and vitality of planktonic species and small fish. However, as mammals, whales have physiological processes and food storage mechanisms that allow them to survive lean years; hence, whales may not indicate slow, incremental changes in habitat quality over time and may not serve as indicators of a declining ecosystem. Rather, they would be expected to respond in some overtly noticeable way only when prey are either absent altogether or present and unavailable due to some abnormal occurrence such as toxic poisoning. An example of this was the mass mortality of whales in the fall and winter of 1987 off Cape Cod after the whales ingested toxic prey. The whales did not become sick slowly over time, or change their behavior; instead, they died, in some cases, with stomachs full of undigested prey. This all-or-nothing response to the availability of food is not an indicator that the quality of a habitat is declining; it would instead suggest that the habitat had become intolerable. Thus, although whales may not be useful gauges of regional trends, their presence or absence from traditional regions may serve as an indicator of global change in the quality of marine habitats.

Perhaps one of the most significant aspects of humpbacks, and all great whales, is that they occupy positions in marine ecosystems that are analogous to top predators in terrestrial habitats. They are the largest creatures on earth and, with the exception of the killer whale (*Orcinus orca*), have no natural predators. Only disease, old age, and humans pose real threats to whales. They compel our respect, our imagination, and our awe. Yet ironically, human activities pose the greatest immediate threat to whales. Fortunately, because of their "charisma," whales are of extreme interest to many people. Although we may not be able to solve all of the problems humans have created for the great whales, our continued efforts to learn more about them, and our concern for their well-being, are the whales' best hope for salvation.

HISTORICAL PERSPECTIVE

Humpback whales were easy prey for shore-based whalers because of their tendency to concentrate near coasts on both summer and winter grounds. Heavy exploitation occurred in the North Atlantic during the late 1800s, leading to low catches after 1900 and giving rise to the realization that few humpbacks remained (Winn and Reichley 1985). An estimated 60,000 humpbacks were killed from 1910 to 1916 in the Southern Hemisphere alone, with other peaks of exploitation occurring in the 1930s and 1950s (Schevill 1974). Exploitation occurred throughout the 20th century in the North Pacific, with peak catches of more than 3,000 whales in 1962 and 1963 (Winn and Reichley 1985).

In 1939, commercial taking of humpbacks was prohibited in the Antarctic and reopened in 1949. But following serious depletion of all stocks, all hunting was banned in 1963 (Mackintosh 1965). In 1956, Antarctic hunting in the North Atlantic was stopped; North Pacific hunting was banned in 1966 following depletion of all stocks. Humpbacks were severely depleted and their recovery has been extremely slow. Some Southern Hemisphere stocks do not appear to have increased appreciably since they were afforded complete protection in 1964 by the International Whaling Commission.

CURRENT TRENDS

As with all great whales, there are scant population data for humpbacks before exploitation began. The worldwide estimate of humpback whales prior to exploitation has been given as 120,000 to 150,000 (Winn and Reichley 1985), while today there are estimated to be fewer than 10,000 animals, or between six and eight percent of the original population (Wolman 1978). Recent studies using photoidentification techniques are providing reasonable estimates for some stocks, particularly in the North Atlantic and North Pacific. The technique is very promising for the study of humpback and other whale species, and may provide better evidence of the species' recovery than previous catch-per-unit-effort statistics that were used when the whales were being exploited commercially. Because the humpback populations are at less than 10 percent of their pre-exploited size, and because of the slow initial recovery of animal populations that grow exponentially, it will take many years before we can expect a significant degree of recovery for many of the existing stocks.

Antarctic Population. The Antarctic population has been studied little since it received protection from commercial whaling, and no recent information is available on whether the humpbacks in this region are recovering from depletion. Estimates of the 19th century pre-exploitation population in the southern oceans number 100,000 whales. But after heavy commercial hunting, there are estimated to be only 2,500 remaining humpbacks (Leatherwood *et al.* 1983).

North Pacific Population. Rice (1978) suggests that the pre-exploitation population in the North Pacific may have numbered 15,000. Baker *et al.* (1986) and Darling and Morowitz (1986) analyzed photoidentification data and estimated that 1,600 to 2,100 humpbacks visited the Hawaiian Islands from the late 1970s to the early 1980s. Estimates for other wintering grounds are in the hundreds.

Baker *et al.* (1985) estimated that 300 to 350 humpback whales are present in Southeast Alaska during the summer and fall, and Rice and Wolman (1982) estimated that approximately 400 whales summer in the Gulf of Alaska and Prince William Sound. Another 300 to 350 may summer near Shumagin and Semidi islands in the Bering Sea, but sightings of humpbacks near the eastern Aleutian Islands are few (National Marine Fisheries Service 1988). Few humpbacks have been seen in the Bering Sea since 1975 (Leatherwood *et al.* 1983).

Aerial surveys from 1980 to 1982 along the West Coast of North America from the Oregon–California border to Point Conception, California estimated 338 whales. As many as 100 individuals are present in the Gulf of the Farallones during the summer and fall (Cubbage *et al.* 1986).

North Atlantic Population. The western North Atlantic stock is relatively healthy; based on analysis of fluke photographs, the total North Atlantic humpback population for the years 1979 to 1986 was from 44,881 ± 3,048 (95 percent CI [Confidence Interval]) to 6,570 ± 148 (95 percent CI) (Katona and Beard 1988). This population consists of at least four and possibly five separate feeding substocks: the Iceland-Denmark Strait; western Greenland; Newfoundland-Labrador; Gulf of St. Lawrence; and Gulf of Maine–Scotian Shelf.

MANAGEMENT

The humpback whale is currently protected from commercial exploitation by the International Whaling Commission (International Whaling Commission 1983). At its 1990 meeting, the commission will undertake a comprehensive status assessment of all whale stocks to determine whether the species' protected status should be changed.

Some humpbacks are still taken by subsistence fisheries in Bequia and Cape Verde islands (International Whaling Commission 1988). Although these takes represent only a few animals, subsistence fisheries can keep local stocks at low levels and delay recovery (Winn and Reichley 1985). Stocks that apparently remain severely depleted include the Okinawa, northern Marianas, and Cape Verde Islands, and several in the Antarctic (Winn and Reichley 1985).

In the United States, humpback whales and their habitats are protected by the Endangered Species Act and Marine Mammal Protection Act. Humpbacks are listed as endangered under both acts and the "taking" by harassment or by direct killing is not permitted. Actions that may pose threats to humpbacks or to their recovery require review by the appropriate government agencies, including the consideration of public comment and the issuance of special permits for the proposed actions.

The Gulf of the Farallones National Marine Sanctuary off central California is the only marine protected area in the United States that encompasses critical habitat—necessary feeding and breeding grounds—for humpback whales. Other areas that should be considered for protected status include portions of the coastal waters of the Hawaiian Islands, the coastal island waters of Southeast Alaska, and the New England coast, particularly the Stellwagen Bank feeding ground off Cape Cod.

The precipitous growth of the whale-watching industry has been accompanied by concern that whale watching may cause both biological problems for the whales and legal problems for whale watchers. The great whales are vulnerable to injury and disturbance by boats, are slow moving, can escape only by diving, and in some locations, such as Hawaii, are confined to limited, shallow areas. Vessel traffic may subject whales to adverse impacts ranging from separation of mothers and calves to increased energy expenditure when feeding or migration is disrupted. Moreover, there is concern that whale watching may "domesticate" wild animals and habituate them to potentially dangerous vessel activity. The extent to which these impacts occur, and whether they adversely effect whale populations are still largely unanswered questions.

Nonetheless, whale watching has the potential to increase public awareness of the plight of the great whales and to foster a growing respect for efforts to prevent undue harrassment and disturbance. An enlightened public, along with enforcement efforts, may benefit the recovery of these endangered species more effectively than regional management efforts.

The National Marine Fisheries Service sponsored a workshop in November 1988 to address the effects of whale watching and other commercial activities on whales. The objectives of the workshop were to evaluate regional whale-watching programs, the biological impacts of such activities on whales, public education programs, and management efforts to mitigate any adverse effects of whale watching. The findings of the workshop are being used by the agency to formulate a new policy initiative for whale watching (Center for Marine Conservation in press.)

PROGNOSIS

Most humpback whale stocks remain seriously depleted. Because of their frequent use of near-shore waters, humpbacks are vulnerable to a variety of human disturbances and loss of habitat from development and pollution.

Human activities that could have detrimental effects on humpback populations include the indirect effects from outer-continental-shelf oil exploration and production, ocean dumping, coastal logging, fishing, resort development, and increasing traffic from pleasure boats and cruise ships. Each of these activities may present a different short-term disturbance to whales or damage their habitat. While short-term disturbances or local destruction of habitat may not pose immediate threats to the whales, the cumulative effect of these events over time may severely threaten the species.

As coastal fishing increases, humpbacks are more frequently becoming fouled in fishing gear, particularly in inshore areas of New England and eastern Canada (Mitchell 1982). Eighteen animals were reported entangled in nets off the northeastern United States from 1975 to 1985—nine were released alive, five died, and four swam off still entangled in the gear (International Whaling Commission 1988).

Marine mammal blubber can serve as a repository for a wide variety of pollutants. Significant levels of DDT, PCBs, chlordane, and dieldrin have been found in humpback whale blubber (Taruski *et al.* 1975). The highest levels of these substances have been found in whales on feeding grounds; lower levels have been found in humpbacks on breeding grounds, probably reflecting the lack of feeding during the breeding season. Because humpbacks feed on massive quantities of prey at lower trophic levels, they accumulate, or concentrate, pollutants. Although the long-term effects of pollutant and heavy metal loads on cetaceans are not presently known, the reported levels of pollutants in humpback tissue are significant enough that a continued monitoring effort for chlorinated hydrocarbons in humpbacks, and in other cetacean species, should be undertaken (Winn and Reichley 1985, International Whaling Commission 1988).

Unusual concentrations of toxic substances, either from natural or human-made sources, could cause a decline in humpback whale prey species and result in the loss of primary feeding areas, or render the prey inedible and possibly even lethal. An example of this was the 1987 deaths of 15 humpbacks—representing perhaps five percent of the Gulf of Maine population—that died and washed ashore along the coast of Cape Cod. The dead whales included all ages of both sexes; the animals appeared to have died quickly. It is believed that abnormal amounts of red tides resulted in extremely high levels of biotoxins in the humpbacks' prey. It is not known if the toxins were the ultimate result of human-made pollution or an unusual natural event. However, this group mortality of large whales demonstrates the impact that a poisoning of coastal waters could have on whales and other marine life.

RECOMMENDATIONS

The humpback whale remains a depleted species worldwide despite its protection from commercial whaling. The humpback's reduction to very low numbers, coupled with its low reproductive rates undoubtedly will slow its recovery time. The North Atlantic humpback whale population has had the best recovery to date and is still growing, although not back to pre-exploitation estimates. But other stocks remain greatly reduced. It will be many years before any of the depleted stocks have recovered to even 50 percent of their pre-exploitation levels.

Protection of the humpback whale must continue in order to encourage its recovery during the initial slow growth period of the stocks. Incidental mortality from fishing activities, pollution, and collisions with ships all will contribute to the slow recovery of this species and should be minimized. Indirect factors impeding humpback recovery include coastal pollution, displacement from preferred habitats, and harassment from human activities. These types of activities must be managed in order to mitigate effects on recovering humpback whale populations.

Management and conservation efforts for humpback whales should be coordinated with research programs to better understand the biological requirements of the species, its behavior, and the importance of specific habitats and resources to populations. Essential areas, such as primary breeding and feeding grounds, deserve special attention. Where feasible, these locations should be designated as marine sanctuaries to ensure that human activities do not degrade them or deter whales from using them. To consider these issues, the National Marine Fisheries Service has developed a recovery plan for the species that is now being reviewed by a team of humpback whale specialists.

Finally, because whales are cosmopolitan, whale conservation is an international issue, as is the responsible management of the oceans. Conservation programs for humpback whales require an understanding of the whales' regional ecosystems and a perception of the total biological context that is not restricted by human-made political boundaries. The principal legal question is how to coordinate conservation programs for this highly migratory species, which lives and moves within the territorial waters of several nations (Stone 1987).

Measures to establish marine protected areas for whales (and other marine species) have been undertaken by Mexico (for gray whales), the United States (U.S. Marine Sanctuary Program), and the Dominican Republic (Silver Bank National Marine Sanctuary). Nations are beginning to recognize that the conservation of migratory marine species is a multinational responsibility as well as a tourist lure. Stone (1987) discusses this problem with respect to humpback whales and suggests that lessons for international protection of marine species and habitats may be drawn from many international programs, such as the Western Hemisphere Convention, International Convention for the Regulation of Whaling, and the Bonn Convention on Highly Migratory Species, each of which regulates international wildlife policy among nations.

The ultimate success of any of these programs is entirely dependent upon multilateral support for conservation treaties. Governments and interested organizations must strive to establish conservation measures and to support and cooperate with similar measures enacted in other countries. If conservation treaties and their mandates are not supported by all nations, and if national domestic law undermines international efforts, then the conservation of species like the humpback whale cannot be realized.

REFERENCES

Baker, C.S., Herman, L.M., Perry, A., Lawton, W.S., Straley, J.M., and Straley, J.H. 1985. "Population characteristics and migration of summer and late-season humpback whales (*Megaptera novaeangliae*) in Southeastern Alaska." *Marine Mammal Science* 1(4):304–323.

————., Herman, L.M., Perry, A., Lawton, W.S., Straley, J.M., Wolman, A.A., Kaufman, G.D., Winn, H.E., Hall, J.D., Reinke, J.M., and Ostma, J. 1986. "Migratory movement and population structure of humpback whales (*Megaptera novaeangliae*) in the Central and Eastern North Pacific." *Marine Ecology Program Service* 31:105–119.

Barnes, L.G. and McLeod. 1984. "The fossil record and phyletic relationships of gray whales," pp. 3–29 in Jones *et al.* eds., *The Gray Whale*, Eschrichtius robustus. Academic Press, Inc. Orlando, Florida. 600 pp.

Chittleborough, R.G. 19865. "Dynamics of two populations of the humpback whale (*Megaptera novaeangliae*)." *Australian Journal of Marine Freshwater Resources* 16:33–128.

Clapham, P.J. and C.A. Mayo. 1987a. "Reproduction and recruitment of individually identified humpback whales, *Megaptera novaeanglia*, observed in Massachusetts Bay, 1979–1985." *Canadian Journal of Zoology* 65:2853-2863.

————. and C.A. Mayo. 1987b. "The attainment of sexual maturity in two female humpback whales." *Marine Mammal Science* 3(3):279–282.

Cubbage, J.C., Calambokidis, J., Steiger, G.H., Balcomb, K.C., and Bloedel, P. 1988. Photoidentification of Humpback Whales (*Megaptera novaeangliae*) in the Gulf of the Farallones, California, With an Analysis of Potential Sources of Sample Bias. International Whaling Commission Special Meeting on Nonlethal Techniques to Estimate Cetacean Population Parameters. La Jolla, California.

Darling, J.D. 1983. Migrations, Abundance, and Behavior of Hawaiian Humpback Whales (*Megaptera novaeangliae*) (Borowski). Ph.D dissertation. University of California. Santa Cruz, California. 147 pp.

————. and D.J. McSweeney. 1985. "Observations on the migrations of North Pacific humpback whales (*Megaptera novaeangliae*)," pp. 359–368 in Payne, R. ed., *Communication and Behavior of Whales.* Westview Press. Boulder, Colorado.

————. and H. Morowitz. 1986. "Census of 'Hawaiian' humpback whales (*Megaptera novaeangliae*)." *Canadian Journal of Zoology* 64:105–111.

Gaskin, D.E. 1982. *The Ecology of Whales and Dolphins.* Heinemann Educational Books, Inc. London, England. 459 pp.

Glockner-Ferrari, D.A. and M.J. Ferrari. 1988. Reproduction in the Humpback Whale (*Megaptera novaeangliae*) in Hawaiian Waters, 1975–1988: Discussion of the Life History, Reproductive Rates, and Behavior of Known Individuals Identified Through Surface and Underwater Photography. International Whaling Commission special meeting on nonlethal techniques to estimate cetacean population parameters. La Jolla, California.

Hain, J.H.W., Carter, G.R., Kraus, S.D., Mayo, C.A., and Winn, H.E. 1982. "Feeding behavior of the humpback whale (*Megaptera novaeangliae*) in the western North Atlantic." *Fishery Bulletin* 80(2):99–108.

Herman, L.M., Forestell, P.H., and Antinoja, R.C. 1980. The 1976/1977 Migration of Humpback Whales Into Hawaiian Waters: Composite Description. Marine Mammal Commission Report MMC-77/19. Washington, D.C. 35 pp.

Ivashin, M.V. and A.A. Rovnin. 1967. "Some results of the Soviet whale marking in the waters of the North Pacific." *Norsk Hvaalfangst-tid* 56(6):123–135.

International Whaling Commission. 1983. *33rd Report of the International Whaling Commission.* 781 pp.

————. 1986. Schedule (for the regulation of whaling). Cambridge, England. 27 pp.

————. 1988. *39th Report of the International Whaling Commission.* 155 pp.

Jurasz, C.M. and V.P. Jurasz. 1979. "Feeding modes of the humpback whale (*Megaptera novaeangliae*) in Southeast Alaska." *Scientific Reprints of the Whales Research Institute* 31:69–83.

Katona, S., Baxter, B., Brazier, O., Kraus, S., Perkins, J., and Whitehead, H. 2979. "Identification of humpback whales by fluke photographs," pp. 33–34 in Winn, H.E. and B. Olla eds., *The Behavior of Marine Mammals, Vol. 3.* Plenum Press. New York.

————. and J.A. Beard. 1988. Population Size, Migrations, and Substock Structure of the Humpback Whale (*Megaptera novaeangliae*) in the western North Atlantic Ocean. Final Contract Report no. 40-EANF 700314 NMFS, NE Region. Woods Hole, Massachusetts. 34 pp.

Leatherwood, J.S., Reeves, R.R., and Foster, L. 1983. *The Sierra Club Handbook of Whales and Dolphins.* Sierra Club Books. San Francisco, California. 303 pp.

Mackintosh, N.A. 1965. *The Stocks of Whales.* Fishing News Books. London, England.

Mattila, D.K. and P.J. Clapham. 1989. "Population cosmopolitan of humpback whales, *Megaptera novaeangliae*, on Silver Bank, 1984." *Canadian Journal of Zoology* 67:0000-0008.

————., L.N. Guinea, and C.A. Mayo. 1987. "Humpback whale songs on a North Atlantic feeding ground." *Journal of Mammalogy* 68(4):880–883.

Mitchell, E. 1982. "Canada: Progress report on cetacean research, June 1980 to May 1981." *International Whaling Commission Report* 32:161–169.

Nemoto, T. 1970. "Feeding pattern of baleen whales in the ocean," pp. 241–152 in Steele, J.H. ed., *Marine Food Chains*. University of California Press. Berkeley, California.

Nishiwaki, M. 1959. "Humpback whales in Ryukyuan waters." *Scientific Reprint of the Whales Research Institute, Toyko*. 14:49–87.

National Marine Fisheries Service. 1988. Status Report on Marine Mammals Involved in Commercial Fisheries. NMFS, NOAA. Washington, D.C. 144 pp.

Norris, K.S. 1969. "The echolocation of marine mammals," pp. 183–227 in Anderson, H.T. ed., *The Biology of Marine Mammals*. Academic Press, Inc. New York.

Payne, R. and S. McVay. 1971. "Songs of the humpback whale." *Science* 173:585–794.

Rice, D.W. and Wolman, A.A. 1982. "Whale census in the Gulf of Alaska, June to August 1980." *International Whaling Commission Report* 32:491–498.

Schevill, W.E. (ed.). 1974. *The Whale Problem*. Harvard University Press. Cambridge, Massachusetts. 419 pp.

Stone, G. 1987. "Humpback whale futures in Silver Bank." *Whale Watcher*. Fall 1987.

Taruski, A.G., Olney, C.E., and Winn, H.E. 1975. "Chlorinated hydrocarbons in cetaceans." *Journal of the Fishery Resources Board of Canada* 32:2205-2209.

Watkins, W.A. 1967. "Air-borne sounds of the humpback whale (*Megaptera novaeangliae*)." *Journal of Mammalogy* 48:573–578.

———. and Wartzok. 1985. "Sensory biophysics of marine mammals." *Marine Mammal Science* 1:219–260.

Winn, H.E. 1972. A Comparison of Mysticete and Odontocete Acoustic Signals and Their Behavioral Consequences. 84th meeting of the Acoustical Society AM. Miami, Florida.

———. and N.E. Reichley. 1985. "Humpback whale, *Megaptera novaeangliae*, (Borowski 1781), pp. 241–273, in Ridgeway, S.H. and R. Harrison eds., *Handbook of Marine Mammals, Vol. 3: The Sirenians and Baleen Whales*. Academic Press. Orlando, Florida.

Wittenberger, J.R. 1981. *Animal Social Behavior*. Duxbury Press. Boston, Massachusetts. 722 pp.

Wolman, A.A. 1978. "Humpback whale," pp. 57–63 in Haley, D. ed., *Marine Mammals*, second edition. Pacific Search Press. Seattle, Washington.

Steve Swartz is the staff marine mammalogist for the Center for Marine Conservation (formerly the Center for Environmental Education). He is working on research programs and legislative issues involving marine mammals and is conducting his own research on the social and breeding behavior of large whales.

The author wishes to thank Scott Baker, a humpback whale expert formerly with the University of Hawaii, and Phil Clapham and Dave Mattilla, humpback whale experts with the Center for Coastal Studies.

The hyacinth macaw, the world's largest and most specialized parrot, makes its home in the large palm trees native to Brazil, Paraguay, and Bolivia. The species is highly sought by international wild-bird traders, who have devastated it in the recent past. Although a worldwide ban on trade in wild hyacinths has been enacted, the species still faces threats from conversion of tropical forests into land for cattle ranching, and illegal capture. *Charles A. Munn/VIREO*

least pressure from bird catchers, meat and feather hunters, and agricultural developers.

The hyacinth macaw's ability to harvest different palm nuts in each part of its range allows it to survive in habitats with extraordinarily different topography, vegetation, and climate. In Pará, for example, the hyacinth lives in seasonally moist eastern Amazonian forest, which is characterized by a broken canopy of Brazil nut trees and an understory of low trees and bamboo (Ridgely 1982); in northeastern Brazil (the intersection of Goiás, Piauí, Maranhão, and Bahía), the species occupies dry, open forest in rocky valleys and plateaus (Ridgely 1982, Munn *et al.*); in Mato Grosso and Mato Grosso do Sul (Ridgely 1982, Munn *et al.* 1987), and in the eastern parts of the Bolivian state of Santa Cruz (Remsen and Ridgely 1980), the hyacinth macaw lives in moist palm groves interspersed with grassy marshes and gallery forests in the Pantanal marshlands of the upper drainage of the Paraguay River, the world's largest freshwater wetland. The climate in all three of these regions features a pronounced dry season that prevents the growth of extensive, tall, closed-canopy tropical forest (see Figure 1).

Diet

Although most other macaw species appear to eat a large variety of seeds, nuts, fruit pulp, nectar, flowers, and leaves (Forshaw 1981, Munn 1988), the hyacinth macaw relies almost entirely on the nutritious, fat-rich meat of very hard palm nuts. Only Sick (1969) and Roth (unpubl.) report that the species occasionally eats other food, such as small seeds, palm sprouts, and snails; palm nuts are by far the species' major food source.

The hyacinth macaw's large bill reflects its food preference; it uses its bill to score and then—in steel-cutter fashion— shear the nuts in two. The hyacinth macaw cuts open palm nuts so cleanly that the cut surfaces resemble the work of a metal-cutting saw or laser rather than of a bird or mammal. Red-and-green macaws and scarlet macaws, which also are endowed with impressive bills, occasionally try to cut open similarly large and hard palm nuts, but these smaller-billed species invariably butcher the nuts with crude gashes and hacking cuts that require many minutes of effort (Munn unpubl.). Their awkward beakwork contrasts markedly with the elegant, efficient shearing of the hyacinth macaws. Only one other macaw—the Lear's macaw—is able to sheer palm nuts so adeptly.

Throughout its range, the hyacinth macaw seems to rely on the nuts of one or two palm species, which vary in different parts of the bird's range. The populations of hyacinth macaw living in the Brazilian state of Pará in the eastern Amazon, for example, rely on the nuts of the palms *Orbignya phalerata* (the famous babaçú) and *Atrocaryum sp.* (locally named "tucumán"). The birds living in the large region at the intersection of the four states of Goiás, Piauí, Maranhão, and Bahía rely on the nuts of the palms *Syagrus coronata* (catolé) and *Atalea funifera* (piaçava); the birds living in the Pantanal region of southern Mato Grosso and Mato Grosso do Sul eat principally the nuts of the palms *Atalea phalerata* (bacurí) and *Acrocomia sp.* (bocaiuva). Because the nuts of these six palm species are of different dimensions and presumably different hardnesses, they would seem to be of potential interest to other macaw species; however, in each part of the hyacinth's range, the large macaws of the genus *Ara* seem to concentrate on a wide variety of other seeds and fruits, leaving the hyacinth's food sources virtually untouched. This avoidance by other macaws may reflect a difference in bill force between the hyacinth and the smaller-billed *Ara* species, but field and laboratory data are required to test this hypothesis.

Breeding

Nest Sites.   In the Pantanal, the hyacinth macaw apparently nests in cavities in large legume trees (*Enterolobium sp.* or *Sterculia striata*), which are the only two trees in the region large enough to provide cavities for the parrots (Yamashita unpubl., Hart unpubl.).

In the drier, rockier habitats occupied by hyacinth macaws in south Maranhão, southwest Piauí, north Goiás, and northwest Bahía, hyacinths nest in cavities of large dead or dying *Buriti* palms (*Mauritia vinifera*) in gallery forests of this large palm, and in natural rock crevices in the tall red cliffs, which are approximately 656 to 1,312 feet (200 to 400 meters) above the flat valleys typical of the region. It appears that trapping has removed the young from so many palms in the region that most of the successful nests are now in the cliffs. Whether the previously palm-nesting pairs have moved to cliff sites or have died out is unknown.

Hyacinth macaws living in the northwestern parts of the their range, such as the Carajas region and the mid-lower Xingu drainage, probably nest in the huge holes that result when large branches fall off the 131 to 164 foot (40 to 50 meters) Brazil nut trees (*Bertolettia excelsa*). These large trees are surprisingly common in those parts of Brazil and, in some sections of the forest north of Carajas, occur in densities of from 0.8 to 4 trees per hectare. Therefore, nest sites should not be a limiting factor for hyacinth macaws in that region. In parts of the rocky valleys of northeast Brazil and in the Pantanal, however, nest sites are probably increasingly scarce and a limiting factor in reproductive success.

Nesting Seasonality. For reasons presumably associated with seasonal differences in food availability, hyacinth macaws, like most South American macaws, nest during the wet season, which typically falls between November and April in regions south of the Equator. To our knowledge, no data currently exist on seasonal availability of palm nuts in the species' range.

Reproductive Rate. Estimates and censuses of hyacinth macaws during the nesting season in the Pantanal suggest that only 15 to 30 percent of the adult population attempts to breed each year (Yamashita unpubl., Hart unpubl.). As small or an even smaller percentage of adult hyacinth macaws in the eastern Amazonian and northeast Brazilian populations may attempt to breed in a given year (Yamashita unpubl.). These data and estimates coincide with data on reproductive rates of blue-and-yellow, scarlet, and red-and-green macaws in the 6,950-square-mile (18,000 square kilometer) Manu Biosphere Reserve in Amazonian Peru, where hunting is not permitted (Munn 1988).

Brazilian observers report that not all hyacinth macaw nests fledge young, and those that do rarely fledge more than one bird. Thus, 100 mated pairs of breeding-age hyacinth macaws may only produce from 7 to 25 young per year—a very low reproductive rate. Although data are required to confirm these estimates, it appears that the species does not have a high enough reproductive rate to withstand any substantial, long-term harvesting for the live animal trade or for hunting for meat and feathers. However, because adults presumably live for decades, a low reproductive rate does not necessarily signify that the species will disappear quickly if nests fail for a few years. Nevertheless, in the absence of good year-to-year data on longevity and reproductive rates, it cannot be assumed that the species will survive in areas where humans frequently destroy nest sites, capture nestlings, or capture or kill adults.

SIGNIFICANCE OF THE SPECIES

The hyacinth macaw's major biological significance is that, as the world's largest and most specialized parrot, it represents an extreme in the avian world. The species's reliance on palm nuts no doubt has influenced the distribution, reproduction, and seed defenses of the many palm species on which the hyacinth macaw depends. It is likely that the hyacinth macaw plays a major role in driving the evolutionary "arms race" between plants and animals, in this case between palms and their seed predators. Presumably, many South American palm species have evolved very hard nut shells to prevent predation by hyacinth macaws. Each time a palm plant produced a harder, better-defended seed, the individual hyacinth macaws with the largest bills probably were disproportionately able to crack the seeds. Hence, they passed their "big bill" genes down to their offspring, leading to larger and larger bills in each generation.

Besides its unique relationship with certain species of palms, the hyacinth macaw may boast a variety of other biological peculiarities that will make it of great interest to evolutionary biologists. These peculiarities may include an apparent ability to thrive—without dying prematurely of arteriosclerosis—on a very limited variety of palm nuts that are exceeding rich in saturated fats; great intelligence (parrots are one of the families of birds with the largest ratio of brain to body weight); and, the possibility of an elaborate social structure within the wild communities of long-lived birds.

Hyacinth macaws are of direct economic value in two ways: (1) as attractions for the rapidly expanding nature tour industry in the Pantanal of Brazil; and (2) as cage birds for the international live-bird trade. Nature tourism, which is exploding in the Pantanal region, could help conserve the Pantanal habitat of the hyacinth, while, ironically, the bird trade has proven to be the principal cause of the recent substantial declines in hyacinth macaws in many parts of Brazil, Bolivia, and Paraguay (Munn *et al.* 1987).

Ultimately, the tour industry may help save the bird. Many international biologists and professionals in nature tourism report that the Pantanal of Brazil is the pre-eminent wildlife spectacle in either North or South America—the New World's closest equivalent to the wildlife spectacles of East Africa. Proper development of this tour potential could provide income and employment for economically troubled Brazil without major environmental disturbance. Given its attributes, the hyacinth macaw could serve as as another attraction for the country's expansive mosaic of marshes and forests.

In contrast to the nature tour industry, which uses the hyacinth macaw in an indirect and virtually harmless manner, the trade in wild-caught hyacinths has rapidly devastated many large populations of the species. Because the species is slow to recover from the extreme pressures of harvest, the hyacinth macaw should be considered a nonrenewable resource. The trade in hyacinth macaws has not only rapidly destroyed wild populations in certain regions, but the bird catchers who live and work in the forests and savannahs of Brazil, Bolivia, and Paraguay, earn only $40 to $60 per bird, whereas middlemen and international dealers subsequently sell and resell the same birds for $300, $900, $1,300, and ultimately $7,000 to $10,000 per bird (Thomsen unpubl.) The final buyers of these wild-caught hyacinth macaws continue to ignore the fact that the birds have been captured illegally in Brazil, thus driving the species closer to extinction.

In 1987, long overdue changes in international laws finally resulted in a worldwide ban of trade in wild-caught hyacinth macaws. However, it still will be legal to sell captive-bred birds, both in the United States and abroad. This production in captivity at least should allow aviculturists to obtain the species without further straining wild populations. In 1987, one breeder reportedly produced eight hyacinth macaw fledglings from the eggs laid by one mated pair of captive birds (G. Jennings pers. comm.). As aviculturists further refine captive-breeding techniques, it is possible that by using incubators and by hand-raising, each year a captive pair of hyacinth macaws might produce more healthy fledglings than they could produce throughout their entire lives in the wild.

Besides the biological and economic value of hyacinth macaws, the birds also are a creature of exceptional aesthetic beauty and a natural choice as a symbol for the conservation of the great forests and savannahs of South America. Conservationists are increasingly recognizing the political and media value that spectacular animal species such as the hyacinth macaw have in saving unique ecosystems.

HISTORICAL PERSPECTIVE

It is impossible to say what the original range and population size of the hyacinth macaw was before the advent of humans to South America approximately 11,000 years ago. Likewise, it is impossible to know the distribution of the species before Europeans arrived in the 1500s. Native Brazilian tribes may have engaged in sizeable trade in hyacinth macaw feathers. It is even possible that hyacinth and other large macaws increased in density throughout South America as European diseases swept across the continent, killing most of the Indians long before Europeans began to penetrate and exploit the resources of the interior (Sweet 1981, Thomsen and Brantigan in press).

It is known, however, that in the early part of the 20th century explorers reported flocks of hundreds of hyacinth macaws at localities in Piauí in northeast Brazil where today the species is totally extirpated (Munn *et al.* 1987, Roth pers. comm.). In reviewing reports of many collecting expeditions between 1930 and the 1960s and from his own personal observation, Yamashita believes that the species formerly existed in many parts of Goiás, Maranhão, and Mato Grosso where none exists today. It is likely that the species originally ranged from just south of the Amazon in Pará to the drainage of the Parana and Paraguay rivers in Paraguay and southern Brazil. To try to estimate the species' world population size prior to the advent of Indians and then Europeans would be difficult, but there were probably between 100,000 and 3,000,000 birds in all.

A combination of habitat destruction for agriculture, capture for the bird trade, and hunting for meat and feathers have brought the world population of hyacinth macaws down to an estimated 3,000 individuals, although the number could range between 2,500 to 5,000 (Munn *et al.* 1987). It seems likely that the destruction of hyacinth macaw habitat—palms and nest trees—and hunting for meat and feathers were the predominant causes of the species decline until the 1960s or early 1970s. Beginning then and continuing until 1988, it appears that a major increase in the international trade in live macaws may have taken a greater toll on the species than either habitat destruction or hunting.

The evidence implicating the live-bird trade as the recent major threat to the hyacinth macaw comes from field surveys, interviews with people living in former hyacinth macaw strongholds (Munn *et al.* 1987), and from analyses of international trade records of the species (Nilsson and Mack 1980, Inskipp *et al.* 1988, Thomsen and Brantgian in press). From these data, scientists have proven that bird catchers systematically and single-handedly harvested entire populations of

Table 1. Minimum Imports of Hyacinth Macaws, 1981 to 1984 (according to CITES records).

Country	1981	1982	1983	1984
Belgium	—	—	—	30
Canada	—	1	14	—
Denmark	—	2	2	—
West Germany	99	7	7	—
Italy	—	10	6	36
France	—	—	—	—
East Germany	—	—	2	—
Japan	—	—	—	2
Kenya	—	—	2	—
Phillipines	8	2	—	—
South Africa	1	11	—	—
Spain	—	—	—	1
Surinam	—	2	—	—
Sweden	—	12	—	—
Thailand	—	4	—	—
Switzerland	1	27	13	7
Great Britain	7	1	—	—
United States	97	318	249	38
(USDA data)	428	522	431	1
U.S.S.R.	—	—	—	—

Source: CITES Annual Reports, Nilsson 1985.

hyacinth macaws to sell to national and international bird dealers (Munn *et al.* 1987, Roth pers. comm., Yamashita unpubl.).

The records of international trade in hyacinths over the last five years also demonstrate that there has been substantial reported trade. Still, actual trade may significally exceed reported trade (see Table 1). In particular, data from U.S. Department of Agriculture quarantine stations at ports of entry into the United States suggest that 1,382 hyacinth macaws entered the United States from 1981 through 1984, while the Convention on International Trade in Endangered Species of Fauna and Flora (CITES) data for the same period indicate only 702 hyacinth macaws were imported into the country (see Table 1) (Inskipp *et al.* 1988). If this discrepancy in import figures also occurs worldwide, two assumptions can be made: (1) CITES data on the hyacinth macaw trade for other countries may be even less accurate and (2) easily two or three times more birds may have been traded than CITES records indicate.

CURRENT TRENDS

Human activities have driven 2 of the 18 macaw species to extinction within the last 100 years: the Cuban macaw (*Ara tricolor*) and the glaucous macaw. Eight of the surviving 16 macaw species are in danger of extinction, while the remaining species, which tend to be the smaller macaws, appear to be declining steadily throughout their range in Central and South America due to habitat destruction, the pet trade, and hunting for meat and feathers.

As mentioned previously, from field surveys and interviews, an estimated 2,500 to 5,000 hyacinth macaws survive in three different populations in Brazil and part of Bolivia. In Paraguay, the species was represented by only two birds in early 1987 (Munn *et al.* 1987).

Hyacinth macaws in the Pantanal of Brazil and Bolivia, are currently not hunted for meat or feathers; the birds have plenty of food but bird catchers continue to capture them and farmers continue to cut down their nest trees. Cattle ranchers in the Pantanal continue to convert patches of forest to pasture. However, ranchers tend to leave all the palm trees standing because their cattle eat palm fruits and their horses reportedly eat palm leaves. After the cattle digest the nutritious outer layers of the fruits, they regurgitate the hard inner nut. As a result, in some extremely well-protected locations where ranchowners actively protect wild hyacinth macaws on their property, the birds forage in cattle pastures and stockyards for the clean palm nuts. Unfortunately, while ranchers leave palms standing, they cut down and burn all other large trees, including the only two tree species that grow large

The hyacinth macaw's powerful bill allows it to shear precisely the hard palm nuts that are the major part of its diet. *John S. Dunning/VIREO*

enough to provide nest sites for the birds. In addition to suffering from the loss of nest sites, in the last two decades—and continuing today despite international protection—thousands of hyacinth macaws from the Pantanal have been captured and sold by professional bird catchers. Unless this capture is halted, the catchers will surely continue to exploit the birds of the Pantanal.

In northeast Brazil, a well-organized professional bird-trading ring is the most severe threat to the species. This ring must be broken if there is to be any hope for the species in this region. Meat hunting by local people is another threat to hyacinth macaws in northeast Brazil. Animal protein is not nearly as abundant in this bleak region as it is in the cattle-rich Pantanal, so the birds are probably killed for food as well as trade. There seems to be much palm-rich hyacinth macaw habitat in the northeast currently devoid of the birds. Although it is possible that future agricultural expansion may threaten the bird's food supply, the threat seems minor compared to major threats from bird catchers and hunters. The number of nest holes in cliffs probably will remain constant and thus are not a factor in the continued loss of the species in northeast Brazil.

Hyacinth macaw populations in Pará are threatened mostly from subsistence hunting by colonists and perhaps from feather trade by some Indian groups. If there are illegal bird-trading rings operating in the region, they are still not as entrenched as in northeast Brazil and in parts of the Pantanal and, thus, are not yet an obvious problem. Furthermore, the Indians of Pará aggressively defend their land and macaws from any outsiders; this will prevent traders from successfully operating in the region. The species' food sources and nest sites are still reasonably intact in Pará, although the rapid, destructive, and unproductive expansion of cattle ranching (on thin soils that will not withstand this type of extensive clearing and use) may be affecting the huge nest trees and palm resources in ways that are not yet known. The environmental changes now taking place in much of Pará are more rapid and generally more devastating and irreversible than those in northeast Brazil or the Pantanal. This destructive development should be replaced with sustainable development in order to protect both forest organisms and the economic health of humans colonizing the region.

Capture or hunting of hyacinth macaws has been illegal for many years in Brazil, Bolivia, and Paraguay, but generally the effectiveness of the governing laws has been minimal. In Brazil, the conservation officials of the state of Mato Grosso do Sul (including the southern half of the Pantanal) have confiscated some illegal shipments of hyacinth macaws, and the federal government of Brazil occasionally captures illegal traffickers with small numbers of birds. Despite these limited successes, until 1987 it remained too easy to capture, buy, and ship the birds for long distances within Brazil, to adjacent countries, and ultimately the world market. But in 1987 and 1988, Brazil stiffened penalties for wildlife trafficking and currently several bird smugglers are being aggressively prosecuted by the Brazilian government.

Further encouraging trends include the report in Munn *et al.* (1987) that some bird dealers were left holding more than 15 birds that had attracted no buyers. The same source reports that ranchowners in the Pantanal region of Brazil and Bolivia repeatedly stated that they were unhappy with the decline of the species on their ranches (constituting approximately 57,900 square miles [150,000 square kilometers] of privately owned ranches) many no longer allow bird catchers on or near their land. Munn *et al.* (1987) also reports similar sentiments from several ranchers in northeast Brazil. Furthermore, all local Brazilian officials and military officers who helped the survey scientists in regions of the Pantanal near the border with Paraguay (one of the areas where the parrot has been hit hardest by bird catchers) were very supportive of the survey efforts and were extremely helpful with information and logistics. Their enthusiasm for scientific studies on the hyacinth macaw seemed to go beyond the usual Brazilian hospitality, extroversion, and friendliness, and indicated a new environmental awareness and sensitivity among *most* Brazilians. Local support is indispensable to the survival of the hyacinth macaw in the wild.

Munn *et al.* (1987) met a number of dedicated Brazilian, Bolivian, and Paraguayan conservation officials and private conservationists who demonstrated the desire and ability to fight for the future of the hyacinth macaw and other endangered species in their countries. Typically working with small budgets and limited support from higher government officials, these people nevertheless are making progress in implementing and enforcing regional and national conservation laws. The question is whether they will be able to act quickly and effectively enough to stabilize the increasingly grim environmental and social situations in their countries.

At the international level, in 1987 the then-96 member countries of CITES voted to outlaw all international trade in wild-caught hyacinth macaws. But despite CITES protection, more than 700 hyacinth macaws were trapped and traded from August 1987 to November 1988 (Tomsen unpubl.). This alarming amount of trade has led to new, sterner measures in Brazil and internationally in an attempt to stem this devastating trade. It is evident that CITES regulations alone cannot be effective in stopping or regulating the trade in the species.

Recently, several groups recognized the hyacinth macaw's decline and teamed up to address it. The CITES Secretariat, Wildlife Conservation International of the New York Zoological Society, TRAFFIC(U.S.A) of the World Wildlife Fund, and the International Council for Bird Preservation joined forces with the Brazilian government's Forestry Development Institute to launch a hyacinth macaw study that is the basis of this chapter. The Brazilian government's mining company, Companhia Vale do Rio Doce, the Brazilian Foundation for the Conservation of Nature, and numerous Brazilian and Bolivian ranchowners were especially helpful to the field survey. With their dedication to the protection of the region's natural heritage, these organizations and people will continue to support efforts to conserve the hyacinth macaw.

PROGNOSIS

The hyacinth macaw will survive if the bird trade can be stopped and its food and nest sites protected from future development. Better data on the volume of illegal trade in the next few years will tell whether the trade has slowed or is continuing unabated. If the trade slows or stops, then the species is virtually assured of survival in the Pantanal region for many decades. Even if the bird trade stops, however, meat hunting and habitat alteration in northeast Brazil remail threats. In

Pará, meat hunting, the sale to tourists of feathers in Indian artisan goods, and forest destruction virtually assure the species' continued decline.

The species will almost certainly decline steadily in northeast Brazil and Pará in the coming years, but it is possible that it will stabilize or increase slowly in the Pantanal if people provide nest boxes and keep nest trees from being cut.

RECOMMENDATIONS

The global survival of the hyacinth macaw requires principally: (1) improved enforcement of existing conservation laws in Brazil, Bolivia, and Paraguay; (2) strict international enforcement of the global trade ban on wild birds; and (3) international pressure on countries that permit smugglers operating within their borders—especially Paraguay, Bolivia, and recently, Argentina, who by far are the worst offenders—and on those countries that allow the import of the birds.

Further study of the species' distribution and biology also would be useful to its conservation. Of particular use would be research on the breeding biology of the birds living in different parts of the Pantanal to determine the possible effect of a shortage of nest sites on reproductive rates. If the data demonstrate a shortage of nest sites, then individuals or organizations should experiment with erecting nest boxes for the birds. Since many palm-forested parts of the Pantanal have lost all their hyacinth macaws to the bird trade, the remaining individuals should have plenty of food to eat and space in which to reproduce. Thus, if food is not limiting, and nest sites are sufficiently abundant, the species most likely could expand its population and reoccupy suitable habitat.

If the bird trade can be discontinued in northeast Brazil and in Pará, then the next step would be to improve the nutritional status of the local people so that they do not have to hunt the birds for food. Likewise, Indian tribes should be prohibited from selling hyacinth macaw feathers commercially (the traditional ceremonial use of such feathers may be relatively harmless).

These suggestions will require implementation of plans for sustained development that currently are not welcomed by many local and national policymakers in Brazil. It can only be hoped that the efforts of all people, whether Brazilians or concerned citizens of other nations, will strengthen the environmental movement in Brazil and Latin America and bring an end to the current policies of environmental, social, and economic destruction for one-time gain. Instead, scientifically sound development policies must be sought to provide sustainable growth and a decent quality-of-life for all citizens. Otherwise, there will be no way to keep the hyacinth macaws of northeast Brazil and Pará from becoming meat for the stew-pot.

REFERENCES

Forshaw, J.M. 1981. *Parrots of the World*. Second Edition. David and Charles Ltd. Newton Abbot, London.

Inskipp, T., S. Broad, and R. Luxmoore. 1988. "Significant trade in wildlife: A review of selected species in CITES Appendix II," in Volume II: *Birds*. IUCN and the CITES Secretariat.

Munn, C.A., J.B. Thomsen, and C. Yamashita. 1987. Population Survey and Status of the Hyacinth Macaw (*Anodorhynchus hyacinthinus*) in Brazil, Bolivia, and Paraguay. Report to the Secretariat of the Convention on International Trade in Endangered Species of Wild Fauna and Flora. Lausanne, Switzerland.

———. 1988. "Macaw biology in Manu National Park, Peru." *Parrotletter* 1:18–21.

Nilsson, G. 1985. Importation of Birds Into the United States, 1981–1984. Animal Welfare Institute. Washington, D.C.

———. and D. Mack. 1980. "Macaws: Traded to extinction?" TRAFFIC(U.S.A.) *Special Report* 2:1–136.

Remsen, V. and R.S. Ridgely. 1980. "Additions to the avifauna of Bolivia." *Condor* 82:69–75.

Ridgely, R.S. 1982. The Distribution, Status, and Conservation of Neotropical Mainland Parrots. Ph.D. dissertation. Yale University.

Sick, H. 1969. "Aves brasileiras ameacadas de extinção e noçoes gerais de conservação de aves do Brasil." *An. Acad. Brasil. Cienc.* 41 (supl.):205–229.

———. 1984. *Ornithologia Brasileira, Uma Introducao*. Editora Universidade de Brasilia. Brasilia, Brazil.

Sweet, D.G. and G.B. Nash. 1981. *Struggle and Survival in Colonial America*. University of California Press. Berkeley, California.

Thomsen, J.B. and C.A. Munn. 1988. "*Cyanopsitta spixii*: A non-recovery report." *Parrotletter* 1:6–7.

———. and A. Brantigan. In press. "Sustainable utilization of neotropical parrots," *in* J.G. Robinson and K.H. Redford eds., *Neotropical Wildlife Use and Conservation*. University of Chicago Press. Chicago, Illinois.

Charles A. Munn is an associate research zoologist for Wildlife Conservation International, a division of the New York Zoological Society. He is a member of the IUBP/SSC Parrot Specialist Group.

Jorgen B. Thomsen is senior program officer at TRAFFIC(U.S.A.), a division of the World Wildlife Fund. He is a member of the ICBP/SSC Parrot Specialist Group and the editor of Parrotletter.

Carlos Yamashita is a member of the IUBP/SSC Parrot Specialist Group. He has studied birds throughout most of South America since the early 1970s, and is currently finishing a graduate degree at the University of Sao Paulo.

As humans settled into the lower Rio Grande Valley, ocelots were perse-cuted as varmints and furbearers. Today, the clearing of brush for grazing, farming, and housing developments has greatly decreased and fragmented the species's prime habitat in southern Texas and Mexico. *Robert W. Parvin*

The Ocelot

David E. Brown
Consulting Wildlife Biologist

SPECIES DESCRIPTION AND NATURAL HISTORY

The ocelot or *tigrillo* (*Felis pardalis*) is a spotted cat about the size of a bobcat (*Lynx rufus*). An adult ocelot weighs from 12 to 25 pounds (5.4 to 11.4 kilograms), and ranges in length (including the tail) from 34 to 50 inches (864 to 1,270 millimeters). As with most cats, the male tends to be slightly larger than the female (Goldman 1943, Laack and Rappole 1986, 1987, Twedt and Rappole 1986). Four to five black parallel stripes are present on the neck, and the tawny-gray fur of the back and flanks is attractively marked with chocolate-colored splotches bordered in black. The striped head is brownish or gray in color and the spotted underparts are whitish.

The ocelot can be identified by its striking spotted and lined markings, relatively long legs, small head, and short tail. When illuminated by artificial light, the eyes reflect a golden rather than green light (Spicer 1988).

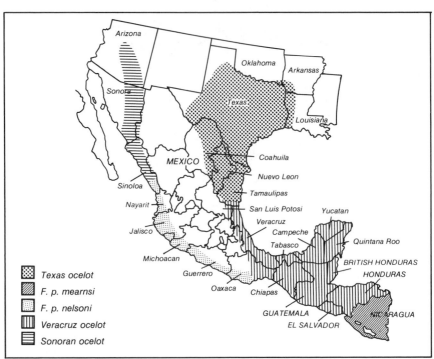

Figure 1. Historic ranges of the five North American races of the ocelot (Hall and Kelson 1959).

Taxonomy and Distribution

Of the four species of native cats still known to reside in the United States[1], the ocelot's distribution is the most restricted. Although this neotropical species is found from Texas to Argentina, breeding ocelots in the United States may now be confined to the four southernmost counties in Texas (Tewes and Everett 1982, Smith 1982, Harwell and Siminski 1985).

Of the five subspecies of *Felis pardalis* recognized by Goldman (1943) (see Figure 1) as occurring in North and Central America, two have been recorded within the boundaries of the United States. The type specimen of the small, pale Texas ocelot (*F.p. albescens*) was collected in 1855

1. The other species are the cougar (*Felis concolor*), also known as the panther or mountain lion; Canada lynx (*Lynx canadensis*); and bobcat. The present status of the jaguarundi as a resident species in the wild is uncertain (Laack and Rappole 1987b). The jaguar, once widely distributed in Texas and Arizona, has now been extirpated from the United States.

in southwest Arkansas, and described as ranging from the Red River drainage southward through Texas and western Louisiana to eastern Coahuila and Nuevo Leon, Mexico, into Tamaulipas; there, it merged with the larger Veracruz ocelot (*F.p. pardalis*) (Hall and Kelson 1959).

The type specimen of the even smaller Sonoran ocelot (*F.p. sonoriensis*) comes from the Rio Mayo drainage in southern Sonora; animals collected from Arizona southward to central Sinaloa have been assigned to this subspecies (Goldman 1943, Hall and Kelson 1959, Hoffmeister 1981). The Texas and Sonoran subspecies are isolated by the highlands of the central Mexican plateau and did not interbreed in historic times. Although both U.S. races are small and pale, the skull of *F.p. albescens* is described as more elongate and thus distinguishable from *F.p. sonoriensis*. Two other subspecies—*F.p. nelsoni* in western Mexico and *F.p. mearnsi* in Central America—have been described as occurring farther south in North America (Goldman 1943).

Because of habitat destruction, the distribution of the Texas ocelot is now much reduced and fragmented (Tewes and Everett 1982, Harwell and Siminski 1985); the only known U.S. populations are restricted to southern Texas (see Figure 2).

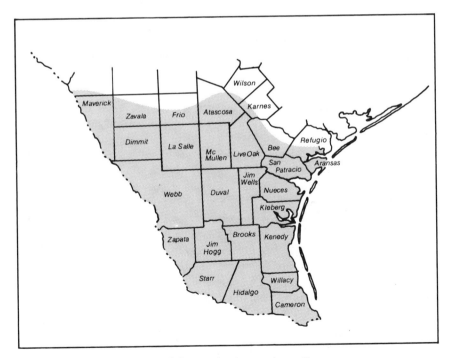

Figure 2. Probable range of the ocelot in southern Texas.

Both the historical and present status of the ocelot in Arizona are somewhat enigmatic. Unlike the jaguar (*Panthera onca*) or *ohshad*, no native Arizonan word for ocelot exists (Saxton and Enos 1983). Definite accounts of ocelots are also absent from the accounts of early explorers (Davis 1982), although E.A. Mearns mentions reports of ocelots in southern Arizona in his unpublished field notes. After Mearns' siting, an ocelot was not recorded again from Arizona until a predator-control agent of the U.S. Biological Survey (now the Animal and Plant Health Inspection Service) reported taking one during fiscal year 1931–1932. No details were given on the animal's sex, location, or the circumstances of its capture and disposition. In 1963, another ocelot was observed near the San Simon River in Cochise County by three seasonal employees of the Bureau of Land Management. In 1964, two hunters killed a large male ocelot in dense oak-pine woodland in the Huachuca Mountains. This animal is the only recently documented ocelot from Arizona.

Additional ocelots may have been taken after 1964, but the protected status, imposed in 1970, made hunters unwilling to report them. There are indications that since 1980 at least four ocelots have been inadvertently caught by trappers (N. Woolsey pers. comm., R. Massey pers. comm.). Two of these were reportedly taken in dense mesquite thickets in the San Pedro Valley; one was reported to be a female that showed evidence of nursing kittens. More recently, another animal was reported taken in the Holbrook–Concho area in northern Arizona.

Although unlikely, ocelots taken in Arizona since 1900 may have been purposefully released and the species cannot yet be considered a "native." A more reasonable explanation for these erratic occurrences is that the animals represent individual incursions of ocelots wandering into Arizona via corridors of subtropical vegetation adjacent to the Yaqui and San Miquel rivers in Sonora, Mexico (Lawler and VanDevender 1984).

Despite a lack of museum specimens, ocelots are known to occur in northern and central Sonora. The same hunter who killed the ocelot in the Huachucas reported killing one in similar habitat around 1966 in the Sierra Azul; a 49-inch ocelot was reported taken in 1974 in the same location. The skins of ocelots taken by trappers have also been observed by biologists near Arizpe in northern Sonora and along the Yaqui River in central Sonora. The possibility exists that the ocelot may be expanding its range as have javelina (*Tayassu tajacu*), coati (*Nasua nasua*), and other recent neotropic invaders to the Southwest. Unless Sonoran populations of the ocelot are depleted through overhunting or habitat degradation, this species may yet become a resident of Arizona via immigration.

Habitat and Home Range

Ocelots prefer humid forests and scrublands of dense, impenetrable cover or rough broken terrain within a tropic-subtropic or warm-temperature environment (Barnes 1899, Bailey 1905, Harwell and Siminski 1985). At the northern edge of their range, they are primarily found in semideciduous forests along streams, in dense thornscrub, and in forests of evergreen oak (*Quercus* spp.) and cedar, or "encinal" (*Juniperus* spp.). Trapping and marking studies in southern Texas have shown that their primary habitats are in dense and varied thickets with a canopy cover composed of greater than 75 percent granjeno (*Celtis pallida*), hogplum (*Colubrina texensis*), wolfberry (*Lycium berlandieri*), shrubby blue sage (*Salvia ballotaeflora*), coyotillo (*Karwinskia humboltiana*), whitebrush (*Aloysia lycioides*), ebony (*Pithecellobium flexicaule*), wild olive (*Cordia boissieri*), brasil (*Condalia obovata*), colima (*Zanthoxylum fagara*), mesquite (*Prosopis glandulosa*), and other trees and shrubs characteristic of the Tamaulipan biotic province (Tewes and Everett 1982). Other important habitats are encinal forests and thickets dominated by live oaks (*Quercus virginiana*) (Twedt and Rappole 1986).

Arizona habitats where ocelots have been reported are mostly riverbottom forests of mesquite (*Prosopis velutina*), hackberry (*Celtis reticulata*), and other subtropical trees and shrubs, or warm-temperature *encinals* of oaks, junipers, and pines (for example, *pinus cembroides* and *P. leiophylla*). Thus, the Texas and Arizona ocelot populations share analogous habitats (Brown 1982).

Preliminary data from two radio-trapped ocelots on Laguna Atascosa National Wildlife Refuge in Texas suggest that ocelots have dumbbell-shaped home ranges averaging slightly more than a square mile, with the male's home range being larger than that of the female (Tewes and Everett 1982). Night hunting forays may cover up to a mile or more. Territories may be smaller in prime habitat. Ocelots have been documented in the 2,000-acre Santa Ana National Wildlife Refuge and the 39-acre Audubon Sabal Palm Grove Sanctuary. In both cases, extensive areas of cleared, cultivated land around the small habitats suggest that native ocelots are confined to these smaller, protected areas.

Breeding

Female ocelots are not sexually mature until their second year (Harwell and Siminski 1985). Most breeding occurs in summer, with the young born in the fall after a gestation period of approximately 80 days (Tewes and Everett 1982, Harwell and Siminski 1985, Laack and

Rappole 1986). The kittens are born blind and nearly hairless; nests are generally in a rocky den, hollow log, or especially dense thicket that is lined with grass or other material (Spicer 1988). The usual litter size is two, but from one to three kittens have been reported (Bailey 1905, Harwell and Siminski 1985). How long young are dependent on their mother is unknown.

Feeding

Ocelots are generally solitary and nocturnal, although mated animals may sometimes hunt in pairs (Tewes and Everett 1982, Spicer 1988). Prey consists of small- to medium-sized mammals—for example, rabbits, and birds, reptiles, and amphibians—that are obtained by stalking and pouncing. Although most hunting is on-the-ground, ocelots are adept at traveling and hunting in trees, where they are sometimes seen stretched out asleep on a limb. Ocelots are good swimmers and individuals may spend considerable time foraging along streams.

Longevity and Mortality

The ages of dead and live-trapped ocelots on Laguna Atascosa National Wildlife Refuge and on private lands in Willacy County, Texas, were estimated to range from two to nine years (Tewes and Everett 1982,

The ocelot can be identified by its striking spotted and lined markings, relatively long legs, small head, and short tail. The eyes reflect a golden light. *Runk/Shoenberger/Grant Heilman Photography*

Twedt and Rappole 1986, Laack and Rappole 1987a). Therefore, it can be assumed that ocelots can live up to, and perhaps exceed, 10 years of age in the wild.

Prior to federal and state protection, ocelots were vulnerable to hunting with hounds (Barnes 1899, Bailey 1905). The species is not particularly difficult to trap and was susceptible to predator-control programs (Spicer 1988). Currently, the most frequently reported deaths are caused by automobiles. The animals are killed when they travel on paved highways between isolated tracts of habitat (Laack and Rappole 1987a).

Diseases and Parasites. Necropsy results from one road-kill and blood smears from five captured ocelots revealed no significant parasitism or exposure to feline pathogens (Harwell and Siminski 1985, Laack and Rappole 1987a). Additional testing for feline distemper and other diseases is needed, however, before any definitive statements can be made regarding the health of Texas populations.

SIGNIFICANCE OF THE SPECIES

In Texas, the ocelot is the largest remaining neotropical predator representative of the Tamaulipan biotic province. As the top-ranking member of the food chain, the ocelot's presence is an important indicator of the health and size of the Tamaulipan semideciduous forest and thornscrub biotic communities. The fact that it also is one of the nation's most attractive and least harmful cats provides additional incentive to acquire and preserve these endangered biomes. If ocelots reside in southern Arizona, they would represent a similar, analogous example of a predatory mammal associated with the Sinaloan biotic province; as in Texas, the presence of this popular animal would facilitate acquisition and preservation of the unique subtropical ecosystem.

HISTORICAL PERSPECTIVE

Ocelots once occurred throughout southern and eastern Texas and may formerly have ranged into southwestern Louisiana (Tewes and Everett 1982). Although most museum specimens are from Tamaulipan semideciduous forest and thornscrub communities in the lower Rio Grande Valley, breeding animals have also been recorded within *encinal* communities of oaks and cedars as far north as the Edwards Plateau and the Palo Pinto Hills (Barnes 1899, Bailey 1905). Constantly persecuted as a varmint and a furbearer, ocelots were steadily reduced in number as human settlement occurred. Since 1900, however, the greatest threat to the species has been "brush" clearing in the Rio Grande Valley and other southern Texas locales for grazing, farming, and housing development. By 1960, 99 percent of prime ocelot habitat in southern Texas had been cleared for agriculture (Cottam and Trefethen 1968). Although begun later, the clearing of brushlands across the river in Tamaulipas, Mexico, has been equally or even more detrimental to ocelots; the removal of the once extensive floodplain forests in the Rio Grande Valley has greatly fragmented the species' available habitat and distribution.

CURRENT TRENDS

In 1982, the U.S. Fish and Wildlife Service (FWS) listed the ocelot as endangered in the United States. The recent status of the ocelot in Texas has been discussed and mapped by Davis (1974), McBride (1976), Smith (1982), and Tewes and Everett (1982). Increases in reported observations after 1985 may be due to greater public awareness, more recreational visits to ocelot habitat, or a recovery in ocelot populations brought on by protective measures and habitat acquisition (G. Homerstad pers. comm.). Ocelots are known to reside in Laguna Atascosa National Wildlife Refuge, where the population in 1988 was estimated at 6 to 7 males, 18 to 20 females, and an unknown number of young animals (Rappole pers. comm.). Ocelots are also known to be present on Santa Ana National Wildlife Refuge and are thought to reside at a number of sites along the lower Rio Grande (for example, Bentsen State Park). Some of these populations may now be isolated as incursions of animals coming into Texas from Tamaulipas are becoming increasingly infrequent due to the almost total elimination of forest and thornscrub along the Mexican side of the Rio Grande[2] in Mexico. Ocelots are already considered extinct in the border state of Nuevo Leon (Guzman 1981). The status of the species in Arizona is unknown.

MANAGEMENT

Since 1981, the Texas Parks and Wildlife Department has mailed annual survey questionnaires to hunters, trappers, biologists, and others

---

2. Rio Bravo is the Mexican name for the Rio Grande from the Rio Grande's confluence with the Rio Conchos to the Gulf.

requesting that they report any ocelot or jaguarundi (*Felis yagou-aroundi*) sightings. When received, these observations are evaluated, rated according to probable validity, and mapped. The most promising areas are visited and surveyed through the use of live traps or camera sets. If ocelots are present, steps can then be taken to protect or acquire their habitat.

FWS intends to expand the Lower Rio Grande Valley National Wildlife Refuge in the four southernmost Texas counties to benefit the ocelot and 114 other wildlife species (Harwell and Siminski 1985); ten district communities will be protected and connected by corridors. The goal of this program is to increase the amount of land under the jurisdiction of federal, state, and private organizations from 33,000 to 107,500 acres. The ocelot recovery program managers are also working to assure that habitats already under federal jurisdiction are preserved and maintained in compliance with Section 7 of the Endangered Species Act. Habitat acquisition and preservation is thus the major thrust of the ocelot recovery effort. Although the official recovery plan is not yet completed, its release is expected in 1989.

In the meantime, the Caesar Kleberg Wildlife Research Institute is conducting studies into the distribution, abundance, and habitat preferences of both the ocelot and jaguarundi in south Texas (Tewes and Everett 1982, Twedt and Rappole 1986, Laack and Rappole 1987b). In addition to collecting basic biological data pertinent to the future management of these endangered felines, the researchers are evaluating the effectiveness of road culverts and other devices in reducing highway mortality.

The only research done on ocelots in Arizona was a preliminary live-trap survey to determine if they were present on the San Pedro River Conservation Area recently acquired by the Bureau of Land Management; no ocelots were found (N. Woolsey pers. comm.).

PROGNOSIS

The prognosis for the future of the ocelot in Texas can be best described as guardedly optimistic. The present population of ocelots on Laguna Atascosa National Wildlife Refuge may be large enough to maintain a viable population, and these cats are believed to still be well distributed in southern Texas. If the long-term plan of wildlife management agencies to acquire and manage at least 100,000 acres of the remaining semideciduous forest and other native habitats in the Rio Grande Valley is successful, the ocelot will probably survive in Texas. Otherwise, the continuing loss of habitat threatens the survival of this cat along with other neotropical species (Harwell and Siminski 1985).

FWS has already acquired 58 parcels at a cost of $39,000,000; the Texas Parks and Wildlife Department has obtained another 13 tracts; and other areas have been acquired as state parks and private refuges.

RECOMMENDATIONS

The principal need of the ocelot in Texas is the continuation and acceleration of the aggressive land-acquisition program being conducted in the lower Rio Grande Valley by FWS, the Texas Parks and Wildlife Department, and private conservation organizations. Special emphasis should be given to acquiring the remaining tracts of Tamaulipan riparian semideciduous forest and areas of dense thornscrub or *encinals* shown to harbor resident ocelots. Land management agencies also should consider increasing the size of tracts already in public ownership. Once acquired, these lands should be managed for ocelots and other species characteristic of Tamaulipan biotic communities, such as white-winged doves (*Zenaida asiatica*) and chachalaca (*Ortalis vetula*). Management practices would consist of protecting existing thickets and allowing cleared areas to revert to brush. Cleared areas should be restocked with native trees and shrubs if necessary. Under no circumstances should brush be cleared from public lands where ocelots are present.

To prevent the isolation of Texas ocelot populations and provide a connecting corridor with other populations farther south, the preservation of at least some remnants of the ocelot's rapidly disappearing habitats in Tamaulipas, Mexico, is urgently needed. Some of these colonies, such as the 100,000-acre Parras de la Fuente Forest and the secluded El Comanche Forest tracts in the central part of the state, undoubtedly contain ocelots. Attempts by The Nature Conservancy's Mexico Borderlands Program and Ducks Unlimited of Mexico to preserve these and similar areas in conjunction with the Mexican government should be strongly encouraged.

In the meantime, the ongoing effort to document the occurrence and status of ocelots should continue with emphasis on verifying the species' presence in areas where it is known to occur. Life-history studies should also be continued as a means of determining the ocelot's habitat requirements and limiting factors. Hunters, trappers, and animal-damage-control agents should be advised of areas where ocelots occur, and leg-hold traps and head snares should be banned in those areas.

It is likely that some lands within the ocelot's historic range are of suitable size and quality to support an ocelot population, but which are presently uninhabited by ocelots due to past extirpation. In these areas a restocking program using wild-trapped ocelots from Laguna Atascosa National Wildlife Refuge or other donor populations should be considered as a restoration measure. Restocking of ocelots is not universally endorsed, however. The few translocations efforts in Texas have met with mixed success. Some cats have attempted to return to their home territories, often at great jeopardy. Critics of translocation also note the risks of transferring disease and genetic inferiority. In addition, in some translocation areas it took years to prove that the restocking effort was successful as shown by the trapping of resident ocelots. Those who oppose translocation would rather focus on habitat acquisition and connecting corridors that allow for natural distribution of young ocelots.

The status of the ocelot in Arizona needs to be investigated. A mail survey of trappers and small-game hunters—coupled with follow-up investigations—as conducted in Texas, would be a logical beginning. Intensive surveys of select subtropical woodland habitats along the lower San Pedro River Valley between Benson and Winkleman should be initiated to determine whether the species is a permanent resident of Arizona. Fecal studies, infrared photography, and live trapping could also be employed. If ocelots are found, key habitats could then be acquired through land exchanges or purchases. If no ocelots are found—and qualified biologists judge that the habitat adjacent to the San Pedro River is suitable for ocelots—a release program using captive-bred Sonoran ocelots might be considered as a method of establishing the species in Arizona.

The status of the ocelot in Sonora also needs to be investigated. Of particular interest is the animal's status along the watersheds of the Yaqui, San Miquel, and Sonora rivers, which provide subtropical travel corridors into Arizona. If ocelots reside along the northern courses of these rivers, a habitat preservation program for select areas would be of scientific interest and possibly benefit ocelots and other wildlife species in both the United States and Mexico.

REFERENCES

Arizona Game and Fish Department. 1988. Threatened Native Wildlife in Arizona. Phoenix, Arizona. 26 pp.

Bailey, V. 1905. "Biological survey of Texas." *North American Fauna 25:* 1–222.

Barnes, S.D. 1899. "Hunting the leopard cat." *Outdoor Life* 3:3 (unnumbered pages).

Brown, D.E. 1982. "Biotic communities of the American Southwest U.S. and Mexico." *Desert Plants* 4:1–342.

Burt, W.H. 1961. "A fauna from an Indian site near Redington, Arizona." *Journal of Mammalogy* 42:115–116.

Convention on International Trade in Endangered Species of Wild Fauna and Flora

(CITES). 1983. CITES Appendices—Mammals. U.S. Department of the Interior. Washington, D.C.

Cottam, C. and J.B. Trefethen (eds). 1968. *Whitewings*. D. Van Nostrand Company. Princeton, New Jersey. 348 pp.

Davis, G.P., Jr. 1982. *Man and Wildlife in Arizona: The American Exploration Period, 1824–1865*. Arizona Game and Fish Department. 232 pp.

Davis, W.B. 1974. "The mammals of Texas." *Texas Parks and Wildlife Department Bulletin* 41:1–252.

Goldman, E.A. 1943. "The races of the ocelot and margay in Middle America." *Journal of Mammalogy* 24:372–385.

Guzman, A.J. 1981. "Especies en peligro y proceso de desaparicion en Nuevo Leon, Mexico." *Centre de Investigaciones Biologicas del lan UANL Bulletin* 8. 2 pp.

Harwell, G. and D.P. Siminski. 1985. Recovery Plan for the Listed Cats of Arizona and Texas (technical draft). U.S. Fish and Wildlife Service. Albuquerque, New Mexico. 31 pp.

Hall, E.R. and K.R. Kelson. 1959. *The Mammals of North America*. Two volumes. Ronald Press Company. New York. 1,078 pp.

Hoffmeister, D.F. 1986. *Mammals of Arizona*. University of Arizona Press. Arizona Game and Fish Department. Tucson, Arizona. 602 pp.

International Union for the Conservation of Nature [RM] (IUCN). 1978. *Red Data Book, I. Mammalia: Ocelot*. IUCN. Morges, Switzerland.

Laack, L. and J.H. Rappole. 1986. Investigation into the Basic Ecology of the Ocelot in Texas. Final report. Caesar Kleberg Wildlife Resources Institute. Kingsville, Texas. 7 pp.

———. and ———. 1987a. Investigation into the Basic Ecology of the Ocelot in Texas. Final report. Caesar Kleberg Wildlife Research Institute. Kingsville, Texas. 19 pp.

———. and ———. 1987b. History of the Jaguarundi road-kill from Cameron County, Texas. Report to the U.S. Fish and Wildlife Service. Caesar Kleberg Wildlife Research Institute. Kingsville, Texas. 5 pp.

Lawler, H. and T. Van Devender. 1984. "Tropical Sonora: Rancho La Brisca." *Sonorensis* 6:5–10.

Leopold, A.S. 1959. *Wildlife of Mexico: The Game Birds and Mammals*. University of California Press. Berkeley, California. 568 pp.

Lindsay, E.H. and N.T. Tessman. 1974. "Cenozoic vertebrate localities and faunas in Arizona." *Journal of the Arizona Academy of Science*. 9:3–24.

McBride, R.R. 1976. Ocelot Survey. Fish and wildlife special report. Albuquerque, New Mexico. 7 pp.

Navarro-Lopez, D., M.E. Tewes, D.D. Everett, and J.H. Rappole. 1984. Historical and pre-Historic Distribution of the Ocelot in North America. *Annual Report* of the Caesar Kleberg Wildlife Research Institute. Kingsville, Texas. 33 pp.

Saxton, D.L. and S. Enos. 1983. *Dictionary: Papago/Pima–English; English–Papago/Pima*. University of Arizona Press. Tucson, Arizona. 145 pp.

Smith, J.C. 1982. Nongame Wildlife Investigations: Feline Status Study. F.A. Project W-103, R-11, personal report. Texas Parks and Wildlife Department. Austin, Texas. 6 pp.

Spicer, R.B. 1988. "Ocelot." *Wildlife Views*. Nongame field notes. Arizona Game and Fish Department. Phoenix, Arizona. 20 pp.

Tewes, M.E. and D.D. Everett. 1982. Studies of the Endangered Ocelot Occurring in Texas. Year-end Report. Contract #14-16-0002-81-229. Caesar Kleberg Wildlife Research Institute. Kingsville, Texas. 52 pp.

Texas Parks and Wildlife Department. 1977. Regulations for Taking, Possessing, Transporting, Exporting, Processing, Selling, or Offering for Sale, or Shipping Endangered Species. Texas Parks and Wildlife Department 127.30.0.001–.006. Austin, Texas.

Tomlinson, R.E. 1987. White-winged Dove Nesting Colonies in Tamaulipas and Nuevo Leon, Mexico. Trip Report, June 1987. U.S. Department of the Interior, Fish and Wildlife Service. Albuquerque, New Mexico. 10 pp.

Twedt, D.J. and J.H. Rappole. 1986. Distribution, Abundance and Habitat Preference of Ocelot and Jaguarundi in South Texas. Final report. Caesar Kleberg Wildlife Research Institute. Kingsville, Texas. 7 pp.

David E. Brown, former game branch supervisor for the Arizona Game and Fish Department, is the author of several books on wildlife, including The Wolf in the Southwest *and* The Grizzly in the Southwest. *He has visited ocelot habitats in Texas, Arizona, Mexico, Belize, and Costa Rica and is presently working on a book about the mountain lions and jaguars of the American Southwest.*

The author wishes to thank Mike Tewes and John Rappole for their useful review comments and additional information.

Its apparent dependence on old-growth trees has placed the marbled murrelet, like the spotted owl, in the center of ongoing controversies regarding the fate of the Pacific Northwest's remaining stands of ancient forest. *Diana Bradshaw*

The Marbled Murrelet

David B. Marshall
Consulting Wildlife Biologist

SPECIES DESCRIPTION AND NATURAL HISTORY

The marbled murrelet (*Brachyramphus marmoratus*) is a robin-sized seabird belonging to the alcid family, which consists of 21 species worldwide (including puffins and auklets); most occur in arctic and Pacific waters. The marbled murrelet differs from the only other member of its genus, Kittlitz's murrelet (*B. brevirostris*), in bill length, plumage color, behavior, distribution, and habitat requirements. Both sexes of the marbled murrelet have identical plumages, but breeding and wintering plumages are distinct. Breeding adults have sooty-brown upperparts with dark wing bars. Underparts are light, mottled brown. Winter adults have brownish-gray upperparts except for a white band below the nape that extends up from white underparts. Fall juveniles are similar to wintering adults except for faint brownish mottling on the chest, breast, and sides. Winter juveniles take on characteristics of adult winter plumage.

Like other alcids, the marbled murrelet presents a dumpy appearance, with its relatively large head, short neck and tail, and heavy compact body. Its stubby wings and rear-placed legs enable the bird to excel underwater in pursuit of fish, but on land the marbled murrelet is awkward and often propels itself in a prone position using both wings and legs. In flight the murrelet's body seems cigar-shaped; it flies at high speeds with a rapid, swift-like wingbeat to compensate for the small wing surface area. While on water both the bill and the short tail point upward. The murrelet's main call-note is a gull-like "keer-keer."

Taxonomy and Distribution

Two subspecies of the marbled murrelet are recognized by the American Ornithologists' Union (American Ornithologists' Union 1957). The two are distinguishable by bill length and body weight (Sealy *et al.* 1982). *B. m. marmoratus* is the North American form and *B. m. perdix* occurs in Asia.

The North American subspecies of the marbled murrelet occurs in summer along the Pacific Coast from the Kenai Peninsula and the Barren and Aleutian islands in Alaska, south to Santa Barbara County in south-central California (see Figure 1). The marbled murrelet winters mostly within the same general area, but tends to vacate the most northern sections of its range and has been recorded as far south as Imperial Beach, San Diego, California. The murrelet breeds throughout

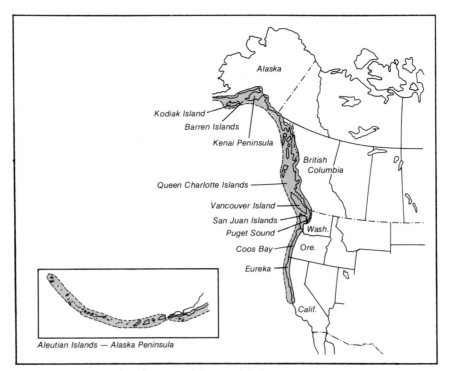

Figure 1. Summer distribution of the marbled murrelet in North America.

its summer range as confirmed by observations of young murrelets off-shore, the finding of grounded young or nests, and collections of adults with brood patches or females with eggs in their oviducts.

The Asiatic form of the marbled murrelet occurs in summer and winter from the Sea of Okhotsk, Kamchatka, and Commander Islands, south to Korea, Japan, and the Kurile Islands.

Foraging

The marbled murrelet occupies a feeding niche in the ocean near shore and in inland saltwater areas—bays, sounds, and saltwater passage-ways—such as those found throughout the Alexander Archipelago of southeast Alaska.

During spring and summer, marbled murrelets are most often seen as singles, pairs, or in small loose aggregations in the ocean immediately offshore and on inland saltwaters such as the Puget Sound–San Juan Islands area and the numerous straits of the inland passage area of British Columbia and Alaska.

The birds tend to gather at the mouths of rivers. During the winter, aggregations can be larger, but overall, marbled murrelets are found closer to shore and tend to flock less frequently than other alcids. Food consists mainly of small fish and invertebrates. The only food habits studies conducted so far have been off the coast of British Columbia and in Kachemak Bay, Alaska (Sealy 1975a, Sanger and Jones 1981, Carter 1984, Sanger 1987). Important forage fish found in these areas include sand lance (*Ammodytes hexapterus*), Pacific herring (*Clupea harengus*), capelin (*Mallotus villosus*), and the invertebrates *Euphausia pacifica* and *Thysanoessa spinifera*. Direct observations of feeding and carrying fish inland at dusk demonstrate that marbled murrelets feed during the day, yet Carter and Sealy (1984) found gill-net mortality occurred almost exclusively at night, indicating nocturnal feeding as well.

The marbled murrelet's feeding habits make it highly subject to mortality in gill-net fisheries. Carter and Sealy (1984) first identified a problem with salmon gill-net mortalities during a study conducted in 1979 and 1980 in Barkley Sound off Vancouver Island, British Columbia. They estimated that in 1980 a total of 380 marbled murrelets were killed by gill nets in the study area, accounting for almost eight percent of the potential fall population in the area. Sealy and Carter (1984) also reported that 600 to more than 800 murrelets are killed yearly in Prince William Sound, Alaska.

Marbled murrelets occasionally occur, and presumably forage, on inland freshwater lakes. Carter and Sealy (1986) analyzed 67 murrelet occurrence records from 33 lakes, 78.6 percent of which were in British Columbia. In May 1984, S.M. Speich (pers. comm.) counted more than 40 marbled murrelets on Lake Quinault, Washington, which is 21 miles (34 kilometers) inland.

Nesting and Flight Behavior

While there are still many missing pieces, some aspects of marbled murrelet reproductive biology are now clear (see "Historical Perspective" for nesting background and chronology). The species nests on the ground where large trees are absent in the northern parts of its range, but farther south nests on large moss-covered branches of old-growth conifers, often many miles from the sea. Like other alcids, only one egg is laid, and sexual maturity is delayed past the first summer after hatching. Subadults, which occur as singles during the period the young are fed, make up 15 percent of the population off Langara Island, British Columbia (Sealy 1975b). From the finding of stranded young and the first appearance of young at sea, it is clear that nesting occurs over an extended period. Egg laying can begin as early as April 15; stranded young have been found as late as September 21 (Carter and

The nesting habits of the marbled murrelet have long been a mystery; however, biologists have concluded that the bird nests both on the ground and in the large, mature trees of the Pacific Northwest. *Diana Bradshaw*

Sealy 1975b, Marshall 1988). Both sexes incubate the egg in 24-hour shifts that are rotated each evening (Simons 1980). Incubation takes about 30 days, and the chick fledges in 28 days (Simons 1980, Hirsch *et al.* 1981). The chick is fed at least once and sometimes twice at dusk by the adults. Usually only one fish is carried to the young (Carter and Sealy 1987a).

Unlike the young of other alcids, which are reared next to the ocean and gain flight after a period at sea, it is generally agreed that marbled murrelet young remain in the nest until they are capable of flying to the sea (Binford *et al.* 1975, Sealy 1975b, Simons 1980). This conclusion is based on four facts: (1) fledglings found at sea can fly; (2) most nests and fledglings found have not been close to streams with adequate water to carry them seaward; (3) an overland journey would be impossible in view of potential predation and considering that murrelets are not anatomically equipped for traveling on land, especially through bushy terrain strewn with downed timber; and (4) there are no reports of fledgling murrelets walking or swimming seaward.

In Washington, Oregon, and California, marbled murrelets are now being located inland through land-based visual and aural detections using transects and fixed-point censuses over forested areas. The activity being recorded consists mainly of flying, which varies from straight courses to circles, figure eights, and other patterns. Generally, one to five birds are observed at a time. The function of the circular and other figured flights is unknown, but the flights occur in known and suspected nesting areas from April or May to September. Peak activity occurs from mid-June to late July in California and from the second week of July to mid-August in Oregon.

Most birds are detected by the "keer-keer" call. They are active 45 minutes before sunrise and up to 1 hour and 45 minutes afterwards. The peak of activity occurs between 20 minutes before and after sunrise. Around sunset, another period of activity erupts, but on a much smaller scale. At present there is no way to translate marbled murrelet detections made at a given location into actual numbers of birds because it is unknown whether the detections represent the same bird or various ones.[1] The function of the morning flights are unknown.

Winter flights inlands are even more of a mystery. Paton *et al.* (1987) detected birds inland every month of the year in California; M.L. McAllister (pers. comm.) also reported winter flights in southeast Alaska and Oregon. H.R. Carter reported that T.G. Sander detected the species on 66 percent of 53 days censused between January 15 and

1. The above description was taken from papers by S. Kim Nelson on Oregon work and by Peter W.C. Paton and C.J. Ralph on California observations that were presented at a workshop in September 1988 conducted by the Marbled Murrelet Technical Committee of the Pacific Seabird Group.

March 11, 1987, at Prairie Redwoods State Park, California (pers. comm.). Carter and Sealy (1986) speculated that the presence of marbled murrelets at inland sites in winter could be related to visitation of nesting areas, possibly involving courtship, pair-bond maintenance, and nest-site prospecting.

One reason for the assumption that the flights relate to nesting comes from at-sea observation. Marbled murrelets are regularly seen in the evening during the nesting season at staging areas at river mouths. Around dusk they either fly up the rivers or gain elevation very rapidly and head overland (Brooks 1926, Jewett *et al.* 1953). Some observers have seen them carrying fish (Guiguet 1956, Drent and Guiguet 1961, Sealy 1975a). Evening activity inland corroborates with the feeding schedule; the change in the 24-hour incubation shifts between male and female occurs at an unknown time of night (Simons 1980).

Habitat Associations

The marbled murrelet's apparent reliance on old-growth forests or forests with old-growth characteristics has been widely recognized (Sowls *et al.* 1980, The Pacific Seabird Group 1982, 1987, Sealy and Carter 1984, Carter and Sealy 1987b). This conclusion is based on the following: (1) all nests found in coniferous forest biomes were in trees possessing old-growth characteristics; (2) downy young have been found only in old-growth forests and fledglings in or near old growth; (3) inland observations of adult marbled murrelets are associated with old-growth and mature forests; and (4) during the nesting season, the species occurs mainly offshore opposite old-growth or mature forest stands in the southern parts of its range. Additional clues suggesting the birds' old-growth preference include their cryptic coloration (breeding plumage matches moss and wood) and a leg structure not adapted for burrowing or extensive walking (Storer 1945).

The species's numbers offshore can be correlated with presence of old growth or trees having old-growth characteristics. For example, in Oregon, the greatest numbers are seen offshore along the central Oregon coast, particularly between Alsea and Coos bays, where most of the Oregon coastal mature and old-growth forests remain (Marshall 1988). Similarly, Sowls *et al.* (1980) reported that marbled murrelets occur in two distinct areas in California—from the Oregon border south to Eureka and from Santa Cruz to Half Moon Bay; the nearly 300-mile (450 + kilometers) section between the two areas has been extensively logged.

The humid forests of the Pacific Northwest in which the marbled murrelet occurs are unique. According to Franklin (1979), "old-growth ecosystems in this region have the greatest biomass accumulations of any plant formations in the temperate zone and, probably the world."

These ecosystems are dominated by coniferous trees, which achieve long lives and large sizes. Dominant species near the coast include Douglas-fir (*Fseudotsuga menziesii*), western hemlock, western red cedar, and Sitka spruce. In southern sections, coast redwood (*Sequoia sempervirens*) is dominant. Old-growth forests consist of many large trees (which show signs of senescence), large snags, numerous downed snags in all stages of decay, and multilayered canopies composed of several tree species. In Oregon, forests begin to exhibit old-growth characteristics at about 175 to 250 years of age. Old growth is preceded by a forest stand described as being "mature" or of the "large saw-timber stage," which begins at about 80 years of age.

It can be concluded that the North American subspecies of the marbled murrelet is a component of the old-growth forests in a major part of its range. From northern British Columbia southward, there is no evidence of nesting, except in trees that are over 150 years old. The possibility also exists that old trees are used for other purposes such as roosting. However, while the marbled murrelet associates with old-growth and mature forests, the possibility exists that it also nests in remnant old-growth trees or groves that are surrounded by younger trees. Such remnants of old-growth forests occur throughout the Pacific Northwest. They are trees that survived fires or were spared by early-day loggers who did not have the equipment or incentives to log every last tree in areas with difficult access. Varoujean tracked a radio-tagged marbled murrelet to a group of scattered old trees in an otherwise young forest during the summer of 1988.

Population Size

Compared to colonial-nesting alcids, the marbled murrelet is difficult to inventory. To date, at-sea inventories have been the only method used for obtaining population estimates. These have been conducted in different ways, according to logistical situations in the area being inventoried. Some inventories have been opportunistic in nature, but others were established specifically for marbled murrelets. Variables in conducting marbled murrelet counts include sea conditions, weather, time, month, tidal conditions—which relate to location of prey, daily movements, inventory techniques (aerial, at-sea, or from shore)—and any mathematical factors used to account for birds present but not seen (including incubating birds). While aerial censuses help overcome the problem of local hourly or daily movements during the census, Speich *et al.* (1988) found that aerial observers overlooked a high percentage of birds actually present, and that sea and lighting conditions affected their observations. This makes establishment of a surface versus aerial visibility factor, as used in other wildlife census work, difficult. All inventory work has been relatively recent; therefore, there has been no opportunity to estimate population changes. Land-based detection—the other inventory method—cannot at present be interpreted to provide population data; however, it does define areas of use.

Alaska.   Alaska and British Columbia, with thousands of miles of shoreline with food resources opposite suitable nesting areas, support most of the marbled murrelets found in North America. Estimates of total number of birds vary widely and reflect the absence of systematic counts. For Alaska there seems to be general agreement as to the major areas of use. M.L. McAllister pointed to three major breeding areas in Alaska with the following marbled murrelet population estimates: Alaska Peninsula, 6,000 to 15,000; Prince William Sound, 15,000 to 20,000; and southeast Alaska, 50,000 to 75,000 (Mendenhall and McAllister 1988). McAllister's figures are much lower than estimates by Islieb and Kessel (1973), who believed that the wintering population in the North Gulf Coast and Prince William Sound region numbered "several hundred thousands, possibly millions." Quinlan and Hughes (1984) cited a publication by Kessel and Gibson (1978), which reported 250,000 marbled murrelets in Prince William Sound; Nelson and Lehnhausen (1983) provided a figure of 250,000 for southeast Alaska.

British Columbia.   While no figures are available for British Columbia in its entirety, Sealy and Carter (1984) estimated a breeding population of 8,640 marbled murrelets in Clayoquot and Barkley sounds on the west coast of Vancouver Island in June 1982. They counted 9,955 individuals on the water and 1,255 birds in flight. On the water they found marbled murrelet population densities to average 21 birds per square mile (8.1 birds per square kilometer).

Washington.   Speich *et al.* (1988) released a current estimate of marbled murrelet numbers of Washington at the 1987 meeting of the Pacific Seabird Group.[2] The data came from both aerial and boat censuses of seabirds. Depending on which sets of assumptions were used, the group estimated that the summer population of marbled murrelets in Washington state stands at between 4,400 and 8,300 individuals, or between 1,900 and 3,500 breeding pairs (if 15 percent were assumed to be subadults). Two-thirds of these birds were in the inland waters of Puget Sound. The group also estimated that an additional 1,000 to 2,000 birds occur during the winter.

Oregon.   In 1986 and 1987, Varoujean and Williams (1987) ran at-sea transects along the Oregon coast between Yaquina and Coos bays.

2. The Pacific Seabird Group is a scientific organization devoted to disseminating information about, and furthering the conservation of, seabirds.

They found marbled murrelet population densities as high as 492 birds per square mile (190 birds per square kilometer). Applying their figures to the entire Oregon coast, they calculated 6,000 individuals (or approximately 2,500 breeding pairs) after removing 15 percent for nonbreeders. However, Varoujean and Williams pointed out that this central stretch of coast between the two bays, which accounts for roughly one-third of the Oregon coastline, is adjacent to most of the state's best remaining marbled murrelet breeding habitat. Data from a 1979 survey of seabird colonies off the Oregon coast also suggest the 2,500-pair figure is an overestimate (Varoujean and Pitman unpubl.).

California. Sowls *et al.* (1980) made 390 sightings of marbled murrelets during the course of seabird surveys conducted in 1980 off California shores. From this sample, they speculated the California summer population to be about 2,000 birds. Coastal waters from Eureka north to the Oregon border and from Santa Cruz north to Half Moon Bay, accounted for 76 percent and 14 percent, respectively, of 185 sightings made during the 1979 breeding season. For all practical purposes, the California birds are considered to be two separately breeding populations. No at-sea surveys have been made off California since 1980, but forest surveys were conducted for murrelets in 1988. C.J. Ralph and P.W.C. Paton found the species to be basically restricted to old-growth forests in state and federal parks and on 20,000 acres (8,100 hectares) of old growth on private land owned by the Pacific Lumber Company. This would provide for the same distribution as reported by Sowls *et al.* (1980).

SIGNIFICANCE OF THE SPECIES

The marbled murrelet is of considerable scientific interest because of its unique and interesting ecological characteristics. This includes nesting in trees many miles from the sea in the southern parts of the murrelet's range as opposed to ground nesting in the north. Juvenile flight to the sea is also unique.

The ecological role of the species is not known, although it is the only alcid along the Pacific Coast that feeds extensively close to shore. The murrelet's presence is dependent on small fish or invertebrates. As an indicator species of its marine environment, King and Sanger (1979) and Manuwal *et al.* (1979) noted that the species has the highest oil:bird-vulnerability index of seabirds in southeastern Alaska and the straits of Juan de Fuca and Georgia in Washington and British Columbia.

From an economic standpoint, protection of the marbled murrelet could mean foregoing some logging of mature and old-growth timber,

The marbled murrelet is a seabird belonging to the alcid family. *Diana Bradshaw*

and could call for changes in gill-net fishing practices. Like the spotted owl (*Strix occidentalis*), the marbled murrelet may be an indicator species for old-growth forests and as such could cause a further restriction on the cutting of old-growth or mature trees in areas of the species' use. (See "The Spotted Owl" chapter in the 1986 *Audubon Wildlife Report.*)

Under the National Management Forest Act, the U.S. Forest Service is required to maintain viable populations of existing native wildlife species on national forests. Preservation needs of the species could have an adverse short-term economic impact on some coastal communities that have mills that still cut large logs. Yet, despite the economic value of ancient forests, such stands also have scientific, aesthetic, spiritual, recreational, and preservation values that provide long-term economic benefits. However, it is too early to predict if the marbled murrelet will affect timber sales, which depends on timely research findings and actions by government agencies. Changes in gill-netting practices may also be necessary, which may entail some cost. Based on work by Carter and Sealy (1984) in Barkley Sound, British Columbia, such change could entail restrictions to gill-net fishing in certain areas and on night gill-netting.

HISTORICAL PERSPECTIVE

Almost unquestionably, the marbled murrelet has declined in Washington, Oregon, and California as older forests are converted into second growth. However, there is a paucity of data on the marbled murrelet population to support this.

Nearly all the terrestrial habitats of Washington, Oregon, and northern and central California within 35 miles (56 kilometers) of the coast and Puget Sound were originally covered with coniferous forests. Except for areas above the timberline, the same situation existed in British Columbia and Alaska. Historical evidence and descriptions show that at least half the area was in old growth. Franklin and Spies (1984) estimated that 60 to 70 percent of the Pacific Northwest's forest area was in old growth before 1800. Occupation of the land by Europeans resulted in an increase in fires, logging of old growth and mature forests, and subsequent replacement by young forest stands.

Nesting Chronology

The nesting behavior and habits of the marbled murrelet are unique and not fully understood. Murrelet nesting location has long been considered one of the big mysteries of ornithology, and the delineation of nesting parameters still represents a challenging area for research.

Early ornithologists, many of whom were egg collectors, soon discovered that marbled murrelets did not nest with other seabirds in colonies on the ground or in burrows on offshore rocks or sea cliffs. The collectors' only sources of murrelet eggs of were females collected with eggs in their oviducts. Observers such as Major Alan Brooks, William Leon Dawson, Joseph Grinnell, and George Willet saw or heard marbled murrelets flying over forests many miles from the ocean or taking off from the ocean and heading inland, sometimes carrying fish (Dawson and Bowles 1909, Brooks 1926). Brooks (1926) mentioned the presence of marbled murrelets year-round at Cowichan Lake in the interior of Vancouver Island, British Columbia. He examined a female collected at Harrison Lake, British Columbia, which was carrying two eggs (only one egg is laid, the other is absorbed) (Brooks 1928); the lake is at least 46 miles (75 kilometers) from saltwater (Carter and Sealy 1986). Speculation emerged at that time that the murrelet nests inland, perhaps on snow-capped peaks or under stumps or rocks in the forest.

In June 1925, E.J. Booth obtained a marbled murrelet egg at a logging camp office 15 miles (24 kilometers) from saltwater on the south fork of the Nooksack River in Washington (Anonymous 1927). There was no mention of a nest other than that the egg was in a bed of moss. Jewett (1934) described how his son and a companion found a flightless, immature bird in a logged area about one mile (1.7 kilometers) from the beach at Devil's Lake in Oregon. Jewett noted that uncut timber was nearby, and his son confirmed that there was an old-growth stand of Sitka spruce "three or four hundred yards away" (pers. comm.). This finding of grounded young was followed by two other discoveries in the forests of Oregon (Gabrielson and Jewett 1940, Barber 1941).

From these early observations has emerged a continuum of similar observations that supports the conclusion that the bird nests in mature and old-growth forests or in forests having residual old-growth trees. Carter and Sealy (1987b) tabulated 10 inland records of 13 downy young and 31 inland records of 31 single fledglings (feathered young) that were found, mostly on the ground. All except 10 of the records were made since 1960.[3] Since then, another fledgling was found in Oregon and one downy young was found in Alaska (Marshall 1988). Carter and Sealy (1987b) also mentioned that "8 out of 10 records of downy young and 20 out of 31 fledglings were obtained in old-growth forests. The remaining records were near old-growth forests."

The finding of young on the ground left open the matter of nest location. A clue denoting possible tree nesting came from Guiguet (1956) and Drent and Guiguet (1961) who reported a "stunned marbled murrelet taken from the debris of a large hemlock [presumably *Tsuga heterophylla*] felled in 1953 by a logger in the Queen Charlotte Islands near Masset, British Columbia. . . . Further search of the debris uncovered the fragments of a marbled murrelet's egg, but no evidence of a nest of any kind was found." This was followed with a similar instance reported by Harris (1971), in which two marbled murrelets dropped out of a cedar (presumably *Thuja plicata*) felled in August 1967 by loggers on Vancouver Island. One of the birds, which was collected, proved to be a young marbled murrelet with primary feathers still sheathed.

These findings still left room for much speculation. The real breakthrough in knowledge came in 1974 with the finding of a nest with a chick in Big Basin Redwoods State Park in the Santa Cruz Mountains, California. The nest was fully described by Binford *et al.* (1975) and Singer and Varado (1975) and remains the most completely described tree nest found to date. The nest was discovered accidentally by Hoyt Foster, a tree surgeon who was removing hazardous limbs from trees in one of the park's campgrounds. The nest was six miles (10 kilometers) from the coast on a large flat limb of Douglas-fir 148 feet (45 meters) above the ground. The tree was described as being 200 feet (61 meters) high and 66 inches (41 centimeters) in diameter, and was covered with bright green moss (*Isothecium cristatum*) at a depth of .20 to .40 inches (5 to 10 millimeters). The nest was simply a depression in the moss. No nesting material had been brought in, and it was suspected that the nest had been used over a period of years because of

3. Breakdown by province and state: Alaska, 4; British Columbia, 9; Washington, 8; Oregon, 3; and California, 17.

wear and excrement around its edges. The site was an old-growth stand of mostly large coast redwoods and smaller Douglas-firs. Binford *et al.* (1975) took particular note of the fact that the site was a virgin forest having an open crown structure with bark colored like the plumage of adult marbled murrelets, and that the nest was positioned high above the ground at a point allowing easy access to the exterior of the forest.

Only one other tree nest has been described for North America. It was found through radio-tagging in 1984 on a hillside 0.8 miles (1.2 kilometers) from Kelp Bay on the northeast side of Baranof Island in southeast Alaska (Quinlan and Hughes 1984). The nest was 51 feet (16 meters) above the ground on a 7-inch (18 centimeter) diameter, moss-covered branch of a mountain hemlock (*Tsuga mertensiana*). The tree was described as being in an open uneven-aged stand. Quinlan and Hughes (1984) and Sealy and Carter (1984) pointed out that lush moss growth does not occur on conifers until the forest is 150 years old or more.

Two marbled murrelet tree nests also have been described from Siberia. The first, found before the Big Basin Redwoods State Park nest, was described by Kuzyakin (1963) as being near the city of Okhotsk about four miles (6 to 7 kilometers) from the sea. It contained one egg and was in a larch (*Latrix dahuria*) in dendroid lichen (*Bryopogon* sp.) on a "branch with a wide flat surface formed by dense intertwining of small twigs situated on almost one plane." A second Siberian nest was found by Nechaev (1986) in 1976 in the broken-off top of a larch on Sakhalin Island.

Travel to and from nesting sites is one explanation of observations made by numerous observers of marbled murrelets in flight in forested areas in coastal portions of Washington, Oregon, and California. Paton *et al.* (1987) and Nelson (1986) have documented how these observations are made almost exclusively over, or in the vicinity of, old-growth and mature forests. Nelson (1986) has detected murrelets up to 29 miles (47 kilometers) from the ocean in Oregon. While this might seem too far from the ocean for daily flights, Brooks (1928) examined a female carrying eggs that was taken nearly 50 miles (75 kilometers) from the sea.

Similar observations have been made of the Asiatic marbled murrelet subspecies. Independently of American workers, Nechaev (1986) wrote of inland observations. Referring to Sakhalin Island in Siberia, he reported that marbled murrelets nest in mountains in coniferous and mixed-stand forests near the coast and inland. He noted the species by sight and sound as far inland as 19 to 25 miles (30 to 40 kilometers) from the Sea of Okhotsk.

Even more enigmatic, marbled murrelet nests have also been found on the ground along the tundra-edged coasts of Alaska, where there are no trees with large, flat, moss-covered branches. Six ground nests in total have been described—the first in 1978 in the Barren Islands. All were discovered in the vicinity of the end of the Kenai Peninsula or on or near Kodiak Island (Simons 1980, Johnston and Carter 1985). One of these nests was in a rocky cavity.

It has been concluded that the marbled murrelet has adapted to ground nesting in treeless or scrub tree regions. Where forest and treeless areas meet it is both a ground nester and tree nester; farther south the marbled murrelet nests only in trees (Marshall 1988). The findings of both nests and stranded young support this conclusion. It is also logical from a standpoint of vegetative characteristics: tundra habitat is sufficiently open to allow murrelets to get on and off the ground, especially on slopes, whereas farther south, where vegetation is heavy, trees offer the best opportunity for marbled murrelets to gain flight.

CURRENT TRENDS

The Pacific Seabird Group (1987) identified three threats to the marbled murrelet: old-growth forest habitat destruction, mortality from gill-net fisheries, and oil pollution. The group's Marbled Murrelet Workshop held in December 1986 identified aquaculture facilities—which use the bird's feeding areas—as a potential fourth threat (Pacific Seabird Group 1987).

The conversion of old-growth forests to managed stands throughout the Pacific Coast states and British Columbia is a major conservation issue. Coastal old growth on private land in Washington, Oregon, and California is virtually gone except in Humboldt County, California. Outside the private land in this area, the old growth that remains is scattered and found mostly in state and national parks, national forests, and Oregon and California Lands (O&C) managed by the Bureau of Land Management. The last remaining old-growth forest stands in Oregon's Coast Range Physiographic Province are largely in the Siuslaw National Forest, on O&C lands, and in state parks. Less than 2,000 acres of old growth within range of the marbled murrelet exists in Oregon state parks. In the Siuslaw National Forest, 34,000 acres of old growth remain (Morrison 1987a). Old growth remaining on O&C lands in western Oregon is estimated at 477,500 acres. An additional 435,500 acres is classified as being in mature forest (Morrison 1987b), but most of these acreages are too far from the coast to be useful to marbled murrelets. Old growth within the range of the marbled murrelet is subject to cutting except the Drift Creek, Cummins Creek, and Rock Creek wilderness areas in the Siuslaw National Forest, Olympic National Park, state parks, viewsheds, riparian zones, research natural areas, and lands set aside for the spotted owl. The areas in the three wilderness areas total 22,431 acres, but only about one-third of this is old growth. Old-growth forests in state parks, at least in Oregon, have been subject to salvage logging in the past and are not yet exempt.

MANAGEMENT

The marbled murrelet is not being afforded protection or provided with special management measures by land-management agencies, except that which may occur through decisions related to other species. The spotted owl has been designated as an indicator species for old-growth forests in the Pacific Northwest, but evidence that preservation of spotted owl habitat meets the murrelet's needs is lacking. Murrelets could require a more open forest crown than the spotted owl, and are obviously limited on the distance they can nest from the ocean. Habitat destruction and gill-net mortality, when combined with the species's low reproductive rate, are particular causes for concern, specifically in those portions of the species's range where population numbers are already low or where remaining nesting habitat is threatened.

On January 15, 1988, the National Audubon Society petitioned to the U.S. Fish and Wildlife Service (FWS) to list the marbled murrelet as threatened in Washington, Oregon, and California under the Endangered Species Act. The petition (and preparation of the status report upon which it was based) was initiated by the Audubon Society of Portland, a local chapter of National Audubon Society. Other groups became co-petitioners, including other Audubon chapters and the Oregon Natural Resources Council. The status report was subsequently published by FWS (Marshall 1988).[4] Simultaneously, the Portland chapter filed a similar petition with the Oregon Fish and Wildlife Commission to list the bird under Oregon's endangered species law. The petition was accepted for review, but listing was subsequently denied. While the Oregon Department of Fish and Wildlife staff publicly stated, "this bird may be in serious trouble because of loss of primary habitat," they could not recommend listing to the Fish and Wildlife Commission because Oregon law strictly requires substantial documentation of a species's status.

The petition directed to FWS was held for a lengthy period, but a finding that the petition presented substantial information and that listing may be warranted was published in the *Federal Register* (53 : 40479) in October 17, 1988. On that date, FWS formally initiated a review of the marbled murrelet's status.

---

4. Most of the material for this chapter was taken directly from the U.S. Fish and Wildlife Service report.

Whether the formal notice of a status review will translate into on-the-ground actions in national forests or on O&C lands remains to be seen, but the petition helped to spark a cooperative research effort on the marbled murrelet.

During summer 1988, research on the species was conducted in Washington, Oregon, and California. Crews in California located all major forest areas used by murrelets in the state. Researchers in Oregon concentrated on further development of techniques for locating inland areas used by murrelets and on development of radio-telemetry techniques. In Washington, volunteers were encouraged to find potential inland murrelet nesting areas, and work progressed on telemetry as well. Financial support for these projects came from a mix of organizations, including state wildlife agencies, the U.S. Forest Service, Bureau of Land Management, FWS, the National Council of the Paper Industry for Air and Stream Improvement, and the National Fish and Wildlife Foundation. The Pacific Seabird Group, in the absence of an interagency technical group, has formed the Marbled Murrelet Technical Committee. The committee provides an information exchange for marbled murrelet researchers and will make research and recommendations to management agencies.

The current absence of protection for marbled murrelet nesting habitat contrasts with the almost full nesting habitat protection provided other seabirds in Alaska, Washington, Oregon, and California via designation of their island nesting sites as national wildlife refuges or other protected areas.

PROGNOSIS

Little information is available and not enough is known about the marbled murrelet in Asia to make predictions. This discussion is therefore limited to North America. The marbled murrelet situation looks much better in Alaska, where nesting occurs on the tundra, than farther south. Population reductions can be expected with the continued removal of old growth in the Tongass National Forest. The long-range future of the species in British Columbia is contingent upon timber management practices and the setting aside of old growth in protected areas. Although there is still too little known to make accurate predictions, the evidence to date indicates that the marbled murrelet could be extirpated from Washington, Oregon, and California in the next 100 years as plans continue to destroy most remaining old growth within the species's range. An expanded research program that dictates on-the-ground management practices for the species needs development. A major problem lies with the difficulty in obtaining information on population trends, biology, and habitat requirements of the species before options are foregone. The situation with the Oregon law illustrates this. The margin for error favors the wood-products industry. While habitat is being destroyed, biologists with insufficient resources attempt to gather the necessary data needed to make a legal decision on whether the bird needs threatened or endangered status that would afford habitat protection. For example, several areas in Oregon in which murrelets were found this summer are slated to be cut within the next five years. Once an area is cut, the possibility of it ever becoming murrelet habitat again is remote. The effects on the population of confining the species only to planned old growth and mature timber set-asides in parks and similar protected areas in national forests cannot be predicted with the information currently available, but would result in a population that would be further fragmented. Fragmentation of habitat and subsequent population isolation is a well-accepted threat to the persistence of any population. Further, there is no assurance that all existing protected areas of old growth will remain marbled murrelet habitat in light of natural environmental catastrophes—such as fire, windstorms, geological phenomenon, and insect attacks—that will continue to shape the forests of the Northwest.

RECOMMENDATIONS

Lack of knowledge, in itself, is a threat to the species. It has taken more than 10 years of intensive research, for example, to find answers to key questions such as amount of old growth required per pair for the spotted owl. The marbled murrelet is far more difficult to study because of its cryptic nesting habits and the fact that it is active in the forest only during poor lighting conditions. Unlike the spotted owl, the marbled murrelet does not respond to recordings of its call and cannot be baited for observation or capture. The Pacific Seabird Group's marbled murrelet technical group management and research recommendations are outlined here.

1. Standardized population monitoring procedures must be developed, implemented, and coordinated between cooperating agencies. Demographic characteristics of the species must be determined. This includes obtaining data on longevity, mortality rates, population numbers, reproductive rates, and reproductive success necessary to sustain the population. Questions on whether birds displaced by habitat loss use replacement habitat, and what effects the fragmentation of old-growth forests has on the population, must be answered.

2. Nesting areas must be located, characterized, and protected. Inland habitat requirements must be better defined. Potential nesting areas can be identified through offshore observations and ground surveys of likely habitat, but a full interpretation of ground observations of the location of more nests appears, at this time, to hinge upon radio-telemetry. Telemetry techniques require further refinement before they can become operational. Securing to an eight ounce (220 grams) seabird an effective radio transmitter that does not cause significant hydrodynamic and aerodynamic drag, and that can withstand the rigors of saltwater, is just one of the challenges ahead.

3. The magnitude and significance of gill-net mortalities for the murrelet population represents still another area of needed research.

For the immediate future, two forms of protection should be considered: (1) setting aside those areas of mature and old-growth forests (or trees) used by marbled murrelets, and (2) providing special protection to at-sea concentration areas by restricting gill-net fishing and future oil development.

REFERENCES

American Ornithologists' Union. 1957. *Check-list of North American Birds.* Fifth Edition. American Ornithologists' Union.

Anonymous. 1927. "Egg of marbled murrelet (*Brachyramphus marmoratus*)." *Murrelet* 8:16.

Barber, O. 1941. "Juvenile marbled murrelet found on Coos River." *Murrelet* 22:38–39.

Binford, L.C., B.G. Elliot, and S.W. Singer. 1975. "Discovery of a nest and the downy young of the marbled murrelet." *Wilson Bulletin* 87:303–440.

Brooks, A. 1926. "The mystery of the marbled murrelet." *Murrelet* 7:1–2.

———. 1928. "Does the marbled murrelet nest inland?" *Murrelet* 9:68.

Carter, H.R. 1984. At-sea Biology of the Marbled Murrelet (*Brachyramphus marmoratus*) in Barkley Sound, British Columbia. Unpublished M.Sc. thesis. University of Manitoba. Winnipeg, Manitoba, Canada.

———. and S.G. Sealy. 1984. "Marbled murrelet mortality due to gill-net fishing in Barkley Sound, British Columbia," pp. 212–220 *in* D.N. Nettleship, G.A. Sanger, P.F. Springer eds., *Marine Birds: Their Feeding Ecology and Commercial Fisheries Relationships.* Canadian Wildlife Service Special Publication.

———. and ———. 1986. "Year-round use of coastal lakes by marbled murrelets." *Condor* 88:473–477.

———. and ———. 1987a. "Fish-holding behavior of marbled murrelets." *Wilson Bulletin* 99:289–291.

———. and ———. 1987b. "Inland records of downy young and fledgling marbled murrelets in North America." *Murrelet* 68:58–63.

Dawson, W.L. and J.H. Bowles. 1909. *The Birds of Washington.* Occidental Printing Company. Seattle, Washington.

Drent, R.H. and C.J. Guiguet. 1961. "A catalog of British Columbia sea-bird colonies." *British Columbia Museum Occasional Papers* no. 12.

Franklin, J.F. 1979. "Vegetation of the Douglas-fir region," in *Forest Soils of the Douglas-fir Region.* A Cooperative Extension, Washington State University. Pullman, Washington. (Reprint by U.S. Forest Service and U.S. Department of Agriculture.)

———. and T.A. Spies. 1984. "Characteristics of old-growth Douglas-fir forests." *Proceedings of the 1983 Convention of the Society of American Foresters.* Bethesda, Maryland.

Gabrielson, I.N. and S.G. Jewett. 1940. *Birds of Oregon.* Oregon State College. Corvallis, Oregon.

Guiguet, C.J. 1956. "Enigma of the Pacific." *Audubon* 58:164–167, 174.

Harris, R.D. 1971. "Further evidence of tree nesting in the marbled murrelet." *Canadian Field-Naturalist* 85:67–68.

Hirsch, K.V., D.A. Woodby, and L.B. Astheimer. 1981. "Growth of a nestling marbled murrelet." *Condor* 83:264–265.

Isleib, M.E. and B. Kessel. 1973. Birds of the North Gulf Coast-Prince William Sound region, Alaska. University of Alaska, biological papers no. 14. Fairbanks, Alaska.

Jewett, S.G. 1934. "The mystery of the marbled murrelet deepens." *Murrelet* 15:24.

———., W.P. Taylor, W.T. Shaw, and J.W. Aldrich. 1953. *Birds of Washington State.* University of Washington Press. Seattle, Washington.

Johnston, S. and H.R. Carter. 1985. "Cavity-nesting marbled murrelets." *Wilson Bulletin* 97:1–3.

Kessel, B. and D.D. Gibson. 1978. "Status and distribution of Alaska birds." *Studies in Avian Biology 1.* Cooper Ornithological Society. Los Angeles, California.

King, J.G. and G.A. Sanger. 1979. "Oil vulnerability index for marine oriented birds," pp. 227–239 *in* J.C. Bartonek and D.N. Nettleship eds., *Conservation of Marine Birds of Northern North America.* U.S. Fish and Wildlife Service, Wildlife Research Report 11.

Kuzyakin, A.P. 1963. "On the biology of the long-billed [marbled] murrelet." *Ornithologiya* 6:315–320.

Manuwal, D.A., T.R. Wahl, and S.M. Speich. 1979. The Seasonal Distribution and Abundance of Marine Bird Populations in the Strait of Juan de Fuca and Northern Puget Sound in 1978. NOAA Technical Memorandum, ERL MESA-44. Marine Ecosystems Analysis Program. Boulder, Colorado.

Marshall, D.B. 1980. "Status of the marbled murrelet in North America: with special emphasis on populations in California, Oregon, and Washington." *Biological Report* 88(30). U.S. Fish and Wildlife Service.

Morrison, P. 1987a. Summary of Existing Old-Growth Inventory Information on Federal Lands in the Douglas-fir Region. Unpublished. Old-Growth forest inventory project. Prepared for The Wilderness Society.

———. 1987b. Summary of Existing Old-Growth Inventory Information on state, private, and nonfederal lands and planned old growth inventory projects on all ownership. Unpublished. Old-Growth forest inventory project. Prepared for The Wilderness Society.

Nechaev, V.A. 1986. "New information on the seabirds of Sakhalin Island," pp. 77–81 *in* N.M. Litvinenko ed., *Seabirds of the Far East.* Akademiya Nauk SSSR. Vladivostok. (English translation by D. Siegel-Causeyl.)

Nelson, J.W. and W.A. Lehnhausen. 1983. Marine Bird and Mammal Survey of the Outer Coast of Southeast Alaska, Summer 1982. Unpublished. U.S. Fish and Wildlife Service, Marine Bird Management Project. Anchorage, Alaska.

Nelson, S.K. 1986. Observations of Marbled Murrelets in Inland, Old-aged Forests of Western Oregon. Unpublished. Contribution no. 54 of the U.S. Department of Agriculture, Forest Service Old-Growth Forest Wildlife Habitat Program. Corvallis, Oregon.

Pacific Seabird Group. 1982. "Consideration of marbled murrelets in old-growth forest management. A resolution of the Pacific Seabird Group." *Pacific Seabird Group Bulletin* 9:62–63.

———. 1987. "Marbled murrelet resolutions." *Pacific Seabird Group Bulletin* 14: 19–20.

Paton, P.W.C., C.J. Ralph, and R.A. Erickson. 1987. Seasonal Changes in Marbled Murrelets at Inland Sites in Northwestern California. Unpublished. U.S. Department of Agriculture, Forest Service, Redwood Science Laboratory. Arcata, California.

Quinlan, S.E. and J.H. Hughes. 1984. Use of Radio-tagging to Locate Marbled Murrelets Nest Sites. Unpublished. Progress report covering May 1, 1983–June 30, 1984. Alaska Department of Fish and Game. Juneau, Alaska.

Sanger, G.A. 1987. "Winter diets of common murres and marbled murrelets in Kachemak Bay, Alaska." *Condor* 89:426–430.

———. and R.D. Jones, Jr. 1981. The Winter Feeding Ecology and Trophic Relationship of Marine Birds in Kachemak Bay, Alaska. Final report to the Outer Continental Shelf Environmental Assessment Program. U.S. Fish and Wildlife Service. National Fishery Research Center, Migratory Bird Section. Anchorage, Alaska.

Savile, D.B.O. 1972. "Evidence of tree nesting by the marbled murrelet in the Queen Charlotte Islands." *Canadian Field-Naturalist* 86:389–390.

Sealy, S.G. 1975a. "Feeding ecology of the ancient and marbled murrelets near Langara Island, British Columbia." *Canadian Journal of Zoology* 53:418–433.

———. 1975b. "Aspects of the breeding biology of the marbled murrelet in British Columbia." *Bird-Banding* 46:141–154.

———. and H.R. Carter. 1984. "At-sea distribution and nesting habitat of the marbled murrelet in British Columbia: problems in the conservation of a solitarily nesting seabirds," pp. 737–756 *in* J.P. Croxall, P.G.H. Evans, and R.W. Schreiber ed., *Status and Conservation of the World's Seabirds.* International Committee for Bird Preservation Technical Publication no. 2.

———., ———., and D. Alison. 1982. "Occurrences of the Asiatic marbled murrelet (*Brachyramphus marmoratus perdix* [Pallas] in North America." *Auk* 99:778–781.

Simons, T.R. 1980. "Discovery of a ground nesting marbled murrelet." *Condor* 82:1–9.

Singer, S.W. and D.R. Verardo. 1975. "The murrelet's nest discovered." *Pacific Discovery* 28:18–21.

Sowls, A.L., A.R. DeGange, J.W. Nelson, and G.S. Lester. 1980. *Catalog of California seabird colonies.* Coastal Ecosystems Project. U.S. Fish and Wildlife Service, Office of Endangered Species. Washington, D.C.

Speich, S.M., T.R. Wahl, and D.A. Manuwal. 1988. "Distribution and abundance of marbled murrelets in Washington marine waters." *Pacific Seabird Group Bulletin* 15:39. Abstract.

Storer, R.W. 1945. "Structural modifications in the hind limb in the alcidae." *Ibis* 87:433–456.

Varoujean, D.H. and W.A. Williams. 1987. Nest Locations and Nesting Habitat of the Marbled Murrelet (*Brachyramphus marmoratus*) in Coastal Oregon. Unpublished. Final report submitted to Oregon Department of Fish and Wildlife. Portland, Oregon.

David B. Marshall is a certified wildlife biologist who was with FWS for 32 years, 8 years with their endangered species program. He prepared the status report on the marbled murrelet that was used as a basis for the petition to list the species as threatened.

The author wishes to thank Lynn Herring of the Audubon Society of Portland and Richard T. Brown, resource specialist for the National Wildlife Federation, Portland, Oregon, for their comments.

Sought by commercial fisheries since the mid-1880s, swordfish are exhibiting signs of overfishing. The species's economic value has triggered disputes concerning stock assessments and harvest limitations. (Swordfish being tagged for migration studies.) *Harold Wes Pratt/NOAA-NMFS*

The Western North Atlantic Swordfish

John J. Hoey, Ramon J. Conser,
and Angelo R. Bertolino

National Marine Fisheries Service

SPECIES DESCRIPTION AND NATURAL HISTORY

Swordfish (*Xiphias gladius* Linnaeus) are large, heavy-bodied predators that are adapted for a wide-ranging, pelagic existence. The bill, or "sword," is long, sharp-edged, and broadly flattened, hence the species's common name "broadbill." The swordfish bill is the longest of all the billfishes and can be one-third or more of total body length. The skull is wide, but shallow in depth, and the head is dominated by large eyes and a large mouth. The dorsal surface of the streamlined body is slate gray to blue or brown, fading to a silvery-white belly. The first dorsal and anal fins are tall, rigid, and triangular in shape. Pectoral fins are rigid and situated low on the sides. Adult swordfish do not have pelvic fins, teeth, or scales. A flattened lateral keel precedes the crescent-shaped tail. Juvenile characteristics, such as rough scales and long dorsal and anal fins, are apparent until swordfish reach an overall length of approximately 30 inches (75 centimeters).

The swordfish's size and strength made it a highly sought trophy for early big-game anglers. The world record on rod and reel is 1,182 pounds (whole body weight) recorded in 1953 off Chile (International Game Fish Association). In the western North Atlantic, the largest verified size is 915 pounds dressed weight[1] (dw) (Tibbo *et al.* 1961). Sex-ratio size sampling of harpooned swordfish (Lee 1942) and longline caught fish (Hoey 1986) indicate that most fish weighing more than 100 pounds dw are female (67 percent), while males are more abundant at sizes less than 100 pounds (60 percent). Males represent 23 percent of the fish greater than 200 pounds dw but only 11 percent of fish greater than 300 pounds. Apparently, sexually dimorphic growth produces larger females and smaller males as is common in fish populations. Recent sampling indicates that smaller males are particularly abundant in warmer, southern areas. Tracking experiments that monitor body temperature and ambient water temperature have provided critical explanations of how swordfish interact with their environment (Carey and Robison 1981). Temperature preferences, which vary by size and seasonal variations in thermal conditions on oceanwide scales, are the dominant features in the life history and ecology of swordfish.

Progress in understanding the life history and biology of swordfish was hampered for many years by the difficulties associated with observing large oceanic predators in the wild. The development of large-scale, wide-ranging fisheries in the late 1950s, and studies associated with these fisheries over the past 30 years, have provided a more complete picture. Information collected from these fisheries allows scientists to assess the status of the resource. National and international management bodies are responsible for regulating harvests.

Taxonomy and Distribution

A powerful animal, the swordfish has been recognized as a single, worldwide species since the days of Aristotle, 450 B.C. The swordfish probably arose as a distinct species in the early Eocene Epoch. It is the sole member of the genus *Xiphias* and the family Xiphiidae. Although sharing many morphological and physiological features with mackerels and tunas (Scombridae), other billfishes (Istiophoridae), and mackerel sharks (Lamnidae), the similarities, such as streamlined rigid bodies with reduced scales, similar patterns in fin shape and positioning, and circulatory adaptations to conserve metabolic heat, reflect convergent evolution.

Swordfish are the most widely distributed of the "billfishes" found throughout the world's tropical, subtropical, and temperate seas. In the North Atlantic, swordfish are found as far north as Newfoundland in the west and off England in the east. In the western Atlantic, swordfish occur from the coast of Newfoundland to Argentina. In the eastern Atlantic, they are reported occasionally in the North Sea and off England and as far south as the coast of South Africa (Cape of Good Hope).

1. Dressed weight is defined as headed, gilled, gutted, and tailed.

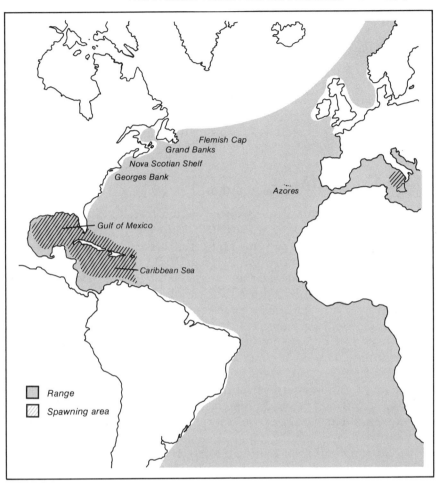

Figure 1. Range and spawning area of the swordfish.

Swordfish are encountered in limited numbers in almost all oceanic areas exploited by the Japanese high-seas tuna fishery. Records from U.S., Spanish, and Canadian fisheries in the North Atlantic indicate that swordfish are more abundant along the edge of the Continental Shelf than in the central Sargasso Sea (see Figure 1).

Habitat

Swordfish preferred habitat occurs along the edge of the Continental Shelf over depths ranging from 100 to 3,000 meters, along frontal zones associated with major ocean current systems (North Atlantic gyre), and where seamounts or mid-ocean islands provide bathymetric relief. Swordfish and other large oceanic predators, such as tunas, other billfish, and pelagic sharks, frequent areas where upwelling and current boundaries increase productivity and concentrate prey. Although some marine predators are found primarily on the warm or cold side of the frontal zone, swordfish appear to be closely associated with, and specialized for, life in areas characterized by the sharpest thermal gradients—the boundary itself. Swordfish have the widest temperature tolerance among the billfish, from about 41° F (5° C) to about 80° F (27° C) (Nakamura 1985), as well as depth range from the surface to at least 2,145 feet (654 meters) (Church 1968).

Seasonal Movements and Segregation

U.S. and Canadian harpoon fisheries, which operated during the late summer and fall from the mid-1880s, exclusively harvested mature, nonripe[2] females north of Cape Hatteras. Swordfish larvae, however, were found only in warm tropical areas. With the advent in the early 1960s of pelagic longline gear and night fishing, small swordfish and particularly males were captured for the first time. Distribution patterns north of Cape Hatteras vary seasonally with sea surface temperature. During the winter months north of Cape Hatteras, swordfish are primarily confined to offshore waters of the Gulf Stream. Expansion of the longline fishery during the 1970s and 1980s in the Straits of Florida, Gulf of Mexico, and the Caribbean increased the known range of swordfish in the western Atlantic. The preferred temperatures for larger swordfish in the southern areas are found at greater depths than farther north. The extent of the southern distributions was not recognized until deeper-fishing longline gear was developed in the late 1970s. Seasonal shifts in fishing effort and landings indicate that the bulk of the population is primarily south of Cape Hatteras in the winter and spring, and farther north and east during the summer and fall. The dominant north-south seasonal migration pattern along the East Coast of North America is supported by approximately 120 recaptures of tagged swordfish.

Male and female swordfish appear to be distributed differentially (at least in the western North Atlantic), probably reflecting size–temperature preferences along a north-south latitudinal gradient. The smaller males have a more southerly center of distribution. As seasonal warming occurs, males and females move northward, with the females moving into the northern feeding grounds before the males. During the summer, overall abundance declines off Cuba and south Florida. Size–temperature segregation is indicated by sex-ratio size

2. "Nonripe" is defined as females that are mature but whose gonads are inactive or at very early stages of egg production.

data, with the percentage of females increasing from approximately 20 percent off Cuba and south Florida, to 85 to 90 percent near Cape Hatteras during winter months (Hoey 1986). In addition to the seasonal shifts for male and female age groups, longer-range migrations would be required of prespawning females. The larger females apparently feed heavily in northern latitudes during the late summer and fall. Their reproductive migrations, either along the Gulf Stream or further offshore through the Sargasso Sea, presumably reflect a search for water temperature optimal for larval survival.

Spawning

Spawning is apparently restricted to warm tropical areas where surface water temperatures are greater than 71° to 74° F (22° to 24° C) (Tanning 1955, Palko *et al.* 1981). Fertilization is external and a single female can produce two to five million eggs over a period of several months. The production of batches of eggs over several months—protracted serial spawning—accounts for larval captures throughout the year. Larval distribution data and records of ripe, spawning females document spawning areas in the Mediterranean and in the tropical Atlantic. In the western Atlantic, larvae are reported in the Gulf Stream south of Cape Hatteras, in the Gulf of Mexico, and in the Caribbean Sea near the Virgin Island–Leeward Island area (Markel 1974). Grall *et al.* (1983) reports that peak larval abundance in the western North Alantic occurs in February, but Arata (1954) indicated that peak spawning occurs from April through September. Apparently, spawning occurs over a broad area in the tropics, and the larvae are transported by Equatorial and Gulf Stream currents.

During spawning, pairs of swordfish are reported. Smaller, supposedly male fish, follow larger, presumably female fish. This rare behavior has been reported in the Caribbean and occasionally off Florida. When the females are captured on pelagic longlines, the males follow them to the boat and are occasionally harpooned and captured. Specimens sampled off the coast of Florida between 1977 and 1980 indicated that males and females mature at different sizes. All males are mature at approximately 90 pounds dw, whereas only 50 percent of females are mature at 100 pounds dw (R. Taylor pers. comm.).

Diet and Feeding

Carey (1982) considered swordfish to be creatures of semidarkness, whose large eyes provide the visual acuity to feed at night near the surface as well as at great depths (600 meters) during the day. The predominance of white muscle tissue indicates that swordfish are stalkers and sprinters that opportunistically feed on available local prey. Swordfish are considered to be primarily diurnal feeders, rising to the surface and near surface waters at night. They feed primarily on squid (Ommastrephidae) and pelagic fish (Atlantic mackerel, herring, bluefish, and butterfish) (Stillwell and Kohler 1985). They are also known to forage from the bottom to the surface over great depths, where they feed on bottom-dwelling species (Gadidae, Sebastes, Ammodytes) and mid-water vertical migrators[3] (Myctophidae and Alepsuridae) (Palko *et al.* 1981). "Basking behavior" during the daylight hours, which makes swordfish vulnerable to harpoon fisheries, may facilitate digestion and allow recovery from feeding at depth in extremely cold water (Carey 1982). Records from the harpoon fishery indicate that most harpooned swordfish had stomachs full of demersal prey (Tibbo *et al.* 1961).

Carey and Robison (1981) noted that the general diurnal pattern (shallow at night and deep during the day) indicates that swordfish respond to light, apparently following a constant light intensity, or "isolume." Their tracking showed a daily cycle of movements between inshore banks during the day and deep water offshore at night. During the day they feed on demersal species moving along the edge of the bank; their preference for shallow offshore waters at night allows them to feed on fish and squid that move to the surface at night. Within this general pattern, frequent vertical excursions probably related to feeding subject swordfish to dramatic temperature changes, as much as 34° F (19° C) in two hours (Carey and Robison 1981).

Physiological and anatomical adaptations for withstanding the diversity of temperatures encountered by swordfish differentially distribute the sexes based on size–temperature preferences along a north-south latitudinal gradient. Temperature preferences reflect an animal's sensitivity to internal temperatures in the face of ambient environmental conditions. Internal temperatures can be maintained (quasi-regulated) by insulating muscle mass or a fat layer (thermal inertia), or by conservation of metabolic heat through circulatory adaptations such as restricted lateral blood flow or countercurrent heat exchange systems. Countercurrent exchangers (retes) have been documented in warm-bodied fish such as bluefin and bigeye tuna, swordfish, and some lamnid sharks (mako, porbeagle, and white) (Carey and Teal 1966, 1969, Carey *et al.* 1971, Carey 1973, Dixon and Brill 1979, Carey *et al.* 1981). In swordfish, the rete heats the brain and protects the central nervous system from rapid cooling during the large temperature changes that are characteristic of its daily routine (Carey 1982). Additionally, the retention of metabolically produced heat in the central

---

3. Deep-water squids and fish that live in the water column and change depth responding to light intensity. They form a deep scattering sonar layer and are called "mesopelagics."

core of the body by restricting lateral blood flow, and the insulation provided by muscle mass, regulates how much time can be spent feeding in colder, productive waters. Size therefore plays a significant role in regulating the rate at which internal temperatures decrease upon movement into colder water. Smaller swordfish are not able to spend as much time feeding in colder water as larger fish. Perhaps this size-related difference in the ability to hunt in cold temperature and the differences in male and female sizes produces the sexual segregation previously discussed.

Life Span

Swordfish growth has been evaluated using mark-recapture data (Anonymous 1987) and marks on skeletal hard parts (Berkeley and Houde 1983). Because of the limited sample size of large swordfish used in these analyses, estimated ages beyond 14 years are unreliable. However, with documented recaptures occurring as long as 15 years after tagging, it is possible that the maximum life span could be 25 years or more. Because verified estimates of age for large males and females are unavailable, we do not know if males live as long as females. Males mature at smaller sizes and do not grow as large as females. Therefore, males either grow slower and have the same life span or have a shorter life span and similar growth rate.

SIGNIFICANCE OF THE SPECIES

Swordfish are part of a complex community of oceanic predators that includes tunas, sharks, billfish, and other large piscivorous fish such as dolphin (Coryphaenidae) and wahoo (*Acanthocybium solanderi*). Larval, juvenile, and very young swordfish are undoubtedly preyed upon by predators of suitable size, but adult swordfish have few natural enemies. Large sharks are the only species ever seen in actual combat with swordfish (Palko *et al.* 1981). Scars apparently resulting from attacks by the cookie cutter shark (*Istius* sp.) have been observed on different sizes of swordfish.

As a top predator, swordfish accumulate heavy metals and pesticides from the prey they consume. Levels of mercury exceeding allowable standard of 0.5 parts per million specified by the U.S. Food and Drug Administration (FDA) were reported in tuna and swordfish in 1970. Consumer reaction and enforcement of FDA regulations reduced U.S. consumption by 96 percent (Lipton 1986). After successful court challenges and additional studies of consumption patterns, FDA in-

The swordfish bill can be one-third or more of total body length. *Duane Raver*

creased the allowable amount of mercury from 0.5 to 1 part per million in 1978. Although this complex and controversial public health issue is still debated, the increased standard allowed for the resumption of the U.S. swordfish fishery, and the North Atlantic harvest increased from 5,000 to 6,000 metric tons in the early 1970s to 15,000 to 16,000 metric tons in recent years.

In 1987 in the North Atlantic (excluding the Mediterranean), approximately 16,500 metric tons (whole body weight) of swordfish—close to 400,000 individuals—were harvested by 10 nations (International Commission for the Conservation of Atlantic Tunas). The United States and Spain alone accounted for 80 percent of the total catch. The 1987 U.S. harvest of about eight million pounds dw had an ex-vessel value[4] of approximately $27 million. Approximate retail value for the U.S. harvest alone was approximately $100 million. The swordfish and related longline fisheries for tuna support valuable fishing and related industries in several countries. Human predation on this wide-ranging species represents a significant international management challenge that has yet to be met and that demands immediate attention to ensure the continued economic viability of this resource (see "Management" and "Prognosis" sections).

---

4. Dollar value that the fishermen receive for the fish.

HISTORICAL PERSPECTIVE

Recognized in Greek, classical, and medieval literature (Goode 1883), swordfish have been hunted by coastal-dwelling people for thousands of years. In the western North Atlantic, swordfish bills have been reported from archaeological excavations of native American dwellings in the northeast United States. Goode (1883) provides considerable detail about early reports concerning swordfish, including a little-known fact about Christopher Columbus: "in the height of his triumphs as a discoverer, he chose to deposit a memento of his first voyage across the seas. . . . It consists of the helmet and armour worn by the discoverer . . . and the weapon of a warrior killed by his party when approaching the American coast—the sword of a swordfish."

Naturalists' letters from the 1750s mention swordfish along the Florida and Carolina coasts. Professor S.L. Mitchell of New York reported in *American Monthly* magazine that a swordfish was harpooned in June 1817 off Sandy Hook, New Jersey, and sold in New York at "a quarter of a dollar the pound" (Goode 1883).

Goode also reported, to the U.S. Commission of Fish and Fisheries, that "for many years from 3,000 to 6,000 of these fish have been taken on the New England Coast." Harpoon gear was the primary method of harvesting. Goode indicated that a well-established U.S. fishery existed by 1840. At an average weight of 250 pounds (apparently dressed weight), "the aggregate weight of a year's catch of Sword-fish [sic] amounts to 1,500,000 pounds, valued at $45,000, the average price being estimated at three cents per pound."

After the harpoon fishery started in New England, it spread into Canada, especially Nova Scotia, where first mention of its development occurs in 1903. By 1909, the Canadian fishery was important enough to be recorded separately in fishery statistics. Total landings fluctuated between one and three million pounds with peak landings periodically exceeding four million pounds (Tibbo *et al.* 1961). Canadian landings predominated after 1939. Landings increased from 3.5 million pounds in 1953 to 7.2 million pounds in 1959. These landings were from the seasonal harpoon fishery and the incidental swordfish catches by trawlers and bottom halibut and tilefish fisheries.

In the early 1960s, incidental catches of swordfish by research vessels and Norwegian and Japanese long-liners prompted Canadian and United States fishermen to use pelagic longline gear for swordfish (Beckett 1971). Long-lining rapidly replaced harpoon gear as the dominant fishing method in the western North Atlantic, and reported landings increased from approximately 4.6 million pounds dw (2,800 metric tons whole body weight) in 1960 to 14.5 million pounds dw (8,800 metric tons) in 1963, reflecting the increased effectiveness of longline gear. Landings then declined and stabilized at approximately

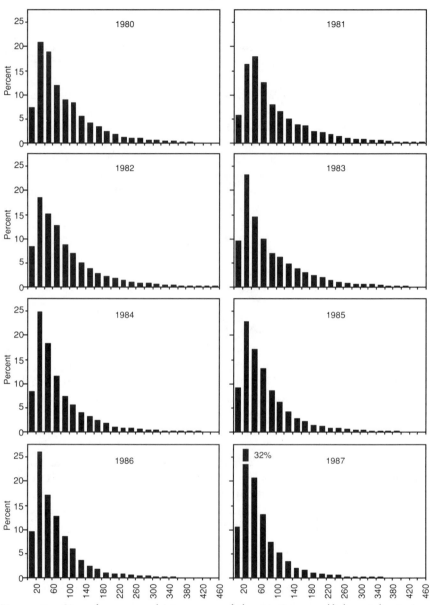

Figure 2a. Size–frequency histograms of the U. S. swordfish catch at size from 1980 to 1987 (in 20-pound DWT increments).

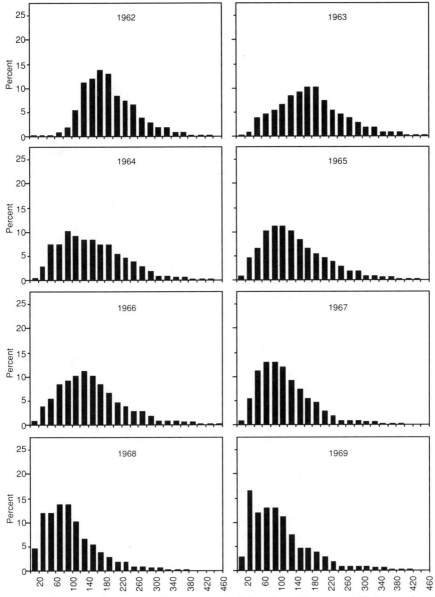

Figure 2b. Size–frequency histograms of the Canadian swordfish catch at size from 1962 to 1969 (in 20-pound DWT increments).

8.3 million pounds dw (5,000 metric tons) through 1971 (Caddy 1976). During this time, the fishery expanded both to the south and east so that by 1969 a year-round fishery exploited Gulf Stream associated waters along the edge of the North American Continental Shelf from Cape Romain, South Carolina, to the Grand Banks and Flemish Cap off Newfoundland.

In 1970, FDA instituted regulations prohibiting the interstate transportation and importation of swordfish containing mercury in excess of 0.5 parts per million. Although these regulations substantially reduced both U.S. and Canadian effort, an "underground" fishery developed, and catch and effort statistics were not reported. During the mid-1970s, a new fishery developed primarily among fishermen in south Florida. Interest in this fishery was undoubtedly stimulated by the seasonal passage of New England long-liners through the Florida Straits and into the Gulf of Mexico for their winter fishery.

In 1978, FDA increased the allowable level of mercury to one part per million. During the late 1970s, the Bahamas, Canada, Mexico, and the United States expanded their territorial jurisdictions, thus displacing many foreign and domestic fishermen from their traditional fishing grounds. Together, these events led to a dramatic increase in the number of vessels participating in the U.S. swordfish fishery. Fishing effort and vessels were concentrated in the U.S. Exclusive Economic Zone, especially in the southern areas. The southern fishermen experimented with gear modifications including a switch from nylon multifilament mainlines and branch lines to complete monofilament construction, increased hook spacing, increasing hook-line and float-line lengths, and the use of chemical light sticks associated with each bait. The southern gear was shown to be two to three times as effective as New England gear in the Straits of Florida (Berkeley *et al.* 1981). The use of the modified gear spread rapidly throughout the southern areas of the fishery. As southern vessels extended their range into traditional New England grounds, experimentation with swordfish continued so that by 1981–1982 the modified gear was accepted and deployed in all areas by the U.S. fleet. Additional fine-tuning has occurred subsequently in conjunction with the increased use of advanced electronics (sea-surface temperature and weather facsimile equipment) and expansion of the fishery to the east of the Flemish Cap. Frontal zones in the area north of the Azores have produced increasing proportions (approximately 28 percent) of U.S. landings from 1985 to 1987.

During winter 1984–1985, 13 vessels expanded operations into the Caribbean and by the following winter that number had increased to about 40 or 45 vessels. Apparently, the winter migrations of swordfish into southern areas protected some portions of the stock in the 1960s and 1970s because year-round commercial exploitation did not occur in southern regions until the early 1980s and the 1984 expansion into the Caribbean.

Because of the changes in the western North Atlantic fishery in the last eight years, historical levels of harvest and associated size-composition data provide an important perspective. During the 1960s, Canada accounted for more than 90 percent of total harvests, whereas current U.S. harvests account for about three-quarters of the total numbers taken. Changes in the size structure of the harvested western North Atlantic swordfish stock(s) can be examined by comparing size–frequency histograms based on the Canadian data from the 1960s (Caddy 1976) and more recent U.S. data from between 1980 and 1987 (Hoey and Nelson 1988) (see Figures 2a and 2b).

The relatively stable landings of approximately 8.3 million pounds dw during the late 1960s (including harvests by Canada, the United States, and Japan) were characterized by size frequencies with modes between 60 and 100 pounds dw. Western North Atlantic landings by the United States alone accounted for 8.1 million pounds yearly in 1986 and 1987. The modes in the resultant size frequences for the last five years have been between 20 and 39 pounds dw. Average sizes have declined continuously from 1978 through 1987 and the number of fish less than 50 pound dw harvested by the U.S. fleet is an all-time high (54 percent in 1987).

CURRENT TRENDS

An assessment of an "assumed" northwest Atlantic swordfish stock was conducted by the National Marine Fisheries Service in 1985 (Conser *et al.* 1985). To assure that the figures were agreed upon, an "open" assessment was held in April 1986 with participants from the Atlantic U.S. Regional Management Councils and the international stock assessment community (Anonymous 1987). The results of the two assessments were similar. There was evidence of growth overfishing, with an excessive number of small fish being taken. However, there was no evidence of recruitment overfishing, that is, fishing to the point where the number of spawners has been reduced so that the ability of the population to regenerate itself is impaired. The analysis of data through 1985 showed increases in levels of recruitment, numbers of juvenile fish, and total stock biomass. The 1985 adult stock—fish weighing 130 pounds dw and larger—was estimated to be within 75 percent of the 1978 level. The population appeared to be building, which was attributed to increasing abundances of young age classes, or recruits. Under those conditions, limitations on the capture of small fish were identified as a management goal that would aid in increasing the stock size of larger fish. The age composition of the population has been substantially changed by recent exploitation, resulting in a population that is currently dominated by smaller, younger, and faster-growing individuals.

The Spanish fishery is now making substantial catches north and west of the Azores. Since 1984, the U.S. fishery has expanded both to the Northeast towards the Azores and to the Southeast through the Caribbean and off the northern coast of South America. The international fishery now exerts pressure on swordfish stocks on a broad scale in the Atlantic. Efforts to determine the extent of Atlantic swordfish fisheries and the status of the stocks on a broad basis were begun at a workshop sponsored by the International Commission for the Conservation of Atlantic Tunas (ICCAT) held in October 1987 in Madrid, Spain. Definitive genetic information on the stock structure of North Atlantic swordfish is currently not available. Because the effectiveness of management relates to influencing harvesting patterns on a stock, knowledge about the extent and magnitude of the stock is critical. Participants at the 1987 ICCAT Swordfish Workshop favored a single North Atlantic stock hypothesis for assessment purposes (Anonymous 1988). Participants noted that it was unclear whether there was one or two stocks (east and west) in the North Atlantic. They recognized that if the two-stock hypothesis was used in assessments, the significant mixing of east and west fish in the central North Atlantic needed to be incorporated in the analysis. At this time there is no information available on how to apportion the large catches in the central Atlantic into eastern and western components. Therefore, rather than arbitrarily dividing the catches, participants at the workshops have chosen as a first step to consider all North Atlantic swordfish as a single group.

A second ICCAT workshop held in September 1988 continued the previous year's work by updating landings, size-frequency samples, and catch-at-age data through 1987. The workshop revised the swordfish growth curve by incorporating all available tag-recapture data to date; evaluating indices of relative abundance developed from commercial catch and effort data from Spanish, Japanese, and U.S. fisheries; and conducting virtual population analyses[5] using accepted analytical techniques. The limitations of time, coupled with problems inherent in combining fisheries data from many nations, prevented this workshop from achieving a final, agreed-upon stock assessment. Preliminary results indicate that fishing mortality rates for young fish and for the fully recruited ages have increased markedly between 1978 and 1987. Qualitatively, the current estimates of trends in population size—ages 0, 1, and from 5 to 10—and age-specific mortality patterns appear simi-

---

5. An analysis of the catches from a given year class over its life in the fishery.

lar to the results from the 1986 assessment (Anonymous 1987). Population size for the mature portion of the stock has declined significantly, with decline estimates ranging from 32 percent to 50 percent between 1978 and 1987.

Stock size estimates are not available for years preceeding 1978. Many harpoon and some long-line fishermen who fished off New England during the 1960s believe the resource is vastly reduced. A rod-and-reel recreational fishery that developed during the late 1970s no longer exists. The large, older component of the population, which specialized in feeding along the edge of the shelf, has clearly been reduced by exploitation; this explains reduced participation in, and landings by, the traditional harpoon fishery. However, many fishermen have reported increased abundances of small fish in recent years, which has also been evident in standardized abundance indices (Hoey *et al.* in press). U.S. longline vessels moving eastward along the edge of the Gulf Stream from the Grand Banks to the Azores and Spanish longline vessels moving westward into the same area between 1983 and 1987 have reported significant catches of intermediate- and large-sized fish. Newly exploited areas in the Caribbean produced substantial catches of large fish between 1985 and 1987. The 1986 and recent ICCAT stock assessments indicate that the stock is heavily exploited and that managing to reduce the catch of small fish and increase the number of older fish in the stock is desirable.

Between 1985 and 1987, U.S. and Spanish fleets overlapped operations north of the Azores, where more than 30 percent of the total number of swordfish harvested in 1986 and 1987 in the North Atlantic were caught (Hoey *et al.* 1988). Apparently, these two dominant fleets in the North Atlantic are shifting from coastal to high-seas operations. An extensive Spanish longline fleet has historically fished in the Mediterranean Sea and in the Northeast Atlantic (Rey *et al.* 1988). In addition to expanding operations to the northwest, the Spanish fleet is also expanding southward into the eastern tropical waters (Caveriviere and Cayre 1986).

Cuban, Brazilian, Venezuelan, and Argentinian fleets have operated in tropical and southern waters of the west Atlantic since the early 1960s. Japan, Korea, and Taiwan have extensive longline fisheries for tunas operating throughout the Atlantic. If market conditions prove favorable, and these fleets expand their effort, more extensive overlapping of fleet operations will occur throughout the equatorial and South Atlantic regions in the near future.

This exploitation pattern is common for oceanic pelagic resources where fleets seek out areas of high abundance, fish out the stock to an economic break-even point, and then look for more productive fishing areas. This pattern agrees with the pattern followed by the U.S. and Canadian harpoon fisheries from the early 1800s through the 1960s, as well as the subsequent evolution of the western North Atlantic long-line fisheries. The Spanish fleet has undergone a similar evolution in the eastern Atlantic, suggesting that most areas of swordfish concentration, if not all, in the North Atlantic are currently exploited. As distant water operations increase in importance with more successful fishermen concentrating in those areas, it is likely that abundance levels of large fish in the North Atlantic will continue to decline and that fishing will shift more to the South Atlantic.

MANAGEMENT

Swordfish management within the U.S. Exclusive Economic Zone is the responsibility of the Secretary of Commerce and the regional fishery management councils established by the Magnuson Fishery Conservation and Management Act of 1976. Management of U.S. vessels operating in international waters beyond 200 miles is also the responsibility of the Secretary of Commerce under the authority of the Atlantic Tunas Convention Act [16 U.S.C. 971–971h]. Limits on swordfish harvest or fishing have not been set. Council efforts, with technical support from NMFS have heightened public and industry awareness of the current decline in the fishery, and encouraged debates on management strategies and their benefits. Management discussions and proposed regulations—never promulgated—emphasize that large catches of small swordfish are wasteful. Mandatory daily logbooks for swordfish catches are required and additional reporting requirements are being considered. Current discussions at the national level are attempting to address problems caused by interrelated swordfish and tuna longline fisheries that are managed through different systems. Swordfish, billfish, and sharks are managed under the Magnuson Fishery Conservation and Management Act of 1976 with responsibility assigned to regional management councils. Tunas are internationally managed through regulations recommended by ICCAT. Those regulations are implemented in the United States by NMFS as authorized under the Atlantic Tuna Convention Act of 1974. Congressional discussions relating to the reauthorization of the Magnuson act will need to consider the relative responsibilities and jurisdiction of the U.S. government and regional management councils for these highly migratory species.

Fleets from the United States, Spain, and Brazil are currently conducting significant swordfish fishing activity in the Atlantic. National fleets from Canada, Cuba, and Venezuela may increase their effort at any time. Existing distant water long-line tuna fleets—Japan, Korea, and Taiwan—currently focusing on tuna could easily and quickly redirect their efforts at swordfish. These nations do not currently impose swordfish regulations, although many are active members of ICCAT. (Although not formally a member, Taiwan is an active participant.) This treaty organization is responsible for managing tuna and billfish in the Atlantic. With the completion of two ICCAT swordfish workshops, international consideration of Atlantic swordfish regulations could take place as soon as late 1989. The rapid expansion of international long-range fishing fleets along the northern and southern boundaries of the North Atlantic currents and further harvest increases represent the greatest potential threat to the resource. Because of the swordfish's highly migratory nature and the wide-ranging fleets that exploit it, the effectiveness of future swordfish regulations rests upon a comprehensive approach adopted by ICCAT or a similar multinational treaty that can regulate catches on an oceanwide basis.

PROGNOSIS

Thus far, the abundance of large swordfish in the North Atlantic has been significantly reduced by commercial long-line fishing for human consumption. Swordfish are a nonschooling ocean pelagic fish and therefore are not as immediately affected by human pollution of the ocean environment as are coastal resources. Naturally occurring environmental changes affect the abundance of swordfish prey and the survival of larvae to juvenile stages. The recent increasing trends in the recruiting year-class numbers in the western North Atlantic, during a period of declining adult stock abundance, offers fertile ground for examining recruitment in a large pelagic species.

It appears certain that all major concentrations of swordfish in the North Atlantic are being exploited. With the certain increase in vessel range and fish-finding technology, swordfish abundance will likely rest upon market demand and the effectiveness of international fishery regulatory agencies, such as ICCAT, to restrict fishing mortality levels. Although market demand is currently high in both the United States and Europe, factors such as restrictions on mercury content and other trade regulations could influence demand. As pointed out by Caddy (1976), the excessive harvesting of small swordfish may be an exploitation pattern that reduces mercury content. If market demand remains unaltered, fleet overcapitalization will occur, creating intense exploitation pressure on large oceanic species. Unfortunately, the history of international management of large oceanic fishes has shown that regulations are usually promulgated *after* abundance is greatly reduced. Recovery of the overfished species is usually slow due to the biological characteristics of these large fish, the degree to which they are reduced, and the high quotas originally set to obtain international agreement on restrictions.

Thus far, an instance where an oceanic pelagic fish stock was driven to commercial extinction or near extinction by fishing has not been documented. However, some species, such as bluefin tuna, have been greatly reduced by extensive exploitation. Swordfish have been exploited in the western North Atlantic since the mid-1800s. Although modern fishing methods catch slightly more than twice the landings of the historical harpoon catches (four to five million pounds dw), and many small juvenile fish, it seems unlikely that commercial extinction will occur in the near future. Swordfish life-history characteristics—such as protracted spawning over large areas, a nonschooling dispersed population, and sex and age segregation—may make the species's population more resistant and resilient to exploitation. The apparent resurgence of the stock when strict mercury restrictions were in effect during the 1970s hints at this. The challenge is to obtain maximum sustainable harvests by effective management instead of allowing unregulated exploitation to threaten the species's long-term economic viability. Historical harvest levels of mature adults, analytical results that indicate a potential for higher total landing (if fishing mortality on young fish is reduced), and the recent abundant year classes highlight the potential that can be realized by conserving young age classes at this time. Progress toward this goal seems likely, considering the current recognition of declining spawning stock size, high fishing mortality levels, and increased reliance on harvests of young immature fish.

RECOMMENDATIONS

Although the United States has formally expressed serious concern about the status of the North Atlantic swordfish stock at the last two ICCAT meetings, no harvest limit has been established due to uncertainty about recent assessment analyses. The United States believes that preliminary estimates suggest a declining resource with high fishing mortality rates and significant reductions in older mature fish. In response, ICCAT has instructed its Standing Committee on Research and Statistics to finalize an analytical assessment of the North Atlantic stock for the 1989 Commission Meeting.

Nationally, the Atlantic regional fishery management councils are considering quota restrictions for swordfish harvested in the western North Atlantic. The potential benefits of minimum catch-size regulations are also being considered. Scientists involved in the process have expressed serious concern about the large number of small swordfish taken, the reduced level of the spawning stock, and the magnitude of total North Atlantic harvests. It is expected that the councils will finalize management decisions and submit regulations to the Secretary of Commerce in mid-1989.

Currently, there are basic biological and fisheries gaps in available Atlantic swordfish data as well as questions regarding the sensitivity of analytical methodologies used by ICCAT scientists. ICCAT's Standing Committee on Research and Statistics recommended short-term investigations of the divergent trends in the catch-at-age and abundance indices. These recommendations raised questions about the reliability of the assessment conducted at the 1988 ICCAT Swordfish Workshop. Additional research is also essential on validated growth models, stock identification techniques, and procedures for evaluating stock-mixing rates. Increased sampling for size and sex by area and month may help address these questions. Analyses are also needed to investigate the sensitivity of currently accepted analytical models to mixing rates for stocks exploited by wide-ranging fisheries, sexually dimorphic growth, different natural mortality rates by age, and changes in age-specific catchability through time.

Considerable progress has been made in recent years on improving the Atlantic swordfish data base. Considering the international interest that has been evident at ICCAT, it seems certain that substantial progress will be made within the next year or two on analytical problems in assessing the fishery. More time will be required to address basic biological questions because of the need for extensive sampling at sea and additional data collection.

REFERENCES

Amorin, A.F. and C.A. Arfelli. 1984. "Estudio biologico pesqueiro do espadarte, *Xiphias gladius* Linnaeus, 1758, no sudestes do sul do Brasil (1971 a 1981)." *B. Inst. Pesca* 11(unico):35–62. Sao Paulo.

Anonymous. 1987. Report of the Swordfish Assessment Workshop. International Commission for the Conservation of Atlantic Tunas (ICCAT). April 1986. Col. Vol. Sci. Pap. XXVI:339–395. Miami, Florida.

———. 1988. Report of the ICCAT Swordfish Workshop. International Commission for the Conservation of Atlantic Tunas (ICCAT). October 1987. Col. Vol. Sci. Pap. XXVII:1–126. Madrid, Spain

Beckett, J.S. 1971. Canadian Swordfish Longline Fishery. International Commission for the Conservation of Atlantic Tunas. Collect. Vol. Sci. Pap. (SCRS-1971) 71/36. 7 pp.

———. 1974. "Biology of the swordfish, *Xiphias gladius* L., in the Northwest Atlantic Ocean," pp. 103–106 *in* R.S. Shomura and F. Williams eds., *Proceedings of the International Billfish Symposium*. Kailua-Kona, Hawaii. August 9–12, 1972. Part 2. Review and Contributing Papers, U.S. Department of Commerce, NOAA technical report, NMFS SSRF 675.

Berkeley, S.A., E.W. Irby, Jr. and J.W. Jolley, Jr. 1981. Florida's Commercial Swordfish Fishery: Longline Gear and Methods. Florida Sea Grant and Cooperative Extension Service.

—— and E.D. Houde. 1983. "Age determination of broadbilled swordfish, *Xiphias gladius*, from the Straits of Florida, using anal fin spine sections," pp. 137–143.

Caddy, J.F. 1976. "A review of some factors relevant to management of swordfish in the Northwest Atlantic." *Canadian Fish. Mar. Serv. Technical Report* 633:1–36.

Carey, F.G. 1982. "A brain heater in the swordfish." *Science* 216(45520):1327–1329.

———. and B.H. Robison. 1981. "Daily patterns in the activities of swordfish, *Xiphias gladius*, observed by acoustic telemetry." *Fishery Bulletin of the United States* 79:277–292.

———., J.M. Teal, J.W. Kanwisher, K.D. Lawson, and J.S. Beckett. 1971. "Warm bodied fish." *American Zoologist* 11:137–145.

———. and J.M. Teal. 1966. "Heat conservation in tuna fish muscle." *Proceedings of the National Academy of Science* 56(5):1464–1469.

Caveriviere, A. and P. Cayre. 1986. "Premiere peches palangrieres de surface a L'espadon (*Xiphias gladius*) au Senegal (1983–1984): prises, rendements et structure en taille des captures." International Commission for the Conservation of Atlantic Tuna. *Col. Vol. Sci. Pap.* XXV:185–196.

Church, R.E. 1968. "Broadbill swordfish in deep water." *Sea Frontier* 14:246–249.

Conser, R., P. Phares, J. Hoey, and M. Farber. 1986. "An assessment of the status of stocks of swordfish in the northwest Atlantic Ocean." International Commission for the Conservation of Atlantic Tuna. *Col. Vol. Sci. Pap.* XXV:218–245.

Dizon, A.E. and R.W. Brill. 1979. "Thermoregulation in tunas." *American Zoology* 19:249–265.

Goode, G.B. 1883. "Materials for a history of the sword-fishes." *Report on U.S. Commercial Fish* (1880)8:287–394.

Grall, C., D.P. DeSylva, and E.D. Houde. 1983. "Distribution, relative abundance, and seasonality of swordfish larvae." *Transactions of the American Fisheries Society* 112:235–246.

Hoey, J.J. 1986. A Review of Sex-ratio Size Data for Western North Atlantic Swordfish. NMFS/SEFC Swordfish workshop working paper 86/10. 21 pp.

———. and W.R. Nelson. 1988. A Review of the U.S. Swordfish Fishery Emphasizing Trends Within the 200 Mile U.S. Exclusive Economic Zone. NMFS/SEFC Oceanic Pelagics Division Contribution ML88-1. 86 pp.

———., J. Mejuto, S. Iglesias, and R. Conser. 1988. "A comparative study of the United States and Spanish longline fleets targeting swordfish in the Atlantic Ocean north of 40 N latitude." International Commission for the Conservation of Atlantic Tunas (ICCAT). *Col. Vol. Sci. Pap.* XXVII:230–239.

———., J. Mejuto, and R. Conser. In press. "CPUE indices derived from combined Spanish and U.S. catch and effort data." International Commission for the Conservation of Atlantic Tunas. *Col. Vol. Sci. Pap.* SCRS/88/22.

Lee, R.E. 1942. "The occurrence of female swordfish-fish in southern New England waters, with a description of their reproductive condition." *Copeia* 1942:117–119.

Lipton, D.W. 1986. "The resurgence of the U.S. swordfish market." *Marine Fisheries Review* 48(3):24–27.

Markle, G.E. 1974. "Distribution of larval swordfish in the northwest Atlantic Ocean," pp. 252–260, *in* R.S. Shomura and F. Williams eds., *Proceedings of the International Billfish Symposium*. Kailua-Kona, Hawaii. August 9–12, 1972. Part 2. Review and contributed papers. U.S. Department of Commerce, NOAA technical report NMFS SSRF-675.

Nakamura, I. 1985. "FAO species catalogue. Vol. 5. Billfishes of the world. An annotated and illustrated catalogue of marlins, sailfishes, spearfishes, and swordfishes known to date." *FAO Fisheries Synop* (125) 5. 65 pp.

Palko, B.J., G.L. Beardsley, and W.J. Richards. 1981. Synopsis of the Biology of the Swordfish, *Xiphias gladius* Linnaeus. U.S. Department of Commerce, NOAA technical report NMFS Circ. 441. 21 pp.

Rey, J.C., J. Mejuto, and S. Iglesias. 1988. "Evolucion historica y situacion actual de la pesqueria Española de pez Espada (*Xiphias gladius*)." International Commission for the Conservation of Atlantic Tunas. *Col. Vol. Sci. Pap.* XXVII:202–213.

Stillwell, C.E. and N.E. Kohler. 1985. "Food and feeding ecology of the swordfish *Xiphias gladius* in the Western North Atlantic with estimates of daily ratios." *Marine Ecology Prog. Serv.* 22:239–247.

Tanning, A.V. 1955. "On the breeding areas of the swordfish (Xiphias)." *Pap. Mar. Biol. Oceanogr., Deep Sea Res., Suppl. to vol.* 3:438–450.

Tibbo, S.N., L.R. Day, and W.F. Doucet. 1961. "The swordfish (*Xiphias gladius* L), its life history and economic importance in the northwest Atlantic." *Fishery Resources Board of Canada Bulletin 130.* 47 pp.

John J. Hoey is a fishery biologist with the National Marine Fisheries Service. He has 10 years experience developing and analyzing data from longline fisheries for sharks, swordfish, and tuna.

Ramon J. Conser is a fishery biologist with primary research interest in the area of population dynamics. He has been actively involved with international tuna and billfish stock assessments since 1977.

Angelo R. Bertolino is a fishery biologist with 14 years experience sampling bluefin tuna, billfish, and swordfish from both commercial and recreational fisheries. He is responsible for the multispecies longline size–frequency data base.

The authors wish to thank Bradford Brown and Walter Nelson, NMFS Southeast Fisheries Center, for reviewing an earlier draft of this manuscript.

The roseate tern's shrinking distribution and concentration in its winter habitat make it extremely vulnerable. But international agreements, such as the Bonn Convention and the Cartagena Convention, provide a means to protect the species in the Western Hemisphere. *Allan D. Cruickshank/VIREO*

The Roseate Tern

Ian C.T. Nisbet

I.C.T. Nisbet & Company

SPECIES DESCRIPTION AND NATURAL HISTORY

The roseate tern (*Sterna dougallii*) is one of the most distinctive of the medium-sized *Sterna* species known as sea terns. Sea terns resemble small gulls, but have a lighter, more graceful flight, longer wings, forked tails, pointed bills, and black caps contrasting with gray upperparts and pale or white underparts. Roseate terns are the palest of the sea terns, with long white tail-streamers, silvery-gray upperparts, and creamy-white underparts. The peach-colored flush on the throat and breast—from which this species derives its common name—usually is concealed by bleached white tips to the feathers, but sometimes is conspicuous on resting birds. The average weight of a breeding adult is about four ounces (124 grams). The sexes are alike in plumage and structure and can be distinguished only by behavior.

In North Atlantic birds, the bill is completely black at the time of egg-laying in the spring, gradually turning red at the base until it is half red by the end of the breeding season. Caribbean roseate terns have more red on the bill.

Roseate terns molt twice a year. Nonbreeding birds lack tail-streamers and have a dark patch on the carpal joint, or "wrist," of the wing; the head is white with a dark patch through the eye and both the bill and legs are black. This plumage is very similar to that of other sea terns and can be distinguished only when the pure white outer tail feathers are noticeable. Molt of the wing feathers probably resembles that of other sea terns—progressing slowly through the nonbreeding season, with overlapping of successive feather generations (Cramp 1985). New flight feathers have a frosty appearance, adding to the bird's overall whiteness.

Downy young are gray or sandy colored above with black speckles and are dull white below; their tufted down gives them a "hairy" appearance. Juveniles are sandy or silvery gray above with an intricate and beautiful pattern of wavy black v's on the mantle and scapulars. Their heads are mostly dark gray with paler, brownish streaks on the forehead, the underparts are white, and the bill and legs are black.

Roseate terns have distinctive structural and flight characteristics that often allow identification at considerable range (Kirkham and Nisbet 1987). The wings are relatively short—about 9.3 inches (23 centimeters) as compared to the 10.3 inches (26 centimeters) of common terns (*Sterna hirundo*). The tail-streamers are very long, ranging from six to eight inches (15 to 20 centimeters) (but occasionally broken off), and the body is relatively narrow. The wing strokes are shallow and rapid, allowing the species to fly much faster than other sea terns. Roseate terns often appear to dive much deeper than common terns (probably as deep as two feet [60 centimeters]), plunging into the water at high speeds from heights of 20 to 40 feet (6 to 12 meters) and remaining submerged for up to 2.5 seconds before re-emerging (Kirkham and Nisbet 1987, Duffy 1986).

Distribution

The roseate tern is an exclusively marine species with a widely scattered distribution throughout the tropical oceans. It breeds in the Bahamas and around the Caribbean Sea; in the Indian Ocean from Madagascar and Kenya to Burma and western Australia; in the Malay Archipelago; and in the western Pacific Ocean from the Philippines to the Solomon and Loyalty islands. It also breeds in several temperate areas, including southern Japan, western Australia, and South Africa, as well as both sides of the North Atlantic Ocean, where it ranges north to western Scotland and southeastern Canada (Nisbet 1980, Cramp 1985) (see Figure 1).

Migration

Both the northeastern and Caribbean populations of the roseate tern are migratory, arriving at breeding areas in early May. Adults and ju-

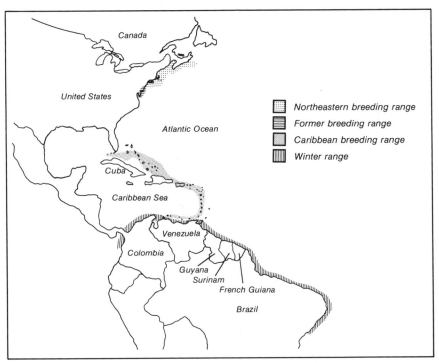

Figure 1. Breeding and winter distribution of roseate terns in the Western Hemisphere.

veniles migrate south between late August and late September. Even birds that breed on islands within 40 miles (65 kilometers) of the South American mainland—typically warm throughout the year—migrate south for the winter. Northeastern birds apparently migrate directly south across the North Atlantic Ocean to the West Indies (Nisbet 1984). Both populations are known to winter in northern South America, but ornithologists have rarely encountered them there (Nisbet 1984).

Banding recoveries suggest that the winter quarters extend all along the north coast of South America, from western Colombia to eastern Brazil. Most three-year-old birds migrate north and breed, but a few birds apparently do not breed until they are four years old (Nisbet 1984). Some two-year-old birds also migrate north; a few of these breed late in the summer.

Breeding

In the Western Hemisphere, roseate terns breed in two discrete areas. The northeastern population breeds on about 20 islands between Jones

Beach, New York, and Sable Island, Nova Scotia. In recent years, small numbers have bred occasionally on islands off Quebec, New Brunswick, New Jersey, and North Carolina. Roseate terns formerly bred in Maryland and Virginia, but have not bred there since about 1930 (Nisbet 1980).

The Caribbean population breeds in the Dry Tortugas and Key West, Florida; in the Bahamas; and around the Antilles chain of islands from the Dominican Republic and Puerto Rico through the Lesser Antilles to the islands off Venezuela (Islas Las Aves and Los Roques, and the Netherlands Lesser Antilles). There are scattered records of nesting on small islands off Cuba, Jamaica, Honduras, and Belize (Nisbet 1980, van Halewyn and Norton 1984) (see Figure 1).

Roseate terns breed almost exclusively on small coastal islands. The Plymouth Beach, Massachusetts, colony is the exception, where the terns are established on a barrier spit that is attached to the mainland (Nisbet 1981). Northeastern roseate terns have been recorded nesting only in colonies of common terns, where they seem to benefit from the aggressive behavior of the latter species toward predators. Northeastern roseates habitually select the more densely vegetated parts of common tern colonies, where they conceal their nests under clumps of beach grass, beach pea, seaside goldenrod, or other herbaceous plants. Caribbean roseates usually nest in mixed colonies with bridled (*S. anaethetus*) or sooty (*S. fuscata*) terns. Some pairs nest under rocks, driftwood, or in artificial sites.

Unlike the Northeastern roseates, Caribbean roseates nest in the open, on bare sand, or among broken coral or limestone. However, many nests are placed near to overhanging rocks or vegetation, which provide shade for the chicks (Burger and Gochfeld 1988). In both areas, roseate terns nest typically at high densities, with nests often located only 18 or 24 inches (45 or 60 centimeters) apart in areas where the rocks or vegetation are suitably patchy (Nisbet 1981).

Roseate terns usually lay one or two eggs in a shallow scrape on bare ground. In the Northeast, most early clutches consist of two eggs, but the average clutch size decreases during the nesting season until late-nesting birds—mostly young birds laying for the first or second time—lay predominantly single eggs (Nisbet 1981, J. Spendelow unpubl.). Clutches of three and four eggs are laid occasionally, probably by female-female pairs as documented in other tern species (Conover 1983).

The eggs are pale brownish or greenish gray, densely marked with clear blackish freckles. The average egg is about 1.6 inches (4.1 centimeters) long, a little over 1 inch (2.9 centimeters) in width, and weighs about 0.7 of an ounce (20 grams) (Nisbet 1981). The eggs are slightly longer and thinner than common tern eggs, more tapered to a point at the small end, and more finely and distinctly spotted. Most northeastern birds lay between mid-May and mid-June, but smaller numbers—mostly younger birds—continue to lay throughout June until late July (Nisbet 1981, J. Spendelow pers. comm.). Caribbean roseates lay a week or two earlier, usually laying smaller clutches, which average about 1.5 eggs at the beginning of the season, and smaller eggs, which average 5 to 10 percent smaller in volume and weight than those of northeastern birds (Nisbet 1981).

Both sexes incubate the eggs, alternating in shifts that last from a few minutes up to six hours. As each shift is completed, the incubating parent adds scraps of vegetation to the nest, so that a substantial nest is built up during the incubation period. On average, the eggs take 23 days to hatch. However, incubation may be extended to 29 to 30 days in colonies subject to nocturnal predation, when adult terns often desert the eggs at night (Nisbet 1981, Nisbet and Welton 1984).

When two eggs are laid, they usually hatch about three days apart. By the time the second egg has hatched, the first chick has grown substantially and remains larger throughout the growth period. When the parents cannot bring enough food for both chicks, the smaller second chick usually starves. However, roseate terns do not show the intense sibling competition for food that characterizes other tern species, and chick starvation is infrequent in the northeastern population (Nisbet 1981).

Northeastern roseate chicks usually remain hidden during the growth period. When they fledge, the parents accompany them closely. On their first flights, the chicks fly out to the edge of the island and usually do not return to the nesting area. In cases in which both chicks are raised, they fledge several days apart. The older chick is then accompanied by one parent while the other parent remains behind to feed the younger chick. Juveniles remain dependent on their parents for at least six weeks after fledging and can often be seen in close company with one or two adults, even in places far from the breeding colony (Nisbet 1981). Juveniles probably migrate south with their parents and may remain dependent on them for part of the first winter.

At several northeastern colonies, roseate terns have been breeding with high success in recent years, commonly fledging more than one chick per pair (Nisbet 1981, unpubl.). Lower breeding success has been reported occasionally in colonies subject to predation (LeCroy and Collins 1972, Houde 1977). Safina *et al.* (1988) found that breeding success may also be limited by the availability of food. Little information is available on the productivity of the Caribbean population, except at Dry Tortugas, where success has been chronically low because of storms and predation (Robertson 1976, pers. comm.).

Diet

Roseate terns feed almost exclusively on small marine fish. They specialize on fish that swim in dense schools in open water. Small schooling fish generally avoid swimming too close to the surface, so roseates can catch them only when a vertical movement of the water or a predator chasing them from below bring the fish near the surface. Northeastern birds feed mainly on American sand lance (*Ammodytes americanus*) and on smaller numbers of various species of herrings (Clupeidae) and Atlantic mackerel (*Scomber scombrus*). They feed occasionally on other species of fish but rarely on shrimps or other invertebrates (Nisbet 1981, Safina pers. comm., Cramp 1985). Caribbean birds feed on schooling "bait" fish such as *Harengula* species (R. Norton pers. comm.).

Roseate terns can dive to greater depths than other plunge-diving terns and commonly feed in deep, turbulent waters, for example, in tidal channels, tide-rips, or places where currents run over coral reefs. Roseates also feed in flocks over predatory fish such as bluefish (*Pomatomus saltatrix*), catching small fish that are driven to the surface by the bluefish; however, roseates appear to be less successful than common terns in these circumstances (Duffy 1986).

Life Span and Mortality

Like most seabirds, roseate terns are long-lived. However, preliminary data from studies at Falkner Islands (Connecticut) suggest that roseate tern adult mortality rates may be higher than those of common terns or other seabirds (Spendelow and Nichols 1988). The oldest banded roseate recovered to date was 14 years old and still breeding successfully (Nisbet unpubl.). However, it is likely that this figure does not represent the species potential longevity, because the bands wear out rapidly and most are lost after 10 to 15 years (Nisbet and Hatch 1983).

The most significant predator on adults at the northeastern breeding colonies is the great horned owl (*Bubo virginianus*). The terns usually respond to the marauding owls by deserting the colonies at night. This behavior minimizes predation on adults, but leaves the eggs and chicks vulnerable to chilling. Other predators include black-crowned night herons (*Nycticorax nycticorax*) and ants, which kill pipping eggs and new chicks. On sites accessible from the mainland, roseates are subject to heavy predation by brown rats (*Rattus norvegicus*), striped skunks (*Mephitis mephitis*), and other terrestrial predators (Austin 1948, Buckley and Buckley 1981, Nisbet 1981). Little is known about predators or other causes of death among Caribbean roseate terns, but predation by cattle egrets (*Bubulcus ibis*), gulls, rats, and land crabs (*Geocarcinus ruvicola*) has been reported (Robertson 1976, Kepler and Kepler 1978, Burger and Gochfeld 1988). Egg collecting by humans is probably an important factor limiting breeding success in the British Virgin Islands as well as elsewhere in the Caribbean (van Halewyn and Norton 1984, van Halewyn 1985).

Killing for human food probably has been the most important mortality factor for wintering roseate tern populations in recent decades. Since 1968, between one and two percent of all roseate terns banded in the Northeast have been recovered in a small area on the northeast coast of Guyana (Hamilton 1981, Nisbet 1984). Investigation revealed that large numbers of terns were being netted at night as they roosted on offshore mudbanks and then were being sold for food in local markets (Trull 1988).

SIGNIFICANCE OF THE SPECIES

As in the case of many other endangered species, the primary reason for expending special efforts to conserve the roseate tern is the value placed on biological diversity. The location of the northeastern population on a coast used intensively for recreation, adjacent to a highly urbanized part of the country, provides both a special impetus for maintaining biological diversity and a difficult challenge for conservationists.

The roseate tern is an indicator species for the problems common to many other seabirds: loss of nesting sites to human development and competing species, predation in the remaining sites, and human exploitation. The species's shrinking distribution is a measure of the deterioration of available habitat for other sensitive species. The roseate tern is especially vulnerable to human predation in the winter quarters, because it is concentrated into limited areas where market trapping is prevalent (Nisbet 1984).

The roseate tern is of considerable scientific interest because of its unusual distribution in both tropical and temperate areas, its specializations for fast flight and deep diving, and its anti-predator adaptations, which enables it to breed more successfully than most other terns. Aesthetically, the roseate tern is widely considered to be the most beautiful of the sea terns.

HISTORICAL PERSPECTIVE

Northeastern roseates were probably more widely distributed in the 19th century, and were reported as numerous in Virginia (Smith 1884) and on Sable Island, Nova Scotia (Dwight 1895). During the 1870s and 1880s, however, large numbers of terns and other seabirds were killed for the millinery trade and eliminated from many parts of the Atlantic seaboard (Drury 1973–1974, Doughty 1975). Roseate terns, protected by the remoteness of their major colonies, were probably less severely affected than other terns (Nisbet 1980). At the end of the 1880s, it is estimated that at least 2,000 pairs of roseates were still nesting at four major colony sites: one on Sable Island, Nova Scotia (Dwight 1895); two off Cape Cod, Massachusetts (Mackay 1895, 1899); and probably one in Long Island Sound (Dutcher 1901). They also may have been nesting at other sites in the same areas, as well as in Virginia (Nisbet 1980).

Early Protective Measures

Breeding terns in the northeast have been subject to various forms of management for nearly 100 years. The great massacres of terns and other birds in the late 19th century constituted one of the early crises of the conservation movement, and led directly to the formation of the Massachusetts Audubon Society and indirectly to the formation of the National Audubon Society. The first active role in stopping the massacres was played by a scientific body, the American Ornithologists' Union (Dutcher 1901). Initially, seabirds were protected primarily by convincing landowners to do so, appointing wardens, and enforcing trespass laws (Dutcher 1902, 1904, Drury 1973–1974). Subsequently, the Migratory Bird Treaty Act of 1918, as well as various state laws, extended legal protection to roseate tern colonies. As these protective measures were enacted, roseate terns and other species quickly regained much of their lost range and many of their lost numbers (Mackay 1895, 1899, Dutcher 1901, Nisbet 1973, 1980).

Between 1929 and 1957, Oliver Austin, Sr., conducted an extensive program to manage the terns breeding around Cape Cod, Massachusetts. The program included acquiring one major colony site (Tern Island, Chatham), managing its vegetation to attract terns, controlling rats on this and other sites, and conducting an extensive banding and trapping program (Austin 1932, 1944, Floyd 1938). Although the primary focus was common terns, Austin's program also maintained inshore sites for roseates. The program lapsed with Austin's death in 1957, but was reactivated by the Massachusetts Audubon Society in 1967. Since then, other governmental and private organizations have developed tern protection programs that entail the posting of tern colonies and protecting them with full-time wardens.

Roseate tern numbers in the Northeast probably reached a peak during the 1930s, when some 8,500 pairs were documented—at least 6,000 of these pairs were in Massachusetts (Nisbet 1980). The population then declined and contracted in range, disappearing from Virginia, Maryland, and New Jersey, and probably from Sable Island. By 1952, the population was limited to its current geographical range, and only 5,000 individuals could be accounted for (Nisbet 1980). Surveys in 1971 and 1972 suggest a population of about 4,700 pairs (Drury 1973–1974, Nisbet 1973, 1980), and surveys indicate 2,600 pairs in 1978 and 1979 (Nisbet 1980, Buckley and Buckley 1981).

Although the historical estimates of numbers vary in completeness and reliability, there is general agreement that the northeastern population has decreased by about two-thirds since 1935 and suffered a "crash" in the early 1970s (Drury 1973–1974, Erwin and Korschgen 1979, Buckley and Buckley 1981, Kress *et al.* 1983, Fish and Wildlife Service 1988).

Little is known of the history of the Caribbean roseate population. The species is now most abundant in the Bahamas, Puerto Rico, and the Virgin Islands. Historical records are insufficient to determine whether any changes have taken place (Cory 1880, Nichols 1943). Smaller groups in the Dry Tortugas and the Netherlands Lesser Antilles have not changed markedly in numbers since 1917 and 1951, respectively (Robertson 1976, pers. comm., van Halewyn 1985). The only other large Caribbean colonies—reported on islands and rocks off Antigua (Danforth 1934)—may have declined (Holland and Williams 1978).

CURRENT TRENDS

In recent years, the northeastern roseate tern population has been stable at about 3,000 pairs (Kress *et al.* 1983, Buckley and Buckley 1984, Fish and Wildlife Service 1988). The total number may be increasing slowly, but difficulties in conducting precise counts make this conclusion uncertain. More importantly, the tendency of the northeastern roseate population to concentrate into a few large colonies has continued. By 1988, about half of the total population was concentrated in one colony, 80 percent in two colonies, and 85 percent in three colonies (Fish and Wildlife Service 1988). Losses of major colony sites have continued during the 1980s.

In the Caribbean, Sprunt (1984) estimated between 1,000 and 2,000 pairs in the Bahamas, and van Halewyn and Norton (1984) estimated about 2,500 pairs in Puerto Rico and the U.S. Virgin Islands. There is insufficient information to determine current trends, but there is no evidence for marked increases or decreases (R. Norton pers. comm.). Current threats to the population include egging, human disturbance, and rat predation (van Halewyn and Norton 1984, van Halewyn 1985).

MANAGEMENT

In recent years, the roseate tern has been designated for special protection in a number of jurisdictions. It is now listed as either endangered or threatened in Maine, New Hampshire, Massachusetts, Connecticut,

New York, and Florida (Fish and Wildlife Service 1988), as well as in Canada (Kirkham and Nettleship 1985). These designations provide for augmented legal protection and give the species priority in the allocation of funds and resources for management. However, in most cases, they do not provide habitat protection for the species or the additional authority to acquire colony sites.

In November 1987, the U.S. Fish and Wildlife Service (FWS) listed the northeastern population of the roseate tern as endangered and the Caribbean population as threatened under the Endangered Species Act. The listing is somewhat unusual because it was *not* based on a specific finding stating that either population is dangerously small or declining. The endangered listing was based primarily on the bird's vulnerability due to the concentration of the small population "within a restricted range, at only a few sites, and with nearly 60 percent of the population confined to one small island off southeastern Massachusetts . . ." (Fish and Wildlife Service 1987). This chapter fully supports this concern: The loss of the colony site at Bird Island, Massachusetts, due to predation, human activity, or natural catastrophe would seriously jeopardize this population, because there are few, if any, secure sites to which the birds could move.

The threatened status for the Caribbean roseate population is based primarily on small population size and disturbance and predation by humans and nonindigenous animals. The listing covers all roseate terns in the Caribbean, including northeastern migrants, and is justified in part by the incompleteness of the available information.

Listing of the species under the Endangered Species Act provides for additional federal protection and enforcement, as well as recovery actions and research. However, as of January 1, 1989, FWS still had not appointed a recovery team for the Caribbean population. A recovery team has been appointed for the northeastern roseate population and has issued a draft recovery plan (Fish and Wildlife Service 1988). The plan recommends a variety of management actions, including continued population monitoring, habitat management and gull control on the breeding grounds, restoration of one or more former colony sites, and investigation of population status and mortality in the terns' wintering areas. The draft plan, however, does not address the need for protection of feeding areas or management of populations of prey species.

In anticipation of the endangered listing, FWS initiated in 1987 a four-year cooperative study of roseate terns on the four largest colonies in the Northeast. The study is designed to investigate productivity, recruitment, survival, dispersal between colonies, and other aspects of population dynamics. The study took advantage of ongoing work on the species at each of these colonies. By the end of the 1988 season, about 20 percent of the breeding adults had been marked with indi-

Audubon biologist Carl Safina bands a roseate tern. *Chris Wille*

vidual color-band combinations, and several thousand chicks had been banded with an FWS aluminum band and color-banded for subsequent study of recruitment (J. Spendelow pers. comm.). However, funding for the continuation of the study through 1989 is uncertain.

Two recent international actions offer potential protection for the species. In 1986, the roseate tern was listed under Appendix C of the Bonn Convention. The convention is an "umbrella treaty" designed to stimulate the development of specific treaties among its parties to protect migratory wildlife. The Bonn Convention listing eventually should lead to international protection of the roseate in Europe and Africa. Unfortunately, few Western Hemisphere countries have signed the Bonn Convention: Jamaica is the only such country within the Western Hemisphere range of the roseate tern.

The most promising vehicle for international activity in the Western Hemisphere is the Cartagena Convention. This treaty is designed to promote the development of specific protocols among its parties to protect the marine environment of the "wider Caribbean region." The Cartagena Convention was enacted in 1986 and has been signed and/or ratified by 18 countries in the region, including the United States, the United Kingdom, France, and the Netherlands. Countries with important populations of roseate terns that have not yet signed the convention include the Bahamas, Dominican Republic, and Guyana. A meeting was held in October 1988 to initiate the development of a protocol under the convention for the designation of specially protected areas. Although it will take several years before such a protocol can be enacted, this is a promising vehicle for protection of areas used by endangered wildlife such as the roseate tern. The species's listing as threatened by the United States may focus attention on it for early action when the protocol is implemented.

Habitat Protection

Great Gull Island, off long Long Island, New York, acquired by the American Museum of Natural History in 1949, is managed for the protection and study of a large tern colony located there (Heilbrun 1970, Hays 1984). Presently, most of the other major colony sites used by roseate terns in the northeastern United States are in secure ownership by either federal, state, or local government agencies and are designated as wildlife refuges or sanctuaries. Most of these sites are actively protected and/or wardened. Human disturbance is no longer a significant problem in these regions. All the larger colonies have been subjected to intensive scientific study requiring the regular presence of biologists in the nesting areas. Consequently, most of the birds in the northeastern population have become habituated to human presence and are very tolerant of casual disturbances by visitors to the islands (Nisbet 1981, Fish and Wildlife Service 1988).

In the U.S. Virgin Islands, most of the colony sites are owned by the Commonwealth Government and have varying degrees of legal protection. There is limited enforcement of laws against egging, but violators are deterred by the presence of biologists (R. Norton pers. comm.). In the Bahamas, roseate terns nest mainly on small inaccessible rocks and do not require much active protection (Sprunt IV pers. comm.). In the Netherlands Lesser Antilles, there has recently been some enforcement of laws against egging, and a wardening program was started in 1983 in Aruba. The program's future, however, is uncertain because of changes in land use (van Halewyn 1985).

Habitat Modification

At some northeastern colonies, habitat management is needed because thick vegetation or other factors limit the number of suitable nest sites. On Bird Island, for example, the nesting area is raked and burned every two to three years to clear away tangles of dead, woody vegetation (Nisbet 1981). On Great Gull Island, the reintroduction in 1981 of meadow voles (*Microtus pennsylvanicus*)—rodents that heavily consume vegetation—resulted in the opening up of many areas that had become too overgrown for the terns to nest in. However, these areas were occupied by common terns; roseates still nest primarily under rocks (Hays 1984). At Falkner's Island, provision of artificial nest sites—by sinking old automobile tires into a pebbly beach—has proved very successful. Roseate terns occupy these sites in preference to natural sites and the number nesting on the island has increased (Spendelow 1982). Since roseates commonly nest under driftwood and other human-made objects, artificially created nest sites could be provided easily in other colonies (Nisbet 1981).

Protection on the Wintering Grounds

Although roseate terns are nominally protected in several countries in which they winter, no specific protection programs in the South American winter quarters have been reported. Recent initiatives in West Africa, however, have demonstrated the possibility for effective action to protect the birds on their wintering grounds.

Gull Control

Since 1930, the primary cause of the progressive loss of roseate and common tern colony sites in the northeast has been the occupation of these sites by expanding populations of herring gulls (*Larus argenta-tus*) and great black-backed gulls (*L. marinus*) (Nisbet 1973, 1980, Kress*et al.* 1983, Fish and Wildlife Service 1988). Attempts to control these gull populations have a long and checkered history (Blodget 1988). Methods used include spraying of eggs with an oil-formaldehyde mixture to prevent hatching (Gross 1938–1952), shooting, poisoning, and various forms of harassment (Nisbet 1980, Drennan *et al.* 1986, Fish and Wildlife Service 1986). Large-scale gull control programs have proved to be very expensive and labor-intensive, and generally have failed (Blodget 1988). Small-scale programs, however, often have proved effective in preventing gulls from taking over small islands or from spreading into tern nesting areas on large islands (Drury and Nisbet 1972, Nisbet 1980, Fish and Wildlife Service 1986). Three former colony sites in Maine have been restored by local gull control programs involving poisoning and harassment (Kress *et al.* 1983, Drennan *et al.* 1986, Anonymous 1986). Overall, gull control programs have been successful in maintaining several of the major roseate tern colonies in the Northeast. As the number of great black-backed gulls continues to increase (Kress pers. comm.), continuation of these programs will be necessary if the last major roseate tern colonies are to be maintained.

Predator Control

Programs to control rats have been conducted at several roseate tern colonies in Massachusetts (Austin 1948, Nisbet 1980) and in the U.S. Virgin Islands (R. Norton pers. comm.). Generally, these programs are effective if started before the rats cause any significant damage. Except in unusually favorable circumstances, control of nocturnal predators, such as great horned owls or black-crowned night herons, has proved to be difficult, expensive, and time consuming.

Conservation of the European Population

The west European population of roseate terns presents conservation problems closely parallel to those of the U.S. northeastern population. The European roseate population has declined in recent decades and now numbers only about 540 pairs (Dunn 1981, Cramp 1985, Hepburn 1986, Cabot 1988). These birds winter in a narrow zone of West Africa, and in recent years up to 2.5 percent of the birds banded in Europe have been recovered in the winter quarters, primarily in Ghana (Langham 1971, Mead 1978, Dunn and Mead 1982, Cabot 1988). An investigation revealed that large numbers of juvenile terns were being trapped along the shore, mostly by small boys for recreation (Dunn 1981, Hepburn 1986). An agreement negotiated among the Government of Ghana (1985), the International Council for Bird Preservation, and the Royal

Society for Protection of Birds provides for an education and conservation program designed to protect seashore resources, placing special emphasis on the roseate tern. The program is funded and advised by the International Council for Bird Preservation and the Royal Society for Protection of Birds, but is implemented by the Ghana Game and Wildlife Department (Hepburn 1986). This unique agreement between private organizations in a developed country and the government of a developing country offers a model for effective conservation of migratory birds in the Western Hemisphere.

PROGNOSIS

Although neither of the Western Hemisphere populations of the roseate terns appears critically endangered at present, the northeastern population could become so quickly if one or more of the remaining large colony sites is taken over by gulls or subject to heavy predation. Alleviation of this threat and provision of new colonies through gull control and predator control will require substantially more management efforts than has been possible in the past. However, if a few more secure colonies can be established, the prospects for this population appear good, provided that the local populations of its prey species remain high. Commercial exploitation of these species has not been proposed, but might pose a threat if it should be undertaken in the future. In the Caribbean, a modest increase in enforcement and management effort in the Virgin Islands should suffice for the maintenance of this population. The Bahamas population appears to be reasonably secure.

In the long run, the future of the species will depend primarily on its fate on the wintering grounds. Increasing human population and deteriorating economic conditions in coastal regions of northern South America will inevitably increase pressures on this and other marginally edible species. The progress made already with an educational program in Ghana, however, offers substantial hope that roseate terns can also be protected in South America.

RECOMMENDATIONS

The most important requirement for long-term maintenance of the roseate tern in the Western Hemisphere is protection on the wintering grounds. Such protection cannot be achieved without greater knowledge of the extent of human predation and other mortality factors. At present, very little is known about the seasonal occurrence of the species in South America and nothing is known about its ecology. Both land-based and sea-based surveys will be required to confirm the roseate's wintering patterns. Such surveys should be designed to identify the importance and geographical occurrence of human predation. Only when this information is obtained will it be possible to plan educational and other programs to reduce the impact of such predation.

In the northeast United States, the primary needs are to increase the number of available colony sites, as well as possibly clearing gulls from one or two former sites, and to eliminate predators from others. A possible option is the creation of new sites by building dredge-spoil islands. Management of existing colonies should continue, with contingency plans for vigorous control of predators if they gain access to any of the existing major colony sites. Investigations should continue on the dependence of the northeastern roseates on local populations of the American sand lance and other prey species. Management or protection of these fish populations may be needed in the future.

In the Caribbean, the greatest need is for more surveys and field research concerning current distribution, breeding success, and limiting factors, including human predation. Depending on the results of such studies, more funding will be needed for management, predator control, and enforcement activities. International promotion of conservation, including educational activities at the grassroots level, will be needed to maintain populations outside U.S. jurisdiction. Development of a protocol under the Cartagena Convention would be an appropriate vehicle for governmental action.

The listing of both populations of the species in 1987 under the Endangered Species Act could have provided an important stimulus for various conservation actions. The failure of FWS to follow up on the listing with even the first step of appointing a recovery team for the Caribbean population is discouraging. Vigorous implementation of the recovery plan for the northeastern population, including its recommendation for studies in the roseate's wintering grounds, would help to promote the recovery of the species. However, budgetary constraints in the federal endangered species program make it unlikely that these recommendations will be implemented fully in the near future, unless conservationists take specific actions to secure funds for roseate tern work.

REFERENCES

Anonymous. 1986. "Arctic tern chick production triples at Matinicus Rock." *Egg Rock Update* 1986: 1
Austin, O.L. 1932. "The status of Cape Cod terns in 1932." *Bird-Banding* 3: 143–156.

———. 1944. "The status of Tern Island and the Cape Cod terns in 1943." *Bird-Banding* 15: 133–139.

———. 1948. "Predation by the common rat (*Rattus norvegicus*) in the Cape Cod colonies of nesting terns." *Bird-Banding* 19: 60–65.

Blodget, B.G. 1988. "The half-century battle for gull control." *Massachusetts Wildlife* 38(2): 12–21.

Buckley, P.A. and F.G. Buckley. 1981. "The endangered status of North American roseate terns." *Colonial Waterbirds* 4: 166–173.

———. and ———. 1984. "Seabirds of the North and Middle Atlantic coast of the United States: Their status and conservation," pp. 101–134 in J.P. Croxall, P.G.H. Evans, and R.W. Schreiber eds., *Status and Conservation of the World's Seabirds.* International Council for Bird Preservation, ICBP Technical Publication no. 2. Cambridge, England.

Burger, J. and M. Gochfeld. 1988. "Nest-site selection by roseate terns in two tropical colonies on Culebra, Puerto Rico." *Condor* 90: 843–851.

Cabot, D. 1988. "The population decline of the roseate tern, *Sterna dougallii,* breeding in NW Europe 1960–1987." Submitted to *Irish Birds.*

Conover, M.R. 1983. "Female-female pairings in caspian terns." *Condor* 85: 346–349.

Cory, C.B. 1880. *Birds of the Bahama Islands.* Charles B. Cory. Boston, Massachusetts. 329 pp.

Cramp, S. (ed.) 1985. *The Birds of the Western Palearctic.* Vol. IV. Oxford University Press. London. 960 pp.

Danforth, S.T. 1934. "The birds of Antigua." *Auk* 51: 350–364.

Doughty, R. 1975. *Feather Fashions and Bird Preservation: A Study in Nature Preservation.* University of California Press. Berkeley, California. 184 pp.

Drennan, M.P., D.C. Folger, and C. Treyball. 1986. Petit Manan National Wildlife Refuge, 1985: Changes in Nesting Seabird Population After Two Years of Gull Management. Unpublished report. College of the Atlantic. Bar Harbor, Maine. 43 pp.

Drury, W.H. 1973–1974. "Population changes in New England seabirds." *Bird-Banding* 44: 267–313; 45: 1–15.

———. and I.C.T. Nisbet. 1972. "The importance of movements in the biology of herring gulls in New England," pp. 173–210 in U.S. Department of Interior, *Population Ecology of Migratory Birds: A Symposium.* Wildlife Research Report 2. Washington, D.C.

Duffy, D.C. 1986. "Foraging at patches: interactions between common and roseate terns." *Ornis scandinavica* 17: 47–52.

Dunn, E.K. 1981. "Roseates on a lifeline." *Birds* 8: 42–45.

———. and C.J. Mead. 1982. "Relationship between sardine fisheries and recovery rates of ringed terns in West Africa." *Seabird Report* 6: 98–104. (1977–1981).

Dutcher, W. 1901. "Results of special protection to gulls and terns obtained through the Thayer Fund." *Auk* 18: 76–104

———. 1902. "Results of special protection to gulls and terns obtained through the Thayer Fund." *Auk* 19: 34–64.

———. 1904. "Report of the A.O.U. Committee on the Protection of North American birds for the year 1903." *Auk* 21(Supplement): 97–208.

Dwight, J., Jr. 1895. "The Ipswich sparrow (*Ammodramus princeps* Maynard) and its summer home." *Memoirs of the Nuttall Ornithological Club* 2: 1–56.

Erwin, R.M. and C.E. Korschgen. 1979. *Coastal Waterbird Colonies: Maine to Virginia, 1977. An Atlas Showing Colony Locations and Species Composition.* U.S. Fish and Wildlife Service, Office of Biological Services, FWS/OBS-79/08. Slidell, Louisiana. 647 pp.

Floyd, C.B. 1938. "Experiments with terns at Tern Island, Chatham, Massachusetts." *Bulletin of the Massachusetts Audubon Society* 21: 2–4.

Government of Ghana. 1985. Save the Seashore Birds project–Ghana. Memorandum of Agreement, June 11, 1985. Accra, Ghana.

Gross, A.O. 1938–1952. Unpublished journals. Bowdoin College. Brunswick, Maine.

Hamilton, J. 1981. "Recoveries of wintering roseate terns." *Journal of Field Ornithology* 52: 36–42.

Hays, H. 1984. "The vole that soared." *Natural History* 93: 7–16.

Heilbrun, L.H. 1970. "Great Gull Island: Its history and biology." *Proceedings of the Linnean Society of New York* 71: 55–79.

Hepburn, I. 1986. "Operation roseate." *Birds* 11: 39–41.

Holland, C.S. and J.M. Williams. 1978. "Observations on the birds of Antigua." *American Birds* 32: 1095–1105.

Houde, P. 1977. "Gull-tern interactions on Hicks Island." *Proceedings of the Linnean Society of New York* 43: 58–64.

Kepler, C.B. and A.K. Kepler. 1978. "The seabirds of Culebra and its adjacent islands." *The Living Bird* 16: 21–50.

Kirkham, I.R. and D.N. Nettleship. 1985. "Status of the roseate tern in Canada." *Journal of Field Ornithology* 58: 505–515.

———., I.C.T. Nisbet. 1987. "Feeding techniques and field identification of arctic, common, and roseate terns." *British Birds* 80: 41–47.

Kress, S.W., E.H. Weinstein, and I.C.T. Nisbet. 1983. "The status of tern populations in northeastern United States and adjacent Canada." *Colonial Waterbirds* 6: 84–106.

Langham, N.P.E. 1971. "Seasonal movements of British terns in the Atlantic Ocean." *Bird Study* 18: 155–175.

LeCroy, M. and C.T. Collins. 1972. "Growth and survival of roseate and common tern chicks." *Auk* 89: 595–611.

Mackay, G.H. 1895. "The terns of Muskget Island, Massachusetts." *Auk* 12: 32–48, 178

———. 1899. "The terns of Muskeget and Penikese Islands, Massachusetts." *Auk* 16: 259–266.

Mead, C.J. 1978. "Tern mortality in West Africa as shown by British and Dutch ringing recoveries." *Ibis* 120: 110.

Nichols, R.A. 1943. "The breeding birds of St. Thomas and St. John, Virgin Islands." *Memorias de la Sociedad Cubana de Historia Natural* 17: 23–27.

Nisbet, I.C.T. 1973. "Terns in Massachusetts: Present status and historical trends." *Bird-Banding* 44: 27–55.

———. 1980. Status and Trends of the Roseate Tern *Sterna dougallii* in North America and the Caribbean. Unpublished report to the U.S. Fish and Wildlife Service, Office of Endangered Species. Massachusetts Audubon Society. Lincoln, Massachusetts.

———. 1981. Biological Characteristics of the Roseate Tern *Sterna dougallii*. Unpublished report to the U.S. Fish and Wildlife Service, Office of Endangered Species. Massachusetts Audubon Society. Lincoln, Massachusetts.

———. 1984. "Migration and winter quarters of North American roseate terns as shown by banding recoveries." *Journal of Field Ornithology* 55: 1–17.

———. and J.J. Hatch. 1983. "Band wear and band loss in roseate terns." *Journal of Field Ornithology* 54: 90.

———. and M.J. Welton. 1984. "Seasonal variations in breeding success of common terns: consequences of predation." *Condor* 86: 53–60.

Robertson, W.B., Jr. 1976. "Birds," *in* H.W. Kale and P.S. Pritchard eds., *Rare and Endangered Biota of Florida.* Volume 2. Florida University Press. Gainesville, Florida.

Safina, C., J. Burger, M. Gochfeld, and R.H. Wagner. 1988. "Evidence for prey limitation of common and roseate tern reproduction." *Condor* 90: 852–859.

Smith, H.M. 1884. "Notes on the birds found on Cobb's Island, Virginia, between July 9 and July 29, 1884. Part II. Water Birds." *Pastime* 3: 37–38.

Spendelow, J. 1982. "An analysis of temporal variation in, and the effects of, habitat modification on reproductive success of roseate terns." *Colonial Waterbirds* 5: 19–31.

————. and J.D. Nichols. 1988. "Annual survival rates of breeding roseate terns (*Sterna dougallii*)." *Auk*. In press.

Sprunt, A., IV. 1984. "The status and conservation of seabirds of the Bahama Islands," pp. 157–168 *in* P.G.H. Evans, and R.W. Schreiber eds., *Status and Conservation of the World's Seabirds*. International Council for Bird Preservation, ICBP Technical Publication No. 2. Cambridge, England.

Trull, P. 1988. "The roseate tern in Massachusetts: endangered and enduring." *Massachusetts Wildlife* 38(3): 22–31.

U.S. Fish and Wildlife Service. 1986. Draft Environmental Assessment: Monomoy National Wildlife Refuge Master Plan. U.S. Fish and Wildlife Service. Newton Corner, Massachusetts. 96 pp.

————. 1987. "Endangered and threatened wildlife and plants: Determination of endangered and threatened status for two populations of roseate tern." *Federal Register* 52: 42064–42071.

————. 1988. Draft Recovery Plan for the Northeastern Roseate Tern. Unpublished draft report. U.S. Fish and Wildlife Service. Newton Corner, Massachusetts. 72 pp.

van Halewyn, R. 1985. Report on 1984 Survey of Marine Birds of Netherlands Lesser Antilles. Unpublished. Research Institute for Nature Management. Arnhem, the Netherlands.

————. and R.L. Norton. 1984. "The status and conservation of seabirds in the Caribbean," pp. 169–222 *in* J.P. Croxall, P.G.H. Evans, and R.W. Schreiber eds., *Status and Conservation of the World's Seabirds*. International Council for Bird Preservation, ICBP Technical Publication No. 2. Cambridge, England.

Ian Nisbet is a freelance scientific consultant and a member of the recovery team for the northeastern U.S. population of the roseate tern. He has been studying roseate and other terns in Massachusetts since 1970.

The author would like to thank Joanna Burger, Michael Gochfeld, Robert W. Norton, Carl Safina, Jeffrey G. Spendelow, and Alexander Sprunt, IV, for helpful discussion and unpublished information on roseate terns. Carl Safina reviewed an earlier draft of this chapter.

In legends, golden eagles were symbols of strength and speed, and considered the carriers of messengers to heaven. More recently, the species has been plagued by DDT poisoning, electrocution by collisions with powerlines, trapping, and shooting. *Leonard Lee Rue III*

THE GOLDEN EAGLE

Thomas C. Dunstan

Western Illinois University

SPECIES DESCRIPTION AND NATURAL HISTORY

The golden eagle (*Aquila chrysaetos*) is a large species of eagle that ranges in weight from 7.8 to 9.6 pounds (3,550 to 4,400 grams) for males and 8.9 to 12.5 pounds (4,050 to 5,720 grams) for females. As in most raptor species, the female is larger. Wingspans range from 6.1 to 6.9 feet (1,890 to 2,125 millimeters) for males and from 7 to 7.6 feet (2,150 to 2,270 millimeters) for females. The tail is relatively long, with the male's averaging from almost 1.8 to 2.1 feet (570 to 660 millimeters.) in length and the female's from 2 to 2.3 feet (625 to 705 millimeters) (Brown and Amadon 1968b).

The species is recognized by its large size, feather pattern, and color (Brown and Amadon 1968b). Adult golden eagles have brown bodies; the nape and crown feathers are edged or tipped with golden-buff or tawny. Body feathers may vary in color from light to dark brown, depending on the age of the plumage and the genes of the individual bird or race. The feet are feathered to the toes, as in other members of the genus *Aquila*, and the tail is dark gray to gray brown. Individual feathers are dark tipped with irregular gray and brown banding. The cere and feet are yellow; the iris is hazel to medium brown; and the beak and claws, or "talons," are black.

Subadult and immature golden eagles are similar in color to adults, only darker; they lack the tawny-edged nape and crown feathers that distinguish the adult and their blackish-brown upper tail is darker than that of the adult. Immature eagles are also characterized by their darker eyes, black beaks, yellow cere and feet, and black talons. Plumage color changes gradually over a four- to five-year period before reaching the adult stage.

Eagles can be heard in the vicinity of the nest during courtship or when they are defending the nest site or food. Young birds are more vocal than adults, except during courtship. The call is a clear yelping sound "weeeo-hyo-hyo-hyo" or a series of "weeo" mewing cries (Brown and Amadon 1968b). Nestlings and young fledglings give a sharp clucking call—"tsyuck-tsyuck"— or emit a high, harsh series of chatter. All of these calls were heard throughout the breeding season during studies in the densely populated Snake River Birds of Prey Area in Idaho (Dunstan pers. observ.). Fewer calling bouts were heard during the nonbreeding season of late fall and winter.

Taxonomy and Distribution

Five races of golden eagle are recognized: *Aquila chrysaetos chrysaetos*, found in Great Britain and northeastern Europe; *A.c. homeryi*, found in Spain and North Africa; *A.c. daphanea*, found from Russian Turkestan, east to Manchuria, southwest China, and south to the Himalayas; *A.c. canadensis*, present in eastern and northeastern Siberia, south to the Sea of Okhotsk, Altai, northern Mongolia, and North America from Alaska to Mexico; and *A.c. japonica*, found in Korea and Japan.

North America. Golden eagles are found in good numbers in the mountainous areas of the western United States. Isolated small populations or individual pairs are found east of the Mississippi River in the mountain ranges. Spofford (1969b) states that golden eagles are widely distributed from the arctic regions of Alaska and Canada, southward into the highlands of central Mexico. A remnant eastern population extends from Quebec into the Appalachians.

Worldwide. The golden eagle is a species of holarctic distribution, present as far south as the Spanish Sahara in North Africa, Arabia and the Himalayas in the Old World, and Mexico in North America (Brown and Amadon 1968b) (see Figure 1). It appears that identifiable characteristics of all races intergrade into one another, and the variations are clinal as a whole.

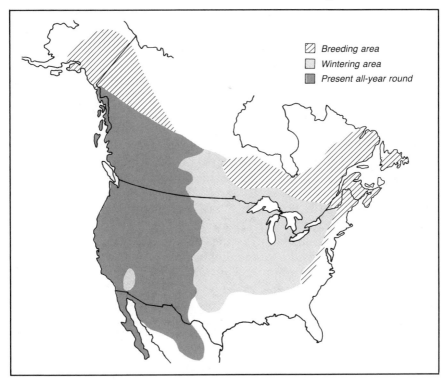

Figure 1. Distribution of the golden eagle in North America.

Home Range

Range sizes vary from 8,000 to 18,000 acres in Scotland (Brown and Watson 1964, Brown 1976), from 2 to 20 square miles for breeding pairs in the Snake River Birds of Prey Area (Dunstan *et al.* 1978), and to anywhere from 19 to 59 square miles in California (Brown and Amadon 1968b).

Breeding

Male-female pairs occupy a home range that includes adequate nesting, feeding, and resting habitat. In many geographic locations, the site is occupied all year. Some degree of territoriality is exhibited and this limits breeding density in a given area. One North American study suggests that the concept of territoriality and the need for adequate breeding structures limits the breeding ability of subadults more so than the availability of food (Steenhof *et al.* 1983). However, breeding attempts by subadult eagles have been recorded in Scotland (Watson

1957, Sandeman 1957), Europe (Novelletto and Petretti 1980), and North America (Steenhof *et al.* 1983).

Breeding and nesting activity begins with elaborate courtship flights by both the male and female. The adult male flies in a series of vigorous undulating dives with a flap-glide wing motion, while calling in the vicinity of the female. Soaring flights by the pair, with dives by the male toward the female, are also seen. Such exaggerated displays are common among many raptors (Brown and Amadon 1968b). Copulation often takes place on a cliff at the nest site.

The golden eagle builds a large nest made primarily of sticks and branches. The nest is often assembled on a rocky ledge or crag rather than in a tree (Brown and Amadon 1968b). Alternative sites and nests often exist within the home range, and a pair may build and refurbish several nests each year before selecting the one to be used for the season. Favored sites and nest structures are repaired and used yearly by the birds; some sites are used for decades.

Two dull-white eggs are laid at two- to four-day intervals (Brown and Amadon 1968b). Egg size varies among the races. The female does most of the incubating, but the male also participates (Brown and Amadon 1968b). Incubation periods have been reported as anywhere from 35 days (Kalmbach *et al.* 1964), to 41 days (Reynolds 1969, Olendorff 1973), to 43 days or more (Hobbie and Cade 1962). (Variation in the length of the reported incubation period may occur because of the difficulty researchers have in determining when an egg was laid and the amount of heat applied.)

Both sexes care for the nestlings. The female broods the young and both the male and female share in bringing food and feeding (Brown and Amadon 1968b). Calopy (1984), however, states that the male's primary role is clearly one of providing food. His studies at the Snake River Birds of Prey Area showed that the male rarely fed or brooded the young. Nestlings are not brooded much after they are three to four weeks old.

The breeding success of undisturbed eagle pairs may vary from 0.5 to 1.4 young per pair per year, averaging 0.8 in Scotland and higher in Montana (Brown and Amadon 1968b). Older studies by Brown and Amadon (1968b) suggest that in 80 percent of the cases when two young are hatched, the older nestling kills the younger. However, detailed studies in the Snake River Birds of Prey Area state that this type of mortality is uncommon (Kochert 1972). Thus, the degree of nestling mortality that can be attributed to sibling aggression remains questionable.

Nestlings fledge at 9 to 10 weeks (Kalmbach *et al.* 1964, Brown and Amadon 1968b, Snow 1973). Fledglings remain in the vicinity of the nest and the parents provide food until they are about 100 days old or older (Snow 1973). Dispersal and migration habits vary within populations (MaGahan 1966, Mead 1973, Steenhof *et al.* 1984). Departure of radio-marked fledglings on the Snake River Birds of Prey Area was irregular (Dunstan *et al.* 1976, 1978). However, immature golden eagles related to the natal area long after the nesting season. Of the recovery or sightings, 75 percent were within 62 miles of the marking locations (Steenhof *et al.* 1984). Steenhof *et al.* (1984) also reports that six eagles marked as nestlings later returned to the study area and established mating territories, demonstrating apparent long-term affinity for the natal area.

Studies conducted by agency, university, or private scientists at scattered areas within the species's range provide productivity trends for certain populations, but there has been no attempt to monitor worldwide population status. Brown (1976) states that the golden eagle is not a rare bird in Great Britain, but with a population estimated at 740 eagles its position is insecure and merits close attention. Brown also estimates that 80 to 90 pairs of eagles are destroyed or fail to breed every year in Scotland and that human interference may reduce productivity from 0.82 young per pair to 0.56 per pair.

Migration

Migration is a function of food supply and climate. Many adult eagles tend to remain on the home range through most of the year with some interrange movements (Brown 1976, Snow 1973). However, some adults and subadults migrate through major raptor-migration corridors (Spofford 1969b). Eagles in the more northern ranges move southward during inclement weather (Brown and Amadon 1968a). Groups of immature eagles are known to gather at food sources such as carrion piles or sheep birthing areas, but they do not remain grouped for roosting on their winter ranges as do bald eagles (*Haliaeetus leucocephalus*). It is generally unknown where immature birds spend their years prior to breeding.

Life Span

Longevity and mortality varies with age class and negative perturbations at specific locations within the species's range. Long-lived eagles in captivity may be 41 to 48 years old (Brown and Amadon 1968a), but because of numerous adverse environmental impacts, it is unlikely that many live that long in the wild.

Diet

Golden eagles are powerful birds of prey and are able to catch and kill many species of large vertebrates. Kalmbach *et al.* (1964) found that golden eagles kill and eat at least 60 species of animals, ranging from full-grown deer and antelope to mice, insects, and frogs. Although their food habits are diverse throughout the year, golden eagles prey primarily on mammals (Olendorff 1976, Brown and Amadon 1968b). Prairie and wood grouse are taken where abundant, and carrion is also eaten when available. Many food-habit studies conducted throughout the world document the species's preference for mammals small enough to transport to feeding perches or nesting structures. In studies at the Snake River Birds of Prey Area, golden eagles were unable to carry food or weight greater than 4.8 pounds (2,208 grams) (Dunstan pers. observ.). According to Snow (1973), the weight that most golden eagles can carry seems to be approximately 2.9 to 3.9 pounds (1,350 to 1,800 grams). The birds require approximately 8.4 to 8.8 ounces (240 to 250 grams) of food daily (Brown and Amadon 1968b).

SIGNIFICANCE OF THE SPECIES

The golden eagle's susceptibility to environmental changes makes it a sensitive and important biological indicator species. Studies of eagles and other large raptors have focused attention on the ecological impacts

In 1963, golden eagles were afforded protection under the Bald Eagle Act of 1940. *Leonard Lee Rue III*

of certain human activities. Case studies since the 1960s have identified the effects that chlorinated-hydrocarbon pesticides have on peregrine falcons and other raptors. Chemical contaminants wind their way through the food web via animals that ingest tainted food and, in turn, are passed on to golden eagles.

Pesticides, such as the now-banned DDT, accumulate to toxic levels in predators. Peregrine falcons that showed traces of these contaminants in their tissue experienced egg-shell thinning and higher chick mortality. Mining and other human development also affect the quality and quantity of golden eagle wintering habitat.

HISTORICAL PERSPECTIVE

According to legend, golden eagles symbolized strength, speed, and mystical powers, and were the carriers of messages from the earth to the heavens. Their images have decorated human artifacts, ceremonial garb, and equipment for generations; eagles are still seen today on flags, banners, coins, and army uniforms. Golden eagles were flown by emperors and royalty in the ancient sport of falconry and are still used today, primarily for taking mammals (Brown and Amadon 1968a, Grossman and Hamlet 1964).

In the United States, most golden eagles are found in the western states (Snow 1973). Population information was spotty prior to the 1960s until Spofford (1964a) published population and mortality data. Spofford estimated that 20,000 golden eagles were shot between 1942 and 1962 in Texas and New Mexico. He estimated a population of 10,000 birds in North America and expressed concern for the impact that human-caused yearly mortality would have on the species's population (Spofford 1964a, 1964b).

Studies published in the 1970s estimated the total population in North America to be between 10,000 and 100,000 golden eagles (Boeker and Ray 1971, Wrakestraw 1972, Snow 1973). A population of 63,242 wintering golden eagles, with an approximate area of 1,762,294 square miles, was estimated to occur in 16 western states (Olendorff *et al.* 1981).

Shooting, poisoning, trapping, and the subtle effects of disturbance from recreational activities on breeding, wintering, and migration areas have all been direct causes of golden eagle mortality. Shooting of eagles has been deliberate, but poisoning has occurred indirectly from tainted carrion placed for coyote control and from insecticides and pesticides used in agriculture. The decline of golden eagles in Quebec has been attributed to poison baits set for wolf control (Spofford 1969b). Trapping has been accidental, involving traps set around open bait for fur taking or predator-control purposes. Electrocution by and collision with powerlines is another cause of death. This type of mortality was strongly documented in the 1970s. It was found that the younger and more inexperienced golden eagles were very susceptible to electrocution (Benson 1981, Olendorff *et al.* 1981). Benson (1981) found 343 golden eagle carcasses under 24 sections of powerlines in six western states—Idaho, Oregon, Nevada, Utah, New Mexico, and Wyoming.

CURRENT TRENDS

The Bald Eagle Act of 1940 made it illegal to "take, possess, sell, purchase, barter, offer to sell, purchase or barter, transport, export or import, at any time or in any manner, any bald eagle, commonly known as the American eagle, alive or dead, or any part, nest or egg thereof." Protection under the act was extended to golden eagles in April 1963. The Migratory Bird Treaty Act placed all migratory birds under federal jurisdiction and protection. State governors, however, can request permission to control golden eagles that threaten livestock (Snow 1973), but they cannot be taken using aircraft or poison. Permits to take eagles for scientific and religious purposes are also allowed under the revised law.

Golden eagle populations in North America appear to be maintaining themselves in the western United States, where population censuses are conducted. Populations in the eastern United States are still difficult to quantify and the eagle's future in the east remains uncertain. Further research of these populations and of Canadian golden eagle populations is still needed.

MANAGEMENT

Raptor management, which has increased greatly since the 1960s, takes many different forms—habitat management, population enhancement, hazard management, controlling human activity in sensitive raptor areas, and education. These methods can be applied specifically for the golden eagle's benefit.

Habitat Management

Habitat management primarily consists of protecting eagle habitat. Areas containing structures used for nesting, resting, or sleeping, or habitat used for foraging by the golden eagle, or any habitat used by the prey base, should be carefully managed (Call 1979).

The Snake River Birds of Prey Area is a fine example of federal habitat management for golden eagles. Established in 1980, the area is 482,640 acres of public land administered by the Bureau of Land Management. The agency's policies are designed for multiple use, with emphasis on management practices that benefit the 14 birds-of-prey species that frequent the area (Kochert and Pellant 1986). Important wildlife habitat along an 80-mile reach of the Snake River is managed for many types of wildlife, including approximately 32 to 37 breeding pairs of golden eagles.

Habitat Enhancement and Manipulation. Placing human-made nests, wire baskets, and nesting platforms on poles at strategic locations provides nesting structures for the species (Olendorff *et al.* 1980). Platforms are used to increase nesting opportunities and facilitate safe nesting by eagles that use transmission towers (Nelson and Nelson 1976). Similar structures have been used where mining operations have eliminated natural nesting sites (Call 1979). Unfortunately, wire baskets and nest platforms generally have had only limited success in attracting birds.

Population Enhancement

Population enhancement through captive breeding, foster parenting, and rehabilitation and reintroduction are feasible techniques where suitable habitat for golden eagles is unoccupied (Snow 1973). In places such as the Appalachian Mountains, where suitable habitat is available, enhancement methods may help re-establish populations. However, in areas where a reservoir of nonbreeding adult eagles exists, population enhancement using these methods would probably be unnecessary. Moving young eagles between occupied nests also can be used in population management (Olendorff and Stoddart 1974).

Hazards Management

Poisoning, trapping, and powerline collision and/or electrocution are human-caused hazards that need to be controlled. As of February 1972, use of poisons on public lands was banned by Executive Order (Snow 1973). Fur-taking groups have established policies against placing leghold traps near open bait, and some states have laws prohibiting open-bait trapping.

To avoid eagle deaths by powerline electrocution or collision, Call (1979) suggests that utility companies consider: (1) situating poles away from roadways (to lessen the chance that eagles will be shot from the road), (2) prohibiting road construction adjacent to powerlines, and (3) shifting to underground power cables where feasible. Eight public utility companies in the western states are active in developing solutions to this environmental hazard (Olendorff *et al.* 1981).

Controlling Human Activity

Like most raptors, golden eagles are likely to abandon their nests during the incubation period if disturbed. Rock climbing and hiking, off-road vehicle traffic, low-flying aircraft, bird watching, photography, and shooting are potential negative disturbances, and are sometimes regulated by limiting human access to sensitive areas used by golden eagles (Call 1979). Placing seasonal restrictions on recreational activities in nesting areas can also minimize the chance of disturbance.

It is also important that scientific research be monitored carefully so that researchers do not create negative impacts (Call 1979). Agency policies and methodology must be adequate and eagle workers should be well trained.

Education

Classroom education about raptorial bird ecology and management has taken place from elementary grades to all levels of higher education. Short training units have been given to agency biologists, conservation groups, and private citizens. Movies, videos, television specials, and newspaper and magazine articles have spotlighted the golden eagle. Many seminars and natural history programs involving various raptor species are given yearly by raptor rehabilitation groups, research centers, wildlife parks, and zoological facilities.

PROGNOSIS

Predicting the future status of the golden eagle worldwide is difficult in light of the continued human population growth and its impact on the earth's resources. However, an optimistic attitude is justified based on the growing international appreciation and general awareness of eagles, especially the golden eagle, which is present in many countries. The golden eagle has become a high-profile species and commands the support of many conservation groups and a large portion of the general public (Brown 1976).

Programs to minimize problems from recreational activities continue to be implemented on public and private lands. Adverse effects by human interference are being identified. Pesticides, heavy metals,

PCBs, and other environmental contaminants are being monitored by scientists and controlled by federal laws.

RECOMMENDATIONS

The degree to which golden eagles can tolerate human disturbance varies; future studies are needed to fine-tune compatibility between humans and golden eagles. Purposeful killing of golden eagles can be controlled under present laws, but success is dependent on efficient law enforcement and prosecution.

Maintaining optimum populations of golden eagles in adequate habitat necessitates the following:

1. Continue to monitor existing populations and to conduct habitat analyses, including prey-base studies (Call 1979).
2. Conduct inventories and breeding eagle surveys in regions of the species's range where adequate habitat is identified.
3. Research the life history of nonbreeding eagles and the relationship of reserve populations to breeding population recruitment.
4. Continue to coordinate and monitor natural resource development in essential breeding and nonbreeding habitat.
5. Acquire and protect critical habitat used by breeding populations.
6. Maximize golden eagle breeding potential on multiple-use areas presently under protective management through strict control of potentially detrimental human-caused perturbations. Call (1979) suggests that it is necessary to recognize the areas most important to the species and then provide these areas with a high degree of protection from human disturbance. This point is critical, considering the increasing pressures on land from a rapidly growing human population.
7. Continue public awareness and educational programs about raptors, emphasizing sound ecological principles. The decrease of natural reserves makes public education a vital component of the species's survival; the future ecological health of the golden eagle, as well as all species, depends upon it.

REFERENCES

Benson, P.C. 1981. Large Raptor Electrocution and Powerpole Utilization: A Study in Six Western States. Unpublished Ph.D thesis. Brigham Young University. Provo, Utah. 98 pp.

Boeker, E.L. and T.D. Ray. 1971. "Golden eagle population studies in the Southwest." *Condor* 73(4): 463–467.

Brown, L.H. and D. Amadon. 1968a. *Eagles, Hawks and Falcons of the World, Vol. 1.* McGraw-Hill. New York, New York. Pp. 1–413.

———. and D. Amadon. 1986b. *Eagles, Hawks and Falcons of the World, Vol. 2.* McGraw-Hill. New York, New York. Pp. 445–856.

Brown, L. 1976. *British Birds of Prey.* Collins Press. London, England. 400 pp.

———. and A. Watson. 1964. "The golden eagle in relation to its food supply." *Ibis* 106(1): 78–100.

Call, M. 1979. *Habitat Management Guides for Birds of Prey.* U.S. Department of the Interior. Bureau of Land Management Technical Note 338. 70 pp.

Calopy, M.W. 1984. "Parental care and feeding ecology of golden eagle nestlings." *Auk* 101: 753–760.

Dunstan, T.C., J.F. Harper and K.B. Phipps. 1976. "Activity hunting patterns, territoriality, and social interactions of birds of prey in the Snake River Birds of Prey Natural Area, Idaho," pp. 63–130 in *Snake River Birds of Prey Research Project 1976 Annual Report.* U.S. Department of the Interior. Bureau of Land Management.

———., J.H. Harper and K.B. Phipps. 1978. *Habitat Use and Hunting Strategies of Prairie Falcons, Red-tailed Hawks, and Golden Eagles.* Final Report. U.S. Department of the Interior. Bureau of Land Management. 177 pp.

Grossman, M.L. and J. Hamlet. 1964. *Birds of Prey of the World.* Clarkson N. Porter. New York. 496 pp.

Hamerstrom, F., B.E. Harrell and R.R. Olendorff. 1974. *Management of Raptors.* Raptor Research Foundation Raptor Research Report no. 2. Vermillion, South Dakota. 146 pp.

Hobbie, J.E. and T. Cade. 1962. "Observations on the breeding of golden eagles at Lake Peters in northern Alaska." *Auk* 64(3): 235–237.

Kalmbach, E.R., R.H. Imler and L.W. Arnold. 1964. *The American Eagles and Their Economic Status.* U.S. Department of Interior. Fish and Wildlife Service, Bureau of Sport Fisheries and Wildlife. Washington, D.C. 86 pp.

Kochert, M.N. 1972. Population Status and Chemical Contamination in Golden Eagles in Southwestern Idaho. M.S. thesis. University of Idaho. Moscow, Idaho. 115 pp.

———. and M. Pellant. 1986. "Multiple use in the Snake Rivers Birds of Prey Area." *Rangeland* 8(5): 217–220.

McGahan, J. 1966. Ecology of the Golden Eagle. M.A. thesis. University of Montana. Missoula, Montana. 78 pp.

Mead, C.J. 1973. "Movements of British Raptors." *Bird Study* 20: 259–286.

Nelson, M. 1980. "Historic overview of raptor-powerline problems and raptor management priorities," pp. 6–8 in *Workshop on Raptors and Energy Development.* Wildlife Society (Idaho chapter). Boise, Idaho.

———. and P. Nelson. 1976. "Power lines and birds of prey." *Idaho Wildlife Review* 28(5): 3–7.

Novelletto, A. and F. Petretti. 1980. "Ecologia dell Aquila reale negli Appennini." *Riv. Ital. Ornithol.* 50: 249–262.

Ohlendorff, R.R. 1973. "The ecology of the nesting birds of prey of northeastern Colorado." *U.S. International Biological Program Technical Report No. 211.* National Resources Ecology Laboratory. Colorado State University. Fort Collins, Colorado. 233 pp.

———. 1976. "The food habits of North American golden eagles." *American Midland Naturalist* 95(1): 231–236.

———., R.S. Motroni and M.W. Call. 1980. *Raptor Management—The State of the Art in 1980.* U.S. Department of the Interior. Bureau of Land Management Technical Note 345. 56 pp.

———., A.D. Miller and R.N. Lehman. 1981. *Suggested Practices for Raptor Research* on *Power Lines—The State of the Art in 1981*. Raptor Research Foundation. St. Paul, Minnesota. 111 pp.

———. and J.W. Stoddart, Jr. 1974. "The potential for management of raptor populations in western grasslands." pp. 47–88 *in* F.N. Hamerstrom, Jr., B.E. Harrell, and R.R. Olendorff eds., *Management of Raptors*. Raptor Research Foundation, Inc. Vermillion, South Dakota.

Reynolds, H.V. III. 1969. Population Status of the Golden Eagle in Southcentral Montana. M.S. thesis. University of Montana. Missoula, Montana. 61 pp.

Sandeman, P.W. 1957. "The breeding success of golden eagles in the southern Grampians." *Scottish Naturalist* 69(3): 148–152.

Snow, C. 1973. "Golden eagle, *Aquila chrysaetos,*" in *Habitat Management Series for Unique or Endangered Species*. U.S. Department of the Interior. Bureau of Land Management Technical Note 239. 52 pp.

Spofford, W.R. 1964a. Golden Eagle in the Trans-Pecos and Edwards Plateau of Texas. *Audubon Conservation Report No. 1*. 47 pp.

———. 1964b. "Recommendations for conservation and control of the golden eagle." *Audubon* 66(1): 46–47.

———. 1969a. "Problems of the golden eagle in North America," pp. 345–347 *in* J.J. Hickey ed., *Peregrine Falcon Populations: Their Biology and Decline*. University of Wisconsin Press. Madison, Wisconsin.

———. 1969b. "Hawk Mountain counts as population indices in Northeastern America," pp. 323–332 *in* J.J. Hickey ed., *Peregrine Falcon Populations: Their Biology and Decline*. University of Wisconsin Press. Madison, Wisconsin.

Steenhof, K., M.N. Kochert and J.H. Doremus. 1983. "Nesting of subadult golden eagles in southwestern Idaho." *Auk* 100(3): 743–747.

———., M.N. Kochert and M.W. Moritsch. 1984. "Dispersal and migration of southwestern Idaho raptors." *Journal of Field Ornithology* 55(3): 357–368.

Watson, A. 1957. "The breeding success of golden eagles in the north-east highlands." *Scottish Naturalist* 69(3): 153–169.

Wrakestraw, G.F. 1972. 1972 Wyoming Bald and Golden Eagle Survey. Wyoming Department of Fish and Game Project No. W-50-R-21. Job No. 31. 7 pp.

Thomas C. Dunstan is a wildlife professor at Western Illinois University's Department of Biological Sciences.

Part Four

Appendices

APPENDIX A

U.S. Forest Service Directory of Key Wildlife and Fisheries Personnel

(As of March 1, 1989)

WASHINGTON HEADQUARTERS

Mailing Address:
Forest Service-USDA
P.O. Box 96090
Washington, D.C. 20013-6090

Public Inquiries
202-447-3957

TITLE	NAME	PHONE
Chief	F. Dale Robertson	202-447-6661
Associate Chief	George Leonard	202-447-7491

National Forest System
Deputy Chief	James Overbay	202-447-3523
Director, Engineering	Sterling Wilcox	202-235-8035
Director, Lands	Gordon Small	202-235-8212
Director, Land Management Planning	Everett Towle	202-447-6697
Director, Minerals and Geology Mgmt.	Buster LaMoure	202-235-8105
Director, Range Management	Robert Williamson	202-235-8139
Director, Recreation Management	John Butruille	202-447-3706
Director, Timber Management	Dave Hessel	202-447-6893
Director, Watershed and Air Management	Gray Reynolds	202-235-8096
Director, Wildlife and Fisheries	Robert Nelson	202-235-8015

TITLE	NAME	PHONE

State and Private Forestry

Deputy Chief	Allan West	202-447-6657
Director, Fire and Aviation Management	Lawrence Amicarella	202-235-8039
Director, Cooperative Forestry	Tony Dorrell	202-235-2212
Director, Forest Pest Management	James Space	202-235-1560

Research

Deputy Chief	Jerry A. Sesco	202-447-6665
Director, Forest Environment Research	Richard Smythe	202-235-1071
Director, Forest Fire and Atmospheric Sciences Research	William Sommers	202-235-8195
Director, Forest Insect and Disease Research	James Stewart	202-235-8065
Director, Forest Products and Harvesting Research	Stanley Bean, Jr.	202-235-1203
Director, Forest Inventory and Economics Research	H. Fred Kaiser, Jr.	202-447-2747
Director, International Forestry	David Harcharik	202-235-2743
Director, Timber Management Research	Stanley Krugman	202-235-8200

Programs and Legislation

Deputy Chief	Jeff Sirmon	202-447-6663
Director, Environmental Coordination	David Ketcham	202-447-4708
Director, Legislative Affairs	Roger Leonard	202-447-7531
Director, Policy Analysis	David Heerwagen	202-447-2775
Director, Program Development and Budget	John Leasure	202-447-6987
Director, Resources Program and Assessment	Thomas J. Mills	202-382-8235

Administration

Deputy Chief	William Rice	202-447-6707

Office of General Counsel-USDA

Assistant General Counsel, Natural Resources Division	James P. Perry	202-447-7121

REGIONAL HEADQUARTERS AND NATIONAL FORESTS

Region 1—Northern Region (Montana, Idaho [northern], North Dakota [Northwestern])

Federal Building
P.O. Box 7669
Missoula, MT 59807
406-329-3511

Regional Forester: John Mumma
Director, Wildlife and Fisheries: Kirk Horn

Region 2—Rocky Mountain (Colorado, Kansas, Nebraska, South Dakota [except northwestern], Wyoming [eastern])

11177 West 8th Ave.
P.O. Box 25127
Lakewood, CO 80225
303-236-9427

Regional Forester: Gary Cargill
Director, Range, Wildlife Fisheries and Ecology: Glen Hetzel

Region 3—Southwestern (Arizona, New Mexico)

Federal Building
517 Gold Ave., SW
Albuquerque, NM 87102
505-842-3292

Regional Forester: Sotero Muniz
Director, Wildlife Management: William Zeedyk

Region 4—Intermountain (Idaho [southern], Nevada, Utah, Wyoming [western])

Federal Building
324 25th Street
Ogden, UT 84401
801-625-5183

Regional Forester: J.S. Tixier
Director, Wildlife and Fisheries Management: William Burbridge

Region 5—Pacific Southwest (California, Guam, Hawaii, Pacific Islands)

630 Sansome Street
San Francisco, CA 94111
415-556-4310

Regional Forester: Paul Barker
Assistant Regional Forester, Fisheries and Wildlife Management: Randall Long

Region 6—Pacific Northwest (Oregon, Washington)

319 S.W. Pine St.
P.O. Box 3623
Portland, OR 97208
503-221-3625

Regional Forester: James Torrence
Director, Fish and Wildlife: Hugh Black, Jr.

*Region 8—Southern (Alabama, Arkansas, Georgia, Kentucky, Loui-
siana, Mississippi, North Carolina, Oklahoma, Puerto Rico, South
Carolina, Tennessee, Texas)*
1720 Peachtree Rd, N.W.
Atlanta, GA 30367
404-347-4177

Regional Forester: John Alcock
Director, Fisheries, Wildlife and Range: Jerry McIlwain

*Region 9—Eastern (Connecticut, Delaware, Illinois, Indiana, Iowa,
Maine, Maryland, Massachusetts, Michigan, Minnesota, Missouri,
New Hampshire, New Jersey, New York, Ohio, Pennsylvania, Rhode
Island, Vermont, West Virginia, Wisconsin)*
310 West Wisconsin Ave.
Room 500
Milwaukee, WI 53203
414-291-3693

Regional Forester: Floyd Marita
Director, Recreation, Range, Wildlife, and Landscape Management: Vacant

Region 10—Alaska
Federal Office Building
P.O. Box 21628
Juneau, AK 99802-1628
907-586-8863

Regional Forester: Michael Barton
Director, Wildlife and Fisheries: Vacant

FOREST AND RANGE EXPERIMENT STATIONS

Intermountain Station
Laurence Lassen, Director
324 25th Street
Ogden, UT 84401
801-625-5412

Northeastern Station
Denver Burns, Director
370 Reed Road
Broomall, PA 19008
215-690-3008

North Central Station
Ronald Lindmark, Director
1992 Folwell Ave.
St. Paul, MN 55108
612-649-5249

Pacific Northwest Station
Charles W. Philpot, Director
P.O. Box 3890
Portland, OR 97208
503-294-2052

Pacific Southwest Station
Ronald E. Stewart, Director
1960 Addison Street
P.O. Box 245
Berkeley, CA 94701
415-486-3292

Rocky Mountain Station
Charles Loveless, Director
240 W. Prospect
Fort Collins, CO 80526-2098
303-498-1126

Southeastern Station
J. Lamar Beasley, Director
200 Weaver Blvd.
P.O. Box 2680
Asheville, NC 28802
704-257-4300

State and Private Forestry Offices
are located in the Regional
Headquarters, except for the Eastern Region,
where it is at:
    Northeastern Area
    Michael T. Rains, Director
    370 Reed Road
    Broomall, PA 19008
    215-690-3125

Southern Station
Thomas Ellis, Director
T-10210, U.S. Postal Service Bldg.
701 Loyola Avenue
New Orleans, LA 70113
504-589-6800

Forest Products Laboratory
John Erickson, Director
One Gifford Pinchot Drive
Madison, WI 53705-2398
608-264-5717

APPENDIX B

U.S. Fish and Wildlife Service Directory of Key Personnel

(As of March 1, 1989)

WASHINGTON HEADQUARTERS

Mailing Address:
Fish and Wildlife Service
Department of the Interior
18th and C Streets, NW
Washington, D.C. 20240

TITLE	NAME	PHONE
Director	Vacant	202-343-4717
Deputy Director	Steven Robinson	202-343-4545
Assistant Director, External Affairs	Sam Marler	202-343-2500
Chief, Legislative Affairs	Owen Ambur	202-343-5403
Chief, International Affairs	Lawrence Mason	202-343-5188
Chief, Public Affairs	Phil Million	202-343-4131
Assistant Director, Refuges and Wildlife	David L. Olsen (acting)	202-343-5333
Chief, Wildlife Support Staff	Leonard Tinsley	202-343-6351
Chief, Division of Refuges	Robert Karges	202-343-4311
Chief, Division of Realty	William Hartwig	703-358-1713
Chief, Office of Migratory Bird Management	Byron K. Williams (acting)	703-358-1714
Chief, Division of Law Enforcement	Clark Bavin	202-343-9242
Assistant Director, Fish and Wildlife Enhancement	Ralph O. Morganweck	202-343-4646
Chief, Division of Endangered Species and Habitat Conservation	William Knepp	235-2771

TITLE	NAME	PHONE
Chief, Division of Federal Aid	Conley Moffett	235-1526
Chief, Office of Management Authority	Marshall Jones	343-4968
Chief, Division of Environmental Contaminants	John Blankenship (acting)	235-1904
Assistant Director, Fisheries	Gary Edwards	202-343-6394
Chief, Division of Fish Hatcheries	Joseph S. Webster	703-358-1715
Chief, Division of Fish and Wildlife Management Assistance	Lynn Starnes	703-358-1718
Assistant Director, Policy, Budget, and Administration	Jay L. Gerst	202-343-4888
Chief, Division of Budget	Kathleen Tynan (acting)	202-343-2444
Chief, Division of Policy and Directives Management	John Carracciolo	202-343-4633

REGIONAL OFFICES

Region 1 (California, Hawaii, Idaho, Nevada, Oregon, Washington, Pacific Trust Territories)

Fish and Wildlife Service
Lloyd 500 Building, Suite 1692
500 NE Multnomah Street
Portland, Or 97232

TITLE	NAME	PHONE
Regional Director	Marvin Plenert	503-231-6118
Deputy Regional Director	E. Wally Steuke	503-231-6122
Assistant Regional Director, Refuges and Wildlife	Robert Shallenberger	503-231-6214
Assistant Regional Director, Fisheries	William Shake	503-231-5967
Assistant Regional Director, Fish and Wildlife Enhancement	Robert Smith	503-231-6159
Deputy Assistant Regional Director, Fish and Wildlife Enhancement	James Teeter	503-231-6150
Deputy Assistant Regional Director, Federal Aid	Donald Friberg	503-231-6128
Chief, Division of Endangered Species	Russ Peterson (acting)	503-231-6131
Regional Wetlands Coordinator	Dennis Peters	503-231-6154
Assistant Regional Director, Law Enforcement	David McMullen	503-231-6125
Assistant Regional Director, Public Affairs	David Klinger	503-231-6121

Region 2 (Arizona, New Mexico, Oklahoma, Texas)

Fish and Wildlife Service
P.O. Box 1306
Albuquerque, NM 87103

Regional Director	Michael Spear	505-766-2321
Deputy Regional Director	Russ D. Earnest	505-766-2322

TITLE	NAME	PHONE
Assistant Regional Director, Refuges and Wildlife	Joseph Massoni	505-766-1829
Assistant Regional Director, Fisheries and Federal Assistance	Conrad Fjetland	505-766-2323
Chief, Division of Federal Aid	Donald Kuntzelman	505-766-2095
Assistant Regional Director, Fish and Wildlife Enhancement	James Young	505-766-2324
Chief, Division of Endangered Species	Steve Chambers	505-766-3972
Regional Wetlands Coordinator	Warren Hagenbuck	505-766-2914
Assistant Regional Director, Law Enforcement	John Cross	505-766-2091
Assistant Regional Director, Public Affairs	Thomas Smylie	505-766-3940

Region 3 (Iowa, Illinois, Indiana, Michigan, Minnesota, Missouri, Ohio, Wisconsin)

Fish and Wildlife Service
Federal Building, Fort Snelling
Twin Cities, MN 55111

Regional Director	James Gritman	612-725-3563
Deputy Regional Director	Marvin Moriarty	612-725-3563
Assistant Regional Director, Refuges and Wildlife	John Eadie	612-725-3507
Assistant Regional Director, Fisheries and Federal Aid	John Popowski	612-725-3505
Chief, Division of Federal Aid	Robert Lang	612-725-3596
Assistant Regional Director, Fish and Wildlife Enhancement	Gerald Lowry	612-725-3510
Chief, Division of Endangered Species	James Engel	612-725-3276
Regional Wetlands Coordinator	Ronald Erickson	612-725-3593
Assistant Regional Director, Law Enforcement	Larry Hood	612-725-3530
Assistant Regional Director, Public Affairs	George Sura	612-725-3519

Region 4 (Alabama, Arkansas, Florida, Georgia, Kentucky, Louisiana, Mississippi, North Carolina, South Carolina, Tennessee, Puerto Rico, and the Virgin Islands)

Fish and Wildlife Service
R.B. Russell Federal Building
75 Spring Street, SW
Atlanta, GA 30303

Regional Director	James Pulliam, Jr.	404-331-3588
Deputy Regional Director	David B. Allen	404-331-3588
Assistant Regional Director, Refuges and Wildlife	Harold Benson	404-331-0838
Assistant Regional Director, Fisheries and Federal Aid	John Brown	404-331-3576
Assistant Regional Director, Fish and Wildlife Enhancement	Warren Olds, Jr.	404-331-6381
Chief, Division of Federal Aid	Cleophas Cooke, Jr.	404-331-5446

TITLE	NAME	PHONE
Chief, Division of Endangered Species	Dave Fleming	404-331-3583
Regional Wetlands Coordinator	John Hefner	404-331-6343
Assistant Regional Director, Law Enforcement	Dan Searcy	404-331-5872
Assistant Regional Director, Public Affairs	Vacant	404-331-3594

Region 5 (Connecticut, Delaware, Maine, Maryland, Massachusetts, New Hampshire, New Jersey, New York, Pennsylvania, Rhode Island, Vermont, Virginia, West Virginia)

Fish and Wildlife Service
One Gateway Center, Suite 700
Newton Corner, MA 02158
617-965-5100

Regional Director	Robert Lambertson	x200
Deputy Regional Director	James Gillett	x200
Assistant Regional Director, Refuges and Wildlife	Donald Young	x222
Assistant Regional Director, Fisheries and Federal Aid	James Weaver	x208
Chief, Division of Federal Aid	William Hesselton	x212
Assistant Regional Director, Fish and Wildlife Enhancement	Ralph Pisapia	x217
Chief, Division of Endangered Species	Paul Nickerson	x316
Regional Wetlands Coordinator	Ralph Tiner	x379
Assistant Regional Director, Law Enforcement	Eugene Hester	x254
Assistant Regional Director, Public Affairs	Inez Connor	x206

Region 6 (Colorado, Kansas, Montana, Nebraska, North Dakota, South Dakota, Utah, Wyoming)

Fish and Wildlife Service
P.O. Box 25486
Denver Federal Center
Denver, CO 80225

Regional Director	Galen Buterbaugh	303-236-7920
Deputy Regional Director	John L. Spinks, Jr.	303-236-7920
Assistant Regional Director, Refuges and Wildlife	Nelson Kverno	303-236-8145
Assistant Regional Director, Fisheries and Federal Aid	William Martin	303-236-8154
Chief, Division of Federal Aid	Jerry Blackard	303-236-7392
Assistant Regional Director, Fish and Wildlife Enhancement	Robert Jacobsen	303-236-8189
Chief, Division of Endangered Species and Environmental Contaminants	Larry Shanks	303-236-7398
Regional Wetlands Coordinator	Charles Elliot	303-236-8180
Assistant Regional Director, Law Enforcement	Terry Grosz	303-236-7540
Assistant Regional Director, Public Affairs	Jack Hallowell	303-236-7904

TITLE	NAME	PHONE

Region 7 (Alaska)

Fish and Wildlife Service
1011 E. Tudor Road
Anchorage, AK 99503

TITLE	NAME	PHONE
Regional Director	Walter Stieglitz	907-786-3542
Deputy Regional Director	John Rogers (acting)	907-786-3543
Assistant Regional Director, Refuges and Wildlife	John Rogers	907-786-3545
Assistant Regional Director, Enhancement	Rowan Gould	907-786-3544
Chief, Division of Fisheries	Randy Bailey	907-786-3466
Chief, Division of Federal Aid	William Martin	907-786-3491
Chief, Division of Ecological Services and Endangered Species	Steve Wilson	907-786-3467
Regional Wetlands Coordinator	John Hall	907-786-3403
Assistant Regional Director, Law Enforcement	David Purinton	907-786-3311
Assistant Regional Director, Public Affairs	Bruce Batten	907-786-3486

Region 8 (Research and Development)[1]

Fish and Wildlife Service
U.S. Department of the Interior
Mail Stop: 725 Arlington Square Building
Arlington, VA 22203

TITLE	NAME	PHONE
Regional Director	Richard Smith	202-343-6394
Deputy Regional Director	John D. Buffington	703-358-1801
Office of Scientific Authority	Charles Dane	703-358-1708
Alaska Fish and Wildlife Research Center 1101 East Tudor Road Anchorage, AK 99503	A. William Palmisano	907-786-3448
Cooperative Fish and Wildlife Research Center Fish and Wildlife Service Mail Stop: 725 Arlington Square Bldg. Arlington, VA 22203	Edward LaRoe	703-358-1709
National Ecology Research Center Creekside One Bldg. 2627 Redwing Road Fort Collins, CO 80526-2899	Vacant	303-226-9100
National Fisheries Contaminant Research Center Route 1 Columbia, MO 65201	Richard Schoettger	314-875-5399
National Fisheries Research Center 7920 N.W. 71st Street Gainesville, FL 32606	James McCann	904-378-8181

1. Responsible for management of research within the Fish and Wildlife Service.

TITLE	NAME	PHONE
National Fisheries Research Center— Great Lakes 1451 Green Road Ann Arbor, MI 48105	Jon Stanley	313-914-3331
National Fisheries Research Center—La Crosse P.O. Box 818 La Crosse, WI 54601	Fred Meyer	608-783-6451
National Fisheries Research Center—Leetown Box 700 Kearneysville, WV 25430	Jan Riffe	304-725-8461
National Fisheries Research Center Building 204, Naval Station Seattle, WA 98115	Alfred Fox	206-526-6282
National Wetlands Research Center 1010 Gause Blvd. Slidell, LA 70458	Robert Stewart	504-646-7564
National Wildlife Health Research Center 6006 Schroeder Road Madison, WI 53711	Milton Friend	608-271-4640
Northern Prairie Wildlife Research Center P.O. Box 2096 Jamestown, ND 58401	Rey Stendell	701-252-5363
Patuxent Wildlife Research Center Laurel, MD 20708	Harold O'Connor	301-956-7300
Office of Information Transfer 1025 Pennock Place, Suite 212 Fort Collins, CO 80524	Richard Gregory	303-493-8401

APPENDIX C

National Park Service Directory of Key Fisheries and Wildlife Personnel

(As of March 1, 1989)

WASHINGTON HEADQUARTERS

Mailing address:
National Park Service
Interior Building
P.O. Box 37127
Washington, D.C. 20013-7127

General Information:
202-343-4747

TITLE	NAME	PHONE
Director	Wm. Penn Mott	202-343-4621
Deputy Director	Denis Galvin	202-343-5081
Program Analysis Officer	Carol Aten	202-343-7456
Chief, Public Affairs	George Berklacy	202-343-6843
Assistant Director, Leg. & Congressional Affairs	Chuck Williams	202-343-5883
Equal Employment Opport. Officer	Marshall Brookes	202-343-6738
Assistant Director, Office of Business and Economic Development	Ramon Cintron	202-343-5477

Natural Resources

Associate Director	Eugene Hester	202-343-3554
Chief, Air Quality Division	John Christiano	303-969-2070
Chief, Water Resources Division	Stan Ponce	303-221-8305

526

TITLE	NAME	PHONE
Chief, Wildlife and Vegetation Division[1]	Michael Ruggiero	202-343-8121
Natural Resources Specialist	Hardy Pearce	
Ecologist	Craig Shafer	202-343-8127
Science Support Staff	Al Greene	202-343-5575
Senior Scientist	Theodore Sudia	202-343-2917

Park Operations

Associate Director	Vacant	202-343-5651
Chief, Land Resources Division[2]	Willis Kriz	202-523-5252

Cultural Resources

Associate Director	Jerry Rogers	202-343-7625

Planning and Development

Associate Director	Gerald Patten	202-343-1264

Budget and Administration

Associate Director	Edward Davis	202-343-6741

1. Created in November 1987.
2. Includes Minerals Resources Section, formerly Energy, Mining and Minerals.

REGIONAL OFFICES

North Atlantic Regional Office (Connecticut, Maine, Massachusetts, New Hampshire, New Jersey, New York, Rhode Island, and Vermont)

Herbert Cables, Jr., Regional Director
National Park Service
15 State Street
Boston, MA 02109
617-565-8800

Chief Scientist: Michael Soukup, 617-565-8805
Natural Resource Contacts: Nora Mitchel, 617-656-8852
Len Bobinchock, 207-288-5456

Mid-Atlantic Regional Office (Delaware, Maryland, Pennsylvania, Virginia, and West Virginia)

James Coleman, Regional Director
National Park Service
143 South Third Street
Philadelphia, PA 19106
215-597-7013

Chief Scientist: John Karish, 814-865-7974
Natural Resource Contact: John Karish, 814-865-7974

National Capital Regional Office (The National Capital Region covers parks in the metropolitan area of Washington, D.C. and certain field areas in Maryland, Virginia, and West Virginia)

Robert Stanton, Regional Director
National Park Service
1100 Ohio Drive, SW
Washington, D.C. 20242
202-426-6612

Chief Scientist: William Anderson, 202-342-1443
Natural Resource Contact: Stan Lock, 703-255-1811

Southeast Regional Office (Alabama, Georgia, Kentucky, Mississippi, North Carolina, South Carolina, Tennessee, and Puerto Rico, and the Virgin Islands)

Robert Baker, Regional Director
National Park Service
75 Spring Street, SW
Atlanta, GA 30303
404-331-5185

Chief Scientist: Dominic Dottavio, 404-331-4916
Natural Resource Contact: Wallace Hilbert

Midwest Regional Office (Illinois, Indiana, Iowa, Kansas, Minnesota, Michigan, Missouri, Nebraska, Ohio, and Wisconsin)

Dan Castleberry, Regional Director
National Park Service
1709 Jackson Street
Omaha, NE 68102
402-221-3431

Chief Scientist: Ron Hiebert, 219-926-7561
Natural Resource Contact: Ben Holmes, 402-221-3475

Rocky Mountain Regional Office (Colorado, Montana, North Dakota, South Dakota, Utah, and Wyoming)

Lorraine Mintzmeyer, Regional Director
National Park Service
12795 West Alameda Parkway
P.O. Box 25287
Denver, CO 80225-0287
303-969-2000

Chief Scientist: Dan Huff, 303-969-2650
Natural Resource Contact: Dan Huff, 303-969-2650

Southwest Regional Office (Part of Arizona, Arkansas, Louisiana, New Mexico, Oklahoma, and Texas)

John Cook, Regional Director
National Park Service
Old Santa Fe Trail
P.O. Box 728
Santa Fe, NM 87504-0728
505-988-6388

Chief Scientist: Milford Fletcher, 505-988-6412
Natural Resource Contact: Milford Fletcher, 505-988-6412

Western Regional Office (Part of Arizona, California, Hawaii, and Nevada)

Stanley Albright, Regional Director
National Park Service
450 Golden Gate Avenue
P.O. Box 36063
San Francisco, CA 94102
415-556-4196

Chief Scientist: Bruce Kilgore, 415-556-4968
Natural Resource Contact: Tom Gavin, 415-556-7664

Pacific Northwest Regional Office (Idaho, Oregon, and Washington)

Charles Odegaard, Regional Director
National Park Service
83 South King Street
Suite 212
Seattle, WA 98104
206-442-5565

Chief Scientist: James Larson, 206-442-4176
Natural Resource Contact: Ed Menning, 206-442-5670

Alaska Regional Office (Alaska)

Boyd Evison, Regional Director
National Park Service
2525 Gambell Street, Room 107
Anchorage, AK 99503-2892
907-271-2690

Chief Scientist: Al Lovaas, 907-257-2568
Natural Resource Contact: Al Lovaas, 907-257-2568

APPENDIX D

Bureau of Land Management Directory of Key Wildlife and Fisheries Personnel

(As of March 1, 1989)

WASHINGTON HEADQUARTERS

Mailing Address:
Bureau of Land Management
U.S. Department of the Interior
18th and C Sts., NW
Washington, D.C. 20240

Robert Burford, Director
Bureau of Land Management
202-343-3801

Dean Stepanek, Assistant Director
Land and Renewable Resources
202-343-4896

J. David Almand, Chief
Division of Wildlife and
Fisheries, BLM
202-653-9202
    Neal Middlebrook, Wildlife Project Manager, 202-653-9202
    William Radtkey, Endangered Species Program Manager, 202-653-9202
    Vacant, Fisheries Program Manager, 202-653-9202

STATE OFFICE DIRECTORS AND BIOLOGISTS

Alaska
Michael Penfold
907-271-5555
[1] Craig Altop, State Office Biologist
Bureau of Land Management
701 C Street, Box 13
Anchorage, AK 99513
907-271-5530

Arizona
D. Dean Bibles, State Director
602-241-5501
Gene Dahlem, State Office Biologist
P.O. Box 16563
Phoenix, AZ 85011

California
Ed Hastey, State Director
916-978-4746
Vacant, State Office Biologist
[1] Butch Olendorff
Bureau of Land Management
Federal Bldg.
2800 Cottage Way, E-2841
Sacramento, CA 95825-1889
916-978-4725

Colorado
Neil Morck, State Director
303-236-1700
[1] Lee Upham, State Office Biologist
Bureau of Land Management
2850 Youngfield Street
Lakewood, CO 80215
303-236-1762

Denver Service Center
Bob Moore, Director
303-236-0161
[1] Allen Cooperrider, Service Center Biologist
[1] Ray Boyd
Bureau of Land Management
Denver Service Center
Denver Federal Center, Bldg. 50
Denver, CO 80225
303-236-6452

Eastern States Office
G. Curtis Jones, Jr., Director
[1] Tom Hewitt, State Office Biologist
Bureau of Land Management
Eastern States Office
350 South Pickett Street
Alexandria, VA 22304
703-274-0194

Idaho
Del Vail, State Director
208-334-1771
[1] Allen Thomas, State Office Biologist
Roger Rosentretter, State Office Botanist
Bureau of Land Management
3380 Americana Terrace
Boise, ID 83706
208-334-1773

Montana (MT, SD, ND)
Marvin LeNoue, State Director (Acting)
Bob Haberchek, State Office Biologist

[1] Dan Hinckley
Bureau of Land Management
222 North 32nd Street
Billings, MT 59107
406-657-6655

Nevada
Ed Spang, State Director
702-784-5451
David Goicoechea, State Office Biologist
[1] Osborne Casey
Bureau of Land Management
P.O. Box 12000
Reno, NV 89520
702-784-5162

New Mexico (KS, NM, OK, TX)
Larry Woodard, State Director
505-988-6231
Jan Knight, State Office Biologist
Bureau of Land Management
Montoya Federal Bldg.
South Federal Place
Santa Fe, NM 87504
505-988-6231

1. Biologist for endangered species.

Oregon (OR, WA)
Charles Luscher, State Director
503-231-6251
Art Oakley, State Office Biologist
503-231-6866
[1]Bill Nietro
503-231-6865
Cheryl McCaffrey, State Office Botanist
Bureau of Land Management
825 NE Multnomah Street
P.O. Box 2965
Portland, OR 97208
503-231-2313

Utah
James Parker, State Director (Acting)
Jerry Farringer, State Office Biologist
801-524-5311
[1]Ron Bolander, State Office Botanist
Bureau of Land Management
324 South State Street
Salt Lake City, UT 84111-2303
801-524-3123

Wyoming (WY, NE)
Ray Brubaker, State Director
307-772-2326
[1]Dave Roberts, State Office Biologist
Bureau of Land Management
2515 Warren Avenue
Cheyenne, WY 82003
307-772-2083

1. Biologist for endangered species.

Environmental Protection Agency Directory of Key Wetlands Management Personnel

(As of March 1, 1989)

HEADQUARTERS

Mailing Address:
U.S. Environmental Protection Agency
401 M St., SW
Washington, D.C. 20460

William K. Reilly, Administrator
202-382-4700

Rebecca W. Hanmer (Acting)
Assistant Administrator for Water
202-382-5700

William Whittington, Deputy Assistant
Administrator for Water
202-382-5700

David G. Davis, Director
Office of Wetlands Protection
202-475-7795

REGIONAL OFFICES

Region 1 (Connecticut, Maine, Massachusetts, New Hampshire, Rhode Island, Vermont)
Michael Deland, Administrator
John F. Kennedy Federal Building
Room 2203
Boston, MA 02203
617-565-3400
Wetlands contacts:
    Matt Schweisberg, 617-835-4422
    Douglas Thompson, 617-835-4422

Region 2 (New York, New Jersey, Puerto Rico, Virgin Islands)
William J. Muszynski, Administrator (Acting)
26 Federal Plaza
Room 900
New York, NY 10278
212-264-2525
Wetlands contact:
    Dan Montella, 212-264-5170

Region 3 (Delaware, District of Columbia, Maryland, Pennsylvania, West Virginia, Virginia)
Stanley L. Laskowski, Administrator (Acting)
841 Chestnut St.
Philadelphia, PA 19107
215-597-9800
Wetlands contact:
    Barbara D'Angelo, 215-597-9301

Region 4 (Alabama, Florida, Georgia, Kentucky, Mississippi, North Carolina, South Carolina, Tennessee)
Greer Tidwell, Acting Administrator
345 Courtland St., N.E.
Atlanta, GA 30365
404-347-4727
Wetlands contact:
    Thomas Welborn, 404-257-2126

Region 5 (Illinois, Indiana, Michigan, Minnesota, Ohio, Wisconsin)
Valdas Adamkus, Administrator
230 S. Dearborn
Chicago, IL 60604
312-353-2000
Wetlands contact:
    Jim Giattina, 312-886-0243

Region 6 (Arkansas, Louisiana, New Mexico, Oklahoma, Texas)
Robert E. Layton, Jr., Administrator
Allied Bank Tower at Fountain Place
1445 Ross Avenue
Dallas, TX 75202
214-655-2100
Wetlands contacts:
    Jerry Saunders, 214-255-2210
    Michael Janski, 214-255-2260

Region 7 (Iowa, Kansas, Missouri, Nebraska)
Morris Kay, Administrator
726 Minnesota Avenue
Kansas City, KS 66101
913-236-2800
Wetlands contact:
    Tom Taylor, 913-757-2823

Region 8 (Colorado, Montana, North Dakota, South Dakota, Utah, Wyoming)
James Scherer, Administrator
999 18th Street, Suite 500
Denver, CO 80202
303-293-1603
Wetlands contact:
    John Peters, 303-564-1585

Region 9 (Arizona, California, Hawaii, Nevada, Pacific Trust Territories)
Daniel McGovern, Administrator (Acting)
215 Freemont Street
San Francisco, CA 94105
415-974-8153
Wetlands contact:
    Clyde Morris, 415-454-8253

Region 10 (Alaska, Idaho, Oregon, Washington)
Robie G. Russell, Administrator
1200 Sixth Avenue
Seattle, WA 98101
206-442-5810
Wetlands contact:
    William M. Reiley, 206-399-1412

APPENDIX F

National Marine Fisheries Service Directory of Key Personnel

(As of March 1, 1989)

Mailing Address:
National Marine Fisheries Service
National Oceanic and Atmospheric Administration (NOAA)
Department of Commerce
1825 Connecticut Avenue, N.W.
Washington, D.C. 20235

TITLE	NAME	PHONE
Assistant Administrator, Fisheries	James W. Brennan	301-427-2239
Deputy Assistant Administrator, Fisheries	James E. Douglas, Jr.	301-427-2239
Executive Director	Vacant	301-427-2239
Chief, Budget and Planning Office	Vacant	301-427-2250
Director, Office of Enforcement	Morris Pallozzi	301-427-2300
Director, Office of Fisheries Conservation and Management	Richard Schaefer (acting)	301-427-2334
Director, Office of Research and Environmental Information	Dr. Glenn A. Flittner (acting)	301-427-2367
Office of Protected Resources	Dr. Nancy Foster	301-427-2332
Office of Trade and Industry Services	Thomas Billy (acting)	301-427-2351
Office of International Affairs	Henry Beasley	301-427-2272

REGIONAL OFFICES

Northeast Region (Connecticut, Delaware, Indiana, Illinois, Maine, Massachusetts, Michigan, Minnesota, New Hampshire, New York, New Jersey, New York, Ohio, Pennsylvania, Rhode Island, Vermont, Virginia, West Virginia, Wisconsin)

Richard Roe, Director
National Marine Fisheries Service
14 Elm Street
Federal Building
Gloucester, MA 01930
617-281-3600

Thomas Bigford, Habitat Conservation Chief
508-281-3600
Douglas Beach, Protected Species
617-837-9154

Southeast Region (Alabama, Arkansas, Florida, Georgia, Iowa, Kansas, Kentucky, Louisiana, Mississippi, Missouri, Nebraska, New Mexico, North Carolina, Oklahoma, South Carolina, Tennessee, Texas)

Dr. Joseph W. Angelovic, Director (acting)
National Marine Fisheries Service
9450 Koger Boulevard
St. Petersburg, FL 33702
813-893-3141

Andreas Mager, Habitat Conservation Chief (acting)
813-826-3503
Charles Oravetz, Protected Species
813-826-3366

Northwest Region (Colorado, Idaho, Montana, North Dakota, South Dakota, Oregon, Utah, Washington, Wyoming)

Rolland Schmitten, Director
National Marine Fisheries Service
7600 Sand Point Way, N.E.
BIN C15700
Seattle, WA 98115-0070
206-526-6150

Merrit Tuttle, Habitat Conservation Chief
206-230-5424
Joe Scordino, Protected Species
206-526-6140

Southwest Region (Arizona, California, Hawaii, Nevada)

E. Charles Fullerton, Director
National Marine Fisheries Service
300 S. Ferry Street
Terminal Island, CA 90731
213-514-6197

James Slawson, Habitat Conservation Chief
213-514-6199
James Lecky, Protected Species
213-795-6664

Alaska Region

Steven Pennoyer, Director
National Marine Fisheries Service
P.O. Box 1668
Juneau, AK 99802
907-586-7221

Theodore Meyers, Habitat Conservation Chief
907-586-7235
Steve Zimmerman, Protected Species
907-586-7233

NMFS FISHERIES CENTERS

Northeast Fisheries Center

Allen Peterson, Jr., Director
NOAA
Woods Hole, MA 02543
617-548-5123

Southeast Fisheries Center

Bradford Brown, Director (acting)
75 Virginia Beach Drive
Miami, FL 33149
305-361-4284

Alaska Fisheries Center

William Aron, Director
7600 Sand Point Way, N.E.
Building 4, BIN C15700
Seattle, WA 98115-0070
206-526-4000

Northwest Fisheries Center

Richard Berry, Director
2725 Montlake Boulevard East
Seattle, WA 98112

Southwest Fisheries Center

Izadore Barrett, Director
8604 La Jolla Shores Drive
P.O. Box 271
La Jolla, CA 92038
619-546-7000

APPENDIX G

U.S. Army Corps of Engineers Directory of Key Personnel

(As of March 1, 1989)

HEADQUARTERS

Mailing Address:
Army Corps of Engineers
Office of the Chief of Engineers
Casimir Pulaski Building
20 Massachusetts Avenue, N.W.
Washington, D.C. 20314

Robert Page
Assistant Secretary, Civil Works
202-697-8986

Lieutenant General Henry J. Hatch
Chief, Corps of Engineers
202-272-0001

Brig. General Patrick J. Kelly
Director of Civil Works (DAEN-CWZ)
202-272-0099

Barry Frankel
Director, Real Estate
202-272-0483

John Wallace
Director, Resource Management
202-272-0077

Bernard N. Goode
Chief, Regulatory Branch
202-272-0199

William Klesch
Chief, Office of Environmental Policy
202-272-0166

DIVISIONS AND DISTRICTS

Lower Mississippi Valley Division
P.O. Box 80
Vicksburg, MS 39180
Leo Max Reed, Chief, Regulatory Branch
601-634-5818

Memphis District
Clifford Davis Federal Building
Rm B-202
Memphis, TN 38103-1894
David Pitts, Regulatory Chief
901-521-3471

Sam Morgan, Field Planning Chief
901-521-3346
William C. Schult, Public Affairs Officer
901-521-3348

New Orleans District
P.O. Box 60267
New Orleans, LA 70160-0267
Ronald Ventola, Regulatory Chief
504-862-2255
Robert Schroeder, Field Planning Chief
504-862-2288
Bruce Sossaman, Public Affairs Officer
504-862-2201

St. Louis District
210 Tucker Boulevard, N
St. Louis, MO 63101-1986
Ronald Messerli, Regulatory Chief
314-263-5703
Jack Rasmussen, Field Planning Chief
314-263-5755
Clyde A. Wilkes, Public Affairs Officer
314-263-5662

Vicksburg District
P.O. Box 60
Vicksburg, MS 39180-0060
Edward McGregor, Regulatory Chief
601-634-5276/89
V.C. Alrich, Field Planning Chief
601-624-5409
Michael H. Logue, Public Affairs Officer
601-634-5052/3/4

Missouri River District
P.O. Box 103 Downtown Station
Omaha, NE 68101
Mores Bergman, Chief, Regulatory Branch
402-221-7290
Don Sedrel, Field Planning Chief (acting)
402-221-7265
Paul T. Johnston, Public Affairs Officer
402-222-7208/9/10

Kansas City District
700 Federal Building
601 E. 12th Street
Kansas City, MO 64106-2896
Mel Jewett, Regulatory Chief
816-374-3645
Phil Rotert, Field Planning Chief
816-426-3671
George Hanley III, Public Affairs Officer
816-426-5241

Omaha District
P.O. Box 5
Omaha, NE 68101-0005
John Morton, Regulatory Chief
402-221-4211
David L. Thomsen, Field Planning Chief
402-221-4575
Betty White, Public Affairs Officer
401-221-3916

New England Division
424 Trapelo Road
Waltham, MA 02254
William Lawless, Chief, Regulatory Branch
617-647-8338
(No district offices)

North Atlantic Division
90 Church Street
New York, NY 10077
Lenny Kotkiewicz, Chief, Regulatory Branch
212-264-7535

Baltimore District
P.O. Box 1715
Baltimore, MD 21203-1715
Don Roeseke, Regulatory Chief
301-962-3670
James F. Johnson, Field Planning Chief
301-962-4900
Harold Kanarek, Public Affairs Officer (acting)
301-962-4616

New York District
26 Federal Plaza
New York, NY 10278-0090
James Mansky, Regulatory Chief
212-264-3996
Simeon Hook, Field Planning Chief (acting)
212-264-9291
Peter H. Shugert, Public Affairs Officer
212-264-9113

Norfolk District
803 Front Street
Norfolk, VA 23510-1096
William Poore, Jr., Regulatory Chief
804-441-3068
Roland Culpepper, Field Planning Chief
804-441-7761
William E. Brown, Public Affairs Officer
804-441-7606

Philadelphia District
U.S. Customs House
2nd and Chestnut Streets
Philadelphia, PA 19106-2991
Frank Cianfrani, Regulatory Chief
215-597-2812
Robert Callegari, Field Planning Chief
215-597-5951
Roy A. Pirritano, Public Affairs Officer
215-597-4802

North Central Division
536 S. Clark Street
Chicago, IL 60605-1592
Mitchell Isoe, Chief, Regulatory Branch
312-353-6379

Buffalo District
1776 Niagara Street
Buffalo, NY 14207-3199
Paul Leuchner, Regulatory Chief
716-876-5454
John Zorich, Field Planning Chief
716-876-5454 x 2274
John Derbyshire, Public Affairs Officer
716-876-5454 x 2209

Chicago District
219 S. Dearborn Street
Chicago, IL 60604-1797
Tom Slowinski, Regulatory Chief
312-353-6428
Dave Hunter, Field Planning Chief (acting)
312-353-6513
Evelyn Shiele, Public Affairs Officer
312-353-6412

Detroit District
P.O. Box 1027
Detroit, MI 48231-1027
Gary Mannesto, Regulatory Chief
313-226-2218
Bill Willis, Field Planning Chief
313-226-6768
Mike Perrini, Public Affairs Officer
313-226-4680

Rock Island District
Clock Tower Building
Rock Island, IL 61201-2004
Steven Vander Horn, Regulatory Chief
309-788-6361

Dudley Hanson, Field Planning Chief
309-788-6361 x 6260
Robert G. Faletti, Jr., Public Affairs Officer
309-788-6361

St. Paul District
1135 USPO & Custom House
St. Paul, MN 55101-1479
Ben Wopat, Regulatory Chief
612-220-0375
Louis E. Kowalski, Field Planning Chief
612-220-0107
Ken Gardner, Public Affairs Officer
612-725-7505

North Pacific Division
P.O. Box 2870
Portland, OR 97208
John Zammit, Chief, Regulatory Branch
503-326-3780

Alaska District
P.O. Box 898
Anchorage, AK 99506-0898
Robert Oja, Regulatory Chief
907-753-2712
Lauren Aimonetto, Field Planning Chief
503-221-6414
Alene Jacques, Public Affairs Officer
503-221-6005

Portland District
Jerry Newgard, Regulatory Chief
P.O. Box 2946
Portland, OR 97208-2946
503-221-6995

Seattle District
P.O. Box C-3755
Seattle, WA 98124-2255
Warren Baxter, Regulatory Chief
206-764-3495
Dwain F. Hogan, Field Planning Chief
206-764-3600
David Harris, Public Affairs Officer
206-794-3750

Walla Walla District
Building 602
City-County Airport
Walla Walla, WA 93362-9265
Dean Hilliard, Regulatory Chief
509-522-6720/24

Vic Armacost, Field Planning Chief
509-522-6588
Orel C. Dugger, Public Affairs Officer
509-522-6660

Ohio River Division
P.O. Box 1159
Cincinnati, OH 45201-1159
Roger Graham, Chief, Regulatory Branch
513-684-3972

Huntington District
508 8th Street
Huntington, WV 25701-2070
Gary Watson, Regulatory Chief
304-529-5487
Bill Sinozich, Field Planning Chief (acting)
304-529-5636
Steven E. Wright, Public Affairs Officer
304-529-5451

Louisville District
P.O. Box 59
Louisville, KY 40201-0059
Don Purvis, Assistant Regulatory Chief
502-582-6461
Neal Jenkins, Field Planning Chief
502-582-5658
Chuck Schumann, Public Affairs Officer
502-582-5736

Nashville District
P.O. Box 1070
Nashville, TN 37202-1070
Charles Huddleston, Regulatory Chief
615-736-5181
Warren Bennett, Field Planning Chief
615-736-5952
Stony Merriman, Public Affairs Officer
615-736-7161

Pittsburgh District
Federal Building
1000 Liberty Avenue
Pittsburgh, PA 15222-4186
Eugene Homyak, Regulatory Chief
412-644-6872
George Cingle, Field Planning Chief
412-644-6817
John A. Reed, Public Affairs Officer
412-644-4130

South Atlantic Division
510 Title Building
30 Pryor St., S.W.
Atlanta, GA 30303
James Kelly, Jr., Chief, Regulatory Branch
404-331-6744

Charleston District
P.O. Box 919
Charleston, SC 29402-0919
Clarence Ham, Regulatory Chief
803-724-4330
Richard Jackson, Field Planning Chief
803-724-4254
Carol S. Todd, Public Affairs Officer
803-724-4201

Jacksonville District
P.O. Box 4970
Jacksonville, FL 32232-0019
John Adams, Regulatory Chief
904-791-3423
A.J. Salem, Field Planning Chief
904-791-2238
Juan A. Colon, Public Affairs Officer
904-791-2235

Mobile District
P.O. Box 2288
Mobile, AL 36628-0001
Ron Krizman, Regulatory Chief
205-690-2658
N.D. McClure, Field Planning Chief
205-690-2777
Samuel R. Green, Public Affairs Officer
205-690-2505

Savannah District
P.O. Box 889
Savannah, GA 31402-0889
Steven Osvald, Regulatory Chief
912-944-5347
Myron Yuschishin, Field Planning Chief
912-944-5271
James N. Parker, Jr., Public Affairs Officer
912-944-5279

Wilmington District
P.O. Box 1890
Wilmington, NC 28402-1890
Charles Hollis, Regulatory Chief
919-251-4629

Larry Saunders, Field Planning Chief
919-343-4925
Marty van Duyne, Public Affairs Officer
919-343-4625

South Pacific Division
630 Sansome Street, Room 1216
San Francisco, CA 94111
Theodore Durst, Chief, Regulatory Branch
415-556-2648

Los Angeles District
P.O. Box 2711
Los Angeles, CA 90053-2325
Charles Holt, Regulatory Chief
213-894-5606
Robert Joe, Field Planning Chief
213-894-7962
Carol Wolff, Assistant Public Affairs Officer
213-894-5320

Sacramento District
650 Capitol Mall
Sacramento, CA 95814-4794
Art Champ, Regulatory Chief
916-551-2275
Walter Yep, Field Planning Chief
916-551-1850
Jim Taylor, Public Affairs Officer
916-551-2526

San Francisco District
211 Main Street
San Francisco, CA 94105-1905
Calvin Fong, Regulatory Chief
415-974-0416
Bill Angelino, Field Planning Chief
415-974-0379
Frank Rezac, Public Affairs Officer
415-974-0355

Southwest Division
1114 Commerce Street
Dallas, TX 75242
Mark King, Chief, Regulatory Branch
214-767-2432

Albuquerque District
P.O. Box 1580
Albuquerque, NM 87103-1580
Andrew Rosenau, Regulatory Chief
505-766-2776

Robert Roumph, Field Planning Chief
505-766-2627
Jim Bryant, Public Affairs Officer
505-766-2738

Fort Worth District
P.O. Box 17300
Fort Worth, TX 76102-0300
Wayne Lea, Regulatory Chief
817-334-2681
Michael Mocek, Field Planning Chief
817-334-2201
Sally Werst, Public Affairs Officer
817-334-3409

Galveston District
P.O. Box 1229
Galveston, TX 77553-1229
Marcos De La Rosa, Regulatory Chief
409-766-3930
William G. Wooley, Field Planning Chief
409-766-3059
Ken Bonham, Public Affairs Officer
409-766-3004

Little Rock District
P.O. Box 867
Little Rock, AR 72203-0867
Louie Cockman, Jr., Regulatory Chief
501-378-5296
David L. Burrough, Field Planning Chief
501-378-5751
Dave McNully, Public Affairs Officer
501-378-5551

Tulsa District
P.O. Box 61
Tulsa, OK 74121-0061
Lou Ringeisen, Regulatory Chief
918-581-7261
Bob Brown, Field Planning Chief
918-581-7314
Ross Adkins, Public Affairs Officer
918-581-7307

APPENDIX H

Budget Information Contacts for Federal Fish and Wildlife Programs

(As of March 1, 1989)

TITLE	NAME	PHONE

Army Corps of Engineers (Wetlands Section 404 Program)

Chief, Programs Division Office	Don Cluff	202-272-0191

Bureau of Land Management

Chief, Office of Budget	Roger Hildebeidel	202-343-8571
Budget Analyst, Fish and Wildlife	Mike Green	202-343-8571
Director, Budget Office	Richard M. Brozen (Acting)	202-475-8340
Budget Analyst, 404 Program	Mark Flory	202-382-4220

Fish and Wildlife Service

Deputy Assistant Director, Policy, Budget, and Administration	James Leupold	202-343-4329
Chief, Budget and Analysis Division	Kathy Tynan (Acting)	202-343-2444

Forest Service

Director, Program Development and Budget	John Leasure	202-447-6987
Branch Chief, Program, Planning, and Development	John Skinner	202-382-9120

544

TITLE	NAME	PHONE

Marine Mammal Commission

Executive Director	John Twiss, Jr.	202-653-6237

National Marine Fisheries Service

Budget Analyst, Office of Policy and Planning	Donald Wickham	301-427-2250

National Park Service

Chief, Budget Division	James Giammo	202-343-8746

APPENDIX I

Federal Fish and Wildlife Program Budgets

Cynthia Lenhart

INTRODUCTION

Five federal agencies are primarily responsible for the management of the nation's fish and wildlife resources: the Fish and Wildlife Service, Forest Service, Bureau of Land Management, National Park Service, and National Marine Fisheries Service. Historically, those with an interest in fish and wildlife management have focused on the policies and actions of these agencies without paying much attention to their budgets. In the past five years or so, however, wildlife interest groups have spent more time in the arcane world of appropriations, analyzing federal agency budgets and advocating changes to them. The environmental community has awakened to the fact that money drives policy, even in the arena of natural resources conservation.

Formulation of the federal budget is a long, complex undertaking in which the primary players are the president, Office of Management and Budget (OMB), federal agencies, and Congress. The process begins some 19 months before the fiscal year begins. The federal fiscal year starts on the first day of October; FY 1989 began on October 1, 1988, and agencies began developing budget projections for FY 1989 in March

1987. All agencies must work with OMB to prepare a budget that is in line with presidential directives and OMB planning targets. In the fall, one year before the fiscal year begins, agencies submit formal budget requests to OMB, which revises these estimates to conform with presidential decisions. (This revision process is often referred to as the "OMB pass-back.") OMB essentially has the final word on agency budget figures and overall budget assumptions and policies.

Traditionally, the president transmits his budget to Congress on the first Monday after January 3. In years when Congress has been slow to complete action on the previous budget, however, the administration has agreed to delay the transmittal of the next budget. The congressional budget process involves three types of committees—budget, authorizing, and appropriations—in both the House and Senate. The process begins with hearings of the budget committees, which have responsibility for setting overall spending, revenue, and other budget targets in a "budget resolution." They base these targets on views and estimates from the authorizing committees. Authorizing committees, as the name suggests, can pass bills to authorize the expenditure of monies, but only the budget and appropriations committees can permit the actual release of federal funds to implement legislation. Appropriations committees deal with the fine detail of each agency's budget, determining how much is to be spent on individual programs and projects.

While the budget committees are developing their resolution on the budget, the appropriations subcommittees are holding hearings and reviewing justifications from each agency. Traditionally, the House Interior and Related Agencies appropriations subcommittee, which has jurisdiction over Fish and Wildlife Service, Forest Service, Bureau of Land Management, and National Park Service budgets, holds a "public witness" hearing in late February. This is the time when private groups can testify as to their proposed changes to the president's budget. (When "add-ons" and "cuts" are mentioned, they are usually in the context of modification to the president's budget.)

If all goes according to schedule (which rarely occurs), the budget resolution is completed by June 15. At this point the appropriations committees receive their spending ceilings, and in turn provide "suballocations" to subcommittees. Only then can the appropriations subcommittees finalize their action, by reconciling their spending bills with the budget resolution.

Under Constitutional law, the House must complete action on its appropriations bills first, theoretically by June 30. The Senate appropriations subcommittees then draft revisions to House bills and reports. After full Senate passage, each appropriations bill goes to a conference committee, where differences between House and Senate versions are resolved; both houses vote on the amended conference version. Finally, each appropriations bill goes to the president for his approval or veto.

If appropriations action is not completed by September 30, or if a presidential veto is not overridden by then, the affected programs are funded in a "continuing resolution" until an appropriations bill is approved by Congress and the president. Continuing resolutions basically maintain programs at current fiscal year levels. They have become common in the recent past because Congress has failed to act in a timely matter on budget reconciliations and appropriations bills.

Appropriations bills themselves reveal little beyond the gross parameters of an agency's budget—one must turn to the reports that accompany the bills to see the fine detail. Appropriations reports show add-ons and cuts to the president's budget—specific line-item actions—and often provide prosaic direction to the agency on how, not just how much, money is to be spent. Reports usually feature a number of discourses on agency policy from the committees' perspective. Appropriations bills and reports are a popular vehicle for congressional policy statements, and allow Congress to prohibit certain activities simply by preventing any expenditure of monies for them.

Appropriations "riders" are common. This practice—attaching unrelated legislation to appropriations bills—allows the rider to pass on the appropriations juggernaut without separate consideration.

FISH AND WILDLIFE SERVICE

The U.S. Fish and Wildlife Service (FWS) is the leading federal agency responsible for the conservation and management of fish and wildlife resources. It has principal authority for migratory birds, threatened and endangered species, and certain marine mammals. FWS manages over 90 million acres of habitat in the 445 refuges that constitute the refuge system.

FWS's FY 1989 budget is $812 million, of which some 44 percent is in permanent and trust funds (see Figure 1). On the whole, the president's proposed FY 1989 budget for FWS was a moderate six percent reduction from the 1988 level. Congressional add-ons resulted in a total increase of nine percent above last year (see Figure 2).

Fish and Wildlife Enhancement

The Fish and Wildlife Enhancement budget category includes certain aspects of the endangered species management program (listing, consultation, permit review, recovery actions on off-refuge lands, and

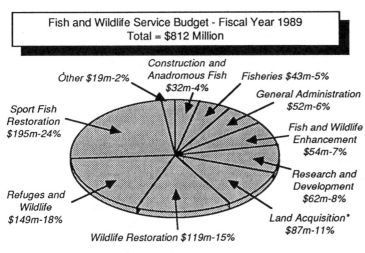

Fish and Wildlife Service Budget - Fiscal Year 1989
Total = $812 Million

Other $19m-2%

Construction and
Anadromous Fish
$32m-4%

Fisheries $43m-5%

Sport Fish
Restoration
$195m-24%

General Administration
$52m-6%

Fish and Wildlife
Enhancement
$54m-7%

Refuges and
Wildlife
$149m-18%

Research and
Development
$62m-8%

Land Acquisition*
$87m-11%

Wildlife Restoration $119m-15%

*Land acquisition includes $57.5 million appropriated from the Land and Water
Conservation Fund (LWCF), and $29.4 million from the Migratory Bird Conser-
vation Account.

Figure 1.

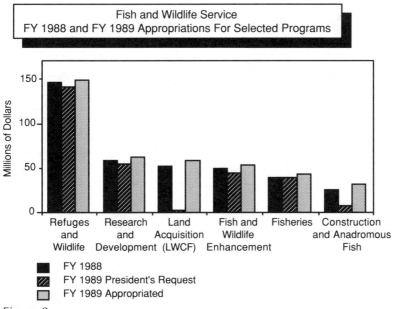

Fish and Wildlife Service
FY 1988 and FY 1989 Appropriations For Selected Programs

Millions of Dollars

150 —

100 —

50 —

0 —

Refuges
and
Wildlife

Research
and
Development

Land
Acquisition
(LWCF)

Fish and
Wildlife
Enhancement

Fisheries

Construction
and Anadromous
Fish

■ FY 1988
▨ FY 1989 President's Request
▦ FY 1989 Appropriated

Figure 2.

grants to states), ecological services, environmental contaminants, and the national wetlands inventory. Congress appropriated $54 million for this program in 1989, about $5 million more than in 1988. Specific congressional add-ons to the president's budget request included $250,000 for listing, which restored funding to the 1988 level. The House report specified that these monies were to be used to assist in "prelisting activities," to help prevent species in peril from requiring listing in the future.

The 1988 funding level for consultation was increased by about $220,000 to accommodate increased workload, generated in part by new listings. Congress once again rejected the administration's proposal to axe federal grants to states for endangered species recovery, instead appropriating $5 million for that program, an increase of $700,000 from the 1988 level.

Endangered species recovery received a total of $1.5 million in add-ons for FY 1989, bringing the total for that activity to about $8.5 million. A number of "high-priority" species were named in the House and Senate reports: the grey and northern Rocky Mountain wolves, Aleutian Canada goose, Puerto Rican parrot, Mount Graham red squirrel, bruneau hot springs snail, Hawaiian forest birds, southern and California sea otter, whooping crane, black-footed ferret, Florida panther, Attwater prairie chicken, sea turtles, and manatee. Also within those funds, $80,000 was earmarked for grizzly bear activities, $100,000 for the red wolf captive-breeding program in Washington state, and $300,000 for the Peregrine Fund. In addition, Congress provided $250,000 for nongame work to be implemented through FWS regional endangered species offices.

Under ecological services, Congress added $1.7 million for Farm Act implementation, bringing the FY 1989 budget for that program to almost $4.7 million. Report language specified that the 1989 add-on is to be used for wetland restoration activities. Congress also added $250,000 to accelerate FWS's National Wetlands Inventory program, which is in the process of mapping wetlands in priority areas and generating scientific information on wetland habitat.

Continuing its focus on refuge contamination problems, Congress added $500,000 to FWS's budget to provide additional field staffing, and directed the agency to develop bioassessment technology with available funds. The total FY 1989 budget for environmental contaminants is about $6.4 million.

Refuges and Wildlife

The Refuges and Wildlife budget category covers expenses related to the administration of the refuge system, migratory bird and marine mammal management, and law enforcement. Congress appropriated $148.6 million for this program in 1989, about $3 million more than in 1988.

Under refuge operations and maintenance, increases to the president's budget included defense of refuge water rights, Alaskan and Hawaiian refuges, firefighting, fishery management plans, Alaska subsistence grants, and challenge grants for projects on refuges.

Law enforcement operations for FY 1989 were funded at $21.5 million. The only congressional increase to the president's request was $500,000 to begin operations at the National Fish and Wildlife Forensics Laboratory in Oregon.

Under migratory bird management, Congress added $250,000 for management and monitoring of nongame species, and directed that use of these funds be coordinated with those provided for nongame under the endangered species program. (See the *Audubon Wildlife Report 1988/1989* for further discussion of nongame program funding.)

Fisheries

The Fisheries account supports operation and maintenance of 71 federal fish hatcheries, management of refuge fish populations, technical assistance to Indian tribes and others, and implementation of the Lower Snake River Compensation Plan. Congress provided $42.8 million for fishery resources in 1989, a nine-percent increase over the 1988 level. Citing the need to upgrade hatcheries and implement deferred maintenance plans, Congress earmarked a $1-million increase for hatchery maintenance. The add-on brought maintenance for hatcheries to just over $5 million, an increase of 65 percent over the 1988 level of about $3 million.

Research and Development

All of FWS's research activities are funded under the Research and Development budget category. Congress appropriated $62 million to the research account in FY 1989, a $3.1-million increase over the 1988 level; the president's budget had proposed a $3.9 million decrease from 1988. Most add-ons to the president's budget served to maintain research programs at the 1988 level, and included $500,000 for nongame species, $650,000 for Alaskan marine mammals, $100,000 for brown tree snake, and $100,000 for purple loosestrife. Fishery research received a boost of $1.9 million above 1988 levels, including $640,000 for start-up costs at the Northeast Anadromous Fish Laboratory, and $600,000 for the Southeast Fish Culture Laboratory.

General Administration

The General Administration budget category covers the costs of running the central office in Washington, D.C., seven regional offices, and research facilities. In the only action with direct bearing on wildlife conservation, Congress provided $5 million to the National Fish and Wildlife Foundation for matching grants.

Construction and Anadromous Fish

Congress appropriated $31.8 million for the Construction and Anadromous Fish account, more than four times the president's request of $7.5 million. As in the past, the administration had proposed no new construction projects on refuges, research labs, and hatcheries, but Congress provided over $22 million for this purpose. Congress rejected the administration's oft-repeated proposal to halt anadromous fish grants to the states, providing $2 million for the program, and continued support for an ongoing striped bass study.

Within the construction account, $1.2 million was earmarked for purchase of water rights for the Stillwater Wildlife Management Area in Nevada. Stillwater, part of the National Wildlife Refuge System, provides critically important wetland habitat for migrating shorebirds. The area was formally included in the Western Hemisphere Shorebird Reserve Network in 1988. Stillwater has had to rely on irrigation overflows for most of its water supply, and recently documented bird deformities and fatalities are believed related to toxic levels of arsenic and boron in the water. In order to avoid another Kesterson-like contamination crisis, the refuge needs clean water to flush the system of these naturally occurring compounds. Although the monies earmarked within available funds are not near enough to purchase all the clean water required, environmentalists regard this congressional action as a positive step in the process of settling water rights disputes on the Carson and Truckee rivers, which flow through California and Nevada. Language in the conference report also designated Stillwater a high-priority wetland, making it eligible for funding under the North American Waterfowl Management Plan.

Land Acquisition

FWS has two main sources of fiscal support for land acquisition: the Land and Water Conservation Fund (LWCF) and Migratory Bird Conservation Account (MBCA). In 1989, the administration, as it has in all but one of the Reagan budgets, requested no monies from the LWCF for land acquisition. It proposed only to spend the $28.9 million in projected MBCA receipts from the sale of duck stamps and

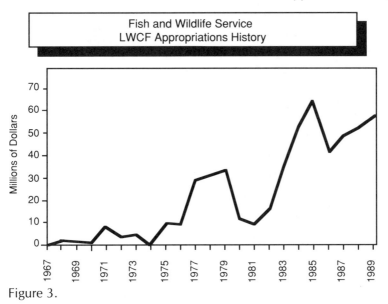

Fish and Wildlife Service
LWCF Appropriations History

Figure 3.

other sources. Congress, however, appropriated $57.5 million from the LWCF, an increase of $5.7 million over the 1988 level (see Figure 3). Notable line items included $10 million for the Lower Rio Grande National Wildlife Refuge—the most ever appropriated in a single year for one refuge. New acquisition projects included Bowerman Basin in Washington and Sunkhaze Meadows in Maine.

FOREST SERVICE

The U.S. Forest Service, with an operating budget of $2.7 billion in FY 1989, is the largest federal natural resource agency. In 1988 the Forest Service employed 36,958 full-time equivalents; just two percent of these, however, were wildlife and fish management personnel.

The National Forest System is made up of some 191 million acres, providing habitat for more than 3,000 wildlife species. Many system areas are critical to big-game populations and to the recovery of threatened and endangered species. National forest lands include or affect most of the nation's premier trout streams and contain more than a quarter of the spawning and rearing habitat for salmon and steelhead in the Pacific Northwest and Alaska. As private lands are converted to other uses, the National Forest System is becoming increasingly important for wildlife- and fish-related recreation.

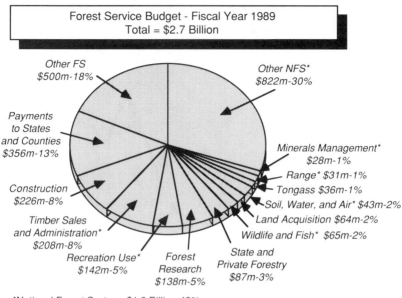

Forest Service Budget - Fiscal Year 1989
Total = $2.7 Billion

Other FS $500m-18%

Other NFS* $822m-30%

Payments to States and Counties $356m-13%

Minerals Management* $28m-1%

Range* $31m-1%

Tongass $36m-1%

Construction $226m-8%

Soil, Water, and Air* $43m-2%

Land Acquisition $64m-2%

Timber Sales and Administration* $208m-8%

Wildlife and Fish* $65m-2%

Recreation Use* $142m-5%

Forest Research $138m-5%

State and Private Forestry $87m-3%

*National Forest System: $1.3 Billion-49%

Figure 4.

The total FY 1989 Forest Service budget is about seven percent higher than in 1988. Roughly one-third of the budget is comprised of permanent and trust funds that support the National Forest System and pay states and counties their share of receipts from commercial activities on forest system lands (see Figure 4).

Wildlife and Fish Habitat Management

Congress appropriated a whopping 44 percent increase to the Forest Service's wildlife and fish program for 1989, a boost of about $20 million from the 1988 level of $45.9 million. The $66-million budget will be split along the following lines: administration—54 percent; fisheries—25 percent; wildlife—11 percent; threatened and endangered species—11 percent.

The fisheries program is based on both direct habitat improvement and mitigation of development impacts for inland and anadromous fisheries. Congress earmarked $3.5 million in increased funding for inland fish habitat improvement in 1989, which brings the budget for that program to $6.2 million. The inland fish habitat improvement program focuses on increasing production of sport fish species such as bass, walleye, and trout. The Forest Service's new national plan, "Rise to the Future," sets the goal of increasing the yearly fish harvest from National Forest System waters from 73 million to 190 million pounds.

Congress also added $6.5 million to the anadromous fish program budget so that $9.3 million will be available in 1989; $1.5 million was specifically targeted for challenge grants. The anadromous fish habitat program places heavy emphasis on restoring habitat in the Pacific Northwest that has been degraded by logging, water resource development, floods, and grazing.

Congress provided an increase of $1.5 million for the wildlife habitat program, resulting in a total of nearly $7 million for that program in 1989. Report language directed the Service to use $1.2 million of those funds to implement the North American Waterfowl Management Plan. Since the Forest Service administers some 12 million acres of waterfowl habitat, the agency could make a significant contribution to the success of the ongoing effort to shore up declining waterfowl populations.

Finally, the threatened and endangered species program of the Forest Service received a $5 million increase above the president's request, for a 1989 funding level of $7.1 million, about $2.7 million more than 1988. Congress specified that $600,000 be spent on plant protection. About one-third of all U.S.-listed species occurs in national forests, including over 1,000 endangered, threatened, and sensitive plants.

Wildlife and Fish Habitat Research

Research for wildlife, range, and fish habitat was funded at $12.8 million in 1989, up three percent from the president's request of $12.4 million, and up five percent from the 1988 level (see Figure 5). Con-

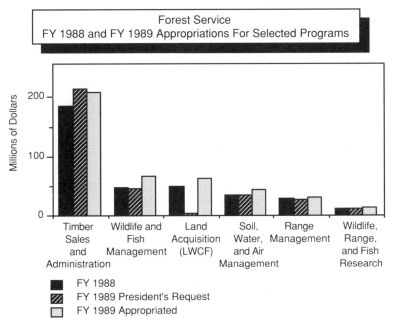

Figure 5.

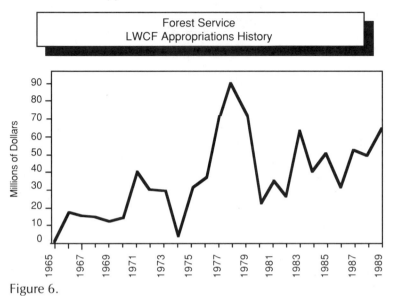

Figure 6.

gress allocated small increases for research on anadromous fish and the spotted owl.

Land Acquisition

Congress once again rejected the administration's proposal to halt new land acquisition and appropriated $64.2 million from the Land and Water Conservation Fund for land additions to the National Forest System. This amount is a 24 percent increase over the 1988 level of $49.1 million (see Figure 6).

BUREAU OF LAND MANAGEMENT

The Bureau of Land Management (BLM) oversees 272 million acres of public land, more than 12 percent of all the land in the United States. The agency also administers mineral leasing and development laws on an additional 300 million acres managed by other agencies and on lands where the subsurface mineral rights are federally owned. BLM lands represent 45 percent of the land managed by the federal government.

Under the Federal Land Policy and Management Act of 1976, BLM manages its lands for multiple uses and benefits. These uses include commodity production—such as livestock grazing (170 million acres in rangeland), energy development, hardrock mining, and timber harvesting (5 million acres in commercial forest)—as well as recreation

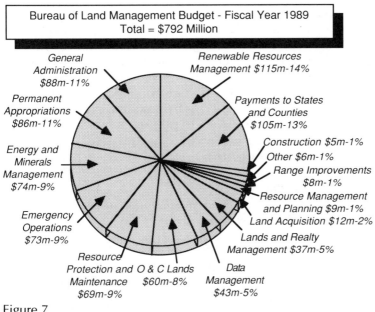

Bureau of Land Management Budget - Fiscal Year 1989
Total = $792 Million

General Administration $88m-11%
Renewable Resources Management $115m-14%
Permanent Appropriations $86m-11%
Payments to States and Counties $105m-13%
Energy and Minerals Management $74m-9%
Construction $5m-1%
Other $6m-1%
Range Improvements $8m-1%
Resource Management and Planning $9m-1%
Land Acquisition $12m-2%
Emergency Operations $73m-9%
Lands and Realty Management $37m-5%
Resource Protection and Maintenance $69m-9%
O & C Lands $60m-8%
Data Management $43m-5%

Figure 7.

and protection of cultural and natural resources. BLM's responsibilities are enormous, yet its budget and staff are modest compared with other federal land management agencies. In FY 1989, BLM will operate on $792 million, with 9,900 personnel. In contrast, the Forest Service, which manages 30 percent less acreage than BLM, has a budget and staff three times as large in 1989.

About half of BLM's budget is allocated to land management programs; the other half goes to general administration, payments in lieu of taxes to states and counties, firefighting, and other miscellaneous activities. BLM's renewable resource management programs, which suffered greater budget cuts under the Reagan Administration than those of any other agency, account for 22 percent of the 1989 budget. Wildlife habitat management is but one aspect of renewable resources management, and accounts for just four percent of the total BLM budget in 1989 (see Figure 7).

Wildlife Habitat Management

The wildlife habitat managed by BLM can be measured not only in terms of its vast acreage, but also in terms of the recreation it provides: an estimated 10 million wildlife observation days, 5 million hunting days, and 3 million fishing days each year. Primary and secondary economic benefits from these activities are measured in hundreds of millions of dollars yearly.

BLM's wildlife program has a broad mandate to protect and enhance habitat, but in recent years its staff has had to focus much of their attention on simply mitigating the adverse impacts of commodity development. Site- or species-specific inventories are gradually replacing costly—but necessary —habitat inventories. For example, in 1989, Colorado's inventory work will focus on bald eagle winter use areas, Uncompahgre fritillary butterfly habitat, and prairie dog colonies. The wildlife program continues to prepare habitat management plans, and monitoring of fish and wildlife habitat trends remains an important aspect of the management program. Research plays a small role in the wildlife habitat management program, accounting for less than five percent of the budget.

Staff shortages continue to be a major problem for the agency's wildlife program. BLM's increasing involvement in endangered species protection and fisheries management has created a growing need for specialized biological expertise. This need has not been met; indeed, the total number of professional wildlife personnel has declined from 363 in 1980 to 259 in 1989. During the Reagan Administration, the number of fisheries biologists declined by 47 percent. In 1989, there are just 30 nationwide, far too few given the agency's ever-growing responsibilities for providing recreational fishing habitat in the West, and managing anadromous fish in Oregon and Alaska and rare fish in the desert regions. At the same time, the number of wildlife biologists has declined by 34 percent. On average, each wildlife biologist is responsible for overseeing one to two million acres of rangeland. Assuring BLM compliance with National Environmental Policy Act (NEPA) requirements for the grazing program and other commodity development on its lands can easily consume most of a biologist's attention. This schedule leaves little time for wildlife management or habitat improvement activities. Likewise, the few BLM field botanists—declining from 17 in 1980 to 15 in 1989—are overwhelmed with work, as the number of rare plant species has skyrocketed. Utah, for instance, has one botanist to manage over 100 rare plants, most of which are candidates for endangered status. The number of endangered plant listings is expected to grow; BLM must hire more botanists if it is to comply with the Endangered Species Act.

The wildlife program suffers from another institutional problem that affects its overall productivity. Simply put, work performed by wildlife program personnel for other programs within the agency is not always reimbursed. Wildlife staff are often called upon to provide input into major planning and environmental assessments that are initiated by other programs, such as oil and gas permits, mine plans, and grazing allotments. This work is supposed to be paid for by the initiating program, but when appropriations for the grazing or mineral programs are cut, funds that should pay for wildlife work are instead used to pay

directly for commodity program activities. The wildlife program—
with limited funds to start with—is, in effect, subsidizing the agency's
commodity programs.

The president's FY 1989 budget once again proposed a significant
cut in BLM's wildlife program, a decrease of $3.6 million and 35 full-
time equivalents from 1988 levels. Congress rejected this proposal and
provided a total of almost $20 million, a 26-percent increase above the
president's request and $1.6 million more than the 1988 appropriation
(see Figure 8). Even though this appropriation is an all-time high for
the program, it is still five percent below the 1981 level in constant
dollars.

About one-third of the congressional add-on, some $1.8 million,
went toward restoration of the wildlife program's 1989 base. (The
"1989 base" is the level of funds required to continue 1988 programs
in 1989, accounting for inflation, salary increases, and the like.) The
base, however, was not entirely restored, and actually shrank by $1.8
million. As in 1989, Congress often has added a significant amount to
the president's budget for the BLM wildlife program, but a large proportion of the increases usually are earmarked for specific projects.
Consequently, the wildlife program's base has eroded each year under
the Reagan Administration.

Specific increases for 1989 included $1 million for threatened and
endangered species protection. A large part of this add-on will go to-

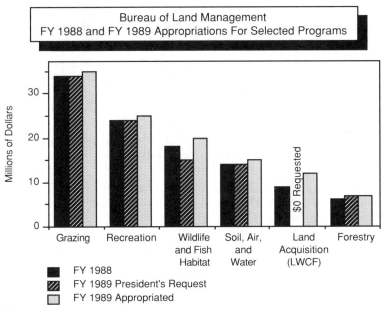

Figure 8.

ward implementation of the new rangewide plan for desert tortoise management. BLM controls over 60 percent of remaining tortoise habitat. While FWS has found listing of the tortoise as an endangered species to be warranted, it has deferred such action, claiming higher priorities. In the meantime, the Utah tortoise population is listed as threatened. Tortoise populations continue to decline due to loss and deterioration of habitat and over-collecting for commercial uses and the pet trade. More research is needed to determine if there are specific cause-and-effect relationships between livestock grazing and the decline of the species. The remaining add-on will be used for other high-priority endangered species needs; Arizona, for example, will address botany staffing needs and peregrine falcon recovery.

BLM administers extensive habitat areas for the northern spotted owl within the Oregon and California (O & C) Grant lands. Under agreement with the Oregon Department of Fish and Wildlife, BLM will provide temporary protection for 110 spotted owl habitat sites. Congress added $100,000 to the O & C account for spotted owl monitoring in 1989. Intensified monitoring of spotted owl habitat areas is necessary to ensure that proper data are used in the development of BLM's resource management plans. Further decline of spotted owl populations could lead to an endangered listing of the species and resultant restrictions on timber harvesting in the owl's range.

Congress added $750,000 to the wildlife program's budget for fisheries management in 1989—about half the amount identified by the states as needed. In Nevada, $25,000 of this add-on will be used to implement the Lahontan cutthroat trout recovery plan. In Oregon, some $10,800 will be spent to inventory 30 miles of the John Day river, important steelhead and chinook salmon habitat. In Wyoming, a new fisheries biologist will be hired. BLM administers over 13,000 miles of anadromous fish streams, mostly on its lands in western Oregon. Congress added $250,000 to the O & C account for anadromous fish habitat improvement in 1989.

BLM's challenge cost-share program, initiated in 1985 as the first federal program of its kind for wildlife purposes, continues to provide a vital boost to implementing on-the-ground habitat improvement projects. Funds appropriated must be matched on a dollar-for-dollar basis by nonfederal entities; a higher percentage of contributions has been the general rule. In 1988, for example, $900,000 was appropriated and $1.5 million was contributed in funds, materials, and labor. Although the President requested no funds for the program in 1989, Congress appropriated $1.5 million; BLM field offices had identified over twice that amount in potential project opportunities. In Arizona, the cost-share program will support, among other things, restoration of riparian habitat along the lower Colorado River for the bald eagle, and radio-telemetry research on the Sonoran pronghorn. In Colorado, the state department of wildlife will contribute to a study of black-footed ferret habitat to determine areas suitable for reintroduction of the species. In California, the Desert Tortoise Preservation Committee, University of California at Los Angeles, and the California Department of Fish and Game will cooperate in research on tortoise disease problems. The California Department of Fish and Game also will contribute to a study of the effect of raven predation on tortoises. In Montana, Trout Unlimited, the state wildlife department and others will cooperate with BLM to acquire about 400 acres of wetland habitat along the Big Hole River. In Nevada, the Nature Conservancy will contribute to a botanical survey of rare plant species. In Oregon, Oregon State University will help support research on fire ecology of native Willamette Valley prairie ecosystems. In Utah, the state wildlife department will help reintroduce otters to the Green River.

BLM oversees about 900,000 acres of riparian zones along waterways in the lower 48 states; these provide important wildlife habitat, especially in the arid west. Management of riparian areas and wetlands has become a higher priority for the BLM wildlife program in recent years, but widespread improvement of such habitat has been slow. For 1989, Congress appropriated an additional $1.5 million for riparian management. Technically, this money was not allocated to the wildlife program, but it may be used for rehabilitation of fish and wildlife resources associated with riparian habitat. In addition, each state has a list of specific habitat improvement projects that will be implemented with base funds. Arizona, for example, plans to construct a total of 14 miles of boundary fence to protect the riparian zones of the Santa Maria, San Pedro, Bill Williams, and Gila Box rivers.

Congress funded three specific projects to be implemented in 1989 for the benefit of wildlife. First, it appropriated $190,000 for research on fire-resistant shrubs in Idaho, where BLM is attempting to restore winter range for wildlife. Fires have allowed non-native cheatgrass to invade, and range managers need to determine which native shrub species are both fire-resistant and palatable to wildlife. Second, Congress added $125,000 to the wildlife program budget for development of a habitat management plan for newly acquired lands along the San Pedro River in Arizona. Third, Congress appropriated an additional $110,000 to continue the Cascade fire rehabilitation project for restoration of deer habitat in Idaho.

Land Acquisition

Since 1980, annual appropriations from the Land and Water Conservation Fund for BLM land acquisition have averaged $3.3 million. Over the years, BLM has acquired important wildlife habitat, including areas critical to the existence of many endangered species. Although the

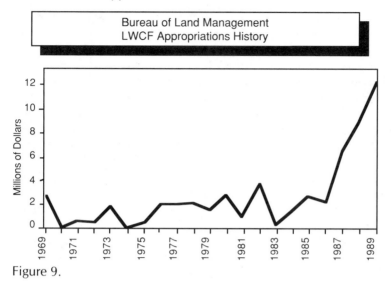

Figure 9.

president's budget proposed no new land acquisition for 1989, Congress appropriated $12.3 million—an all-time high for this program (see Figure 9). This amount included a total of $2.3 million for acquisition of desert tortoise habitat—$1.3 million for the Chuckwalla Bench Area of Critical Environmental Concern and $1 million for the Desert Tortoise Natural Area, both in California. Congress earmarked $5 million of the total for acquisition in the Carrizo Plain of California, which provides habitat for five endangered species, most notably the San Joaquin kit fox and the blunt-nosed leopard lizard.

NATIONAL PARK SERVICE

The National Park Service manages some 80 million acres of land, or less than three percent of the total area of the United States. The park system, consisting of 354 units, serves to protect a wide variety of cultural and natural resources, ranging from small historic sites to vast wildernesses. Most of the major ecosystems in the country, including several of international significance, are represented in the park system.

Along with protecting some of the nation's most spectacular scenic treasures, parks play a major role in the conservation of wildlife habitat in the United States. The prominent status given wildlife in NPS promotions, however, is not matched by monetary or personnel support for wildlife programs. Over the years, the Park Service has shifted emphasis from single-species management to more of an ecosystem approach, but this refined policy remains somewhat over-whelmed by the agency's strong development orientation. While the 1916 Organic Act established resource conservation as a primary pur-pose of the park system, recreation also is a primary purpose, setting the stage for management and budget conflicts. The emphasis on visi-tor services, construction and maintenance is to be expected with heavy use of the parks—projected visitation in 1988 is 375 million people—but this is not especially conducive to resource conservation.

The NPS budget reflects the decentralized character of the agency itself. Presented in a "programmatic" format to Congress, the budget is really a composite of budgets from 354 park units, 10 regional of-fices, a few support centers, and a variety of Washington office and Park Service-wide programs. In fact, there does not appear to be much, if any, centralized programming or budgeting.

Congress appropriated a total of $1.1 billion for NPS in FY 1989, roughly 18 percent higher than the 1988 level of $931 million. This figure includes funding for a wide variety of programs managed by the Park Service, including several that do not have anything to do with natural resources management, such as the John F. Kennedy Center and the Historic Preservation Fund (see Figure 10).

Natural resource programs, as evidenced in the NPS budget, are unintegrated, and the lack of systematic analysis makes it difficult to track wildlife-related expenditures on an agency-wide basis. Most Park Service wildlife activities are funded under "Operations of the Na-tional Park System," within the natural resources subactivity of the

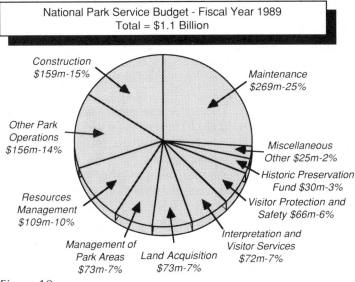

National Park Service Budget - Fiscal Year 1989
Total = $1.1 Billion

Construction $159m-15%

Maintenance $269m-25%

Other Park Operations $156m-14%

Miscellaneous Other $25m-2%

Historic Preservation Fund $30m-3%

Visitor Protection and Safety $66m-6%

Resources Management $109m-10%

Interpretation and Visitor Services $72m-7%

Management of Park Areas $73m-7%

Land Acquisition $73m-7%

Figure 10.

park management activity. There are four sources of money for natural resources management: park base funds, regional base funds, service-wide programs, and the new fee account.

Almost half of the monies spent on natural resources programs comes from individual park budgets. Funds are allocated at the park level to carry out objectives identified in park Resource Management Plans. Park superintendents are thus allowed autonomy in how they spend money on natural resource management, which provides for much-needed flexibility. However, the actual amount of money spent and the accomplishments derived from it are largely unknown.

At the regional level, funding is provided for short-term monitoring, research, and mitigation projects. These projects often are geared to benefit several parks with a common problem. Programming for these activities at the regional level allows NPS to react to unanticipated events, and to shift funds from park to park as priorities change. The regional base funds also support the regional chief scientists and their staff. In general, regional natural resource funding levels are far below estimated needs.

There are 10 NPS-wide natural resource management programs, including ones for fire, acid rain, air quality, mining and minerals. Large, long-term wildlife projects are supported by the NPS-wide Natural Resources Preservation Program. For example, in 1988 program funds supported a study of natural and human-made influences on the declining deer population on Cape Cod, and a study of lake fish at Gates of the Arctic.

The final source of funding for NPS natural resource programs is the new fee account. The 99th Congress provided permanent entrance fee authority to NPS, with fee monies returned by formula to the parks. These funds were earmarked in the legislation for interpretation, resource protection, and research and maintenance related to resource management, reflecting congressional concern for these programs. In 1989, the amount available for enhanced park operations is equal to the total fee revenue in 1988, estimated at $52 million.

The president's FY 1989 budget, reflecting the fee legislation and fiscal limitations, proposed a radical change in priorities for the Park Service. Substantial decreases in maintenance programs contrasted with large increases for interpretation, visitor services, and resource management. Congress objected to this realignment, citing a recent General Accounting Office study that detailed deficiencies in park maintenance and estimated the Service-wide maintenance shortfall at almost $2 billion. The final appropriation for 1989 maintenance was $270 million, about $25 million above the president's request.

As it has in the past, the administration proposed to zero out the Historic Preservation Fund, but Congress appropriated $30.5 million for that program (see Figure 11). In the end, the natural resources management program was funded at a level of nearly $59 million in 1989,

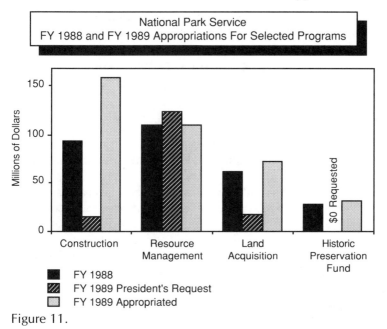

Figure 11.

about the same as in 1988. Despite congressional intent to augment it with new fee income, this program remains a relatively insignificant part of the overall NPS budget picture, constituting just five percent of the agency's budget in 1989.

A few wildlife-related add-ons were included in the final budget report. Most notably, the conference committee agreed to earmark $200,000 for drafting of an Environmental Impact Statement (EIS) on the reintroduction of wolves to Yellowstone National Park. Conference report language detailed the following issues to be included in the EIS: (1) control of wolves inside and outside of park boundaries; (2) effect of reintroduction on Yellowstone's prey base and on big-game hunting outside the park; (3) effect of reintroduction of wolves on grizzly bears in the vicinity; (4) delineation of management zones; and (5) assignment of a FWS wolf coordinator to work with NPS.

The conference report also included language stating that no funds may be used in 1989 to issue a permit for seismic exploration in Big Cypress National Preserve until an EIS has been completed; the committee specified a two year deadline for the EIS. In 1988 Shell Western was issued a permit to conduct such activity in Big Cypress; the permit was withdrawn after environmentalists filed suit, claiming that impact to wildlife and hydrology of the preserve had not been adequately addressed in NPS's environmental assessment.

Congress cut funds requested by the president for a study on the feasibility of restoring the Hetch Hetchy Valley in Yosemite National Park. Senate report language (deleted in conference) included a discourse on the current debate over whether such language is binding. Although the Office of Management and Budget maintained throughout much of the 1989 budget process that report language was not binding, the agency eventually agreed to accept congressional direction in reports.

Land Acquisition

Land and Water Conservation Fund appropriations are used to acquire additional acreage for the National Park System and for matching grants to states for outdoor recreation programs. Congress added more than $40 million to the president's request for federal land acquisition, bringing the 1989 total to $52.6 million. Ignoring the administration's proposal to zero-fund state grants, Congress appropriated about $20 million to that account. (Both figures include acquisition management.) The 1989 appropriation for federal and state accounts is well below historic levels; park acquisition was funded at an average of $290 million in the late 1970s, but declined steadily and precipitously during the Reagan years (see Figure 12).

In one final action with ramifications for wildlife, Congress appropriated $350,000 for the National Academy of Sciences to review and report within 18 months on the land-acquisition criteria and programs of the four federal land management agencies in order to determine the effectiveness of those criteria and programs in achieving policy objectives.

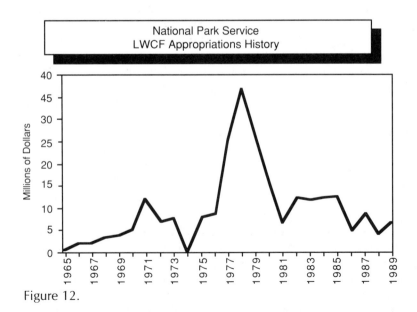

Figure 12.

NATIONAL MARINE FISHERIES SERVICE

The National Marine Fisheries Service (NMFS) has authority over more than two million square miles of the territorial waters of the United States. This Exclusive Economic Zone (EEZ), extending seaward 200 miles from the coast, provides habitat for more than 15 percent of the world's marine resources.

NMFS is charged with a mission as immense and complex as the area it must manage, "to achieve a continued optimum utilization of living marine resources. . . ." (From FY 1989 budget justification, page 61.) The statutory backbone of the agency dictates two, often conflicting, goals—promoting the commercial and recreational use of fisheries while conserving marine ecosystems. In addition to managing economically important finfish and shellfish, NMFS has responsibility for more than 100 species of protected marine mammals and 21 marine species listed as threatened or endangered. The agency's mandate has evolved over the two decades since NMFS was established, from a primary focus on industry service, to a multifaceted role in resource conservation.

Unfortunately, the NMFS budget has not undergone a similar metamorphosis and the agency is currently beset with a number of problems. NMFS is criticized for allowing the overharvest of some 19 economically important fish groups, and for paying inadequate attention to the endangered species and marine mammals under its purview. The agency's primary weakness may be institutional, and a major

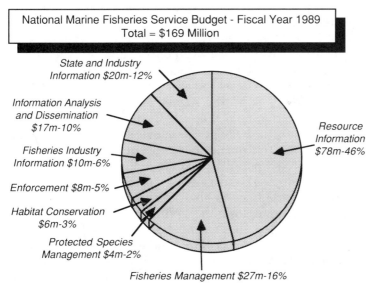

Figure 13.

policy overhaul may be needed to get to the root cause of many of its problems. A number of its difficulties, however, could be appropriately addressed with an infusion of money and staff.

The Reagan budget years have been particularly debilitating to the agency. The NMFS budget has been targeted again and again for significant reductions that Congress, for the most part, has restored. The president's budget for FY 1989 continued this trend, proposing a 45 percent reduction overall, or $65 million less than the 1988 budget of $162 million. Congress largely restored the proposed cuts, and earmarked about $5.5 million in add-ons, bringing the 1989 NMFS budget to over $167 million (see Figure 13).

Information Collection and Analysis

Information Collection and Analysis funds the agency's data collection on composition, abundance, and distribution of marine resources. The data are used to develop management strategies for fisheries and protected species. NMFS also funds habitat research, focusing on the value of, and effects of pollution on, coastal wetlands. The president's FY 1989 budget proposed a 35 percent decrease in funding for information collection and analysis. Such a reduction would have resulted in the cancellation of several ongoing research projects. Congress restored funding for all of these projects.

Of particular note, the president's budget proposed to virtually eliminate the $1.2 million protected species research program, which in 1988 included surveys of sea turtle populations, field trials of turtle excluder devices, and research on Hawaiian monk seals, bowhead whales, and other cetaceans. Marine mammal research, a $1.5-million program, would also have been significantly reduced. Gear entanglement studies in the Pacific would have been terminated, as would right whale studies in the Atlantic. The conference report included specific language regarding research on bowhead whales, earmarking $400,000 for aerial surveys and $350,000 to the Alaska Eskimo Whaling Commission for research, International Whaling Commission representation, and implementation of a cooperative management agreement with the National Oceanic and Atmospheric Administration.

Congress also restored funding for habitat studies cut in the president's FY 1989 budget proposal, most notably research on the impact of pollution on fishery resources in the Northeast. Pollution, along with the pressures of habitat loss and commercial fishing, is seriously threatening marine life in the Northeast's coastal waters. In 1989, NMFS will spend about $3 million studying the physiological and biochemical impacts of contaminants in the Northeast, a program which—even with restoration of the 1989 base—remains underfunded.

The president's budget also proposed termination of NMFS Chesapeake Bay research, begun in 1988 at the direction of Congress. Congress provided the $1.6 million required to continue studies on the response of Bay fish populations to pollution and to other human impacts.

Conservation and Management Operations

The Conservation and Management Operations part of the NMFS budget supports species management, habitat conservation, and law enforcement. Given the agency's almost sole responsibility for protection of many species of marine mammals and 21 endangered or threatened marine species, its limited budget for protected species management and habitat conservation is of great concern to the environmental community. Funding for both programs has declined substantially in recent years.

NMFS is responsible for developing strategies to reduce mortality of whales, porpoises, seals, and sea lions from commercial fishing, oil development, and other activities. NMFS also is responsible for implementing several international agreements concerning marine mammals, including the International Convention for the Regulation of Whaling. In addition, the agency must develop recovery plans for en-

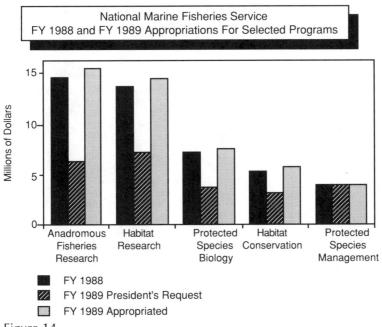

Figure 14.

dangered and threatened species such as the Hawaiian monk seal, California harbor porpoise, sea turtles, and humpback and right whales. The budget for such activities has decreased by 60 percent in constant dollars since 1982. The president's budget proposed to cut funding for this program in 1989, but Congress restored monies to support continued work on Oregon harbor seals and sea lions, and endangered species recovery plans.

The president's FY 1989 budget proposal also included a 35 percent reduction in habitat conservation funding (see Figure 14). Under this program, NMFS provides federal agencies with information and recommendations concerning the environmental effects of proposed actions that would affect marine, estuarine, and certain anadromous fish populations. Typical subjects for review are projects requiring Army Corps of Engineers permits for dredging and filling of wetlands, Federal Energy Regulatory Commission licenses for hydropower plant construction, and Environmental Protection Agency permits for contaminant discharge. NMFS also assesses potential impacts of outer-continental-shelf oil and gas development and Bureau of Reclamation construction projects. Funding for this important program has decreased by 14 percent in constant dollars since 1982. In 1989, NMFS's national program will have just $3.3 million to carry out this program, including evaluating and monitoring more than 6,600 Corps permits and investigating another 500 violations. While lack of money is a distinct problem, the habitat conservation program also suffers from a lack of regulatory veto power over the agencies it advises. Consequently, development continues while NMFS can only warn of the consequences.

Cynthia Lenhart is a wildlife specialist in Audubon's Washington, D.C., office.

Index